What They Said
in 1992

What They Said
In 1992

The Yearbook Of World Opinion

Compiled and Edited by

ALAN F. PATER

and

JASON R. PATER

MONITOR BOOK COMPANY

To

The Newsmakers of the World . . .

May they never be at a loss for words

Preface to the First Edition (1969)

Words can be powerful or subtle, humorous or maddening. They can be vigorous or feeble, lucid or obscure, inspiring or despairing, wise or foolish, hopeful or pessimistic . . . they can be fearful or confident, timid or articulate, persuasive or perverse, honest or deceitful. As tools at a speaker's command, words can be used to reason, argue, discuss, cajole, plead, debate, declaim, threaten, infuriate, or appease; they can harangue, flourish, recite, preach, discourse, stab to the quick, or gently sermonize.

When casually spoken by a stage or film star, words can go beyond the press-agentry and make-up facade and reveal the inner man or woman. When purposefully uttered in the considered phrasing of a head of state, words can determine the destiny of millions of people, resolve peace or war, or chart the course of a nation on whose direction the fate of the entire world may depend.

Until now, the *copia verborum* of well-known and renowned public figures—the doctors and diplomats, the governors and generals, the potentates and presidents, the entertainers and educators, the bishops and baseball players, the jurists and journalists, the authors and attorneys, the congressmen and chairmen-of-the-board—whether enunciated in speeches, lectures, interviews, radio and television addresses, news conferences, forums, symposiums, town meetings, committee hearings, random remarks to the press, or delivered on the floors of the United States Senate and House of Representatives or in the parliaments and palaces of the world—have been dutifully reported in the media, then filed away and, for the most part, forgotten.

The editors of *WHAT THEY SAID* believe that consigning such a wealth of thoughts, ideas, doctrines, opinions and philosophies to interment in the morgues and archives of the Fourth Estate is lamentable and unnecessary. Yet the media, in all their forms, are constantly engulfing us in a profusion of endless and increasingly voluminous news reports. One is easily disposed to disregard or forget the stimulating discussion of critical issues embodied in so many of the utterances of those who make the news and, in their respective fields, shape the events throughout the world. The conclusion is therefore a natural and compelling one: the educator, the public official, the business executive, the statesman, the philosopher—everyone who has a stake in the complex, often confusing trends of our times—should have material of this kind readily available.

These, then, are the circumstances under which *WHAT THEY SAID* was conceived. It is the culmination of a year of listening to the people in the public eye; a year of scrutinizing, monitoring, reviewing, judging, deciding—a year during which the editors resurrected from almost certain oblivion those quintessential elements of the year's *spoken* opinion which, in their judgment, demanded preservation in book form.

WHAT THEY SAID is a pioneer in its field. Its *raison d'etre* is the firm conviction that presenting, each year, the highlights of vital and interesting views from the lips of prominent people on virtually every aspect of contemporary civilization fulfills the need to give the *spoken* word the permanence and lasting value of the *written* word. For, if it is true that a picture is worth 10,000 words, it is equally true that a verbal conclusion, an apt quote or a candid comment by a person of fame or influence can have more significance and can provide more understanding than an entire page of summary in a standard work of reference.

The editors of *WHAT THEY SAID* did not, however, design their book for researchers and scholars alone. One of the failings of the conventional reference work is that it is blandly written and referred to primarily for facts and figures, lacking inherent "interest value." *WHAT THEY SAID*, on the other hand, was planned for sheer enjoyment and pleasure, for searching glimpses into the lives and thoughts of the world's celebrities, as well as for serious study, intellectual reflection and the philosophical contemplation of our multifaceted life and mores. Furthermore, those pressed for time, yet anxious to know what the newsmakers have been saying, will welcome the short excerpts which will make for quick, intermittent reading—and rereading. And, of course, the topical classifications, the speakers' index, the subject index, the place and date information—documented and authenticated and easily located—will supply a rich fund of hitherto not readily obtainable reference and statistical material.

Finally, the reader will find that the editors have eschewed trite comments and cliches, tedious and boring. The selected quotations, each standing on its own, are pertinent, significant, stimulating—above all, relevant to today's world, expressed in the speakers' own words. And they will, the editors feel, be even more relevant tomorrow. They will be re-examined and reflected upon in the future by men and women eager to learn from the past. The prophecies, the promises, the "golden dreams," the boastings and rantings, the bluster, the bravado, the pleadings and representations of those whose voices echo in these pages (and in those to come) should provide a rare and unique history lesson. The positions held by these luminaries, in their respective callings, are such that what they say today may profoundly affect the future as well as the present, and so will be of lasting importance and meaning.

ALAN F. PATER
JASON R. PATER

Beverly Hills, California

Table of Contents

PART THREE: GENERAL

Editorial Treatment

ORGANIZATION OF MATERIAL

Special attention has been given to the arrangement of the book—from the major divisions down to the individual categories and speakers—the objective being a logical progression of related material, as follows:

(A) The categories are arranged alphabetically within each of three major sections:

Part One:	"National Affairs"
Part Two:	"International"
Part Three:	"General"

In this manner, the reader can quickly locate quotations pertaining to particular fields of interest (see also *Indexing*). It should be noted that some quotations contain a number of thoughts or ideas—sometimes on different subjects—while some are vague as to exact subject matter and thus do not fit clearly into a specific topic classification. In such cases, the judgment of the Editors has determined the most appropriate category.

(B) Within each category the speakers are in alphabetical order by surname, following alphabetization practices used in the speaker's country of origin.

(C) Where there are two or more quotations by one speaker within the same category, they appear chronologically by date spoken or date of source.

SPEAKER IDENTIFICATION

(A) The occupation, profession, rank, position or title of the speaker is given as it was *at the time the statement was made* (except when the speaker's relevant identification is in the past, in which case he is shown as "former"). Thus, due to possible changes in status during the year, a speaker may be shown with different identifications in various parts of the book, or even within the same category.

(B) In the case of a speaker who holds more than one position simultaneously, the judgment of the Editors has determined the most appropriate identification to use with a specific quotation.

(C) The nationality of a speaker is given when it will help in identifying the speaker or when it is relevant to the quotation.

THE QUOTATIONS

The quoted material selected for inclusion in this book is shown as it appeared in the source, except as follows:

(A) *Ellipses* have been inserted wherever the Editors have deleted extraneous words or overly long passages within the quoted material used. In no way has the meaning or intention of the quotations been altered. *Ellipses* are also used where they appeared in the source.

(B) *Punctuation and spelling* have been altered by the Editors where they were obviously incorrect in the source, or to make the quotations more intelligible, or to conform to the general style used throughout this book. Again, meaning and intention of the quotations have not been changed.

(C) *Brackets* ([ ]) indicate material inserted by the Editors or by the source to either correct obvious errors or to explain or clarify what the speaker is saying. In some instances, bracketed material may replace quoted material for sake of clarity.

(D) *Italics* either appeared in the original source or were added by the Editors where emphasis is clearly desirable.

Except for the above instances, the quoted material used has been printed verbatim, as reported by the source (even if the speaker made factual errors or was awkward in his choice of words).

Special care has been exercised to make certain that each quotation stands on its own and is not taken "out of context." The Editors, however, cannot be responsible for errors made by the original source, i.e., incorrect reporting, mis-quotations, or errors in interpretation.

DOCUMENTATION AND SOURCES

Documentation (circumstance, place, date) of each quotation is provided as fully as could be obtained, and the sources are furnished for all quotations. In some instances, no documentation details were available; in those cases, only the source is given. Following are the sequence and style used for this information:

Circumstance of quotation, place, date/Name of source, date:section (if applicable), page number.

Example: *Before the Senate, Washington, Dec. 4/The Washington Post, 12-5:(A)13.*

The above example indicates that the quotation was delivered before the Senate in Washington on December 4. It was taken for *WHAT THEY SAID* from *The Washington Post*, issue of December 5, section A, page 13. (When a newspaper publishes more than one edition on the same date, it should be noted that page numbers may vary from edition to edition.)

(A) When the source is a television or radio broadcast, the name of the network or local station is indicated, along with the date of the broadcast (obviously, page and section information does not apply).

(B) An asterisk (*) before the (/) in the documentation indicates that the quoted material was written rather than spoken. Although the basic policy of *WHAT THEY SAID* is to use only *spoken* statements, there are occasions when written statements are considered by the Editors to be important enough to be included. These occasions are rare and usually involve Presidential messages and statements released to the press and other such documents attributed to persons in high government office.

INDEXING

(A) The *Index to Speakers* is keyed to the page number. (For alphabetization practices, see *Organization of Material*, paragraph B.)

(B) The *Index to Subjects* is keyed to both the page number and the quotation number on the page (thus, 210:3 indicates quotation number 3 on page 210); the quotation number appears at the right corner of each quotation.

(C) To locate quotations on a particular subject, regardless of the speaker, turn to the appropriate category (see *Table of Contents*) or use the detailed *Index to Subjects*.

(D) To locate all quotations by a particular speaker, regardless of subject, use the *Index to Speakers*.

(E) To locate quotations by a particular speaker on a particular subject, turn to the appropriate category and then to that person's quotations within the category.

(F) The reader will find that the basic categorization format of *WHAT THEY SAID* is itself a useful subject index, inasmuch as related quotations are grouped together by their respective categories. All aspects of journalism, for example, are relevant to each other; thus, the section *Journalism* embraces all phases of the news media. Similarly, quotations pertaining to the U.S. President, Congress, etc., are in the section *Government*.

MISCELLANEOUS

(A) Except where otherwise indicated or obviously to the contrary, all universities, organizations and business firms mentioned in this book are in the United States; similarly, references made to "national," "Federal," "this country," "the nation," etc., refer to the United States.

(B) In most cases, organizations whose names end with "of the United States" are Federal government agencies.

SELECTION OF CATEGORIES

The selected categories reflect, in the Editors' opinion, the most widely discussed public-interest subjects, those which readily fall into the over-all sphere of "current events." They represent topics continuously covered by the mass media because of their inherent importance to the changing world scene. Most of the categories are permanent; they appear in each annual edition of *WHAT THEY SAID*. However, because of the transient character of some subjects, there may be categories which appear one year and may not be repeated the next.

SELECTION OF SPEAKERS

The following persons are always considered eligible for inclusion in *WHAT THEY SAID*: top-level officials of all branches of national, state and local governments (both U.S. and foreign), including all United States Senators and Representatives; top-echelon military officers; college and university presidents, chancellors and professors; chairmen and presidents of major corporations; heads of national public-oriented organizations and associations; national and internationally known diplomats; recognized celebrities from the entertainment and literary spheres and the arts generally; sports figures of national stature; commentators on the world scene who are recognized as such and who command the attention of the mass media.

The determination of what and who are "major" and "recognized" must, necessarily, be made by the Editors of *WHAT THEY SAID* based on objective personal judgment.

Also, some persons, while not generally recognized as prominent or newsworthy, may have nevertheless attracted an unusual amount of attention in connection with an important issue or event. These people, too, are considered for inclusion, depending upon the specific circumstance.

SELECTION OF QUOTATIONS

The quotations selected for inclusion in *WHAT THEY SAID* obviously represent a decided minority of the seemingly endless volume of quoted material appearing in the media each year. The process of selecting is scrupulously objective insofar as the partisan views of the Editors are concerned (see *About Fairness*, below). However, it is clear that the Editors must decide which quotations *per se* are suitable for inclusion, and in doing so look for comments that are aptly stated, offer insight into the subject being discussed, or into the speaker, and provide—for today as well as for future reference—a thought which readers will find useful for understanding the issues and the personalities that make up a year on this planet.

ABOUT FAIRNESS

The Editors of *WHAT THEY SAID* understand the necessity of being impartial when compiling a book of this kind. As a result, there has been no bias in the selection of the quotations, the choice of speakers or the manner of editing. Relevance of the statements and the status of the speakers are the exclusive criteria for inclusion, without any regard whatsoever to the personal beliefs and views of the Editors. Furthermore, every effort has been made to include a multiplicity of opinions and ideas from a wide cross-section of speakers on each topic. Nevertheless, should there appear to be, on some controversial issues, a majority of material favoring one point of view over another, it is simply the result of there having been more of those views expressed during the year, reported by the media and objectively considered suitable by the Editors of *WHAT THEY SAID* (see *Selection of Quotations*, above). Also, since persons in politics and government account for a large percentage of the speakers in *WHAT THEY SAID*, there may exist a heavier weight of opinion favoring the philosophy of those in office at the time, whether in the United States Congress, the Administration, or in foreign capitals. This is natural and to be expected and should not be construed as a reflection of agreement or disagreement with that philosophy on the part of the Editors of *WHAT THEY SAID*.

Abbreviations

The following are abbreviations used by the speakers in this volume. Rather than defining them each time they appear in the quotations, this list will facilitate reading and avoid unnecessary repetition.

AAUW:	American Association of University Women
ABC:	American Broadcasting Companies
ACLU:	American Civil Liberties Union
ACT:	Action for Children's Television
AFDC:	Aid to Families With Dependent Children
AFL-CIO:	American Federation of Labor-Congress of Industrial Organizations
AFSC:	American Friends Service Committee
AFSCME:	American Federation of State, County and Municipal Employees
AIDS:	acquired immune deficiency syndrome
AMA:	American Medical Association
ANC:	African National Congress
AT&T:	American Telephone & Telegraph Company
BAC:	British Airways Corporation
CAFE:	corporate average fuel efficiency
CBS:	Columbia Broadcasting System (CBS, Inc.)
CD:	compact disc
CEO:	chief executive officer
CFC:	chlorofluorocarbons
CIA:	Central Intelligence Agency
C.I.S.:	Commonwealth of Independent States
CNN:	Cable News Network
CPA:	certified public accountant
C-SPAN:	Cable-Satellite Public Affairs Network
DNA:	deoxyribonucleic acid
EC:	European Community
EMS:	European Monetary System
EPA:	Environmental Protection Agency
ERA:	earned run average
ERM:	exchange rate mechanism
FBI:	Federal Bureau of Investigation
FCC:	Federal Communications Commission

FDA:	Food and Drug Administration
F.D.R.:	Franklin Delano Roosevelt
FMLN:	Farabundo Marti National Liberation Front
GDP:	gross domestic product
GE:	General Electric Company
GM:	General Motors Corporation
GNP:	gross national product
GOP:	Grand Old Party (Republican Party)
HDTV:	high definition television
HIV:	human immunodeficiency virus (AIDS virus)
HUD:	Department of Housing and Urban Development
IAEA:	International Atomic Energy Agency
IBM:	International Business Machines Corporation
ICAO:	International Civil Aviation Organization
ICBM:	intercontinental ballistic missile
IMF:	International Monetary Fund
INS:	Immigration and Naturalization Service
IRA:	individual retirement arrangement
IRS:	Internal Revenue Service
KGB:	Soviet State Security Committee
KLM:	Royal Dutch Airlines
L.B.J.:	Lyndon Baines Johnson
MBA:	Master of Business Administration
MFN:	most favored nation (trade status)
MGM:	Metro-Goldwyn-Mayer, Inc.
MIA:	missing in action
MIT:	Massachusetts Institute of Technology
MPLA:	Popular Movement for the Liberation of Angola
MTV:	Music Television
NAACP:	National Association for the Advancement of Colored People
NAFTA:	North American Free Trade Agreement
NASA:	National Aeronatics and Space Administration
NATO:	North Atlantic Treaty Organization
NBA:	National Basketball Association
NBC:	National Broadcasting Company
NCAA:	National Collegiate Athletic Association
NEA:	National Endowment for the Arts
NFL:	National Football League
NGO:	non-governmental organization
NHL:	National Hockey League

NIH:	National Institutes of Health
NRA:	National Rifle Association
OAS:	Organization of American States
OAU:	Organization of African Unity
PAC:	political action committee
PBS:	Public Broadcasting Service
PCS:	personal communications services
PLO:	Palestine Liberation Organization
POW:	prisoner of war
PTA:	Parent-Teachers Association
R&D:	research and development
RNC:	Republican National Committee
ROTC:	Reserve Officers' Training Corps
SAC:	Strategic Air Command
SAT:	Scholastic Aptitude Test
SDI:	Strategic Defense Initiative
SEC:	Securities and Exchange Commission
S&L:	savings-and-loan association
SSI:	Supplemental Security Income
TV:	television
UAW:	United Automobile Workers of America
U.K.:	United Kingdom
UN:	United Nations
U.S.:	United States
U.S.A.:	United States of America
USIA:	United States Information Agency
U.S.S.R.:	Union of Soviet Socialist Republics
VCR:	video cassette recorder
WPA:	Works Progress Administration

Party affiliation of United States Senators, Representatives, Governors and state legislators:

       D: Democratic
       I: Independent
       R: Republican

The Quote of the Year

Cynicim is a luxury and is something that people who have real needs can't afford. I can't afford to be cynical because it is hope that keeps the people alive. When your job is gone, and your electricity is turned off, and your loved ones are injured or dead, and your job is gone, and you are down to your irreducible essence, only hope stands between you and collapse. It can't collapse. That's why we have to keep hope alive. It's so fundamental to the human spirit. The very least that leaders can do, when they can't supply the material goods yet, is to sustain imagination and hope.

—JESSE L. JACKSON
Civil-rights leader.
In an interview in May.

PART ONE

National Affairs

The State of the Union Address

Delivered by George Bush, President of the United States, at the Capitol, Washington, January 28, 1992.

Mr. Speaker, Mr. President, distinguished guests and fellow citizens:

Thank you very much for that warm reception. You know, with the big buildup this address has had, I wanted to make sure it would be a big hit, but I couldn't convince Barbara to deliver it for me. I see the Speaker and the Vice President are laughing. They saw what I did in Japan. They're just happy they're sitting behind me.

Great Changes

I mean to speak tonight of big things; of big changes and the promises they hold, and of some big problems and how together we can solve them and move our country forward as the undisputed leader of the age.

We gather tonight at a dramatic and deeply promising time in our history, and in the history of man on Earth.

For in the past 12 months the world has known changes of almost biblical proportions. And even now, months after the failed coup that doomed a failed system, I'm not sure we've absorbed the full impact, the full import of what happened. But Communism died this year.

And even as President, with the most fascinating possible vantage point, there were times when I was so busy managing progress, and leading change, that I didn't always show the joy that was in my heart.

But the biggest thing that has happened in the world in my life—in our lives—is this: By the grace of God, America won the Cold War.

I mean to speak this evening of the changes that can take place in our country now that we can stop making the sacrifices we had to make when we had an avowed enemy that was a superpower. And now we can look homeward even more, and move to set right what needs to be set right.

End of the Cold War

And I will speak of those things. But let me tell you something I've been thinking these past few months. It's a kind of roll call of honor. For the Cold War didn't "end," it was won.

And I think of those who won it, in places like Korea, and Vietnam. And some of them didn't come back. And back then they were heroes, but this year they were victors.

The long roll call—all the G.I. Joes and Janes, all the ones who fought faithfully for freedom, who hit the ground and sucked dust and knew their share of horror.

This may seem frivolous—and I don't mean it so—but it's moving to me how the world saw them.

The world saw not only their special valor but their special style—their rambunctious, optimistic bravery, their do-or-die unity unhampered by class or race or region. What a group we've put forth, for generations now—from the ones who wrote "Kilroy Was Here" on the walls of the German stalags, to those who left signs in the Iraqi desert that said, "I Saw Elvis." What a group of kids we've sent out into the world.

And there's another to be singled out—though it may seem inelegant. And I mean a mass of people called the American taxpayer. No one ever thinks to thank the people who pay a country's bills, or an alliance's bills. But for half a century now the American people have shouldered the burden, and paid taxes that were higher than they would have been to support a defense that was bigger than it would have been if imperial Communism had never existed.

But it did. Doesn't anymore.

And here's a fact I wouldn't mind the world acknowledging: The American taxpayer bore the brunt of the burden, and deserves a hunk of the

23

glory.

And so now, for the first time in 35 years, our strategic bombers stand down. No longer are they on 'round-the-clock alert. Tomorrow our children will go to school and study history and how plants grow. And they won't have, as my children did, air raid drills in which they crawl under their desks and cover their heads in case of nuclear war. My grandchildren don't have to do that, and won't have the bad dreams children had once, in decades past. There are still threats. But the long, drawn-out dread is over.

Desert Storm and U.S. Power

A year ago tonight I spoke to you at a moment of high peril. American forces had just unleashed Operation Desert Storm. And after 40 days in the desert skies, and four days on the ground, the men and women of America's armed forces, and our allies, accomplished the goals that I declared, and that you endorsed: We liberated Kuwait.

And soon after, the Arab world and Israel sat down to talk seriously, and comprehensively, about peace—an historic first. And soon after that, at Christmas, the last American hostages came home. Our policies were vindicated.

Much good can come from the prudent use of power. And much good can come of this: A world once divided into two armed camps now recognizes one sole and preeminent power: the United States of America.

And they regard this with no dread. For the world trusts us with power—and the world is right. They trust us to be fair, and restrained; they trust us to be on the side of decency. They trust us to do what's right.

And I use those words advisedly. A few days after the war began I received a telegram from Joanne Speicher, the wife of the first pilot killed in the Gulf, Lt. Commander Scott Speicher. Even in her grief she wanted me to know that someday, when her children were old enough, she would tell them ". . . that their father went away to war because it was the right thing to do."

And she said it all. It was the right thing to do.

And we did it together. There were honest differences right here in this chamber. But when the war began, you put partisanship aside, and supported our troops.

And this is still a time for pride—but this is no time to boast. For problems face us, and we must stand together once again and solve them—and not let our country down.

Defense Cuts

Two years ago I began planning cuts in military spending that reflected the changes of the new era. But now, this year, with imperial Communism gone, that process can be accelerated.

Tonight I can tell you of dramatic changes in our strategic nuclear force. These actions we are taking on our own—because they are the right thing to do.

After completing 20 planes for which we have begun procurement, we will shut down further production of the B-2 bomber. We will cancel the small ICBM program. We will cease production of new warheads for our sea-based ballistic missiles. We will stop all new production of the Peacekeeper missile. And we will not purchase any more advanced cruise missiles.

This weekend I will meet at Camp David with Boris Yeltsin of the Russian Federation. I have informed President Yeltsin that if the Commonwealth—the former Soviet Union—will eliminate all land-based multiple-warhead ballistic missiles, I will do the following:

We will eliminate all Peacekeeper missiles. We will reduce the number of warheads on Minuteman missiles to one, and reduce the number of warheads on our sea-based missiles by about one-third. And we will convert a substantial portion of our strategic bombers to primarily conventional use.

President Yeltsin's early response has been very positive, and I expect our talks at Camp David to be fruitful.

I want you to know that for half a century, American Presidents have longed to make such decisions and say such words. But even in the midst of celebration, we must keep caution as a friend.

For the world is still a dangerous place. Only the dead have seen the end of conflict. And though yesterday's challenges are behind us, tomorrow's are being born.

The Secretary of Defense recommended these

cuts after consultation with the Joint Chiefs of Staff. And I make them with confidence. But do not misunderstand me:

The reductions I have approved will save us an additional $50-billion over the next five years. By 1997 we will have cut defense by 30 percent since I took office. These cuts are deep, and you must know my resolve: this deep, and no deeper.

To do less would be insensible to progress— but to do more would be ignorant of history.

We must not go back to the days of "the hollow army." We cannot repeat the mistakes made twice in this century, when armistice was followed by recklessness, and defense was purged as if the world were permanently safe.

I remind you this evening that I have asked for your support in funding a program to protect our country from limited nuclear missile attack. We must have this protection because too many people in too many countries have access to nuclear arms. And I urge you again to pass the Strategic Defense Initiative, SDI.

There are those who say that now we can turn away from the world, that we have no special role, no special place.

But we are the United States of America, the leader of the West that has become the leader of the world.

And as long as I am President I will continue to lead in support of freedom everywhere—not out of arrogance, and not out of altruism, but for the safety and security of our children.

This is a fact: Strength in the pursuit of peace is no vice; isolation in the pursuit of security is no virtue.

The Economy

Now to our troubles at home. They are not all economic, but the primary problem is our economy. There are some good signs: Inflation, that thief, is down; and interest rates are down. But unemployment is too high, some industries are in trouble, and growth is not what it should be.

And let me tell you right from the start and right from the heart: I know we're in hard times, but I know something else: This will not stand.

In this chamber, in this chamber, we can bring the same courage and sense of common purpose to the economy that we brought to Desert Storm.

And we can defeat hard times together.

I believe you'll help. One reason is that you're patriots, and you want the best for your country. And I believe that in your hearts you want to put partisanship aside and get the job done—because it's the right thing to do.

The power of America rests in a stirring but simple idea: that people will do great things if only you set them free.

Well, we're going to set the economy free, for if this age of miracles and wonders has taught us anything, it's that if we can change the world, we can change America.

We must encourage investment. We must make it easier for people to invest money and create new products, new industries, and new jobs. And we must clear away the obstacles to growth—high taxes, high regulation, red tape and, yes, wasteful government spending.

None of this will happen with a snap of the fingers—but it will happen. And the test of a plan isn't whether it's called new or dazzling. The American people aren't impressed by gimmicks; they're smarter on this score than all of us in this room. The only test of a plan is: Is it sound, and will it work?

We must have a short-term plan to address our immediate needs and heat up the economy. And then we need a long-term plan to keep the combustion going and to guarantee our place in the world economy.

President's Economic Plan

There are certain things that a president can do without Congress, and I am going to do them.

I have this evening asked major Cabinet departments and Federal agencies to institute a 90-day moratorium on any new Federal regulations that could hinder growth. In those 90 days, major departments and agencies will carry out a top-to-bottom review of all regulations, old and new, to stop the ones that will hurt growth and speed up those that will help growth.

Further, for the untold number of hard-working, responsible American workers and businessmen and women who've been forced to go without needed bank loans: The banking credit crunch must end. I won't neglect my responsibility for sound regulations that serve the public good, but regulatory overkill must be stopped.

And I have instructed our government regulators to stop it.

I have directed Cabinet departments and Federal agencies to speed up pro-growth expenditures as quickly as possible. This should put an extra $10-billion into the economy in the next six months. And our new transportation bill provides more than $150-billion for construction and maintenance projects that are vital to our growth and well-being. And that means jobs building roads, jobs building bridges and jobs building railways.

I have this evening directed the Secretary of the Treasury to change the Federal tax-withholding tables. With this change, millions of Americans from whom the government withholds more than necessary can now choose to have the government withhold less from their paychecks. Something tells me a number of taxpayers may take us up on this one. This initiative could return about $25-billion back into our economy over the next 12 months, money people can use to help pay for clothing, college or to get a new car.

And finally, working with the Federal Reserve, we will continue to support monetary policy that keeps both interest rates and inflation down.

Congress and the Economy

Now, there are the things I can do. And now, members of Congress, let me tell you what you can do for your country. You must pass the other elements of my plan to meet our immediate economic needs.

Everyone knows that investment spurs recovery.

And I am proposing this evening a change in the alternative minimum tax and the creation of a new 15 percent minimum tax and the creation of a new 15 percent investment tax allowance. This will encourage business to accelerate investment and bring people back to work.

Real estate has led our economy out of almost all the tough times we've ever had. Once building starts, carpenters and plumbers work, people buy homes and take out mortgages.

My plan would modify the passive loss rule for active real-estate developers, and it would make it easier for pension plans to purchase real estate.

For those Americans who dream of buying a first home but who can't afford it, my plan would allow first-time home buyers to withdraw savings from [Individual Retirement Accounts] without penalty and provide a $5,000 tax credit for the first purchase of that home.

Capital Gains

And finally, my immediate plan calls on Congress to give crucial help to people who own a home, to everyone who has a business or a farm or a single investment.

This time, at this hour, I cannot take no for an answer. You must cut the capital-gains taxes on the people of our country.

Never has an issue been more demagogued by its opponents. But the demagogues are wrong—they're wrong and they know it. Sixty percent of the people who benefit from lower capital gains have incomes under $50,000. A cut in the capital-gains tax increases jobs and helps just about everybody in the country. And so I'm asking you to cut the capital-gains tax rate to a maximum 15.4 percent.

And I'll tell you, those of you who say, "Oh no, someone who's comfortable may benefit from this." You kind of remind me of the old definition of the Puritan, who couldn't sleep at night worrying that somehow, someone, somewhere, was out having a good time.

The opponents of this measure—and those who've authored various so-called soak-the-rich bills that are floating around this chamber—should be reminded of something: When they aim at the big guy they usually hit the little guy. And maybe it's time that stopped.

This, then, is my short-term plan. Your part, members of Congress, requires enactment of these common-sense proposals that will have a strong effect on the economy—without breaking the budget agreement and without raising tax rates.

While my plan is being passed and kicking in, we've got to care for those in trouble today. I have provided for up to $4.4-billion in my budget to extend Federal unemployment benefits. And I ask for Congressional action right away. And I thank the committee.

And let's be frank. Let's be frank. Let me level

with you.

I know, and you know, that my plan is unveiled in a political season. I know, and you know, that everything I propose will be viewed by some in merely partisan terms. But I ask you to know what is in my heart. My aim is to increase our nation's good. I am doing what I think is right; I am proposing what I know will help.

I pride myself that I am a prudent man and I believe that patience is a virtue, but I understand that politics is, for some, a game—and that sometimes the game is to stop all progress and then decry the lack of improvement.

But let me tell you, let me tell you: Far more important than my political future—and far more important than yours—is the well-being of our country. And members of this chamber are practical people and I know you won't resent some practical advice: When people put their party's fortunes, whatever their party, whatever side of this aisle, before the public good, they court defeat not only for their country but for themselves. And they will certainly deserve it.

And I submit my plan tomorrow. And I am asking you to pass it by March 20. And I ask the American people to let you know they want this action by March 20.

From the day after that, if it must be: the battle is joined.

And you know, when principle is at stake I relish a good fair fight.

Long-Term

And I said my plan has two parts and it does. And it's the second part that is the heart of the matter. For it's not enough to get an immediate burst—we need long-term improvement in our economic position.

We all know that the key to our economic future is to ensure that America continues as an economic leader of the world. We have that in our power.

Here, then, is my long-term plan to guarantee our future.

First, trade: We will work to break down the walls that stop world trade. We will work to open markets everywhere.

And in our major trade negotiations I will continue pushing to eliminate tariffs and subsidies that damage America's farmers and workers. And we'll get more good American jobs within our own hemisphere through the North American Free Trade Agreement and through the Enterprise for the Americas initiative.

But changes are here, and more are coming. The workplace of the future will demand more highly skilled workers than ever—more people who are computer literate, highly educated.

Education

And we must be the world's leader in education. And we must revolutionize America's schools.

My America 2000 education strategy will help us reach that goal. My plan will give parents more choice, give teachers more flexibility, and help communities create New American Schools.

Thirty states across the nation have established America 2000 programs. Hundreds of cities and towns have joined in.

And now Congress must join this great movement: Pass my proposals for New American Schools.

That was my second long-term proposal. And here's my third:

We must make common-sense investments that will help us compete, long-term, in the marketplace.

We must encourage research and development. And my plan is to make the R&D tax credit permanent, and this year alone—for people who will explore the promise of emerging technologies.

Crime

And fourth, we must do something about crime and drugs.

And it is time for a major, renewed investment in fighting violent street crime. It saps our strength and hurts our faith in society, and in our future together.

Surely a tired woman on her way to work at 6 in the morning on a subway deserves the right to get there safely. Surely it's true that everyone who changes his or her life because of crime—from those afraid to go out at night to those afraid to walk in the parks they pay for—surely these people have been denied a basic civil right.

It is time to restore it. Congress, pass my comprehensive crime bill. It is tough on criminals and supportive of police—and it has been languishing in these hallowed halls for years now.

Pass it. Help your country.

And fifth, I ask you tonight to fund our HOPE housing proposal—and to pass my Enterprise Zone legislation which will get businesses into the inner city. We must empower the poor with the pride that comes from owning a home, getting a job, becoming a part of things.

My plan would encourage real-estate construction by extending tax incentives for mortgage revenue bonds and low-income housing.

And I ask tonight for record expenditures for the program that helps children born into want move into excellence: Head Start.

Health Care

Step six—we must reform our health-care system. For this too bears on whether or not we can compete in the world.

American health costs have been exploding. This year America will spend over $800-billion on health. And that's expected to grow to $1.6-trillion by the end of the decade. We simply cannot afford this.

The cost of health care shows up not only in your family budget, but in the price of everything we buy and everything we sell. When health coverage for a fellow on an assembly line costs thousands of dollars, the cost goes into the products he makes—and you pay the bill.

We must make a choice.

Now some pretend we can have it both ways. They call it "play or pay"—but that expensive approach is unstable. It will mean higher taxes, fewer jobs and, eventually, a system under complete government control.

Really, there are only two options: We can move toward a nationalized system—which will restrict patient choice in picking a doctor and force the government to ration services arbitrarily. And what we'll get is patients in long lines, indifferent service, and a huge new tax burden.

Or we can reform our own private health-care system—which still gives us, for all its flaws, the

best quality health care in the world.

Well, let's build on our strengths.

My plan provides insurance security for all Americans—while preserving and increasing the idea of choice. We make basic health insurance affordable for all low-income people not now covered. And we do it by providing a health-insurance tax credit of up to $3,750 for each low-income family. And the middle class gets new help too. And, by reforming the health-insurance market, my plan assures that Americans will have access to basic health insurance even if they change jobs or develop serious health problems.

We must bring costs under control, preserve quality, preserve choice, and reduce the people's nagging daily worry about health insurance. My plan, the details of which I will announce very shortly, does just that.

The Budget and the Deficit

Seventh, we must get the Federal deficit under control.

We now have in law enforceable spending caps and a requirement that we pay for the programs we create.

There are those in Congress who would ease that discipline now. But I cannot let them do it—and I won't.

My plan would freeze all domestic discretionary budget authority—which means. "No more next year than this year." I will not tamper with Social Security, but I will, would, put real caps on the growth of uncontrolled spending. And I would also freeze Federal domestic government employment.

And with the help of Congress, my plan will get rid of 246 programs that don't deserve federal funding. Some of them have noble titles, but none of them are indispensable. We can get rid of each and every one of them.

You know, it's time we rediscovered a "home truth" the American people have never forgotten: Their government is too big and spends too much.

And I call upon Congress to adopt a measure that will help put an end to the annual ritual of filling the budget with pork-barrel appropriations. Every year the press has a field day making fun of outrageous examples—Lawrence Welk museums, research grants for Belgian endive.

We all know these things get into the budget. And maybe you need someone to help you say no. I know how to say it. And you know what I need to make it stick. Give me the same thing 43 Governors have: The line-item veto. And let me help you control spending.

We must put an end to unfinanced Federal government mandates. These are the requirements Congress puts on our cities, counties and states—without supplying money. And if Congress passed a mandate, it should be forced to pay for it, and to balance the cost with savings elsewhere. After all, a mandate just increases someone else's burden—and that means higher taxes at the state and local level.

Step Eight: Congress should enact the bold reform proposals that are still awaiting Congressional action—bank reform, civil-justice reform, tort reform, and my national energy strategy.

The Family

And finally: We must strengthen the family—because it is the family that has the greatest bearing on the future. When Barbara holds an AIDS baby in her arms, and reads to children, she is saying to every person in this country, "Family matters."

And I'm announcing tonight a new Commission on America's Urban Families. I've asked Missouri's Gov. John Ashcroft to be chair, former Dallas Mayor Annette Strauss to be co-chair. You know, I had Mayors, leading Mayors from the League of Cities in the other day, and they told me something striking. And they said that everyone of them, Republicans and Democrats, agreed on one thing: That the major cause of the problems of the cities is the dissolution of the family.

And they asked for this commission, and they were right to ask, because it's time to determine what we can do to keep families together, strong and sound.

There's one thing we can do right away: ease the burden of rearing a child. I ask you tonight to raise the personal exemption by $500 per child for every family. For a family with four kids, that's an increase of $2,000. And this is a good start, in the right direction, and it's what we can afford.

It's time to allow families to deduct the interest they pay on student loans. I am asking you to do just that. And I'm asking you to allow people to use money from their IRA's to pay medical and educational expenses—all without penalties.

Welfare System

And I'm asking for more. Ask American parents what they dislike about how things are in our country, and chances are good that pretty soon they'll get to welfare.

Americans are the most generous people on earth. But we have to go back to the insight of Franklin Roosevelt who, when he spoke of what became the welfare program, warned that it must not become "a narcotic" and a "subtle destroyer" of the spirit.

Welfare was never meant to be a lifestyle; it was never meant to be a habit; it was never supposed to be passed from generation to generation like a legacy.

It's time to replace the assumptions of the welfare state, and help reform the welfare system.

States throughout the country are beginning to operate with new assumptions: That when able-bodied people receive government assistance, they have responsibilities to the taxpayer. A responsibility to get their lives in order, a responsibility to hold their families together and refrain from having children out of wedlock, and a responsibility to obey the law.

We are going to help this movement. Often, state reform requires waiving certain Federal regulations. I will act to make that process easier and quicker for every state that asked our help.

And I want to add, as we make these changes, as we work together to improve the system, that our intention isn't scapegoating or finger-pointing. If you read the papers or watch TV you know there's been a rise these days in a certain kind of bitterness, racist comments, antisemitism, an increased sense of division.

Really, this is not us. This is not who we are. And this is not acceptable.

And so you have my plan for America. I am asking for big things—but I believe in my heart you will do what's right.

Need for Action

You know, it's kind of an American tradition to show a certain skepticism toward our democratic institutions. I myself have sometimes thought the aging process could be delayed if it had to make its way through Congress.

You will deliberate, and you will discuss, and that is fine.

But, my friends: the people cannot wait. They need help now.

There is a mood among us. People are worried; there has been talk of decline. Someone even said our workers are lazy and uninspired.

And I thought, really. Go tell Neil Armstrong standing on the moon. Tell the men and women who put him there. Tell the American farmer who feeds his country and the world. Tell the men and women of Desert Storm.

Moods come and go, but greatness endures. Ours does.

And maybe for a moment it's good to remember what, in the dailyness of our lives, we forget:

We are still and ever the freest nation on Earth; the kindest nation on Earth; the strongest nation on Earth.

And we have always risen to the occasion.

And we are going to lift this nation out of hard times inch-by-inch and day-by-day, and those who would stop us had better step aside. Because I look at hard times and I make this vow: This will not stand.

And so we move on, together, a rising nation, the once and future miracle that is still, this night, the hope of the world.

Thank you. God bless you. And God bless our beloved country.

The American Scene

Patrick J. Buchanan
Political commentator;
Candidate for the 1992
Republican Presidential nomination

1

[Comparing America's resources with those of its competitors]: Those little dinky countries can't beat us. You know, you take Germany, East and West Germany, put them together, that's about the size of Oregon and Washington. It's a little dinky country. You take Japan. It's a pile of rocks over there. You could put the whole thing in California.

Campaigning, Gulfport, Miss.,
March 7/
Los Angeles Times, 3-9:(A)19.

2

I'll tell you how you make America Number 1: You get away from this insane, idiotic notion of advancing people on the basis of color, ethnicity, creed or where their grandparents came from and you advance them on the basis of excellence, merit, ability and character. When you do that, you come out with the best.

Interview/
USA Today, 4-16:(A)13.

3

The United States is now undergoing the greatest invasion in history, a mass immigration of millions of illegal aliens yearly from Mexico. The invasion is eroding our tax base, swamping social services and undermining the social cohesion of the Republic. Our government seems paralyzed.

The Christian Science Monitor,
5-15:2.

George Bush
President of the United States

4

Don't listen to all those gloomsayers around this country saying that we are a nation in decline. We are, once again, the respected leader of the entire world. We are going to make the life of every single American better.

Before American Farm Bureau Federation,
Kansas City, Mo., Jan. 13/
Los Angeles Times, 1-14:(A)12.

Robert C. Byrd
United States Senator,
D-West Virginia

5

[Saying proficiency in English should be considered when deciding who should be allowed to immigrate to the U.S.]: I pick up the telephone and call the local garage. I can't understand the person on the other side of the line. I'm not sure he can understand me. They're all over the place, and they don't speak English. Do we want more of this? . . . [With high unemployment in the U.S.,] what are we doing, opening up another door here for more immigrants who can't speak English?

Before the Senate,
Washington, D.C./
The Washington Post,
6-26:(A)4.

Herb Caen
Columnist,
"San Francisco Chronicle"

6

[On San Francisco in the 1940s and '50s]: I owned this town then . . . You read Oscar Wilde and Kipling and Twain and Jack London—all those writers were fascinated by this town. It had some special quality. I don't find it now. There was a bustling waterfront, a party atmosphere, prostitutes and crooked cops and politicians.

Interview,
San Francisco, Calif./
USA Today, 4-9:(B)5.

WHAT THEY SAID IN 1992

Bill Clinton
Governor of Arkansas (D);
Candidate for the 1992
Democratic Presidential nomination

1

When we [as a nation] have been divided, distracted, when we have our head looking over our shoulder at yesterday instead of the future, we have been in deep trouble. But when we have been together as one nation . . . we have been unstoppable.

Campaigning in New Hampshire,
Feb. 13/
The Washington Post, 2-14:(A)1.

2

The basic institutions that held our country together—the family, the school, the church, the neighborhood—all have been savagely weakened in a rising tide of drugs and violence. Families break down, and in so many places and in so many ways, gangs have moved in to fill the void created when people have nothing else to which they can belong, no other unit in which they are the most important person in the world. What are we to do about this, my fellow Americans? I could give you the best economic policy this country has ever seen, and to be sure, if elected President, that is exactly what I will try to do. But how can we revitalize America when one 8-year-old steals his brother's gun in Chicago and takes it to school and shoots another 8-year-old?

Speech, Birmingham, Ala.,
April 30/
Los Angeles Times, 5-26:(A)5.

Bill Clinton
Governor of Arkansas (D);
1992 Democratic
Presidential nominee

3

Underneath all the incredible diversity of America, there is a core of common caring and concern; we're a lot more alike than I think we think we are. That's the real tragedy of all these racial problems. The American people are so much more alike at a human level than they think they are, from how much they love their kids to

how badly they want to be safe, how concerned they are about their jobs and their futures. I'd like to be remembered for making people really believe that we're all better off when we define our lives in terms of our common purposes, for really helping to re-establish a sense of community and bridging the troubled water of race— particularly race—and all the other things dividing this country. I think life is lonelier than it ought to be in America because we are so isolated from one another.

Interview/
U.S. News and World Report,
7-20:36.

Albert Gore, Jr.
United States Senator,
D-Tennessee;
1992 Democratic
Vice-Presidential nominee

4

The deeper crisis in this country is a crisis of meaning. Many people feel that their lives no longer have a sense of purpose. And part of the reason for that is this culture of distraction that we have which constantly falls in 15- and 30-second bursts of commercial activity toward this, that or the other extraneous matter. Many people come home at night and just flip on the television, and that's it.

Interview/Time, 10-19:36.

John E. Jacob
President,
National Urban League

5

Many of us [blacks] grew up in devout, proud black families whose powerful values helped us survive a Jim Crow society. We were nurtured on the biblical values that guided our behavior and molded us into responsible adults . . . Traditional American values—getting an education, holding a job and raising a family—are in danger. If the government is really concerned about family values, it has to create the political and economic environment to allow those values to flourish.

At National Urban League convention,
San Diego, Calif., July 26/
Los Angeles Times, 7-27:(A)3,20.

Sharon Pratt Kelly
Mayor of Washington, D.C.

1

[The U.S. has gotten] away from our basic values in the last decade. We became a self-serving, hedonistic country. We basically lost any commitment to saving, which was part of the American ethic when I was growing up. We're a mortgaged country now. Corporations are mortgaged, the Federal government's mortgaged, the local government's mortgaged. We used to be a country that really took pride in, for example, research and development. [Now] everything is what will the next quarterly report look like. We used to be a country that took pride in its public education system. We talk it. We aren't willing to invest in it. We used to be a country that took pride in our work product. Work ethic. That's a missing ingredient in any aspect of America now. We see the neglect reflected in the infrastructure of our communities, be it roads, bridges, buildings. We, above all, see it in the next generation. The very neglected generation. The ones nurtured with the absence of values, the American values. I think that's the most troubling dynamic any of us are up against as we try to turn the corner for the next century.

Interview, Washington, D.C./
Los Angeles Times, 6-14:(M)3.

Madeleine M. Kunin
Visiting scholar,
Radcliffe College;
Former Governor
of Vermont (D)

2

The anxiety facing this country is as great as your childhood anxieties over nuclear war. Only this time, the enemy is not external, it is internal, right here, within ourselves. And the weapons of destruction are not identifiable, they are elusive, because they have to do with such things as an erosion of morality, justice, compassion and generosity of spirit. You . . . have no choice, whether or not to lead lives that can make a difference. That is a luxury given to prior generations.

At Lesley College commencement/
The Christian Science Monitor, 6-22:11.

Lee Kuan Yew
Former Prime Minister
of Singapore

3

Americans emphasize the rights of the individual. Take drug testing. Test an American either through his urine or his blood to see whether he's consumed drugs, and you'd have a suit for battery and assault and a huge claim for damages. Indeed, an American case went up to the Supreme Court where they held that as the initial arrest was unlawful, the fact that he subsequently was found to have drugs did not support the conviction. That's an American view of how things should be—the primacy and privacy of the individual. But nobody in Singapore complains that we have laws which enable our police to require anybody, without giving any reasons, to take your urine sample for testing. If the sample is proved positive, then you undergo treatment. That's the law, and it's kept our drug problem under control. But it's completely unthinkable in America. What is one society's good is another society's bugbear.

Interview, Singapore/
Los Angeles Times, 5-19:(H)15.

Joseph E. Lowery
President, Southern Christian
Leadership Conference

4

It is not our economy we need to be worried about. What's imperiled today in America is her soul. We can deal with the economy. If we lose our souls, what, then, is there for us? There is no sanctuary for the soul from the sorrow of the society in which we live.

Sermon at Cascade United
Methodist Church,
Atlanta, Ga., June 14/
The Washington Post, 6-15:(A)8.

Edward N. Luttwak
Foreign-policy specialist,
Center for Strategic and
International Studies,
Georgetown University

5

Our political community is unique in the world. A voluntary association based exclu-

WHAT THEY SAID IN 1992

sively on abstract ideas and principles, such as liberty, equal opportunity, separation of church and state . . . [It] continually wavers between furious internal struggles about "values" and the unifying presence of an [external] enemy.

World Press Review,
February:40.

Robert H. Michel
United States Representative,
R-Illinois

1

We need radical change—not change for the sake of change but change for the sake of the people and our country. The world itself is in a time of great and historic transition. Old ways of doing things are dying out, and new ways are waiting to be born. From education to the economy, from health care to trade, we stand between two ages. And what the country needs at a critical time like this is a government that will make democracy work.

At Capitol Hill Club
Headliner Breakfast,
Washington, D.C., May 21/
The Washington Post, 5-22:(A)25.

Kiichi Miyazawa
Prime Minister of Japan

2

For various reasons, U.S. society, and I must say I believe the U.S. society is a great society, but there are homeless people, there is a problem with AIDS, and so on, and for various reasons education is not as high as in the past. And U.S. industries are not as competitive [as] in the past for various reasons. Americans are pointing to these problems. And since Americans themselves are aware of these problems, I am convinced they will overcome these problems.

News conference,
Tokyo, Japan, Jan. 9/
The New York Times,
1-10:(A)4.

David Murphy
Architect, Nebraska State
Historic Preservation Office

3

[On the abandoned farmsteads across the U.S.]: They're skeletons. They symbolize a time when everything was used and nothing wasted. They were passed down through generations. There is a sense in them of the value of the earth and land as an inheritance.

The New York Times, 4-2:(A)1.

Colin L. Powell
General, United States Army;
Chairman, Joint Chiefs of Staff

4

We must remember that America is a family. There may be differences and disputes in our family, but we must not allow [it] to be broken into warring factions . . . We must all work together to pull our people, to pull all Americans, out of the violence, out of the dark and soul-damning world of drugs, out of the turmoil of the inner cities. As we climbed on the backs of others, so must we allow our backs to be used for others to go even higher than we have.

At Fisk University commencement/
The Christian Science Monitor,
6-22:10.

Marilyn Quayle
Wife of Vice President
of the United States
Dan Quayle

5

I came of age in a time of turbulent social change. Some of it was good, such as civil rights; much of it was questionable. But remember, not everyone joined the counter-culture. Not everyone demonstrated, dropped out, took drugs, joined in the sexual revolution or dodged the draft. Not everyone concluded that American society was so bad that it had to be radically remade by social revolution. Not everyone believed that the family was so oppressive that women could only thrive apart from it. The majority of my generation lived by the credo our parents taught us: We believed in God; in hard

(MARILYN QUAYLE)

work and personal discipline; in our nation's essential goodness; and in the opportunity it promised those willing to work for it. And so most of us went to school, to church and to work. We married and started families. We had a stake in the future, and though we knew some changes needed to be made, we did not believe in destroying America to save it.

At Republican National Convention,
Houston, Texas, Aug. 19/
The Washington Post, 8-20:(A)34.

Richard Scher
Professor of political science,
University of Florida

1

[On Florida]: This is the ultimate post-World War II state. It didn't really exist until after 1945. It was a small, sleepy southern state. Now we're—what?—the fifth largest in the country. It all happened rather suddenly . . . Florida is like an overgrown 13-year-old. Awkward and self-conscious and emotional.

The Washington Post, 3-6:(A)14.

Paul E. Tsongas
Candidate for the 1992
Democratic Presidential nomination;
Former United States Senator,
D-Massachusetts

2

Ultimately, a society is only as strong as its culture. I want to start a discussion about what is

the value system that bonds us. It's time to heal and, beyond that, it's time to have a discussion of what is important. A society that does not bond, it will not survive. So what we have to do, in my judgment, is create an environment where we're all part of one team. We're talking . . . I was born Greek so I have a sense of myself. What we have to do is create a situation where a child born in this country, whatever race, whatever ethnic group, has the sense that being an American gives me the same strength. Look at Jews in America. With all the discrimination there is a bondedness, a sense of identity that I think is an enormous advantage.

Interview/
USA Today, 2-4:(A)9.

Lowell P. Weicker
Governor of Connecticut (D)

3

We [the U.S.] don't gain our strength from what we achieve worldwide; we get it from the way we build ourselves up as to the best educated, best housed, best in terms of health care. That's the strength of the nation. And then if called upon to confront a crisis, we're in a position to do so. Right now we've got a big name and a big reputation on what we've done in the outside world. But too many people have been left in the gutter, and the U.S. can't survive that way.

Interview, Hartford, Conn./
Time, 4-13:17.

Civil Rights • Women's Rights

Robert Blauner
Sociologist,
University of California, Berkeley

1

Whites and blacks have developed two different languages of race, and central to the differences of the language are different definitions of racism. In these two different languages of race, the black language of race sees race and racism as absolutely central to American culture and the way society is organized, whereas whites . . . don't see racism as central.

The Washington Post, 6-8:(A)7.

Bill Bradley
Unites States Senator,
D-New Jersey

2

Even though our American future depends on finding common ground, many white Americans resist relinquishing the sense of entitlement skin color has given them throughout our national history. They lack an understanding of the emerging dynamics of "one world," even in the United States, because to them non-whites always have been "the other." On top of that, people of different races often don't listen to each other on the subject of race. It's as if we're all experts, locked into our narrow views and preferring to be wrong than risk changing those views. Black Americans ask of Asian Americans, "What's the problem? You're doing well economically." Black Americans believe that Latinos often fail to find common ground with their historic struggle, and some Latino Americans agree, questioning whether the black civil-rights model is the only path to progress. White Americans continue to harbor absurd stereotypes of all people of color. Black Americans take white criticism of individual acts as an attempt to stigmatize all black Americans. We seem more interested in defending our racial territory than recognizing that we could be enriched by another race's perspective.

Speech, March 26/
The Washington Post, 3-30:(A)15.

Patrick J. Buchanan
Political commentator;
Candidate for the
1992 Republican
Presidential nomination

3

[Criticizing President Bush]: We've had enough of a President who caves in . . . on [racial] quotas. Quotas of any kind are wrong. You don't change the invidious nature of quotas simply by reversing the color of the skin of the beneficiaries. And if I am elected, all forms of reverse discrimination in the Federal government will be eliminated.

Campaigning, Feb. 21/
Los Angeles Times, 2-22:(A)18.

4

How would I unite the American people? I would do away with this idiotic thing called group rights [affirmative-action programs] and get back to rights that inhere to individuals. You've got to get back to judging people not by race and color but by consideration of excellence and ability.

At Whittier (Calif.) College,
May 13/
Los Angeles Times, 5-14:(A)11.

George Bush
President of the United States

5

[Arguing against abortion]: The most compelling legacy of this nation is Jefferson's concept [in the Declaration of Independence] that all are created equal. It doesn't say "born" equal. He says "created." From the moment the miracle of life occurs, human beings must cherish that life, must hold it in awe, must preserve, protect and defend it.

Telephone speech
to anti-abortion advocates,
Washington, D.C., Jan. 22/
The New York Times,
1-23:(A)1.

(GEORGE BUSH)

1

[Saying he is not wavering on his anti-abortion stance]: No matter the political price—and they tell me in this [election] year that it's enormous—I am going to do what I think is right. I am going to stand on my conscience and let my conscience be my guide when it comes to matters of life . . . The President should try to set a moral tone for this country. And if you're looking to restore America's moral fiber, why buy synthetic [his Presidential opponent Bill Clinton] when you can get real cotton? . . . In some places, a 13-year-old girl cannot get her ears pierced without parental permission . . . But some believe that the same girl should be able to get an abortion without parental consent. I think most Americans believe this idea is crazy.

Before Knights of Columbus,
New York, N.Y.,
Aug. 5/USA Today, 8-6:(A)4.

2

[Saying he would stand by his granddaughter if she became pregnant and wanted an abortion, an act he personally opposes]: If my granddaughter said, "I've done something terrible, I've robbed, I've stolen something," I'd stand by her. I think that's what the Vice President [Dan Quayle] was saying [when he was asked the same question about his own daughter. It] didn't mean he condoned the act [of abortion]. But he said he'd stand by his child. Of course I'd do that. My granddaughter, my son, my daughter, whoever it is. We've done that all our life as a family . . . Would I support my child? I'd put my arm around her and say, if she was trying to make that decision, encourage her to not do that, but of course I'd stand by my child. I'd love her and help her, lift her up, wipe the tears away, and we'd get back in the game . . . I'd like to be able to influence [her] for the [anti-abortion] belief I have. You see, I'm offended by 1.5 million abortions. I'm offended by that lack of respect for life . . . But your question was if she went ahead and did it, what would I do? . . . I'd . . . love her.

Broadcast interview/
"Dateline NBC,"
NBC-TV, 8-11.

3

[On suggestions that he does not have enough women in key positions in his Administration]: You don't see [State Department spokesman] Margaret Tutwiler sitting in there with me today? . . . I happen to think she's a key person . . . I think our Cabinet members are key people. I think the woman that works with me, Rose Zamaria, is about as tough as a boot out there and can make some discipline and protects the taxpayer. Look at our Cabinet—you talk about somebody strong. Look at [U.S. Trade Representative] Carla Hills. Look at [Labor Secretary] Lynn Martin, who's fighting against this "glass ceiling" [that allegedly keeps women out of top spots in industry and government] and doing a first-class job on it. Look at our Surgeon General, Dr. [Antonia] Novello. You can look all around and you'll see first-class strong women . . . We've got a very good record appointing women to high positions and positions of trust, and I'm not defensive at all about it. What we got to do is keep working—as the Labor Department is doing a first-class job on—to break down discrimination, to break down the glass ceiling, and I'm not apologetic at all about our record with women.

At Presidential candidates' debate,
East Lansing, Mich., Oct. 19/
The New York Times,
10-20:(A)14.

Clarence Carter
Director of
African-American affairs,
Republican National Committee

4

Black Americans are looking for an alternative solution to their problems—teenage pregnancy, the fact that more black men are in jail than in college, poor economic performance . . . Blacks are saying that whatever we've been doing in not working. We want to try something else. What the Republican Party has not done is present itself as that alternative. We have an unprecedented opportunity to do that now.

The Christian Science Monitor,
10-6:7.

WHAT THEY SAID IN 1992

Jimmy Carter
Former President of the United States

1

I think [it's] a mistake that is made by many news reporters to equate the African-American community with [civil-rights leader] Jesse Jackson. Jesse Jackson is a powerful spokesman who's attractive and who puts himself forward, and he's a master at projecting himself as the primary spokesperson for the black community. That's not accurate . . . I think that most Americans who happen to be black look at the candidates [in an election] and say "which one will be best for me and my children," and not listen to leaders, whether it's the Mayor of a great city or a member of Congress or Jesse Jackson to tell them how to vote.

Broadcast interview/
"MacNeil-Lehrer News Hour,"
PBS-TV, 7-14.

Bill Clinton
Governor of Arkansas (D);
Candidate for the 1992
Democratic Presidential nomination

2

[On the recent Supreme Court decision upholding the *Roe v. Wade* abortion-rights ruling, with certain restrictions]: You have four judges plainly committed to repeal *Roe v. Wade,* three others nibbling around the edges and a brave Justice [Harry] Blackmun saying he doesn't know how much longer he can hang on. This is one of the things this Presidential election is about, and I hope the American people will say in clear, unambiguous terms we do not want to go back [to the days when abortion was illegal].

News conference, Little Rock, Ark.,
June 29/
Los Angeles Times, 6-30:(A)10.

Bill Clinton
Governor of Arkansas (D);
1992 Democratic
Presidential nominee

3

Hear me now: I am not pro-abortion. I am pro-choice. I believe this difficult and painful deci-

sion should be left to the women of America. I do not want to go back to the time when we made criminals out of women and their doctors.

Accepting the Presidential
nomination at Democratic
National Convention,
New York, N.Y.,
July 16/
The New York Times, 7-17:(A)13.

4

The National Women's Political Caucus gave me an award, one of their good-guy awards, for my involvement of women in high levels of government. And I've appointed more minorities to positions of high level in government than all the Governors in the history of my state combined before me. So that's what I'll do as President. I don't think we've got a person to waste, and I think I owe the American people a White House staff, a Cabinet and appointments that look like America but that meet high standards of excellence, and that's what I'll do.

At Presidential candidates' debate,
East Lansing, Mich., Oct. 19/
The New York Times, 10-20:(A)14.

Hillary Clinton
Wife of Arkansas Governor
and 1992 Democratic
Presidential candidate
Bill Clinton

5

[On her being a lawyer]: I suppose I could have stayed home, baked cookies and had teas, but what I decided was to fulfill my profession, which I entered before my husband was in public office . . . You know, the work that I've done as a professional, as a public advocate, has been aimed in part to assure that women can make the choices that they should make—whether it's full-time career, full-time motherhood, some combination, depending upon what stage of life they are at—and I think that is still difficult for people to understand right now, that it is a generational thing.

To reporters, Chicago, Ill.,
March 16/
The Washington Post, 3-17:(A)6.

(HILLARY CLINTON)

1

As women today, you face tough choices. You know the rules are basically as follows: If you don't get married, you're abnormal. If you get married but don't have children, you're a selfish yuppie. If you get married and have children, but work outside the home, you're a bad mother. If you get married and have children, but stay home, you've wasted your education. And if you don't get married, but have children and work outside the home as a fictional newscaster, then you're in trouble with the Vice President [Dan Quayle, who criticized the out-of-wedlock pregnancy of fictional TV character Murphy Brown].

At Wellesley (Mass.) College commencement/ The Christian Science Monitor, 6-22:11.

Elizabeth Fox-Genovese
Professor of the humanities, Emory University; Director, Institute for Women's Studies

2

I do not like the argument for abortion on the grounds of an absolute right. I'm very uncomfortable with it and I think some American women are as well. Some American women who favor choice aren't entirely clear about or comfortable with the argument for the reason that at a certain point a fetus becomes a potentially viable life—it begins to look like a socially meaningful one. I am not arguing that it does at the moment of conception. But if you don't moderate your argument for abortion to take account of the claims of life, you put the terminally ill and the handicapped and even the elderly at risk. Individual right is closely related to an argument for abortion for personal convenience.

Interview/Humanities, Jan.-Feb. 5.

Wanda Franz
President, National Right to Life Committee

3

We [anti-abortionists] believe that we have always had the majority of Americans. We believe that the polls continue to support that. Americans do not approve of abortion on demand for nine months, abortion being used for purposes of birth control, abortion being advocated for young children behind the back of their parents. These are the common practices in this country today and are part of the reason why abortion is such an insidious social problem.

Interview/USA Today, 1-7:(A)7.

Betty Friedan
Women's-rights advocate

4

The media and even, to some degree, leaders of women's organizations are thinking of the women's movement as it looked 15 years ago. They don't understand that the women's movement is an absolute part of society now. It is in the consciousness, it is taken for granted. It is part of the way women look at themselves, and women are looked at . . . There are some die-hard male chauvinist pigs and there are some Neanderthal women who are threatened by equality—but the great majority, polls say 65 per cent to 75 per cent of women in America, of all ages, absolutely identify with the complete agenda of the women's movement: equal opportunity for jobs, education, professional training, the right to control your own body—your own reproductive process, freedom of choice [in abortion], child care—the whole agenda.

Interview, Marina del Rey, Calif./ Los Angeles Times, 4-26:(M)3.

Henry Louis Gates, Jr.
Chairman, department of Afro-American studies, Harvard University

5

I see the racial divisions [in the U.S.] as metaphors for deeper economic differences unlike we have seen in this country before. Look at the black community; simultaneously we have the largest black middle class that we have ever had along with the largest black underclass we've ever had. None of [this year's Presidential] candidates has given a sufficient explanation as to why this is the case. There's been a lot of

WHAT THEY SAID IN 1992

jibberish about racism, but no systematic analysis of what caused this problem, and no analysis leading to a systematic solution.

Interview, Cambridge, Mass./
The Christian Science Monitor, 4-10:11.

William H. Gray III
President,
United Negro College Fund;
Former United States Representative,
D-Pennsylvania

1

There is compelling evidence that in the years just ahead, the fulfillment of the aspirations of black and other minority Americans will be fundamental to the continued success of the American dream itself.

At Fairleigh Dickinson University
commencement,
May 17/
The New York Times, 5-18:(C)11.

James D. Griffin
Mayor of Buffalo, N.Y.

2

[On his anti-abortion stance]: We have three people running for President proclaiming pro-choice. You got [Bill] Clinton and [Jerry] Brown in the march in Washington, D.C., for pro-choice. You've got [industrialist Ross] Perot for pro-choice. You've got the wife of the head of CNN [actress Jane Fonda] who is going around yelling and screaming about pro-choice and staying out of her womb and all this other stuff. [CNN head] Ted Turner, he's probably pro-choice; 80 per cent of the media is pro-choice, as far as I'm concerned. So why not the Mayor of Buffalo being pro-life? . . . Just think what we're missing as a society by those kids [terminated by abortion] not living. We might be missing one of the greatest scientists that could have lived, one of the greatest musicians that could have lived, one of the greatest athletes that ever came around. We have a "throwaway society," and that's a problem that's going to haunt us in years to come.

Interview, Buffalo, N.Y./
Los Angeles Times, 4-29:(A)5.

Lee H. Hamilton
United States Representative,
D-Indiana

3

[The abortion issue] is tearing this country apart. My record on abortion, I think, is exactly where most Americans are. I must concede to you I have some ambivalence about it. I don't want to ban abortions, but neither do I want to encourage them. I don't want to criminalize them. I want to see government not play a major role with regard to abortion, either. I don't want it to ban the abortion and I don't want to encourage it through the providing of funds.

Broadcast interview/
"Meet the Press," NBC-TV, 7-5.

Bernadine P. Healy
Director, National Institutes
of Health of the United States

4

Often, when women get into leadership positions, they're embarrassed or shy or unwilling or afraid to take on women's issues because they don't want to be seen only as a leader of women . . . I view myself in my role as responsible for more than women's issues—but I also will not shy away from coming out on women's issues, because if I don't, how can I expect a man to?

Los Angeles Times, 4-14:(E)2.

Spencer Holland
Director,
Center for Educating
African-American Males

5

I say to our [black] children all the time that if it hadn't been for white citizens of good standing, slavery would not have ended. If it hadn't been for white citizens of good standing, the civil-rights movement wouldn't have taken hold the way it did. So white people should let their children know that white people who do things like [police brutality against blacks] are wrong, just like black people in the ghetto who sell drugs are wrong.

At forum sponsored by "Newsweek" magazine/
Newsweek, 5-11:44.

Benjamin L. Hooks
Executive director,
National Association
for the Advancement of Colored People

1

There was one time when I was bitter about the criticism [of the NAACP], very bitter, until I looked at the critics . . . I feel sorry for them. They deserve my sympathy, empathy, compassion, education and training. We shall continue to be as relevant as tomorrow morning's news, as nutritious as a good breakfast and as sure as the rising of the morning sun.

News conference, Feb. 19/
The Washington Post, 2-20:(A)8.

2

I've been through it. I've seen it all. I've spent about half my life in segregation, half my life in integration. And believe me, integration is better . . . The NAACP has helped every black in the nation, every one, use the water fountain, get a job, use the hotel, treat us as human beings. We have a varied membership, from people with Ph.D.s to people who dropped out in third grade. There are 500,000 of them. They're devoted and their love of liberty is the same . . . You've got to believe that tomorrow somehow can be and will be better than today.

Interview, Baltimore, Md./
The Christian Science Monitor,
2-24:9.

Roy Innis
Chairman,
Congress of Racial Equality

3

I'm convinced that the romance America had with overt racism is over. The justice system has protected and shielded us from the worst effects of prejudice and hate in the '50s and '60s. The judiciary has been the bulwark of black freedom in this country. Black America, and the rest of America, needs to hear from honest black leaders who will not attempt to alibi for the pillagers [blacks who rioted in Los Angeles after a not-guilty verdict in the trial of police officers in the Rodney King brutality case]. There should be a legitimate protest at the way the trial was conducted, a protest to insist that the Federal government move quickly and with great determination. But the only thing those riots are about is criminals acting like criminals.

At forum sponsored by
"Newsweek" magazine/
Newsweek, 5-11:48.

Patricia Ireland
President,
National Organization for Women

4

The reality is that we're [women] tired of begging men in power for our rights. If the courts won't protect them, then Congress has got to enact laws to protect a woman's rights. And if Congress doesn't, then we're going to elect pro-choice [on abortion] women to Congress.

Interview, April 5/
The New York Times, 4-6:(A)11.

Jesse L. Jackson
Civil-rights leader

5

It is time now for blacks and Jews and Hispanics and Asians to get into the real significance of multicultural education. You can't have people living that close together who have no operative appreciation of each other . . . Multicultural education ceases to be a debatable theory. It becomes a necessity for surviving in the multicultural arrangement. We have to have an appreciation of how we each got here—the suffering of Jewish displaced persons and Japanese in American concentration camps. We have to stop viewing others as parasites. The fact is—all of us are hosts, and none of us are parasites.

Interview/
Los Angeles Times, 5-15:(T)8.

Franklyn G. Jenifer
President,
Howard University

6

Some people tend to worry that when black people start talking about excellence that somehow that means that we are not talking about where we came from . . . I say it's just the opposite. If you look far enough back, you will see that we have *never* been a people who have been afraid of change or challenge.

Ebony, May:122B.

Barbara Jordan
Former United States Representative,
D-Texas

1

We are one, we Americans, and we reject any intruder who seeks to divide us by race or class. We honor cultural identity. However, separatism is not allowed. Separation is not the American way. And we should not permit ideas like political correctness to become some fad that could reverse our hard-won achievements in civil rights and human rights. Xenophobia has no place in the Democratic Party. We seek to unite people, not divide them, and we reject both white racism and black racism. This Party will not tolerate bigotry under any guise. America's strength is rooted in its diversity.

At Democratic National Convention,
New York, N.Y., July 13/
The New York Times, 7-14:(A)12.

Sharon Pratt Kelly
Mayor of Washington, D.C.

2

We [blacks] are such a part of the history and ethic of this country. How are you not, if you're here before the Pilgrims arrive? How are you not, when you helped define the culture of the country? How are you not, if you gave America her first music? How are you not a part of the ethic of America? Yet America remains so conflicted on it. I think it expresses itself more now along economic class divisions. Part of that, though, clearly is a strong component of racism. Case in point: An African-American in this country is defined by the person who is most troubled. If you are educated, if you are successful, if you own your own business, if you listen to the majority of the media, you cease to be a reflec-

tion of the African-American community. Yet, if you look back over what happened over the last 15 years, once there was any window of opportunity, more African-Americans became a part of that middle class than any other segment of America . . . But when you have a majority media defining African-Americans as the most troublesome element, then there's no way to describe it other than racism.

Interview, Washington, D.C./
Los Angeles Times, 6-14:(M)3.

C. Everett Koop
Former Surgeon General
of the United States

3

I'm not talking to either side of the abortion issue until they sit down and talk to each other. I think we've had 18 years of rhetoric, with very few people changing sides. The time has come to get rid of abortion—which I am convinced both sides would at least like to see reduced—by attacking the cause of abortion, which is unwanted pregnancy. And that can only come about by the understanding of contraception—and a commitment to it.

Interview, Washington, D.C./
Los Angeles Times, 2-23:(M)3.

Arthur J. Kropp
President,
People for the American Way

4

America is becoming very intolerant. That didn't happen overnight. Americans are angry. There's a lot of fear about the future our young people will have. So we're picking our villains here. Blacks, feminists, gays, liberals—all the good villains are becoming targets.

USA Today, 9-2:(A)9.

Joseph E. Lowery
President,
Southern Christian
Leadership Conference

5

I think the race issue is now, more than it's ever been, a national issue. The whole country is

(JOSEPH E. LOWERY)

South. It's down South, up South, over South and out South.

The New York Times, 11-10:(A)7.

Ruth Mandel
Director,
Center for Women and Politics,
Eagleton Institute,
Rutgers University

1

[On Democratic Presidential candidate Bill Clinton's wife, who has a strong personality and a successful law career]: Hillary Clinton's life and behavior represents the changes that have taken place in women's lives and marriages, and yet she is faced with the dilemma of not confronting the public with the extent of those changes. When it comes to women, people are not ready to take more than a teaspoonful of change at a time.

The New York Times, 5-18:(A)8.

Jack McDevitt
Associate director,
Center for Applied Social Research,
Northeastern University

2

Hate crimes tend to go up in more economically difficult times. We know from polling that what seems to motivate people most, frighten them, is fear of losing their jobs, their homes. Combine that with frustration when you can't alter the situation you're in. Then you get into the feeling of resentment, then scapegoating. You look for someone who seems to be getting preferential treatment and blame your problems on that.

Interview/
USA Today, 9-2:(A)9.

Gordon McQuillen
President,
Wisconsin American
Civil Liberties Union

3

[On the ACLU]: We have been in with strange bedfellows before. We have represented the [Ku

Klux] Klan in the past. We have represented the American Nazi Party. We are not ideologically based. We think we are the most conservative organization in America devoted to the preservation of the Constitution, so we don't judge our clients—or those who come to us—on ideological or any other political grounds. It's whether or not we believe they have a Constitutional question.

Interview/
USA Today, 2-5:(A)9.

Kate Michelman
President, National Abortion
Rights Action League

4

We need to really begin to highlight for the American public how grave a risk women face with the [possible] impending overturn of *Roe v. Wade* [the Supreme Court ruling legalizing abortion]. It is very difficult for people to understand the grave consequences . . . I don't want to sound overly dramatic here, but I really do envision political and social upheaval. I envision a nation where women are faced with the choice between a forced, unwanted pregnancy or an illegal abortion. Poor women at risk for their lives and health. Families losing mothers. I really believe that it's a devastation to our country.

Interview/
USA Today, 1-7:(A)7.

Zell Miller
Governor of Georgia (D)

5

[Saying the Confederate battle symbol should be eliminated from Georgia's state flag]: What we fly today is not an enduring symbol of our heritage, but the fighting flag of those who [in 1956] wanted to preserve a segregated South in the face of the civil-rights movement . . . It is time we shake completely free of that era. We need to lay the days of segregation to rest, to let bygones be bygones and rest our souls.

May 28/
The New York Times, 5-29:(A)8.

Ross Perot
Industrialist

1

[On affirmative-action programs]: I stand on the fact that everybody in this country is an American . . . an equal partner . . . Now then, if you have to fall back to laws to force it, those laws, while they do create a fair channel for a minority that might not have it, they create a tremendous amount of stress if a less-talented person is promoted over a more-talented person, and that's just Human Nature 101. So we'll have to walk both paths probably for a while, but my goal [if elected President of the U.S.] would be I'll define success as when you can shut down the legal side and everybody does the right thing.

News conference, June 23/
USA Today 6-25:(A)9.

Ross Perot
Industrialist;
1992 independent
Presidential candidate

2

Our [racial] diversity is a strength; we've turned it into a weakness. Now, again, the White House is a bully pulpit. I think whoever is in the White House should just make it [racism] absolutely unconscionable and inexcusable . . . See, our differences are our strengths. We have got to pull together. In athletics we know it. See, divided teams lose; united teams win. We have got to unite and pull together, and there's nothing we can't do. But if we sit around blowing all this energy out the window, on racial strife and hatred, we are stuck with a sure loser because we have been a melting pot. We're becoming more and more of a melting pot. Let's make it a strength, not a weakness.

At Presidential candidates' debate,
St. Louis, Mo., Oct. 11/
The New York Times, 10-12:(A)15.

Colin L. Powell
General, United States Army;
Chairman, Joint Chiefs of Staff

3

Too many African-Americans are trapped in a cycle where poverty, violence, drugs, bad hous-

ing, inadequate education, lack of jobs and loss of faith combine to create a sad human condition. A human condition that cannot be allowed to continue if this nation is to hold its rightful place in the world . . . We must remember that America is a family. There may be differences and disputes in our family, but we must not allow [it] to be broken into warring factions . . . We must all work together to pull our people, to pull all Americans, out of the violence, out of the dark and soul-damning world of drugs, out of the turmoil of the inner cities. As we climbed on the backs of others, so must we allow our backs to be used for others to go even higher than we have.

At Fisk University commencement/
U.S. News & World Report,
5-18:17.

Dan Quayle
Vice President
of the United States

4

There is no question that this country has had a terrible problem with race and racism. The evil of slavery has left a long legacy. But we have faced racism squarely, and we have made progress in the past quarter century. The landmark civil-rights bill of the 1960s removed legal barriers to allow full participation by blacks in the economic, social and political life of the nation. By any measure, the America of 1992 is more egalitarian, more integrated and offers more opportunities to black Americans and all other minority-group members than the America of 1964. There is more to be done. But I think that all of us can be proud of our progress.

Before Commonwealth Club,
San Francisco, Calif., May 19/
The New York Times, 5-20:(A)11.

5

I've just returned from a week-long trip to Japan . . . In the midst of all of [our] discussions of international affairs, I was asked many times in Japan about the recent [riots by minority groups] in Los Angeles. From the perspective of many Japanese, the ethnic diversity of our culture is a weakness compared to their homo-

(DAN QUAYLE)

genous society. I begged to differ with my hosts. I explained that our diversity is our strength. And I explained that the immigrants who come to our shores have made, and continue to make, vast contributions to our culture and our economy. It is wrong to imply that the Los Angeles riots were an inevitable outcome of our diversified society.

Before Commonwealth Club,
San Francisco, Calif., May 19/
The Wall Street Journal, 5-20:(A)14.

1

[Addressing anti-abortionists]: People like yourselves don't just talk about the value of human life. You reflect it in your lives and enshrine it in your homes. Contrast that with the orientation of the cultural elite. It avoids responsibility and flees from the consequences of its self-indulgence. If, as a result of one's own actions a child is conceived, they have a simple solution: Get rid of it [by abortion]. Our opponents treat God's greatest gift—new life—as an inconvenience to be discarded.

Before National Right to Life Committee,
Arlington, Va., June 11/
The New York Times, 6-12:(A)11.

2

[President Bush] will have a policy of nondiscrimination [against homosexuals]. But, obviously, the gay and lesbian activists are a constituency of the Democratic Party, and [1992 Democratic Presidential nominee] Bill Clinton has made a pledge that he will hire gays and lesbians, and the only way that he can do that, to have [that] kind of a situation, is to ask someone their sexual orientation. We [in the Bush Administration] don't think it's anybody's business.

Broadcast interview/
"This Week With David Brinkley,"
ABC-TV, 9-13.

Marilyn Quayle
Wife of Vice President
of the United States Dan Quayle

3

Like many of you [women], I chose to have a career. I became a lawyer. Believe me, having a

profession is not incompatible with being a good mother or wife. But it isn't easy. Women's lives are different from men's lives. We make different trade-offs. We make different sacrifices. And we get different rewards. Watching and helping my children as they grow into good and loving teenagers is a source of daily joy for me. There aren't many women who would have it any other way . . . In our generation, women have carved out a new public life. And frankly, nothing offends me more than attempts to paint Republicans as looking to turn the clock back for women. When Dan married me, he married a budding lawyer. He wanted a partner—and he has one. Political liberals hold no monopoly on respecting women's abilities . . . [Liberals are] disappointed because most women do not wish to be liberated from their essential natures as women. Most of us love being mothers or wives, which gives our lives a richness that few men or women get from professional accomplishment alone. Nor has it made for a better society to liberate men from their obligations as husbands or fathers.

At Republican National Convention,
Houston, Texas, Aug. 19/
The Washington Post, 8-20:(A)34.

Neil L. Rudenstine
President, Harvard University

4

I am often asked why is it that ethnic, racial and other relations among students today seem to be so tense and even hostile on this campus. My own view is that [the] human race has tended throughout history to be quite tribal and sectarian.

At Harvard University commencement,
June 4/
The New York Times, 6-5:(A)9.

Donna Shalala
Chancellor,
University of Wisconsin,
Madison

5

I think it's clear that the admission of women to the Ivy League [colleges] was highly influential.

(DONNA SHALALA)

For the first time, corporate leaders sent their daughters to those places. The women came out with first-class degrees, went into MBA programs, and went to work on Wall Street, on the floors of the exchanges. So with daughters of the *Fortune* 500 down there, a lot of sexist behavior had to disappear.

Interview, New York, N.Y./
Lear's, May:18.

James Steele
Political scientist,
Howard University

1

What is "black racism"? If [it] means that some blacks hold prejudiced views against whites, I agree . . . But that's not racism. Racism is power. Under what guise can blacks exercise power to hurt the white population? What institutions do we [blacks] control to deny whites jobs or housing or social advancement?

July 15/
Los Angeles Times, 7-16:(A)6.

Shelby Steele
Professor of English,
San Jose (Calif.) State University

2

You hear a lot of blacks screaming that racism is dripping off the trees, and you hear a lot of whites screaming "I'm not racist! I have no animosity toward blacks." Well, the truth is somewhere in-between.

The Washington Post, 6-8:(A)7.

Gloria Steinem
Women's-rights activist;
Former editor,
"Ms." magazine

3

If you measure things in the only way this country seems to provide us to measure, which is public-opinion polls, there's been a fairly steady growth in support for feminist issues, although that goes contrary to popular wisdom. One of the

things I find so frustrating is the fact that you turn on the television set and nine-tenths of the national news is about so-called women's issues . . . The women's movement is alive and well; it's just not being called the women's movement.

Interview/
Vanity Fair, January:139.

4

Education for women is, by and large, an undermining process. There is a reason our self-esteem goes down with every additional year of schooling. The higher up we go, the less likely we are to be learning about what women do, or to have women in our textbooks or women of authority in our classrooms or in the administration— or to have a cooperative atmosphere, which women are generally more comfortable with. The longer we are in that structure, the more undermined we are.

Interview/
Working Woman,
January:68.

5

Throughout the 1970s, the [women's] movement was more consciousness-raising in the classic sense. People were enunciating new issues. There were speakouts and demonstrations. That still goes on, but now that we have majority support, we're ready for institutional change. Women are beginning to connect our everyday lives to changing work patterns and even the government. It's a big leap to think that what happens to you every day—in the secretarial pool, at the shopping center—has anything to do with who is in the Senate or the White House. The connection is just beginning to be forged. We are only 25 years into what by all precedent is a century of feminism. But once you get a majority consciousness change, you also get a backlash. It's both an inevitable tribute to success and a danger. The future depends entirely on what each of us does every day. After all, a movement is only people moving.

Interview,
New York, N.Y./
Time, 3-9:57.

Barbra Streisand
Actress, Singer

1

We've [women] come a long way. Not too long ago we were referred to as dolls, tomatoes, chicks, babes, broads. We've graduated to being called tough cookies, foxes, bitches and witches. I guess that's progress. Language gives us an insight into the way women are viewed in a male-dominated society . . . A man is commanding—a woman is demanding. A man is forceful—a woman is pushy . . . He shows leadership—she's controlling. He's committed—she's obsessed. He's persevering—she's relentless. He sticks to his guns—she's stubborn. If a man wants to get it right, he's looked up to and respected; if a woman wants to get it right, she's difficult and impossible . . . I look forward to a society . . . that accepts that a woman can be many things: strong *and* vulnerable, intelligent *and* sexy, opinionated *and* flexible, deep thinking as well as deep feeling. They can get Ph.D.s *and* manicures. They can contain the masculine and feminine. Of course, all this applies to men as well.

> *Speech, upon being inducted into*
> *Women in Film's Hall of Fame,*
> *June 12/*
> *Los Angeles Times, 6-15:(F)2.*

George C. Wallace
Former Governor
of Alabama (D)

2

[On his anti-school-integration stance when he was Governor in the 1960s]: Every Governor who ran [for election] in 1962 had to face the race question, or they would have been defeated. [Former President and former Georgia Governor] Jimmy Carter told me if he had run when I ran and I'd run when he ran, I might have been the Vice-Presidential nominee, but he never would have been the Presidential nominee, because he would have had to face that question [about segregation]. These New South Governors all were elected after the race question was settled, and they didn't have to face it. But if they had run when I ran and had had to face it, they wouldn't have been elected. Our platform was simply this: I will do all I can to maintain segregation within the law without violence . . . [But] if I had ever said anything in the race for Governor that reflected [poorly] on black people other than being for the segregation of the school system, [blacks] would never have voted for me. Some of the Governors used to say [blacks] were inferior in mind and all that kind of stuff. If I had ever said anything like that, no decent black person would have ever voted for me, and I wouldn't blame them, because all those things aren't true.

> *Interview, Montgomery, Ala./*
> *Time, 3-2:10.*

Faye Wattleton
President,
Planned Parenthood Federation
of America

3

There is nothing new about [President] Bush's guidelines to implement the gag rule, which censors speech [by counsellors] about abortion at federally funded family-planning clinics. They merely affirm Mr. Bush's intent to prevent health-care professionals from giving poor women full information about all their reproductive options. The gag rule is not only an affront to free speech, it is a government-sanctioned medical malpractice.

> *Interview, Washington, D.C./*
> *Los Angeles Times, 4-12:(M)3.*

Eddie N. Williams
President,
Joint Center for Political and
Economic Studies

4

Racism has nothing to do with power. It has to do with attitudes. I know white racists and I know black racists. To say that blacks can't be racist is to excuse a lot of black behavior without holding them accountable for it.

> *Los Angeles Times, 7-16:(A)6.*

Walter E. Williams
Professor of economics,
George Mason University

5

Most Americans would support what was called affirmative action back in the '60s, programs where efforts were made by companies and colleges to go outside the mainstream in their

WHAT THEY SAID IN 1992

(WALTER E. WILLIAMS)

recruiting, for example. They did this to recognize that in our history, blacks had been kept out of a lot of things. Most Americans can support this. But that's an entirely different thing from having hard and fast racial quotas—hiring people according to their numbers in society.

Interview/ USA Today, 3-2:(A)9.

The black leaders say one thing, and the [black] people say something else. Black people have more in common with [white evangelist] Jerry Falwell, while black leaders like Jesse Jackson and [U.S. Representative] Maxine Waters have more in common with white hippies.

Los Angeles Times,
8-6:(A)14.

Commerce • Industry • Finance

Robert E. Allen
Chairman,
American Telephone &
Telegraph Company

1

[On the breakup of AT&T into various independent companies several years ago]: The best thing is really the evidence . . . that the marketplace works. The whole concept here was to separate the competitive business from the monopoly business. It has not been easy for AT&T to make the transition. But I think the transition has been worth it. And I think people will look back on that event sometime in the future and say: That was the right thing for this country.

Interview/
The Christian Science Monitor,
2-10:7.

Michael H. Armacost
United States Ambassador
to Japan

2

In a global market, the companies that flourish are the companies that have a feeling for particular markets—and you acquire a feeling for markets by being in them.

Los Angeles Times, 5-19:(H)12.

Arthur Blank
President, Home Depot, Inc.

3

We [at Home Depot] have an ongoing commitment to running scared. If you attended any of our meetings, you would never believe that this company is the size it is or is doing as well as it is. We spend very little time talking about all the things we are doing well. We spend 80 to 90 per cent of our time focusing on the issues and problems, what what the competition is doing, what our customers are looking for, what they are not finding in our stores, what stores are having problems. The whole focus of the company is to

take today's standards and accept them for what they are but say we have to improve upon them for the future. Maintaining what we do today is just not going to cut it.

Interview/
Nation's Business, February:33.

Nicholas F. Brady
Secretary of the Treasury
of the United States

4

[The drop in farm population from 25 per cent to 2 per cent over the last century] must have been an enormously painful thing when [this country] was going through it for people on the farms. But the point is, we got through it, and I don't think anybody would go back and change what happened. Today [a similar situation is happening] in our largest, most well-advertised companies—AT&T, General Motors, Ford, IBM: contractions which allow them to get their cost structures in line with international cost structures, so that they can come back and build the thing up with export sales. And I think they will. At the same time, we've got to make sure that the job-generating mechanism in this country, which is small businesses, isn't hindered [by taxes], which is what the [Democratic Presidential nominee Bill] Clinton program does.

Interview/
The Christian Science Monitor, 8-25:4.

William H. Brandon, Jr.
President,
American Bankers Association

5

[Suggesting that relaxation of government banking regulations would help stimulate the economy]: The logic is that there are loans out there that we are not making that we would normally make. If we could move the regulatory environment from the most conservative back toward normal, we could generate four per cent more loans in six months' time.

Interview, Dec. 16/
The New York Times, 12-17:(C)1.

49

WHAT THEY SAID IN 1992

Richard C. Breeden
Chairman,
Securities and Exchange Commission
of the United States

1

I do not believe the stocks of small companies are inherently suspect. I do not believe that stocks below $5 are inherently evil.

April 10/
Los Angeles Times, 4-11:(D)3.

2

[Calling for better disclosure of executive compensation for the information of company shareholders]: Why should executives who don't bring home the bacon get paid as if they did? . . . The best protection against abuses in executive compensation is a simple weapon: the cleansing power of sunlight and . . . an informed shareholder base.

USA Today, 10-16:(B)1.

Arnold Brenner
Executive vice president
in charge of Japanese business,
Motorola, Inc.

3

Japan is not only a big market, but it is also a very important market in that you can't allow the Japanese to nurture their products there without being challenged, as a kind of sanctuary. That's why it's so important to crack the barriers that exist and make the effort . . . It takes an enormous commitment from the chief executive and the whole board of directors [of a U.S. company] because you have to be ready to lose money [in Japan] for several years. That's obviously a very scary tactic for a lot of companies. But the question is how do you get U.S. companies to do that? . . . Americans tend to work better with their backs to the wall. There are a whole lot of Americans waking up to the fact that their country is not healthy. One of the ways I think we're going to get healthy is to be able to compete with the Japanese on their own turf.

The New York Times,
2-24:(C)4.

William E. Brock III
Former United States
Trade Representative

4

[On the competition faced by the U.S. from countries and foreign companies that provide for more government involvement in private-sector business, government-business cooperation and different relationships between business and the community]: You can argue whether one [system] is better than the other, but the fact that they are different is going to create a potential for conflict. In the short term, we [the U.S.] are doomed to a lot of problems because we just have not advanced politically as fast as we moved economically. That is going to force us to be much more effective in linking politically and creating international systems that allow us to do business in the world.

Los Angeles Times, 6-8:(A)8.

Edmund G. "Jerry" Brown, Jr.
Candidate for the 1992
Democratic Presidential nomination;
Former Governor
of California (D)

5

The welfare king is the former president of General Motors, Roger Smith . . . All he did was help drive General Motors into the ground, and he gets $1.2-million [pension] for the rest of his life. That's the kind of privilege that is at the heart of what's ailing America.

USA Today, 3-4:(B)2.

George Bush
President of the United States

6

[On government regulations on business]: Every regulation that reduces efficiency slaps a hidden tax on the consumer. From the tab on a bag of groceries at the checkout line to the sticker price on the showroom floor, every American takes a hit when the government over-regulates.

Speech/
Nation's Business, June:52.

(GEORGE BUSH)

1

We entered the '80s with a 50-year-old banking system designed for the days when tellers wore green eyeshades, not for an era when billions, billions of investment dollars crossed borders at the speed of light. In the late '70s, record interest rates and inflation rates rocked this anachronistic system. The less-efficient institutions could not survive, obligating the Federal government to protect the savings of millions of Americans. Now this process of paying debt down is nearing its end. Our financial system will become more flexible and efficient, but for now lenders are cautious, and despite low interest rates, small business can still find it hard to get the credit.

Before Detroit Economic Club,
Detroit, Mich., Sept. 10/
The New York Times, 9-11:(A)12.

2

Most of our industries are transforming themselves from old-style hierarchies into flatter organizations with fewer layers between customer and executive. The new organizations emphasize a skill-based work-force, lean production, shorter cycles, from castings to computers. This is a revolution as dramatic as the one made earlier this century when Henry Ford led the country from craft-based production to mass manufacturing.

Before Detroit Economic Club,
Detroit, Mich., Sept. 10/
The New York Times, 9-11:(A)12.

3

[On the government bail-out of the savings-and-loan industry's debacle]: We paid in this savings-and-loan mess for excesses. People—private businesses did too much. They went out and loaned money that they shouldn't have loaned. And the taxpayer ends up getting burned, except I vowed we must protect every single depositor, and we've done that. Not a bail-out [for] some institution. Protect the depositor.

Broadcast interview,
New York, N.Y., Sept. 21/
The New York Times, 9-22:(A)12.

Bill Clinton
Governor of Arkansas (D);
Candidate for the 1992
Democratic Presidential nomination

4

The average CEO at a major American corporation is paid about 100 times as much as the average worker . . . And our government today rewards that excess with a tax break for executive pay, no matter how high it is. That's wrong . . . There should be no more deductibility for irresponsibility.

USA Today, 3-4:(B)2.

5

The banking system in this country is fundamentally sound, with some weak banks. I think that our goal ought to be first of all not to politicize it, not to frighten people. Secondly, to say that we have to enforce the law in two ways. We don't want to over-react, as the Federal regulators have in my judgment, on good banks so that they've created credit crunches that have made our recession worse in the last couple of years. But we do want to act prudently with the banks that are in trouble. We also want to say that insofar as is humanly possible, the banking industry itself should pay for the cost of any bank failures; the taxpayers should not. And that will be my policy and I believe we have a good balanced approach. We can get the good banks loaning money again, end the credit crunch, have proper regulation on the ones that are in trouble. And not over-react.

At Presidential candidates' debate,
East Lansing, Mich., Oct. 19/
The New York Times, 10-20:(A)15.

John Cregan
President, United States
Business and Industrial Council

6

[Some politicians have an] unabashed statist approach toward U.S. business—lumping big government, big labor and big business together. And it has a very negative connotation to the average American. The past 12 years have been about a reaction against big government . . . We

51

WHAT THEY SAID IN 1992

don't have to put government in the boardroom. What we must do is get government to recognize that it must look at business strategically.

The Christian Science Monitor,
2-20:8.

Jeff Faux
President,
Economic Policy Institute

1

Industrial policy [by government] is as American as apple pie . . . Look at the development of the airline industry. In the 1920s, we were far behind. But the U.S. Postal Service offered lucrative contracts to U.S. air services if they scheduled more flights. Airmail subsidized passenger service, and we built the most productive, most successful air-travel sector in the world. That is, until we deregulated it in the 1980s.

The Christian Science Monitor,
2-20:8.

Donald Frey
Former chief executive officer,
Bell & Howell Company

2

A good [board] director is the best friend of the CEO and his best critic.

The Christian Science Monitor,
8-3:7.

Robert M. Gates
Director of Central Intelligence
of the United States

3

The most senior policy-makers of the government clearly see that many of the most important challenges through and beyond the end of this decade are in the international economic arena—and they have fleshed out that insight with a detailed set of requirements for the intelligence community . . . [But U.S. intelligence] does not, should not and will not engage in industrial espionage . . . Plainly put, it is the role of U.S. business to size up their foreign competitors'

trade secrets, marketing strategies and bid proposals. Some years ago, one of our clandestine service officers said to me: "You know, I'm prepared to give my life for my country, but not for a company." That case officer was absolutely right.

Before Economic Club of Detroit,
Detroit, Mich., April 13/
The Washington Post, 4-14:(A)5.

4

We will not do commercial spying. Period. But we can be helpful on economic intelligence, by identifying foreign governments that are involved in unfair practices, or where they are violating agreements, either bilateral or multilateral, with the U.S., or where they are colluding with businesses in their country to the disadvantage of the U.S. We are following high-technology developments around the world that may have national-security implications: computers, telecommunications, new materials. Counter-intelligence is also going after those foreign-government intelligence organizations that are targeting American businesses.

Interview, Washington, D.C./
Time, 4-20:62.

Stephen Gillers
Professor of legal ethics,
New York University Law School

5

[On the settlement by which the accounting firm of Ernst & Young will pay the Federal government $400-million for improper auditing of banks and S&Ls that failed and were Federally insured]: This is going to be pointed to as a watershed event in the altered view of professional responsibility. This represents a new magnitude of exposure for professional firms. Now maybe we'll get auditors who audit and lawyers who put their foot down when they see wrongdoing.

Nov. 23/
The Washington Post,
11-24:(A)1.

Otis Graham
Professor of history,
University of California,
Santa Barbara

1

[President] Bush knows he's knee-deep in sectoral-specific policies, but he won't admit it, because he's afraid of the political heat . . . Since [then-President] Ronald Reagan denounced industrial policy in 1980, Republicans have denied that we've had such a policy. Fact is, we've always had one. Policies are sector-specific, tax policies aren't uniform, and we're always picking winners and losers. For example, steel production doesn't get [government] research-and-development assistance, but electronics manufacturing does.

The Christian Science Monitor, 2-20:8.

James Grant
Financial analyst

2

At times, I think I have been too moralistic about debt. Debt is not an evil potion, nor is it an elixir. It is a kind of hamburger helper or extender.

U.S. News & World Report,
6-8:56.

Donald Hambrick
Professor of business,
Columbia University

3

[On criticism that U.S. executives are overpaid]: Straightening out executive pay is not going to be the centerpiece of what it's going to take to make us globally strong. But it's symbolic. There has to be much more of a sense of shared fate [between executives and workers].

The Christian Science Monitor, 2-13:8.

Paul Hirsch
Professor of strategy
and organization,
School of Business,
Northwestern University

4

The newspaper says the banking industry will lose 100,000 jobs this year. That's 100,000 middle-class people who thought they were going to be in control of their lives. Manhattan is filled with 40-year-olds out of work, deep in debt and over-extended on their apartments. They never thought it would happen to them.

Newsweek, 1-13:22.

William Hoglund
Executive vice president,
General Motors Corporation

5

[On GM's new style of decision-making]: It's a face-to-face, give-and-take system of making decisions, instead of the old style, writing up a report and sending it to a whole series of committees. We have all the chiefs, of manufacturing, marketing, financial, purchasing—all the major disciplines—in on decisions from the word "go." It's amazing. When an issue comes up, bam! It's scheduled for a meeting right now. And when it's all over, it's all over. There's a decision made, and we all go!

Interview, New York, N.Y./
Newsweek, 11-23:47.

Thomas D. Hopkins
Professor of economics,
Rochester (N.Y.)
Institute of Technology

6

[On government regulations on business]: When a business person has to spend time figuring out the compliance routine and what he's got to do, it just saps the effort that otherwise could be going into strategic planning or just running the business. There are just not enough hours in the day to handle all of the regulatory requirements and really do justice to the ordinary business-planning activities of the firm.

Nation's Business, June:53.

Lawrence Hrebiniak
Professor, Wharton School,
University of Pennsylvania

7

[On the financial troubles of some U.S. business giants]: When you're on top of the heap,

(LAWRENCE HREBINIAK)

there's a disdain for change, a disdain for new ideas. It just goes with the territory, because you are Number 1.

Time, 12-28:28.

Elmer Johnson
Former executive vice president,
General Motors Corporation

1

[On General Motors' new policy of holding executives accountable for their job performance]: [GM's managers must understand that] the higher you rise in the organization, the tougher the standards of performance are going to be. That's a very good message to send out when you are eliminating 74,000 jobs [as GM is doing]. You can't have the moral authority to make those decisions unless there is accountability.

The New York Times, 4-8:(C)7.

Louis Lataif
Dean, Boston (Mass.)
University School of Management

2

[On the financial troubles of some U.S. business giants]: Nothing is forever. None of us today could name the 50 largest companies in America in 1900, but everyone alive at the time thought they would all go on forever.

Time, 12-28:28.

Robert L. Lattimer
Managing director,
Diversity Consultants, Inc.

3

There is a growing sentiment that diverse employee teams tend to outperform homogeneous teams of any composition. Managers tell us that homogeneous groups may reach consensus more quickly, but often they are not as successful in generating new ideas or solving problems, because their collective perspective is narrower.

The New York Times, 12-15:(C)2.

Jim Leach
United States Representative,
R-Iowa

4

[Criticizing proposals for the Federal government to invest in and help ailing banks and S&Ls regain their health]: Propping up sick institutions may look politically appealing in the short term for Presidential politics, but in the long term it could too easily result in an increase in taxpayer liabilities and undercut a major pinion of conservative economic philosophy. It is ironic that the more conservative econonomic party [the Republicans] is toying with a "Father Knows Best" policy, intervening in the market to decide which thrifts will be allowed to stay afloat with government funds and which will be taken over for lack of them.

Washington, D.C., Feb. 25/
The Washington Post, 2-26:(G)1.

Frank Lourenso
Executive vice president
in charge of middle-market lending,
Chemical Bank, New York, N.Y.

5

The main reason for sluggish loan demand has been lack of demand by businesses, not that they find it tough to borrow or that the banks are too regulated. The loan window is open here, but I can't push my customers to borrow.

The New York Times, 12-17:(C)1.

Robert Monks
Official,
Institutional Shareholder Partners

6

Pay [of corporate leaders] masks a much bigger problem. The real problem is the lack of accountability. CEOs are today's absolute monarchs and their boards are the House of Lords, and they feel they can thumb their noses at us shareholders without fear of being held accountable. But I guarantee you, the days of corporate royalty are over.

Time, 5-4:47.

William Morin
Director,
Council on High Technology,
National Association
of Manufacturers

1

Companies are taking a harder look at how they spend their research dollars. That's not necessarily bad if you accept the fact that companies in this country need to focus less on the revolutionary leaps in [product] technology and more on the step-by-step, incremental improvements like the Japanese do.

The Christian Science Monitor,
4-7:7.

William Ouchi
Professor of management,
University of California,
Los Angeles

2

There is fundamentally a competitive marketplace that governs the behavior of both the U.S. and Japanese auto-makers. I think people in business know that politics [government] in the end cannot solve the problems of management.

Los Angeles Times, 5-18:(D)1.

Ross Perot
Industrialist

3

The quickest way to stimulate the economy and have a growing, dynamic job base is to stimulate small business. You'll create more jobs faster by going through small business than through the huge industries.

Interview, Dallas, Texas/
Los Angeles Times, 6-5:(A)24.

4

In Japan, they have an intelligent, supportive relationship between government and industry ... We [in the U.S.] have an adversarial relationship . . . [The U.S.] government seems to be preoccupied with trying to break industry's legs . . . The first thing you'll hear back from the [U.S.] car companies . . . is we have made the strangest trade agreements in the world with our international competitors. They have picked our pockets. Why? [Because our foreign competitors] knew how to negotiate. The people we sent over didn't. And the people we sent over to negotiate know that, if they keep their noses clean, that in a short period of time they [can leave government and] be hired for $30,000 a month as a Japanese lobbyist [in Washington].

Interview/
Los Angeles Times, 6-11:(A)26,27.

5

We need to take the shackles off of American business. Our foreign competitors, Germany and Japan, the two economic superpowers, have an intelligent, supportive relationship between business and government. We need that. Then once we put that in place, then the next step is to industry by industry, company by company, to develop long-term plans, not 30-minute plans, not quarter-to-quarter plans, long-term plans. Last step. Target the industries of the future. Have an alliance between government and business to make sure that the industries of the future that will pay our people the highest standard of living are in this country. Why must we do this? Well, we must do it for our people, but forget that if you want to. We have to do it to get the taxes to pay our bills, to make our country work. Pretty basic stuff.

Viewer call-in broadcast/
"Today," NBC-TV, 6-11.

6

My dad said, "Son, nobody ever went broke with money in the bank. So, think about something you want. Save your money. And when you got enough money, pay for it. But don't ever borrow money for anything." If you look at my business career, that's what I've done. I would make a little money, reinvest it and make a little more. That imposes a discipline. You don't take risks by leveraging yourself. That's what destroyed so many of our companies in recent years.

Interview/
U.S. News & World Report, 6-29:25.

(ROSS PEROT)

1

My philosophy of running a company is this: Bring me people who are smart, tough, self-reliant. Bring me people who would have to be the best at whatever they do. Bring me the guys who love to win and women who love to win . . . When you run out of those, bring me people who hate to lose. You often have to go through 1,000 people to find one who has those traits.

Interview/
U.S. News & World Report,
6-29:27.

Harold Poling
Chairman,
Ford Motor Company

2

[The Japanese car companies have] got everything going for them. My God, the press [in the U.S.] just supports them every step of the way. I mean, [people] talk about "Japanese bashing" in this country. My God, [U.S. car-makers] get clobbered every time we open our mouths. And it isn't just [Chrysler's] Lee Iacocca. I mean, [the press says,] "Hit these guys [in Detroit]. They look like they're coming up for air."

Interview/
USA Today, 4-30:(B)2.

Dan Quayle
Vice President
of the United States

3

[Saying there is not much the government can do to encourage banks to step up lending to home-buyers and small-business following recent years of bad loans]: How are you going to regulate stupidity? How are you going to regulate mistakes? How are you going to regulate bad judgment? Now they are going the other way, saying: "Boy, let's not get risky here. Take the safe way. Take the safe course." But we're saying, risk is part of the American way. Let's get out and do business.

Campaigning for the
New Hampshire primary, Jan. 9/
The New York Times, 1-10:(A)9.

John Rosenblum
Dean, Graduate School
of Business Administration,
University of Virginia

4

Business schools grew up in a period of relative tranquility. One could settle on a winning strategy and ride it for years. Now what's *not* changing in the business world? Change and complexity are the rule.

The Christian Science Monitor,
11-16:13.

Arnold D. Scott
Senior executive vice president,
Massachusetts Financial
Services Company

5

[Criticizing proposed changes in SEC regulations that would expand the services mutual funds could offer and increase competition in the mutual-fund field]: Over the past four or five years, we have seen the savings-and-loan industry go down the chute, the insurance industry has been hurt and the banking industry has taken its hits. The mutual-fund sector is the only one that has not been tattered. I have to wonder what gain the world at large is going to achieve in exchange for the risk of unsettling a system of distribution that has been in place and worked well for 50 years.

The New York Times, 5-22:(C)5.

Walter Scott
Professor,
Kellogg Graduate School
of Management,
Northwestern University

6

Big companies find that the challenges of keeping up with what's going on in the marketplace become infinitely greater as the companies get larger. The layers of management and perks isolate executives too much . . . Doing well means continually challenging the premises of your business. It means having a vision and being restless and discontented with the status quo.

Time, 12-28:28.

Allen Sinai
Chief economist,
The Boston Company

1

[Suggesting that relaxation of government banking regulations would help stimulate the economy]: In the current situation, the biggest effort should be made looking for the so-called freebies, measures that help growth without causing the Federal government to spend money . . . If the [banking] regulators ease up, and the economy gets better, banks put out more credit, the country grows faster—with no cost to the [Federal] budget deficit. And as the economy grows, it generates more tax revenues that can actually reduce the deficit.

The New York Times, 12-17:(C)1.

Bill Spencer
President,
Sematech (government-industry
consortium for the
semiconductor industry)

2

The little corner of the world that I'm interested in changing is manufacturing capability. The United States has lost its ability to manufacture competitive products today. It's particularly true when we're talking of high-volume, low-cost manufacturing, the kind of thing that has made TVs and VCRs so popular today. We don't know how to design a product. We don't know how to manufacture it once it's designed. This is our biggest technological problem. The answer is to get a group of companies together, involve the government and cooperate in systemic and generic manufacturing. If we don't rebuild our industry, we can't remain a leading country. We can't do it with nuclear weapons now. We have to do it with manufacturing.

Interview/
The New York Times, 2-5:(A)8.

Tim Sponsler
Director,
United for State Action

3

It has become increasingly clear that political involvement by business on the state level is a necessary management function. The people we elect to our state legislatures have a tremendous impact on the way we [in the corporate world] can conduct business.

Nation's Business, January:55.

Robert C. Stempel
Chairman,
General Motors Corporation

4

[On criticism that Japanese executives make less money than their U.S. counterparts]: Our executives have had a tremendous downturn in their earnings for the past two years. We did not pay any bonuses at GM last year, and the way earnings are headed I can't see any bonus on the horizon this year either. But I don't really feel sorry for any Japanese chief executive. He enjoys a very good lifestyle. I'll be happy to exchange pay with any Japanese CEO.

Interview, Detroit, Mich./
Time, 1-27:46.

Robert C. Stempel
Former chairman,
General Motors Corporation

5

[Saying he resigned from GM in October because disagreements among management and board members were made public]: If it's internal, a CEO can handle it—you have honest differences with management. [But] once you get into the situation where I was in this summer and fall, where you're dealing with innuendoes and things being tossed across the transom, that becomes virtually unmanageable.

Interview/
USA Today, 12-2:(B)2.

William Taylor
Chairman, Federal Deposit
Insurance Corporation

6

You've got a very, very large chunk of the [banking] industry earning quite a bit of money, actually more than has historically been the case. More sobering, a significant portion of the industry is not doing well at all. To put it another

WHAT THEY SAID IN 1992

(WILLIAM TAYLOR)

way, the winners are winning big and the losers
are losing big.

Before Institute of International Bankers,
Washington, D.C., March 9/
The New York Times, 3-10:(C)3.

Stansfield Turner
Former Director
of Central Intelligence
of the United States

1

[On whether the CIA should be involved in
foreign spying on behalf of U.S. companies]:
Today, our economic well-being is probably
more a factor in our national security than our
military strength. And economic spying is no
more immoral than military spying.

USA Today, 7-2:(B)9.

Peter V. Ueberroth
Businessman;
Chairman,
Rebuild Los Angeles Committee

2

[On the business community's response to the
increasing minority populations in states like
California]: The private-sector community is
smart, and demographic studies are not hidden
away in vaults. Their customer base is going to be
a customer base of color in the state of California.
If they're not part of an involved employee base
that matches as close as they can to their
customer base—they're pretty much out of business. They might as well move to Japan or move
to some other country and send some product in.
Global companies, whether they be in Japan,
Germany, they're going to access this marketplace which is the 6th or 7th largest marketplace
in the world. They'd better be part of the solution.
They'd better understand how to make and how
to offer opportunities to all kinds of people, or it
will hurt their business. There are sheep in every
part of society, and you need good leadership.
And good leadership will follow good leadership
in a company system.

Interview, Los Angeles, Calif./
Los Angeles Times, 5-17:(M)3.

Linda Wachner
President,
Warnaco Group, Inc.

3

You can lose money while increasing sales
figures. Sales aren't as important as the quality of
sales. If a manager expects lower sales this year,
then he needs to reduce expenses. There's a
rhythm to expenses, earnings and sales—you
have to get them all working together, like an
orchestra.

Interview/
Working Woman, May:73.

Robert Waterman, Jr.
Business consultant

4

There are two ways to learn—trial-and-error,
and role-modeling. As an ex-ski instructor and a
sometimes artist, an awful lot of real learning is
done by role-modeling. In business, we haven't
done it enough.

USA Today, 11-27:(B)7.

Jack Welch
Chief executive officer,
General Electric Company

5

[On GE's increased use of input from employees in its decision-making]: We believe right
to our toes that we've got to engage every mind in
this place. They've got to feel good about being
here. They've got to feel their contributions are
respected. That doesn't mean our standards
aren't higher than ever in terms of productivity;
we just happen to think [this] is the right way to
do it. Breaking down boundaries, taking away
hierarchy. The idea is to liberate people . . .
There is a cynicism about this stuff in our society.
But I think the people who run a lot of today's
corporations believe in it. What are we doing this
for? To be competitive. To win. Tell me, is
engaging every mind a good idea? Is getting
everyone involved in the idea flow a good idea?

Interview/
Newsweek, 11-30:63.

B. Joseph White
Dean, School of Business,
University of Michigan,
Ann Arbor
1

Business is about results. It's not fundamentally about ideas. There are a lot of good ideas out there, but if you don't have the leadership, communication and negotiation skills to put ideas into action, you can't produce results.
The Christian Science Monitor,
11-16:13.

Ralph Whitworth
President,
United Shareholders of America
2

There's a populist wind that's sweeping through this country with people saying, "We're fed up with special deals for special people."

There's a different mood now than there was five years ago. There's less willingness to accept the status quo, whether it's in Congress or in a corporation.
The Washington Post, 7-1:(F)8.

Ron Wyden
United States Representative,
D-Oregon
3

[CPAs are] called certified "public" accountants because they're accountable to the public. But accountants are not living up to their public duty. If they find wrongdoing, they have an obligation to come forward . . . Accountants didn't cause the S&L crisis. But they could have saved taxpayers a lot of money if they did their jobs properly and set off enough warning alarms for regulators.
Time, 4-13:49.

Crime • Law Enforcement

James Jay Baker
Chief lobbyist,
National Rifle Association

1

[Arguing against various gun-control measures]: Instead of asking law-abiding people to change what they are doing, why not keep the people that are committing the crimes [with guns] in jail? . . . I haven't seen a gun proposal in the 13 years that I've been here that had any potential for reducing the homicide rate. The law-abiding people will obey the law, and the criminals will not.

The New York Times, 4-3:(A)11.

William P. Barr
Attorney General
of the United States

2

I believe that the first duty of government is providing for the personal security of its citizens. Therefore I would naturally place the highest priority on strengthening law enforcement. I think public servants should respond to the citizens' most pressing concern, and right now people are threatened by violent crimes and they are right to be worried about it.

The New York Times, 3-3:(A)12.

3

Traditionally, the Federal government's role in dealing with violent crime has been quite limited because 95 per cent of violent crime is committed and handled at the state and local level. Nevertheless, this (Bush) Administration believes that the Federal government, working in close partnership with state and local law enforcement, can have a positive and substantial impact on violent crime . . . Over the past year, we have doubled Federal prosecutions of firearms offenders in the Federal system. We have charged over 6,400 individuals nationally. We are convicting them at a rate of over 90 per cent. The average sentence for that whole group so far has been seven years without parole, and

the average sentence for the armed career criminals—that is, three-time losers—has been 18 years without parole . . . Most serious felons will get firearms regardless of what the gun-control laws are . . . Our position is that part of any attack on firearm violence has to be targeting these felons who repeatedly commit acts of violence and getting them off the street.

News briefing,
Washington, D.C., July 29/
The Washington Post, 7-31:(A)22.

4

[On the Justice Department after President-elect Bill Clinton takes office in 1993]: I think there's a potential for many setbacks for what was accomplished during the [Ronald] Reagan and [George] Bush Administrations. The big difference is going to be in the philosophy of approaching crime, and generally speaking we say that part of the solution of dealing with crime has to be holding individuals accountable. I am talking about violent crime and making violent criminals pay by sending them to prison for a long period of time. I am doubtful the approach [of the Clinton Justice Department] will be [the] same.

Interview, Washington, D.C.,
Nov. 19/
The New York Times, 11-23:(A)9.

Robert J. Beatty
Chief of Inspection Services,
New York City
Police Department

5

[On corruption in the police force]: There has never been a time in this job when we've been presented with more corruption hazards than in the last five years, because of the drug situation. I don't care if you go back to the Roaring '20s, there's never been more of an opportunity [for police officers] to make so much money so easily, so fast and so undetected as now . . . How do you deal with those situations? It's mind boggling. You can't even believe this.

The New York Times, 6-20:16.

Tom Bradley
Mayor of Los Angeles, Calif.

1

[On the recent street riots by minorities in Los Angeles following not-guilty verdicts in the trial of police officers in the Rodney King brutality case]: The jury's verdict will never outlive the images of the savage beating [of King] seared forever into our minds and souls . . . I understand full well that we must give voice to our great frustration. I know that we must express our profound outrage. But we must do so in ways that bring honor to ourselves and our communities.

Broadcast address to the city,
Los Angeles, Calif., April 29/
Los Angeles Times, 5-15:(A)32.

Lee Brown
Commissioner of Police
of New York City

2

Excessive force [by police] is unacceptable. Police are not in business to use excessive force. Therefore our agreement, our understanding, is police forces must do that which is necessary to ensure that police officers do not overstep their authority and use excessive force on the citizens. It's unacceptable and cannot be tolerated.

At meeting of Mayors and police chiefs,
Houston, Texas, June 20/
The Christian Science Monitor,
6-22:9.

Haywood Burns
Dean, City University of New York
Law School

3

[Criticizing a jury's verdict of not guilty in the trial of Los Angeles police officers in the Rodney King brutality case]: I wouldn't condemn the whole jury system, but I don't have an explanation for the verdicts except that the jury must have been on another planet.

USA Today, 5-1:(A)4.

George Bush
President of the United States

4

[On the recent street rioting by minority groups in Los Angeles]: All of us saw sickening sights in Los Angeles of criminals breaking windows and burning buildings and looting businesses. But even worse was the looting of something harder to replace than merchandise, the stealing of something precious—stealing hope, promise, the future. This we cannot allow . . . We must show less compassion for the criminal and more for the victims of crime.

At law-enforcement
memorial ceremony,
Washington, D.C., May 15/
The Washington Post, 5-16:(A)14.

5

[On criticism that it is racism and playing politics when he calls for tough law enforcement following the recent streets riots in Los Angeles by minority groups]: There is nothing racist, there is nothing divisive about protecting decent people from crime. Some say it's playing politics. Well, they're wrong. Playgrounds overrun by gangs, senior citizens locked behind triple-bolted doors, or mothers shot through open kitchen windows—this isn't the America we want.

At Town Hall of California,
Los Angeles, Calif., May 29/
Los Angeles Times, 5-30:(A)1.

6

I've been fighting for very strong anti-crime legislation. *Habeas corpus* reform so you don't have these endless appeals, so when somebody gets sentenced, hey, this is for real. I've been fighting for changes in the exclusionary rule so if an honest cop stops somebody and makes a technical mistake, the criminal doesn't go away. I'll probably get into a fight in this room with some, but I happen to think that we need stronger death penalties for those that kill police officers . . . I am not for national registration of firearms. Some of the states that have the toughest anti-gun laws have the highest levels of crime.

At Presidential candidates' debate,
Richmond, Va., Oct. 15/
The New York Times,
10-17:11.

Joseph A. Califano, Jr.

*Director, Center on Addiction
and Substance Abuse,
Columbia University;
Former Secretary of Health,
Education and Welfare
of the United States*

1

You can put 100,000 more cops on the street and you're still going to have a major drug problem. The trick is to stop the pipeline from filling up with new drug abusers. And that means prevention programs and treatment programs.

The New York Times, 10-22:(A)14.

Bill Clinton

*Governor of Arkansas (D);
1992 Democratic
Presidential nominee*

2

[On the drug problem]: First, we ought to prevent more of this on the street. Thirty years ago there were three policemen for every crime; now there are three crimes for every policeman. We need 100,000 more police on the street. I have a plan for that. Secondly, we ought to have [drug] treatment on demand. Thirdly, we ought to have boot camp for first-time non-violent offenders so they can get discipline and treatment and education and get re-connected to the community before they are severed and sent to prison where they can learn how to be first-class criminals. There is a crime bill that lamentably was blocked from passage once again, mostly by Republicans in the United States Senate, which would have addressed some of these problems. That crime bill is going to be one of my highest priorities next January, if I become President.

*At Presidential candidates' debate,
St. Louis., Mo., Oct. 11/
The New York Times, 10-12:(A)15.*

3

I support the right to keep and bear arms. I live in a state where over half the adults have hunting or fishing licenses or both. But I believe we have to have some way of checking handguns before they're sold—to check the criminal history, the mental-health history and the age of people who are buying them. Therefore I support the Brady bill, which would impose a national waiting period unless and until a state did what only Virginia has done now which is to automate its records. Once you automate your records, then you don't have to have a waiting period. But at least you can check. I also think we should have, frankly, restrictions on assault weapons whose only purpose is to kill. We need to give the police a fighting chance in our urban areas.

*At Presidential candidates' debate,
Richmond, Va., Oct, 15/
The New York Times, 10-17:11.*

Richard Cullen

*United States Attorney for the
Eastern District of Virginia*

4

[On soft gun-sales laws in Virginia that have resulted in that state being the origin of handguns that are used throughout the Northeast]: [Gun-runners] come into the state and go into a store and buy handguns by the dozens, with hardly a question asked. Then they haul the guns north and sell them on the street for cash or drugs at profits of 300 and 400 percent. No other East Coast state has gun laws as lax as Virginia's laws—not South Carolina, not Georgia, not Florida. Nobody. This has to stop . . . Virginia used to be the state that shook its head sadly about all the bad things happening up in Washington and New York. Now Washingtonians and New Yorkers are shaking their heads sadly about what's going on down in Virginia.

The New York Times, 12-23:(A)8.

Mathea Falco

*Former Assistant Secretary
for International Narcotics,
Department of State
of the United States*

5

We're losing the war against drugs. Heroin and cocaine are cheaper and more freely available now. I think the important measure is not the amount of drugs seized, but the quality-of-life questions, such as the number of addicts, how

(MATHEA FALCO)

safe people feel in their communities, the numbers of drug-affected babies and the spread of AIDS through drug use. These are the things that really matter . . . [The problem is] here in the families, schools and communities of America [not in the drug-supplying countries]. We should be putting our law-enforcement resources in more community policing, more cops on the streets to help engage the neighborhoods in keeping the dealers out.

The Christian Science Monitor,
8-27:1,4.

Clifford Fishman
Professor of law,
Catholic University of America

1

[Criticizing a jury's verdict of not guilty in the trial of Los Angeles police officers in the Rodney King brutality case]: I am ashamed and embarrassed that our system could produce this result. [But] what is the alternative? You can't have trial by TV viewers or polls, and if you did away with juries and put it before a panel of judges, it would be anti-democratic and you might get many more racially tainted verdicts than you have now . . . The facts were easy this time because of the videotape [of the police beating of King]. But why those 12 people [on the jury] fooled themselves into deciding there was nothing morally wrong with the facts is beyond me.

USA Today, 5-1:(A)4.

Patrick S. Fitzsimons
Chief of Police
of Seattle, Wash.

2

We're [the police] sort of like the court of last resort for a lot of people who need help. We're being asked to intercede and find shelter, to take people out of squatters' situations. We're in the middle on something created by the economy. You have to take a humane approach.

The New York Times, 8-8:9.

James Alan Fox
Dean,
College of Criminal Justice,
Northeastern University

3

[Committing] murder is plunging to a much younger age group. What is so dangerous about this is that a 15-year-old with a gun in his hand is a much more volatile individual than a 40-year-old or even an 18-year-old . . . They don't think about the consequences, and they don't have a long-term perspective. They face death every day on the street and even at school, so why should they be afraid that maybe the police will catch them and maybe they will be executed?

The New York Times, 10-19:(A)8.

James M. Fox
Assistant director in charge
of the New York office,
Federal Bureau of Investigation

4

[On the conviction of John Gotti, a top organized-crime figure, on murder and racketeering charges]: The don is covered with Velcro, and every charge stuck. This was really a crossroads, the most important crossroads [in fighting organized crime]. I'm not saying it's going to happen in a year, but the mob as we know it in New York City and the country is on its way out.

New York, N.Y., April 2/
The New York Times, 4-3:(A)1.

Daryl F. Gates
Chief of Police
of Los Angeles, Calif.

5

[On misbehavior of police officers, such as brutality toward suspects, which has been recorded on amateur video tape]: It would be nice if we videotaped every occasion so that you get a running picture of how police conduct themselves on a regular basis. People would have a different idea of what police officers have to put up with . . . As far as ferreting out those officers who are consistently causing problems, I don't know of a police department in the country that hasn't been doing that as long as I can remem-

WHAT THEY SAID IN 1992

(DARYL F. GATES)

ber. People forget there are job protections of all kinds, police unions, rights you can't trample on . . . incidents that were reviewed and nothing came of them.

Interview, Los Angeles, Calif./
The Christian Science Monitor,
3-30:8.

Richard H. Girgenti
Director of Criminal Justice
of New York State

1

As the century is coming to a close, we are on the verge of having DNA technology as important as fingerprinting was at the beginning of the century. We are going through the same kind of debate and resistance that people had 100 years ago over the value of fingerprints as evidence.

The New York Times, 5-12:(A)13.

Reuben Greenberg
Chief of Police
of Charleston, S.C.

2

[Criticizing a jury's verdict of not guilty in the trial of Los Angeles police officers in the Rodney King brutality case]: That decision knocked us in the chops about 40 years backwards. How could [police] be applauding that verdict? How could they think that verdict will be good for law enforcement? We gain nothing . . . We can salvage this situation and hold our heads up in public by saying this incident, regardless of the criminal implications, is definitely beneath [police] standards . . . This is not a standard we endorse.

USA Today, 5-1:(A)4.

Maynard Jackson
Mayor of Atlanta, Ga.

3

There are too many guns [on the streets in the U.S.], and there's too much dope and too much violence. The guns are not regulated, they're not licensed and our children are getting killed . . .

The guns, and the guns, and the guns keep coming.

At memorial to the late civil-rights
leader Martin Luther King, Jr.,
Atlanta, Ga., Jan. 17/
The Washington Post 1-18:(A)12.

George Kelling
Fellow, criminal-justice program,
Kennedy School of Government,
Harvard University

4

A lot of police departments are going through soul-searching after the Rodney King [police-brutality] incident in Los Angeles. I think most chiefs knew that the outbreak [of police brutality] could happen in almost every police department in the United States . . . I think we have allowed a police culture to develop that is oftentimes quite at odds with the management culture. One of the primary problems is when we constantly think in terms of wars: wars on crime, wars on drugs, wars on violence. You shouldn't be surprised when you get warriors.

The Christian Science Monitor, 4-20:9.

Mark Kleiman
Associate professor
of public policy,
Harvard University

5

"Are we winning the war against drugs?" is not a coherent question. A war is something that happens for a while, and then you win or lose. Drug policy isn't like that; in five years, the war against drugs will not be over. It's a constant problem, and that calls for policies which are sustainable over time. So the crisis mode is probably not the way to go.

The Christian Science Monitor, 8-27:4.

Melvyn Levitsky
Assistant Secretary
for International
Narcotics Matters,
Department of State
of the United States

6

[Saying the fight against international drug trafficking will not be won soon]: We view this

(MELVYN LEVITSKY)

effort as a long-term one, and there will be no instant success against a deeply rooted problem . . . If we do not have the patience and the stamina to persevere, we will not only lose the ground we have gained, we will fail in the goal of reducing the threat to this country and to our friends and allies from drugs.

Los Angeles Times, 2-26:(A)6.

Dennis Luther
Warden, Bradford, Pa.,
Federal Prison

1

[On his prison]: It is the people who make the difference here, how people treat people . . . I have never met anyone who is irredeemable.

The Christian Science Monitor,
8-11:12.

Bob Martinez
Director, Federal Office
of National Drug Control Policy

2

[On probable independent Presidential candidate, industrialist Ross Perot]: I salute Mr. Perot for his good intentions when it comes to the drug war. At least he wants to win. But his proposals in this area, as in others, illustrate why he is not fit to be President of the United States. Mr. Perot apparently believes that Draconian quick fixes will rid the nation of drugs. He has talked about cordoning off entire inner-city neighborhoods and treat[ing] all who live there as guilty until proven innocent. He says we ought to declare civil war. He advocates reckless, Wild West covert operations. And he apparently regards the Bill of Rights as little more than an antique inconvenience.

At U.S. Conference of Mayors,
Houston, Texas, June 23/
Los Angeles Times, 6-24:(A)13.

Victor A. McKusick
Professor of medical genetics,
Johns Hopkins University

3

We [a National Academy of Sciences panel he chairs] confirm the general reliability of using

DNA typing in forensic science. When performed properly, the technique is capable of providing strong evidence for solving crimes. We think it is a powerful tool for criminal investigation and for exoneration of innocent individuals . . . But there are certain standards that need to be met consistently from a technical point of view, and aspects of the statistical interpretation of the findings that need to be taken into account in reporting the results of tests.

News conference, April 14/
Los Angeles Times, 4-15:(A)17;
The Washington Post, 4-15:(A)16.

Joseph D. McNamara
Research fellow,
Hoover Institution,
Stanford University;
Former Chief of Police
of San Diego, Calif.

4

The [police] chief has to be a person with vision, a manager, a leader and an interpreter of political policy.

The New York Times, 8-8:9.

Francois Mitterrand
President of France

5

[On the recent street riots by minorities in Los Angeles following a not-guilty verdict for police officers in the Rodney King brutality case]: [The riots were] above all a racial conflict and racial conflict is always wed to poor social programs. [President] George Bush is a generous man, who embodies an extremely conservative political ideology, and American society is conservative and economically capitalist. Here are the results.

Los Angeles Times 5-2:(A)8.

Terrie Moffitt
Associate professor
of psychology,
University of Wisconsin

6

Where you really learn delinquency from is from your family . . . A criminal is made when

(TERRIE MOFFITT)

the mother drinks and smokes or uses drugs and causes her baby to grow up with a learning disorder. A criminal is made when a 3-year-old isn't given consistent discipline, or a 7-year-old doesn't get help with his homework because the parents are not good parents . . . You don't learn to become a criminal only at 17 when someone teaches you to steal a car.

The New York Times, 1-31:(A)1,8.

Mark H. Moore
*Professor of
criminal-justice policy,
Kennedy School of Government,
Harvard University*

1

You come to the important point of view that the causes of [violent crime] are complex and therefore elusive. The hope that we might be able to base policy on definite knowledge of the causes of violence is receding . . . The [political] right is saying, "All we need are more prisons and police." The [political] left says, "That is a stupid waste of money. What we really need is to abolish poverty and racial discrimination."

The New York Times, 11-13:(A)7.

Ross Perot
Industrialist

2

[On what he would do about the drug problem if he ran for and became President]: Everything we need to do, we can do within the Constitution. I could just make one of these mindless statements that I'm against drugs, that we ought to declare war on drugs. Anybody who can get up in the mornings and dress themselves understands that if we get rid of this stuff, it won't be pretty. Once you decide what needs to be done, you go to the American people. It's up to you, folks. The point is whether the American people want to talk about it or do it. All Washington does is talk about it. If you want to talk about it, I'm not your man. If you just want more show business, fine. I don't want to waste my time. I don't want to waste the country's time.

*Interview, Dallas, Texas/
Newsweek, 4-27:27.*

Ross Perot
*Industrialist;
1992 independent
Presidential candidate*

3

If any human being in this country ever uses a gun to intimidate others . . . we ain't going to see him on the street anymore ever. You say, "That's pretty harsh." Well, do you want to fix it or not?

USA Today, 11-2:(A)4.

Barbara Price
*Dean, graduate program,
John Jay College
of Criminal Justice*

4

[On public anti-police attitudes]: When you give people [the police] the power to use force, in extreme cases deadly force . . . then you're going to have incidents, no matter how professional we make the training and how stringent the standards. That's the price of having police in any society.

*The Christian Science Monitor,
7-23:3.*

Dan Quayle
*Vice President
of the United States*

5

[The recent racial rioting in Los Angeles was] directly related to the breakdown of family structure, personal responsibility and social order in too many areas of our society . . . Instead of denouncing wrongdoing, some have shown tolerance for rioters. Some have enjoyed saying, "I told you so." Who is to blame for the riots? The rioters are to blame. Who is to blame for the killings? The killers are to blame. Yes, I can understand how people were shocked and outraged by the verdict [of not guilty for police officers] in the Rodney King [police-brutality] trial. But there is simply no excuse for the mayhem that followed.

*Before Commonwealth Club,
San Francisco, Calif., May 19/
Los Angeles Times,
5-20:(A)14.*

J. Michael Quinlan
Director,
Federal Bureau of Prisons

1

[On the crackdown on the granting of furloughs to prisoners in the Federal prison system]: There's heightened sensitivity to the fact that we only want to put people on furlough who . . . are not going to put people in jeopardy. Certainly, [the Willie Horton case, in which a convicted murderer committed assault while on furlough,] was a factor . . . Hopefully, I'm not immune from general common sense here.

The Washington Post, 3-9:(A)15.

Fred Romero
Official,
National Rifle Association

2

[On the recent street riots by blacks in Los Angeles following a not-guilty verdict for police officers in the Rodney King brutality case]: What you saw in Los Angeles is the most graphic example of what we've [the NRA] been saying for years: that in times of anarchy, the only people without guns will be the people that need them the most. I can't wait to see how the gun-control people rationalize this one.

USA Today, 5-4:(A)4.

Robert S. Ross, Jr.
Former Director,
Office of International Affairs,
Department of Justice
of the United States

3

[On a recent Supreme Court ruling allowing the U.S. to kidnap criminal suspects in foreign countries and bring them to the U.S. for trial]: This sort of thing has got to be a tool of official law enforcement when you have officially sanctioned terrorism or drug trafficking [in foreign countries]. [But] it's not in the foreign-policy interest of the U.S. to go willy-nilly around the world grabbing people.

The Washington Post,
6-17:(A)2.

Kenneth F. Schoen
Former Corrections Commissioner
of Minnesota

4

[On alternatives to prison for certain crimes]: States will never have enough money for these lower-cost programs until Governors and legislators bite the political bullet. They have got to change all those mindless get-tough crime laws and mandatory-minimum-sentencing statutes that they passed in recent years, because these laws and policies are what's creating the explosion in the prison population.

The New York Times, 8-7:(B)8.

Charles E. Schumer
United States Representative,
D-New York

5

[On the conviction in Miami of former Panamanian leader Manuel Noriega on drug-trafficking charges]: I think that the government has won a great victory in bringing Noriega to justice. The question is, did they pay too high a price? And what I am specifically talking about is the various plea bargains that were made up and down the line to murderers, major drug dealers and other assorted bad people in order to get them to testify against Noriega . . . The Noriega conviction certainly sends a signal to some types of people—the international outlaws, the [Libyan leader Muammar] Qaddafis—that if you mess with the United States you could be in for trouble; and that's good. But it also sends a signal to major drug dealers in America that if you are fortunate enough to rat on a major big person, you're going to get off easy.

News conference, April 10/
The Washington Post, 4-15:(A)24.

Stanley K. Sheinbaum
President,
Los Angeles Police Commission;
Former chairman,
American Civil Liberties
Union Foundation

6

I don't think the [Los Angeles Police] Department is any more racist than the society around it.

(STANLEY K. SHEINBAUM)

The real problem is that, to the extent that the society is racist, you're going to find pockets of racism in the Department. Don't expect the people on the force to be pure, when the community around them has racist impulses . . . [The police] are there to protect law and order, to protect the community against itself—and that creates a self-righteousness that they are doing something good. Self-righteousness is a trap for anybody—and it becomes a rationale for over-stepping. That is the tendency on the police side that has to be held in check. They still have a responsibility to observe the rights of the people, some of whom may be uncontrollable. But it is the police obligation to protect those rights.

Interview/
Los Angeles Times, 3-22:(M)3.

Darrel Stephens
Executive director,
Police Executive Research Forum

1

A good 40 per cent of [police chiefs] either resign or are fired under pressure. A lot of the other people, after they've been in the job two or three or four years or so, start feeling the conflicting pressures, and they just retire, drop out. Very few grow old in the job.

The New York Times, 8-8:9.

Rita Walters
Los Angeles City Councilwoman

2

[On the recent street riots by minorities in Los Angeles following not-guilty verdicts in the trial of police officers in the Rodney King brutality case]: Here was a black man [King], beaten by a horde of white rogue policemen, tried in an all-white town, practically all-white town, by a practically all-white jury and acquitted—the policemen were acquitted of any wrongdoing and declared it wasn't excessive force. We had another case here of a young black girl being shot in the back of the head by a shopkeeper. You take both of these incidents with all the rest of the

disenfranchisement that occurs in minority communities, and this [riot] is what you get.

Broadcast interview/
"Crossfire," CNN-TV, 4-30.

Willie L. Williams
Commissioner of Police
of Philadelphia, Pa.;
Chief of Police-designate
of Los Angeles, Calif.

3

The African-American community wants strong, tough, honest, fair policing. There is no African-American community in America that does not want to see police there. The people want to be treated fairly. They want to be treated honestly and with dignity. I think that even in the city of Los Angeles [which recently experienced street rioting in black neighborhoods], with all its strife, people say, "Hey, wait a minute. These people are robbing and stealing and looting. They are not our community; they are not our friends. They are gang members, or they are hoodlums, and they are bums, and they belong in jail." Crime also has a long-term effect on the community because it drives out the mom-and-pop businesses, the corner stores, where a lot of shopping is done. It drives out the source of income for the teenagers and the young adults who don't have a lot of skills or are just going to school to learn skills. It often drives out the source of income for the one or two parents who may be living and working at home and working in the area. The cost of crime in the African-American community cannot be underestimated.

Interview/
Time, 5-11:37.

Willie L. Williams
Chief of Police
of Los Angeles, Calif.

4

The police department is the largest social-service agency in the city in addressing non-criminal needs on a seven-day, 24-hour basis. Recessionary budget cuts across the board impact policing at every level—more welfare and homeless people on the street, fewer parks and

(WILLIE L. WILLIAMS)

recreation, fewer health services, abandoned vehicles and all the rest. All these add to the number of police calls, levels of expectation and stress level.

The Christian Science Monitor, 9-14:14.

James Q. Wilson
Professor of political science,
University of California,
Los Angeles

1

[While violent crime as a whole has been going down in the U.S. since the mid-1980s,] the rate hasn't gone down as much as you would have predicted in relation to the aging population. And that's because the average young male today is more apt to commit a violent crime than the average young male was in the 1950s. No one knows why, but you can make some guesses: first, the pervasive spread of the drug culture, and second, a kind of value shift in American culture that makes people more inclined to do their own thing and less inclined to worry about their reputation in the eyes of older people.

Los Angeles Times,
2-5:(A)8.

Pete Wilson
Governor of California (R)

2

[On a Governor's right to grant clemency in a death-penalty case]: Clemency, by definition, is an act of executive mercy. It doesn't go either to the question of guilt—that is long since settled—nor does it go to the wisdom of capital punishment. It is purely and simply an act of executive mercy.

News conference,
Santa Rosa, Calif., March 23/
The New York Times, 3-24:(A)6.

Marvin Wolfgang
Professor of criminology and law,
and director of the
Sellin Criminology Center,
University of Pennsylvania

3

[On youngsters becoming involved in violent crimes]: What we're seeing is the loss of childhood. These kids are growing up too fast into the subculture of violence. They are learning at an ever-younger age that violence is not only tolerated, but often expected and sometimes required. If you don't respond agressively to a slur on your mother or your manhood, you're a coward.

The New York Times, 10-19:(A)8.

Defense • The Military

Gordon Adams
Director,
Defense Budget Project

1

[On cutbacks in defense spending resulting from the end of the Cold War]: If you make helicopters, aircraft, missiles, ships, look out, because you're going to get a lot smaller a lot faster than you think. It will be a substantially smaller [defense] industry, one that emphasizes the inputs to the weapons platform rather than production of the platform itself. It's an industry without a lot of production workers and with a heavy emphasis on research and design teams.

The New York Times, 1-30:(C)2.

Les Aspin
United States Representative,
D-Wisconsin

2

[Calling for a "ground-up" rebuilding in the military]: If we reduce our forces from the top down, by simple subtraction, we will get a smaller defense budget and smaller forces, but the chances are good that neither the budget nor the forces will be the right ones.

Speech, Jan. 24/
The Washington Post, 6-24:(A)6.

3

The biggest news about [U.S.] high-tech weaponry is that they . . . did perform beyond really anybody's expectations [during 1991's Persian Gulf war], even under the revised estimates, and performed in a way that was much better than anything that we have seen in any war that the Americans have had previously. And it's part of a continued trend. The trend is that starting back in World War II, according to best available estimates, it took about 9,000 bombs to destroy a single target . . . In Vietnam the number changed to about 300 bombs. In [the Persian Gulf war], the precision weapons . . . under the revised estimates, took

two to destroy a target. So it is, first of all, part of a trend, but secondly, a significant trend . . . So regardless of the arguments about whether the revisionists are right or the original estimates were right, or whether anybody . . . had their numbers right at the time or not . . . the overall point is this trend, and this trend has significantly changed the way battles are fought and the way things need to be thought of in the future.

News conference,
Washington, D.C., April 23/
The Washington Post, 4-24:(A)26.

4

[Saying there is a place for the use of "limited" U.S. military force]: If we say it is "all or nothing" and then walk away from the use of force in the Balkans [for instance, where limited U.S. force is advocated by some to help the Bosnians against the Serbs], we are sending a signal to other places . . . We are not deterring anybody . . . Those [like us] who disagree with the all-or-nothing school are unwilling to accept the notion that military force can't be used prudently short of all-out war.

Speech/The New York Times,
9-28:(A)6.

Les Aspin
United States Representative,
D-Wisconsin;
Secretary of Defense-designate
of the United States

5

President-elect [Bill Clinton] has included two sets of big challenges with [my nomination as Defense Secretary]. The first set involves maintaining the superb quality of our [military] forces and our high technology edge as we go about the inevitable downsizing of our forces. We know the men and women in uniform today comprise the finest military force in the world, and we know that the American technological know-how that we saw in [1991's Persian] Gulf war will mean

(LES ASPIN)

fewer casualties all around if and when we must use force again . . . Our high quality in people, high technology and technological equipment—that force must be maintained. The second set of challenges involves meeting the demands of the new post-Cold War, post-Soviet world. In this new world the definition of national security has been changed and it has been broadened. It now includes not only the threat from regional powers, but it also includes the new nuclear danger of proliferation and the possibility of the reversal of reforms in the former Soviet Union with untold consequences. It even includes [U.S.] economic [factors].

News conference,
Little Rock, Ark., Dec. 22/
The New York Times, 12-23:(A)10.

Donald J. Atwood, Jr.
Deputy Secretary of Defense
of the United States

1

We're faced now with a different world situation, in which we are no longer being chased by the Soviets or by the Russians in the development of new technology. We have weapons which have proven themselves to be the finest in the world. And we don't have to get into production on new ones just because we're chasing someone or they're chasing us.

The Washington Post,
1-30:(A)10.

Norman R. Augustine
Chairman,
Martin Marietta Corporation

2

[On his decision that his company buy General Electric's aerospace division]: I see the defense industry as the nation's fifth armed service. Without the defense industry we can't win. And the path we've been on has been one of a shrinking industry, with weaker competitors. The only solution I could see was to merge. The whole industry must consolidate.

USA Today, 11-25:(B)4.

Robert Barrow
Major,
United States Marine Corps

3

[On the Marines]: We are the general practitioners of the armed forces. People need to understand we are neither Gomer Pyles nor Rambos—we are something in-between, trained for everything from peacekeeping to all-out combat.

The Christian Science Monitor,
12-11:7.

Joseph R. Biden, Jr.
United States Senator,
D-Delaware

4

[Criticizing the Bush Administration for demanding too much from the Russians in talks aimed at reducing nuclear arsenals]: The Administration continues to see only a few trees instead of the forest. We have the opportunity to achieve drastically deep cuts in the Russian arsenal if we are willing to make cuts ourselves. Yet the Administration focused solely on weapons systems where the United States cuts would be minimal. [The U.S. position] appears driven by antiquated Cold War theories and a desire to achieve unilateral advantage. At this moment of opportunity, trying to push Moscow over the threshold from cooperation to unilateral disarmament is dangerously shortsighted. Our goal should be the deepest possible mutual cuts compatible with nuclear stability.

The New York Times, 6-8:(A)1.

Patrick J. Buchanan
Political commentator;
Candidate for the 1992
Republican Presidential nomination

5

This country has to remain first militarily. That means first on land, first on sea, first in the air, first in technology. We must still build a land-based missile defense system, as well as deploy the Strategic Defense Initiative to ensure our security. I will not *ask* our allies who have been freeloading off us for the entire Cold War to carry

(PATRICK J. BUCHANAN)

more of the burden of their own defense, I will *tell* them they have to carry more of the burden of their own defense because American troops are coming home. Why do we need 200,000 American troops in Bavaria when the Red Army is going home?

Los Angeles Times, 3-17:(H)6.

George Bush
President of the United States

1

[Russian President Boris Yeltsin and I] have agreed to eliminate the world's most dangerous weapons [from the two countries' arsenals]— heavy ICBMs and all other multiple-warhead ICBMs—and dramatically reduce our total strategic nuclear weapons. Those dramatic reductions will take place in two phases. They will be completed no later than the year 2003 and may be completed as early as the year 2000, if the United States can assist Russia in the required destruction of ballistic-missile systems. With this agreement, the nuclear nightmare recedes more and more for ourselves, for our children and for our grandchildren.

News conference,
Washington, D.C.,
June 16/
The New York Times, 6-17:(A)6.

2

[On charges by some families that he has not made public relevant information the government has on the whereabouts of POWs and MIAs from the Vietnam-war era]: To suggest that the Commander-in-Chief that led this country into its most successful recent effort [the Persian Gulf war] would condone for one single day the personal knowledge of a person held against his will, whether it's here or anyplace else, is simply totally unfair.

Before National League
of POW/MIA Families,
Virginia, July 24/
Los Angeles Times, 7-25:(A)18.

3

I'm old enough to remember [the] Vietnam [war], and I'm old enough to remember World War II . . . and I learned lessons from both. The first one in World War II was get the job done. Win it. Don't tie the hands of the military. Do what it takes. And the second one in Vietnam is don't get bogged down in a guerrilla war where you don't know what the hell you're doing and you tie the hands of the military. If I send a kid into battle, the force is going to be there to be sure he, or her, are on the winning side and fast.

Interview, Aug. 4/
USA Today, 8-5:(A)9.

4

Don't commit your [military] forces unless you see how it's going to end. And [then] go all out. Don't do it halfway. It is not right that a single soldier have anything but all-out support of his Commander-in-Chief. One Vietnam is enough. We put ourselves through an era of self-doubt, and we sent the signal around the world: The United States may not have the will to do what it has to do to finish the job. I'm still convinced that that false signal [sent by U.S. peace demonstrators just before the Persian Gulf war] led [Iraqi President] Saddam Hussein to believe that we would never use force against him. I'll feel that way as long as I'm alive. He said to himself: "How can a President [of the U.S.] move against this public opinion? How can he move when the Congress is telling him what he can't do? How can he move when you see all these demonstrations in front of the White House and all these editorials telling him he hasn't made his case?"

Interview/
U.S. News & World Report,
8-17:22.

5

Sending a son or daughter into combat, believe me, is the toughest part of the Presidency. Does this mean that if you've never seen the awful horror of battle that you can never be Commander-in-Chief. Of course not. But it does mean that we must hold our Presidents to the

(GEORGE BUSH)

highest standard, because they might have to decide if our sons and daughters should knock early on death's door . . . Why do these questions even matter [in a Presidential election campaign]? Why are they part of our national debate? They matter because, despite all our problems at home, we can never forget that we ask our Presidents to lead the military, to bear the awful authority of deciding to send your sons and daughters in harm's way.

Before National Guard Association,
Salt Lake City, Utah, Sept. 15/
USA Today, 9-16:(A)6.

1

[Referring to a letter written during the Vietnam war by Bill Clinton, Bush's Democratic opponent in this year's Presidential election]: I do not "loathe" the military. When Governor Clinton wrote and said "loathe the military," I said, "That's a shame." [U.S. soldiers in Vietnam] served their country with distinction and honor. We ought to salute them, not loathe them.

Campaigning,
Newark, N.J., Sept. 30/
The New York Times, 10-1:(A)14.

2

When anybody has a spending program they want to spend money on at home, they say, "Well, let's cut money out of the Defense Department." I will accept, and have accepted, the recommendations of two proven leaders—[Joint Chiefs Chairman] General Colin Powell and [Defense] Secretary Dick Cheney. They feel that the levels we're operating at and the reductions that I have proposed are proper . . . We are the sole remaining superpower, and we should be that. And we have a certain disproportionate responsibility . . . I don't want to see us make reckless cuts. Because of our programs, we have been able to significantly cut defense spending. But let's not cut into the muscle.

At Presidential candidates' debate,
St. Louis, Mo., Oct. 11/
The New York Times, 10-12:(A)12.

James T. Bush
Associate director,
Center for Defense Information

3

[On the arms-reduction agreement reached in just-held talks between U.S. President Bush and visiting Russian President Boris Yeltsin]: What this treaty does is remove the weapons that are most dangerous, the ones most likely to lead to a pre-emptive strike . . . their SS-18s and our MXs. Both sides will be left primarily with submarine-based missiles, which are not accurate enough to provide a first-strike capability, and bombers, which are so slow and easy to detect that you don't have a first-strike capability with them either. What you are left with essentially are retaliatory forces on both sides, and this greatly reduces the hair-trigger environment that we lived in for so long.

June 16/
The New York Times, 6-17:(A)7.

Dick Cheney
Secretary of Defense
of the United States

4

[On cutting the defense budget in the wake of the end of the Cold War]: There will be a debate [in Congress], certainly, in [an election] year that will suggest that . . . instead of cutting the number [President Bush] will announce . . . we could cut two or three times that. That's hogwash . . . Our military force is a very, very fragile and unique being, if you will. If we make the wrong decisions, then the next time we go to war, there will be a lot more of our people who don't come home again when it's over with.

Before Foreign Policy Association,
New York, N.Y.,
Jan. 27/Los Angeles Times, 1-31:(A)16.

5

There's only one reason to have a Department of Defense. We're not a social-welfare agency. We are there for one reason and one reason only—that's to be prepared to fight and win when called upon to do so.

March/
The Washington Post, 9-3:(A)12.

(DICK CHENEY)

1

Congress cannot have it both ways. They cannot tell us to cut the defense budget and then object every time we move to cut the defense budget. All I hear from my friends on the [Capitol] Hill is, "Not in *my* back yard; don't close *my* armory; don't shut down *my* production line." We can't operate on that basis.

News conference,
Washington, D.C., March 26/
Los Angeles Times, 3-27:(A)20.

2

[On the Navy scandal involving sexual harassment by male officers of female officers at last year's Las Vegas meeting of the Tailhook Association]: I think it would be a mistake to look at these events as somehow indicating there's some kind of fundamental problem with the United States Navy. For the nation, or the press, or anyone else to judge men and women in uniform based upon what a handful of individuals did in Las Vegas would be absolutely, totally unfair and irresponsible.

News conference,
Washington, D.C., July 7/
The Washington Post, 7-8:(A)2.

Bill Clinton
Governor of Arkansas (D);
Candidate for the 1992
Democratic Presidential nomination

3

[On the controversy about his avoiding the draft during the Vietnam war]: The way I got back into the [draft] lottery [after being classified 1-D because he planned to enter an ROTC program at college] was, at the end of the summer [of 1969], I just decided [ROTC] was not a good thing to do. I'd already had one good year at Oxford [University in England], but by then four of my classmates had died in Vietnam, including a boy that was one of my closest friends when I was a child. So I asked to be put back in the draft. I didn't know anything about the lottery [system], and I sure as hell didn't know what my number was. And the guy that was the head of the ROTC

unit really tried to talk me out of it. He said, "I've done a tour in Vietnam, and I did Korea, and I did World War II and you don't need to do this." I said, "Yeah, I just can't put it off. Call me. Let's go."

Interview/
The Washington Post, 1-18:(A)10.

4

[Calling for an end to the ban on homosexuals serving in the armed forces]: We can't afford to waste the capacities, the contributions, the hearts, the souls, the minds of the gay and lesbian Americans . . . As soon as the Pentagon issued a study . . . which said there was no basis in national security for discriminating based on the sexual orientation of Americans who wish to serve in the military, I said I would act on [it, if elected President]. It seemed to me elemental that if a person, a man or woman, wanted to serve their country, they ought to be able to do it.

May 19/USA Today, 11-18:(A)4.

5

We need to define the defense we need. What will it take for us to be the strongest country in the world still? And we need to pay for that. We know we don't need as many troops in Europe. We know the Germans and the Japanese should pay more of their own way. We know we may not need 12 carrier groups. We may not need all the weapon systems. What do we need?

Broadcast question-and-answer session/
"This Morning," CBS-TV, 6-15.

Bill Clinton
Governor of Arkansas (D);
1992 Democratic
Presidential nominee

6

It is time to take a fresh look at the basic organization of our armed forces. We have four separate air forces—one each for the Marines, Army, Navy and Air Force. Both the Army and Marines have light-infantry divisions. The Navy and Air Force have separately developed, but similar, fighter aircraft and tactical missiles.

(BILL CLINTON)

While respecting each service's unique capabilities, we can reduce redundancies, save billions of dollars and get better teamwork.

Speech,
Los Angeles, Calif., Aug. 13/
The New York Times, 12:31:(A)10.

1

[On whether someone like himself, who opposed the Vietnam war and avoided the draft, could be a good Commander-in-Chief]: I was opposed to the war, I couldn't help that. I felt very strongly about it and I didn't want to go at the time. It's easy to say in retrospect I would have done something differently. President [Abraham] Lincoln opposed the war and there were people who said maybe he shouldn't be President. But I think he made us a pretty good President in wartime. We got a lot of other Presidents who didn't wear their country's uniform and had to order our young soldiers to the battle, including President [Woodrow] Wilson and President [Franklin] Roosevelt. So the answer is I could do that. I wouldn't relish doing it, but I wouldn't shrink from it. I think that the President has to be prepared to use the power of the nation when our vital interests are threatened. When our treaty commitments are at stake. When we know that something has to be done that is in the national interest. And that is a part of being President. Could I do it? Yes, I could.

At Presidential candidate's debate,
East Lansing, Mich., Oct. 19/
The New York Times, 10-20:(A)13.

Bill Clinton
Governor of Arkansas (D;
President-elect
of the United States

2

We know there have always been gays in the military, and we know, according to the study which was released near the end of [this year's Presidential-election] campaign, that it costs the United States taxpayers about $500-million to get fewer than 17,000 gays out of the military over the last 10 years. And so the issue therefore is not whether there are gays in the military. It is whether they can be in the military without lying about it, as long as there is a very strict code of conduct, which if they violate it would lead to dismissal from the service or other appropriate sanctions. There is a great deal of difference between somebody doing something wrong and their status, condition in life.

News conference,
Little Rock, Ark., Nov. 16/
The New York Times, 11-17:(A)12.

John Conyers, Jr.
United States Representative,
D-Michigan

3

[On reports that the U.S. Patriot anti-missile missile may not have performed as well as initially thought in last year's Persian Gulf war]: In future conflicts, we could unnecessarily endanger soldiers' lives if we deploy the Patriot based on overly optimistic assessments of its capabilities. If American soldiers think that they can depend on Patriot battalions destroying nine out of 10 enemy missiles, when the actual defense capability may be closer to one out of 50, it would be a disaster. If we know that, but refuse to admit it, then the offense is criminal.

April 7/
Los Angeles Times, 4-8:(A)12.

Paula Coughlin
Lieutenant,
United States Navy

4

[On her charges of sexual harassment by fellow officers during a convention of the Tailhook Association]: The honorable thing, in my mind, is to come forward. You come forward and you let those who are not guilty—all those naval officers who are good officers who resent this black eye should be given the opportunity to perform their job and be proud of being in the Navy without having those guilty parties among their ranks. I think at all levels, in and out of the Navy, civilian and military, that there's not a clear understanding of the terrible side effects of sexual

(PAULA COUGHLIN)

harassment, sexual assault. And I think that's why I kind of needed to come forward and put a face to this terrible incident. And it's not a glamorous thing to come forward with a very humiliating and degrading experience. But if somebody can understand what I suffered and appreciate why it shouldn't happen again, then it's worth it, then that's part of the evolution.

Broadcast interview/
"Newsmaker Sunday," CNN-TV, 6-28.

J. James Exon
United States Senator,
D-Nebraska

1

[Criticizing the Administration's warnings about Congress cutting military spending more than recommended by President Bush]: There is an artful, emotionally charged, yet inherently dishonest snow job going on as the future of our nation's military is debated. [Deeper cuts than Bush's can be achieved] without pink-slipping troops by the tens of thousands, as many in the Administration would have Congress believe if we dare cut a penny below the President's number.

The Washington Post, 4-10:(A)10.

Thomas C. Foley
Major General,
United States Army;
Commander, Armor School,
Fort Knox, Ky.

2

[On the current scaling down of the military in the wake of the end of the Cold War]: This transition period is potentially dangerous. I don't want to say there is a bogey man behind every tree, but you have to admit [that] when the American people say, "Our interests are being threatened, let's do something about it," we have got to be ready to go, on a much reduced scale maybe, but ready to go.

The New York Times,
2-3:(A)6.

John R. Galvin
General,
United States Army;
Supreme Allied Commander/Europe

3

NATO of the Cold War was a push-button organization. It was aimed at an immediate and unified response to a short-term attack by a very powerful force. NATO of the future will not be that kind of organization. It's going to be a pool of capabilities—many nations capable of responses in a lot of different ways. All NATO [could] jump up together [to deal with] some kind of crisis. Or NATO could send forces from a variety of different countries. This has been done in the past couple of years.

Interview/
U.S. News & World Report,
6-1:40.

Albert Gore, Jr.
United States Senator,
D-Tennessee;
1992 Democratic
Vice Presidential nominee

4

In the aftermath of the Cold War, the definition of strong national defense has obviously changed somewhat . . . We believe that we can make savings in our defense budget and at the same time improve our national security. Now, for those who are affected by the cutbacks, whether they come from [President George Bush] or [Democratic Presidential nominee] Bill Clinton and me, the difference is Bill Clinton and I have a defense conversion program, so that those who won the Cold War will not be left out in the cold. We want to put them to work building infrastructure and an economy here in this country for the '90s and the next century.

At Vice-Presidential candidates' debate,
Atlanta, Ga., Oct. 13/
The New York Times, 10-14:(A)13.

Phil Gramm
United States Senator,
R-Texas

5

[Saying the Defense Department should determine how much it can cut back now that the Cold

(PHIL GRAMM)

War is over]: I believe that even in a world where the lion and lamb are about to lie down together, I want to be sure we're the lion.

News conference,
Washington, D.C., Jan. 6/
USA Today, 1-7:(A)13.

J. Daniel Howard
Acting Secretary of the Navy
of the United States

1

[On recent revelations of sexual harassment of female members of the Navy by men within the service, such as at the Tailhook Association convention]: Those things happened right under our noses. [The abuses] were committed by a few, but ladies and gentlemen, they were excused by far too many, and by all the leaders over the years who turned a blind or bemused eye to the crude, alcohol-inspired antics of a few idiots in our ranks.

Speech to senior leadership of Navy
and Marine Corps,
at the Pentagon, July 1/
The Washington Post, 7-3:(A)9.

Edward M. Kennedy
United States Senator,
D-Massachusetts

2

It is inconsistent for the President [Bush] to claim we won the Cold War and then reduce defense spending only to normal Cold War levels when we face other urgent needs. Either the Cold War is over, or it is not.

At Senate Armed Services
Committee hearing,
Washington, D.C., Jan. 31/
Los Angeles Times, 2-1:(A)15.

3

[Supporting legislation to ban U.S. nuclear-weapons testing]: We have been preaching [nuclear] non-proliferation to other nations for years. We have to let them know we practice what we preach.

Aug. 3/USA Today, 8-4:(A)1.

Henry A. Kissinger
Former Secretary of State
of the United States

4

[On implications now by those in Congress that he and others in the Administration of President Richard Nixon did not try sufficiently or lied or covered up in their attempts to bring home all U.S. POW/MIAs as the Vietnam war wound down in the 1970s]: From the day we entered office, we had no more consistent goal than the release of the brave Americans held prisoner throughout Indochina, and a full accounting of their missing colleagues. The negotiating record makes clear that this matter was insistently raised with the Vietnamese. Despite Hanoi's protestations, we demanded that Hanoi guarantee the release of American POWs in Laos and Cambodia, and assist in accounting for MIAs. There was no issue on which American officials from the President on down were more adamant . . . Here we are, 20 years later, being pilloried in leaks, without a shred of evidence, for the unforgivable libel that we knowingly abandoned the very group whose suffering was the biggest single incentive for our exertion . . . Just as I was leaving for the final negotiations in January, 1973, the [U.S.] House and Senate Democratic [Party] caucuses each passed, by very large margins, resolutions calling for legislation to cut off all funds for the war. I challenge those flaunting their 20-20 hindsight [today] to say how they could have gotten better terms in that charged political atmosphere. What, precisely, would they have been willing to do to achieve what particular changes and at what cost? Moreover, since Congress removed both incentives and penalties for Hanoi's compliance, how exactly would any achievable amendment have changed Hanoi's behavior? . . . What has happened to this country that a Congressional committee could be asked [today] to inquire whether any American official of whatever Administration would fail to move heaven and earth to fight for the release of American POWs and an accounting of the missing? Can anyone seriously believe that any honorable public official would neglect American servicemen, and especially those who suffered so much for their country, or, even worse, arrange for a conspiracy to

WHAT THEY SAID IN 1992

obscure the fate of the prisoners left behind? . . . In theory we had three sources of leverage available [against Hanoi for a POW/MIA accounting]— bombing the north, offering economic aid to Hanoi, and giving military and economic aid to Saigon to deprive Hanoi of the hope of military victory. The U.S. Congress took all three levers away, denying us both the carrot and the stick. When the Congress eliminated our leverage, we were trapped in the classic nightmare of every statesman. We had nothing to back up our tough words. But more tough words. Under such conditions, we had no bargaining position left.

Before Senate Select Committee
on POW/MIA Affairs,
Washington, D.C., Sept. 22/
The New York Times, 9-23:(A)12.

Dennis H. Long
Colonel, United States Army;
Director of Total Force Readiness,
Fort Knox, Ky.

1

[On the end of the Cold War]: For 50 years, we [the military] equipped our football team, practiced five days a week and never played a game. We had a clear enemy [the Soviet Union] with demonstrable qualities, and we had scouted them out. [Now] we will have to practice day in and day out without knowing anything about the other team. We won't have his playbook, we won't know where the stadium is, or how many guys he will have on the field. That is very distressing to the military establishment, especially when you are trying to justify the existence of your organization and your systems.

The New York Times, 2-3:(A)6.

Robert S. McNamara
Former Secretary of Defense
of the United States

2

The danger is not that some group of nations will engage in conflict that will endanger the military structure of the great powers. The danger is that the great powers will fail to follow through on

the vision. If the United States will give leadership in that direction and the other great powers will follow, then I believe it should be possible to cut military expenditures in the world roughly in half. The residual role for the military is to deal with the conflicts that can't be deterred.

Interview/
The New York Times, 2-3:(A)6.

Merrill A. McPeak
General and Chief of Staff,
United States Air Force

3

[On the dismantling of SAC]: There is a sense in which you could say . . . that the Strategic Air Command won the war that it was established to fight, the Cold War. So, with the rearrangement of global . . . circumstances, we simply had to take another look and see are we organized properly for the new world order . . . We're making history today. We are present at the creation of a new and better Air Force . . . We are instituting basic changes here, not just tinkering at the margins.

Omaha, Neb., June 1/
Los Angeles Times, 6-2:(A)13.

4

Even though logic tells us that women can [conduct combat operations] as well as men, I have a very traditional attitude about wives and mothers and daughters being ordered to kill people. I take some solace in thinking that not all human problems yield to strict logic.

Before House Armed Services Committee,
Washington, D.C., July 30/
Los Angeles Times, 7-31:(A)20.

John J. Mearsheimer
Professor of political science,
University of Chicago (Ill.)

5

Nuclear weapons have helped keep the peace for 45 years. The best way to prevent war between great powers is to make them secure and cautious . . . [and] nuclear weapons do that.

Los Angeles Times, 6-9:(A)16.

Jack Mendelsohn
Deputy director,
Arms Control Association

1

[On the arms-reduction agreement reached in just-held talks between U.S. President Bush and visiting Russian President Boris Yeltsin]: We are talking about a very good deal. On paper, it looks like the two forces will be reduced equally, but in fact the Russians will be giving up the backbone of their arsenal—land-based multiple-warhead missiles—while we [the U.S.] will be retaining the area of our greatest strength, sea-based ballistic missiles.

June 16/The New York Times, 6-17:(A)7.

Sam Nunn
United States Senator,
D-Georgia

2

[Criticizing duplications and redundancies in the armed services]: As former Senator Barry Goldwater frequently said, we are the only military in the world with four air forces. We have a Marine Corps and an Army with light infantry divisions. Both the Navy and the Air Force design, build, test and field cruise missiles. Both the Navy and the Air Force build and operate satellites. Each of the military departments has its own huge infrastructure of schools, laboratories, industrial facilities, testing organizations and training ranges. We have at least three, and in some instances four, separate chaplain corps, medical corps, dental corps, nursing corps and legal corps. In certain cases Navy radios can't operate interchangeably with Army radios. Navy aircraft require different types of aerial refueling equipment than Air Force aircraft. Air Force aircraft use chaff and flares that can't be used by the Navy. The list goes on and on.

Before the Senate,
Washington, D.C., July 2/
The Washington Post, 7-3:(A)21.

Sean O'Keefe
Secretary of the Navy
of the United States

3

One of my primary concerns is ending the rivalries and jealousies between the key war-fighting communities of the Navy. Our approach is very simple. We believe that there can be no jealousy among the fingers of a strong fist.

News conference,
Washington, D.C., July 22/
The Washington Post, 7-23:(A)3.

Ross Perot
Industrialist;
1992 independent
Presidential candidate

4

If we learned anything in Vietnam it's you first commit this nation before you commit the troops to the battlefield. We cannot send our people all over the world to solve every problem that comes up . . . It is inappropriate for us, just because there's a problem somewhere around the world, to take the sons and daughters of working people—and make no mistake about it, our all-volunteer armed force is not made up of the sons and daughters of the beautiful people, it's the working folks who send their sons and daughters to war, with a few exceptions. It's very unlike World War II when F.D.R.'s sons flew missions, everybody went. It's a different world now and very important that we not just, without thinking it through, just rush to every problem in the world and have our people torn to pieces.

At Presidential candidates' debate,
St. Louis, Mo.,
Oct. 11/
The New York Times, 10-12:(A)14.

Colin L. Powell
General, United States Army;
Chairman, Joint Chiefs of Staff

5

[Criticizing those in Congress who have called for sweeping cuts in defense spending]: I get a little annoyed sometimes at being accused of not seeing the new world—"You Colonel Blimps in the Pentagon have got to get with it." Well, we have definitely got with it . . . Though we can still plausibly identify some specific threats—North Korea, something in Southwest Asia—the real threat is the unknown, the uncertain. In a very real sense, the primary threat to our security

(COLIN L. POWELL)

is . . . being unprepared to handle a crisis or war that no one expected or predicted . . . I categorically reject this idea of no-threat, no-sweat, cut the forces. It's a simplistic idea. It is historically wrong.

Before Senate Armed Services Committee,
Washington, D.C., Jan. 31/
The Washington Post, 2-1:(A)4.

1

[On his philosophy when using the U.S. military in situations such as a possible strike against Iraqi mass-destruction weapons and facilities]: If we are called upon to be a part of this solution, we will perform our role in an absolutely professional way with desired results . . . The only recommendations I give are for decisive action: overwhelming use of power when necessary with as little risk [to U.S. forces] as possible.

Before Senate Armed Services Committee,
Washington, D.C., March 20/
Los Angeles Times, 3-21:(A)8.

2

[On the dismantling of SAC]: For 46 years, SAC held in its hands the ultimate weapons of war and the essential key to peace. Their job complete [with the end of the Cold War], their war won, we bid farewell to SAC . . . Thank you, Strategic Air Command. Job well done! Enjoy your retirement.

Omaha, Neb., June 1/
Los Angeles Times, 6-2:(A)13.

3

[Saying he is not a fan of "limited" use of military force without clear-cut objectives]: As soon as they tell me it is limited, it means they do not care whether you achieve a result or not. As soon as they tell me "surgical" [strike], I head for the bunker . . . [Those who call for limited or graduated use of U.S. forces in a particular situation] are the same folks who have stuck us into problems before that we have lived to regret. I have some memories of us being put into situations like that which did not turn out quite the way

that the people who put us in thought—i.e., Lebanon, if you want a more recent real experience, where a bunch of Marines were put in there as a symbol, as a sign. Except those poor young folks did not know exactly what their mission was. They did not know really what they were doing there. It was very confusing. Two hundred and forty-one of them died as a result.

Interview, Washington, D.C./
The New York Times, 9-28:(A)1,6.

4

[On President-elect Bill Clinton's proposal to lift the ban on homosexuals serving in the armed forces]: This is a judgment that will have to be made by political leaders. The military leaders in the armed forces of the United States—the Joint Chiefs of Staff and the senior commanders—continue to believe strongly that the presence of homosexuals within the armed forces would be prejudicial to good order and discipline. And we continue to hold that view.

To reporters, Argentina, Nov. 12/
The New York Times, 11-14:8.

Dan Quayle
Vice President
of the United States

5

We won the Cold War because we invested in national security. We won the Cold War because we invested in our military. We won the Cold War because America had the political will and made the right decisions. Yes, we can make the cuts in defense, and we have. [But Democratic Presidential nominee] Bill Clinton wants to cut defense another $60-billion . . . We would not have won the Cold War if we had listened to [Democratic Vice-Presidential nominee] Senator [Albert] Gore and his crowd and had supported a nuclear freeze. If you would have supported that attitude, we would not have won the Cold War. We won the Cold War because we invested and we went forward.

At Vice-Presidential candidates' debate,
Atlanta, Ga., Oct. 13/
The New York Times, 10-14:(A)13.

Paul Roush
Colonel, United States
Marine Corps (Ret.);
Leadership professor,
U.S. Naval Academy

1

Women as professionals [in the military] will not be fully legitimized until the combat exclusion . . . is eliminated. Its continuation perpetuates second-place status and expectations of substandard performance for women. It reinforces bigotry as a learned behavior for men.

Before Presidential Commission
on Women in the Armed Forces/
The Washington Post, 7-14:(A)3.

James R. Sasser
United States Senator,
D-Tennessee

2

[Calling for deeper cuts in U.S. defense spending than those proposed by President Bush]: If it indeed is as low as we can go, we are putting a very low ceiling on the kind of investment we can make in America . . . Something less than seizing the day is going on here. The reward for peace [seems to be] a modest sliver.

At Senate Budget Committee hearing,
Washington, D.C., Feb. 3/
Los Angeles Times, 2-4:(A)14.

David Scheffer
Senior fellow,
Carnegie Endowment
for International Peace

3

[On U.S. concern that its involvement with UN forces and the resulting joint command structure will result in loss of control over its own forces]: The command issue is a canard—the fear has been exaggerated . . . We've got to recognize the utility of joint command structures and joint armed forces. The U.S. is simply not going to [use its military power] unilaterally anymore, and you can't have your cake and eat it too.

The Christian Science Monitor,
6-22:3.

Paul C. Warnke
Former Director,
Arms Control and
Disarmament Agency
of the United States

4

Getting [the defence budget] down to about $150-billion rather than $300-billion by the end of the decade is readily doable. The problem is we are now finding other reasons for maintaining a defense budget. One of them is to keep people employed. That's the only conceivable reason for having something like 20 B-2 bombers. You couldn't possibly find any scenario in which you need 20 B-2s. You find the same phenomenon with the Seawolf submarine, which essentially is a jobs program for Connecticut and Rhode Island. The Seawolf was designed to search out and destroy Soviet nuclear submarines; and, again, the threat is gone. So it really is a question of biting the bullet. As a result of the end of the Cold War, you just don't need all of these companies manufacturing missiles, airplanes, you name it. So some of those companies will disappear.

Interview/USA Today, 6-17:(A)13.

Boris N. Yeltsin
President of Russia

5

The Cold War confrontation has become a thing of the past, but we have inherited from it mountains of weapons, huge armies and entire defense-oriented industries employing millions of people. In the most dramatic terms, the gap that separates the new political realities and the military-technological situation finds expression in the fact that the strategic forces of nuclear powers . . . remain targeted on each other's countries. The absurdity of such a situation is evident.

Message to UN Conference
on Disarmament, Feb. 12/*
Los Angeles Times, 2-13:(A)10.

6

Saying that U.S.-Russian arms-control negotiations may result in U.S. nuclear superiority]: Parity is of another era . . . If the resulting

(BORIS N. YELTSIN)

arsenals turn out to be different in size, then so be it.

During talks with U.S. President Bush,
Washington, D.C.,
June 16/Los Angeles Times, 6-17:(A)6.

John Young
Former president,
Hewlett-Packard Company

1

Historically, the government share [of investment] that has gone to defense R&D has been about half [with the other half going to civilian R&D]. That, of course, has been built up so that it's about 60 per cent [for defense] right now . . . So if we just go back to 50-50, we would free up $7-billion that could be deployed to other commercially relevant technologies. Given the economic warfare in the years ahead that I foresee, as opposed to the real shooting warfare that we've been used to, maybe that needs to be upside down. Maybe 60 per cent of that over time needs to be on commercially relevant R&D, and only 40 per cent on defense.

Interview/
The Christian Science Monitor,
11-19:8.

The Economy • Labor

Henry J. Aaron
Economist,
Brookings Institution

1

If the Federal deficit remains just an abstraction, a number too large for human comprehension, a quantity that floats unconnected with human loss and frustration that it inevitably causes, we are never effectively going to deal with it . . . The calls for increased [Federal] spending and for tax breaks . . . are endless. These claims are tangible and easily understood and many of them are deserving of approval. But unless the public recognizes that the excessive Federal deficits affect the economic hopes and aspirations of U.S. businesses and U.S. workers, the deficit and the pain it inflicts are going to persist indefinitely. The United States needs more *private* investment, not less. That means, I think, that all new government spending should be paid for by either cutting other spending or by raising taxes, not by even more borrowing.

At economic conference convened
by President-elect Bill Clinton,
Little Rock, Ark., Dec. 15/
The New York Times, 12-16:(A)10.

Alex Alexiev
Personal economic adviser to
Prime Minister of Bulgaria
Philip Dimitrov

2

In a Western nation, if your GNP is falling and unemployment is rising, then that is cause for serious concern. But in a Communist country, neither one of those measures means a thing. Let's take GNP. In a capitalist country, only goods produced and sold end up in GNP. But in any Communist or socialist country it includes goods produced but not sold. They do not deduct the goods not sold like they do in a capitalist country, so the GNP from a Communist country usually contains about 30 per cent junk, things that you have spent raw materials for, skilled labor, expensive energy, and produced junk,

something that cannot be sold at any price. So if you have an economy like that, and if your production of junk declines by 30 per cent [as you move toward a market economy], then you're doing something extremely useful.

USA Today, 11-30:(Our World)16.

Akhil Reed Amar
Professor of constitutional law,
Yale Law School

3

[Supporting the idea of a Constitutional amendment that mandated a balanced Federal budget]: Not every provision of the Constitution is fully enforceable. Even if this proposed amendment weren't a cleanly workable political rule, it might give some moral status and strength to the fundamental idea that it is wrong for us to finance current benefits on the backs of our children and grandchildren who, of course, aren't able to vote now.

The New York Times, 6-11:(A)10.

Richard K. Armey
United States Representative,
R-Texas

4

[Supporting a proposed Constitutional amendment aimed at forcing a balanced Federal budget]: The most important reason for passing the amendment is to force members of Congress to set priorities. Do we spend scarce resources on farm subsidies or children's nutrition? Do we spend money for national defense or public television? Currently, we're simply pushing these tough decisions into the future. The White House would also be dealt back into the process. Administration officials will play a much larger role in crafting what is actually in the budget. Congress could not simply deem the Administration budget "dead on arrival."

The Washington Post, 6-2:(A)17.

William P. Barr
Attorney General
of the United States

1

[On the Justice Department's decision to expand antitrust laws to cover foreign business practices that are detrimental to U.S. interests]: Applying the antitrust laws to remove illegal barriers to export competition makes sense as a matter of law and policy. Our antitrust laws are designed to preserve and foster competition, and in today's global economy competition is international.

April 3/The Washington Post, 4-4:(C)1.

Peter L. Bernstein
Economic consultant

2

The whole history of capitalism is that you overdo expansion, as we did from 1967 until 1982, and then overdo the cutback until you fall short of capital stock.

The New York Times, 12-1:(C)2.

Charles Black
Senior adviser
to the re-election campaign
of President George Bush

3

[On Paul Tsongas, candidate for the 1992 Democratic presidential nomination]: The economics he's talking right now [are] pretty close to the President and it's a repudiation of what the [tax-writing] Ways and Means Committee and these Democrats in Congress are doing. He's even said it's not necessary to tax the rich; what's necessary is investment incentives to get growth. Sounds like George Bush. Even sounds like [HUD Secretary] Jack Kemp.

Interview, Feb. 21/
The Christian Science Monitor, 2-24:8.

John W. Bligh, Jr.
Minister-Counselor
for Commercial Affairs,
United States Embassy,
Bonn, Germany

4

If a weaker dollar is the solution to our trade problems, then why don't we have a trade surplus, since the dollar has been weak for years and reached a new historical low during the past few months? You can only sell so much grain or so many service products. Large sectors of our manufacturing industry do not have competitive products right now. If you have nothing to sell, its price is irrelevant.

The New York Times, 12-1:(C)1.

Alan Blinder
Professor of economics,
Princeton University

5

America's first response to the productivity slow-down problem actually worsened the inequality problem. And I refer, of course, to supply-side economics or trickle-down economics or whatever you'd like to call it . . . Fortunately there's an alternative strategy to trickle down and I call it percolate up. That is, if you work to raise the quality of the workforce, and if you succeed, then the productivity of capital in our economy will be higher, the returns earned by the owners of capital will be higher, and there is nothing that will boost investment more than higher returns to capital.

At economic conference convened
by President-elect Bill Clinton,
Little Rock, Ark., Dec. 14/
The New York Times, 12-15:(A)14.

Henryka Bochniarz
Former Minister of Industry
of Poland

6

I believe in the wisdom of the common man. But when it comes to economics, sometimes the only way to get things moving is not to take too much notice of what people say.

U.S. News & World Report,
3-23:50.

Joseph Boskin
Director, urban-studies
public-policy program,
Boston (Mass.) University

7

[President-elect Bill] Clinton's first priority should be job creation. I'd like to see such efforts

(JOSEPH BOSKIN)

as Job Corps programs connected with universities and colleges, so that there are some long-term development of skills going on, and not just cleaning the streets.

The Christian Science Monitor,
12-2:8.

Michael J. Boskin
Chairman,
Council of Economic Advisers
to President of the United States
George Bush

1

For the first time in many years, more capital is flowing back into the Americas for new investment than is flowing out as flight capital. In nearly every nation in the Americas, real growth has returned, often after a very difficult decade. Barriers to trade and investment are coming down, and one of the most exciting regions for world growth and investment is Latin America, an increasingly important market for U.S. exports . . . A North American Free Trade Agreement will benefit the American [U.S.] economy. NAFTA will create an enormous market of 360 million consumers with total output of more than $6-trillion. In joining in a free-trade area with Canada and Mexico, we will be joining in a barrier-free area with our first and third leading trade partners.

Washington, D.C., June 24/
The Washington Post, 7-1:(A)22.

Emmett Boyle
Chairman,
Ravenswood Aluminum Corporation

2

[Criticizing a proposal that Congress enact a ban on companies' hiring permanent replacements for striking workers]: If an employer did not have the right to replace its work force, it could be held hostage by organized labor with unreasonable demands. [If such a ban is enacted,] you will see a lot more strikes and you will see a lot more companies fail.

Wheeling, W.V./
The Christian Science Monitor, 4-9:6.

Nicholas F. Brady
Secretary of the Treasury
of the United States

3

If your view in the United States economy is slow-growing and the only thing you can do is increase taxes to get that job done, then I don't think you're going to get the private economy energized. But if you indicate you have pro-growth plans that induce more industrial activity, give people a chance to buy houses, provide, in the case of [reductions in] the capital-gains tax, a freeing up of assets and an opportunity for small- and middle-income people to make a profit, then that'll happen. But it's the private economy that gets the job done.

Interview/
USA Today, 2-11:(A)11.

4

Lowering interest rates—a more optimistic view by everybody, investors, consumers and industrial people—is the way to work our way out of this [recessioin]. If you are worried about the banking system . . . the single thing that would help most is more optimism, and that would come with lower interest rates. It has been a mystery to me why that has been so hard to understand.

Interview/
The Washington Post, 6-17:(F)1.

5

[On 1992 Democratic Presidential nominee, Arkansas Governor Bill Clinton]: If he can't have more success with Arkansas in bringing it out of the absolute rear end of every economic statistic, what in heaven is he going to do [as President] with the United States?

The Washington Post, 7-31:(F)3.

Edmund G. "Jerry" Brown, Jr.
Candidate for the 1992
Democratic Presidential nomination;
Former Governor
of California (D)

6

[On the proposed U.S.-Canada-Mexico free-trade agreement]: While we have to integrate

WHAT THEY SAID IN 1992

(EDMUND G. "JERRY" BROWN, JR.)

Canada, Mexico and America, we shouldn't do it overnight, and we shouldn't do it at the expense of [U.S.] jobs or the environment or the fabric of our community. We need to have people representing the interests of average American workers because those people are getting trampled as the big corporate executives steamroll down the fast track.

Los Angeles Times, 3-17:(H)6.

1

A flat tax makes it understandable. It takes out loopholes. It reduces disincentives. The problem we have now is that we have a theory of graduated income tax, but because that deters investment and interferes with a lot of things that people like, you then have to carve it up into lots of little loopholes—investment tax credit, deductions for business in various ways, loss carry forward, capital-gains reduction, innumerable items which people are asking for. So then you defeat the whole purpose because the tax code then distorts economic activity. What is required is the simplest tax possible.

Interview/
USA Today, 5-7:(A)11.

John Bryan
Chairman,
Sara Lee Corporation

2

[On the current recession]: You can't spend eight years priming the pump and getting all your growth through debt in the private, corporate and public sectors and expect to come out of it overnight. We're not going to get any momentous return to growth anytime soon.

Time, 1-13:36.

Patrick J. Buchanan
Political commentator;
Candidate for the 1992
Republican Presidential nomination

3

Like GM, the U.S.A. has been downsized by smirking competitors in Europe and Asia. My

resolution: to put America first, to make America first and keep America first. We must put an end to the economic disarmament of our country. We must be as tough in trade talks with new rivals as we were in arms talks with old enemies. We need a new patriotism. The time when America could ship off $300-million a week in foreign aid to Third World regimes, and not miss it, is over. Americans need work, not welfare.

Interview/
Newsweek, 1-6:24.

4

First thing I'd do [as President] is freeze Federal spending . . . cut regulations across the board, cut Federal salaries and go for tax cuts across the board. In the longer term . . . we have got to make America competitive again . . . You have got to take money away from the government and give it back to people and to businesses and their institutions if they're going to start creating jobs . . . As for trade barriers . . . we're not going to let foreign governments target one [U.S.] industry after another, knock it off with subsidies and dumping and then move on and target another.

Broadcast interview/
"Good Morning America,"
ABC-TV, 2-4.

George Bush
President of the United States

5

Protectionism isn't a prescription for prosperity. Boil away all the tough talk, all the swagger and all the patriotic posture, and protectionism amounts to a smoke screen for a country that is running scared.

Speech announcing his candidacy
for re-election,
Washington, D.C., Feb. 12/
The New York Times, 2-13:(A)10.

6

Some politicians don't share our views on the value of free trade. They want to address this issue from both sides of their mouths, and they

(GEORGE BUSH)

suggest that we can hide in the cocoon of protection and still benefit from the fresh air of competition. That is simply not possible. You can pander to the protectionists or you can promote free trade. You cannot have it both ways.

To National Association
of Hispanic Journalists,
via satellite from Washington, D.C.,
April 24/The New York Times, 4-25:8.

1

I would remind the people that Congress appropriates every dime and tells me how to spend every dime. It's the Congress that does that. But, sure, I'll accept my share of the responsibility for this long recession, and so will the Congress. But the question isn't blame. The question is what you do about it . . . It's a question of . . . challenging the Congress to help us help the American people.

News conference,
Washington, D.C., June 4/
The New York Times, 6-5:(A)10.

2

I think [people are] disenchanted with the economy. And . . . all kinds of people . . . want to capitalize on that in order to be elected. People are angry and they want to think something can be different . . . It's not all economic. You've got [concerns about] education. You have crime in the neighborhoods. All of this contributes. But economics contributes the most, because if people think that they have no chance or that their chances are much less, in terms of home-ownership or in terms of educating their kids, why, it results in a churning around and a discouragement.

Interview, Washington, D.C./
The Atlantic, August:24.

3

Americans want jobs. On January 28, I put before Congress a plan to create jobs. If it had been passed back then, 500,000 more Americans would be at work right now. But in a nation

that demands action, Congress has become the master of inaction.

At Republican National Convention,
Houston, Texas, Aug. 20/
The New York Times, 8-21:(A)16.

4

There's an old saying: "Good judgment comes from experience, and experience comes from bad judgment." Two years ago, I made a bad call on the Democrats' tax increase. I underestimated Congress's addiction to taxes. With my back against the wall, I agreed to a hard bargain: One tax increase one time, in return for the toughest spending limits ever. Well, it was a mistake to go along with the Democratic tax increase. But here's my question for the American people: Who do you trust in this [fall's Presidential] election? The candidate [himself] who raised taxes one time and regrets it, or the other candidate [Arkansas Governor Bill Clinton] who raised taxes and fees 128 times, and enjoyed it every time?

At Republican National Convention,
Houston, Texas, Aug. 20/
The New York Times, 8-21:(A)16.

5

[On 1992 Democratic Presidential nominee Bill Clinton]: My opponent says America is a nation in decline. Of our economy he says, we are somewhere on the list beneath Germany, heading south toward Sri Lanka. Well, don't let anyone tell you that America is second-rate, especially somebody running for President. Maybe he hasn't heard that we are still the world's largest economy. No other nation sells more outside its borders. The Germans, the British, the Japanese—can't touch the productivity of you, the American worker and the American farmer. My opponent won't mention that. He won't remind you that interest rates are the lowest they've been in 20 years, and millions of Americans have refinanced their homes. And you just won't hear that inflation—the thief of the middle class—has been locked in a maximum-security prison.

At Republican National Convention,
Houston, Texas, Aug. 20/
The New York Times, 8-21:(A)16.

WHAT THEY SAID IN 1992

(GEORGE BUSH)

1

We start with a simple fact: Government is too big and spends too much. I've asked Congress to put a lid on mandatory spending, except Social Security. And I've proposed doing away with over 200 programs and 4,000 wasteful projects and to freeze all other spending. The gridlock Democrat Congress has said, "No." So, beginning tonight, I will enforce the spending freeze on my own. If Congress sends me a bill spending more than I asked for in my budget, I will veto it fast . . . After all these years, Congress has become pretty creative at finding ways to waste your money. So we need to be just as creative at finding ways to stop them. I have a brand new idea. Taxpayers should be given the right to check a box on their tax returns, so that up to 10 percent of their payments can go for one purpose alone: to reduce the national debt. But we also need to make sure that Congress doesn't just turn around and borrow more money, to spend more money. So I will require that, for every tax dollar set aside to cut the debt, the ceilings on spending will be cut by an equal amount. That way, we'll cut both debt and spending, and take a whack out of the budget deficit.

At Republican National Convention,
Houston, Texas, Aug. 20/
The New York Times, 8-21:(A)16.

2

[Criticizing 1992 Democratic Presidential nominee Bill Clinton's proposal to increase tax collections from foreign-owned businesses operating in the U.S.]: He should understand what is at stake here, and if he doesn't, let me tell him. Those are American jobs he's playing with, those are American workers he's putting at risk, and the American people simply won't buy it. The proudest people on Earth have never stooped to fear mongers before, and we must not stoop now to fear mongers . . . By attacking the bogeyman of foreign investors, Governor Clinton hopes to exploit the darker impulses of this uncertain age: fear of the future, fear of the unknown, fear of foreigners.

Campaign speech,
St. Louis, Mo., Aug. 27/
Los Angeles Times, 8-28:(A)20.

3

In our country we've always prized an entrepreneurial capitalism that grows from the bottom up, not the top down, a prosperity that begins on Main Street and extends to Wall Street, not the other way around . . . Our nation has never been seduced by the mirage that my opponent [in this year's Presidential election, Bill Clinton] offers of a government that accumulates capital by taxing it and borrowing it from the people and then distributing it according to some industrial policy. We know that the clumsy hand of government is no match for the uplifting hand of the marketplace.

Before Detroit Economic Club,
Detroit, Mich., Sept. 10/
The New York Times, 9-11:(A)12.

4

[There] is the emergence of a global economy. No nation is an island today. One out of every six manufacturing jobs is directly tied to exports. The crops sown from one out of every three acres of farmland are sold abroad. Consider some implications of this global economy. When growth slows abroad, as it has recently, our own growth slows as well. And America will only grow in the next century if we can compete globally in every part of the world.

Before Detroit Economic Club,
Detroit, Mich., Sept. 10/
The New York Times, 9-11:(A)12.

5

According to some studies, just 2 per cent of you will work the same job from now until retirement. The average worker can expect to change jobs 10 times during the course of his career. You need real-world security, skills you can put to work now and 10 years from now. But just as you can't drive a nail without a hammer, you can't build a dream without a job. And you're here at Job Corps because you know that it takes more and better skills to earn good jobs. And you decided you were going to do something about that. Well, America has work to do. And we can't let your drive go to waste. Maybe 50 years ago a strong back might have been enough to get a good

(GEORGE BUSH)

job. In our changing economy it's not enough anymore. What you earned yesterday with sweat you got to earn tomorrow with skills.

To Job Corps students and employees,
Excelsior Springs, Mo., Sept. 11/
The New York Times, 9-12:7.

1

At a decisive moment in history comes your choice about who should lead the American economy—the government planner or the entrepreneur, the risk-taker. I stand with the private sector and with the risk-taker . . . From Mexico to Eastern Europe, from Russia to South China, command-and-control economies have been dismissed as failures. At the exact moment that the rest of the world is going our way, why should we want to go their [his Democratic Presidential opponent Bill Clinton's] way?

At rally, Enid, Okla., Sept. 17/
The Washington Post, 9-18:(A)9.

2

[Saying the news media plays up the nation's economic problems excessively]: I think [the American people are] feeling negative about the economy because they hear 92 per cent of the coverage on the television—where a lot of people get their news from—on the economy has been negative. There are some good things [in the economy]. Interest rates are down. People aren't being robbed by inflation anymore. Inventories are down. A lot of people think we're in a deep recession in this country. The irony is we are growing and we've grown for five quarters. Now, don't tell that to a guy that's worrying about his job tomorrow, but I am telling you, the fact that they've hammered into them that things are a total disaster is influencing people's judgments.

Broadcast interview,
New York, N.Y., Sept. 21/
The New York Times, 9-22:(A)13.

3

[On Bill Clinton, his Democratic opponent in this fall's Presidential election]: I think the

American people have a right to know what they're buying into because, remember, if you buy what candidate Clinton is selling, there's no refund, there's no rebate. Actually it's more like a permanent payment plan, and I don't think we need that for the United States of America. On one issue, and I think it's the fundamental issue in this campaign, my opponent and I have just agreed to disagree. It's a question of how our economy grows and how our country works, and it's kind of like [the TV game show] *Jeopardy.* It all comes down to how you ask the question. And my opponent asks, what makes the economy grow? And his answer, and look at his program, is government planners and projects and programs.

At Pennsylvania State University,
University Park, Sept. 23/
The New York Times, 9-24:(A)12.

4

[On his veto of family-leave legislation for company employees]: I'm not going to do what the liberal Congress wants me to do, slap another mandate on business's back. I am not going to do that. I believe in family leave, and I believe our approach to facilitate family leave through tax credits is a far better way than putting new mandates on a guy [businessman] who is struggling to make ends meet.

Campaigning for re-election,
Sept. 23/
The New York Times, 9-24:(A)14.

5

[On his Presidential opponent Bill Clinton]: I think he said that the country is coming apart at the seams. Now, I know the only way he can win is to make everybody believe the economy is worse than it is. But this country's not coming apart at the seams, for heaven's sakes. We're the United States of America. In spite of the economic problems we are the most respected economy around the world. Many would trade for it. We've been caught up in a global slowdown. We can do much, much better, but we ought not try to convince the American people that America is a country that's coming apart at the seams. I would hate to be running for President and think that the only way I could win would be to convince everybody how horrible things are. Yes, there are big problems. And yes, people are hurting. But I believe that this agenda for American renewal I have is the answer to do it.

At Presidential candidates' debate,
St. Louis, Mo., Oct. 11/
The New York Times, 10-12:(A)12.

1

[On his Presidential opponent Bill Clinton]: Governor Clinton says 200,000 [will be the triggering point in income when his tax increase would go into effect], but he also says he wants to raise 150 billion. Taxing people over 200,000 will not get you 150 billion. And then when you add in his other spending proposals, regrettably you end up socking it to the working man. That old adage that they use—We're going to soak the rich; we're going to soak the rich—it always ends up being the poor cab driver or the working man that ends up paying the bill. And so I just have a different approach. I believe the way to get the [Federal] deficit down is to control the growth of mandatory spending programs and not raise taxes on the American people. You got a big difference there.

At Presidential candidates' debate,
St. Louis, Mo., Oct. 11/
The New York Times, 10-12:(A)12.

2

[Democratic Presidential nominee Arkansas Governor Bill Clinton] always talks about Arkansas having a balanced budget, and they do. But he has a balanced-budget amendment—[he has] to do it. I'd like the [Federal] government to have that. And I think it would discipline not only the Congress, which needs it, but also the Executive Branch. I'd like to have what 43 Governors have—the line-item veto, so if the Congress can't cut, [if] we've got a reckless-spending Congress, let the President have a shot at it by wiping out things that are pork-barrel.

At Presidential candidates' debate,
Richmond, Va., Oct. 15/
The New York Times, 10-17:10.

3

[Criticizing the economic plan of his Presidential opponent Bill Clinton]: I don't see how you can grow the [Federal] deficit down by raising people's taxes. You see, I don't think the American people are taxed too little, I think they're taxed too much. I went for one tax increase, and when I make a mistake I admit it . . . Two-thirds of the [Federal] budget I, as President, never get to look at; never get to touch. We've got to control that growth [of mandatory-spending programs] to inflation and population increase. But not raise taxes on the American people now. I just don't believe that would stimulate any kind of growth at all.

At Presidential candidates' debate,
Richmond, Va., Oct. 15/
The New York Times, 10-17:10.

4

The thing that saved us in this global economic slowdown is in our exports. And what I'm trying to do is increase our exports. And if, indeed, all the jobs were going to move south [to Mexico] because of lower wages, there are lower wages now and they haven't done that. And so I have just negotiated with the President of Mexico the North American Free Trade Agreement, and the Prime Minister of Canada. I want to have more of these free-trade agreements. Because export jobs are increasing far faster than any jobs that may have moved overseas . . . We want to have more jobs here, and the way to do that is to increase our exports. Some believe in protection. I don't. I believe in free and fair trade, and that's the thing that saved us.

At Presidential candidates' debate,
Richmond, Va., Oct. 15/
The New York Times, 10-17:10.

5

Go back to what it was like when you had a Democratic President and a Democratic Congress. You don't have to go back to Herbert Hoover. Go back to Jimmy Carter [in the 1970s]. And interest rates were 21 per cent. Inflation was 15 per cent. The misery index— unemployment and inflation added together—it

(GEORGE BUSH)

was invented by the Democrats—went right through the roof. We've cut it in half. And all you hear about [today] is how bad things are. You know, remember the question: "Are you better off?" Well, is a home buyer better off [today] if he can refinance the home because interest rates are down? Is the senior citizen better off because inflation is not wiping out their family's savings? I think they are. Is the guy out of work better off? Of course he's not. But he's not going to be better off if we grow the government, if we invest, as [Democratic Presidential nominee] Governor [Bill] Clinton says, in more government.

At Presidential candidates' debate,
East Lansing, Mich., Oct. 19/
The New York Times, 10-20:(A)12.

Robert C. Byrd
United States Senator,
D-West Virginia

1

[Saying he does not support a proposed Constitutional amendment requiring a balanced Federal budget]: What we really need is a Constitutional amendment that says [when it comes to a balanced budget], "There shall be some spine in our national leaders."

The Washington Post, 6-11:(A)8.

Shirley Carr
Former president,
Canadian Labor Congress

2

[On her being a Democratic Socialist]: We oppose totalitarianism and believe completely in democracy. But our guiding assumption is that a democratic government can and should secure full employment, a comprehensive social safety net for all and a recognition of basic labor rights . . . Neo-conservatives like [former U.S. President Ronald] Reagan and [current U.S. President George] Bush and our [Canadian] Prime Minister [Brian] Mulroney argue that full employment, the welfare state and strong [labor] unions undermine growth and competitiveness. Privatization, deregulation and promotion of a

so-called market economy and free trade became the order of the day when they took power . . . When I look around the world, I find that the most successful economies are not those most fervently committed to the so-called free market . . . but rather those which remain committed to full employment, social justice and worker rights. The Social Democratic countries of Northern Europe have demonstrated that it is indeed possible to reconcile the goals of economic efficiency and social equity.

Interview/
Los Angeles Times, 6-28:(M)3.

Joseph Carson
Chief economist,
Dean Witter Reynolds, Inc.

3

There are two speeds in the global economy. [If] they [the U.S.'s trading partners] don't grow, we don't grow at all . . . A number of companies in Europe canceled orders [for U.S. exports] at the last minute because of currency turmoil. Those goods have yet to be delivered and are backing up in the pipeline. It's the developed countries—Canada, Japan, Western Europe—that are our weak spots. Our biggest problems are in our biggest markets. And those markets are probably getting weaker.

The Washington Post, 10-17:(A)5.

Bill Clinton
Governor of Arkansas (D);
Candidate for the 1992
Democratic Presidential nomination

4

[On his proposal for a middle-class tax cut]: Don't let people tell you it's bad for the economy if you try to restore the middle class. How are you going to reduce poverty if there's no middle class to move into? Don't let people tell you we're waging class warfare. Class warfare is what we had in the '80s, when middle-class people worked harder for less money.

Campaigning, Miami, Fla.,
March 3/
Los Angeles Times, 3-4:(A)12.

(BILL CLINTON)

1

I am pro-worker. I am not anti-union. [But] I believe that most people in the workforce work in non-union jobs, so I have to address union and non-union. This is a false fight. We get into the choice of union and non-union. This is the choice of the people in the workforce.

Chicago, Ill., March 12/
The New York Times, 3-13:(A)11.

2

A central failing [over the past 12 years] is that we were the only major economy in the world that had no national economic strategy . . . We didn't have an automobile strategy, a strategy for maintaining a high wage base, a strategy for revitalizing our cities. We didn't have an overall strategy because Presidents Reagan and Bush believed that the Federal government would mess up anything it got into, and that the main thing to do was to keep taxes low, especially on upper-income people and corporations, and basically to let the market take its course. That course does not work. We need a national economic strategy as well as a human-development strategy that recognizes we are living in a world in which what people earn depends largely on what they can learn and whether their economies are organized for change.

Debate with former U.S. Senator
Paul Tsongas, Chicago, Ill./
Time, 3-23:16.

3

All these countries we are competing with, they're working in partnership, hand in hand, government, business, labor, education, to stake a position for their workers of the future. Only the United States is saying we don't have to do that . . . We have not had the kind of partnership we need to compete in the global areas.

Campaigning, San Diego, Calif./
Los Angeles Times, 5-20:(A)10.

4

If I were President, I would submit a balanced-budget plan over a five-year period. I don't think you can go from $400-billion [deficit] to zero in a year. In this recession, you'd have to raise taxes and cut benefits; you'd make the economy worse. The reason I opposed the [proposed] balanced-budget [Constitutional] amendment is I thought it was a gimmick and a put-off so nobody'd have to really make any decisions for six years, and because it did not make a distinction between investment and consumption. That is, most of you have borrowed money for homes, for cars, for businesses, right? If the government borrows money to put us to work and we'll get it back, that's okay. But we're eating our seed corn, as we say in the farming country. We're borrowing money to go to dinner at night. That's what's wrong.

Call-in question-and-answer broadcast,
Pittsburgh, Pa./NBC-TV, 6-12.

5

We ought to change the tax system. We ought to say to business and to wealthy people, we want you to have more tax incentives, but only if you invest in this country. So here are more incentives for new plant and equipment, for new businesses, for housing. But we're going to take all those ridiculous incentives out of the tax bill that are there now that actually encourage people with your tax money to shut plants down and move them overseas.

Call-in question-and-answer broadcast,
Pittsburgh, Pa./NBC-TV, 6-12.

6

I will always have a preference for free trade. I'm always going to be working for expanded trade, but I'm going to be doing it with a view toward maintaining a competitive, high-wage economy in America and integrating other countries in a pattern of growth . . . The world needs to know that America is serious about us being an exporting power and about opening markets, and before we adopt protectionist strategies, we must do everything we can do to meet the competition on our own terms.

Interview,
New York, N.Y./
The Washington Post, 6-17:(A)25.

Bill Clinton
Governor of Arkansas (D);
1992 Democratic
Presidential nominee

1

I was raised to believe that the American dream was built on rewarding hard work. But the folks in Washington have turned that American ethic on its head. For too long, those who play by the rules and keep the faith have gotten the shaft. And those who cut corners and cut deals have been rewarded. People are working harder than ever, spending nights and weekends on the job instead of at the Little League or the Scouts or the PTA. But their incomes are still going down, their taxes are going up, and the costs of housing, health care and education are going through the roof. Meanwhile, more and more people are falling into poverty—even when they're working full time.

Accepting the Presidential nomination
at Democratic National Convention,
New York, N.Y., July 16/
The New York Times, 7-17:(A)12.

2

[President Bush] is still in the grip of a failed idea, still believing the only way to make an economy grow in a tough global environment is to cut taxes on the wealthiest 1 percent, raise them on the middle class, let the deficit grow, reduce investment in our future and stay out of the economic battleground with other nations. He still believes that, when it comes to offering opportunity for ordinary men, the best policy for the government is to do nothing.

At rally, New Orleans, La., July 29/
Los Angeles Times, 7-30:(A)21.

3

[In the U.S.,] we have stubbornly refused to develop the kind of partnership for growth and opportunity in this country that the global economy requires, a partnership which will require us, in my judgment, to adopt an across-the-board investment tax credit for new plant and equipment so that we can continually have incentives to reinvest and modernize our plants here

and our small businesses; a partnership that requires, in my judgment, the infusion of new amounts of venture capital into new ventures, and therefore we ought to have a long-term capital-gains treatment for investment in new ventures in America; a partnership that requires a comprehensive and permanent research-and-development tax credit and significant housing incentives to revitalize the construction industry in this country; and more importantly, a partnership that requires us to make a comprehensive long-term commitment to the education and training of all of our people and to creating a climate in this country that supports the development of new technologies, supports the revitalization of our manufacturing sector, supports and strengthens our effort to promote small business.

News conference,
Chicago, Ill., Sept. 21/
The New York Times, 9-22:(A)12.

4

We [in the U.S.] have gone from first to 13th in the world in wages in the last 12 years, since [Presidents] Bush and Reagan have been in. Personal income has dropped while people have worked harder. In the last four years there have been twice as many bankruptcies as new jobs created. We need a new approach. The same old experience is not relevant. We're living in a new world after the Cold War and what works in this new world is not trickle-down [economics], not government for the benefit of the privileged few, not tax and spend, but a commitment to invest in American jobs and American education, controlling American health-care costs and bringing the American people together.

At Presidential candidates' debate,
St. Louis, Mo., Oct. 11/
The New York Times, 10-12:(A)12.

5

I've known a lot of people who've lost their jobs because of jobs moving overseas . . . [We should] change the tax code. There are more deductions in the tax code for shutting plants down and moving overseas than there are for modernizing plant and equipment here. Our

(BILL CLINTON)

competitors don't do that. Emphasize and subsidize modernizing plant and equipment here, not moving plants overseas. Stop the Federal government's program that now gives low-interest loans and job-training funds to companies that will actually shut down and move to other countries, but we won't do the same thing for plants that stay here. So more trade, but on fairer terms and favor investment in America.

At Presidential candidates' debate,
Richmond, Va., Oct. 15/
The New York Times, 10-17:10.

1

[On the proposed U.S.-Canada-Mexico free-trade agreement]: I'm the one who's in the middle on this. [U.S. independent Presidential candidate Ross] Perot says it's a bad deal. [U.S. President] Bush says it's a hunky dory deal. I say on balance it does more good than harm if we can get some protection for the environment so that the Mexicans have to follow their own environmental standards, their own labor-law standards and if we have a genuine commitment to re-educate and retrain the American workers who lose their jobs [because of the agreement] and reinvest in this economy. I have a realistic approach to trade. I want more trade. And I know there are some good things in that agreement. But it can sure be made better.

At Presidential candidates' debate,
East Lansing, Mich., Oct. 19/
The New York Times, 10-20:(A)13.

2

My plan says that we want to raise marginal [tax rates] on family incomes above $200,000 from 31 to 36 per cent; that we want to ask foreign corporations simply to pay the same percentage of taxes on their income that American corporations pay in America. That we want to use that money to provide over $100-billion in tax cuts for investment in new plant and equipment, for small business, for new technologies and for middle-class tax relief. Now, I'll tell you this: I will not raise taxes on the middle class to pay for

these programs [in his plan]. If the money does not come in there to pay for these programs, we will cut other government spending or we will slow down the phase-in of the programs. I am not going to raise taxes on the middle class to pay for these programs. Now, furthermore, I am not going to tell you "read my lips"—on anything. Because I cannot foresee what emergencies might develop in this country . . . But I can tell you this: I'm not going to raise taxes on the middle-class Americans to pay for the programs I recommended.

At Presidential candidates' debate,
East Lansing, Mich., Oct. 19/
The New York Times, 10-20:(A)15.

Bill Clinton
Governor of Arkansas (D);
President-elect
of the United States

3

As we address short-term business-cycle issues, we must never forget that the most profound problems of our economy are longer-term and structural. Many of the problems did not develop overnight. We cannot expect to solve them overnight.

At economic conference he convened,
Little Rock, Ark., Dec. 14/
The New York Times, 12-15:(A)1.

Robert L. Crandall
Chairman, AMR Corporation
(American Airlines)

4

Until the government makes some major changes, our economy won't rebound as fast or as far as any of us would like. For the first time in U.S. history, young Americans entering the workforce cannot count on having a higher standard of living than their parents did. The public understands all this, and its confidence about the future is low. And when confidence is low, people are both slow to buy and intent on getting the most for their money.

USA Today, 4-15:(B)2.

Charles Craypo
Professor of economics,
University of Notre Dame

1

If it's just a sheer power struggle . . . the [labor] union will probably lose more . . . than [it] will win. There's no question that the total environment today gives employers advantages . . . The public still seems to accept the argument that lower labor costs are critical to American competitiveness . . . Until that [attitude] changes, I don't think we'll see a lot of sympathy for things that strengthen labor's hand.

The Christian Science Monitor,
5-7:6.

Mario M. Cuomo
Governor of New York (D)

2

It would be bad enough if we could say this is . . . a terrible but only a temporary recession. But this is more than a recession. Our economy has been weakened fundamentally by 12 years of conservative Republican's supply-side policy. Supply side proved to be a form of "free enterprise for the few," paid for by higher taxes on the rest of us. It operated from the naive Republican assumption that if we fed the wealthiest Americans with huge income-tax cuts, they would eventually produce "loaves and fishes" for everyone. In fact, it was just another version of the failed economic fundamentalism of 65 years ago—then called "trickle down"—which led to the Great Depression. And it has failed again! . . . And that, ladies and gentlemen, is the legacy of the [President] Bush years: The slowest economic growth for any four-year Presidential term since World War II. An economy crippled by debt and deficit. The fading of the American dream. Working-class families sliding back down toward poverty, deprivation, inexplicable violence . . . The ship of state is headed for the rocks. The crew knows it. The passengers know it. Only the captain of the ship, President Bush, appears not to know it. He seems to think that the ship will be saved by imperceptible undercurrents, directed by the invisible hand of some cyclical economic god, that will gradually move the ship so that at the last moment it will miraculously glide past the rocks to safer shores. Well, prayer is always a good idea. But our prayers must be accompanied by good works. We need a captain who understands that and who will seize the wheel, before it's too late. I am here tonight to offer America that new captain with a new course.

Nominating Bill Clinton for President
at Democratic National Convention,
New York, N.Y., July 15/
The New York Times, 7-16:(A)12.

Richard T. Curtin
Director,
Consumer Research Center,
University of Michigan

3

[The U.S. economy] faces changes in the underlying structure of expectations and aspirations. These concerns reflect a deep-seated sense of apprehension among consumers about their future economic situation, accompanied by a lack of confidence in the ability of government to deal effectively with the problems. In short, there now exists an enduring sense of malaise among consumers, a sense of frustration and despair about economic opportunities that is not likely to fade even when the economy rebounds.

Speech, January/
The Washington Post, 2-26:(A)1.

4

There has been a certain resurgence in fond memories of inflation. Our surveys show that the kind of animosity that we have had toward inflation in the past decade is weakening at the edges. People are starting to associate more inflation with more jobs and greater wealth.

The New York Times, 11-17:(C)2.

Herman Daly
Economist,
International Bank for
Reconstruction and Development
(World Bank)

5

[On the world economy]: When something grows, it gets quantitatively bigger; when it

95

(HERMAN DALY)

develops, it gets qualitatively better. Quantitative growth and qualitative development follow different laws. Our planet develops over time without growing. Our economy, a subsystem of the finite and non-growing Earth, must eventually adapt to a similar pattern of development.

Los Angeles Times, 4-12:(M)2.

Richard G. Darman
Director, Federal Office
of Management and Budget

1

From what I see in the polls, if you give people a list of things that should be done to help the economy, controlling [government] spending and reducing the [Federal] deficit comes out near the top or at the top. So the public understands the importance of it. The problem is people are opposed to most of the particulars. If you go back and say: "Would you like to cut spending for this or that" and it's concrete—education, transportation, Medicare, Medicaid, welfare benefits—people don't want to decrease it. In fact, they frequently want to increase it at the same time they want to reduce the deficit. At the same time, they don't want to increase taxes.

Interview/
USA Today, 3-18:(A)11.

Walter Dellinger
Professor of law,
Duke University

2

[Arguing against a proposed Constitutional amendment aimed at forcing a balanced Federal budget]: It would be wonderful if we could simply declare by Constitutional amendment that henceforth the air would be clean, the streets free of drugs and the budget forever in balance. But merely saying those things in the Constitution does not make them happen. Putting false promises in the Constitution is not a trivial matter. It breeds disrespect for the rule of law. The proposed Constitutional amendment specifies no mechanism for accomplishing its goal . . . Proposing a balanced-budget amendment would

not be a step toward a balanced budget, but a diversion from that goal. Its adoption would cut no spending and raise no revenue. Because it provides an excuse for avoiding real steps to reduce the deficit, its proposal by Congress would disserve both the Constitution and the goal of fiscal responsibility.

The Washington Post, 6-2:(A)17.

Pete V. Domenici
United States Senator,
R-New Mexico

3

The principal problem with the Federal government now is that everybody wants a balanced budget and nobody wants to sacrifice. Everybody wants us to get the budget under control, and they're all certain that if somebody else will just give, the budget will be balanced. Well, we've reached a point in time where there's nothing more dangerous to our children and grandchildren . . . I think we will have sustained recessions, sustained recessions, some time out in the not-to-distant future, unless we get the deficit under control because the vitality of the country is being sapped. The principal vitality is net savings. That's what causes a capitalistic society to grow, and the debt is getting so big that it gobbles up the net savings of all our people and our corporations. And if you don't have net savings, you don't have the energizer for the capitalist growth machine.

Washington, D.C., June 22/
The Washington Post, 6-23:(A)20.

William C. Dunkelberg
Chief economist,
National Federation
of Independent Business

4

[The economic] news isn't all bad—if you look behind the 7.5 per cent [unemployment] number. We did create more jobs, but even more people decided they wanted one and started looking. This is consistent with the nature of the recovery. The economy has grown since April, 1991, but not by enough to absorb new entrants to the labor

(WILLIAM C. DUNKELBERG)

force, much less to re-hire those who became unemployed during the recession.

June 5/The Washington Post,
6-6:(A)6.

Donald V. Fites
Chairman, Caterpillar, Inc.

1

[Arguing against protectionism]: We always tell the U.S. government, "For heaven's sake, don't try to help us by putting up protective barriers, because as soon as you do that, your costs go up and you're that much less globally competitive." The other fallacy of protectionism is that if we think we can protect the automobile industry in this country or any other industry. In this day and age, in this world, I can't see protectionism working.

Interview, Peoria, Ill./
The New York Times, 4-13:(A)11.

Richard Florida
Associate professor of management,
Heinz School of Public Policy
and Management,
Carnegie-Mellon University

2

The American heartland—ignored by government, abandoned by large parts of business—has become the real cornerstone of the American economy.

The Christian Science Monitor,
11-4:7.

Thomas S. Foley
United States Representative,
D-Washington;
Speaker of the House

3

The standard of living of the American people is a first and fundamental measure of the state of the American union. So the urgent, overriding task of 1992 is to restore growth and jobs . . . For too long, we were told to wait—that things would get better on their own. There was even an effort

to talk us out of the recession—or to tell us that it wasn't really happening at all. But the truth finally became all too painful—and all too clear . . . When we say a middle-class tax cut, we mean exactly that . . . We will insist that this time the benefits must go to working families, not to the privileged. We will insist that a middle-class tax cut be paid for, not by taking money that should go to schools and health care, but by calling on the richest of our citizens at long last to pay their fair share.

Broadcast Democratic response to
President Bush's State of the Union
address, Washington, D.C.,
Jan. 28/USA Today, 1-29:(A)11.

4

[Arguing against a proposed Constitutional amendment aimed at forcing a balanced Federal budget]: The President [Bush] and his predecessor [Ronald Reagan] have had it in their power to submit balanced budgets for many years and they have not done so. Our present deficit problem is relatively short-lived, reaching its present proportions only during the last decade or so. It's cure is also clear: cut spending and/or increase taxes. We do not need to amend the Constitution to do that.

At National Press Club,
Washington, D.C., June 9/
Los Angeles Times, 6-10:(A)8.

Barbara Hackman Franklin
Secretary of Commerce
of the United States

5

American workers are the most productive and innovative in the world. A study released just last week by the McKinsey Global Institute reports that the average American worker produces $49,600 worth of output—goods and services—annually, and that's the highest in the world. This compares to $44,200 for the German worker and $38,200 for the Japanese. The study has said that one of the secrets of our success is that our companies are not overburdened by government intervention in the markets. Competition . . . not government mandates or misguided attempts at protectionism, keeps our businesses in the lead. More than anywhere else, our entrepreneurs have the liberty to invest, to innovate, to excel and are making impressive strides in quality.

At Commerce Department U.S.-Japan
Business Council symposium, Oct. 19/
The Washington Post, 10-20:(A)18.

Robert Fullinwider
Senior research scholar,
Institute for Philosophy
and Public Policy,
University of Maryland

1

When you become middle class, you become a home-owner, a property-owner, someone aspiring to send your kids to good schools and college, and you're keenly interested in property taxes and the quality of schools . . . You become very conservative in lots of ways.

The Christian Science Monitor,
9-22:7.

Karl H. Gerlinger
President,
BMW of North America

2

[On why a low dollar hasn't resulted in a great leap in U.S. exports and a large drop in imports]: The United States is the most competitive market in the world. If you base your prices here only on [currency] exchange rates, you will be out of the market immediately. You have to look at currency movements as a long-term factor and figure your costs and prices from there.

The New York Times, 12-1:(C)1.

Albert Gore, Jr.
United States Senator,
D-Tennessee;
1992 Democratic
Vice-Presidential nominee

3

[On a family-leave bill he supports, but which the Bush Administration does not]: It's written in

a way that minimizes any hardship on employers. The leave is unpaid. Small businesses are exempted. The amount of leave that is required is limited to a relatively short period of time. There have to be the circumstances that absolutely warrant it. Now, you talk about the hardships that would be faced by an employer, even with all those conditions. What about the hardship faced by families who suddenly are facing a crisis that requires them to be in a hospital with a child or to help a spouse who has suddenly had an accident or a serious illness? What about the hardship on the families? What about the hardship on the taxpayers who end up paying billions of dollars a year in extra welfare and food-stamp costs for people who are fired from their jobs simply because of a family crisis leading to them having to take a little time off? This [bill] is good for families. It's good for the taxpayers. And I believe that it's good for business too. Japan, Germany, every other industrial country in the world, already has this law.

Lexington, Ky./
The New York Times, 9-11:(A)13.

4

We don't believe our nation can stand four more years of what we've had under [President] George Bush and [Vice President] Dan Quayle. When the recession came, they were like a deer caught in the headlights—paralyzed into inaction, blinded by the suffering and pain of bankruptcies and people who were unemployed . . . The "experience" that George Bush and Dan Quayle have been talking about includes the worst economic performance since the Great Depression. Unemployment is up, personal income is down, bankruptcies are up, housing starts are down. How long can we continue with trickle-down economics when the record of failure is so abundantly clear.

At Vice-Presidential candidates' debate,
Atlanta, Ga., Oct. 13/
The New York Times, 10-14:(A)12.

5

[Democratic Presidential nominee] Bill Clinton's top priority is putting America back to

(ALBERT GORE, JR.)

work. Bill Clinton and I will create good high-wage jobs for our people the same way he has done in his state [Arkansas, where he is Governor]. Bill Clinton has created high-wage manufacturing jobs at 10 times the national average. And in fact, according to the statistics coming from the Bush-Quayle Labor Department, for the last two years in a row Bill Clinton's state has been Number 1 among all 50 in the creation of jobs in the private sector. By contrast, in the nation as a whole during the last four years, it is the first time since the Presidency of Herbert Hoover that we have gone for a four-year period with fewer jobs at the end of that four-year period than we had at the beginning.

At Vice-Presidential candidates' debate,
Atlanta, Ga., Oct. 13/
The New York Times, 10-14:(A)12.

Lyle Gramley
Chief economist,
Mortgage Bankers
Association of America;
Former Governor,
Federal Reserve Board

1

Sometimes Administration [economic] forecasts have what I call an element of political optimism. You stretch as much as you can without straining the bounds of credibility.

The New York Times, 5-22:(C)10.

William H. Gray III
President,
United Negro College Fund;
Former United States Representative,
D-Pennsylvania

2

America's prosperity, productivity, competitiveness and wealth are going to depend on the competence and skill of people that today we call disadvantaged. If we don't begin to provide wider doorways of opportunities for women, minorities and new immigrants, then we're not going to be a global power in the 21st century.

Interview/
The Christian Science Monitor,
10-20:3.

Alan Greenspan
Chairman,
Federal Reserve Board

3

I and others have long argued before this Committee that bolstering the supply of savings available to support productive private investment must be a priority for fiscal policy. In that regard, reducing the call of the Federal government on the nation's pool of savings is essential . . . I urge you to adhere to a budgetary strategy for fiscal 1993 and beyond that is geared to the longer run needs of the U.S. economy . . . Maintaining a commitment to the elimination of the structural budget deficit over the coming years will help enormously to alleviate the concerns of the American people about our economic future.

Before House Budget Committee,
Washington, D.C., Feb. 4/
The Washington Post, 2-6:(A)26.

4

If our measures are at all accurate, the rate of job losses in this recession are well below where they were in the recession of 1982, or 1975, yet we have a degree of concern about job security that is as great or greater than we had then. I think that reflects a growing concern for the long-term economic health of the country.

Before Senate Banking, Housing
and Urban Affairs Committee,
Washington, D.C., Feb. 25/
Los Angeles Times, 2-26:(A)13.

Tom Harkin
United States Senator,
D-Iowa;
Candidate for the 1992
Democratic Presidential nomination

5

It's time for a new Democratic [Party] economic program that focuses on jobs and putting people back to work in this country. And we can do it. I have a plan, "A Blueprint to Build a New America"—five points where I point out how we can get the money down to these local communities . . . to get people back to work, working on

WHAT THEY SAID IN 1992

(TOM HARKIN)

our infrastructure, roads and bridges, sewer and water systems, school improvement programs. The plans are on the shelf. They're there ready to go. But the money isn't. It's time to get the money down and put people to work. And guess what happens when people like that go to work. They go downtown and they shop through stores. They buy clothes for their kids. They buy a carpet for the floor, and furniture for their house. They may buy a new car. They spend their money and the economy gets going again. And what do we get out of it? We get a better infrastructure that allows the private sector to be more efficient and more productive. That's a Democratic economic program.

Campaign speech, Boscawen, N.H., Feb. 13/
The Washington Post, 3-2:(A)10.

J. Brooke Hern
Economic Spokesman,
Department of Commerce and
Economic Development
of New Jersey

1

Manufacturing is the base of real jobs that . . . generates more economic activity and more jobs. Services can't survive without a sound manufacturing base, for that is who they provide services for. We cannot build an economy just shining each others' shoes.

The Christian Science Monitor,
10-16:4.

Hiroshi Hirabayashi
Acting Japanese Ambassador
to the United States

2

[On Chrysler Corporation chairman Lee Iacocca, who has criticized Japan for its trade policies which he says is a cause of the large trade imbalance between the U.S. and Japan]: Iacocca is blaming others while laying off workers and getting hefty bonuses. I'm not an America-basher; an Iacocca-basher, maybe. He is the symbol of U.S. protectionism, of America's crybaby syndrome.

Interview/
USA Today, 3-23:(A)9.

Robert Hormats
Vice chairman,
Goldman Sachs International

3

[On the drop of the U.S. dollar on international markets]: If you [Americans] buy imported goods—shoes, sweaters, imported books, imported bananas—it's all going to cost more . . . [The Bush Administration is] hoping it will help stimulate [U.S.] exports and thereby stimulate growth in a very lackluster economy. [But that also] makes you poorer as a nation. It debases your currency. A German who buys American goods pays less. An American who sells goods to Germany receives less for them. What puzzles me is that the Administration seems to be nonchalant about the decline of the dollar.

The Washington Post, 8-22:(A)7.

Lee A. Iacocca
Chairman,
Chrysler Corporation

4

If you want to continue being leaders in the world, start by getting some of that [Federal] debt off your backs. Debtors can't be leaders. It's the guy holding the IOUs who calls the shots; the other guy is called a hostage.

At Johns Hopkins University commencement/
The New York Times, 5-26:(C)3.

5

[On wholesale layoffs by many companies as a cost-cutting measure]: I worry, because as we all restructure, if we lay off enough people, there'll be nobody to buy the cars or the houses. So we've got to watch that this isn't a downhill spiral.

Broadcast interview, November/
The New York Times, 12-17:(C)2.

John E. Jacob
President,
National Urban League

6

Every indicator of economic well-being shows that African-Americans are doing far worse than whites. We [blacks] were in a recession before

(JOHN E. JACOB)

this [current national] recession hit, and now we are in a deep economic depression . . . I have heard that middle-class people are angry, and what we are seeing is the rebelling of middle-class people to their plight. I will tell you that if middle-class people are angry because of 18 months of recession, they ought to try being black with 400 years of oppression. This country cannot deal with her productivity issues, her competitiveness issues, unless we deal with people who have the greatest need.

Washington, D.C., Jan. 21/
The New York Times, 1-22:(A)9.

Karlyn Keene
Resident fellow
and public-opinion specialist,
American Enterprise Institute

1

[On the Federal deficit]: The Republicans beat the Democrats over the head with it for years and it didn't work. The Democrats then beat the Republicans over the head with it, and that didn't work either . . . [The public] can't relate to it. It's [the deficit] too big. It doesn't touch their lives personally. It's one of those big numbers and it's hard to wrap your arms around it. And nobody knows how to deal with it.

The Washington Post, 9-29:(A)12.

Jack Kemp
Secretary of Housing
and Urban Development
of the United States

2

The question of the post-Reagan conservative world is what are the great transcendent issues of the day? They are economic—both domestic and global—trade, jobs, education, helping families fighting poverty . . . Equality is a word that seldom comes into the lexicon of the conservative movement, but it's a very important word. Not equality of earnings but equality of opportunity—and frankly, we've [conservatives] got a way to go. You can't have equality of opportunity in an economy where there is 7 per cent

[overall unemployment] and 40-50 per cent unemployment among minorities.

Los Angeles Times, 7-4:(A)23.

Edward M. Kennedy
United States Senator,
D-Massachusetts

3

[On recent Senate approval of legislation providing job leave for employees of most companies in the event of childbirth or serious family illness]: Working Americans have waited far too long for this very important piece of legislation. When a child is born or a serious illness strikes a family member, working Americans should be guaranteed the right to take a reasonable amount of time off, without fear that they will lose the job.

Los Angeles Times, 8-12:(A)12.

Dean Kleckner
President,
American Farm Bureau Federation

4

Our government's economic policy, if you could call it that, refuses to recognize the need to reduce spending. We have developed a clear message to those who seek office in 1992. First, scrap the 1990 [Federal] budget deal. We didn't get a balanced budget from the budget deal. We all got snookered once again.

At American Farm Bureau
Federation convention,
Kansas City, Mo., Jan. 13/
Los Angeles Times, 1-14:(A)13.

Paul R. Krugman
Economist, Massachusetts Institute
of Technology

5

I think that we have been crossing an intellectual watershed in economic policy, away from a belief in the magic of the marketplace toward a belief that markets are very good but not perfect things and they sometimes need a little help from government.

The New York Times, 11-21:23.

Robin Leigh-Pemberton
Governor, Bank of England

1

I know there are some who argue that the costs of disinflation, especially when inflation is low, outweigh the benefits of price stability. Consequently, they argue, we should settle for low and stable inflation. I am afraid I do not believe that such an option exists. Whenever inflation is viewed as acceptable, it is possible to settle for an alternative rate which is just a little higher. The end result is an inflation rate which is high and rising, and is costly to reduce.

Speech at London School of Economics,
London, England, Nov. 11/
The New York Times, 11-12:(C)2.

Jay Levy
Chairman,
Forecasting Center,
Levy Economics Institute,
Bard College

2

When the government puts [spends] more money into the economy than it takes out, it is stimulating activity . . . By cutting down net flow of government money into the economy, you're reducing personal and business purchasing power, you increase unemployment and the need for social safety nets, and you wind up with as big a [Federal budget] deficit as you started with, and you've hurt the economy in the process.

The Christian Science Monitor,
10-30:6.

William Lucy
Secretary-treasurer,
American Federation of State,
County and Municipal Employees

3

State and local governments are in the worst shape they have been in since the Great Depression. We will not get out of this recession without spending money, and the Federal government alone has the ability to provide the needed economic jolt.

Before House Budget Committee,
Washington, Feb. 12/
Los Angeles Times, 2-13:(A)22.

Lynn Martin
Secretary of Labor
of the United States

4

There was a time, and it's not a time to diminish or demean, when job security was your union. Your union protected you. Your security was your company. You stayed with the company. Maybe you worked there all your life. For women, it was your husband, mainly. It worked for [American workers] after World War II. It did. But it's not 1950 now. You cannot change the world out there at the gates. You can't. But you can take some of those same skills that made that joy of life and ability to change that has been part of the American frame of mind and see that we are going to have this again. Times are tough right now, but I believe that we are looking at a chance literally for a miracle. We're at the chance for a kind of [labor-management] peace that 10 years ago no one could have thought of. [Thus,] we can redirect our energies and intentions. Nothing can stop us.

Interview, Washington, D.C./
The Christian Science Monitor,
3-6:13.

5

The [labor] union movements' decline . . . has been, to some extent, because they don't fit into changing jobs. Unions . . . today are trying really far more outreach for the first time. If you look at apprenticeship programs, they overwhelmingly were all white male. So they didn't serve a lot of people. Now they're trying to make changes, too, so that an apprenticeship program can actually reflect more of the population . . . If you look at the AFL-CIO board of directors—I think there are two women and two African-Americans . . . It's the job of the Labor Department to represent people . . . whether or not they belong to a union, and to make sure that what happens to working men and women is as positive as possible. That means new jobs, it means retraining, it means pensions . . . That's why we're moving in far more directly . . . If 84 per cent of the people aren't unionized, you have to find other routes to get to them.

Interview, Washington, D.C./
Los Angeles Times, 3-15:(M)3.

(LYNN MARTIN)

1

We've done a lousy job of helping students make the transition from school to the workplace. Fifty per cent of our kids don't go to college. They are a hidden, ignored resource.

Interview/
USA Today, 5-14:(A)9.

Mark Mellman
Democratic Party
public-opinion analyst

2

There's a fundamental "dissensus" in this country on how to achieve [Federal] deficit reduction, and no politician, whether running for President, Senator or Congress, wants to walk into the middle of that kind of dissensus. Given a choice between running on an 80-20 issue or a 50-50 issue, people will campaign on an 80-20 issue every time.

The Washington Post, 9-29:(A)12.

Alan Meltzer
Economist,
Carnegie-Mellon University

3

[On the recent economic conference in Little Rock, Ark., convened by President-elect Bill Clinton]: The big thing that was not done in Little Rock was to address economic problems in terms of trade-offs. [According to the prevailing attitude at the conference,] everything pays for itself. We can have investment without saving. We can have [trade] protection without retaliation. We can have the expansion in all sorts of command-and-control regulation—environmental, labor, whatever—without any effects on the economy. That's baloney.

The New York Times, 12-21:(C)3.

George J. Mitchell
United States Senator,
D-Maine

4

The notion has grown up in this country that if you do anything to restrict trade, it's protec-

tionist. That's a profound mistake. What you need is reciprocity [from trading partners], but you don't need to defeat your own interests by creating the impression that no matter what others do, you will not respond in any way.

Interview/
The Christian Science Monitor,
11-12:4.

Kiichi Miyazawa
Prime Minister of Japan

5

[In the 1980s,] American college graduates landed high-paying jobs on Wall Street, and as a result you and I have seen that the number of engineers able to make products has fallen year after year . . . [The U.S. tradition of] producing things and creating value has "loosened" too much in the past 10 years or so . . . I have thought for some time that they may lack a work ethic. [Some Americans have forgotten how] to live by the sweat of their brow.

At debate in Japanese Parliament,
Feb. 3/
The New York Times, 2-4:(A)6.

Stephen Moore
Director of
fiscal policy studies,
Cato Institute

6

If massive growth of government and multi-billion-dollar deficits were the solution to America's economic problems, the nation would be basking in unprecedented prosperity, and [President] Bush would be widely acclaimed as an economic miracle worker.

The Christian Science Monitor,
10-30:7.

Brian Mulroney
Prime Minister of Canada

7

[Criticizing new U.S. tariffs on Canadian exports of Honda automobiles and softwood lumber]: [Mexico's] President [Carlos] Salinas is very much interested in [the proposed U.S.-

(BRIAN MULRONEY)

Canada-Mexico free-trade agreement] as is [U.S.] President Bush, as am I. And hopefully, we'll be able to put one together. But you know, if cases like softwood lumber and Honda don't give the Mexicans pause . . . I can tell you they're having a substantial impact on the Europeans and the Japanese. The attitude being, well, if the Americans do this to their best friends . . . what in the hell do you think they're going to do to us?

Interview, Ottawa, Canada/
U.S. News & World Report,
5-25:50.

Lyn Nofziger
Former Special Assistant
for Political Affairs
to the President
of the United States
(Ronald Reagan)

1

[President Bush is] in trouble [in this year's Presidential election] because these guys over at the White House don't understand the American people. They never had to worry about a job, and they don't understand people who have to really worry about a job. As a result, they came at this matter of the economy rather casually . . . I've been saying for weeks the best thing the President could do for his campaign is fire [Federal Budget Director] Dick Darman. That would send a message that the President's finally begun to understand he's got to do something about the situation in the country. I'd make [Darman] Ambassador to New Zealand.

Interview, February/
Newsweek, 3-2:28.

Janet L. Norwood
Senior fellow,
Urban Institute;
Former Commissioner,
Bureau of Labor Statistics,
Department of Labor
of the United States

2

Unless we create more jobs, the college-educated are going to crowd out the people below

them. The college-educated can at least go down, but the people below them have nowhere to go.

The New York Times, 5-14:(A)1.

Karen Nussbaum
Executive director, 9 to 5,
the National Association of
Working Women

3

Everyone knows [that] women work to support our families and, without our wages, family incomes would have plunged even further in the past 20 years; that the workplace has got to change and give some slack to working parents; that low wages and few benefits are killing us and the economy as well. [President-elect] Bill Clinton was elected for just these reasons . . . I hope to come out of 1993 with policies that establish new social values and make real changes in the lives of most people.

Interview/
USA Today, 12-30:(A)11.

Norman J. Ornstein
Fellow,
American Enterprise Institute

4

Under normal circumstances, [a Constitutional amendment mandating a balanced Federal budget] would not go anywhere because people by and large recognize that, although it has great political appeal, it is a stupid, self-defeating and meaningless thing to do . . . [Because] until Congress is willing to tackle the entitlement problem, which is the tapeworm eating the budget alive, it will always find ways to get around even a Constitutional amendment.

Los Angeles Times, 4-21:(A)24.

Leon E. Panetta
United States Representative,
D-California

5

[Criticizing White House Budget Director Richard Darman for blaming the country's economic problems on a number of factors other than President Bush]: It is disingenuous at best to

(LEON E. PANETTA)

say after four years in office that everybody else is to blame—the Federal Reserve, [Iraqi President] Saddam Hussein, the Congress, the press. My God, he's [Bush] President of the United States. Does he not have any power? Is it just p.r. events from day to day?

At House Budget Committee hearing,
Washington, D.C., July 28/
The New York Times, 7-29:(A)8.

Ross Perot
Industrialist

1

If anybody will listen, I have said there is one priority that faces this country. That is to stop the decline in the job base. Because if we continue to lay off tens of thousands of people, we lose taxpayers and get welfare users. A welfare user gets more money from the government than a blue-collar worker pays in taxes every month. So it's more than a double kill. We take in a trillion dollars a year. We spend a trillion four . . . The way out of debt is the expanded job base. If you don't have that, you can't make this country work.

Interview, Dallas, Texas/
Newsweek, 4-27:27.

2

Our current tax system is a very ineffective, inefficient tax system basically put together by special interests over a period of many years, and it's got a thousand patches on it, all by the special interests. You've got to change the tax system, and it has to have several characteristics. One, it's got to be fair. The current tax system is not. And two, in my judgment, it should be paperless for most of the people, and get rid of this giant, ineffective bureaucracy we have around the IRS.

Interview, Dallas, Texas/
Time, 5-25:37.

3

Do we need to make clothing in this country? Of course we do. Do we need to make shoes in this country? Of course we do. We have places in our country where people would be delighted to work in a shoe factory for reasonable wages. When I think of shoes, I think of Valley Forge [where, in the American Revolutionary War, George Washington's soldiers used rags and bandages on their feet]. My mind bounces back and forth between the world I hope we have and the world that might be. We might be fighting barefooted.

Interview, Dallas, Texas/
Los Angeles Times, 6-5:(A)24.

4

Raising taxes is like taking dope, for politicians. You've got to stop raising taxes. You've got to bring discipline. So unless there's some kind of incredible emergency that I can't envision, absolutely not [to raising taxes]. It has to be a last-ditch decision, because the more you give these boys [in government] to spend, the more they'll spend. So you've got to make money a critical resource, not a resource that allows everybody just to throw it everywhere at a whim . . . If we don't raise taxes we have to cut spending. Now [if elected President I] will go carefully across the board. We throw more money away than you can print almost right now. And we will go through it piece by piece. Now, you may not need me but you need a businessperson. You need a person who can go in, look at the waste, communicate that back to the American people. We've got to build a consensus. Now, if you can't stand a little pain and you can't stand a little sacrifice and you can't stand a trip across the desert with limited water, we're never going to straighten this country out.

Viewer call-in broadcast/
"Today," NBC-TV, 6-11.

5

[The U.S. is] $4-trillion in debt, and we don't have anything to show for it. Let's assume every [American] city looked like Singapore—spotless, clean, beautiful. Let's assume we had the greatest industrial base in the world and we had spent all that extra money to get it. We'd say: "Gee, we shouldn't have gone that far in debt, but look at what we have." But we've got the worst of all worlds now: a declining industrial base, declining schools, and the most violent, crime-ridden country in the world. What did that $4-trillion buy?

Interview/
U.S. News & World Report,
6-29:32.

Ross Perot
Industrialist;
1992 independent
Presidential candidate

1

It's very important that we not continue to let our industrial base deteriorate. Someone . . . in the President's [Bush] staff said he didn't care whether he made potato chips or computer chips [in the U.S.]. Well, anybody who thinks about it cares a great deal. Number one, you make more making computer chips than you do potato chips. Number two, 19 out of 20 computer chips we have in this country now come from Japan; we've given away whole industries. So as we phase these industries over, there's a lot of intellectual talent in these industries; a lot of these people and industries can be converted to the industries of tomorrow. And that's where the high-paying jobs are. We need to have a very carefully thought-through phase-over. See, we practice 19th-century capitalism; the rest of the world practices 21st-century capitalism.

At Presidential candidates' debate,
St. Louis, Mo., Oct. 11/
The New York Times, 10-12:(A)13.

2

[On the proposed U.S.-Canada-Mexico free-trade agreement and whether it will result in U.S. companies moving their manufacturing to less-expensive Mexico]: To those of you . . . who are business people, pretty simple: If you're paying $12, $13, $14 an hour for factory workers and you can move your factory south of the border . . . pay a dollar an hour for your labor, have no health care . . . have no environmental controls,

no pollution controls and no retirement [benefits], and you don't care about anything but making money, there will be a giant sucking sound going south . . . I called the Who's Who of the folks who've been around it and I said, "Why won't everybody go south [to Mexico]?" They say, "It'd be disruptive." I said, "For how long?" I finally got them up from 12 to 15 years. And I said, "Well, how does it stop being disruptive?" And that is when they're [Mexico's] jobs come up from a dollar an hour to six dollars an hour, and ours go down to six dollars an hour, and then it's leveled again. But in the meantime, you've wrecked the [U.S.] with these kinds of deals.

At Presidential candidates' debate,
Richmond, Va., Oct. 15/
The New York Times, 10-17:10.

3

Our principal need now is to stabilize the tax base, which is the job base, and create a growing dynamic base. Now, please, folks, if you don't hear anything else I say, remember—millions of people at work are our tax base. One quick thought: If you confiscate the *Forbes* 400 wealth, take it off, you cannot balance the [Federal] budget this year. It kind of gets your head straight about where the taxes, year in and year out, have got to come from: millions and millions of people at work.

At Presidential candidates' debate,
East Lansing, Mich., Oct. 19/
The New York Times, 10-20:(A)13.

Shirley Peterson
Commissioner,
Internal Revenue Service
of the United States

4

We believe most of our citizens will comply with the [tax] law if they know what their duties are. For example, we are convinced that red tape makes it very hard sometimes for small businesses to meet their tax obligation. We should like to find a way to be there when they start out in business and to educate them to "this is what you have to do, and if you need help, we'll help you fill out the forms." If you're not able to meet your

(SHIRLEY PETERSON)

obligation, we'll work out an installment arrangement. Basically, we're trying to help people get in the system and stay in the system.

Interview/
USA Today, 3-31:(A)11.

Michael Porter
Professor, Harvard University
Business School

1

There's a new paradigm of international competition and that paradigm is based on dynamism, on the capacity of firms to innovate and upgrade the sophistication of how they compete. Now success depends on relentless investment by companies . . . not just in physical assets, but also in less tangible assets such as research and development, training, supplier relationships, and the losses required to gain access to foreign markets. What's the problem? We [in the U.S.] invested a significantly lower rate in plant and equipment than our major international rivals. We simply don't have a large enough pool of investment capital. We're not saving enough, either in households or in government. In addition to this inadequate pool of capital, our policies are too erratic. We keep changing the tax code. We keep changing the rules. And this instability causes companies to waiver, to hold back from investment.

At economic conference convened
by President-elect Bill Clinton,
Little Rock, Ark., Dec. 14/
The New York Times, 12-15:(A)14.

Clyde V. Prestowitz, Jr.
Chairman,
Economic Strategy Institute

2

[On Democratic Presidential candidate Bill Clinton's and probable independent Presidential candidate Ross Perot's suggestions that government work more closely with business to help the U.S. economy compete in the world]: When it was just the Democrats saying these things, it was easy for the Republicans to say it's more Democratic claptrap. [But] when you have a very successful businessman [Perot] saying it, it makes it harder for the Republicans to dismiss it. Nobody doubts Perot is committed to capitalism, so you can't call it socialism.

Los Angeles Times, 6-27:(A)14.

Dan Quayle
Vice President
of the United States

3

Let us look at this great city [New York]. It attests to what becomes of those who put their faith in the benevolence of the state. In what should be a liberal paradise, what do we find instead? Honest, ambitious, hard-working New Yorkers struggling to pay the highest local taxes in America—about $1,600 per person. A business tax three times greater than that paid by businesses in Chicago and Los Angeles. One in every eight people on the dole. Taxpayers investing $7,000 a year for each public-school student, compared to $3,000 per student in private schools. The taxpayers' investment in education gets a high-school graduation rate of 38 percent. That means 62 per cent don't finish on time. Liberal economics may prevail here, but it sure doesn't work here. It's estimated that by 1994, a total of 320,000 private-sector jobs will be lost in New York City. When the taxpayers meekly protest these high taxes, the liberal deep-thinkers snap back that we lack "compassion" for the working man. But the working man is usually the one most hurt by this kind of thinking . . . You don't build economic strength by taxing economic strength. If you tax wealth, you diminish wealth. If you diminish wealth, you diminish investment. The fewer the investments, the fewer jobs.

Before Economic Club of New York,
Feb. 27/
The New York Times, 2-28:(A)7.

4

[Criticizing Democratic Presidential candidate Bill Clinton's economic plan]: Despite the Democrats' new rhetoric, the American people know the substance. They remember it well from

(DAN QUAYLE)

that golden era known as the [Jimmy] Carter-[Walter] Mondale era—that time of double-digit inflation, double-digit unemployment and interest rates approaching 20 per cent . . . I'm sure that during [Clinton's] slick bus trip through the area, our opponents never mentioned their idea to put new taxes on everything from gas and coal to paper and packaging. Well, what about all the jobs and money these plans will cost? What about the Ohio steelworker, the West Virginia coal miner or the Michigan auto worker thrown out of work?

Before Citizens for a Sound Economy,
Columbus, Ohio, Aug. 7/
Los Angeles Times, 8-8:(A)14.

1

[Democratic Presidential nominee] Bill Clinton's economic plan and his agenda will make matters much, much worse. He will raise your taxes. He will increase spending. He will make government bigger. Jobs will be lost . . . President Bush wants to hold the line on taxes. Bill Clinton wants to raise taxes. President Bush is for a balanced-budget amendment. Bill Clinton is opposed to it . . . [Clinton's] proposal is to raise $150-billion in taxes to raise $200-billion in new spending. How is raising taxes going to help small business? How is raising taxes going to help the farmer? How is raising taxes going to help the consumered America? I submit to you that raising taxes will make matters much, much worse.

At Vice-Presidential candidates' debate,
Atlanta, Ga., Oct. 13/
The New York Times, 10-14:(A)12.

Richard D. Recchia
Executive vice president,
Mitsubishi Motor Sales
of America

2

I don't think there's anything wrong with the average American worker. If you put him in the proper atmosphere to work, he's going to create quality that is world class . . . But the process has to be world class. You could take a Japanese worker, move him over here and put him in some of the operations in the United States that are building cars that are a lousy quality, and they will still be a lousy quality. The worker can't change the process that builds a lousy car. He can only do his part of whatever function he is responsible for.

Interview/
Los Angeles Times, 2-24:(D)2.

Robert B. Reich
Professor of public policy,
Harvard University

3

A large gap between people at the top [the rich] and average workers demoralizes Americans, who have always clung to the ideal of upward mobility . . . When the working poor feel the game is rigged, they simply lose interest [in such things as productivity].

U.S. News & World Report,
3-23:53.

4

The economy suffers from two separate maladies. There's a short-term flu—it's a recession from which it's very difficult to emerge . . . [The] long-term disease is related primarily to America's failure to invest adequately in our future productivity. It is also a failure both in the public sector and the private sector, a failure to invest in factories and equipment, a failure to invest in education, training and infrastructure, and a failure to invest well and wisely.

Interview/
USA Today, 11-25:(A)13.

Robert B. Reich
Secretary of Labor-designate
of the United States

5

I heard people beginning to frame a conversation around a supposed choice between [Federal] deficit reduction and public investment. You know, it's a little bit like that false choice between jobs or the environment. Only a very tiny propor-

(ROBERT B. REICH)

tion of the Federal budget actually goes to anything that any of us around this table would call public investment. The General Accounting Office did a study recently that [showed] only 9 per cent—9 per cent—of the Federal budget went to . . . infrastructure, childhood health and education and welfare, training, education . . . Only 9 percent.

*At economic conference convened
by President-elect Bill Clinton,
Little Rock, Ark., Dec. 15/
The New York Times, 12-16:(A)10.*

Ann Richards
Governor of Texas (D)

1

[Saying President Bush should not be given credit for current indications of economic recovery]: This uptick belongs to [Federal Reserve Chairman] Alan Greenspan, who, after years of inflated real interest rates, did his damndest to produce the usual pre-election bonanza. And if it was a little late, well, he can console himself with the fact that it was overdue anyway . . . that most Americans still recognize a Hail Mary pass when they see one.

*To Gannett Co. managers,
Washington, D.C., Dec. 8/
USA Today, 12-9:(A)4.*

Alice M. Rivlin
*Visiting professor of economics,
George Mason University;
Former Director,
Congressional Budget Office*

2

[On the country's large Federal deficit]: The real problem is that such deficits gnaw at the standard of living and slowly reduce its growth. If Americans are to live better in the future, they need to save more and channel those savings into productivity-enhancing investment. If, instead, they continue to use their relatively low private savings to finance ongoing expenses of government, they are likely to get low investment, stagnant productivity growth, continued trade deficits and growing obligations to send interest, dividends and profits overseas.

*Before House Economic
Stabilization Subcommittee,
Washington, D.C., April 7/
Los Angeles Times, 4-8:(A)12.*

Felix G. Rohatyn
*Senior partner,
Lazard Freres & Company,
investment bankers;
Chairman, Municipal Assistance
Corporation of New York*

3

The reason that I feel that public [Federal government] investment [in the economy] is so important isn't necessarily to stimulate the economy, but because we're about $2-trillion under-invested in the public sector. And most of the public investment is done at the state and local government level, and those state and local governments are tapped out in terms of debt service. And I think people are underestimating the drag on the economy of the state of the cities and the state of the states.

*At economic conference convened
by President-elect Bill Clinton,
Little Rock, Ark., Dec. 15/
The New York Times, 12-16:(A)10.*

Christina Romer
*Economist,
University of California,
Berkeley*

4

[On the recent economic conference in Little Rock, Ark., convened by President-elect Bill Clinton]: What we didn't see at the Little Rock conference is a sense of caution about where government weighs in [in helping the economy]. Government may screw up. It may choose the wrong industry or encourage tons of lobbying. I'd be much happier with across-the-board research-and-development tax credits than with government setting up a bunch of Sematechs or saying one industry's R&D is the right kind of R&D.

The New York Times, 12-21:(C)1.

Dan Rostenkowski
United States Representative,
D-Illinois

1

Here we are with the President [Bush] saying: "I won't sign [an economic] bill with increased tax rates in it" . . . Well, if the President will not sign legislation that has anything to do with higher taxes, and we're [Congress] not going to give him anything that doesn't have higher rates, we might do what all the economists suggested: We might not do anything; and in my opinion, that is not all bad.

Interview/
USA Today, 3-19:(A)11.

Warren Rudman
United States Senator,
R-New Hampshire

2

There can be no doubt that sustained record [Federal] budget deficits, high real interest rates, and the devotion of an increasing portion of the economy to pay interest on the skyrocketing national debt is the primary factor. And there can also be no doubt that the blame for this lies with the Congress and the President, with Democrats and Republicans alike, most all of whom have been unwilling to make the hard choices or to explain to the American people that there is no such thing as a free lunch.

Before the Senate,
Washington, D.C., March 12/
The New York Times, 3-25:(A)8.

3

Congress is not addressing fundamental issues. The one I've talked about the most is the [Federal] deficit, and the fact that we are about to enter an era of annual $400-billion to $500-billion deficits, which will truly wreck the country. I mean, we will be facing a situation at the end of this century that will be not very pretty to look at financially. We will have foreign governments in a position to dictate terms and conditions of money they will loan us. Interest rates will go higher. The economy will be seriously impaired.

The standard of living will decline. And this Congress just seems unable to deal with it. And quite frankly, the last several Administrations haven't either.

Interview/Time, 4-6:20.

4

We're going to be close in the next [few] years of probably having less than 5 [to] 6 per cent of the [Federal budget] for what we all traditionally call government. We're heading toward 60-65 per cent entitlement programs, 13 or 14 per cent defense, 17 per cent interest [on the debt]. If you want to do things for education and for health research, and for law enforcement—there's no money.

Interview/Newsweek, 4-6:28.

Larry J. Sabato
Professor of government,
University of Virginia

5

People [in New Jersey who voted in a Republican state Senate and Assembly after Democratic Governor Jim Florio increased taxes] just didn't like the tax increases, and they didn't buy Florio's explanations for them . . . Voters want it all, and they don't want to pay for it; that's the basic problem in the nation and all 50 states.

The Christian Science Monitor,
8-11:6.

Stan Schultz
Social historian,
University of Wisconsin

6

I don't think people study the economic indicators and decide they ought to be gloomy. We bring home the paycheck, pay the bills and realize that we can't buy as many goodies. Given that we've come to view the acquisition of goodies as the purpose of life, we conclude that things are terrible.

Newsweek, 1-13:22.

Charles L. Schultze
Senior fellow,
Brookings Institution

1

[Arguing against a proposed Constitutional amendment aimed at forcing a balanced Federal budget]: Once the amendment is enforced, by whatever means, the performance of the U.S. economy could be seriously damaged. One of the features of our economy, which has kept modern business cycles less violent than was true earlier in American history, is the automatic stabilizing character of the Federal budget. When recessions occur, budget revenues automatically fall and spending rises, helping to sustain the economy through the period of weakness. Under the amendment, a determined minority in either chamber of Congress could force highly depressing spending cuts—or less likely, tax increases—during recessions, driving the economy deeper into trouble.

The Washington Post, 6-2:(A)17.

John Sculley
Chairman, Apple Computer

2

I believe that we're at a turning point in the world economy today, not unlike transformation from the agricultural economy in the 19th century to the industrial economy that we've had for most of this century. The biggest change in this decade is going to be the reorganization of work itself. In this new economy, the strategic resources are no longer just the ones that come out of the ground, like oil and wheat and coal, but they are ideas and information that come out of our mind.

At economic conference convened
by President-elect Bill Clinton,
Little Rock, Ark., Dec. 14/
The New York Times, 12-15:(A)14.

Allen Sinai
Chief economist,
The Boston Company

3

The 1973 period marked the beginning of the decline of the American standard of living. The Reagan years interrupted that trend by borrowing and spending, which led to the retrenchment that has deepened the current slump.

Time, 1-13:36.

George A. Sinner
Governor of North Dakota (D)

4

I think you could tax the wealthy a lot more. If we continue into this sewer of debt, our children and the families that are suffering today, that's nothing compared to what these families of tomorrow will suffer. I for one will stand and say, "Yes, I think we should raise [taxes].

Speech to state Governors,
Washington, D.C., Feb. 3/
The Washington Post, 2-4:(A)6.

Robert C. Stempel
Chairman,
General Motors Corporation

5

What I did see in this period of time [since he became chief at GM] was a challenge coming from Japan that indicated they weren't going to stop. They weren't interested in a portion of this [U.S. car] market; they were interested only in the total market. I became convinced that we were targeted, just like television, just like video cameras, radios and cameras. I don't mind sharing the market. I do object to being told that "we're going to take you out." I'm not asking for sympathy. I just want to compete fair and square . . . What really focused our attention during this [economic] downturn was the fact that all manufacturers brought their production in line with demand. Only one group, the Japanese, didn't do it that way. Only one group [the Japanese] steadily increased its inventory of vehicles. I'm sure those vehicles aren't going to get thrown in the ocean—they're going to get sold. And so there's no question about it—their penetration of the U.S. market is going to increase. We told the President [Bush] and his people back last March that we could see the trend developing. That kind of behavior, in my view, really shouldn't continue.

Interview, Detroit, Mich./
Time, 1-27:45.

James B. Stockdale
1992 independent
Vice-Presidential candidate;
Admiral,
United States Navy (Ret.)

1

I think America is seeing right now the reason this nation is in gridlock. The trickle-downs and the tax-and-spends, or whatever you want to call them, are at swords' points; you can't get this economy going. Over here [on my right], we've got [Vice President] Dan [Quayle], whose President [Bush] is going to take eight years to balance the budget; and on my left, [Democratic Vice-Presidential nominee] Senator [Albert Gore, Jr.], whose boss [Democratic Presidential nominee Bill Clinton] is going to get it halfway balanced in four years. Ross Perot has got a plan to balance the budget five years in length from start to finish . . . The lifeblood of our economy is investment. And right now when we borrow $350-billion a year, it saps the money markets, and the private investors are not getting their share. What we do is work on that budget by an aggressive program, not a painful program, so that we can start borrowing less money and getting more investment money on the street through entrepreneurs who can build factories, who will hire people, and maybe we'll start manufacturing goods here in this country again.

At Vice-Presidential candidates' debate,
Atlanta, Ga., Oct. 13/
The New York Times, 10-14:(A)12.

James Tobin
Professor emeritus
of economics,
Yale University

2

We believe that cutting income taxes is exactly the wrong approach [to stimulate the economy]. It would promote consumption, not investment. And although there is a case for a quick, temporary tax cut, history tells us it would be almost impossible to reverse.

News conference,
Washington, D.C., March 30/
The Washington Post, 3-31:(C)4.

3

The country needs some fiscal stimulus [from the government] in the short run. I would be willing to see something like 1 per cent of GDP stimulus, which would be about $60-billion a year, and for a couple of years. Other people may prefer a smaller amount. Now, fiscal policy for recovery is bound to raise the [Federal] deficit temporarily. And we're fooling ourselves if we think there's a way of having a fiscal stimulus that doesn't have that result. The thing to do, I believe, is to combine the short-run fiscal stimulus with credible deficit-reduction policies that will be phased in at a later time . . . In today's weak economy, fiscal austerity would be counter-productive and would actually reduce investment in plant and equipment, in technology and human capital for the future. So it actually would damage the prospects of our children and grandchildren, rather than improving them.

At economic conference convened
by President-elect Bill Clinton,
Little Rock, Ark., Dec. 15/
The New York Times, 12-16:(A)10.

James A. Traficant, Jr.
United States Representative,
D-Ohio

4

[On President Bush's veto of the "family leave" bill]: While politicians flap their mouths about "family values," jobs and financial security have gone to hell. And what's the political response? The President of the United States has just vetoed the family medical leave bill. Now, that's what I call a "kinder and gentler America" [the words Bush used in his campaign for President four years ago]. I think it's time the Congress tells the President to shove his veto pen up his deficit.

Before the House,
Washington, D.C., Sept. 24/
The Washington Post, 9-25:(A)23.

Laurence H. Tribe
Professor of constitutional law,
Harvard University

5

[Arguing against a current proposal for a Constitutional amendment that would mandate a

(LAURENCE H. TRIBE)

balanced Federal budget]: Congress is saying, "Once we have tied ourselves to the mast with this amendment, we will have the courage to not listen to the sirens of spending and won't get ship-wrecked on another deficit budget." But the problem is that this amendment has no ties that bind.

The New York Times, 6-11:(A)10.

Alexander Trotman
President-designate,
worldwide automotive operations,
Ford Motor Company

1

We [the U.S.] are being slowly turned from a manufacturing society into a service society with lower-paid jobs and lower-technology jobs. It has changed America's wealth-generating capability. It has changed our technology base and changed our place in the world as a leading-industry coun-try. It has to be arrested and turned around.

Interview/
The Christian Science Monitor,
12-2:9.

Paul E. Tsongas
Candidate for the
1992 Democratic Presidential nomination;
Former United States Senator,
D-Massachusetts

2

[On how to help the economy]: My view of life is that you have an enormous river that runs, called self-interest. What I have to figure out is how I take that river and not create a new river, but channel it. If I know how this economy works, and I think I do, then my job is simply to shift the channel—to see that this river is flowing in the right direction. That's what I propose to do with my capital-gains tax [reduction]. It's how to get people to invest. It's how to get people in cor-porations to think differently. If I can readjust those markers, that river is going to flow in the right direction.

Interview/
The Christian Science Monitor, 2-11:19.

3

The core of my message is that you cannot be pro-jobs and anti-government at the same time. You cannot love employees and despise em-ployers. You cannot redistribute wealth that you never created. No goose, no golden egg.

Upon winning the New Hampshire
Democratic primary, Feb. 18/
Los Angeles Times, 2-19:(A)11.

4

We are becoming an economic colony. Amer-ica is up for sale. One per cent of Japan's manu-facturing base is foreign-owned; 2 per cent of Germany's is; 3 per cent of France's. Our is 18 per cent and growing rapidly.

Los Angeles Times, 3-17:(H)6.

5

If you wish to live well, you must produce well. That's the core, so the entire focus of my effort basically is: How do you end up with a viable, profitable, competitive manufacturing base? There is no other foundation for economic growth, long term. If you lose manufacturing, everything else falls apart. So you either have an investment strategy or a consumption strategy . . . [President] George Bush's economic philosophy is purist *laissez-faire*: Go out and compete; good luck, I hope you make it. The purist *laissez-faire* approach does not work. You have to under-stand where the engine is. The engine is manufac-turing. So you take whatever bullets you have and you expend them to get the engine run-ning . . . If we don't end up with a national ethic that values investment over consumption, we are not going to survive against nations that are reso-lute in their commitment to savings and invest-ment. We need a President who recognizes that absent a viable manufacturing base, there is no U.S. economy.

Debate with Arkansas Governor Bill Clinton,
Chicago, Ill./Time, 3-23:17.

Thomas J. Usher
President,
United States Steel Corporation

6

[On labor-management relations]: Our long-term interests are exactly the same. Whether you

113

(THOMAS J. USHER)

are a manager or a member of the union, everyone wants to do a good job, and they want to provide for their families. But I think there is a growing realization that we are not going to make it without the union and the union is not going to make it without us.

Interview, Pittsburgh, Pa./
The New York Times, 4-3:(C)1.

William Vickrey
Professor of economics,
Columbia University;
President,
American Economics Association

1

[The economics profession is] not really coming up with sound solutions to basic problems. Too many economists are basically astronomers, admiring our wonderful free-market system, or weathermen, predicting what the economy is going to do.

Interview/
The New York Times, 1-4:17.

Paul A. Volcker
Former Chairman,
Federal Reserve Board

2

After having been rich and strong, people have begun losing sight of what's necessary to maintain efficiency and strength. We seem to be in a mood as a nation that consumption is the all-important thing. [But] the more you consume and the less you invest, the less efficient and productive you're likely to be.

Interview, New York, N.Y./
The New York Times, 6-8:(C)2.

Linda Wachner
President,
Warnaco Group, Inc.

3

A woman's job has been to run the family—to seek the love and respect of children and a spouse. Out in the workplace, you can make

a business your family—as I have done—but employees are not your children. You judge each member of your corporate family for their work. You have to cast a colder eye on them and be very goal-oriented. It doesn't matter if people think you're tough or difficult, if you do it with a quality of human decency.

Interview/
Working Woman, May:105.

Lowell P. Weicker
Governor of Connecticut (I)

4

[We've] been subjected to 12 years of the highest authority in the land saying you can spend it and you don't have to pay for it. We can have wars, and we don't have to tax for it. But now we have to take a look at the domestic devastation in the U.S. We have no financial credibility at all, and we're going around the world begging for other nations to accommodate us. Why should they? This nation has turned its back on children, the disabled, the poor; it's a horrible record out there. I've long said that if you want to cut through all the bullshit of politicians, take a look at a budget. It tells you exactly what your priorities are. We spent a lot on the military. Now it shouldn't come as any mystery as to why we have difficulties given the budgets of the past 12 years.

Interview, Hartford, Conn./
Time, 4-13:16.

William Julius Wilson
Professor of sociology and
public policy,
University of Chicago

5

[I] have in mind the creation of some international economic policy whereby various countries would reach agreement on economic strategies that would maximize stability and growth in all nations. Our economies are so interdependent it's no longer possible for a modern nation to take steps to confront economic downturns without taking into account economic policies in other countries.

Interview/
The New York Times, 2-7:(A)7.

Timothy E. Wirth
United States Senator,
D-Colorado

1

What do you use tax policy for—growth or fairness? It's an enormously important question, but we never get to it. Another thing we should be debating is, what are we going to tax? We now tax investment and production. We tax labor; we tax capital. But the world out there is changing, and we probably should be looking at a value-added tax or a consumption tax. We ought to be looking at taxing environmental evils—a carbon tax or something like that. But because we say, "Read my lips, no new taxes," you don't get into any of this, either. And such things are the stuff of government. We decide what's important to us by putting programs in the budget and raising taxes—these steps reflect our values. But we never talk about these things.

Panel discussion, Washington, D.C./
Time, 6-8:68.

Raymond Worseck
Chief economist,
A. G. Edwards & Sons, Inc.

2

For decades it was a badge of honor for corporations to brag about the number of people they employed. Now it seems to be the reverse as restructuring becomes the key word. There is great unease [that] these . . . [unemployed] Americans will be permanently unemployed.

The Christian Science Monitor,
3-19:6.

Education

Lamar Alexander
*Secretary of Education
of the United States*

1

Those who support [large Federal spending increases for state and local school-improvement] believe that fundamentally the American education system is okay; all we need to do is dribble a little more money into it and everything would be fine. President Bush, and those who support his approach [of using vouchers to help send students to the schools of their choice, public or private], believe that there are a lot of good people, most of them working hard, in an educational system that is fundamentally flawed and needs dramatic change. And so we want to give poor families more choices of the schools that rich families already have.

*Jan. 21/
The New York Times, 1-22:(A)13.*

2

For too long we have not expected all of our children to learn to the same high standards, and so some of them—a disproportionate number of them minority students—end up unprepared for the workplace and they are left out and understandably frustrated when they find themselves there.

*Interview, Sydney, Australia/
The Christian Science Monitor,
5-7:2.*

3

The teaching profession needs to make special efforts to attract more minorities. What it most needs are the best possible teachers who include minorities, and the fastest way to do that of course is just to go out in the local school district and raise the salary until you get them. See, we go through all these laborious meetings, and baloney is what a lot of it is, thinking of ways within the existing system to think now about attracting people who are 10 years old to be teachers 30 years from now, when we have talented Hispanics, talented African-Americans, who are somewhere, who could go teach physics in the classroom if we'd just go pay them to do it . . . But we can't get through our existing ways of doing things to do that. Alternative certification programs are the fastest way to move people into teaching who are high quality or special needs or willing to go teach in a particular place, or bring something to the table that others don't.

*Before American Association
of State Colleges and Universities,
Washington, D.C., June 15/
The Washington Post, 6-17:(A)24.*

4

Our debate about education too often boils down to whether we're spending enough money. We are all in favor of investing more money to make our schools the best in the world, but these numbers [that show more being spent on education than ever before and yet also show a mixed or worse student performance] remind us that money alone is not the answer for better schools. We should spend our money on changing our schools: breaking the mold, higher standards, better tests, getting government off the backs of teachers, and giving families more choices of all schools.

*The Christian Science Monitor,
9-4:3.*

Gregory R. Anrig
*President,
Educational Testing Service*

5

[On a survey showing U.S. students lagging their foreign counterparts in math and science]: International assessment does give us a good picture of what being first would mean. It shows where we have to be. Until we know what we are shooting for, we are going to have a tough time being first in anything.

*Feb. 5/
Los Angeles Times, 2-6:(A)16.*

Albert Beaton
Former director of research,
National Assessment of
Educational Progress

1

The largely curriculum-free SAT became useful as a predictor of applicants' success in college. The SAT succeeded by including questions based on fairly basic to higher-order reasoning skills that should be answerable without the detailed knowledge that comes from studying specific high-school subjects. The SAT . . . does not directly measure specific student learning and proficiency in school subjects. A different test is needed to accomplish the purposes of education reform.

The Washington Post,
9-15:(A)23.

Ernest L. Boyer
President, Carnegie Foundation
for the Advancement
of Teaching;
Former Chancellor,
State University
of New York

2

[On college presidents]: The job has been powerfully diminished, and I think the nation is the loser. We need people who are able to interpret historically, ethically and socially the issues of the day. But because [college presidents] are under such pressure financially, it becomes risky to be prophetic. There is a hazard in offending.

The Washington Post,
6-15:(A)4.

Marvin Bressler
Professor of sociology,
Princeton University

3

The egalitarian conception that everyone has a right to an education appropriate to his potential is a highly democratic and compassionate standard.

Time, 4-13:59.

Anne Bryant
Executive director,
American Association
of University Women

4

[On a report indicating bias against girls in education]: This is truly a wake-up call to the nation's education and policy leaders, parents, administrators and guidance counselors that unless we pay attention to girls' needs today, we will find out 15 years from now that there is still a glass ceiling [against the advancement of women in society].

The New York Times, 2-12:(A)1.

George Bush
President of the United States

5

My opponent [Democratic Presidential nominee Bill Clinton] and I both want to change the way our kids learn. He wants to change our schools a little bit—and I want to change them a lot. Take the issue of whether parents should be able to choose the best school for their kids. My opponent says that's okay, as long as the school is run by the government. I say every parent and child should have a real choice of schools—public, private or religious.

At Republican National Convention,
Houston, Texas, Aug. 20/
The New York Times, 8-21:(A)16.

Gerhard Casper
Provost,
University of Chicago;
President-designate,
Stanford University

6

Faculty, students, staff, presidents have to always be reminded that universities are first of all about the pursuit of knowledge and that pursuit of knowledge has, as a condition, that we all respect one another for what we say, or criticize one another for what we say, but do not deal with one another on the basis of [cultural] stereotypes.

News conference/
The Wall Street Journal, 4-27:(A)16.

(GERHARD CASPER)

1

University bashing is not the same as criticizing universities. Universities make mistakes, and the mistakes should be criticized. But it's quite a different thing to bash, and I think we have seen a fair amount of bashing in the last year or so. We have come to expect an awful lot of universities . . . The demands are increasing all the time, and one of the dangers I see is that we are . . . going to divert universities from what they are primarily about, which is to teach the next generation and to do research. And those two things go together. I have never seen a conflict between teaching and research. I think they are just two sides of the same coin.

Interview, Chicago, Ill./
The Christian Science Monitor,
4-27:12.

Bob Chase
Vice president,
National Education Association

2

[Saying there is a shortage of minority and male teachers]: It's very disheartening to see that we have not made significant progress in these areas of teacher recruitment. Students learn lessons about life both through formal instruction and what they see around them. We need more male elementary-school teachers and more people of color at all grade levels.

The Washington Post, 7-7:(A)4.

John Chubb
Senior fellow,
Brookings Institution

3

[On the Bush Administration's proposal for a voucher system to enable parents to send their children to the public, private or religious school of their choice]: This is the kind of bill with direct appeal to poor constituents. If you're unhappy with your kids' school, if it's dangerous and if the quality of education is poor, here's a thousand bucks, choose a new school. The worst of public schools will be run out of business . . . so what?

The Christian Science Monitor,
6-29:9.

Bill Clinton
Governor of Arkansas (D);
Candidate for the 1992
Democratic Presidential nomination

4

Just as there are opportunity gaps in education, there are also responsibility gaps as well, places where our system failed because people didn't do their part. Politicians who posture instead of act on education. Schools where turf battles get more attention than gang battles. Bureaucrats who'd rather shuffle paper than change lives. Teachers who are burned out and given up and are just going through the motions. Parents who treat school as government-financed child care. Citizens who couldn't care less about education so long as they keep their local taxes down. And students who sometimes act more like kids in [the TV show] *Beverly Hills 90210* than the kids in [the film] *Stand and Deliver.*

At East Los Angeles (Calif.) College,
May 14/
Los Angeles Times, 5-15:(A)26.

Bill Clinton
Governor of Arkansas (D);
1992 Democratic
Presidential nominee

5

[I want] an America in which the doors of college are thrown open once again to the sons and daughters of stenographers and steelworkers. We'll say: "Everybody can borrow the money to go to college. But you must do your part. You must pay it back, from your paychecks, or better yet by going back home and serving your communities." We'll have millions of energetic young men and women, serving their country, policing the streets, teaching the kids, caring for the sick, helping young people stay off drugs and out of gangs, giving us all a sense of new hope and limitless possibilities.

Accepting the Presidential nomination
at Democratic National Convention,
New York, N.Y.,
July 16/
The New York Times,
7-17:(A)13.

Bill Clinton
Governor of Arkansas (D);
President-elect
of the United States

1

[On his plans for improving the student-loan program for college education]: How much money should everybody be able to borrow a year? What contributions should people's families be expected to make, if any? If you put this into effect, how are you going to keep the colleges and universities of this country from using it as an excuse to explode tuition even more? I mean, there are lots of factual questions.
News conference, Nov. 12/
The New York Times, 11-25:(A)12.

Robert L. Crain
Professor of sociology
and education,
Teachers College,
Columbia University

2

[On New York City's system of magnet schools]: Among the big cities, this is the most egalitarian I know and probably the most exciting set of choices for a student in high school. All the chronic problems big cities have are as bad here as anywhere else, but at the same time there are these experimental schools. It's like a swamp— there are these mangrove trees growing out of it that are quite amazing.
The New York Times, 4-20:(A)1.

William E. Dannemeyer
United States Representative,
R-California

3

The last 30 years in America, we have educated a whole generation of kids in what can be called the permissive philosophy that says you can do anything you want to, there are not standards anymore . . . We Californians will have a measure on the ballot this November that I think will make a revolutionary change in how we educate the next generation. We're going to do the novel thing in California of giving parents a choice as to what school their kids will go to

school . . . When we kicked the voluntary prayer out of public schools in 1962, we kicked out of the educational process the creator of the standards, and that's in my judgment the most significant step of changing the quality of public education in America that we badly need.
Broadcast interview/"Crossfire,"
CNN-TV, 4-30.

Richard G. Darman
Director,
Federal Office of Management
and Budget

4

We believe, and statistics demonstrate, the national education system is extraordinarily uniform and it's fairly uniform in its poor performance compared with other countries. That has to be changed. We can't compete successfully in the 21st century with other countries that are training workers for a more complicated work environment requiring statistical skills, computer literacy and other kinds of technical skills for high productivity. We will not be able to compete if there's a very wide gap between our performance and theirs. We've got to change.
Interview/
USA Today, 3-18:(A)11.

James J. Davis
Interim chairman,
department of foreign languages,
Howard University

5

I advise students to study a foreign language regardless of which one it is, because foreign-language study is not just about learning a second language but about opening your mind to a larger world . . . Students usually think that foreign-language study is only about conjugating verbs and memorizing vocabulary, and I try to dispel that misconception at the outset. Language is really about culture. If I could have any influence in teaching foreign languages at Howard, I would work toward getting culture taught as a primary goal, and the other things such as grammar and vocabulary will fall into place.
Interview/
Humanities, Jan.-Feb:25,26.

Erik Devereux
Assistant professor
of political science,
Heinz School of Public Policy
and Management,
Carnegie-Mellon University

1

In the past, [college] faculty members who expressed concerns about public-private tension [in the universities] did so from a position of strength. Now everyone knows this is not the case. The state colleges are the backbone of the job market, and they're in deep trouble. One of the lasting legacies of [former President] Ronald Reagan and [current President] George Bush is a wide acknowledgment of the role of the private sector [in higher education], and [President-elect] Bill Clinton never disputed that. In light of that, universities are going to be more reliant on the private sector and that is not going to change. When universities ask where money is coming from, it's going to be coming from the private sector.

The Christian Science Monitor,
11-23:13.

Joseph Duffey
President,
American University,
Washington, D.C.

2

By the year 2000, American higher education will no longer be dominant in the world. Our general belief in education and our ability to finance it are running out.

Time, 4-13:60.

Chester E. Finn, Jr.
Member, President's Education
Policy Advisory Committee;
Member, National Assessment
Governing Board

3

There is a fundamental difference between what a Governor and a President can do [about education]. A Governor is responsible for education in the state, while the President is a national leader, a figure who persuades people to do something differently on the state and local level.

The Christian Science Monitor,
4-13:11.

4

[On President Bush's current proposals to provide government money to help send children to private schools]: There's absolutely no doubt that over four years Bush has changed on this issue. The continuing decrepitude of American [public] education between 1989 when Bush was inaugurated and the present—and the mounting evidence that the reforms of the '80s have not worked—has radicalized me. I wouldn't be at all surprised if it's had a similar effect on Bush.

The Christian Science Monitor,
8-25:4.

Leon D. Finney
Former member,
Board of Education
of Chicago, Ill.

5

[On the rise in enrollment in Christian schools]: Parents are looking for alternatives. There's a sense that the public schools may be doing somewhat of a job on the three Rs. But on the issue of values, there's much to be desired . . . This is cutting across class lines. These [Christian] schools tend to instill responsibility and discipline. And they market that.

The Washington Post, 10-17:(A)8.

Richard Florida
Associate professor
of management,
Heinz School of Public Policy
and Management,
Carnegie-Mellon University

6

[On partnerships between corporations and universities]: Xerox and companies like it are drastically reducing their supplier lists and developing longer-term relations with a smaller number of suppliers. Those suppliers provided on-time delivery and a product tailored to meet

(RICHARD FLORIDA)

the needs of the customer. The next step is to demand this of the universities, and what they supply is people.

The Christian Science Monitor, 11-23:12.

Henry Louis Gates, Jr.
Chairman, department of
Afro-American studies,
Harvard University

1

All issues of multi-culturalism go by-the-by if we have a society of illiterates. Our concern has to be basic literacy as well as changing the curriculum on the higher end of things. The two are not necessarily unconnected. I think we can use non-traditional materials, say Afro-American materials, in the teaching of literacy. Many scholars have pointed out over and over again that the dominant theme in Afro-American literature is the relationship between freedom and literacy. In a way it's fair to say that we [blacks] have always been a people of the book too, but this heritage is being lost out there in the inner city, and perhaps more variegated subject matter could make for more compelling lesson plans. There is a process of mediation between scholarship and social change. Sometimes it takes decades. For instance, here's Thomas Paine, and [many years] later, here's the American Revolution.

Interview, Cambridge, Mass./
The Christian Science Monitor, 4-10:11.

William F. Glavin
President, Babson College

2

I do not believe that academic institutions have got to be run by academics. They need to be run like a business, more cost-effective and efficient.

The Washington Post, 6-15:(A)4.

Hannah Holborn Gray
President,
University of Chicago

3

In the end, what we hope we are doing for our students is not simply teaching them history, or physics, or this, or that. We hope that we're teaching them to think. We hope that we're enabling them to become more independent-minded, more capable of critical judgment, more inquiring, not taking things for granted so much, and above all, looking toward integrating apparently disparate areas of experience and ideas.

Interview, Chicago, Ill./
The Christian Science Monitor,
2-25:14.

Vartan Gregorian
President, Brown University

4

The [communal campus life] and the American university have become identical in people's minds. In America it is assumed that a student's daily life is as important as his learning experience.

Time, 4-13:60.

David Hamburg
President,
Carnegie Corporation

5

The original idea of junior high school was to ease the transition from childhood to adulthood. Unfortunately, junior high has become a replica of high school. There are no distinctive social relationships or curriculum. It's actually wound up forcing children to make the transition to adulthood even earlier.

Interview/Time, 3-23:59.

Walter Haney
Researcher, Center for the
Study of Testing,
Boston (Mass.) College

6

The pressure to prep kids for tests comes from school boards and building principals and just an awareness of how the school is going to be judged by the scores reported in newspapers. In some cases, [teachers] are told to raise their test scores or lose their jobs.

USA Today, 9-16:(A)7.

Theodore M. Hesburgh
President emeritus,
University of Notre Dame

1

There are some college presidents who can't hire or fire athletic directors or coaches. That power is held by a board of trustees. We won't rest until every president has that power. If the president is responsible for upholding the integrity of the institution, he has to have that power.

News conference,
Washington, D.C., March 17/
The New York Times, 3-18:(D)3.

2

Fund-raising has become the name of the game [for college presidents]. You can have the greatest vision in the world, but if you don't have money, you're up a creek.

The Washington Post, 6-15:(A)5.

Michael Hooker
President,
University of Massachusetts

3

The role of the research university in the 21st century is to transfer technology or ideas out of our labs into the commercial world. Those companies that compete most effectively will be those that bring products to market quickly. The University of Massachusetts has only begun to lay out a vision for the future . . . to marshal resources of our five campuses to contribute to the economic development of the state.

The Christian Science Monitor,
11-23:12.

Franklyn G. Jenifer
President, Howard University

4

Ensure that every youngster's education needs are not just addressed between 9 and 5. Education is a 24-hour-a-day job. It requires parental input. In some instances, we have to think about residential schools with individuals who care for youngsters and love them.

Interview/
Los Angeles Times, 5-15:(T)7.

Leroy Keith
President, Morehouse College

5

We've been so successful in educating black males and our graduates have such a high degree of self-esteem that people think there is something of a mystery at Morehouse. And, in fact, there is something in the air here. There is an air of expectancy that students, once prepared here, will be able to achieve whatever their goals might be. The brotherhood that exists here, where people feed each other with encouragement and reinforcement, has been a trademark and credo of Morehouse for years. And it results in a kind of spirit and a kind of feeling that does not exist on any other campus that I have been affiliated with or that I have visited. And that exuberance carries over once the student graduates, giving him the feeling that "I am a Morehouse Man and I am expected to do certain things."

Interview, Atlanta, Ga./
Ebony, June:34.

Edward M. Kennedy
United States Senator,
D-Massachusetts

6

[Criticizing the Bush Administration's "GI Bill for Children," a voucher system to enable parents to send their children to the public, private or religious school of their choice]: The Administration has given a souped-up name to its school-voucher scheme, but it's the same old warmed-over proposal that Congress has already rejected. It is a serious mistake to use Federal tax dollars to support private schools . . . Our goal in education reform is to improve the public schools, not abandon them.

The Christian Science Monitor,
6-29:9.

Bernard Knox
1992 Jefferson lecturer
in the humanities;
Former professor,
Yale University

1

I haven't taught in universities for a long time, but what I read is not very reassuring. All these attempts to break down the common culture that we've always had—at least since English-speaking people have had any kind of common culture. It is hard, even now, to give students more than a superficial acquaintance with the main documents of the Western tradition; all we can do is try to give them enough so that they will want to read on for themselves later. But if we add Asian, African and other literatures, I'm afraid that no one will get more than a smattering not only of the new additions but also of the texts that have defined our identity since the Renaissance.

Interview/Humanities, May-June:36.

Jonathan Kozol
Educator

2

[Criticizing the Bush Administration's proposal for school vouchers to help families send their children to the school of their choice, public or private]: I'm bitterly opposed to vouchers. The concept is as sinister as can be. [Education Secretary Lamar] Alexander has a seductive formula for selling vouchers to the public. He says rich people already have the choice to send their child to private schools; why don't poor parents have the same choice? One would think he was ready to send poor black children in Harlem to Exeter [Academy in New Hampshire]. But he's only talking about vouchers of a couple thousand dollars. That might be part of the tuition at the lowest-level private school. Rich people will use it as a subsidy for the best schools. The only way it would be just is if every child in America got an equal voucher pegged for the best private schools in America. The Bush Administration is never going to do that.

Interview/Essence, August:108.

3

[Saying permitting parents to choose the school their children will attend, such as is allowed in a number of states, is resulting in "white flight" from schools that racial minorities attend]: This justifies the worst fears of urban school districts. How can one possibly ignore the implications? These parents are not fleeing ugly schools with leaky roofs, classes of 45 students or rock-bottom funding like in New York, or gang warfare like in Los Angeles. What are they fleeing? I'm afraid the answers are self-evident. In theory, choice allows parents to make pedagogic decisions for children. In fact, they are not picking the more fitting school for their children, but the more fitting schoolmates . . . White parents, once passionately opposed to busing for integration because it was unfair to keep children on a bus for an hour, are now putting their children on two-hour bus rides to get away from black and Hispanic children. The bus ride was never the issue. The destination was the issue.

The New York Times, 12-16:(A)15.

Francis L. Lawrence
President, Rutgers University

4

Teaching without research is empty, [and] research without teaching is sterile.

At Rutgers University commencement,
May 21/
The New York Times, 5-22:(A)12.

Arthur Levine
Professor,
Graduate School of Education,
Harvard University

5

All universities are like department stores. In the next few years [due to budget cuts] many institutions will move from department stores to boutiques.

The Christian Science Monitor,
11-16:10.

Glenn Linden
Professor of history,
Southern Methodist University

6

Some shift of the money is essential [to help students in poor districts get good educations.

(GLENN LINDEN)

But] presently there isn't any willingness to share the burden of public education. The people with the money are opting out. We say the future is children, but we're not going to support the black kids, brown kids. We've got to say they're not my kids or your kids but the nation's kids. If not, we're a Third World country down the road.

The Christian Science Monitor,
12-8:2.

H. William Lurton
Chairman, United States
Chamber of Commerce

1

Our country's economic health depends on continued investment in plants and equipment, research and development, and infrastructure. But even more so, our ability to compete at home and in world markets depends on the most vital capital investments of all: the one we make not in things but in people. We must upgrade the quality of education in this country, and business must continue taking the lead in this crucial effort.

Before Kansas Chamber of Commerce/
Nation's Business, April:44.

Ann Lynch
Member,
Education Advisory Committee
to President of the United States
George Bush;
Former president,
National Parent-Teacher
Association

2

School has not been taken seriously for a long time. And school has not changed in conception since it started. Still the same number of hours, the same number of days. We never really changed the structure . . . We need to really sit back and ask, "How do people learn? What is the best atmosphere for their learning? What do we want them to learn?" Most people don't realize one of the things President Bush did was to direct the [state] Governors—who are responsible for education in this country—to set goals. We've

never had goals for education. So let's sit down and say what we expect when a child graduates.

Interview/USA Today, 1-6:(A)7.

David Noble
Co-founder,
Coalition for Universities
in the Public Interest

3

Places like MIT are [becoming] conduits for public subsidy for private industry. In a nutshell, the universities are getting out of the education business. We've found that it's not unusual for university presidents to make more from their corporate board fees than from their university salaries. They're cutting back on curricular offerings, jacking up tuition, restricting access while spending madly in building new laboratories and beefing up their commercially viable enterprises. That is visible on every campus in America: impoverishment of the educational mission and expansion of the commercial one.

The Christian Science Monitor,
11-23:13.

Ross Perot
Industrialist

4

If we've got to cough up more [money for education by increasing taxes], we cough it up, because this is very precious money. If you have to spend more to help these tiny little children become productive, successful, tax-paying citizens, it's the cheapest money you'll ever spend. Now, it's pennies compared to having them on welfare or keeping them in prison.

Broadcast interview/
"Both Sides with Jesse Jackson,"
CNN-TV, 5-30.

5

In those days [when he was going to school] the parents were allies of the teachers. Nowadays, if you're a teacher and you try to discipline a student, you face a class-action suit from the parents. In those days, the worst thing was to cross a teacher. I knew when I did wrong that

EDUCATION

(ROSS PEROT)

whatever was done to punish me in school was nothing compared to the problem I faced at home ... The secret of the public-school system then was the alliance between these wonderful ladies [the teachers] and the kids' mothers. All the moms got their little charges by the ears, set them down and helped them—or forced them—to do their [school] work.

Interview/
U.S. News & World Report,
6-29:25.

Dan Quayle
Vice President
of the United States

1

One reason our schools are in crisis is because they have, in many ways, lost their moral bearings. When eighth-graders are squandering the gift of youthful innocence in premarital sex, the solution is not to give them a condom. The solution is to give them a value-based education, to teach them what is right and wrong, to teach them that they alone are responsible for their actions. Public-school educators should be less concerned with promoting lifestyles curricula and more concerned with teaching basic values: personal integrity, responsibility, hard work and morality.

Before Manhattan Institute,
New York, N.Y., June 15/
Los Angeles Times, 6-16:(A)21.

Diane S. Ravitch
Assistant Secretary
for Educational Research
and Improvement,
Department of Education
of the United States

2

[Criticizing those who say U.S. schools are as good as in the past]: The critics are wrong in saying the schools are just as good as they ever were. That is deeply damaging; it inspires complacency and a false sense of self-esteem. To say we do as well today as we did 20 years ago—our

kids today are not going to be competing with their parents, but with children being educated in other countries.

The New York Times, 4-8:(B)8.

3

[On a new program that replaces multiple-choice tests with tests requiring students to analyze and explain their answers]: This is probably the biggest, most important thing happening in education. There has been a lot of criticism about multiple-choice tests, but it is the first time the Department of Education has lent its prestige and support for the need for change.

The Washington Post, 5-18:(A)1.

Roy Romer
Governor of Colorado (D)

4

To set goals doesn't make anybody an "education President." It's what you do to help people achieve the goals ... Anybody who claims to be the "education President" is probably riding on the reputation of what the Governors of states are doing.

The Christian Science Monitor,
10-1:8.

Jeffrey A. Ross
National campus-affairs director,
Anti-Defamation League
of B'nai B'rith

5

In the past, what we had were [college] campuses that were basically white, essentially mono-cultural. They have become diverse, but the arrival of diversity provides opportunities and challenges. It provides for a social richness, an enriched cultural mix. It also presents dangers of a withdrawal into group enclaves. Rather than a cosmopolitan atmosphere, we could create a series of ghettos.

Los Angeles Times, 1-4:(A)16.

Neil L. Rudenstine
President, Harvard University

6

[On the increased difficulty for students in paying college tuition]: What has changed is not

125

(NEIL L. RUDENSTINE)

so much the relationship between tuition and inflation. The real change has been more recent: Family incomes have been growing more slowly [than tuition has been rising].

At National Press Club,
Washington, D.C., Nov. 30/
The New York Times, 12-1:(A)11.

Sam Sava
Executive director,
National Association of
Elementary School Principals

1

[On cuts in government funding for inner-city schools]: All we're doing is establishing a permanent underclass in our nation because they won't receive the education they need to break out of this cycle of poverty. You need smaller class sizes, more bilingual teachers. These are the children that need the best education and they're taking a terrible beating.

USA Today, 9-3:(A)2.

Benno C. Schmidt, Jr.
President, Yale University

2

The future of the country really depends on the quality and vitality of our educational system. We have the best system of higher education in the world . . . but I think most Americans feel that our system of elementary and secondary education is not working well.

Interview, New Haven, Conn./
The Christian Science Monitor,
5-28:7.

Patricia Schroeder
United States Representative,
D-Colorado

3

Among the 100 public colleges where the tuition went up the most, the amount of teaching time went down and the class size went up. The costs are hidden behind a "magical" field of research, where professors are freed up from their classes and given more money for travel, research assistants and laboratories.

Sept. 14/
The Washington Post, 9-15:(A)3.

4

When it comes to college education, American families are paying more and getting less. Since 1980, the cost of sending our kids to college, a key part of the American dream, has doubled or tripled the rate of inflation every single year.

The Christian Science Monitor,
11-16:10.

Albert Shanker
President,
American Federation of Teachers

5

In the old days, people used to go to doctors to get cured. But for several centuries doctors were actually harming their patients, indeed sometimes resulting in deaths, because they didn't realize they had to wash their hands and sterilize their instruments. In other words, in the normal course of practice, doctors were doing things out of ignorance that were harmful to their patients. We need to ask whether schools in the normal course of education do things that are harmful to students.

The Atlantic, May:26.

John R. Silber
President, Boston University

6

[At American colleges, there is] an increasing number of too-small classes and too many courses. We have about 150 courses that study the human mind. But all that we know about the human mind could be taught in 30. A course on the effect of Anna on Sigmund Freud is fine. But it's part of the waste that is commonplace at big research universities. Small colleges cannot afford that kind of narcissism.

Time, 4-13:58.

Herbert A. Simon
Nobel Prize-winning economist;
Member of the faculty and board,
Carnegie-Mellon University

1

A decade from now, we're [universities] going to look a lot like the way we look now. Maybe we'll be a bit leaner, maybe a little poorer, maybe the elbow patches on our tweed jackets will be a little more patched, but essentially we'll be what we are now.

The New York Times, 2-3:(A)12.

Theodore R. Sizer
Professor of education,
Brown University;
Chairman,
Coalition of Essential Schools

2

[On a new program that replaces multiple-choice tests with tests requiring students to analyze and explain their answers]: I think the new tests are first-rate. But I think it is exceedingly unwise to tie them into a national set of standards. Who sets the standards and by what right do they do it? It's very hard for some kids to compete against a national standard if some kids are in good schools and some kids are in poor schools.

The Washington Post, 5-18:(A)8.

Peter Syverson
Director of information,
Council of Graduate Schools

3

[On the master's degree]: We call it the "connected degree" because, of all degrees, the master's is the most connected with the students and their careers. It's the practitioner's degree, the degree where people learn to do and apply research.

The Washington Post, 7-6:(A)9.

Chang-Lin Tien
Chancellor,
University of California,
Berkeley

4

[Calling for increases in funding for higher education]: I would like to suggest an alternative

to "buy American." How about: "Invest in America today; compete worldwide tomorrow." Although this slogan might lack emotional punch, it comes much closer to addressing the pivotal issues in the decade ahead . . . The worst thing we could do is put on blinders that limit our vision and restrict our courses of action. But that is exactly what we are doing when we buy into the "buy American" craze.

Before Comstock Club,
San Francisco, Calif., Feb. 24/
Los Angeles Times, 2-25:(A)19.

Marc Tucker
Co-founder,
New Standards Project

5

[On new methods of student testing that rely on more than specific correct answers]: You want to know how kids perform when they are given a goal but not a clear problem statement. When there's no one right answer but a lot of answers, some of which are better than others . . . A diploma certifies that you've been there 12 years. It does not certify to any particular level of performance. [A goal should be that] every kid who meets world-class performance standards gets a certificate of mastery, regardless of age.

USA Today, 9-16:(A)8.

Herbert J. Walberg
Professor of education,
University of Illinois

6

[On the rise in enrollment in Christian schools]: The marketplace tells us a lot. [Those who send their children to Christian schools are frequently] very poor parents who in essence are paying twice . . . But they can see that their children are not getting an effective education in public schools.

The Washington Post, 10-17:(A)8.

Chris Whittle
Educator; Founder,
Channel One

7

[On his projected Edison Project, a chain of nationwide private schools with high educational standards]: Let's not be locked into the standard student-teacher ratios. That rigidity—twenty-to-one, thirty-to-one, with the teacher in front—is part of the problem. With technology in place, the idea of "teacher" will be expanded. Yes, we may have fewer paid teachers. Parents and students may do the great bulk of running the cafeteria—that's a big cost. Kids run McDonald's—why can't they run the cafeteria? Critics say, "You want kids to work for the school?" Well, they clean schools in Japan. I say that by having students work and by getting each parent to give just two hours a week to the school, you're giving teachers much more time to meet with kids one-on-one. That's a *radical* improvement right there.

Interview/Vanity Fair, August:174.

Walter E. Williams
Professor of economics,
George Mason University

1

A black kid who graduated [from high school] with 1,100 on an SAT is not going to have a problem getting into any college. It's the black student who gets 500; the question is, "How did he manage to get through high school with such a poor achievement record?" You can't say it's discrimination, because some of the worst schools for black kids are in the cities where the Mayor is black, the school superintendent is black, most of the prinicpals are black.

Interview/USA Today, 3-2:(A)9.

Miriam Williford
Associate provost for
continuing education and
public service,
University of Massachusetts,
Amherst

2

I think there are going to be more and more providers of continuing education. We are learning it is not now possible to get a bachelor's degree in a particular field and think we are set for life. We're probably going to have six different

careers. Very few will not require some sort of upgrading education.

The Christian Science Monitor,
9-15:4.

Marshall Witten
Member, board of trustees,
Vermont State College

3

The four-year, ivy-covered [college] campus, to some extent, is a hairy mastodon on its way out . . . A four-year, straight-from-high-school, cloistered experience on campus will be reserved for the very wealthy and the very able. Everyone else is going to catch post-secondary education on the job, after work, at home, and at local institutions that may not look like a traditional college setting.

The Christian Science Monitor,
11-16:10.

Robert Wood
Professor of
democratic institutions
and the social order,
Wesleyan University

4

In the past five years, we have generally had two counsels on curriculum [at American colleges]. Allan Bloom and others basically say, "Don't read anything after the Age of Enlightenment." Then we have our present multicultural movement saying every culture should be explored. We need some consensus on this. What we should do is concentrate on how to train competent Americans . . . We've got to teach economics to every student. It conveys a rigor and quantitative skill that all students should understand before they look at political or social institutions. We should require the study of communications, especially visual ones, and not just with some tired old journalist teaching students how the front page is put together. And third, we need to offer real science courses to the non-science student.

Time, 4-13:58.

Robert Zemsky
Director,
Institute for Research
in Higher Education,
University of Pennsylvania

1

What you are getting is a rapid shift toward defining higher education as a service industry [for business] and making it subject to market demands. The university becomes more a holding company for entrepreneurs and less a cohesive institution pursuing a way of life.

The Christian Science Monitor,
11-23:13.

The Environment • Energy

Donald Barry
Vice president,
World Wildlife Fund

1

The Endangered Species Act is the pit bull of environmental laws. It's short, compact and has a hell of a set of teeth. Because of its teeth, the act can force people to make the kind of tough political decisions they wouldn't normally make.

The New York Times, 5-26:(A)14.

Christopher S. Bond
United States Senator,
R-Missouri

2

[On the trainload of garbage that was sent from New York City to the Midwest for dumping but was rejected and sent back to New York]: While some of my colleagues had the opportunity of enjoying New York City, the Big Apple, over the recess, the state of Missouri was threatened with the apple cores . . . Forty cars of rotten, maggot-filled trash [were hauled around Kansas, Illinois and Missouri]. For two weeks, it simmered and boiled in the hot sun with plenty of rain to moisten it and keep it nice and juicy. Fortunately, the trash train kept on moving. Ultimately, it went back to New York City, where it should have been dumped in the first place.

Senate debate, Washington, D.C./
The Washington Post, 7-23:(A)8.

Edmund G. "Jerry" Brown, Jr.
Candidate for the 1992
Democratic Presidential nomination;
Former Governor
of California (D)

3

Don't tell me that we don't have the money [for energy and environmental programs]. Don't tell me that the [Federal] deficit's too big. When it comes to pay raises, when it comes to bailing out the S&L industry, and when it comes to fighting a [Persian] Gulf war, the deficit never stands in the

way. And it shouldn't stand in the way for energy efficiency, human health, protecting the environment and putting America in the forefront of innovation and energy creativity.

At Earth Day rally,
Washington, D.C., April 22/
The Washington Post, 4-23:(A)18.

Lester R. Brown
President, Wordwatch Institute

4

Every major global indicator of the Earth's environmental health shows dramatic deterioration since 1972. The forests are smaller. The deserts are larger . . . Two great issues of our time are going to converge there [at the forthcoming environmental summit in Rio de Janeiro]—the environmental degradation of the planet and the spread of poverty. What I see is the industrial countries trying to get developing countries to focus on these [worldwide environmental] issues, but the political reality within many Third World countries is that what people are overwhelmingly concerned about is how to survive to the next harvest.

Interview/
Los Angeles Times, 5-26:(H)10.

Carol M. Browner
Administrator-designate,
Environmental Protection Agency
of the United States

5

The problem we have had in the states with the EPA, and one that the President-elect [Bill Clinton] is very familiar with, is the lack of certainty in any of the Agency's decisions. The EPA too frequently just does not bring an issue to a close. And that contributes to the lack of credibility with the public, with business and with others affected by what the EPA does. You can't have environmental protection without having people believe in what you are doing. The public wants answers in a timely manner and business

(CAROL M. BROWNER)

needs answers for their planning. I've found business leaders don't oppose strong environmental programs. What drives them crazy is a lack of certainty. We can change that.

Interview/The New York Times, 12-17:(A)13.

George Bush
President of the United States

1

I came to this office committed to extend America's record of environmental leadership and I've worked to do so in a way that is compatible with economic growth, because this balance is absolutely essential, and because these are twin goals, not mutually exclusive objectives.

At NASA research center,
Greenbelt, Md., June 1/
The New York Times, 6-2:(A)5.

2

Let's face it, there has been some criticism of the [environmental record of the] United States. But I must tell you, we come to Rio proud of what we have accomplished and committed to extending the record on American leadership on the environment. In the United States, we have the world's tightest air-quality standards on cars and factories, the most advanced laws for protecting lands and waters, and the most open processes for public participation. And now for a simple truth. America's record on environmental protection is second to none. So I did not come here to apologize. We come to press on with deliberate purpose and forceful action, and such action will demonstrate our continuing commitment to leadership and to international cooperation on the environment. We believe that the road to Rio must point toward both environmental protection and economic growth, environment and development. And by now it's clear. To sustain development, we must protect the environment; and to protect the environment, we must sustain development.

At United Nations Conference
on Environment and Development,
Rio de Janeiro, Brazil, July 12/
The New York Times, 6-13:5.

3

[Defending his environmental record]: Some will look at the record and say it isn't enough. I have a surprise for them: I couldn't agree more. Take a look at what I've asked for from Congress, and then take a look at what we've got . . . I could [list all the funding the Administration asked for and the Congress turned down], but the very trees around us might get nervous. [Indeed,] all of us ought to be a little nervous. Congress has met a fork in the road now, and they have a choice. On one hand they can gut these proposals, they can stuff them with pork and perks and then turn around and complain about the environment . . . I'm asking Congress to do the right thing: full funding for our land, our trees, our waters and our parks . . . [While] we all want a more beautiful America, some flaunt their commitment with these sound bites, and I've proven mine through, I believe, sound policy proposals. Some have sent entire forests to their death to fill books with propaganda—short on facts and long on fiction.

To reporters,
Sequoia National Forest, Calif.,
July 14/
The Washington Post, 7-15:(A)9.

4

[On 1992 Democratic Vice-Presidential nominee Senator Albert Gore, Jr.]: This guy is so far off in the environmental extreme, we'll be up to our necks in owls and out of work for every American. This guy is crazy. He is way out, far out, man.

Oct. 29/
USA Today, 10-30:(A)2.

George Carey
Archbishop of Canterbury
(England)

5

No hope of heaven should be used as a pretense to neglect Earth. We must nurture, not consume and destroy the intricate and beautiful life systems which make up God's creation.

April 19/
The Washington Post, 4-20:(A)14.

Fidel Castro
President of Cuba

1

It is necessary to point out that consumer societies are the main ones responsible for the atrocious destruction of the environment. They were born from the old colonial metropolises and from imperial policies, which in turn generated the backwardness and poverty that today lash the majority of humankind. With only 20 per cent of the world population, they consume two-thirds of the metals and three-forths of the energy produced in the world. They have poisoned the air, weakened and perforated the ozone layer, saturated the atmosphere with gases that change climatic conditions with catastrophic results that we now are beginning to suffer.

*At UN Conference on Environment
and Development,
Rio de Janeiro, Brazil, June 12/
Los Angeles Times, 6-13:(A)23.*

Roger B. Clegg
*Deputy Attorney General,
Environmental Division,
Department of Justice
of the United States*

2

In the last three years, there have been more fines levied and longer jail terms handed out in environmental criminal cases than in the previous 18 years that EPA has been in existence. We believe we have an extraordinarily successful record in the Bush Administration.

The Washington Post, 9-10:(A)6.

Bill Clinton
*Governor of Arkansas (D);
Candidate for the 1992
Democratic Presidential nomination*

3

I've spent the last decade, and then some, as Governor of a poor state, fighting to keep jobs . . . I also faced the old short-term tradeoffs between jobs and the environment, tradeoffs that were made tougher by Federal cutbacks in aid to clean up the environment and the lack of clear national policies in areas which allowed states to be played off against one another in jobs-versus-the-environment conflicts. And in that context, I've made the choice, from time to time, for jobs because my state was a poor one without either enough jobs or enough Federal help to clean up the environment.

*At Drexel University, April 22/
The New York Times, 4-23:(A)10.*

4

If I had been President over the last year, today's ceremonies [at the Earth Summit in Rio de Janeiro] would have capped a year of energetic United States leadership [in environmental matters] rather than a year of grudging participation and general denial of the problems that exist and the phenomenal opportunities before us to create a real new world order rooted in economic prosperity and environmental protection.

*News conference,
Washington, D.C., June 12/
The New York Times, 6-13:5.*

5

[Democratic Vice-Presidential candidate Senator] Al Gore has spent the last decade working on the global environmental challenges we desperately need to address: global warming, ozone depletion, energy conservation. He has written a magnificent book on his thoughts and recommendations. He has asked me to join in his commitment to preserve not only the environment of America but to preserve the environment of our globe for future generations, and together we will finally give the United States a real environmental Presidency.

*News conference,
Little Rock, Ark., July 9/
The New York Times, 7-10:(A)8.*

Bill Clinton
*Governor of Arkansas (D);
1992 Democratic
Presidential nominee*

6

We ought to have a goal of raising the fuel-efficiency standards [of automobiles] to 40 miles a gallon. I think that should be a goal. I've never

(BILL CLINTON)

said we should write it into law if there is evidence that that goal cannot be achieved. The National Science Foundation did a study which said it would be difficult for us to reach fuel-efficiency standards in excess of 37 miles per gallon for the year 2000. I think we should try to raise the fuel efficiency. And let me say this: I think we ought to have incentives to do it. I think we ought to push to do it. That doesn't mean we have to write it into law.

At Presidential candidates' debate,
East Lansing, Mich., Oct. 19/
The New York Times, 10-20:(A)13.

Dan R. Coats
United States Senator,
R-Indiana

1

How do you make a decision between a better environment and the jobs it will cost? The dignity of employment and our stewardship over creation both demand moral attention. Is a cleaner river worth regulations that eliminate 30 jobs, 300 jobs, 3,000 jobs? How do you weigh cleaner air against the broken spirit of the unemployed?

At Wheaton (Ill.) College commencement/
Christianity Today, 7-20:27.

James N. Corbridge, Jr.
Chancellor,
University of Colorado, Boulder

2

Let us realize the fragility of the planet, and our obligations to it. This involves, at the very least, the need for each one of us to think about *respect* for our environment . . . And that respect must translate to action—every day, in every personal act . . . Buckminster Fuller . . . said: "The most important fact about spaceship Earth—an instruction book didn't come with it." He was right. So it is up to us to make the instruction book . . . and then to follow it . . . But considering the consequences of our every action is a good place to begin.

At University of Colorado-Boulder commencement/
The Christian Science Monitor, 6-22:10.

John Cregan
President,
United States Business
and Industrial Council

3

Spending money is the only means of addressing [environmental] degradation. Only a growing economy, unencumbered by costly regulations, can produce enough wealth and technology to deal with these problems.

The Christian Science Monitor,
6-3:2.

Michael R. Deland
Chairman,
Federal Council on
Environmental Quality

4

[Saying the U.S. supports programs dealing with all "greenhouse" gases around the world, not just carbon dioxide emissions as some people have urged]: We have been unwilling to subscribe to the politically popular program of timetables and targets [for the limitation of greenhouse emissions by industrialized countries] that focus only on CO_2 when there are several others that are of substantial importance in the equation. We think that is a very short-sighted approach . . . You could have one nation make reductions in methane gas and another nation make reductions in CO_2 and do so in a cost-effective manner that makes both environmental and economic sense.

USA Today, 2-18:(A)7.

5

[On Senator Albert Gore's criticism of the Bush Administration's environmental record]: I'm tired of seeing you [Gore] seek out every soap box you can find to deliver this "gospel according to Gore," which is nothing other than a trashing of the environmental record of the American people, a record that's second to none in the world.

Broadcast interview/
"Newsmaker Sunday," CNN-TV, 6-7.

Charles Ebinger
Senior fellow,
Center for Strategic and
International Studies

1

The [Bush] Administration hasn't addressed the primary question of whether we face a national-security threat due to our dependence on oil imports or whether we are putting our economy at risk. [And Democratic Party strategists] haven't made energy policy an issue, except with opposition to the gas tax and a vague mention of support for renewable energy sources.

The Christian Science Monitor,
9-3:1.

Paul Erlich
Demographer,
Stanford University

2

There's no question that population growth is eventually going to come to a halt. The question is whether it's going to end because we manage to humanely lower birthrates or because we exceed the Earth's carrying capacity.

The Christian Science Monitor,
7-8:16.

Fabio Feldman
Brazilian Congressman

3

[Criticizing the U.S. for not doing enough to help the environment]: The mood [at the forthcoming UN environmental conference] in Brazil is that the United States will be the biggest villain of the conference. U.S. intransigence is recreating the polarized atmosphere of the 1960s: all civil society and the press against the U.S.

June 1/
The New York Times, 6-2:(A)5.

George Gallup, Jr.
Public-opinion analyst

4

Unlike the situation just two decades ago, the state of the environment is no longer an exotic, elitist issue, a periphery issue in the minds of most people, but an issue of real concern to people in developing nations, as well as developed nations, and to people in upscale groups within nations, as well as to people in downscale groups. It is becoming a truly global concern, reaching all levels of society and nations around the world . . . Citizens in both developing and developed nations accept a share of responsibility for environmental problems, so the situation appears to be much less polarized than perhaps is assumed . . . We were surprised to discover the high level of concern in all nations surveyed to date, as well as a relatively high rate of awareness of environmental problems.

At National Press Club,
Washington, D.C., May 4/
The Washington Post, 5-6:(A)28.

Albert Gore, Jr.
United States Senator,
D-Tennessee

5

Just as an alcoholic denies the existence of his problems, and sees a series of auto accidents as an unrelated set of unfortunate coincidences, so we [incorrectly] see the ozone hole, Alaskan oil spill and garbage crisis as isolated, unconnected events . . . People look at [his "global Marshall Plan" to save the environment] and think it is impossible—it can't be done. But what if I had suggested two years ago that the Soviet Union would disappear, that Russians would embrace capitalism and people would gather in the Budapest city square and sing "We Shall Overcome"? What happened is that people realized that Communism was stupid, looked around and found others agreed, and they reached a critical mass. That's the change I expect to occur in respect to the environment. And when that happens, the political system will fall all over itself to respond.

Interview, Washington, D.C./
Los Angeles Times, 2-6:(E)5.

6

The idea that [human beings] are separate from the Earth, disembodied intellects entitled to behave with impunity toward the natural world—

(ALBERT GORE, JR.)

that idea is under increasing pressure from a new conception, from our connectedness, our place within the web of life ... There has been a steady increase in the level of concern expressed by the American people. You can go into any elementary school in this nation and ask the kids there what they think is the most important issue and they'll quickly tell you the threat to the global environment.

Interview, Boston, Mass./
The Christian Science Monitor,
2-27:11.

1

The task of saving the Earth's environment must become the central organizing principle of the post-Cold War world. Our [the U.S.'s] ability to lead the world depends on our being a part of this new consensus and helping to point the way to how we can successfully confront this challenge.

Interview/USA Today, 4-28:(A)13.

Albert Gore, Jr.
United States Senator,
D-Tennessee;
1992 Democratic
Presidential nominee

2

We can create millions of new jobs by leading the environmental revolution instead of dragging our feet and bringing up the rear. You know, Japan and Germany are both openly proclaiming to the world now that the biggest new market in the history of world business is the market for the new products and technologies that foster economic progress without environmental destruction ... This is an issue that touches my basic values. I'm taught in my religious tradition that we are given dominion over the earth, but we're required to be good stewards of the earth, and that means to take care of it. We're not doing that now under the Bush-Quayle [Administration] policies ... We cannot stick our heads in the sand and pretend that we don't face a global environmental crisis. Nor should we assume that

it's going to cost jobs. Quite the contrary. We are going to be able to create jobs, as Japan and Germany are planning to do right now, if we have the guts to lead.

At Vice-Presidential candidates' debate,
Atlanta, Ga., Oct. 13/
The New York Times, 10-14:(A)13.

3

[On charges that his pro-environment views are too extremist]: I believe that the extremist view is held by those who are willing to tolerate the doubling of carbon dioxide in a single generation, the loss in a single lifetime of more than half the living species God put on Earth, the destruction of a large percentage of the protective ozone shield in only a few decades, the loss of more than an acre of tropical rain forest every second, the addition of an entire China's worth of people every decade, the poisoning of our air and water resources, the serious erosion of our cropland. Those of us who are attempting to rally this nation to lead a worldwide response to this crisis are responding in a common-sense way.

Interview/Time, 10-19:36.

Tim Hermach
Founder, Native Forest Council,
(Oregon)

4

A study came out of Oregon State University last year that said the little old-growth, primary, native forests—whatever you like to call them— regardless of age, size or condition left across the U.S. are far too precious to continue logging. All we've advocated is Federal lands not be converted to tree farms, be taken out of the market competing with the private sector ... [As far as the loss of logging jobs is concerned,] we're talking about short-term jobs that are going to be gone anyway. Why? Because the trees are almost gone. Not because of environmental protection. Not because of anything sensible that we've done. It's because we've done the unsensible things, the unintelligent things, and we've liquidated almost this nation's entire forest.

Interview/
USA Today, 5-13:(A)11.

Saburo Kato
Director General,
Global Environment Department,
Environment Agency of Japan

1

In recent years, [the environmental] attitude [of Japanese companies] has dramatically changed. They want to survive in the 21st century and they well know that in the 21st century, the most important requirement of any company will be to be friendly to the Earth.

The New York Times, 7-31:(A)7.

Andy Kerr
Director of conservation
and education,
Oregon Natural Resources Council

2

[U.S.] Interior Secretary Manuel Lujan, Jr., is working to clear the way for timber cutting in seven square miles of forest that the Fish and Wildlife Service has found to be critical to the spotted owl. The owl essentially would be isolated and cut off from a significant portion of its range . . . It would mean the owl has less chance of continued existence . . . Life will go on without the owl. But the owl is like a canary in a coal mine: It is telling us there is something very wrong with the way we are managing our forests. And besides, these public forests belong to all the people. They aren't just for the local benefit of the timber industry.

Interview/USA Today, 5-13:(A)11.

Richard Leakey
Paleoanthropologist

3

Unless we change [our environmental ways], we are likely over the next three decades to lose 50 per cent of the species we know on this planet . . . One of the sadnesses that I feel is that the Rio de Janeiro [Earth Summit in June of this year] came up with such a big agenda with such a huge budget, and that much of it won't happen because people are afraid of something [that big and expensive]. If we could simply take a few small steps at a time, I think we could stop the

worst scenario—that loss [of species] over three decades.

At luncheon sponsored by
National Geographic Society,
Washington, D.C./
The Christian Science Monitor,
9-29:14.

Warren Lindner
International coordinator,
'92 Global Forum

4

No country, no matter how industrially powerful or weak, politically powerful or weak, large or small, has the unfettered freedom to set its own [environmental] destiny or set its own [environmental] policy. There are too many of us.

The Christian Science Monitor, 6-3:3.

John Major
Prime Minister
of the United Kingdom

5

There will be people who will decry the achievements of this [environmental] conference. But this conference is proof of a dramatic shift over the last decade: The environment is no longer the specialist concern of a few—it has become the vital interest of us all . . . Much of the damage that we have done to our environment has been inflicted not out of greed ar malice, but out of ignorance. What every child knows today few scientists knew the day before yesterday. I suspect that for many of us it was not until we saw the pictures of the Earth taken from outer space that we realized just how small, fragile and precious our globe is.

At United Nations Conference
on Environment and Development,
Rio de Janeiro, Brazil, June 12/
Los Angeles Times, 6-13:(A)23.

Julian Martin
Executive director,
Texas Independent (oil)
Producers and Royalty Owners

6

The development of the National Energy Strategy is a strong indication that the [Bush]

(JULIAN MARTIN)

Administration still counts on oil flow from the Middle East as the center point of energy supply. It's the cheapest source in the world and keeps prices down, but there are tremendous costs for [U.S.] defense and transportation. The closer to home energy is developed, the better.

The New York Times, 8-22:21.

Roger McManus
Biologist; Director,
Center for Marine Conservation

1

The [environmental] risk [in offshore oil drilling] is not huge, but is it a risk you want to take? [The oil industry] has never learned to recognize and respect other people's values in the offshore environment. The industry has largely insisted that they can drill anywhere they want to, and repeatedly—through Congress and through administrative action—have found out that other people disagree.

The Christian Science Monitor,
4:23:12.

George Miller
United States Representative,
D-California

2

When [U.S.] President Bush flies to the [current] Earth Summit [in Rio de Janeiro], he will find that the "new world order" looks a lot more like Rio than [it does] the [Persian] Gulf war. The Earth Summit is perhaps the most formidable attempt at international cooperation in history, utilizing not F-16s and smart bombs [as in the Gulf war] but scientific analysis, mutual respect and reasoned debate. [We are] struck by the palpable resentment toward our country both from the developed nations and the developing world. The anger is especially strong toward President Bush for his well-publicized efforts to dilute the global-warming convention and his refusal to sign the agreement on biological diversity.

Rio de Janeiro, Brazil/
Los Angeles Times, 6-10:(A)6.

3

The most important signal the new President [President-elect Bill Clinton] can send—and I think will send—is that there really is a public trust and public stewardship of the land—that these are the public resources of the people of America, not just there to be auctioned off, and ruined, and left behind. [Such a Clinton Administration attitude would] set an entirely different tone in how Congress deals with those issues.

Interview,
Washington, D.C./
The Christian Science Monitor,
12-10:11.

Kamal Nath
Minister of Environment
and Forests of India

4

[The developed countries] say, "Yes, we are the major polluters, so we must pay [for global environmental cleanup]. But now that we pay, we must also dictate." That is the ridiculousness of it. I don't think you can shove the environment down anybody's throat.

The Washington Post,
6-1:(A)1.

William O'Keefe
Chief operating officer,
American Petroleum Institute

5

We [the U.S.] are the world's preeminent oil industry in terms of technology, safety and performance. But the significant drop in crude-oil prices during the 1980s, the Federal government's undercutting of the energy industry's development, and costly environmental regulations have had a devastating effect . . . We'll consume more energy as the economy grows. By the end of the decade, we should see up to a 2 per cent increase in energy consumption—oil, natural gas and coal. But if we don't increase domestic production, then we'll see imports climb from our current 50 per cent to near 70 per cent.

The Christian Science Monitor,
9-3:4.

Michael Oppenheimer
Senior scientist,
Environmental Defense Fund

1

[On the current UN environmental conference in Rio de Janeiro]: With over 100 heads of state here and many other countries represented, a message has been sent to every government, every bureaucrat, every minister, that environmental protection resides at the top of the political agenda for the 21st century. I expect the process to go on for another 20 years.

Rio de Janeiro, Brazil/
The Christian Science Monitor,
6-11:5.

Bob Packwood
United States Senator,
R-Oregon

2

[On the loss of jobs because of restrictions on logging in the Northwest to protect the spotted owl]: I think it comes down to this: Are you for people or for the bird? . . . People [should] finally get the same consideration as owls.

Los Angeles Times, 5-15:(A)16.

Dan Quayle
Vice President
of the United States

3

Our [Bush Administration] record on the environment is stronger than any record in the history of America when it comes to the environment. We've reduced CO_2, we've reduced carbon monoxide, CFCs are going to be phased out, lead has been phased out of gasoline. We have a very good environmental record, and we're proud of it. It does take some. But there's a way to do it and there's a way not to do it. And we're doing it in a balanced way. We are doing it to make it as least costly and least burdensome to the private sector. If you let [Democratic Presidential candidate] Bill Clinton and [Vice-Presidential candidate] Al Gore, who will probably be in charge of the EPA, run the environmental laws in this country, you will not have balance. It will not be a choice between jobs and environment, it will only be environmental regulation, and jobs will simply be out the window, because too much regulations cost jobs.

Broadcast interview/
"This Week With David Brinkley,"
ABC-TV, 9-13.

4

What is going to be [Democratic Presidential and Vice-Presidential candidates Bill Clinton and Al Gore's] position when it comes to the environment? . . . You want to ask somebody in Michigan, a UAW worker in Michigan, if they think increasing CAFE standards, the fuel economy standards, [to] 45 miles a gallon is a good idea. 300,000 people out of work. You ought to talk to the timber people in the Northwest, where they [Clinton and Gore] say that, well, we can only save the [endangered spotted] owl; forget about [logging] jobs. You ought to talk to the coal miners about putting a coal tax on; [Clinton and Gore] are talking of taxing utilities; a tax on gasoline, home heating oil; all sorts of taxes. No, the choice [shouldn't be] environment and jobs. With the right policies, prudent policies, we can have both.

At Vice-Presidential candidates' debate,
Atlanta, Ga., Oct. 13/
The New York Times, 10-14:(A)13.

William K. Reilly
Administrator,
Environmental Protection Agency
of the United States

5

There is a certain amount of posturing by developing countries to try to get us and other developed countries to contribute more funds [for environmental purposes]. At this economic moment for industrialized nations, those contributions are not in the cards.

The Washington Post, 6-3:(A)21.

6

One of the real marks of growing democratization in Latin America—in fact, one of the groups that has been a leadership element behind that—

(WILLIAM K. REILLY)

is the growth of environmental organizations. That was true in Brazil, under the previous government. That was true in Chile. It's something that I think is a mark of societal maturity and growth. And it's a very important wedding of democratic principles with environmental protection. They almost always go together. If the people have influence, they want health and protection for their environment.

The Christian Science Monitor,
6-15:3.

1

[His advice to the new head of EPA in the forthcoming Clinton Administration]: Take [environmental groups and lobbyists] seriously; keep the lines of communication open. But . . . get them to understand the budget. Make them aware of trade-offs . . . I think when an honest tally is rendered, this [Bush] Administration will have the most distinguished environmental record ever . . . [But President Bush] just got continually lambasted [by his critics] . . . and that had a sobering, discouraging effect on people [in the White House].

To reporters,
Washington, D.C., Dec. 16/
USA Today 12-17:(A)2.

Mark Rey
Executive director,
American Forest Resource Alliance

2

[Criticizing restrictions on logging in the Northwest in order to protect the spotted owl]: What we're doing is essentially creating an Appalachia in the Pacific Northwest . . . If you spend a lot of time in the woods, you'll see one endangered species, the spotted owl. But if you're driving through town, you can see another endangered species: an 8-year-old girl. Her father's an out-of-work logger. An 8-year-old's well-being ought to count for as much as the value of a spotted owl.

USA Today, 5-13:(A)11.

William D. Ruckelshaus
Former Administrator,
Environmental Protection Agency
of the United States

3

What I really think is at stake [in the environmental movement] globally is the future of free institutions. I think that suddenly democracies . . . have been thrust into the forefront and given the responsibility of grappling with these very complex [environment and development] problems. If we wait for the chronic issues to become acute before we do anything about them, I think the first thing to go will be free institutions. It really is an open question in my mind of whether we can cope with these chronic problems— problems that you don't need to solve tomorrow in order to survive—within the context of freedom.

Interview/
Los Angeles Times, 5-26:(H)10.

Stephan Schmidheiny
Swiss industrialist

4

Environmental thinking is bringing a new industrial revolution. It is the most forceful trend in my lifetime. It will reshape business because it will redefine the rules of the economic game . . . We have all made mistakes, we all pollute, we all have given too little consideration to nature; but this is a new era . . . We are now learning to think of the environment in economic terms. We are changing our accounting principles to insert environmental costs into industry. And we are now in the early stages of understanding the mechanisms.

Interview, Geneva, Switzerland/
The New York Times, 6-2:(C)1,7.

C. J. "Pete" Silas
Chairman,
Phillips Petroleum Company;
Chairman,
American Petroleum Institute

5

We still don't know what [President-elect] Bill Clinton really has in mind for oil and gas. What is

WHAT THEY SAID IN 1992

(C. J. "PETE" SILAS)

shaping up so far is an Administration with contradictions built in on the ground floor.

The Christian Science Monitor,
12-18:9.

James Gustave Speth
President,
World Resources Institute

1

[Criticizing President Bush's lukewarm attitude toward the forthcoming UN environmental
conference in Brazil]: It would be hard to imagine
a more important event for the future of the global
environment than this one. And so it's been one
of the most discouraging experiences of my 10
years of working on international environmental
issues to see my government fail to give the kind
of leadership that it gave 20 years ago.

The New York Times, 5-7:(A)5.

Wallace Stegner
Author

2

It is impossible to be unconscious of or indifferent to [open] space in the West. At every city's
edge it confronts us in Federal lands kept open by
aridity and the custodial bureau; out in the
boondocks it engulfs us. And it contributes to
individualism, if only because in that much
emptiness people have the dignity of rareness and
must do much of what they do without help.
For clerks and students, factory workers and
mechanics, the outdoors is freedom, just as
surely as it is for the folkloric and mythic figures.

Interview/
U.S. News & World Report, 3-16:65.

James B. Stockdale
1992 independent Vice-Presidential
candidate (running mate of
Presidential candidate
Ross Perot);
Admiral,
United States Navy (Ret.)

3

I read Senator [and Democratic Vice-Presidential nominee Albert] Gore's book about the

environment and I don't see how he could possibly pay for his proposals in today's economic
climate. You know, the Marshall Plan of the
Environment and so forth. And also, I'm told by
some experts that the things that he fears most
may not be all that dangerous, according to some
scientists. You know, you can overdo, I'm told,
environmental cleaning up. If you purify the
pond, the water lilies die. You know, I love this
planet and I want to stay here; but I don't like to
have it the private property of fanatics that want
to overdo this thing.

At Vice-Presidential candidates' debate,
Atlanta, Ga., Oct. 13/
The New York Times, 10-14:(A)13.

Maurice Strong
Secretary General,
United Nations Conference
on Environment and Development

4

You cannot solve our environmental problems
without business. Business is the prime actor in
which we through our economy impact on the
environment. And we, as consumers, cannot
divorce ourselves from business. Every one of us
is part of the system. We have to change the full
system, change individual behavior. And business has to be an important part of that change.
The way to mobilize business is to ensure
that their basic motivation for profit will cor-
respond with society's motivation for a better
environment.

Interview, Geneva, Switzerland/
The Christian Science Monitor,
5-29:3.

5

[On the just-concluded UN environmental
conference in Rio de Janeiro]: As a conference,
Rio was clearly a great success, but whether or
not it succeeds in its purpose of setting the planet
on a new track remains to be seen. I sat at a
podium [at the environmental conference] in
Stockholm 20 years ago. I heard most of the
same things. Most were not translated into
action . . . As a bureaucrat, I don't always use the
hottest words to describe things, but now we have

(MAURICE STRONG)

to push like hell to make sure implementation takes place.

To reporters,
Rio de Janeiro, Brazil, June 14/
The New York Times, 6-15:(A)5.

Russell Train
Chairman, World Wildlife Fund;
Former Administrator,
Environmental Protection Agency
of the United States

1

Unless this country takes bold steps now to marry environmental and economic prosperity, the risks of continued environmental deterioration and long-term economic decline are grave.

The Christian Science Monitor,
12-11:8.

Ben Wattenberg
Senior fellow,
American Enterprise Institute

2

Why should we worry [about increases in the world's population growth]? We've gone from 1 [billion] to 5 billion while living standards have gone up exponentially. There's no evidence that population growth diminishes or dilutes development.

The Christian Science Monitor,
7-8:9.

Robert E. Wycoff
President,
Atlantic Richfield Company

3

At the moment, at least, Saudi Arabia controls any excess of crude-oil supply and in effect controls the world's supply of oil and its price. Fortunately, I think they have been champions [of price stability].

Los Angeles Times, 6-7:(D)8.

Clayton K. Yeutter
Assistant to President
of the United States
George Bush
for Domestic Policy

4

[On whether President Bush will attend the Earth Summit in Brazil in June]: The definition of a productive meeting is whether it's in the best interests of the United States. Hopefully, what's in the best interests of the United States is also in the best interests of the world, but we have to make this judgment call on whether what's going to happen or not happen in Rio [de Janeiro] is in the best interests of this country . . . I have not seen any arguments yet that would persuade me that the United States ought to agree to definitive targets and timetables [for emissions standards in fighting global warming]. I believe we would do this country a major disservice if we were to make commitments that could cost this nation billions of dollars, when those commitments were to be made on the basis of dubious scientific evidence.

Interview, March 27/
The Washington Post, 3-28:(A)8.

Government

George Allen
United States Representative,
R-Virginia

1

[On the scandal involving Congressmen who had overdrafts at the House bank]: There's nothing more important to this institution [the House] than the public trust . . . This is a coverup and everybody in the House knows it . . . Members who have bounced only a few checks can explain them to their constituents and they'll understand. Members who have bounced [many checks] can try to explain.

The Washington Post, 3-12:(A)25.

Lititia Baldridge
Newspaper columnist;
Former White House aide
to Jacqueline Kennedy,
wife of the late President
John F. Kennedy

2

The First Lady treads a delicate path. She can't be perceived by other people in the White House or the public or the press as interfering, because then she'd be fried in oil. She can get things done, but by means other than the direct means reported by the press. You don't do it openly. You don't do it brazenly. You do it behind the scenes.

The New York Times, 11-16:(A)10.

Gordon Black
Public-opinion analyst

3

The government of the United States has succeeded in alienating between 60 and 75 per cent of the voters in this country. More than three-quarters [of Americans] believe that Congress is bought, paid for and owned by PACs; that money has so dominated the political process that they [the people] have no role in it any longer, and their right to choose has been taken away from them.

The Christian Science Monitor,
7-13:3.

William S. Broomfield
United States Representative,
R-Michigan

4

[On his decision not to run for re-election in the fall]: The partisanship [in Congress] is so bitter that it's very difficult to get anything through. Everyone is trying to get the political advantage and everyone is suffering . . . I just felt I didn't want to continue in the minority, getting old and not being able to do any more.

Interview, April 21/
The Washington Post, 4-22:(A)1.

Edmund G. "Jerry" Brown, Jr.
Candidate for the 1992
Democratic Presidential nomination;
Former Governor
of California (D)

5

Those who spend a lot of time in Washington don't have the same appreciation as those out among the states, the grass roots, of the need for more basic change . . . When you run a frontal assault on what you call a decrepit, corrupt status quo [in the Federal government] that no longer serves the American people, you can't be surprised if people in that neighborhood band together in a mutual-protection defense.

Milwaukee, Wis., March 26/
The Washington Post, 3-27:(A)16.

John Bryant
United States Representative,
D-Texas

6

"Pressure" around here [in Congress] is the Speaker [of the House] asking: "Are you going to vote for this bill? Oh, no? Why not? Oh, that's okay." That's why nothing happens around here. The Speaker should say, "This bill is important to me—I need your vote."

Washington, D.C., Feb. 27/
The New York Times, 2-28:(C)4.

George Bush
President of the United States

1

We must put an end to unfinanced Federal government mandates. These are the requirements Congress puts on our cities, counties and states without supplying the money. And if Congress passes a mandate, it should be forced to pay for it and balance the cost with savings elsewhere.

State of the Union address,
Washington, D.C., Jan. 29/
The New York Times,
3-24:(A)10.

2

[Because of] one-party [Democratic] control [of Congress for almost four decades], the Party's lack of supervision, lack of new blood, lack of change, there isn't the competition to make these institutions in the Congress more efficient. I'm not talking here about barber shops [for Congressmen], or perks, or calligraphers or parking spaces [for Congressmen]. It's about the government mental process, its potential to help or hinder the public good. It's about the changes that are sweeping the rest of the country but are not being made in Washington.

Before Federalist Society,
Philadelphia, Pa., April 3/
The New York Times,
4-4:7.

3

There will be so many new members of Congress after this [year's] election that regardless of which party ends up with control, I think we have a chance to move things forward. I think there will be over 100 new members in the House. I will be taking the case forcefully to the American people that if you really want substantive change, then change the one institution that hasn't changed—Congress. I think it's been 36 years of control for Democrats in the House of Representatives.

Interview/
U.S. News & World Report,
8-17:20.

4

Four years ago, [Vice President] Dan Quayle and I teamed up, and I told him then, speaking from some personal experience, that the job of Vice President was a real character builder, and I was not exaggerating. But look, this guy stood there, and in the face of those unfair critics he has never wavered. And he simply told the truth and let the chips fall where they may . . . He has been a super Vice President, and he will be for another four years.

At rally, Houston, Texas, Aug. 17/
The New York Times, 8-18:(A)6.

5

I served in Congress 22 years ago. Back then, we cooperated; we didn't get personal. We put the people above everything else. At my first inauguration [as President], I said that people didn't send us to bicker. I extended my hand to the Democratic leaders—and they bit it. The House leadership [by the Democratic Party] has not changed in 38 years. It is a body caught in a hopelessly tangled web of PACs, perks, privileges, partisanship and paralysis. Every day, Congress puts politics ahead of principle and above progress.

At Republican National Convention,
Houston, Texas, Aug. 20/
The New York Times, 8-21:(A)16.

6

[I've] decided not to . . . wring my hands about this being the loneliest job in the world. I've not done that, and I don't plan to start now. I think I've upheld the honor of this office. We've had a good, clean Administration. Our ethical standards are high. Also, I've learned I can take the heat. It goes back to what your mother taught you: Do your best, try your hardest.

Interview/Washington, D.C./
Time, 8-24:24.

7

I think people don't recognize the difference in how [a President can] handle a foreign-policy issue, where you can just take action on your

(GEORGE BUSH)

own, and how you handle a domestic issue, where in almost every instance you have to get help from what has proved to be a very recalcitrant Congress . . . I think the people know that I've held out my hand to Congress and it's been a very frustrating experience.

Interview, Washington, D.C./
Time, 8-24:22.

1

Today the Federal government spends nearly 24 cents of every dollar, 24 cents of every dollar of the nation's income. And that's the fact. Government is too big and spends too much. And the size and structure of government are relics of a different age—artifacts more suited to the dilemmas of 50 years ago than the problems of today. Every institution in our society has learned that by pushing power down through organizations, by using technology to speed the flow of information, you don't just save money, you improve productivity. And it's time for the government to do the same. And I will streamline the government, consolidating agencies, tightening budgets and cutting the salaries of highly paid Federal employees. And I'll start by cutting the White House budget 33 per cent if the Congress cuts its own budget by the same amount.

Before Detroit Economic Club,
Detroit, Mich., Sept. 10/
The New York Times, 9-11:(A)12.

2

Let me tell you a little what it's like to be President. In the Oval Office, you can't predict what kind of crisis is going to come up. You have to make tough calls. You can't be on one hand with this way and one hand another. You can't take different positions on these difficult issues . . . I hope as President that I've earned your trust. I've admitted it when I make a mistake, but then I go on and help try to solve the problems. I hope I've earned your trust because a lot of being President is about trust and character.

At Presidential candidates' debate,
St. Louis, Mo., Oct. 11/
The New York Times, 10-12:(A)15.

3

I strongly support term limits for members of the United States Congress. I believe it would return the government closer to the people . . . The President's terms are limited to two—a total of eight years; what's wrong with limiting the terms of members of Congress to 12? Congress has gotten kind of institutionalized. For 38 years one party [the Democrats] has controlled the House of Representatives, and the result—a sorry little [House] post office that can't do anything right and a [House] bank that has more overdrafts [by House members] than all the Chase Bank and Citibank put together. We've got to do something about it, and I think you get a certain arrogance—bureaucratic arrogance—when people stay there too long. And so I favor—strongly favor—term limits.

At Presidential candidates' debate,
Richmond, Va., Oct. 15/
The New York Times, 10-17:11.

4

Most of the people that are lobbying are lobbying the Congress. And I don't think there's anything wrong with an honest person who happens to represent an interest of another country from making his case. That's the American way. And what [critics are] assuming is that that makes the recipient of the lobbying corrupt, or the lobbyist himself corrupt. I don't agree with that. But if I found somebody that had a conflict of interest that would try to illegally do something as a foreign registered lobby, the laws cover this.

At Presidential candidates' debate,
East Lansing, Mich., Oct. 19,/
The New York Times, 10-20:(A)13

Robert C. Byrd
United States Senator,
D-West Virginia

5

[Arguing against giving the President a line-item veto over Congressional bills]: The power over the purse is the taproot of the tree of Anglo-Saxon liberty. The [line-]item-veto debate, when shorn of all of its fancy trappings, is a debate

(ROBERT C. BYRD)

about power, and control of the purse is the bone and sinew of power.

Before the Senate,
Washington, D.C., February/
The New York Times, 11-18:(A)13.

Arne Carlson
Governor of Minnesota (R)

1

[Criticizing Federal regulations on state and local governments]: Every time state and local governments get creative, they have to stand in line and petition Congress and the Executive Branch [in Washington] for permission to solve the problem. It's a silly system . . . If Congress can't send cash, then [it should] at least send permission.

At National Governors'
Association meeting,
Princeton, N.J./
The Christian Science Monitor, 8-5:8

Thomas R. Carper
United States Representative,
D-Delaware

2

Republicans who want to be in the majority will do anything they can to run down the institution [of Congress]. Democrats are willing to do anything we can to hamstring the President. [This gridlock] threatens to make Congress and the President almost irrelevant.

The Washington Post, 3-4:(A)21.

Dick Cheney
Secretary of Defense
of the United States;
Former United States Representative,
R-Wyoming

3

[On the House-bank scandal tainting many Congressmen]: [We former House members now] see the institution pass under a cloud. We see its reputation sullied. For those of us who

love the House, this is deeply painful to watch. When occasion demands, this House will rise again, and we and our fellow citizens will once again understand it for what it is: the greatest legislative assembly of the greatest nation on Earth.

At gathering of former House members,
Washington, D.C., April 2/
The Washington Post, 4-3:(A)15.

Warren M. Christopher
Director of President-elect
Bill Clinton's transition team

4

[Saying new ethics guidelines issued by the Clinton team barring senior government officials from lobbying within five years after leaving government would not keep good, capable people from wanting to serve in government]: It's possible to imagine that people who are in Washington and had intended to go in government for a short time and then come back out and practice will be discouraged by that, or appear in Washington as lobbyists. That's exactly the kind of vice we're trying to get at, and if some of those people are excluded, I would think that really is the price of these rules, and we think it's a fair price to pay.

News conference, Little Rock, Ark.,
Dec. 9/
The New York Times, 12-10:(A)18.

Bill Clinton
Governor of Arkansas (D);
Candidate for the 1992
Democratic Presidential nomination

5

Most politicians are not candid with people. They try to act like they hate politics—and, "Oh, this is a burden, I just had to do it." When the truth is most of them love it and wouldn't do anything else on a dime if they could avoid it. I'm just more candid than that. I decided when I was a young man that my best use in life would be in public life, that I had some gifts at it and I wanted to make a difference. To me politics is the only area of human life where it's bad form to be ambitious.

Interview/Newsweek, 3-9:36.

(BILL CLINTON)

1

If I become President, it is my solemn duty to try to provide more opportunity for the people of this country. But if I become President, you [the people] have responsibilities too. For no politician can do anything for a people they are not willing to do for themselves.

Campaigning, Brooklyn, N.Y.,
April 5/
The New York Times, 4-7:(A)16.

2

Everybody wants it both ways. They want to attack you for not spending more and then attack you when you won't run a deficit. They want to attack you if you raise taxes for investing in education, and they want to attack you if you under-spend in education. It's time that we grew up and recognized that we have to make tough choices.

At fund-raising luncheon,
Little Rock, Ark., April 20/
The New York Times, 4-21:(A)8.

3

There is a role for government, but it has to be carried out through grass-roots community organizations [rather than through bureaucrats and Federal agencies]. The government does not always know what is best or how to do it.

Before American Newspaper
Publishers Association,
New York, N.Y., May 5/
The New York Times, 5-6:(A)14.

4

I am a proud member of this union [AFSCME]; I am a dues-paying member of this union. When [President] George Bush runs against government day in and day out, it's a hypocritical thing because he has done more to break it than anybody else. I promise you I will never bash public employees. I will challenge us all to change in a partnership that will restore the confidence of the American people in their government.

Before American Federation of State,
County and Municipal Employees,
Las Vegas, Nev., June 17/
The Washington Post, 6-18:(A)18.

5

I want a leaner bureaucracy and more investment. Most of that will go into private hands. If you build roads and bridges and high-speed rail networks, that money winds up being spent on contracts in the private sector. I've always supported increased investment targeted to areas that would promote economic growth and education, but I've tried to restrict the growth of what you might call the permanent government.

Interview, Little Rock, Ark./Time, 7-20:27.

Bill Clinton
Governor of Arkansas (D);
1992 Democratic Presidential nominee

6

People want change, but government is in the way. It has been hijacked by privileged, private interests. It has forgotten who really pays the bills around here. It's taking more of your money and giving you less in service. We have got to go beyond the brain-dead politics in Washington and give our people the kind of government they deserve: a government that works for them. A President ought to be a powerful force for progress. But right now I know how President Lincoln felt when General McClellan wouldn't attack in the Civil War. He asked him, "If you're not going to use your army, may I borrow it?" [President] George Bush, if you won't use your power to help people, step aside. I will . . . We need a new approach to government. A government that offers more empowerment and less entitlement, more choices for young people in public schools and more choices for older people in long-term care. A government that is leaner, not meaner; that expands opportunity, not bureaucracy; that understands that jobs must come from growth in a vibrant and vital system of free enterprise. I call it a New Covenant, based not simply on what each of us can take, but on what all of us must give to make America work again.

Accepting the Presidential nomination
at Democratic National Convention,
New York, N.Y., July 16/
The New York Times, 7-17:(A)13.

7

[On the idea of term limits for members of Congress]: I know they're popular but I'm

(BILL CLINTON)

against them. I'll tell you why. I believe, Number 1, it would pose a real problem for a lot of smaller states in the Congress, would have enough trouble now making sure their interests are heard. Number 2, I think it would increase the influence of unelected staff members in the Congress who have too much influence already. I want to cut the size of the Congressional staffs, but I think you're going to have too much influence there with people who were never elected who have lots of expertise. Number 3, if the people really have a mind to change, they can. [In this year's election,] you're going to have 120 to 150 new members of Congress.

At Presidential candidates' debate,
Richmond, Va., Oct. 15/
The New York Times, 10-17:11.

Bill Clinton
Governor of Arkansas (D);
President-elect
of the United States

1

I've pledged to the American people that my Cabinet will look more like America than those of previous Administrations. I intend to look and am now aggressively looking among not only people of different racial and ethnic backgrounds, and men and women, but also people of different political backgrounds.

News conference,
Little Rock, Ark., Nov. 12/
USA Today, 11-13:(A)1.

2

[On his recent meeting with former President Ronald Reagan]: He said he thought [my wife] Hillary [and daughter] Chelsea and I should make ample use of [the Presidential retreat at] Camp David [Md.]. He said that it's about the only place where you can really walk freely, you know, and be alone, virtually unencumbered. He said, "It will help you keep your peace of mind."

Los Angeles, Calif., Nov. 27/
The New York Times, 11-28:6.

3

People who come to work in my Administration are going to have to sign an agreement not to go to work for other interests and lobby the government and make a profit out of their public service.

Campaigning for U.S. Senate candidate
from Georgia Wyche Fowler/
The New York Times, 11-28:6.

4

[On women's groups who are criticizing him for not appointing enough women to Cabinet-level posts in his forthcoming Administration, but instead appointing them to lower positions]: I believe that if I had appointed white men to those [below-Cabinet-level] jobs, those people, those same people [who are criticizing me now] would have been counting those jobs in a very negative way. They would have been counting those positions against our Administration, those bean counters who are doing that, if I had appointed white men to those positions . . . They are playing quota games and math games. I think what the American people want me to do is to give them the most diverse Cabinet I can consistent with a real commitment to excellence, and they want me to be satisfied that in each case when I make an appointment, I have appointed someone I think is superbly qualified to serve.

News conference,
Little Rock, Ark., Dec. 21/
The New York Times, 12-22:(A)11.

5

[On the appointments he has made to his forthcoming Presidential Cabinet]: They come from all across America. From the state capitals and the U.S. Capitol, from the city halls and the board rooms, and the classrooms. They come from diverse backgrounds and we will all be better and stronger for that diversity. I can say with pride that I believe this Cabinet and these other appointees represent the best in America.

News conference,
Little Rock, Ark., Dec. 24/
The New York Times,
12-25:(A)1.

Hillary Clinton
*Wife of Arkansas Governor
and 1992 Democratic
Presidential candidate
Bill Clinton*

1

[On what a First Lady is]: A partner. A partner who represents for all of us a view of who her husband is, as well as a symbol of women's concerns and interests at a particular time.

*Interview/
Working Woman, August:72.*

James Coyne
*Director,
Americans to Limit
Congressional Terms;
Former United States
Representative, D-Pennsylvania*

2

[Supporting term limits for members of Congress]: The reason that the 30-year veteran of the [Federal] bureaucracy has power is because he's been a buddy for 30 years of an entrenched Congressman and a powerful lobbyist. The people have no power to throw out the lobbyists or the power to fire the bureaucrats, but we do have the power to keep the Congressmen from becoming entrenched.

*The Christian Science Monitor,
10-29:4.*

John C. Danforth
*United States Senator,
R-Missouri*

3

I have never seen more Senators express discontent with their jobs . . . Deep down in our hearts, we know that we have bankrupted America and that we have given our children a legacy of bankruptcy.

*The Christian Science Monitor,
3-30:1.*

Pete V. Domenici
*United States Senator,
R-New Mexico*

4

Essentially I believe we [in Congress] have a system that minimizes the opportunity to be courageous. It diminishes the opportunity to lead and clearly it wilts the will-power—too many committees, overlapping jurisdiction, complicated bills that have to go to four or five committees.

*The Christian Science Monitor,
3-30:4.*

Thomas J. Downey
*United States Representative,
D-New York*

5

Barney's [the New York department store] used to have an ad: "You can select; you don't have to settle." Unhappily, taxes are not like men's haberdashery. Here [in Congress] we have to settle.

*Before the House,
Washington, D.C., Feb. 27/
The New York Times, 2-28:(C)4.*

Kenneth M. Duberstein
*Former Chief of Staff
to the President
of the United States
(Ronald Reagan)*

6

[On the transition period between a new President's election victory and his officially taking office]: All the attention, all the media focus, all the political focus all flows to the incoming guy. And you're [the current President] kind of left there taking care of business. It's as if you knew it was time to move off center-stage, but you were still onstage when all of a sudden the new soprano was front and center. Even if the soprano's act didn't begin till tomorrow.

The New York Times, 11-19:(A)12.

Pierre S. (Pete) du Pont
*Former Governor
of Delaware (R)*

7

The trouble with the 1980s is not a product of what happened, but what did not happen. The growth of taxes was slowed, and that was good. But the growth of taxation was not reversed. That

(PIERRE S. (PETE) DU PONT)

is the problem. The regulatory knot was loosened
from the neck of American enterprise, and that
was good. But the rope was not removed from our
necks. That is the problem. The defense America
needed to protect itself and deter its enemies in
the 1980s was built, and that is good. But the
defense we need for the 21st century has not been
built. That is the problem. The growth of government bureaucracy has slowed, its virus mo-
mentarily contained, and that is good. But the
growth was not reversed; the virus was not killed.
That is the problem . . . Why were the obvious
mandates of the '80s pursued so tentatively? It
is not because America's majority lost its
principles, its vision, its understanding or its
numbers. No, the problem has been that our
leaders have lost the self-confidence that should
be so easily maintained by those chosen to implement the majority will. And as their confidence
has waned, our influence has eroded.

Before Heritage Foundation,
Jan. 16/
The Wall Street Journal,
4-21:(A)18.

Julie Nixon Eisenhower
Daugher of former President
of the United States
Richard M. Nixon

1

Being First Lady is like being a minister: You
give and give and give, and it takes great faith and
courage to continue in that role.

USA Today, 11-27:(A)11.

Susan Estrich
Professor of law,
University of Southern California

2

[On Hillary Clinton, wife of President-elect
Bill Clinton]: Most Americans look for her to do
more than curate the White House. If that's all
she did, it would be an unfortunate waste of
talent. Most feminists are delighted to see a
strong women in the White House.

The New York Times, 11-16:(A)10.

Edward F. Feighan
United States Representative,
D-Ohio

3

[On his decision not to run for re-election in the
fall]: I have never had to endure such a mean-
spirited, ugly and dehumanizing atmosphere as
the one which now prevails in Washington. For
the first time in memory, there is a small group of
partisan extremists in the House who have set
out to destroy this institution in the name of
reforming it.

The Washington Post, 4-22:(A)4.

Thomas S. Foley
United States Representative,
D-Washington;
Speaker of the House

4

We're looking at the so-called perks on Capitol
Hill. Both the House and Senate are doing that.
I've taken the lead in seeing to it that gymnasium
fees are quadrupled, that we've eliminated free
medical care for members [of Congress] at the
Capitol, that we've looked at every other aspect
of job performance . . . [As for the Executive
Branch,] I don't think anybody questions the fact
that a Cabinet officer probably should have an
automobile and driver, but we see limousines by
the dozens coming up to the Hill with deputy
assistant secretaries, chauffeur-driven secretaries. There's medical care provided for, not
[only for] the President and Vice President, but
White House staff, free medical care. There are
1,360 aircraft maintained by the government,
some of them militarily operated, for non-military
purposes, some of them civilian, and I think it's
just appropriate to look and see if those are being
used appropriately. If they are, fine. If not, then
they should be eliminated as all other unnecessary government perks should be.

Broadcast interview/
"Good Morning America," ABC-TV, 3-31.

5

[On criticism of Congressional perks]: The last
person who should raise the question of perks and
so forth is the President [Bush], who is the king of

WHAT THEY SAID IN 1992

(THOMAS S. FOLEY)

perks in the United States government, and the Vice President [Quayle] who is the crown prince of perks.

To reporters,
Washington, D.C., April 3/
The Washington Post, 4-4:(A)7.

1

[On the anti-government feeling across the U.S.]: There's a chorus trying to stimulate anger, too; political candidates [and] radio talk shows have a vested interest in creating angry responses. So there's a kind of crusade, almost, a sermonizing of discontent that's going on in the country, steaming people up and calling into question everybody's private and public ethical standards, creating in part a vortex of dissatisfaction . . . I think it has great dangers for this society—because it, one, isn't true! It's fine to look at reality and to look at serious problems that exist; but the fact that people are, in effect, being told that their institutions are corrupted and that their officials are not interested in public values, that there is a cynicism about power and position, that people [in government] are living gilded and separate lives . . . All untrue! All untrue!

Interview,
Washington, D.C., April 3/
The Christian Science Monitor,
4-7:2.

Gerald R. Ford
Former President
of the United States;
Former United States Representative,
D-Michigan

2

I really do believe, and I say it very sincerely, that we've got to reduce the number of Congressional committees, and especially subcommittees. We've got to redefine or rationalize committee jurisdictions. They've gotten out of control, in my judgment. We've got to increase the power of the leadership, whether it's Democrat or Republican. You can't run an institution—

and I had eight or nine years of that experience— if you don't have some power over the members of your party on critical and crucial issues. I feel sorry and sad for [House Speaker] Tom Foley and [House Republican leader] Bob Michel. They need the help in order to run the institution instead of having 435 prima donnas up there who have no allegiance to their party or to their leadership.

At National Press Club,
Washington, D.C., June 1/
The Washington Post, 6-10:(A)21.

R. Scott Fosler
President,
National Academy
of Public Administration

3

[On attempts to cut the Federal bureaucracy]: The old-fashioned tendency is to just hack it. But it's like looking for fat in a piece of steak—you won't find it all in one place. It's marbled throughout the whole piece of steak.

The Washington Post, 7-14:(A)11.

Anthony M. Frank
Postmaster General
of the United States

4

[On why he does not favor privatization of the Postal Service]: Because this is not a business. This is a business-like public service. The charter is that all Americans, no matter where they live, get the same service at the same price. If you privatize it, the cost would go up for a lot of Americans. Twenty-nine cents [postage for a first-class letter] compared to anywhere else is an incredible bargain. It's 67 cents in Germany, 47 cents in Japan and 42 cents in Canada. And they don't have any overnight service. This is a very amazing national treasure that I'm afraid people don't appreciate or even understand . . . They don't understand we don't use taxes. They don't understand we don't set our own prices. They don't understand that we have 535 people looking over our shoulder every day up on Capitol Hill. But it's a pretty amazing operation. Could it be better? Sure. Will it be better? Abso-

(ANTHONY M. FRANK)

lutely. It's really on the road to excellence in both efficiency and service.

Interview/
USA Today, 1-8:(A)7.

Newt Gingrich
United States Representative,
R-Georgia

1

[On recent Congressional scandals]: This is about systemic, institutional corruption, not personality. To ask the Democratic leadership to clean things up would be like asking the old Soviet bureaucracy under [Leonid] Brezhnev to reform itself. It ain't going to happen . . . Until someone is prepared to lay out the systemic problem, we will simply go through cycles of finding corruption, finding a scapegoat, eliminating the scapegoat and relaxing until we find the next scandal.

Interview/
The New York Times, 3-17:(A)12.

Albert Gore, Jr.
United States Senator,
D-Tennessee

2

I personally feel a large part of the problem is we've had divided government for so long that both sides have learned to play the game too well. The creative tension that existed between [former President Ronald] Reagan and Congress has become just tension under [President] Bush. There's nothing creative about it.

The Washington Post, 3-16:(A)10.

Albert Gore, Jr.
United States Senator,
D-Tennessee;
1992 Democratic
Vice-Presidential nominee

3

Discussions of the Vice Presidency tend sometimes to focus on the crisis during which a Vice President is thrust into the Oval Office [to take over as President]—and indeed, one third of the Vice Presidents who have served have been moved into the White House. But the teamwork and partnership [between Vice President and President beforehand] . . . how you work together is critically important. The way we've [he and Presidential running mate Bill Clinton] worked together in this campaign is one sample.

At Vice-Presidential candidates' debate,
Atlanta, Ga., Oct. 13./
The New York Times, 10-14:(A)12.

Porter Goss
United States Representative,
R-Florida

4

[On perks available to members of Congress]: Through the years, Congress has accumulated services and powers and benefits that go well beyond what the Founding Fathers had in mind. Some Congressmen do have a mentality that when they win election, they've won the lottery.

The Christian Science Monitor,
3-13:4.

Willis D. Gradison, Jr.
United States Representative,
R-Ohio

5

[On proposed term limitations for members of Congress]: We have to decide if we really trust the people. If we do, the Congress will eventually submit a Constitutional amendment for Congressional term limitations to the states with or without recommendation—and then abide by the results. To continue the present situation could well lead to the Congress being one of a diminished number of legislative bodies in the country without term limits and yet afraid to let the people decide if they want term limits for the Congress. In my view, this would only intensify the feeling that the Congress is out of touch. But worse still, it further undermines the sense of legitimacy of our actions without which representative government could be viewed as a mere slogan used by those whose overriding concern is maintaining power, not serving the public.

The Washington Post, 1-2:(A)23.

Gary Hart
Former United States Senator,
D-Colorado

1

Most people go about the Presidency in the wrong way; they figure out how to win, then how to govern. I don't think George Bush went into the Presidency with the foggiest notion of an agenda. I think he makes it up as he goes along.

Interview, Denver, Colo./
The New York Times, 2-3:(A)8.

Vaclav Havel
Former President
of Czechoslovakia

2

I have found that good taste, oddly enough, plays an important role in politics. Why is it like that? The most probable reason is that good taste is a visible manifestation of human sensibility toward the world, environment, people. I came to this castle and to other governmental residences inherited from Communism, and I was confronted with tasteless furniture and many taste-less pictures. Only then did I realize how closely the bad taste of former rulers was connected with their bad way of ruling. I also realized how important good taste was for politics. During political talks, the feeling of how and when to convey something, of how long to speak, whether to interrupt or not, the degree of attention, how to address the public, forms to be used not to offend someone's dignity and on the other hand to say what has to be said, all these play a major role. All such political behavior relates to good taste in a broader sense. What I really have in mind is something more than just knowing which tie to match a particular shirt.

Interview, Prague, Czechoslovakia/
Time, 8-3:48.

Carla A. Hills
United States Trade Representative

3

[On whether her successor in the forthcoming Clinton Administration should be a technocrat and lawyer as she is]: Why do you want to pigeon-hole [me]? Having served as a Cabinet officer before, why don't you think of me as a politician? Why don't you? Who happens to be knowledgeable about her portfolio? Why is it either you're a technocrat or you have political sense—why is it disjunctive and not conjunctive?

The New York Times,
12-18:(C)2.

Lawrence Hunter
Chief economist,
United States Chamber of Commerce

4

An overwhelming majority of businesses say that anything that government will do—about the economy, slow productivity growth, the environment—anything it will do will be the wrong thing.

Newsweek, 1-13:22.

Henry J. Hyde
United States Representative,
R-Illinois

5

[A Congressman] has to decide to *be* somebody or *do* something. Congress is a following institution, a poll-taking, weather-vane kind of enterprise. You will not see an awful lot of profiles in courage.

Interview, Washington, D.C./
Christianity Today, 3-9:30.

Craig T. James
United States Representative,
R-Florida

6

[On the scandal involving Congressmen who had overdrafts at the House bank]: The House-bank scandal is a stain on this Congress . . . [that affects everyone], including members like me who never bounced checks and those who bounced a check for 20 bucks . . . Full disclosure [of those involved] is the only way to clear the name of the House

The Washington Post, 3-12:(A)25.

Nancy L. Johnson
United States Representative,
R-Connecticut

1

People are angry at Congress. They see this body as out of touch, as incompetent, and I tell them, "If you are not angry now, democracy is brain dead."

Washington, D.C., Feb. 27/
The New York Times, 2-28:(C)4.

Hamilton Jordan
Adviser to industrialist
Ross Perot on his
probable 1992 independent
Presidential campaign;
Former Assistant to the
President of the United States
(Jimmy Carter)

2

I doubt if there has been a time in the recent history of our country where there has been a greater disparity between what the American people want and expect from their government and what both political parties provide for them.

News conference, Dallas, Texas,
June 3/
The New York Times, 6-4:(A)10.

Jerry Lewis
United States Representative,
D-California

3

[On the tensions that have built up in members of Congress]: I have observed all kinds of stresses and strains and frustrations in legislative bodies for years now, but I have never seen anything like this. It's almost a pall hanging over the place . . . It's a negative mood so thick you could cut it with a knife.

Los Angeles Times, 4-13:(A)1.

Paul Light
Professor of political science,
University of Minnesota

4

[The Vice Presidency is] a much better job than it used to be. Is it a good job for an aspiring politician to have? The answer is definitely yes. Nine of our last 18 Presidential candidates have been former Vice Presidents. You make the contacts. You get the exposure that puts you in the front-runner's spot almost automatically in the future. [President] George Bush is proof of that. [The Vice Presidency is] a good job, and it comes with a set of perks and access points that didn't exist 20 years ago . . . We have [former Vice Presidents] Nelson Rockefeller and Walter Mondale to thank for that. They got guaranteed access to the policy process. There's no piece of paper that a Vice President now can't see, no meeting the Vice President can't attend. You have an opportunity to make a difference. So, from that perspective, it has evolved to be a substantial, attractive position.

Interview/USA Today, 7-9:(A)13.

Joseph Malone
State Treasurer of Massachusetts

5

[Advocating term limitations for members of Congress and state legislatures]: I think all too often we are getting young people into government who remain in government one term after another, after another and before you know it, they have been there 30, 40 years only talking to lobbyists, politicians and bureaucrats. Well, there's a whole big world outside of the [Washington] Beltway. There's a whole big world outside of [the Massachusetts State Capitol on] Beacon Hill.

The Christian Science Monitor,
5-15:3.

Will Marshall
Director,
Progressive Policy Institute

6

The great story of 1992 is the degree to which voters feel disconnected from their political system by the insulation of a professional political class, comprising politicians, the press and the pressure elite. People are yearning to be part of a democratic conversation with their government, their leaders, and they now feel they are isolated by the political class, which has arrogated the conversation to itself.

The New York Times, 6-6:8.

John McCain
United States Senator,
R-Arizona

1

I [rise again this year] to strongly oppose many of the add-ons, unauthorized and authorized, [to Congressional bills such as the current defense authorization bill] which we can frankly no longer afford, I find them, again, totally unacceptable. I also want to admit from the start that I am not without sin in casting the first stone. All of us have had to accept legislation that contains items we wish had not been added to our bills. Further, all of us have to fight hard for our state and constituent interests. If we do not, the end result is inevitably to see our programs lose funding, regardless of their merit, and add-ons and pork take their place. There is no man or woman in this body who can point the finger at others in innocence. In fact, it is one of our key functions to fight for the interests of the constituents we serve . . . [But] there is no such thing as a free lunch and there is no such thing as free pork.

Before the Senate, Washington, D.C./
The Washington Post, 10-13:(A)19.

Daniel Patrick Moynihan
United States Senator,
D-New York

2

The most important thing to observe at this moment is that we [government] have no resources [to deal with social and urban problems]. If resources are an issue, we do not have any. And it is no accident that we do not have any, but a deliberate act of government in which this body acquiesced, which this body to this day seemingly cannot understand . . . In 1981, people came to [Washington] and deliberately set about destroying the capacity of the Federal government to respond to these issues with anything like the resources that might be needed . . . This is a very important subject. If we do not get this straight, all the rest is flawed.

Before the Senate,
Washington, D.C., May 13/
The Washington Post,
5-18:(A)19.

David R. Nagle
United States Representative,
D-Iowa

3

If public opinion is right, you need to follow it. If public opinion is wrong, you need to change it.

USA Today, 5-8:(A)9.

Lyn Nofziger
Former Special Assistant
for Political Affairs to the
President of the United States
(Ronald Reagan)

4

Somehow they've got to get [President Bush] back on a pedestal where Presidents belong. You can't send the President out to buy socks. They've got to get him back up on a level where he's doing and saying things that are Presidential. They've had him out there trying too hard to be one of us, and there's nothing wrong with *not* being one of us. The American people are getting more sophisticated about these sorts of things.

Interview, February/
Newsweek, 3-2:28.

Jim Nussle
United States Representative,
R-Iowa

5

Between members of Congress . . . we don't have the opportunity any more to just communicate, one to another, to talk about the issues that are important, to set the priorities and goals for the country. For instance, we don't spend much time on the floor of the House or, for that matter, in committee or in subcommittee, talking about the important goals of whatever piece of legislation or priority we happen to be working on at the time. What that creates, then, is crisis management. An issue will boil over. We'll run to the floor, barely know each other's names or know what our fortes are and then jump to a conclusion without a lot of thought . . . The way to [avoid crisis management] is to put into effect a form of Congressional planning . . . First, you provide and you stimulate communication be-

(JIM NUSSLE)

tween members of Congress by, for instance, simply requiring attendance at subcommittee, committee and floor meetings. Second, you establish a period of time during the Congressional session where you set clearly the goals and the priorities for the country . . . Next you put together a strategic plan or action plan for each one of the goals. And finally, you put together a mechanism to review each one of those plans, to determine how well you're doing and what changes need to be made every other or every two or five years . . . If you put that plan together, you will have the ability to lead the country.

July 7/
The Washington Post, 7-8:(A)28.

Norman J. Ornstein
Fellow,
American Enterprise Institute

1

[On the scandal involving what many see are too many perks for members of Congress]: The story is not only overblown, but involves some of the most deliberately distorted coverage I've ever seen. It is hyped beyond belief. The description of perks has been wildly exaggerated by people who know better.

The Washington Post, 4-9:(A)4.

Ross Perot
Industrialist

2

This city [Washington] has become a town filled with sound bites, shell games, handlers and media stuntmen, who posture, create images and talk, shoot off Roman candles, but don't ever accomplish anything. And if they want to debate that, I'll buy them an hour of television time.

At National Press Club,
Washington, D.C., March 18/
The Washington Post, 3-19:(A)14.

3

We attract to government . . . people with tremendous egos. These are not the people we

want. We want people who go to serve. Does it make sense for the servants of the people to have retirement programs that pay two to three times what the people's programs pay? . . . My advice [to government officials]: Go to the airport, fly commercial, get in line, lose your baggage, eat a bad meal, face reality.

Before American Society
of Newspaper Editors,
Washington, D.C., April 10/
The Washington Post, 4-11:(A)10.

4

[On his possible run for the presidency this year]: Everybody likes to point out that I haven't spent any time in Washington. But the fascinating thing to me is that I may be the only guy that ever read the Constitution, and I understand that Congress and the White House are equal and that the White House can't throw rocks at Congress and expect to get much done, because they need one another. So you would see me buried with the leaders of Congress, buried with Cabinet members who would be the best of the Democrat and Republican parties and others who may be independent. We would be working night and day to fix these problems . . . We'll have the hood up and we'll be working on the engine, and we'll get the car back on the road and not just talk about it.

Broadcast interview/
"Face the Nation," CBS-TV, 4-26.

5

[On his possible run for the Presidency this year]: If I ever get stuck up there [in Washington], I can't stay inside the Beltway. It's like living in a bubble. If you don't see, feel and taste the real America, you could be up there and not know there's a recession. I don't mean that the President's [Bush] a villain. I'm just saying he has been put in the bubble. If Sam Walton hadn't stood in the aisles of his [Walmart] stores talking to customers, he would never have built the empire he built. If you want to serve the people, you've got to listen to real people. If you stay inside the Beltway, the special interests become the real people.

Interview, Dallas, Texas/
Newsweek, 4-27:27.

(ROSS PEROT)

1

[On how he would handle the Presidency if he were elected]: We look at the plans, whether it's health care, whether it's rebuilding the schools or what have you. We come with the best plans. We take them to the people. We explain them. We build a consensus. And always take a little bit of time to do pilot programs, even after everybody's wildly enthusiastic, to debug it, optimize it, improve it. And then, and this is kind of unthinkable in our country, when you pass it into law, leave the people who run this program a lot of freedom to optimize and improve it and don't freeze it by so much legislation that it's locked in time. That's our biggest problem with a lot of our social programs.

News conference, June 23/
USA Today, 6-25:(A)9.

2

We have an election system [for President] now that attracts people with huge egos, with huge power drives, who are willing to take all this punishment and abuse [of running for President] so that they can have the motor cavalcades, have someone play "Hail to the Chief" and go around on Air Force One. And that has totally disoriented us from having our elected officials as servants of the people.

Interview/
U.S. News & World Report,
6-29:32.

Ross Perot
Industrialist;
1992 independent
Presidential candidate

3

If I get there [the Presidency] it will be a very unusual and historical event because the people, not the special interests, put me there. I will have a unique mandate. I have said again and again, and this really upsets the establishment in Washington, that we're going to inform the people in detail on the issues through the electronic town hall so that they really know what's going on. They will want to do what's good for our country. Now, all these fellows with $1,000 suits and alligator shoes, running up and down the halls of Congress, that make policy now—the lobbyists, the PAC guys, the foreign lobbyists and what have you—they'll be over there in the Smithsonian [Institution], you know, because we're going to get rid of them, and the Congress will be listening to the people, and the American people are willing to have fair-shared sacrifice. They're not as stupid as Washington thinks they are.

At Presidential candidates' debate,
St. Louis, Mo., Oct. 11/
The New York Times, 10-12:(A)15.

4

If the American people send me up to do this job [being President], I intend to be there one term. I do not intend to spend one minute of one day thinking about re-election. and as a matter of principle—and my situation is unique and I understand it—I would take absolutely no compensation. I'd go as their servant . . . If you put term limits in [for members of Congress], and don't reform government, you won't get the benefit you thought. It takes both. So we need to do the reform and the term limits, and after we reform it, it won't be a lifetime career opportunity. Good people will go serve and then go back to their homes. They're all nice people; they're just in a bad system. I don't think there are any villains, but, boy, is the system rotten.

At Presidential candidates' debate,
Richmond, Va., Oct. 15/
The New York Times, 10-17:11.

5

As a private citizen, believe me, you are looked on [by Congress] as a major nuisance. The facts are, you now have a government that comes *at* you and you're supposed to have a government that comes *from* you . . . Now, you've got to have a government that comes *from* you again; you've got to reassert your ownership in this country and you've got to completely reform our government. And at that point, they'll just be like apples falling out of a tree—the programs will be good because the elected officials

(ROSS PEROT)

will be listening to [you] . . . You pay for it; why shouldn't you get what you want as opposed to what some lobbyist who cuts a deal, writes the little piece in the law and it goes through. That's the way the game's played now.

At Presidential candidates' debate,
Richmond, Va, Oct. 15/
The New York Times, 10-17:12.

1

[Criticizing Congressional perks]: Who can give themselves a 23 percent pay raise anywhere in the world except Congress? Who would have 1,200 airplanes worth $2-billion a year just to fly around in? I don't have a free reserved parking place at National Airport; why should my servants [the Senators]? I don't have an indoor gymnasium and an indoor tennis court, an indoor every other thing they can think of. I don't have a place where I can go make free TV to send to my constituents to try to blame Washington—to elect me the next time . . . I'm going to show how much they have increased this little stuff they do for themselves, and it is silly putty, folks, and the American people have had enough of it.

At Presidential candidates' debate,
East Lansing, Mich., Oct. 19/
The New York Times, 10-20:(A)15.

Roger Pilon
Director,
Center for Constitutional Studies,
Cato Institute

2

Constitutions are efforts to write in stone for eternity what we haven't the will or discipline to write in sand at the moment.

The New York Times, 6-11:(A)10.

William Proxmire
Former United States Senator,
D-Wisconsin

3

[On Congressional "pork-barrel" projects]: I put a lot of the blame on Congress. There's an easy answer about what you can do—and that's the line-item veto [for the President]. It's disgraceful we don't have a line-item veto [for the President]. [State] Governors have a line-item veto overwhelmingly. It's something that is long, long overdue . . . The line-item veto would also put the monkey on the President's back. Then you can go directly to the President and say: "Mr. President, it's one thing for a member of Congress to want a Lawrence Welk museum back in his district or in his state. But it's something else when the President doesn't veto it." And that would undoubtedly save millions of dollars.

Interview/USA Today, 3-11:(A)11.

Dan Quayle
Vice President
of the United States

4

[On his desire to reduce government regulation]: The future of the country is at stake, because if you can't figure out a way to basically tame that bureaucracy, and if we can't do it on our watch . . . then who's going to do it? . . . The bureaucrats are smart; they've been here; they've got more ways to skin a cat than you can think of, [and] they've got the press primarily on their side . . . I am doing what the President [Bush] wants me to do. That is to make sure that "regulatory creep"—to use his words—does not get back into his Administration.

Interview/
The Washington Post, 1-9:(A)1.

5

From my conservative viewpoint and my conservative ideology, the more Congress is messed up, the better off the country is.

USA Today, 4-28:(A)6.

6

When you're the President or the Vice President, you're going to have your whole life out there for inspection. Now, the question is, what is relevant and not relevant? Well, what a person does privately is a very good indicator of what he's going to do publicly. What a person is like personally will give you an indication of where he's going to take the country. And if you have somebody who wants to be President or Vice President, why would they want to hide, to keep things private? Why wouldn't they want to be open and say, here's what I'm all about? I've always believed that you should practice what you preach. And If you're preaching something different than you're practicing, we ought to know about it.

Interview/
Christianity Today, 6-22:30.

1

Almost 16 years ago, in my first speech as a member of the House of Representatives, I proposed limiting the terms of Congress. The Democratic Congress tells us that it is good for the country to limit [Republican Presidents] Ronald Reagan and George Bush to two terms as President. I say to them, if it is good for the country to limit Ronald Reagan and George Bush to two terms, then it would be great for the country to limit the terms of Senators like [Democrats] George Mitchell and Ted Kennedy, and the rest of that liberal Democratic Congress.

At Republican National Convention,
Houston, Texas, Aug. 20/
The New York Times, 8-21:(A)10.

2

Teamwork and partnership may be fine in the Congress. That's what Congress is all about. But when you're . . . Vice President [of the U.S.] and you have to fill in [for a disabled President], you've got to make a decision. You've got to make up your [own] mind [in a crisis].

At Vice-Presidential candidates' debate,
Atlanta, Ga., Oct. 13/
The New York Times, 10-14:(A)12.

William J. Roberts
Chief lobbyist,
Environmental Defense Fund

3

Getting a law enacted is arduous, complex and controversial. But it really gets you to only about

the third inning of the ball game. There are a lot more innings to play, some in courtrooms, some in the political arena, some locally and some nationally. Whether it's the best way to make policy or not is an open question, but all of us take it as a given.

The New York Times, 4-25:6.

Paul Roche
Poet-in-residence,
Centenary College

4

We're all ignorant in different ways. But poets' antennae are on to things way before they strike politicians or the populace. We need a poet attached to every government department as social lookouts.

Interview, Hackettstown, N.J./
The New York Times, 12-18:(A)24.

Dana T. Rohrabacher
United States Representative,
R-California

5

People [in Congress] are very depressed [about the way Congress operates[. I will tell you, many times lately I've thought about ditching this and going surfing for the rest of my life.

The Christian Science Monitor,
3-30:1.

Warren Rudman
United States Senator,
R-New Hampshire

6

[In Congress,] you have to take some political risks. An English politician once said there are two ways you can lose an election: You can lose it because you do nothing; or you can lose it because you do something. I would rather lose it doing something. I like to see this place function and do constructive things . . . People want to talk about [how] Congress needs to be reorganized—and it does, I agree—but that isn't the fundamental problem. The problem is lack of will to do what has to be done.

Interview/Newsweek, 4-6:28.

(WARREN RUDMAN)

1

[Washington is] a phony city. That's one of the problems with Congress. Though most members of this body are very dedicated and honest, there are some, who shall remain nameless, who have become thoroughly enthralled with life in Washington and are truly out of touch with the rest of the country. Personally, I find the social scene here very boring. I'm not much interested in sitting next to someone at a function who is there because they gave 6 trillion dollars and make widgets in Omaha.

Interview, Washington, D.C./
People, 4-20:70.

2

[On his decision not to seek re-election to the Senate this year]: [The Senate used to be] a place in which major issues facing the country would be deliberately and carefully debated and decisions made. And the first three or four years [of my term] were like that. [But with today's increased partisanship,] the Senate is now less than the sum of its parts. I guess that's the best way I can put it, which is really sad . . . I've read often of the lives of [earlier Senators] Mike Mansfield and Everett Dirksen. Those two men had some very fundamental disagreements about a lot of things, but they were able to . . . work out compromises that would advance the interests of the country because they had some control over their respective sides of the aisle. I mean, right now [Senate majority leader] George Mitchell and [Senate minority leader] Robert Dole preside over a group of independent contractors, to a large extent.

Interview, Washington, D.C./
The Christian Science Monitor,
6-19:7.

Larry J. Sabato
Professor of government,
University of Virginia

3

[On President-elect Bill Clinton's plans for call-in shows, frequent radio addresses and other ways of dealing more directly with the people]: It makes it appear that he's keeping in touch, and it's a very populist innovation that enables him to short-circuit the news media. Clinton is bound to totally dominate that kind of format and come off smelling like a rose every time he does it. It would be a shame if this becomes the prime cross-examination of the President. Instant democracy is not the way to make decisions.

The New York Times, 11-21:7.

Patricia Schroeder
United States Representative,
D-Colorado

4

We have lost confidence in our government and in those who serve in it. But the power to change is only limited by the desire to act.

At Bryn Mawr College commencement,
May 17/
The New York Times, 5-18:(C)11.

5

If we could break through these two glass ceilings of not having more than two women in the Senate and never having more than 20-something women in the House, people [would] say, "It's terrific—the Year of the Woman." But you're not anywhere near what sociologists have told us is a critical mass, which is about 25-30 per cent. When you get to critical mass, then you can start to be able to change the institution [of Congress].

Interview, Denver, Colo./
The Christian Science Monitor,
8-27:7.

Samuel K. Skinner
Chief of Staff to President
of the United States
George Bush

6

[On an understanding in the Bush Administration not to ask the President to resolve any but the most important disputes]: Why bother the President if you don't have to? Number one, you might lose . . . Number two, you're burdening him with something that he does not like to be burdened

(SAMUEL K. SKINNER)

with. He wants people to work it out. The gentlemen's agreement is, try to work it out before it gets to him. [The President says,] "I don't want to have to decide between Cabinet members." Everybody understands that's what the President wants . . . Anybody that's loyal to the President is going to do it that way.

The Washington Post, 1-9:(A)16.

Merrie Spaeth
Former Special Assistant
to former President
of the United States
Ronald Reagan

1

The First Lady's job is more than a full-time job. It's the responsibility of using the White House to represent the country. It's not just state dinners. It's youth concerts, the Easter-egg roll, the White House tours, the recognition of the volunteer ladies who work on art-history week. An effective First Lady is the eyes and ears of her husband. She's a reality check, as in, "Dear, you haven't been reading the newspapers lately." Second, she serves as a route for the senior staff to reach her husband. It isn't an up-front role.

The New York Times, 11-16:(A)10.

George Stephanopoulos
Communications director for
President-elect Bill Clinton

2

Bill Clinton is going to have an open Presidency, and he's got an open inaugural [coming in January]. We want to make sure that people understand that they are truly in charge of the government, that the government is accessible to them, that the President isn't someone who is out of touch with their problems and concerns.

The Christian Science Monitor,
12-9:9.

3

[On whether Hillary Clinton, wife of President-elect Bill Clinton, will participate in decision-making sessions at the White House]: I don't know how many she'll attend, but certainly she'll

be free to attend when she feels she can make an addition, and that's probably a lot. She obviously can contribute on a number of issues having to do with children, family, but I wouldn't want to limit in any way or expand on it in any way right now.

News briefing,
Little Rock, Ark., Dec. 18/
The New York Times, 12-19:8.

Sheila Tate
Former White House
Press Secretary
to Nancy Reagan,
wife of former President
Ronald Reagan

4

Americans want to love their First Lady. They always have. But the American people are very conflicted about First Ladies. They want whoever she is to represent American womanhood without spending a lot of money on clothes, and to preserve and protect the historic national treasure known as the White House—again without spending undue sums of money. And they want her to carve out her own niche without becoming power-hungry and forgetting that she really simply arrived there because she is married to the man who was elected. Brutal as it sounds, Americans have lines they draw.

The New York Times, 11-16:(A)10.

Charles Taylor
United States Representative,
R-North Carolina

5

[Criticizing excessive Congressional perks]: The public pays for my office expenses, telephone expenses and mailings that are necessary for me to carry on the activities that represent them. But the public shouldn't pay for my care and feeding. If I want to belong to a gym, I should pay for it.

USA Today, 3-26:(A)4.

James A. Traficant, Jr.
United States Representative,
D-Ohio

6

How can America return to greatness if Congress continues to vote on bills that are at

(JAMES A. TRAFICANT, JR.)

best half good and half bad? Where I come from, half good and half bad is mediocre. The problem with our country is we have enacted mediocre laws and we have a mediocre economy and we have a mediocre Congress that leads a mediocre government.

Washington, D.C., Feb., 27/
The New York Times, 2-28:(C)4.

Henry A. Waxman
United States Representative,
D-California

1

[On the scandals and frustrations building up in Congress]: I can well understand why many good people are getting fed up and are leaving. There are a lot of good people here who want to do the right thing and make the tough decisions, and they are taking a lot of abuse . . . It makes me very worried. I worry about what kind of people are going to run for public office in the future and what kind of people are going to stay.

Los Angeles Times, 4-13:(A)14.

Stephen J. Wayne
Professor of government,
Georgetown University

2

[On the public's anger at the perks available to Congressmen and other government officials]: The people in government are not a privileged class, and once they begin acting like one, we get mad as hell. The reaction is: "Who the hell do you think you are? You work for us."

The New York Times, 3-31:(A)8.

Vin Weber
United States Representative,
R-Minnesota

3

[The U.S.] can't and probably shouldn't go to a full-fledged parliamentary system. We set up

this system of checks and balances and separation of powers partially to protect against the growth of government. But we now have a big government. So that argument is settled. The question is, can we change our very large government that affects people in so many ways? We're preventing government from getting more responsive because we can't change the institutions that we built up over 200 years.

Panel discussion,
Washington, D.C./
Time, 6-8:68.

Sheila Rabb Weidenfeld
Former White House
Press Secretary to Betty Ford,
wife of former President
Gerald R. Ford

4

The White House is a very chauvinist place. There's no understanding of what to do with the First Lady. The people in the West Wing know there is pillow talk, and they resent it. I look at the roles as a head-heart distinction. The President is elected. He's the head. The East Wing is the heart. For an Administration to be successful, it has to have both. When [former President Jimmy Carter's wife] Rosalyn Carter sat in at a Cabinet meeting, there was a lot of criticism, and rightly so. It was the wrong symbolism. It made people wonder, "Where's the heart? Where's the compassion?" She was doing something she wasn't elected to office to do.

The New York Times, 11-16:(A)10.

William F. Weld
Governor of Massachusetts (R)

5

The issue [underlying privatization of government functions] is not public versus private. The issue is monopoly versus competition. We've learned in Massachusetts that letting the profit motive and competition in on the process of government . . . can greatly benefit the state.

Speech, Washington, D.C., April/
Nation's Business, August:23.

Charles Wilson
United States Representative,
D-Texas

1

[On the scandal involving Congressmen, including himself, who had overdrafts at the House bank]: [It's] no big deal . . . It's not like molesting young girls or young boys. It's not a show-stopper. In the words of Abraham Lincoln, this too shall pass. But we are not going to get any badges of honor. It's one more anti-incumbent thing. It might be a show-stopper. If it is, *c'est la vie.*

Interview/
The Washington Post,
3-13:(A)10.

Law • The Judiciary

William P. Barr
Attorney General
of the United States

1

[Saying he does not support the use of independent prosecutors or counsels, unaccountable to the Justice Department, to investigate wrongdoing in the Federal government]: Part of the constraints that exist in the Department of Justice are a set of policies, an institutional ethos about the proper role of a prosecutor, and the fact that we have here experienced prosecutors who see many cases and well understand the proper functioning of a prosecutor. What the statute [authorizing independent counsels] does is set someone outside that milieu, not necessarily controlled by policies, not controlled or influenced by the ethos of the Department, and with no accountability. No supervisor or anyone to make sure there's no abuse of power going on. And unlimited resources. I think that any person concerned about civil liberties should be concerned about that kind of structure.

Interview, Washington, D.C./
Los Angeles Times, 6-21:(M)3.

2

I think people [investigated and prosecuted by the special independent prosecutor] in the Iran-contra [scandal] have been treated very unfairly, many of them . . . People in this Iran-contra matter have been prosecuted for the kind of conduct that would not have been considered criminal or prosecutable by the Department of Justice, applying standards that we have applied for decades to every citizen.

Interview, Dec. 16/
USA Today, 12-17:(A)2.

Joseph R. Biden, Jr.
United States Senator,
D-Delaware

3

[The] current collapse of the confirmation process [for Supreme Court nominees is due to the Bush] Administration's campaign to make the Supreme Court the agent of an ultra-conservative social agenda which lacks support in the Congress or in the country. [In this context, the] prospects for anything but conflagration with respect to a Supreme Court nomination this year are remote. If the President does not restore the historical tradition of genuine consultations [with Congress on nominees] . . . or instead restore the common practice of Presidents who chose nominees who strode the middle ground between the divided political branches, then I [as Chairman of the Senate Judiciary Committee] shall oppose his future nominees, immediately upon their nomination.

Before the Senate,
Washington, D.C., June 25/
The Washington Post, 6-26:(A)21.

Jay Bloom
Municipal-court judge,
San Diego, Calif.;
Former Deputy Attorney General
of California

4

The appellate process is very disconcerting. At a trial you're dealing with right or wrong, guilt or innocence. Suddenly you get up on appeal and it seems like you're trying everything but the defendant's guilt or innocence. Did the prosecution do something wrong? Did the judge say the magic words? Sometimes you wonder if the whole appellate process hasn't lost sight of what the whole thing is all about—criminal justice . . . [In the appellate process,] we [aren't] worried about truth or falsity or guilt or innocence. We [are] involved in this technical morass of things, of procedures . . . So many steps removed from the crime. The emotion and the trauma of the event [are] often lost in the blur of technical issues . . . No one ever [thinks] about the victims or the culpability.

Los Angeles Times,
4-20:(A)18.

Howard Brockman
Judge, Superior Court,
Visalia, Calif.

1

[On his reputation for unusual sentencing]:
When you are a judge, there is no bank of ideas.
You cannot go to your friends and ask them what
they think you should do. That would be wholly
unethical. I sit and read the cases and read what
other judges have done in similar situations and
try to think of what is fair and reasonable and
what makes sense. Sometimes I'll think of the
answer while I'm driving my car.
Interview, Visalia, Calif./
Time, 3-9:16.

Edmund G. "Jerry" Brown, Jr.
Candidate for the 1992
Democratic Presidential nomination;
Former Governor
of California (D)

2

[As Governor,] I appointed 850 judges, and
guess what—they're all lawyers. You know who
comes to fund-raisers and gets into politics and
gets elected? Lawyers. Half the people in politics
are lawyers. And those people, all of them, want
to be judges. Do I think the system is bad? You
bet I do, and that's why I've limited [contribu-
tions to his Presidential campaign] to $100.
Democratic candidate debate,
New York, N.Y., April 5/
The Washington Post, 4-6:(A)16.

George Bush
President of the United States

3

I see something happening in our towns and in
our neighborhoods. Sharp lawyers are running
wild: Doctors are afraid to practice medicine,
and some moms and dads won't even coach Little
League anymore. We must sue each other less,
and care for each other more. I'm fighting to
reform our legal system, to put an end to crazy
lawsuits. If that means climbing into the ring with
the trial lawyers, well, let me just say, Round 1
starts tonight.
At Republican National Convention,
Houston, Texas, Aug. 20/
The New York Times, 8-21:(A)16.

4

[Announcing his granting of pardons to former
Secretary of Defense Caspar Weinberger and
others who have been implicated in the Iran-
contra scandal]: I am pardoning him not just out
of compassion or to spare a 75-year-old patriot
the torment of lengthy and costly legal pro-
ceedings, but to make it possible for him
to receive the honor he deserves for his
extraordinary service to our country . . . I have
also decided to pardon five other individuals for
their conduct related to the Iran-contra affair:
Elliott Abrams, Duane Clarridge, Alan Fiers,
Clair George and Robert McFarlane. First, the
common denominator of their motivation—
whether their actions were right or wrong—was
patriotism. Second, they did not profit or seek to
profit from their conduct. Third, each has a
record of long and distinguished service to this
country. And finally, all five have already paid
a price—in depleted savings, lost careers,
anguished families—grossly disproportionate to
any misdeeds or errors of judgment they may
have committed. The prosecutions of the individuals I am pardoning represent what I believe
is a profoundly troubling development in the
political and legal climate of our country: the
criminalization of policy differences. These differences should be addressed in the political
arena, without the Damocles sword of criminality
hanging over the heads of some of the com-
batants. The proper target is the President, not
his subordinates; the proper forum is the voting
booth, not the courtroom. In recent years, the use
of criminal processes in policy disputes has
become all too common. It is my hope that the
action I am taking today will begin to restore
these disputes to the battleground where they
properly belong.
Washington, D.C., Dec. 24/*
The New York Times, 12-25:(A)10.

5

[On suggestions in the press that his granting
pardons to six people implicated in the Iran-
contra scandal shows that high government officials are above the law]: No, it should not give
any such appearance. Nobody is above the law.
And I believe when people break the law, that's a

(GEORGE BUSH)

bad thing. I've read some stupid comment to the contrary . . . But the Constitution is quite clear on the powers of the President, and sometimes the President has to make a difficult call, and that's what I've done . . . I've read some rather frivolous reporting that I don't care about the law. I pride myself on 25 or more years of public service, of serving honorably, decently and with my integrity intact. And certainly I wouldn't feel that way if I had a lack of respect for the law. And I don't think there is one single thing in my career that could lead anybody to look at my record and make a statement of that nature.

News conference,
Washington, D.C., Dec. 30/
The New York Times, 12-31:(A)8.

Jesse H. Chopper
Dean, University of California-Berkeley
Law School

1

[On President Bush's appointments to the Supreme Court]: He has had strong political considerations in mind, as have his predecessors. He has made no bones about that. That is, he's got certain criteria that he wants fulfilled. Basically, he wants people who are not very activist, who are tending to be sort of strict interpreters of the law and the Constitution, to play a relatively restrained role in the making of law . . . My general prediction is that they are going to be much more inclined to find in favor of government against individual rights. In my judgment, if they do that in as aggressive a way as they could, I don't think that will be good for the country.

Interview/
The New York Times, 7-1:(A)9.

Bill Clinton
Governor of Arkansas (D);
Candidate for the 1992
Democratic Presidential nomination

2

I want to appoint [to the Supreme Court] somebody who has an expansive view of the Bill of Rights and believes in the right to privacy . . . I

think that there ought to be some balance on the Court. I don't want to appoint somebody who has far-out liberal views or left-wing views or to do any kind of litmus test like that. I just believe that the personal liberties of the American people have been subject to some severe politicization as a result of this [current] Supreme Court, and I think that we ought to have somebody on the Court who respects past decisions and traditions.

Interview, Little Rock, Ark./
Newsweek, 7-20:29.

Bill Clinton
Governor of Arkansas (D);
President-elect
of the United States

3

[On President Bush granting pardons for a number of those implicated in the Iran-contra scandal, including former Secretary of Defense Caspar Weinberger]: I am concerned by any action that sends a signal that if you work for government, you're beyond the law, or that not telling the truth to Congress under oath is somehow less serious than not telling the truth to some other body under oath.

News conference,
Little Rock, Ark., Dec. 24/
The New York Times, 12-25:(A)10.

Mary Coombs
Professor of criminal law,
University of Miami
Law School

4

[On Florida's judicial system which permits acquitted defendants to recover certain trial costs from the court]: The Florida system is a fair system if you don't look at a case involving a [wealthy-family member such as a] Kennedy, but instead think about one with your average Joe Schmo who's not poor enough to use Legal Aid. He mortgages his home, uses several thousand in savings, is falsely accused and then acquitted. It's a cost that the state should bear. I know the state can't afford it, but neither can many of the people caught in one of these cases.

The New York Times, 1-10:(B)9.

Alan M. Dershowitz
Professor of law,
Harvard University
Law School

1

[On Florida's judicial system which permits acquitted defendants to recover certain trial costs from the court]: The Florida approach is too simple-minded. An acquittal doesn't mean that he's innocent, it just means he's not found guilty beyond a reasonable doubt. That shouldn't be enough reason to charge the cost to taxpayers. The rule, if enforced, would discourage certain types of cases, like date rape, that are hard to win. Close cases ought to be prosecuted.

The New York Times, 1-10:(B)9.

Lloyd Doggett
Justice,
Supreme Court of Texas

2

[Saying too many civil cases involving product liability are sealed from public view after adjudication]: A wide range of consumer products have a tendency to cause injury. Information that is hidden in one state may have consequences that literally result in people being killed and maimed in other states because you can't have accident avoidance and recognition of dangers if you never hear about the danger in the first place . . . The only way to alter it is by changing the rules and changing the laws to require specifically that judges do their job of balancing the interest between secrecy and the public's right to know. And it's definitely a balancing process. There's no guarantee that in every situation . . . the public has a right to know everything. But what's happening is the public is losing by default because judges aren't doing the job of balancing; they're just signing off on what the parties agree. And that's got to be changed.

Interview/USA Today, 1-30:(A)9.

Hamilton Fish, Jr.
United States Representative,
R-New York

3

[Backing a Bush Administration proposal aimed at reducing frivolous and unnecessary

lawsuits]: [This legislation] is not intended as an attack on our nation's legal system or the legal profession. The fact is that the American people sense that something is wrong with our legal system. They believe there are too many lawsuits, too many excessive damage awards. They believe that there is too much litigation, and this is hurting the American economy.

Washington, D.C., Feb. 4/
The New York Times, 2-5:(A)11.

Steven Gillers
Professor of legal ethics,
New York University
Law School

4

[On law firms' reluctance to address the issue of their legal ethics]: Partly it's arrogance. Law firms think, "It won't happen to us" [being charged with ethics violations]. Partly it's self-deception: "We think we know it already and we don't need someone to tell us." Partly it's complacency: "We have insurance." And partly it's distraction: Lawyers spend all their time worrying about how the law applies to their clients, and don't think of themselves as clients. It's only after they get stung that they pay heed.

The New York Times, 3-13:(B)11.

Ernest F. Hollings
United States Senator,
D-South Carolina

5

[Criticizing Washington's corporate lawyers]: If you can ever find out how much the corporate lawyers are paid for sitting on their duffs around this town and making a call to a Senator, you will find out the real cancer in the law practice—the fixers in this place.

Before the Senate, Washington, D.C./
The Washington Post, 10-13:(D)21.

Vernon E. Jordan, Jr.
Lawyer; Former president,
National Urban League

6

We [in the legal profession] must measure our success by higher standards than winning law-

(VERNON E. JORDAN, JR.)

suits, closing real-estate deals, writing legislation . . . We, as lawyers, must be concerned with the larger issues that imperil our society, issues such as discrimination, poverty, homelessness, crime, education, housing and a host of others. For unless we labor to help others achieve a reasonable stake in society, we may find ourselves losing the society in which we have so great a stake.

At District of Columbia Bar Association,
Washington, D.C., June 25/
The Washington Post, 7-3:(A)22.

Don C. Keenan
National president,
American Board
of Trial Advocates

1

The thing that saddens me is that people don't look at the justice system the way Thomas Jefferson said was justice by the people. They look at it as the "lawyer system"—and it is. The lawyers determine what the schedule is going to be. They determine when the jury has to go out and sit in a little cramped room for three or four hours while they haggle over small points. The ability of lawyers to spend two to three weeks to choose a jury is ridiculous, and it's absolutely outrageous to ask some of the personal questions that are on those questionnaires. I would absolutely refuse.

Interview/
USA Today, 12-21:(A)11.

Helena Kennedy
British Queen's Counsel

2

[Saying there is bias against women working in the legal profession]: Historically the law has been one of the tools to keep women in their place. It seems to me there is a particular failure when one of our central institutions, which is supposed to give remedies to those who experience discrimination, not only hasn't got it right but is so badly erring. This is not just about jobs for girls. It's actually about democracy not working for more than half of the population.

Interview/
The New York Times, 12-11:(B)12.

George Kuhlman
Counsel, Center for
Professional Responsibility,
American Bar Association

3

[On judges who are involved in personal scandals]: Judges have been disciplined even for being seen publicly going on weekend vacations with their mistresses. If the public sees that judges seem to think that laws are fine for people who come before them but need not necessarily be enforced for themselves, that clearly sends a very bad signal. It tends to undermine the sense the public should have that justice is administered fairly.

The Christian Science Monitor,
11-12:8.

David O'Brien
Professor,
University of Virginia

4

One of the hallmarks of the [former President Ronald] Reagan and [President] Bush [-appointed] judges was that they were young. They wanted to lock in the revolution. By no means in his first term can [President-elect Bill] Clinton reverse the legacy.

USA Today, 11-9:(A)2.

Ben Overton
Justice,
Supreme Court of Florida

5

Juries rarely make mistakes on what is presented to them. What *isn't* presented is something else.

U.S. News & World Report,
5-25:38.

Dan Quayle
Vice President
of the United States

6

The American Bar Association's position is this: They want to increase taxpayer financing for litigation; they want to increase a new

(DAN QUAYLE)

bureaucracy in the Justice Department to hire more lawyers; and they want more grants for lawyers. Well, that may be the reform package of the American Bar Association, but that is not the reform package of the American people. I'm telling you, the American people are on my side on this issue.

News conference,
Washington, D.C., Feb. 4/
The New York Times, 2-5:(A)11.

1

Our legal system is spinning out of control. The explosion of frivolous lawsuits burdens our economy and weakens our system of justice. America has 5 per cent of the world's population and 70 per cent of the world's lawyers. I have nothing against lawyers—at least most of them. I'm a lawyer; I'm married to one . . . I looked forward with pride to becoming part of the finest legal system in the world. But today our country has a problem: Our legal system is costing consumers $300-billion a year. The litigation explosion has damaged our competitiveness; it has wiped out jobs; it has forced doctors to quit practicing in places where they are needed most. Every American knows the legal system is broken—and now is the time to fix it.

At Republican National Convention,
Houston, Texas, Aug. 20/
The New York Times, 8-21:(A)10.

Kathleen Sampson
Director of information
and program services,
American Judicature Society

2

We need educational programs to demystify the judicial branch. It's just as visible a branch of government as the other two. So unless you're a juror or litigant, you may know very little about what a courtroom looks like or what goes on in a courtroom.

The Christian Science Monitor,
6-9:12.

Thomas S. Smith
Director of daily operations,
New Jersey State
Public Defender's Office

3

I probably receive anywhere between 10 and 12 resumes a week from people who want to come here [and be Public Defenders]. Because, if you want to learn how to try a criminal case, this is the place to be. If you come here as a young lawyer, we are going to have you on your feet in front of a judge and a jury very quickly. This place is not like the large law firms, where they keep you in the office, handling interrogatories.

The New York Times, 10-19:(A)13.

Willian D. Smith
President,
National Union
Fire Insurance Company

4

[On costly legal settlements paid by many law firms resulting from malpractice suits]: During this litigation onslaught, one of the techniques used to keep the [malpractice] insurance afford-able was for the firms to take slightly higher deductibles. [But] the number of claims each firm is facing and the fact that significant values are now attaching to each of these cases clearly has the potential of straining the financial resources of many law and accounting firms . . . This has not been a great time for law firms. They're paying people off, and now they're faced with sig-nificant cash outlays. And I think you may see more partnerships dissolve just because they're not going to be able to pay the bills.

The New York Times, 4-1:(C)6.

John Paul Stevens
Associate Justice,
Supreme Court
of the United States

5

In Great Britain, 1991 [was] the year in which the re-examination of the convictions of alleged Irish terrorists has reminded us that trusted police officers sometimes fabricate confessions to obtain convictions. In this country [the

(JOHN PAUL STEVENS)

U.S.] ... an extraordinarily aggressive Supreme Court has reached out to announce a host of new rules narrowing the Federal Constitution's protection of individual liberties. [For example,] the prosecutor's use of a coerced confession—no matter how vicious the police conduct may have been—may now constitute harmless error [and not reflect in the accused's favor].

Speech,
University of Chicago (Ill.) Law School/
The Washington Post, 1-18:(A)23.

Geoffrey Stone
Dean, University of Chicago (Ill.)
Law School
1

[On the trend toward law schools offering courses that link law with specific social issues, rather than staying exclusively based in teaching law]: Legal training must stay rooted in law. Some law schools seem to be too enamored of the scholarship of professors who aren't really interested in teaching lawyers.

The Christian Science Monitor,
11-30:13.

Robert S. Strauss
United States Ambassador
to Russia
2

[Saying the new non-Communist Russia could use U.S. legal expertise]: I found the only place in the world that can use 500 lawyers. If we could take 500 lawyers out of our own and move them into this [Russian] government, it would be one of the great bonanzas of all time for both countries.

To reporters,
Moscow, Russia, Feb. 19/
The Christian Science Monitor,
2-20:3.

Laurence H. Tribe
Professor of constitutional law,
Harvard University
3

[On the Supreme Court's recent ruling upholding the Court's earlier *Roe v. Wade* abortion-

rights decision, but with some restrictions]: You're going to be getting lots of people on the pro-choice side giving you spin that this [the new restrictions] is terrible news. I do not regard it as terrible news. This decision is far more persuasive in explaining why women should have this right [to abortion] than *Roe* was. And the fact that [this new ruling] was written by three [Presidents] Reagan-Bush appointees underscores how it reflects not a marginal view of extremists or an ideologically committed group of people, but a central tradition of American democracy.

USA Today, 6-30:(A)2.

Lawrence E. Walsh
Independent Counsel
investigating the Iran-contra
scandal;
Former president,
American Bar Association
4

[Criticizing President Bush's granting pardons to former Secretary of State Caspar Weinberger and others who have been implicated in the Iran-contra scandal]: President Bush's pardon of Caspar Weinberger and other Iran-contra defendants undermines the principle that no man is above the law. It demonstrates that powerful people with powerful allies can commit serious crimes in high office—deliberately abusing the public trust without consequence. Weinberger, who faced four felony charges, deserved to be tried by a jury of citizens. Although it is the President's prerogative to grant pardons, it is every American's right that the criminal-justice system be administered fairly, regardless of a person's rank and connections ... Weinberger's concealment of notes is part of a disturbing pattern of deception and obstruction that permeated the highest levels of the [former President Ronald] Reagan and Bush Administrations. This office was informed only within the past two weeks, on December 11, 1992, that President Bush had failed to produce to investigators his own highly relevant contemporaneous notes, despite repeated requests for such documents. The production of these notes is still ongoing and will lead to appropriate action. In light of President Bush's own misconduct, we are gravely concerned about his

(LAWRENCE E. WALSH)

decision to pardon others who lied to Congress and obstructed official investigations.

Dec. 24/
The New York Times, 12-25:(A)10.

Caspar W. Weinberger
Former Secretary of Defense
of the United States

1

[On his just-announced indictment in connection with the Iran-contra scandal of the 1980s]: The decision to indict me is a grotesque distortion of the prosecutorial power and a moral and legal outrage . . . In order to avoid this indictment I was not willing [to] accept an offer by the Office of the Independent Counsel to plea to a misdemeanor offense of which I was not guilty, nor was I willing to give them statements which were not true about myself or others. I would not give false testimony nor would I enter a false plea. Because of this refusal, which to me is a matter of conscience, I have now been charged with multiple felonies.

News conference,
Washington, D.C., June 16/
The New York Times, 6-17:(A)1,14.

2

[On his being indicted in connection with the Iran-contra scandal a few days before the recent Presidential election, which he says may have been influenced by the indictment, causing President Bush to lose]: It is unfortunate that my family has to go through this terrible ordeal not because of anything I have done but rather because I have become a pawn in a clearly political game as is shown by the return of the indictment only days before the Presidential election.

To reporters after pleading
not-guilty at the Federal courthouse,
Washington, D.C., Nov. 24/
The New York Times, 11-25:(A)7.

Politics

Bella Abzug
Former United States Representative,
D-New York

1

The [political] parties say, "We don't discriminate; women can run [in elections]." But we're running against the tide of history. It's not enough to say "We don't discriminate." Women advanced professionally partly because of affirmative action, the argument goes; they may not advance politically without it.

The Atlantic, July:62.

Rob Andrews
United States Representative,
D-New Jersey

2

For a while it looked as if the [just-held national] election would be a referendum on Congress. A lot of members worked hard to shift the ground away from whether or not people liked Congress, which they didn't, to themselves and their opponents. You had to shift the field of battle. You have to de-rascalize yourself.

Nov. 4/
The New York Times, 11-5:(B)6.

Roone Arledge
President, ABC News

3

[National political conventions are] irrelevent. Nothing of significance happens at them. Almost every decision of any importance happens out of sight. I don't think we should try to pretend that conventions are what they used to be.

The New York Times, 7-6:(A)10.

Warren Beatty
Actor

4

I see nothing wrong with an actor becoming a politician—and I think an actor has many tools to be effective in politics. Everybody knows I don't agree with his politics, but [former President and actor] Ronald Reagan is a good example of the citizen politician. It would be good if we would all, as citizens, be interested in giving years of public service the way Ronald Reagan did.

Interview, New York/
Los Angeles Times, 3-1:(M)3.

William J. Bennett
Former Director,
Federal Office of National
Drug Control Policy;
Former Secretary of Education
of the United States

5

[On President Bush's re-election defeat this year]: We [Republicans] ran out of steam in the second half of the second [President Ronald] Reagan Administration. We've been in office for 12 years. We got tired. We forgot why we came. It's generational. George Bush genuinely believed that the major job he had was to win the peace and end the Cold War [rather than tackle domestic problems].

Nov. 4/
The New York Times, 11-5:(A)1.

Richard N. Bond
Chairman,
Republican National Committee

6

[On industrialist Ross Perot, who will probably announce his independent candidacy for President shortly]: I just don't think that the risk that Ross Perot presents to the American people out there is a risk that they're going to take. He doesn't have the temperament to be President. His greatist proclivity, when he runs into opposition, is to take his ball and bat and go home, and I don't think you want that in the President of the United States.

Broadcast interview/
"Face the Nation,"
CBS-TV, 6-14.

(RICHARD N. BOND)

1

When the Perot people [those who supported industrialist Ross Perot, who recently pulled out of the Presidential race] now, as they've been talking about the last couple of days, focus on the Congress, they're going to find out what [President] George Bush and the rest of us have been saying is totally true: that it is the Democratic Congress that has obstructed for 3½ years George Bush's program, and if you make the change in Congress, you will have changed the country.

Broadcast interview/
"This Week With David Brinkley,"
ABC-TV, 7-19.

2

[On 1992 Democratic Presidential nominee Arkansas Governor Bill Clinton]: He hasn't been a very good Governor of a small state. We've got to establish a couple of common-sense points with voters and convince them that you wouldn't elect Clinton the Governor of your state, [so] why in the world would you elect him President.

The Washington Post, 8-22:(A)12.

Barbara Boxer
United States Representative,
D-California;
1992 Democratic nominee
for U.S. Senator from California

3

I believe that if ever we were going to see this, if you will, revolution [of women in government], it will be this year, because . . . people are ready for a domestic agenda. And that's what we women talk about. We talk about the family, we understand the needs of our people. We hurt when we see the unemployment rate, we hurt when we see kids in trouble . . . And that women's agenda is becoming the nation's agenda.

Broadcast interview,
New York, N.Y./
"Larry King Show,"
CNN-TV, 7-14.

Bill Bradley
United States Senator,
D-New Jersey

4

The evidence of this [Bush] Administration's willingness to inflame the wounds that it should heal is everywhere. And the spectacle of social crises that can be seen right through the windows of the White House does not seem to trouble our leaders' sleep. They lead the most idealistic nation in history, but they are themselves without idealism. Fear, division and the death of hope: These are the fruits of Republican [Party] rule.

At Democratic National Convention,
New York, N.Y., July 13/
The New York Times, 7-14:(A)12.

Edmund G. "Jerry" Brown, Jr.
Candidate for the 1992
Democratic Presidential nomination;
Former Governor
of California (D)

5

The reason why I believe so many people don't vote anymore is because they don't feel that their vote will actually add any difference to their lives—either good or bad. It's just another empty ritual that comes along and they don't want to take part. And I think that's a very damning statement about the state of politics. Now, when everything goes along fine and people are having economic security and opportunity, maybe that voter participation doesn't have the same significance. But when, as we see [in] . . . so many other places in the country, a real decline in opportunity and real hardship and people losing their jobs, then we look to the political system for some kind of redress, for some kind of sustenance and leadership to do what isn't being done.

Campaigning, Merrimack, N.H.,
Jan. 11/
The Washington Post, 3-3:(A)11.

6

[On Arkansas Governor Bill Clinton who is running for the 1992 Democratic Presidential nomination]: I think he has got a big electability problem . . . He's funneling money to his wife's

(EDMUND G. "JERRY" BROWN, JR.)

law firm for state business . . . His wife's law firm is representing clients before the state of Arkansas agencies, his appointees. And one of the keys is the poultry industry which his wife's law firm represents. There's 270 miles of Arkansas rivers that are polluted with fecal coliform bacteria that are unsafe for humans or fish. So it's not only corruption, it's an environmental disaster, and it's the kind of conflict of interest that is incompatible with the kind of public servant that we expect in the President of the United States.

At Clinton-Brown debate,
Chicago, Ill., March 15/
The Christian Science Monitor,
3-19:2.

1

I believe that in this [Democratic] Party we have to divide before we can determine where is our soul here. I mean, what is this Party? Is this a bunch of lollipops for business, lollipops for something called the middle class—or is it about social justice?

Interview/Newsweek, 3-16:28.

2

[Disagreeing with those who say he should stop his attacks on Bill Clinton, his opponent and front-runner in the current Democratic Presidential primaries]: What is this, the [Soviet] Politburo? There is only the candidate picked by the power structure? I'm not the spoiler. Slick Willie's the spoiler. If he gets the nomination, he's going to ruin the whole Democratic Party.

Interview/
The New York Times, 3-23:(A)11.

3

[On Bill Clinton, who is also running for the Presidential nomination]: The thing with Clinton is that you have a scandal a week. He's got everybody fronting for him. I think our own [Democratic] Party chairman does a disservice by telling everyone to somehow cover it up and keep quiet about what's going on with Clinton. The

truth about Bill Clinton is that he's not electable and he's taking the Democratic Party for a ride.

News conference,
Green Bay, Wis., March 27/
Los Angeles Times, 2-28:(A)18.

4

Crisis has been triggered by the collapse of our two-party system. In reality, there is only one party: It's the Incumbent Party. There are, of course, two major political organizations with different names, but at their core they are the same. They share the same world view and they serve the power of the same private interests which, in return, finance the campaigns of both.

The Christian Science Monitor,
4-13:8.

5

Many people in politics and government, they are well meaning men and women. But tragically, most have become captive to a degenerate system, which forces them to rely not on the people, but on those whose money and organized influence is wrongly thought essential to success. I'd rather lose than participate in it.

Speech, Philadelphia, Pa., April 27/
The New York Times, 4-28:(A)10.

6

[On formulating the Democratic Party platform for the 1992 national election]: I want to make sure this process is open, and I don't want to get to [the convention in] New York and see this whole platform a rigged deal, just a lot of verbal cellophane that is wrapped around a [Presidential] candidate [Bill Clinton] who has already been sprinkled with holy water and delivered to the American people packed in ice.

News conference,
Cleveland, Ohio, May 19/
Los Angeles Times, 5-20:(A)16.

7

[On the political popularity of industrialist Ross Perot, who may run for President this year

(EDMUND G. "JERRY" BROWN, JR.)

as an independent]: Because [the major-party] candidates are not representing identifiable constituencies with clear agendas that are really intended to be implemented and will make an impact, our politics has degenerated into gesture, photo opportunity and ambiguous utterances and images that people know are meaningless. Therefore, people are looking for a man on a white horse.

Interview, Albuquerque, N.M.,
May 20/
Los Angeles Times, 5-21:(A)27.

Ron Brown
Chairman,
Democratic National Committee

1

[On the current Democratic primary campaigns]: Frankly, I don't remember a campaign in my lifetime where candidates have been more specific about what their plans are for America, more specific in laying out economic recovery plans for America—some of them in books, all of them in major papers, saying exactly what they would do. A lot of folks involved in politics think they're being too specific, opening themselves up to criticism that this [Bush] Administration would never open itself up to, because this Administration isn't about leading, isn't about spending political capital to do what's in the interest of the nation but rather about hoarding political capital, not about providing leadership to the people of this country.

Before American Federation of Teachers,
Washington, D.C., March 17/
The Washington Post, 3-19:(A)26.

2

[On the popularity of industrialist Ross Perot, who may run for President this year as an independent]: I think there is an irrational obsession with Ross Perot. Ross Perot has not yet faced one voter in one state [primary]. He hasn't had anybody run against him yet. He's gotten a virtual free ride. Nobody can seriously run for President of the United States when voters know little or nothing about him and don't know what his stands are on issues. We're just moving to a new stage in this contest, where tough questions will be asked and answers ought to be expected.

June 2/
The Washington Post, 6-3:(A)15.

Patrick J. Buchanan
Political commentator;
Candidate for the
1992 Republican
Presidential nomination

3

[On charges that he is racist, sexist, anti-Semitic and homophobic]: Look, there are people who don't like me. Who *really* don't like me. Who feel that Pat Buchanan has to be kept away from wherever the power lies . . . They are going to keep hammering me and hammering me and hammering me for the rest of my life. People want me to apologize, and other folks want me to crawl. But I wasn't raised that way.

Interview, New Hampshire/
Los Angeles Times, 2-6:(A)12.

4

[On his strong second-place showing so far against President Bush in the Republican Presidential primaries]: We didn't have $50-million and Air Force One and all the surrogates and the attack ads and all those kennel-fed conservatives up in Washington. We just had . . . Asphalt One [his campaign bus]. We are winning because we got energy and we got ideas and we got vision and they got none. We are fresh and they are tired and they are yesterday and we are tomorrow.

Campaigning,
Atlanta, Ga., March 3/
Los Angeles Times, 3-4:(A)10.

5

If the Republican Party doesn't get back to the conservative views and conservative values in 1992, and they stay a one-party government with Democrats and Republicans conspiring with one another and collaborating with one another against the national interest of the American

(PATRICK J. BUCHANAN)

people, then in 1996 you will have a brand-new third party. I guarantee you that.

> *To young voters, Midland, Mich.,*
> *March 14/*
> *The New York Times, 3-16:(A)12.*

1

Anti-Communism was really the glue that held [the Republican Party] together. Now that issue has faded away. It's like Alexander the Great's death now—suddenly his generals are dividing up the empire. And the great coalition that elected [former President Ronald] Reagan is cracking apart . . . [President] George Bush is the last of the World War II generation, and I think he is still living in a sense in the past. I mean, they're not going to keep 150,000 troops in Germany. It's just not going to happen.

> *Los Angeles Times, 7-4:(A)22.*

Barbara Bush
Wife of President
of the United States
George Bush

2

[On critics of her husband]: The ugly scapegoating that divides our country is the problem, not the solution. Budget-busting spending is the problem, not the solution. Political posturing is not governing, and naysaying is not leadership.

> *Speech,*
> *Peterborough, N.H., Jan. 23/*
> *The Washington Post, 1-24:(A)8.*

3

Character's an issue [in election campaigns] if you're talking about cheating, lying, deceiving, maybe not keeping vows—I don't know, those are important things. But you don't come out when there's no proof and you don't smear good men and good women when there's no proof. That's just ugly, and it's not all the news that's fit to print.

> *Interview/Newsweek, 8-24:27.*

George Bush
President of the United States

4

[On the 1992 Presidential-election campaign]: I'm certainly going into this as a dog-eat-dog fight, and I will do what I have to do to be re-elected.

> *Newsweek, 1-13:17.*

5

I think the two-party system has really given us the most stable political system in the world. And, yes, we're going through an unusual period [when independent businessman Ross Perot tops both Bush and Democratic frontrunner Bill Clinton in polls for this year's Presidential election]. But the two-party system has provided us fantastic historical stability. And you look around the world and compare this system with any other democratic system, and I think that would avail. I'm sure the Brits take great pride in their Parliamentary system. But I think our two-party system has provided us with the stability that heretofore we've simply taken for granted. So my view, as the campaign unfolds, as all of us spell out our position on the issues, people are going to recognize that, and the two parties will be strong when this election is over.

> *News conference,*
> *Washington, D.C., June 4/*
> *The New York Times,*
> *6-5:(A)10.*

6

[Saying he is not being given proper credit, in this election year, for his accomplishments as President]: We had [Russian President Boris] Yeltsin standing here in the [White House] Rose Garden, and we entered into a deal to eliminate the biggest and the most threatening intercontinental ballistic missiles—the SS-18s of the Soviet Union—and [in the country] it was almost, "Ho-hum, what have you done for me recently?" . . . [On the economy,] there is a gap between reality and perception, and part of my job when I do get into a [re-election] campaign mode is to try to close that gap and be sure that we are judged on reality, not on these erroneous perceptions that are being portrayed in the political process.

To agricultural journalists,
Washington, D.C.,
June 30/
The New York Times, 7-1:(A)10.

1

[On industrialist Ross Perot's decision not to run as an independent candidate for the Presidency this year]: Today I have a message for anyone who supported Ross Perot, and any American who identifies with that frustration that brought them together: I hear you, and you've come through loud and clear. I hear the voices, in so many accents, say that attention must be paid to our jobs, our schools, our families. Attention must be paid to our future. And I hear that call. And more than that, I share your frustration.

Jackson Hole, Wyo., July 17/
The New York Times, 7-18:9.

2

[On why he should be re-elected this year]: Because I think I've been a good President in difficult times. I think [the people] know me to be a man of honor and integrity. I think they've seen that our leadership has helped change the world. And I think they'll recognize that my appeal is a good one: Now help me change America . . . I've tried to serve with a sense of decency. I think people look at that. I think we've tried to talk about family values. We try to live them. We talk about my caring, and I do. And I think those things come through . . . I think [the American people] say, "Hey, these times have been rough, but the President's doing his best, and I disagree with him on this or that, but he's a good man."

Interview, Washington, D.C./
The Atlantic, August:28.

3

I have been trying [to stand] up against the one institution that hasn't changed for 38 years: the Democratically controlled House of Representatives—and also the Senate, [Democratically controlled] except for six. My opponent [Presidential candidate Bill Clinton] is out there talking about change, change, change. And yet the one thing that is blocking significant change—change the way the American people want it, whether it's in education or a strong crime bill or whatever—is an old-thinking United States Congress.

Interview, Aug. 4/
USA Today, 8-5:(A)9.

4

The [Democratic Party] leadership in Congress made a calculated decision—certainly this is true for the last year—that they were going to deny my getting passed the domestic initiatives that I am convinced would have helped this economy long before now. It was purely partisan. For the most part, they wanted to impose on me certain things I said I oppose philosophically . . . In a [Bill] Clinton [his opponent in this year's Presidential election] Administration, we'd have a repeat of the [former President] Jimmy Carter years. Clinton has made so many promises to so many different people, changed his position on so many things that I think we'd have a repeat of the misery index going right through the roof and into outer space. We ought to try something that hasn't been tried in a long, long time. That is: a Republican President, whose values, policies are much more in accord with the American people, and give those policies a chance by changing control of the House and Senate [to Republican].

Interview/
U.S. News & World Report,
8-17:20,21.

5

[On Bill Clinton, Bush's Democratic opponent in this year's Presidential election]: The minute you start to define Clinton's record, they call it "negative campaigning." And I'm not going to be deterred by that. [The Clinton side has] been dishing it out for nine months. Now they are going to have an opportunity to take it [from the Bush side]. It's not so much [my] anger as it is the determination to set the record

(GEORGE BUSH)

straight. He hasn't begun to see anything hard-hitting like he's going to see.

Interview/
U.S. News & World Report,
8-17:21.

1

The Democratic leaders of the United States Congress don't like our [Administration] ideas. They are the sultans of the status quo. They are the only people in America who could drive to work with a blindfold every morning because they've been going the same way, controlling that Congress for 38 years. You're darn right. You talk about gridlock [in government]. We know where the gridlock is: It's under those leaders that control the Congress, both the Senate and the House, and we're going to change it . . . I am going to take that message to change the Congress all across the country. I've held out my hand to those crazy guys—I've held out my hand to them only to have it bitten off. And I'm tired of it.

At rally, Houston, Texas, Aug. 17/
The New York Times, 8-18:(A)6.

2

[1992 Democratic Presidential nominee Bill] Clinton and Congress know that you've caught on to their lingo. They know when they say "spending" you say "oh, oh." So now they have a new word: "investment." They want to "invest" $220-billion more of your money—but I want you to keep it. Governor Clinton and Congress want to put through the largest tax increase in history, but I won't let it happen. Governor Clinton and Congress don't want kids to have the option of praying in school, but I do. Clinton and Congress don't want to close legal loopholes and keep criminals behind bars, but I will. Clinton and Congress will stock the judiciary with liberal judges who write laws they can't get approved by the voters.

At Republican National Convention,
Houston, Texas, Aug. 20/
The New York Times, 8-21:(A)16.

3

[On this year's Presidential election]: I'm going to win. Nobody believes that, but it's the truth. I'm very confident I'm going to win, not over-confident. And the reason is I think what I've done and what I want to do for this country will prevail. And I think also I've demonstrated I can make tough decisions. And the people are going to say, "Who do you trust to do those things?" That's why I have this rather quiet confidence in the face of some of the darndest criticism I've ever seen.

Interview, Washington, D.C./
Time, 8-24:24.

4

My agenda keeps faith with the crusade we called the Reagan Revolution. It will decrease what government must do, and increase what individuals may do. It shows what the differences are in the 1992 election. Two candidates [he and Democratic Presidential opponent Bill Clinton]. Two philosophies. Two agendas. A Grand Canyon of a divide. On the one hand—the left hand, naturally—stands my opponent. A man who started in politics with the McGovern campaign, a politician nearly all of his adult life, a man who has known virtually no avocation beyond getting elected. On the other hand, you're looking at a man proud to have spent half my life in the private sector, built a business, met a payroll. From my own experience, I know that [former President] Ronald Reagan had it right: "The American people aren't under-taxed, the government in Washington is over-fed."

At rally, Anaheim, Calif., Sept. 13/
The New York Times, 9-14:(A)14.

5

[On his Presidential opponent Bill Clinton's anti-war activities during the Vietnam war]: I think it's wrong to demonstrate against your own country or organize demonstrations against your own country in foreign soil [England, when Clinton was at Oxford University]. I just think it's wrong. Maybe they say, well, it's a youthful indiscretion . . . But demonstrating—it's not a question of patriotism. It's a question of character and judgment . . . I just find it impossible to understand how an American can demonstrate against his own country in a foreign land, organizing demonstrations against it, when young [American] men are held prisoner in Hanoi [Vietnam] or kids out of the ghetto were drafted. Some say, well, you're a little old-fashioned. Maybe I am, but I just don't think [what Clinton did was] right . . . How could you be Commander-in-Chief of the armed forces and have some kid say when you have to make a tough decision as I did in Panama or in Kuwait, and then have some kid jump up and say, "Well, I'm not going to go. The Commander-in-Chief was organizing demonstrations halfway around the world during another era."

At Presidential candidates' debate,
St. Louis, Mo., Oct. 11/
The New York Times, 10-12:(A)12.

1

The other night, on character, [Democratic Presidential nominee] Governor [Bill] Clinton said it's not the character of the President [that's important], but the character of the Presidency. I couldn't disagree more. Horace Greeley said that the only thing that endures is character. And I think it was [Supreme Court] Justice [Hugo] Black who talked about great nations like great men must keep their word. And so the question is, who will safeguard this nation? Who will safeguard our people and our children?

At Presidential candidates' debate,
East Lansing, Mich., Oct. 19/
The New York Times, 10-20:(A)15.

2

[Saying Democratic Presidential nominee Bill Clinton waffles on issues]: [On the proposed North American Free Trade Agreement, he says,] "On the one hand it's a good deal, but on the other hand I'd make it better" . . . You can't do that as President. You can't do it on the [1991 Persian Gulf] war, where he says, "Well, I was with the minority [in Congress against the war], but I guess I would have voted with the majority."

This is my point tonight. We're talking about two weeks from now you've got to decide who's going to be President. And there is this pattern that has plagued [Clinton] in the primaries and now about trying to have it both ways on all these issues. You can't do that . . . He says, "On the one hand I'm for it—on the other I may be against it."

At Presidential candidates' debate,
East Lansing, Mich., Oct. 19/
The New York Times, 10-20:(A)13.

3

[On the record of Arkansas Governor Bill Clinton, his Democratic opponent in this year's Presidential election]: Arkansas ranks 50th in the quality of environmental initiatives, 50th in the percentage of adults with college degrees, 50th in percentage—per capita spending on criminal justice, 49th in per capita spending on police protection. And Governor Clinton said the other night, "I want to do for the country what I've done for Arkansas." We cannot let him do that.

Campaigning,
Kannapolis, N.C., Oct. 21/
The New York Times, 10-22:(A)1.

4

[On his re-election loss to Bill Clinton]: It's very important that we not be begrudging during the transition . . . Let us all finish the job with the same class with which we served. I [leave] without bitterness, without hindsight and without regret.

To his Cabinet,
Washington, D.C., Nov. 5/
USA Today, 11-6:(A)5.

Patrick Caddell
Political strategist

5

Politics is disconnected from the country. We were already seeing signs of protest in 1990—[unconventional political candidates like] David Duke, Dianne Feinstein, Clayton Williams and Bernie Sanders were all supping out of the same pot. And it wasn't about ideology. For the last 25 years, the politicians in this country have pre-

(PATRICK CADDELL)

sided over a decline, and it is impossible for them to acknowledge it. Because to change, to turn the country toward what has to be done, they would first have to tell the truth. And to do that would be to risk their own power, because, in a democracy, that means standing up and saying, "We have failed." And the track record of people who do that is not very good. So the Democratic Party lives a lie, the Washington Establishment lives a lie: "Nothing's really wrong. Don't worry about the $400-billion deficit. Just elect us."

Interview, Los Angeles, Calif./
Los Angeles Times, 4-5:(M)3.

Jimmy Carter
Former President
of the United States

1

[On industrialist Ross Perot, who is considering running for the Presidency as an independent this year]: Eventually, he's going to have to let the American people know what he stands for. He can't hide all the way through the season when people are actually going to be addressing him as a potential leader of our nation. He's been evasive so far, deliberately so. He brags on the fact that he doesn't get specific about what he's going to do about anything. He either doesn't have ideas clearly in mind now or he is ashamed and doesn't want to share his ideas with the public because they might be unpopular. I think that can go on only so long.

News conference,
Atlanta, Ga., May 20/
The New York Times, 5-21:(A)11.

James Carville
Senior strategist,
Bill Clinton's 1992 Democratic
Presidential-election campaign

2

[On President Bush]: He reeks of yesterday. He will do anything except trade wives to get re-elected. He has a mouth like a catfish. He can talk out of both sides and whistle out the middle at the same time.

Interview, New York, N.Y./
The New York Times, 7-16:(A)9.

3

[Saying the Clinton campaign can't rest on its laurels even though it has a sizeable lead in the polls with the election a couple of weeks away]: We have to go out and work hard every day. In the poultry business, when you sit on an egg it hatches. In the political business, you sit on a lead and it rots.

USA Today, 10-19:(A)5.

Robert P. Casey
Governor of Pennsylvania (D)

4

[Criticizing the Democratic Party for its pro-choice abortion stance]: I just made the decision I'm not going to remain silent any longer, because there is a litmus test for [Democratic] Presidential candidates [to be pro-choice] and I think it's destructive and self-defeating for the national Party. If you're pro-life [anti-abortion], you don't qualify. You can be a Mayor, you can be a Congressman, you can even be a Governor; but just go away, don't talk about it.

Washington, D.C., April 22/
The Washington Post, 4-23:(A)16.

5

[On Bill Clinton, frontrunner for the 1992 Democratic Presidential nomination]: We have to recognize reality. The primary process is not producing someone who has a good crack at winning in November . . . We've got a tiny minority of Democrats voting for Bill Clinton, and he's winning every [primary] race without generating any sparks, any enthusiasm, any momentum . . . People have a tremendous unease about him. He's got a tiny, fly speck of support . . . Maybe he can turn this around; I hope he can. But if he can't, convention rules provide for the selection of an alternative candidate. Let's pick a winner.

Interview, Philadelphia, Pa.,
April 23/The New York Times, 4-24:(A)1.

Torie Clarke
Press Secretary for
the re-election campaign
of President George Bush

6

[On whether Patrick Buchanan, who has been running against President Bush for the 1992

(TORIE CLARKE)

Republican Presidential nomination, will be allowed to speak at the upcoming Republican National Convention]: He has to get down on his hands and knees and grovel on broken glass with his mouth open and his tongue hanging out—and then we'll talk.

Newsweek, 6-15:17.

1

[On why probable independent Presidential candidate Ross Perot does not have as much support among women as he does among men]: The theory is that women tend to find him a little bit erratic, a little bit unpredictable, a little bit scary. Chicks don't like that.

Newsweek, 6-22:21.

Alan Clem
Professor of political science,
University of South Dakota

2

[On the public's judging of political candidates]: This is meant to be the age in which politics is essentially image, not issues, not ideology, not political parties. So we want to know not only if this guy has a nice smile and a good haircut, we want to know purely personal things, from his marital record to his military record. A war record, I think, is part of a candidate's *vita,* in the same way our students at the university fill out their *vitae* and have to identify the important things they've done in their lives. A war record is simply one of the things you look for.

Los Angeles Times, 3-5:(A)16.

Bill Clinton
Governor of Arkansas (D);
Candidate for the 1992
Democratic Presidential nomination

3

[On questions being raised about his integrity and past indiscretions]: [Americans] have a right to be worried about being lied to. But there's not a single shred of evidence in my public career that

I've been dishonest. Even people who dislike me would tell you that I wouldn't take a nickel to see the cow jump over the moon. I'm getting a little sick and tired about being asked those kinds of questions.

Interview, New Hampshire/
U.S. News & World Report,
2-10:35.

4

One of the things I've learned in this business is make your own strategy, try to stick to it, hope for the best, assume the worst, and go on.

Interview, March/
The New York Times, 11-5:(B)3.

5

[On his victories in the South in the Super Tuesday primaries]: The people of the South heard the worst about me but they saw the best. They know that the true measure of character in politics can never be perfection, because, if it were, no one could pass. The true measure is genuine commitment that lasts day in and day out, through failures and disappointment and defeat and setback.

Campaign speech,
Chicago, Ill., March 10/
Los Angeles Times, 3-11:(A)12.

6

[On accusations by Democratic Presidential rival Jerry Brown that Clinton's wife's law practice benefited from his being Governor of Arkansas]: Let me tell you something, Jerry. I don't care what you say about me . . . but you ought to be ashamed of yourself for jumping on my wife. You're not worth being on the same platform with my wife . . . Jerry comes here with his family wealth and his $1,500 suit and makes a lying accusation about my wife. I never funneled any money to my wife's law firm—never!

At Clinton-Brown debate,
Chicago, Ill., March 15/
The Washington Post, 3-16:(A)11.

(BILL CLINTON)

1

[Criticizing Jerry Brown's campaign against him for the Democratic Presidential nomination]: He's got nothing to lose. He'll say anything. He's always been one of these guys who would hurt anybody, say anything, think only of himself . . . He can be a lightning rod for whatever resentments are out there.

Broadcast interview/
"MacNeil-Lehrer NewsHour,"
PBS-TV, 3-20.

2

[On those who have questioned his character and ambition in running for President]: If I were dying of ambition, I wouldn't have stood up and put up with all this crap I've put up with over the past six months. I'm tired of snotty-nosed remarks [questioning his character]. That's bull and I'm tired of it. I've had about enough of this. I have listened to all these attacks, attacks, attacks on me that's just a bunch of bull. Don't you understand that one of the problems in this country is we all devalue each other? We've got to go back to putting some value on the integrity of people's lives.

Campaigning,
New York, N.Y., March 26/
USA Today, 3-27:(A)4.

3

Abraham Lincoln said that a house divided cannot stand. [But] we have been gripped by a politics which says, "As long as a house is divided, we get re-elected, so what do we care?" The wreckage of that political theory can be seen every time a child is shot or stabbed in a school, every time a neighborhood is inflamed over ethnic division or racial strife.

At New York Historical Society,
March 27/
The New York Times, 3-28:8.

4

If I become President, we will keep a glatt kosher kitchen in the White House.

Before Council of Jewish Organizations
of Borough Park, Brooklyn, N.Y.,
March 29/The New York Times, 3-31:(A)12.

5

[Saying he wants his wife, Hillary, to play a major role in his Administration if he wins the Presidency in November]: I think what we will do if I am the nominee and if I am elected, we will try to decide what it is she ought to do, and then discuss it with ourselves and then tell the American people, and give them time to get adjusted to it . . . I would hope that the American people would support that, because I certainly would want her involved in some very clear and high-level way . . . I'll sure try to get her in there at some high level. But you've got to get me in first before I can get her in.

Campaigning, Milwaukee, Wis.,
March 30/
The Washington Post,
3-31:(A)6.

6

[On the day's Democratic Presidential primaries in New York, Kansas and Wisconsin, all of which Clinton won by varying degrees]: Tonight every person who voted in the Democratic primary—every person—voted for change. Every vote for Jerry Brown was a vote that recognized the power of technology through his first-derided and now-respected 800 [phone] number, that the power of technology can give dignity to ordinary people and can give the average voter a say. Every vote for Paul Tsongas tonight was a vote for change—a vote that respected his courage in getting into this race when [President] George Bush was at over 70 per cent in the approval polls, a vote that recognizes these are serious economic problems we face that require a serious response. Tonight, I ask you to reach out to those who did not vote for me but voted for change. We want to be their campaign, too. From Manhattan, Kansas, to Manhattan Island, people said tonight: "We want Americans to be able to earn a decent living, to walk on safe streets, to educate their children and to have them do better than they did. We want our country to win again and to be one again."

Primaries victory speech,
New York, N.Y.,
April 7/
The New York Times, 4-9:(A)11.

(BILL CLINTON)

1

The truth is that I've gotten a little bit of a bum rap on this [personal] character issue. Maybe some of it was of my own making. I'm not sure when I got into this race I understood that there would be a different set of rules applied now than in any previous Presidential campaign, and perhaps applied to me [more] than any other Presidential candidate. I'm doing the best I can to be as candid as I can about every relevant issue with the American press and the American people. I've done a good job in my public life, I believe character is very relevant in this election and I believe that as the issues are raised and the campaign unfolds, the American people will feel that Bill Clinton has the character to be President.

To National Association of
Hispanic Journalists,
via satellite from Columbus, Ohio,
April 24/
The Washington Post, 4-25:(A)18.

2

[On possible Presidential candidate, industrialist Ross Perot]: I think as we go along, he'll have a hard time being elected without being able to answer everything on where he stands on the issues. And if he hates Washington so much, what is his relationship with the United States Congress? Has he, in fact, lobbied and made vast contributions to Congressmen to get special deals for himself through the Congress? . . . He'll have a contribution to make. But he's been as political as anybody else has been . . . The best thing to be in American politics today is famous and totally unexamined.

Columbus, Ohio, April 24/
The New York Times, 4-25:8.

3

I've watched the Republicans divide our country in election after election with the politics of division and denial and destruction. And they are good at it. They're better at it than we [Democrats] are. Let's 'fess up. We're not near as good [at] destroying people as they are.

Campaigning, San Diego, Calif., May 18/
The New York Times, 5-20:(C)19.

4

I refuse to let this [Democratic] Party be boxed into the categories of the past which have killed us repeatedly in Presidential elections . . . I believe we can be pro-business and still pro-labor. I believe we can be pro-growth and pro-environment. I think we can be tough on crime and pro-civil rights. I think we can be pro-family and pro-choice [on abortion].

Broadcast question-and-answer forum,
Pittsburgh, Pa., June 11/
The Washington Post, 6-13:(A)12.

5

[On the ill-will between President Bush and Ross Perot, the industrialist who is a probable independent candidate for President this year]: It's obvious that you've got two people here who just can hardly bear each other, they can't stand each other and they've turned this thing into a kind of personal vendetta. That's fine with me . . . I think the American people can see that here are two people who really intensely dislike each other. It's obvious that they've got an almost obsession with one another. I'll let them play it out. I'm going to get out here to fight for the people.

Boston, Mass., June 25/
The Washington Post, 6-26:(A)18.

6

[On his choice of Senator Al Gore to be his Vice-Presidential running mate]: I asked [my Vice-Presidential selection committee] to look for a candidate who met three tests. I said I wanted a Vice President who really understood what had happened to ordinary Americans in the last 12 years, someone who was committed to making government work again for the average, hard-working American families. I said I wanted a Vice President who would complement me and my own experiences and bring other experiences, knowledge and understanding to our common endeavor. And above all, I said I wanted a Vice President who would be ready, should something happen to me, to immediately assume the office of President of the United States.

News conference, Little Rock, Ark.,
July 9/The New York Times, 7-10:(A)8.

(BILL CLINTON)

1

I think a lot of this personal stuff [criticism by his opponents of his private behavior] can be way overblown. I've been reclined on the national couch. In some ways this obsession with the personal, to a far greater extent than in any Presidential campaign in history, is partly because people can't imagine what an effective Presidency would be like anymore. They don't know how to believe government can make a difference in their lives, so let's just vote on all this personal stuff. If you do that, you may wind up voting for somebody who's either lucky or dishonest . . . Questions of *public* character ought to be the keystones of this [Presidential] election. If you look back in history, our best Presidents were not blameless but were subject to a totally different standard and demonstrated public character, a commitment to certain things that got done that made a difference. So I don't mind discussing all this. But there is certainly no reward for being candid.

Interview/
U.S. News & World Report,
7-20:36.

2

One reason I ran for President this year is I knew that I wasn't obsessed with winning it anymore. I didn't want to get into the race when the only thing in the world was winning. I think that's one of the things that's killing [his opponent, President] Bush. He says, "I'll do whatever it takes to win" . . . If you look at how Presidents have to live today, anybody that would turn down the life I've got for the life I'm going toward just to hold the job would be nuts. The only purpose of having the job [of President] is to change the country. When I got into this race, I realized, well, I'm going to do the very best I can. And if I get taken out, I'll find something else to do. You may only be fit to be President when you're not obsessed with it.

Interview/
U.S. News & World Report, 7-20:30.

3

I have been more trustworthy as a political leader than [President Bush] has. I kept more of my commitments than he has. If I were George Bush, I wouldn't be out here running on trust, not after "Read my lips [no new taxes]" and "I promise you 15 million new jobs." [The Republicans] can't re-elect *him,* so they want to defeat *me.* You're dealing with people who basically have no soul, no passion for this country, no concern, whose only desire is to stay in power and the only way they know how to do it is destroy other people. These are very cynical, manipulative people.

Interview, Little Rock, Ark./
Newsweek, 7-20:28.

Bill Clinton
Governor of Arkansas (D);
1992 Democratic
Presidential nominee

4

The choice you face [in the coming Presidential election] is clear. [President] George Bush talks a good game. But he has no game plan to compete and win in the world economy. I do. He won't take on the big insurance companies to lower costs and provide health care to all Americans. I will. He won't streamline the Federal government and change the way it works; cut 100,000 bureaucrats and put 10,000 more police on your streets. I will. He never balanced a budget. I have; eleven times. He won't break the stranglehold special interests have on our elections and lobbyists have on our government. I will. He won't give mothers and fathers a chance to take some time off from work when a baby's born or a parent is sick. I will. He doesn't have a commitment to keep family farms in the family. I do. He hasn't fought a real war on crime and drugs. I will. He won't crack down on polluters, clean up the environment and take the lead on creating jobs in environmental technologies. I will. He doesn't have [Democratic Vice-Presidential nominee Senator] Al Gore. I do. And he won't guarantee a woman's right to choose [abortion]. I will.

Accepting the Presidential nomination at
Democratic National Convention,
New York, N.Y.,
July 16/
The New York Times, 7-17:(A)12.

183

WHAT THEY SAID IN 1992

(BILL CLINTON)

1

Your plan and my plan—let us be clear—do not involve liberal versus conservative, left versus right, big government versus little government. That's a load of bull we've been paralyzed with for too long. Your plan and my plan are about big ideas versus old ideas . . . You know, sometimes you've got to change just to survive. Change is the law of life. Change is necessary to preserve our basic values. Change today is the order not just for people who think of themselves as liberal—that is, open and reaching out and inclusive—but for people who think of themselves as conservatives. How can you conserve the basic values, how can you conserve the fabric of your life if you do not have the courage to change when what you're doing is tearing the heart out of your country?

Before National Urban League,
San Diego, Calif., July 27/
The New York Times, 7-28:(A)9.

2

Four years ago, this President [Bush] promised 15 million new jobs, no new taxes and a kinder and gentler nation. But most important, he promised to be President, to accept responsibility. The mission was an America "moving forward, always forward." Four years later, we're moving backward. We are not moving forward, always forward, and all Mr. Bush has to offer is the politics of blame and more of the same . . . Beyond the trust issue, beyond the broken promises, beyond the bad economic policies, underneath all this is an even more fundamental issue—that is the failure of the President to accept responsibility for the future of this country.

To group of his supporters,
New Orleans, La., July 29/
Los Angeles Times, 7-30:(A)21.

3

[Criticizing the Bush Administration's behavior in the current Presidential campaign]: These people are desperate to hold onto the White House. They cannot imagine what life would be like if they didn't have Camp David and they didn't have the dinners at the White House and they didn't have all the perks and the power of the Presidency. The national Bush crowd thinks it belongs to them. They will do anything to hold it.

Detroit, Mich., Aug. 21/
The Washington Post, 8-22:(A)12.

4

[On the controversy surrounding his answers to current questions regarding why he did not serve in the military during the Vietnam war]: I think I could have handled it [answering the questions] a lot better, but I haven't ever tried to mislead anybody. There were a lot of things that were asked that I honestly couldn't remember, and I was dumbfounded at the way it was being treated, largely because I had been in so many campaigns here [in Arkansas] when so many more people who were there and who remembered what happened were around and it was fresh in their memories and no one ever suggested anything wrong was done. It's been very frustrating to me, and I'm sure to the people.

Broadcast interview,
Little Rock, Ark., Sept. 14
The Washington Post, 9-15:(A)8.

5

[Criticizing his Presidential opponent, President Bush, for questioning his anti-war activities during the Vietnam war]: You [Bush] have questioned my patriotism. You even brought some right-wing Congressmen into the White House to plot how to attack me for going to Russia in 1969-1970 when over 50,000 other Americans did. Now, I honor your service in World War II . . . and the service of every man and woman who ever served, including Admiral [William] Crowe who was your Chairman of the Joint Chiefs [of Staff] and who is supporting me. But when [the late Senator] Joe McCarthy went around this country attacking people's patriotism, he was wrong. He was wrong. And a Senator from Connecticut stood up to him named Prescott Bush. Your father was right to stand up to Joe McCarthy. You were wrong to attack my

(BILL CLINTON)

patriotism. I was opposed to the [Vietnam] war but I love my country.

At Presidential candidates' debate,
St. Louis, Mo., Oct. 11/
The New York Times, 10-12:(A)12.

1

[On a suggestion that Arkansas is too small a state to qualify him as experienced enough to be President]: I think [being Governor of Arkansas is] highly relevant; and I think that a $4-billion budget, with state and Federal funds, is not all that small. And I think the fact that I took a state that was one of the poorest states in the country and had been for 153 years and tried my best to modernize its economy and to make the kind of changes that had generated support from people like the presidents of Apple Computer and Hewlett Packard, and some of the biggest companies in this country, 24 retired Generals and Admirals and hundreds of business executives are highly relevant . . . [And] the people who have jobs and educations and opportunities that didn't have them 10 years ago don't think it's irrelevant at all.

At Presidential candidates' debate,
East Lansing, Mich., Oct 19/
The New York Times, 10-20:(A)12.

Bill Clinton
Governor of Arkansas (D);
President-elect of the United States

2

[On his winning the recent Presidential election with a large electoral-vote count but only a popular-vote plurality]: In terms of whether I got a mandate or not, having a 100-vote electoral majority more than you need is not too bad. There are only a couple of Democrats in this century who've gotten a bigger percentage vote. But arguably, the greatest President we ever had, Abraham Lincoln, was elected with under 40 per cent of the vote. So I think the American people will all now evaluate what I do and whether I do it well and whether they support it.

News conference,
Little Rock, Ark., Nov. 12/
The New York Times, 11-13:(A)8.

Hillary Clinton
Wife of Arkansas Governor
and 1992 Democratic
Presidential candidate Bill Clinton

3

Bill's candidacy stands for something bigger than him. That is the overriding message to me, that this is not just about letting Bill Clinton live in the White House. If that was all this was about, I wouldn't be working as hard as I'm working. [In a political campaign,] people can overlook and ignore a whole lot of stuff that is thrown out into the atmosphere if they view it as irrelevant, tangential and just downright stupid and nasty. If you don't have a view of the world that is bigger than yourself, if the only reason that you're doing something is to fulfill your own personal ambition, then you can't sustain a campaign against that kind of concerted campaign [by your opponents]. I think we're ready on all those counts.

Interview/Newsweek, 2-3:23.

Ernesto Cortes
Director, Texas division,
Industrial Areas Foundation

4

Politics is best done by groups of people. They've got to become involved, they've got to take some ownership. They can't do it by themselves. They've got to do it in connection with some other institutions, with a church, or neighborhood association. They need to understand that, until we restore an appreciation for and an understanding of politics, we're in big trouble. And what politics is about is not electing candidates; it's about debate and discussion. Politics is those decisions that have to do with how you allocate resources.

Interview/
The Christian Science Monitor,
7-7:14.

Mario M. Cuomo
Governor of New York (D)

5

President Bush cannot tell you he will deliver anything because, even if he were to win [re-election this year], he has to face a Democratic

WHAT THEY SAID IN 1992

Congress. [But Democratic Presidential candidate Bill Clinton can say,] "If I win, here's the outlines of the health-care bill they're going to pass the first day I'm there. Here's the urban agenda . . . When I win, they pass it, I sign it." You have effective government for the first time in years and years and years. If he [Bush] wins, you're right back to where you are, everybody running around in wild circles, achieving nothing.

To reporters, Washington, D.C./
The Christian Science Monitor,
5-22:3.

1

I think that what Americans desperately want [in Presidential candidates] is sweet strength. They want someone who is very strong and very sure and throws off that self-assured confidence of his own truth. But they want it to be sweet. They don't want it to be ugly. They don't want it to be antagonistic. They don't like negatives. We've got to make this a positive, sweet-strength campaign. You don't run against [probable independent Presidential candidate Ross] Perot. You don't run against President Bush. You do run against policies. But you have to finish your talk by saying: "Here's what we do that's positive."

Interview/
The Christian Science Monitor,
6-9:18.

Robert Dallek
Professor of history,
University of California,
Los Angeles

2

[On Bill Clinton, candidate for the 1992 Democratic Presidential nomination]: This is a man who passionately wants the White House. My sense of Clinton is that he has demonstrated a kind of strength and durability that reminds me of people like [former Presidents Lyndon] Johnson and Richard Nixon, and even Franklin Roosevelt. These are people who go through the wringer and then pop back up ready to do battle again.

Los Angeles Times, 3-19:(A)14.

John C. Danforth
United States Senator,
R-Missouri

3

I am upbeat about the future of the Republican Party. The [recent] Presidential election [in which Democrat Bill Clinton was elected] was a vote for change. It wasn't a vote against core Republican principles, nor was our loss an endorsement of the Democratic Party. It should be noted that Governor Clinton took care to associate himself as often as possible with Republican themes, including American leadership in the world, a responsible national defense, holding the line on taxes and not going back to tax-and-spend policies. The first rule for the GOP is, therefore, don't panic. The Republican message is sound. The way to revive the Party's position is to sharpen and clarify the core messages.

Interview/
USA Today, 11-19:(A)13.

Walter De Vries
Director,
Institute of Political Leadership

4

[On politicians who lie to the public]: You don't know you're being misled until after [it's happened]. I think there is a difference between the intent to deceive, making a mistake and admitting it, or deciding I'm just going to lie about this particular thing. These are all different shades. But I think anybody in politics who engages directly in telling a lie and knows it consciously [has] got to be pretty stupid to do that, and I'm not even talking about the morality or ethics of it.

Interview
The Christian Science Monitor,
2-20:12.

John Patrick Diggins
Author, Historian

5

The New Left was the most influential of all the radical movements in this century. It played a central role in awakening America's consciousness to poverty, racism, the fragility of the

(JOHN PATRICK DIGGINS)

environment and the exclusion of women. Moreover, I believe that the war in Vietnam would have dragged on indefinitely had there not been opposition in the streets [of the U.S.] instigated by the New Left. Yet the movement never felt that it achieved very much, probably because its expectations were so high . . . The one area where I have deep reservations about the impact of the [New] Left is in the academy [the schools]. Many in the "lyrical" as well as the Old Left believed in the value of classical education and in the future of Western civilization. But many in the academic [New] Left think that classical education is elitist and that Western civilization is oppressive to the rest of the world.

Interview/
U.S. News & World Report,
7-20:59.

John DiIulio, Jr.
Professor of politics and public affairs,
Princeton University

1

There is always a gap between voter anger picked up on surveys and how voters actually behave. I don't believe in the House elections in 1992 that you're going to have any massive change in the control of the House. Everybody hates Congress, but loves their Congressman.

The Christian Science Monitor,
4-9:7.

Linda DiVall
Republican Party
political analyst

2

[On the better-than-expected showings for commentator Patrick Buchanan against President Bush in the primary elections for the 1992 Republican Presidential nomination]: The message here is not that people want to support Pat Buchanan [and his conservative views]—when you look at the exit polls, he's getting almost the same support from liberals, moderates and conservatives. What people are demanding of President Bush is leadership and a sense of what direc-

tion he's going to take his Presidency. Voters don't want to keep hearing [from Bush], "I got your message." They want to hear what the President is going to do.

The Washington Post, 3-5:(A)24.

Robert J. Dole
United States Senator,
R-Kansas

3

[Criticizing a Democratic Party proposal for public financing of election campaigns]: The last thing the American people want to hear from Washington is a bunch of incumbent politicians demanding even more money from the taxpayers so they can stay in office. Take your political tin cup to the taxpayers on that one and see what you come back with. My guess is, a black eye and a fat lip.

April 3/
The Washington Post, 4-4:(A)4.

4

The Republican Party is not on life-support and does not need to be "revived" [following its loss of the Presidency in the recent election]. The Republican Party was *not* wiped out at the polls on Election Day. We gained seats in the House, held our own in the Senate and made dramatic gains in state legislatures across America . . . [But] we must continue to broaden the base of our Party. It doesn't take a wizard to determine that we're not going to win elections if we create litmus tests for Party membership. But don't get me wrong—while we must be inclusive, we can't lose our mainstream identity in the process. There is no appetite in America for a flavorless political party. I'm confident our Party's best days are yet to come.

Interview/USA Today, 11-19:(A)13.

Robert K. Dornan
United States Representative,
R-California

5

[Saying President Bush must start his re-election campaign soon and forcefully to counter

(ROBERT K. DORNAN)

Democratic opponent Bill Clinton who is leading in the polls]: We may have a Catch-22 here, where the advisers are not asking the President to lead any charges and the President's not ordering them to create any battle plans and we just sit there on a mountaintop and watch the Clinton forces occupy village after village that we're going to have to retake once the combat starts.

The New York Times, 7-30:(A)8.

Michael S. Dukakis
Former Governor
of Massachusetts (D);
1988 Democratic
Presidential nominee

1

[On 1992 Democratic Presidential nominee Bill Clinton's use of bus trips as opposed to flying during his campaigning]: The bus trips pep you up. There's nothing that dulls you more than that plane routine. Being out there in small-town America with folks and real people [on a bus] is better. In a plane, you're down and you're up, you're up and you're down; you look out a window, you're not seeing townspeople, you're looking at air. And let me tell you, it's boring and it's dulling.

Interview, Boston, Mass./
The Christian Science Monitor,
9-30:9.

Alan Ehrenhalt
Executive editor,
"Governing" magazine
(published by
"Congressional Quarterly")

2

[On politicians who lie to the public]: We agree to buy the Brooklyn Bridge from politicians. They keep selling it to us because we're willing to buy it . . . [Politicians] never say, "I'm not sure there is a solution to that problem." There are many problems in which . . . there are no easy solutions. No politician likes to say, "Look, our state's 49th out of 50 in all important economic indicators. If I do the best possible job, maybe we

can be 48th in four years" . . . All that [then-President Richard] Nixon had to do at some point in the [Watergate scandal] process was say, "Look, we really made a terrible mistake. There was a burglary, and I found out about it." I think it really would have been accepted. People will put up with all sorts of personal failings as long as people tell the truth.

The Christian Science Monitor,
2-20:12.

Susan Estrich
Professor of political science,
University of Southern California

3

[On the possibility that there will be two women U.S. Senators from California after this year's election]: The old conventional wisdom was people wouldn't vote for any woman; the new conventional wisdom is they will only vote for one woman. This comes from the conventional way of looking at politics, which says it's a man's game . . . The assumption is women are so unique and disfavored that the most you can expect is people will vote for one. I'm not sure it's true for male voters, and I'm pretty sure it's not true for women voters.

Los Angeles Times, 5-27:(A)12.

Amitai Etzioni
Sociologist,
George Washington University

4

[The "liberal" and "conservative" political labels] are outmoded. When it comes to freedom of speech, enforcement of law, public safety, the family and schools, we find it better to talk about "authoritarians" who want to impose their moral solution on everybody, "libertarians" who oppose any voice other than that of the individual, and "communitarians" who want new moral standards reached through consensus.

Interview/
USA Today, 4-23:(A)13.

Mervin D. Field
Director, the California Poll

5

[On Jerry Brown, candidate for the 1992 Democratic Presidential nomination and former

(MERVIN D. FIELD)

Governor of California]: The perfect spot for Jerry Brown would be the Senate. The Senate needs to be shaken up. He'd be 1 in 100. He wouldn't hurt the government process. He'd shake things up without having disproportionate power . . . I see in Jerry two conflicting streaks. He's a real political animal. He knows politics and goes for the jugular. But he's also a real seminarian. He wants to save souls. A lot of politicians make 180-degree turns, but Jerry is "the 180-degree kid." All politicians have to be chameleons. But Jerry stretches the definition to the limit. When I contemplate the possibility [of a Brown Presidency], I almost get apoplectic—it would be a disaster. He's so mercurial, so changeable, so extreme. All that comforts me is the fact that it won't happen.

Interview/
The New York Times, 4-2:(A)15.

1

There may be a strong desire among women to elect more women to higher office, but I'm not sure it is a compelling desire. In the final analysis, for women and men, the chief criteria will be competence and whether a candidate is aligned with the voters' views.

Time, 5-4:35.

Gerald R. Ford
Former President
of the United States

2

[On the imminent entry of popular industrialist Ross Perot into the Presidential race as an independent]: What worries me . . . is that on election day not one of the three [Presidential candidates] will get the 270 electoral votes, which is essential to become President, and then the race or selection for President will go to the House of Representatives, where we have 50 states, and each state gets one vote. Alaska gets one vote, Delaware gets one vote, California with 52 Congressmen gets one vote; that could be a real Constitutional crisis, because the three candidates there also have to get a majority, the

50 votes, and you can't tell at this point—you could have a lot of very difficult decisions made by the newly elected Congress.

Broadcast interview/CNN-TV, 5-20.

J. William Fulbright
Former United States Senator,
D-Arkansas

3

The country's very fortunate to have someone with [President-elect and Arkansas Governor] Bill Clinton's ability. When I was young, we [in Arkansas] used to say, "Thank God for Mississippi," because it was the only state poorer than we were. But economic conditions are much better, relatively, than they used to be, and I think Clinton deserves much of the credit. He's been a good Governor. He's very bright. When he gets to the White House, he'll use his head.

Interview, Washington, D.C./
The Christian Science Monitor,
11-27:14.

Curtis B. Gans
Director,
Committee for the Study
of the American Electorate

4

[On the current downward trend in voter turnout on election day]: There are a lot of factors: the conduct of our campaigns; the weakening and lack of clear advocacy of the political parties; the lack of anticipation, and responsiveness, perceived by the people, of government. Things like "Read my lips [no new taxes]"—and then new taxes. People doubt their leaders will deliver on their promises once elected . . . We're different from 20 or 30 years ago when there were a lot of pillars of the party in Congress. That has a lot to do with the consultant revolution and the decline of the political parties. Now we have a politics of free-lance operatives rather than a politics of any sort of collective leadership. Advocacy is determined by polling rather than by values. Our politics is suffering from that.

Interview/
USA Today, 3-12:(A)7.

WHAT THEY SAID IN 1992

Jack Germond
Political columnist,
"The Baltimore Sun"

1

[On the current trend of Presidential candidates appearing on TV call-in shows rather than facing media questioners]: The difference clearly is the voter doesn't have the fund of knowledge to ask detailed follow-up questions. That is why candidates like these formats, and I don't blame them.

Los Angeles Times, 6-13:(A)15.

Newt Gingrich
United States Representative,
R-Georgia

2

I believe the [1992] Democratic [Presidential] nominee will by the end of the [primary and nomination] process be a surprisingly effective person, or he wouldn't have been nominated. The process, which I think is actually pretty healthy, of not having an immediate front-runner, but instead having to work their way to nomination, actually will strengthen the final nominee. They will be better known, they will be more tested, their skills and their teamwork will be better.

Interview,
Washington, D.C., Feb. 27/
The Christian Science Monitor,
2-28:3.

3

[On political commentator Pat Buchanan, who is running for the 1992 Republican Presidential nomination]: Buchanan's view of the ethnic mix of America is explicitly and totally wrong; I would vehemently repudiate it. Buchanan's view of [trade] protectionism and isolationism is explicitly wrong, and I would repudiate it. He does not represent the future of the conservative movement. He represents a personality. I don't in any way take him seriously for 1996. Because once you examine Buchanan and not ask the question, "Do you want to send [President] George Bush a signal?" but instead ask the question, "Is this a future that America is capable of achieving?" I don't think there is 8 per cent of the

American people who would consider his vision of the future one that is workable.

To reporters, Washington, D.C./
The Christian Science Monitor,
3-10:18.

4

[In this election year,] there's an anti-incumbent, anti-Washington, very significant vote out there. The burden of proof used to be on the challenger, but now the burden of proof is on the incumbent.

USA Today, 8-6:(A)4.

Barry M. Goldwater
Former United Senator,
R-Arizona;
1964 Republican
Presidential nominee

5

[On President Bush's re-election defeat in the recent Presidential election]: [Bush ran] a hell of a bad campaign . . . If he had continued to campaign after the [1991] war in the Persian Gulf, he would have won [re-election], but he quit campaigning. He had a bunch of idiots in the White House advising him . . . A party is good for about 20 years and then they run out of people and they run out of money. And that's about where the Republican Party was a year ago, but they didn't realize it.

Broadcast interview/
"Good Morning America,"
ABC-TV, 11-17.

Lugenia Gordon
President,
Freedom Republicans

6

[Saying blacks are not represented enough in important Republican Party positions]: We are ignored—as if we didn't exist, as if Abraham Lincoln didn't exist, as if Frederick Douglass didn't exist. We want the Federal Election Commission to hold back every dime of the money it gives to the Republican National Committee until blacks are more fairly represented in the Party.

The New York Times, 4-8:(A)9.

Albert Gore, Jr.
United States Senator,
D-Tennessee

1

Our founders talked openly about posterity. But in politics today, if you stand on a podium and express concern about what's going to happen in 200 years, it doesn't strike many sparks.

Interview, Washington, D.C./
Los Angeles Times, 2-6:(E)5.

Albert Gore, Jr.
United States Senator,
D-Tennessee;
1992 Democratic
Vice-Presidential nominee

2

[The Bush Administration has] had their chance and they have failed. They have taxed the many to enrich the few. It is time for them to go. They have given us false choice, bad choices and no choice. It is time for them to go. They have ignored the suffering of those who are victims— of AIDS, of crime, of poverty, of hatred and harassment. It is time for them to go. They have nourished and appeased tyrannies and endangered America's deepest interests while betraying our cherished ideals. It is time for them to go. They have mortgaged our children's future to avoid the decisions they lack the courage to make. It is time for them to go. They embarrassed our nation when the whole world was asking for American leadership in confronting the environmental crisis. It is time for them to go. They have demeaned our democracy with the politics of distraction, denial and despair. It is time for them to go. The American people are disgusted with excuses and tired of blame.

Accepting the Vice-Presidential nomination
at Democratic National Convention,
New York, N.Y., July 16/
The New York Times, 7-17:(A)13.

3

If we [he and Democratic Presidential nominee Bill Clinton] win [the election], we will change the psychology of how this country views the future and how we work together as a nation toward common goals in far less than 100 days [in office]. We will start doing that on Day One, and you will see a burst of productive activity throughout that 100-day period.

Interview/
Time, 10-19:36.

Lewis L. Gould
Historian, University of Texas

4

[On industrialist Ross Perot's sudden decision not to run for the Presidency as an independent this year after encouraging his many supporters]: He stared American politics in the eye and he blinked . . . For a man who started out to reduce the disillusion in American politics, instead he compounded it. Like many businessmen, he thought it would be easy. He found out that politics is a profession and it takes a great deal of skill to go through the agony these people go through. We expect them [politicians] to have the skin of a rhinoceros. He had the skin of a butterfly.

Los Angeles Times, 7-24:(A)26.

Paul Green
Director,
Institute for Public Policy,
Governors State University

5

[President Bush has kept his promises] as well as any candidate. [Political election] campaigns are basically competing wish lists. Whether you like him or dislike him, he basically hasn't changed. He's what he said he would be. He has done as well as expected. He has basically done a satisfactory job.

Interview/
The New York Times, 6-25:(A)12.

Judd Gregg
Governor
of New Hampshire (R)

6

The public does not trust the President, the Congress, the two parties—and I think they are right. Both parties have fallen in love with this miserable game of politics.

At truckers forum/
The New York Times, 10-1:(A)16.

Tom Harkin
United States Senator,
D-Iowa

1

[Saying he will support whoever is the Democratic nominee for President in this year's election]: I will pay any price, bear any burden, learn to speak Greek [if Paul Tsongas is nominated], develop a Southern accent [if Bill Clinton is nominated], or learn to wear a turtleneck [if Jerry Brown is nominated] to insure that a Democrat is elected President in 1992.

On his withdrawal from the race
for the nomination,
Washington, D.C., March 9/
The New York Times, 3-10:(A)16.

Gary Hart
Former United States Senator,
D-Colorado

2

[On Bill Clinton and Paul Tsongas, who are running for the 1992 Democratic Presidential nomination]: Within the Democratic Party, there is always an establishment party and an anti-establishment party. Bill managed in late 1991 to become the establishment candidate, and Paul, running an insurgency out of sheer necessity, has now become, rather by default, the non-establishment man.

Interview,
Moscow, Russia, March 4/
The New York Times, 3-5:(A)10.

Peter Hart
Democratic Party
public-opinion analyst

3

[Saying he doesn't think the 1992 Presidential-election campaign will be different from 1988

when it comes to candidate evasions, dishonesty and "negative campaigning"]: I always used to believe that there was a pendulum that swung from negative to positive. I've come to believe there's no such thing as a pendulum anymore. It continues to swing one way, and the American public never says enough is enough.

The Washington Post, 1-2:(A)6.

Michael A. Hess
Deputy chief counsel,
Republican National Committee

4

[On charges that minority groups are not represented enough in important Republican Party positions]: It's the failure of minorities to participate in the Party that accounts for their relatively low numbers in the [national] convention and the Republican National Committee. Any representative body reflects the pool from which it is selected. The Republican Party has been actively and aggressively seeking participation by blacks, Hispanics, Asian-Americans and members of other minority groups.

The New York Times, 4-8:(A)9.

Stephen Hess
Senior fellow,
Brookings Institution

5

This is the year in which women started to reach their rightful rung on the political ladder. It's not the year of the women because of . . . Anita Hill [who brought allegations of sexual harassment against Supreme Court Justice-designate Clarence Thomas last year]. It's the year of the women because they've served their apprenticeships.

USA Today, 11-4:(A)3.

Jack Hilton
Political consultant

6

[On Jerry Brown's low-spending campaign for the 1992 Democratic Presidential nomination]: In making it possible for someone to run for President without a massive treasury, Jerry

(JACK HILTON)

Brown may be a trailblazer . . . Because of his shoestring campaign, Brown has availed himself of every opportunity in TV and radio, returning phone calls and getting his messages across for nothing, which is clever as hell. He calls talk-radio stations. He finagles himself on the air. He has never shunned a camera crew here in New York for the last two weeks.

New York, N.Y./
Los Angeles Times, 4-4:(F)1.

Ellen Hume
Executive director,
Barone Center on the Press,
Politics and Public Policy,
Harvard University

1

[On attacks on the personal character of Democratic Presidential candidates Bill Clinton and Jerry Brown]: Clinton and now Brown are being killed by a thousand cuts without anyone ever pretending to look at the whole record. Is marital infidelity as important as policies [of the Bush Administration] that have led to the savings-and-loan debacle? I don't understand why this country's afraid to talk about what is really at stake in this election. We're constantly sidetracked on character issues that no President—not F.D.R., not Richard Nixon, certainly not Jack Kennedy or Lyndon Johnson—could have endured.

The New York Times, 4-13:(A)9.

Molly Ivins
Political columnist,
"Fort Worth (Texas)
Star-Telegram"

2

[On Presidential-election campaigning in the South]: The operating assumption seems to be that all Southerners are slack-jawed, slope-browed ridge runners and you must talk to them very slowly in words of one syllable and play to their well-known prejudices. You must, of course, promise to have a strong national defense, coura-geously defend traditional family values and

promise never to raise taxes under any circum-stances. But look at who won five Southern states on Super Tuesday in 1988: [black civil-rights leader] Jesse Jackson, which is logical since it makes no sense. With Southerners, you just never know.

Interview/
USA Today, 3-9:(A)9.

3

If you set aside the war in Vietnam . . . [the late President] Lyndon Johnson undoubtedly would have gone down as one of the greatest Presidents in the history of this country. And Lyndon Johnson could not have passed any character test devised by the human imagination.

Interview, Austin, Texas/
The Christian Science Monitor,
11-2:13.

4

[On 1992 independent Presidential candidate industrialist Ross Perot]: It may be yet another symptom of our political decline that a man who's never been elected to anything by any-body was at one point leading in the polls for the Presidency based on six appearances on televi-sion. If that doesn't strike you as weird, it probably should . . . This is a man who's bought his way into the election. If Perot were, instead of being a multibillionaire, just your standard right-wing millionaire car dealer from Kansas City, we'd all think he was the greatest joke in the world.

Interview, Austin, Texas/
The Christian Science Monitor,
11-2:13.

Jesse L. Jackson
Civil-rights leader

5

[On his decision not to run for the 1992 Democratic Presidential nomination]: I don't see this as stopping my run for the Presidency. We went around the track twice. Now we're changing our tires and getting a bigger motor. Now instead

193

(JESSE L. JACKSON)

of running for President, I'm running to change the environment for politics in the country.

Interview/
Mother Jones, Jan.-Feb.:15.

1

There has been a real obsession [by Democratic Presidential candidate Bill Clinton's campaign] with regaining the white conservative vote. But it takes two wings to fly. [Black voters] are crucial for the Democratic Party because in the South there are more white Republicans than there are white Democrats. The only reason the Party has not become extinct in the South is the black vote. So it is, in fact, a vote that must be respected.

Interview,
Washington, D.C., July 9/
Los Angeles Times, 7-10:(A)29.

2

We [minority-group voters] have a lot riding on [1992 Democratic Presidential nominee Bill] Clinton and the people surrounding him. We have no such leverage on the Republican side. There are many who feel they are without . . . sufficient enthusiasm, and they're in this anybody-but-[President] Bush frame of reference. [They feel] that we may not like this or that tactic [by the Democrats] but we must defeat the Reagan-Bush cycle. The success the [Clinton] ticket is now enjoying [in the polls] has a lot to do with economic conditions more than [party] strategy.

Interview, Sept. 24/
The Christian Science Monitor,
9-25:3.

Sharon Pratt Kelly
Mayor of Washington, D.C.

3

There's enormous frustration with the status quo. I think there's [a] gut-level feeling amongst the American people that things aren't working right, that the last thing we need is a traditional politician—somebody who tries to figure out which way the winds are blowing. People [want someone] who will speak up based upon conviction, whether you agree with them or not. Very often women, particularly, are perceived as a part of that new order, because we've not been invited into the corridors of power in the past. But you'll see it at many levels. Independent candidates all across this country will hold a new attraction for the American people, because people know that we are a morally unanchored nation now, and that we need people to speak, driven on the basis of conviction, rather than what's politically smart.

Interview, Washington, D.C./
Los Angeles Times, 6-14:(M)3.

Jack Kemp
Secretary of Housing
and Urban Development
of the United States

4

I don't think conservatism should be allowed to be portrayed as bashing Japan, bashing Mexico, bashing immigrants, bashing Israel, bashing the poor or bashing low-income people for the problems of America. A country can't base leadership on a negative. It's not what you are against that determines what you are—it is what you are for.

Los Angeles Times, 7-4:(A)23.

Edward M. Kennedy
United States Senator,
D-Massachusetts

5

[Supporting proposed legislation that would require election ballots and materials to be provided in various languages for specific minorities who speak little or no English]: Those who oppose this legislation think it will lower the incentive for Americans to learn English. That is just plain wrong. Bilingual elections do not promote separatism but instead help to integrate non-English-speaking minorities into our democracy.

Los Angeles Times, 8-8:(A)11.

Bob Kerrey
United States Senator,
D-Nebraska;
Candidate for the 1992
Democratic Presidential nomination

1

In the Republican Party, [Vice President] Dan Quayle and President Bush are trying to distance themselves from [Republican Presidential candidate David Duke, who has a racist background]. Well, they've been watering that tree for the last 24 years with hatred and divisive rhetoric, talking about quotas, talking about race as if this nation should not strive to provide equal opportunity for all of us! And now that tree has borne the fruit of David Duke, and in this campaign we'll make sure that Americans understand that if your policy is based upon hatred, that hatred indeed is what you'll yield.

At fund-raising party,
Los Angeles, Calif./
Vanity Fair, January:131.

2

[On Arkansas Governor Bill Clinton, who is running for the 1992 Democratic Presidential nomination]: I will tell you today, Bill Clinton should not be the nominee because he will not be able to win [the Presidential election this fall]. This is a truth that is largely unspoken. But it is a truth almost universally believed. [Against the Republicans,] I think he is going to get opened up like a soft peanut.

At Spelman College,
Atlanta, Ga., Feb. 26/
Los Angeles Times, 2-27:(A)1.

Laurence J. Kirwan
Former chairman,
New York State
Democratic Party

3

[On the current Democratic Presidential primary campaign between frontrunners Bill Clinton and Jerry Brown]: Thousands of people you'd have hoped to have energized and involved in this campaign just aren't there, because it's a failure. There's great disillusionment with a process that brings us a Brown and a Clinton as the choice. People have no confidence that that's the best the Democratic Party has to offer, and they feel let down. Brown's an anybody-but-Clinton candidate, and Clinton is rapidly dissipating all the big advantages he started with. [Clinton says he once smoked but] didn't inhale marijuana! If my son told me that, I'd tell him, "Come on, you've got to get serious."

The New York Times, 4-4:8.

Everett Ladd
Professor of political science,
University of Connecticut;
Executive director,
Roper Center for Public
Opinion and Research

4

When I talk about Presidential candidates, I sometimes talk about Class I, Class II and Class III candidates . . . A class I candidate is someone who enters the campaign as a major, established national figure. I'm not talking about incumbent Presidents. Ronald Reagan in 1980 had established that kind of major position. Class II candidates are people who have substantial national followings and who have been thought about for some time in terms of the Presidency. I would think George Bush in 1980 as a Class II candidate or Walter Mondale in 1984 . . . This [the 1992 Presidential campaign] is the first campaign in modern American life, at least since the New Deal, in which a major party [the Democrats] has entered into the campaign without one contender for its nomination who's a reasonably established national figure.

Interview/
USA Today, 1-14:(A)11.

W. Anthony Lake
Foreign-policy adviser to
1992 Democratic Presidential
candidate Bill Clinton;
Former Director
of Policy Planning,
Department of State
of the United States

5

In the 1970s and 1980s, every four years [at election time] we refought the Vietnam war

(W. ANTHONY LAKE)

within the [Democratic] Party. Every position a candidate took was a victory for either the conservative wing or the liberal wing. With the end of the Cold War, those ideological arguments are finally over. This means the center has widened enormously—in the Party and in the country—and we want to keep expanding that middle.

The New York Times, 3-28:8.

Ann F. Lewis
Former political director,
Democratic National Committee

1

If a woman runs for Governor and says, "I'm gentler, nicer and like children better [than a man]," she sounds as if she's running for day-care supervisor. On the other hand, what she can say is, "I know what real life is like. I know what budgets are like, what it is like to pay hospital bills and try to make ends meet. And when I go to the Governor's office, I'll bring that knowledge with me."

The Atlantic, July:65.

Theodore Lowi
Political scientist,
Cornell University

2

There is a dirty little secret that sophisticates have been hiding from the masses for three or four decades. The secret is that the two-party system is dying. [It] has failed to make the adjustment to the requirements of modern, 20th-century democratic government.

The Christian Science Monitor,
7-13:3.

G. Terry Madonna
Director, Center for Politics
and Public Affairs,
Millersville (Pa.) University

3

Abortion is not and never has been a salient [political] issue in this state [Pennsylvania] . . . If *Roe v. Wade* [the Supreme Court ruling

upholding abortion rights] is overturned completely, that would be a different story, here and nationwide. But in two straight polls, the last one this week, abortion makes hardly a blip when you ask open-ended questions about what matters most. Pennsylvanians put jobs first. The economy in general comes after that, then health care, then education.

The New York Times, 4-27:(A)10.

Thomas E. Mann
Director of governmental studies,
Brookings Institution

4

[On Bill Clinton emerging as the frontrunner for the 1992 Democratic Presidential nomination]: It was a very weak field of Democratic candidates. But easily the most qualified and able . . . emerged as the apparent nominee. That says something about the good sense of the American people. As for [President] Bush, what you see is what you get. He has never been a great visionary. He is smart, able, decent, but has no great mission other than doing the right thing. So the choice is between someone who wants to do the right thing [Bush] and someone who wants to do what the voters want [Clinton]. It's not so awful.

The Christian Science Monitor,
3-25:4.

Lynn Martin
Secretary of Labor
of the United States

5

The [Republicans] can be a majority party . . . We should be reaching out to young women and men who see a changing world and want confidence in our ability to focus on the future. We need to represent those fighting to own a home or business and those who have worked to enjoy retirement. We need Americans who are selecting a variety of roles in their lives and respect that they, like all of us, will have a variety of beliefs on perplexing and often contentious issues. So, we can be elected as Republicans, whether we're pro-life or pro-choice [on abortion], as long as we're pro-people. We must pursue ideas power-

(LYNN MARTIN)

fully and clearly so that Americans know we are on their side and can deliver what we promise.

Interview/
USA Today, 11-19:(A)13.

Bob Martinez
Director, Federal Office
of National Drug Control Policy

1

[Criticizing probable independent Presidential candidate industrialist Ross Perot]: This nation didn't gain a hard-won victory in the Cold War only to surrender its Constitutional liberties to a secretive computer salesman with a penchant for skullduggery.

At U.S. Conference of Mayors,
Houston, Texas, June 23/
The New York Times, 6-24:(A)10.

Bill McInturff
Republican Party
public-opinion analyst

2

The painful secret is it's very hard to hold the Republican coalition [together] during a tough economy [when there is a Republican President]. The Republican coalition of the '80s was built on economic good news, and it frays very hard around the edges in a tough economy.

USA Today, 1-16:(A)6.

Gordon McQuillen
President, Wisconsin
American Civil Liberties Union

3

[Saying David Duke has the right to be on Republican Presidential primary ballots, even though the Party rejects him because of his racial views]: As far as we know, a person becomes a Republican by saying, "I'm a Republican." We don't know of any formal procedures that the Republican National Committee has for expelling a person from the Party. If that were possible, the RNC, which presumably favors the incumbent President, could declare [Presidential candi-

date] Pat Buchanan was not a Republican and obviate the need for primaries anywhere . . . [It's] very difficult to argue that [Duke is] not a Republican. I understand they think he's an offensive cockroach, and I may agree with that. But that has nothing to do with the fact that he's an offensive *Republican* cockroach. The Democrats had to deal with George Wallace, [and today] they have to deal with Lyndon LaRouche. That's the nature of the beast.

Interview/
USA Today, 2-5:(A)9.

Adam Meyerson
Editor, "Policy Review,"
the magazine of the
Heritage Foundation

4

It's a long way to [the] November [Presidential election], but at this point many conservatives would not be disturbed by a [Democratic candidate Bill] Clinton Administration because Clinton seems to have moved the Democratic Party back to the center on foreign policy, and because [President] Bush has not yet returned to the [conservative] Reagan economic policies he ran on in 1988.

The Washington Post, 7-29:(A)11.

Robert H. Michel
United States Representative,
R-Illinois

5

[On industrialist Ross Perot, who may run for the Presidency this year as an independent]: Ross Perot is one of the most amazing political phenomena of our time. And in himself, he's not all that important. It's what he represents. He isn't the first, not going to be the last, to say that democracy isn't working and that if you trust me with power I'll solve your problems. That message, sometimes sinister, sometimes just downright silly, has been heard all over the world at various times in this century. That siren call has enchanted good, decent people who are frustrated and disillusioned, and on every occasion, people are attracted to such simplicity and ignorance because of genuine grievances with

197

(ROBERT H. MICHEL)

their government . . . Ross Perot is the wake-up call for all those who believe that democratic government must be made to work and who are willing to spell out the ways it can work, in the old-fashioned American way, before the elections . . . It may turn out that the big story in this campaign is how Ross Perot awakened both political parties, and if so, then I'd say he's done his country a great service.

At Capitol Hill Club Headliner Breakfast,
Washington, D.C., May 21/
The Washington Post, 5-22:(A)25.

Zell Miller
Governor of Georgia (D)

1

[On industrialist and probable independent Presidential candidate Ross Perot]: Sounds to me like, instead of shaking the system up, Mr. Perot's been shaking it down. Ross says he'll clean out the barn, but he's been knee deep in it for years. If Ross Perot's an outsider, folks, I'm from Brooklyn. Mr. Perot's giving us salesmanship, not leadership . . . So the choice [among President Bush, Perot and Democrat Bill Clinton] is clear: We've got us a race between an aristocrat, an autocrat and a Democrat.

At Democratic National Convention,
New York, N.Y., July 13/
Los Angeles Times, 7-14:(A)14.

George J. Mitchell
United States Senator,
D-Maine

2

I've said hundreds, probably thousands of times that I believe the Democratic Party did well nationally when it was in fact and was perceived as the party of economic growth and of opportunity . . . Without exception, every step toward creating opportunity, reducing discrimination, breaking down barriers in this country, in this century, has been instigated by Democrats who passed legislation frequently, not always, frequently over Republican opposition.

Interview, New York, N.Y./
The Christian Science Monitor,
7-17:6.

Walter F. Mondale
Former Vice President
of the United States;
1984 Democratic
Presidential nominee

3

[On popular 1992 independent Presidential candidate Ross Perot]: It's alarming to me that this man could skip most of the accepted methods of determining a candidate's readiness to be President. Perot didn't run in any primary. He avoided the experienced and seasoned reporters in the field and appeared only on entertainment talk shows of his choosing. He used a mountain of money and double-speak to try to make it appear that he was selected by the people. It's almost Orwellian in proportion.

The New York Times, 11-3:(A)10.

Sheffield Nelson
1990 Republican nominee
for Governor of Arkansas

4

[On 1992 Democratic Presidential nominee Arkansas Governor Bill Clinton, against whom he ran for Arkansas Governor in 1990]: [If Clinton wins the Presidency this year,] you're going to be, just quite truthfully, buying you a dope-smoking, draft-dodging womanizer; and if that's what the people want to head this country, it's an indictment of the United States of America.

USA Today, 10-30:(A)11.

Richard M. Nixon
Former President
of the United States

5

Politics is the greatest sport there is. It's competitive. People win, people lose, people come back.

Broadcast interview/C-SPAN, 2-23.

Peggy Noonan
Former speechwriter for
President of the United States
George Bush

6

Sound bites are less relevant [during the Presidential election campaigns] this year than

(PEGGY NOONAN)

anybody knows yet, because the American people have become so sophisticated in the ways of politics and the media. When Harold and Mary sit back watching the Democrats debate and one of them says something short and pithy and strong, Harold will not say to Mary, "What a great leader he'll make." He'll say, "What a great sound bite." They'll be impressed by the candidate's technique, that's all. And that's not enough.

The New York Times,
1-23:(A)10.

1

[On President Bush's re-election defeat this year]: He was a doomed President because he simply misunderstood, as a pol with ego, what had happened to him in [his election in] 1988. He thought that the American people elected him resoundingly in a landslide because of his own charming, gallant, ambivalent self. They [really] elected him because of·what he said he was: a continuance of [previous President Ronald] Reagan-ism.

Nov. 4/
The New York Times, 11-5:(B)5.

Michael Osborn
Professor of communications arts,
Memphis (Tenn.) State University

2

The most striking statements and forms of [political] rhetoric are no longer verbal, they are now visual. Much of the art of modern political campaigning is finding ways to transform verbal forms of expression into visual forms . . . Some people claim that much of the greatness of the speakers in Greece was a product of the high quality of their audiences. As this critical sensitivity develops in our audience, we'll see a response to that in the political campaign utterances on television. Our political rhetoric will become visual as well as verbal.

The Washington Post,
8-20:(A)17.

Ross Perot
Industrialist

3

If voters in all 50 states put me on the ballot—not 48 or 49 states, but all 50—I will agree to run [for the Presidency this year as an independent].

Broadcast interview/
"Larry King Live," CNN-TV, 2-20.

4

[On whether he will decide to run for President this year]: I have no desire to be President. My personal feelings are [that] anybody intelligent enough to be able to do the job would not want the toughest, dirtiest, most thankless job in the world, that is absolutely brutal on your family and everybody you love. [But] it's up to the people.

Broadcast interview/
"This Week With David Brinkley," ABC-TV, 3-22.

5

[On his possible run for the Presidency this year]: I didn't realize the system was so rotten. The thing that leaps out at you as a newcomer is that the process to select a President is totally irrelevant and disconnected from selecting a good person. It has everything to do with sound bites, whispers and innuendo.

Interview, April/
The New York Times, 7-17:(A)15.

6

[On the kind of campaign he would wage if he decided to run for President this year]: If you ever see me doing photo opportunities, have me led away. Just put on the front page of your paper, "This guy has lost it" . . . I will not be one of these guys that they wind up in the morning, handing me a speech of the day, giving me these three-by-five cards. You ever see me with one of those, shoot me and call it a mercy killing.

Interview, Dallas, Texas/
The Washington Post, 5-5:(A)4.

7

[On his possible run for the Presidency this year]: We need to worry about how things are and

(ROSS PEROT)

how to make things better and how to fix things and how to correct the mistakes we've made and to leave our children a stronger, better country so that the American dream still exists for them and they can dream great dreams and have those dreams come true. That's worth my spending several very unpleasant, miserable years of my life [as President], after all the good things that have happened to me in my life.

Broadcast interview/
C-SPAN, 5-17.

1

We have a political system that's driven by getting money. Running up and down the halls of Congress all day, every day, are the organized special interests who have the money that makes it possible to buy the television time to campaign to get re-elected next year. There are no villains here. It's just something that has evolved.

Interview, Dallas, Texas/
Time, 5-25:36.

2

[Saying he may come up with a platform if he decides to run for President this year, but he may not implement it as President]: I'm sick and tired of having everybody want to know what my positions are, so it's not for the people. This is for the media, who apparently can't breathe without it [a platform] . . . Democrats and Republicans always have platforms—never implement much from the platform . . . The people want action, not talk.

Broadcast interview/
The Washington Post, 5-29:(A)10.

3

[On criticism of him in connection with his possible run for the Presidency this year]: The part that's the real Silly Putty category is that I'm autocratic and dictatorial. If I treated my people [employees and associates] the way that folks are claiming, they wouldn't stay with me for 10 minutes. Talk to any of the people who've worked

with me, and they'll tell you that I thrive on controversy and debate. I make decisions after a lot of discussion, and my goal is always consensus. What's most unique about me and my companies is that after the process of making a decision, we really focus on execution. I see my mission as solving problems. Leadership is this: Have a goal; have a vision; assemble a talented team; get it done; go on to the next one. These charges that I want to win at any price are dead wrong. I run a very ethical business. In my whole life, I can think of just three or four times I've used private investigators. I never wiretapped anybody. It's a feeding frenzy by the press. I'm interested in what stories will come out next. Tomorrow someone will have me meeting with extraterrestrials.

Interview/
U.S. News & World Report,
6-29:24.

4

[On his decision to pull out of the race for President which he was pursuing as an independent]: Now that the Democratic Party has revitalized itself, I have concluded that we cannot win in November and that the election [would] be decided in the House of Representatives. Since the House of Representatives does not pick the President until January, the new President will be unable to use the months of November and December to assemble the new government. I believe it would be disruptive for us to continue our program since this program would obviously put it in the House of Representatives and be disruptive to the country.

News conference,
Dallas, Texas, July 16/
The New York Times, 7-17:(A)15.

Ross Perot
Industrialist;
1992 independent
Presidential candidate

5

[Announcing his candidacy for President after abandoning the idea last July]: I thought that both political parties [Democratic and Republi-

(ROSS PEROT)

can] would address the problems that face the nation. We gave them a chance. They didn't do it. The American people are concerned about a government in gridlock. Our people are good, but our government is a mess . . . Everybody in Washington makes excuses, but nobody takes responsibility . . . We will create a new political climate where the system does not attract ego-driven, power-hungry people.

News conference,
Dallas, Texas, Oct. 1/
The Washington Post, 10-2:(A)1.

1

I think the principal issue that separates me [from his Presidential opponents Bill Clinton and George Bush] is that five-and-a-half million people came together on their own and put me on the ballot. I was not put on the ballot by either [of] the two parties. I was not put on the ballot by any PAC money, by any foreign-lobbyist money, by any special-interest money. This is a movement that came from the people. This is the way the framers of the Constitution intended our government to be, a government that comes from the people. Over time we have developed a government that comes *at* the people, that comes from the top down, where the people are more or less treated as objects to be programmed during the [election] campaign with commercials and media events and fear messages and personal attacks and things of that nature. The thing that separates my candidacy and makes it unique is that this came from millions of people in 50 states all over this country who wanted a candidate that worked and belonged to nobody but them. I go into this race as their servant. And I belong to them.

At Presidential candidates' debate,
St. Louis, Mo., Oct. 11/
The New York Times, 10-12:(A)12.

2

Can we win [the Presidential election]? Absolutely we can win . . . You gotta stop letting these folks in the press tell you you're throwing your vote away [when people vote for him]. You gotta

start using your own head. Then the question is: Can we govern? I love that one. The "we" is you and me. You bet your hat we can govern, because we will be in there together and we will figure out what to do and you won't tolerate gridlock, you won't tolerate endless meandering and wandering around, and you won't tolerate non-performance. And believe me, anybody that knows me understands I have a very low tolerance for non-performance.

At Presidential candidates' debate,
East Lansing, Mich., Oct. 19/
The New York Times, 10-20:(A)15.

3

[On Arkansas Governor and 1992 Democratic Presidential nominee Bill Clinton's qualifications to be President as measured by his being Governor]: Let's put it in perspective. It's a beautiful state; it's a fairly rural state; it has a population less than Chicago or Los Angeles, about the size of Dallas and Fort Worth combined. So I think probably we're making a mistake night after night after night to cast the nation's future on a unit that small . . . It's irrelevant . . . I could say that I ran a small grocery store on the corner, therefore I extrapolate that into the fact that I could run Walmart; that's not true.

At Presidential candidates' debate,
East Lansing, Mich., Oct. 19/
The New York Times, 10-20:(A)12.

4

[Saying he decided not to run for President in July because of reports he received that the Republicans were going to smear his daughter and disrupt her wedding]: I want to spend one minute telling you the reason why I dropped out in July . . . I received a report of a high-level Republican meeting where they said: "We have thrown everything we can make up on Perot and he just keeps going up in the polls. Isn't this guy sensitive to anything?" . . . I got that from a source away from government, and then about a week or 10 days later I got a report from a person very close to the Republican process who said: "Ross, I just cannot tolerate this. I have got to tell

(ROSS PEROT)

you." And it was identical. So I had three flares go up . . . I looked the situation over, and I realized that this was a risk I did not have to take. I could keep my commitment and my adoration to her, and I could keep my commitment to you [the public], and I stepped back . . . I cannot prove that any of that happened. I just got these reports. It was a risk I could not take.

At campaign rally,
Pittsburgh, Pa., Oct. 25/
The New York Times, 10-26:(A)10.

Burton Yale Pines
Senior vice president,
Heritage Foundation

1

[On commentator Patrick Buchanan, who is a candidate for the 1992 Republican Presidential nomination]: If you're taking a look at the starting lineup for [the 1996 Republican Presidential nomination], at who's going to have the funding bases and the grass-roots support, it's only Buchanan and the Vice President [Dan Quayle]. In effect, as of last week Buchanan was really no longer running against [President] Bush [in this year's primaries] but running against all the other contenders in 1996.

Los Angeles Times, 3-28:(A)20.

2

[On President Bush's recent re-election loss]: Many conservatives [warned] Bush that he was heading for re-election disaster. Many conservatives pleaded with George Bush to change course and to re-embrace the "Reaganaut" policies and populism that won three Presidential elections [for the Republicans]. By refusing to do this, George Bush and his White House aides broke faith with America's conservative majority . . . [President-elect Bill Clinton] now has the chance to build a majoritarian Democratic Party, if he realizes that [former Republican President] Ronald Reagan was not a fluke, that there was a conservative tide in the country.

The Christian Science Monitor,
11-12:4.

Samuel Popkin
Political scientist,
University of California,
San Diego

3

There is something worse than money in politics, and that's no money in politics. You have to spend a lot of money to get to the people who don't understand as much, who are busy. It takes a lot more money to get to a single mother than it does to get to . . . the rich and successful [who have] the time to pay attention to everything.

The Christian Science Monitor,
3-5:9.

Dan Quayle
Vice President
of the United States

4

The only real question facing us [conservatives] is whether our President [Bush] will enter the general election campaign [this year] from a position of strength or from a position of weakness. As conservatives, we believe in acting responsibly; and starting today, it is our job to act responsibly to ensure that our conservative President is strong for the fall campaign . . . Let's not allow our movement to be divided [by other conservatives such as Patrick Buchanan, who decided to run against Bush for the Republican nomination]. Let's not allow ourselves to play into the hands of those who wish to weaken the President—the liberal Democrats . . . Today we face a choice of building on 12 years of conservative governance or going back to the old bickering over who is 90 per cent or who is 100 per cent pure.

At Conservative Political Action Conference,
Washington, D.C., Feb. 21/
The Washington Post, 2-22:(A)1.

5

We're [Republicans] accused of having a gender gap that favors males. The Democrats are accused of having a gender gap that favors females. I don't really buy that argument very much. I know that we make a concerted effort to be inclusive, not exclusive. Unless you have it at

(DAN QUAYLE)

exactly 50-50, you're always going to be able to make the argument. I know that our Party includes all, and we are very inclusive, we're not exclusive.

Interview/
USA Today, 4-22:(A)15.

1

[On the possible independent Presidential candidacy of industrialist Ross Perot]: Electing Ross Perot wouldn't fix the deadlock between the elected branches [of government], it would make this worse. So let us return to the tried and true. Let us elect a President—Republican or Democrat—and give him a Congress that responds to Presidential leadership. Give one party the authority and responsibility to govern . . . There's no doubt that [Perot] has tapped into a deep well of frustration in this country. He draws his appeal largely from the claim that he is a man who can "get things done," even if he's reluctant to say exactly what "things" he has in mind—other than nullifying representative democracy with a bizarre scheme of government by polls [electronic gathering of public opinion].

Before Federalist Society,
Washington, D.C., June 12/
The New York Times, 6-13:1,9.

2

[Saying the Republican Party welcomes pro-choice people even though the Party's platform is anti-abortion]: I talk about the "pro-life big tent." I know where I stand; I know where the President [Bush] stands; I know what the platform is going to be. The tent on the abortion issue is pro-life. The overall tent is Republican—you have pro-life Republicans and you have pro-choice Republicans. I am not going to ride people out of the Republican Party who happen to disagree with me on the issue of abortion. In fact, I want them to be included. The Democrats are the ones who are actually excluding pro-life Democrats and making them feel uncomfortable. You ought to go back and take a look at [Democratic] Pennsylvania Governor Robert Casey's recent

speech to the National Press Club. He said, "I am pro-life and I'm feeling very uncomfortable in the Democratic Party." They have a much bigger problem than we [Republicans] do.

Interview/
Christianity Today, 6-22:31.

3

[1992 Democratic Presidential nominee] Bill Clinton talks about "change," but he can't really change America because the special interests won't let him. He can't say a word—not a single word—about legal reform, because the trial lawyers won't let him. He can't support school choice for parents, because the education lobby in Washington won't let him. He will not join the majority of Americans in supporting [Congressional] term limits, because the Democratic Congress won't let him. And he can't fight for the traditional family, because his supporters in Hollywood and the media elite won't let him.

At Republican National Convention,
Houston, Texas, Aug. 20/
The New York Times, 8-21:(A)10.

4

[On questions regarding his and 1992 Democratic Presidential nominee Bill Clinton's not serving in the Vietnam war]: I chose to serve in the Indiana National Guard. Bill Clinton chose not to serve. I answered all the questions that the media put to me in 1988. I answered every single last one of them. Bill Clinton is going to have to answer those questions too.

The Washington Post,
9-3:(A)14.

5

[Saying that, although he has grown in the Vice Presidency since taking office in 1989, the press still covers him as if he were a bumbling neophyte]: Either they haven't seen it or, more importantly, they don't want to see it. There is not one person that's been with me in 1992 since 1988 that says there is not a world of difference. Not one. It's the inability for us to get any kind of fair shake from the media that's been the most frustrating thing about this [re-election] campaign.

Interview/
The New York Times, 10-12:(A)11.

WHAT THEY SAID IN 1992

(DAN QUAYLE)

1

At some time during the next four years, there is going to be a crisis. There will be an international crisis. I can't tell you where it's going to be. I can't even tell you the circumstances, but it will happen. We need a President who has the experience, who has been tested, who has the integrity and qualifications to handle the crisis. [President Bush] has been tested. The President has the integrity and the character. The choice is yours [the voters]. You need to have a President you can trust. Can you really trust [Democratic Presidential nominee] Bill Clinton?

At Vice-Presidential candidates' debate,
Atlanta, Ga., Oct. 13/
The New York Times, 10-14:(A)12.

2

This is a fundamental problem with [Democratic Presidential nominee] Bill Clinton—is trust and character. It is not the issue of how he avoided military service 20 some years ago; it's the fact that he does not tell the truth about it. He first said he didn't get an induction notice; then we find out that he did. He said he didn't have an ROTC slot; then we find out he did. He said he didn't use [then-Senator J. William] Fulbright's office for special influence; then we find out that he did. These are inconsistencies.

At Vice-Presidential candidates' debate,
Atlanta, Ga., Oct. 13/
The New York Times, 10-14:(A)13.

3

[On whether Vice Presidential candidates matter in Presidential elections]: The American people vote for the President. The American people vote for the top of the ticket, where obviously the Vice Presidents . . . can help—they can help with the core constituency out there. [But] the bottom line is, people vote for Presidents, not Vice Presidents.

Interview/Time, 10-19:37.

4

[On President-elect Bill Clinton, who defeated the President Bush-Vice President Quayle re-election ticket in 1992's election]: If he runs the country as well as he ran his campaign, we'll be all right.

The Christian Science Monitor,
11-5:4.

Ronald Reagan
Former President
of the United States

5

I heard those speakers at that other [recent Democratic Party] convention saying "We won the Cold War," and I couldn't help wondering, just who exactly do they mean by "we"? And to top it off, they even tried to portray themselves as sharing the same fundamental values of our [Republican] Party. What they truly don't understand is the principle so eloquently stated by Abraham Lincoln: "You cannot strengthen the weak by weakening the strong. You cannot help the wage-earner by pulling down the wage-payer. You cannot help the poor by destroying the rich. You cannot help men permanently by doing for them what they could and should do for themselves." If we ever hear the Democrats quoting that passage by Lincoln and acting like they mean it, then, my friends, we will know that the opposition has really changed.

At Republican National Convention,
Houston, Texas, Aug. 17/
The New York Times, 8-18:(A)6.

6

To hear the Democrats talk, you'd never know that the nightmare of nuclear annihilation has been lifted from our sleep. You'd never know that our standard of living remains the highest in the world. You'd never know that our air is cleaner than it was 20 years ago. You'd never know that we remain the one nation the rest of the world looks to for leadership. It wasn't always this way. We mustn't forget, even if they would like us to, the very different America that existed just 12 years ago: an America with 21 per cent interest rates and back-to-back years of double-digit inflation; an America where mortgage payments

(RONALD REAGAN)

doubled, paychecks plunged and motorists sat in gas lines; an America whose [Democratic Party] leaders told us it was our own fault, that ours was a future of scarcity and sacrifice and that what we really needed was another good dose of government control and taxes.

At Republican National Convention,
Houston, Texas, Aug. 17/
The New York Times, 8-18:(A)6.

Ralph Reed
Director,
Christian Coalition

1

[On the many victories by conservative Christian candidates in state and local races in this year's elections, despite the fact that Democrat Bill Clinton won the Presidency]: We focused on where the real power is: in the states and in the precincts and in the neighborhoods where people live and work. On the one hand, [President] George Bush was going down to ignominious defeat in a landslide. On the other hand, the anecdotal evidence is that at school boards and at the state legislative level we [conservative Christians] had big, tremendous victories.

The New York Times, 11-21:8.

Leo Ribuffo
Historian,
George Washington
University

2

[Former Democratic President Jimmy] Carter was to the right of [the Democratically controlled Congress] on Capitol Hill. He emphasized efficiency, deregulation, while most of the Democrats wanted to expand the welfare state and national health care. Even if he had been the greatest schmoozer in the world, there would have been problems . . . but he wasn't.

The Christian Science Monitor,
11-13:4.

Felix G. Rohatyn
Senior partner,
Lazard Freres & Company,
investment bankers;
Chairman,
Municipal Assistance Corporation
of New York

3

There are reasons besides winning for running for high office. There's also the challenge of affecting the direction in which the nation is going by laying out an alternative. If tennis players had to win all the time, nobody would go to Wimbledon.

The Washington Post, 1-2:(A)23.

Edward J. Rollins
Co-chairman, National
Republican Congressional Committee

4

My great fear in American politics is that we are going to have an accidental President one of these days. We are going to . . . elect somebody who is very charismatic, who understands the process very, very well, but who has some very significant flaws because he is a total unknown.

To college students, February/
Newsweek, 6-15:17.

Edward J. Rollins
Former co-chairman,
National
Republican Congressional Committee

5

[On the causes of President Bush's re-election defeat this year]: It's him. He's a guy who thought he was a great politician because he had been the national Party chairman and because he knew the name of every national committeeman and state Party chairman. But he never understood what was going on in the country. [Former President] Ronald Reagan was never a state Party chairman and he didn't know the names of any committeemen, but he always knew where the country was.

Nov. 4/
The New York Times, 11-5:(B)5.

Roy Romer
Governor of Colorado (D)

1

We all come at things with our own set of rose-colored glasses. I'm white. I'm Protestant. I'm rural. I'm middle class. So I'm going to see things one way. Someone of a different background can look at the very same circumstances and see it another way. It means [as a politician] you've got to listen very hard to what someone is saying.

Interview, Denver., Colo./
The New York Times, 3-30:(A)8.

Dan Rostenkowski
United States Representative,
D-Illinois

2

The President [Bush] has said that he recants the '90 tax increases. He's sorry that he misled the country, that he said: "Read my lips, no new taxes." I feel bad for the President because I think he becomes weaker and weaker as he changes his mind so often. You know, if you don't have a vision, rent one for a while.

Interview/USA Today, 3-19:(A)11.

Tim Russert
Host, "Meet the Press,"
NBC-TV

3

[On Democratic Presidential candidate Bill Clinton's appearance on a TV show playing the saxophone]: The candidates have decided that they prefer to communicate in an unfiltered way, more their personality than their positions on issues. But in the long run, there is no substitute for discussing the tough issues they're going to have to handle as President. If people really thought you could get elected by playing the saxophone, there would be a lot more musicians running for President.

June 4/
The New York Times, 6-5:(A)12.

Robert Rutland
Former historian,
University of Virginia

4

Of the two [political] parties, the Democrats are still the party of individual liberties . . . The

key is that the Party has remained tied to the old moorings of getting a better deal for the common man. Farmers who were in debt and city people who had few possessions could both look to the Democratic Party and find help.

The Christian Science Monitor,
7-13:4.

Larry J. Sabato
Professor of government,
University of Virginia

5

The debate to abolish PACs is the most nonsensical debate in the modern era. If we abolish them, industry, labor and trade groups will merely find other ways of using their influence.

The Christian Science Monitor,
3-5:11.

6

[On Bill Clinton, Governor of Arkansas and candidate for the 1992 Democratic Presidential nomination]: I don't think any candidate has ever had more brickbats thrown at him for less reason than Clinton [has had during the current Presidential primary campaign]. Some of them are ridiculous, and some of them are accurate but give a distorted picture because they only focus on a small piece of his record. The average reader or viewer could be excused for believing that Bill Clinton was among the worst and sleaziest of American Governors. But scholars who have studied Governors' records—I did a book looking at 300 of them myself—will tell you that he's easily in the top 10 per cent. Whether or not you like him or his politics, it's unfair that the casual viewer is reaching a conclusion that is precisely the opposite of the truth.

The New York Times, 4-2:(A)14.

Oscar Luigi Scalfaro
President of Italy

7

Nothing does greater harm to democracy than the turbid brew of politics and business. To get involved in politics, it is not enough to have a

(OSCAR LUIGI SCALFARO)

clean criminal record. One's dealings must be transparent.

Before Italian Parliament,
Rome, Italy, May 28/
The New York Times, 5-29:(A)4.

Arthur M. Schlesinger, Jr.
Historian

1

The [Democratic Party] has held together because it has remained a party of outsiders against the party of business [the Republicans]. What [its factions] have had in common is the notion that business shouldn't run the country.

The Christian Science Monitor,
7-13:4.

Alan K. Simpson
United States Senator,
R-Wyoming

2

[Saying the press should pursue and question Ross Perot, popular industrialist who may run for the Presidency this year, just as they have done with President Bush and Democratic Presidential candidate Bill Clinton]: Give this guy what you've given Bush for 12 years and what you've given Clinton for 12 months, and he'll begin to shrivel like squashed vines in the wintertime.

Broadcast interview/
USA Today, 5-29:(A)13.

3

[Arguing against proposed legislation that would require election ballots and materials to be provided in various languages for specific minorities who speak little or no English]: I fear that what we're doing is simply for a temporary, feel-good effect. We need to bring people into the mainstream of our society. Treating them specially, differently or separately does not further that goal.

Los Angeles Times, 8-8:(A)11.

4

[Criticizing Republicans who have deserted President Bush in the current Presidential-election campaign]: You have to push back your pettiness and pride and perhaps your petulance and just remember there's a very fine and decent man running for re-election as President. If George Bush gets beat, it won't be the Democrats that did it to him. It will be the Republicans.

To Montana Republicans/
USA Today, 10-19:(A)5.

Samuel K. Skinner
Chief of Staff to
President of the United States
George Bush

5

[On Senate Majority Leader George Mitchell]: He's the most partisan Majority Leader we've had this century. He makes Lyndon Johnson look like a statesman . . . I have the benefit, coming from Chicago, to know what strong-arm tactics are. Having grown up in Chicago, and watched Chicago politicians, watched the first Mayor [Richard] Daley and watched everything that went on in Illinois for so many years, I can smell a crass politician when I see one. And I can smell someone who puts politics above his country . . . I'm not saying Senator Mitchell smells; I don't want the headline to be "Mitchell Smells." But I would put him in the category of people who are playing crass politics with the American people's pocketbooks.

Interview, March 5/
The Washington Post, 3-6:(A)9.

Theodore H. Sorensen
Former speech writer
for the late President
of the United States
John F. Kennedy

6

The first rule of Presidential speech writing is, or should be, that saying so doesn't make it so. For someone such as [President] Bush, who has represented the political establishment his entire career, to try to pretend that he's a revolutionary won't fly. He can say it 700 or 7,000 times and

(THEODORE H. SORENSEN)

people will not think that a jack rabbit who calls himself a horse is a horse.

The New York Times, 4-25:1.

Stuart Spencer
Republican Party
political strategist

1

In four years of any Presidency, you get breaks and you get downers. [Former President Ronald] Reagan had all his downers at the front end. [President] Bush got all his breaks at the front end and the downers now [at re-election time].

Los Angeles Times, 1-31:(A)26.

James Squires
Spokesman for the developing
independent Presidential campaign
of industrialist Ross Perot

2

When they say Perot won't talk about specifics, what they're really complaining about is that Perot doesn't want to fall into the polarized positions by which we judge people. Even if we write long stories, and it's done by intelligent thoughful people, we still take these basic positions that have been staked out as the party line of one party or another, or one special interest or another, and we apply them to individuals. It's like the world is a huge box chart, and the issue can actually be described by one word or one phrase: the Brady bill; Roe versus Wade; enterpise zones.

Interview, Dallas, Texas/
The Washington Post, 6-10:(B)8.

James Squires
Former spokesman
for the 1992 independent
Presidential campaign
of industrialist Ross Perot

3

[President-elect Bill Clinton] can't pay [Perot's voters] off just by going after lobbyists or the Japanese. You have to go after the [Federal budget] deficit and debt. If you look at the Perot coalition, you find that it contained people from the far left and far right. They were a political zoo representing every trend. We found that the one thing, the only thing, that they could all agree on was dealing with the debt and the deficit. [Clinton's] trying to attract them [for the 1996 Presidential election] with anything else will be folly.

The New York Times. 11-28:6.

George Stephanopoulos
Communications director
for President-elect Bill Clinton

4

[On whether President-elect Clinton will form some of his strategy as President to satisfy those who voted for 1992 independent candidate Ross Perot in order to woo them for 1996 Presidential election]: I can't believe I am talking about 1996 before Governor Clinton has even been inaugurated [as President in 1993]. But assuming that 1996 will be a two-person race, then the Perot voters will be central to that election. They have to be part of our thinking. They will be the difference between winning and losing.

The New York Times, 11-28:1.

James B. Stockdale
1992 independent
Vice-Presidential candidate
(running mate of Presidential
candidate Ross Perot);
Admiral (Ret.),
United States Navy

5

Who am I? Why am I here? I'm not a politician, everybody knows that. So don't expect me to use the language of the Washington insider. Thirty-seven years in the Navy and only one of them up there in Washington. And now I'm an academic. The centerpiece of my life was the Vietnam war. I was there the day it started. I led the first bombing raid against North Vietnam. I was there the day it ended. And I was there for everything in-between . . . I look back on those years as the beginning of wisdom, learning everything a man can learn about the vulnerabilities and the strengths that are ours as Americans.

(JAMES B. STOCKDALE)

Why am I here tonight? I am here because I have in my brain and in my heart what it takes to lead America through tough times.

At Vice-Presidential candidates' debate,
Atlanta, Ga., Oct. 13/
The New York Times, 10-14:(A)12.

Robert M. Teeter
Chairman of President
George Bush's
re-election campaign

1

[On the public popularity of Ross Perot, an industrialist who may run independently for President this year]: One of the questions about Perot is how the public takes to a guy who is going to go outside and play by a different set of rules, whether it's money or the rules of law. Perot is a guy who's been noted in his public career for doing a lot of things outside the rules. And I'm not sure the public likes the idea—they haven't up to now in my lifetime—or Presidents going outside the rules. It's greatly popular to go out and say, "Look, here's a guy who gets things done." But I think the electorate, by the time you get to September and October, starts focusing on the fact we're going to put somebody in the White House. And I don't think they're going to want to see as President of the United States a guy who thinks he's above or outside the rules or the law.

To reporters, May 27/
Los Angeles Times, 5-28:(A)16.

Paul E. Tsongas
Candidate for the 1992
Democratic Presidential nomination;
Former United States Senator,
D-Massachusetts

2

I want to win [the Presidency] if I can have a mandate. If I can't have a mandate, I don't want the goddam job. If I'm the President in a country that does not want to do this, to save more, invest more and be competitive, I will have four miserable years.

New Hampshire, January/
USA Today, 3-20:(A)5.

3

[On his Presidential campaign]: I have two choices: I can be the most charismatic leader you ever had or I can tell you the truth. Apparently the first option is closed to me. So I tell you the truth.

Interview/
USA Today, 2-4:(A)9.

4

The only poll that counts is what happens election day. The worst thing that can happen to a candidate is to become obsessed with polls. [If I would have paid attention to my early popularity showings,] I would have been for 10 months in the fetal position.

News conference,
Manchester, N.H., Feb. 11/
The New York Times, 2-12:(A)13.

5

[Accusing Bill Clinton, who is running against him for the 1992 Democratic Presidential nomination, of pandering to audiences during his campaign]: There are those who believe the American people are not intelligent, that you can be Santa Claus, that you can pander and give middle-class tax cuts. I'm going to tell you something, Bill Clinton: You're not going to pander your way into the White House as long as I'm around.

Campaign speech, Lowell, Mass.,
March 10/
Los Angeles Times, 3-11:(A)12.

6

[Announcing his withdrawal from the race for the Presidential nomination]: This journey had two missions. The first was to redefine the Democratic Party, to combine economic growth with our traditional social compassion. America needs such a Democratic Party. I believe the force of our message and our sheer survival has caused people all over this country to see a new path. It is a steeper and harder path, but it is more compelling and more noble. It is the path of America's future. At the end of that path lies a

WHAT THEY SAID IN 1992

(PAUL E. TSONGAS)

prosperous and humane America. More importantly, it is the path of our generational responsibility. Our young deserve our willingness to make hard choices. Their fate lies in our resolve. To turn away from that sacred responsibility is to violate the legacy of our ancestors. That message, that sacredness, that resolve, was my mission, and I feel deeply fulfilled. The obligation of my survival has been met . . . But the hard fact is that the nomination process requires resources, and last evening it was clear that we did not have the resources necessary to fight the media war in [the forthcoming] New York [primary]. We simply did not have the resources. I would have been defined by others, and have been unable to defend myself. Worse, my message would have been wounded, and all that we worked for, for this past year, would have been put at risk. The message must endure.

News conference,
Boston, Mass., March 19/
The New York Times, 3-20:(A)12.

Lane Venardos
Director, special events unit,
CBS News

1

[On the TV networks' planned cutbacks in coverage of this year's Democratic and Republican conventions]: We are driven by a desire to have the amount of coverage have some bearing on the news value. Increasingly, the parties have squeezed every ounce of controversy and potential news out of the convention to provide a seamless event for their candidates. They've ceased to become news events, and have become theatre.

The New York Times, 6-29:(A)13.

Richard A. Viguerie
Chairman,
United Conservatives

2

[Arguing against President Bush dropping Vice President Dan Quayle from his re-election ticket because of Quayle's low opinion-poll ratings]: Bush doesn't have a Quayle problem.

Bush has a Bush problem. Dan Quayle mustn't be scapegoated in the President's re-election strategy. President Bush's troubles are a direct result of his failed economic policies.

The New York Times, 7-23:(A)10.

George Voinovich
Governor of Ohio (R)

3

The lesson of the last election [in which Democrat Bill Clinton recently defeated President George Bush] is that the American people want results, and they expect their government leaders to work together to get results. They're not going to be tolerant of grand posturing or ideological outbursts.

USA Today, 11-30:(A)4.

Nicholas von Hoffman
Author, Journalist

4

All my life I've been labeled a member of the left. In fact, most of my life I've voted Republican. I abhor bureaucracy, which I associate with liberalism, and have always been virulently anti-Communist. But I've also been, I hope, the kind of person who does not deny that a problem exists. There were conservatives years ago who said, "What do you mean, black people can't vote in Mississippi?" Calling yourself a conservative doesn't absolve you from serving the interests of justice.

Interview, New York, N.Y./
Publishers Weekly, 9-21:72.

Larry Wachtel
Vice president,
Prudential Securities

5

[1992 Democratic Presidential nominee Bill] Clinton led the polls in July, he retained his lead in August and September and he's still out front in October. His election won't put [Wall Street] in a tank. He's not a wild-eyed Bolshevik; this is a very well-prepared candidate who has hundreds of corporate executives and economists behind him.

The Christian Science Monitor,
10-19:7.

Richard Wald
Senior vice president,
ABC News

1

When the [TV] networks covered [the national political conventions] at great length, it was a . . . time when primaries didn't carry so much weight. The political process was changed by the [George] McGovern reforms. The Democratic Party gave the weight of choice for the nominee to primaries and away from the convention. The result: The networks now cover more of the primaries, less of the conventions . . . The old idea of conventions no longer holds; the public knows it and no longer watches. I believe it is essential for the parties to reinvent conventions, for their own benefit, and so they'll be more interesting for the public to watch.

The Christian Science Monitor,
7-10:4.

Henry A. Waxman
United States Representative,
D-California

2

[On Jerry Brown, candidate for the 1992 Democratic Presidential nomination and former Governor of California]: It's impossible to know what a Brown Administration would be like. He was very unpredictable as Governor. He did some pretty good things when Governor, but a lot of his behavior in those days was quite erratic. He did a good job bringing in women and minorities, but seemed very hostile to the University of California. I think he has a fundamental belief in civil liberties and civil rights and protection of the environment. But he's got a lot of flexibility on some major questions of our time, which I find very disturbing.

Interview/
The New York Times, 4-2:(A)15.

Vin Weber
United States Representative,
R-Minnesota

3

I think the erosion of the political parties is to blame for much of what's wrong. Certainly, par-

ties were once corrupt and needed reform. But now they are unable to play the role they *should* play—as filters between special-interest groups and individual office-holders. I think you need to try to strengthen the parties.

Panel discussion,
Washington, D.C./
Time, 6-8:65.

4

[Saying Republican Congressmen are worried that the Bush Administration's low standing in public-opinion polls may hurt their own re-election chances in this year's election]: Members are beginning to see the impact of the national polls on their own states and their own districts. It should not have surprised them. But it is one thing to say there is a hurricane coming; it is another to see your basement flooding.

July 29/
The Washington Post, 7-30:(A)1.

William F. Weld
Governor of Massachusetts (R)

5

I think [Vice President] Dan Quayle—I don't expect any of you to agree with this—I think he's got the best political mind in the White House.

Newsweek, 8-3:15.

John White
Former chairman,
Democratic National Committee

6

[On Presidents, such as President Bush, who use their position to grant government favors to interest groups during a re-election campaign]: It's a typical pattern. We did it in 1980 [during Jimmy Carter's re-election campaign], emphasizing our involvement in states and cities that were then sorely needed [politically]. [Richard] Nixon did it in 1972—he was an easy winner with dairy and grain price supports. Even Harry Truman did it.

The Christian Science Monitor,
9-9:4.

John White
Former issues coordinator
for the 1992 independent
Presidential campaign
of industrialist Ross Perot

1

The Perot voters are people who are very skeptical and hard to convince. I don't mean this as a criticism, but they tended to be a little naive. These are people who were attracted to simple solutions, and that is why the Perot thing worked. [President-elect Bill Clinton's] appealing to them with anything other than black-and-white solutions for the [Federal] debt and deficit is not going to be easy.

The New York Times, 11-28:6.

L. Douglas Wilder
Governor of Virginia (D)

2

[Criticizing Democratic Presidential candidate Bill Clinton for golfing at an all-white country club, which Clinton admits]: Governor Clinton, a man besieged with stories about his personal life in the past few months, has taken to lecturing Americans about personal responsibility. All I can say to Governor Clinton is, doctor, heal thyself. It is inconceivable to me that a sitting Governor would either accept membership or recreate in a club that openly discriminates against blacks and other minorities.

March 19/
The New York Times, 3-21:8.

Roger Wilkins
Professor of history
and American culture,
George Mason University

3

The Democratic Party, every four years [at Presidential election time], becomes very arrogant and high-handed with respect to blacks. Its campaigns are invariably run by some new wave of young white men. One of the attitudes is that we blacks have nowhere else to go. The attitude is, really, that we should shut up, stay out of the

way, not make waves, but show up at the polls in November.

The New York Times, 7-11:7.

Pete Wilson
Governor of California (R)

4

[Speaking to business executives, saying they should not support Democrats who have not supported business]: Support those who are supportive . . . Don't support the people who have not been friends—those who have in fact been indifferent . . . We've got to change the laws. If the present lawmakers won't change them, I tell you you're damn fools to support the present lawmakers. [Change] doesn't just happen . . . Your success depends on meeting the needs of your customers. That should be a proper measure of success for government as well. We've got to say to those who ask for campaign contributions, that they have to have justified those campaign contributions by performance. If in fact they have been part of the problem rather than part of the solution, then I see no point in enabling them to continue.

Before California Manufacturers Association,
Sacramento, Calif.,
March 17/
Los Angeles Times, 3-18:(A)3.

Timothy E. Wirth
United States Senator,
D-Colorado

5

Congress is awash in money. Interests have emerged that have enormous amounts of cash and that stand between the Congress and its constituency. In my 18 years in Congress, I have seen the denominator of debate get lower and lower, and I think much of that is explained by fear—fear that you will be unable to raise money from a certain group; or worse, that the interest group will give the money to the other guy; or worse still, that the money will go to a third party as a so-called independent expenditure. We need reform that would do three things: provide shared

(TIMOTHY E. WIRTH)

public-private [election] funding, similar to the current system for Presidential campaigns; second, limit how much a candidate can spend; and third, ensure non-incumbents of enough money to be competitive—which would, by the way, ensure better members of Congress.

Panel discussion,
Washington, D.C./
Time, 6-8:64.

Betsey Wright
Fellow, Institute of Politics,
Kennedy School of Government,
Harvard University

1

Who are the women who are advising [the 1992 Presidential candidates]? Not peripherally but in the center core on issues, on strategy and on raising money? If they're there, they are invisible.

The Christian Science Monitor, 4-7:8.

Social Welfare

David Blankenhorn
President,
Institute for American Values

1

Fatherlessness is a special concern. Tonight, more than one-third of our nation's children will go to sleep in homes in which their fathers do not live. Before they reach age 18, more than half of our nation's children will spend a significant portion of their childhood living apart from their fathers. Fatherlessness is now approaching a rough parity with fatherhood as a defining feature of American childhood. If I had to pick the most important family issue facing the nation today, it would be fatherlessness.

Interview/USA Today, 7-8:(A)9.

Robert Bray
Director of public information,
National Gay and Lesbian
Task Force

2

Family diversity is one of the cutting-edge social issues in this country. We live in a country that has a vibrant and textured mosaic of loving unions, ranging from elderly families to single parents to gay and lesbian families. Unfortunately, the Ozzie and Harriet family myth drives social policy in this country. What's not messed up are family values. What's messed up is society's reaction to diverse families. The problem for us isn't who's in the kitchen and who's at work. The problem for us is homophobia and racism which threaten to undermine those loving unions.

Interview/USA Today, 7-8:(A)9.

Edmund G. "Jerry" Brown, Jr.
Candidate for the 1992
Democratic Presidential nomination;
Former Governor
of California (D)

3

[The underclass] is becoming institutionally embedded in the cities of America in a way

that is destroying our democracy. And it isn't that human nature has changed. It's just that the concentration of institutional neglect, despair and poverty is overwhelming whatever good-will normal human beings start out in life with . . . You need a fundamental shift in our national priorities. You have to create a reason not to be drug dependent, not to have children out of wedlock, and you do that through economic security, a living family wage. That is the moral imperative that this society must commit itself to, or we are going to degenerate and rot like the Holy Roman Empire.

Campaign debate,
New York, N.Y., March 29/
The Washington Post, 3-30:(A)8.

Wayne R. Bryant
New Jersey State Assemblyman (D)

4

Until the needs and the problems of the family are confronted in a comprehensible way, welfare will continue its course of entrapping one generation after the next in a modern form of slavery.

Nation's Business, August:32.

Gary Burtless
Senior fellow of economic studies,
Brookings Institution

5

For some people, when you say the word "welfare," you are also indicating people of color or mothers who are members of racial minorities. So it occasionally does have a racist tinge to it. But still, the majority of people collecting AFDC are white. And for many people of good will, including people who are themselves members of racial minorities, welfare is regarded as a narcotic or something that is bad.

Interview/USA Today, 2-27:(A)11.

George Bush
President of the United States

6

Think of the way that the world looks right now to the single mother on welfare. Government

(GEORGE BUSH)

provides you just enough cash for the bare necessities. Government tells you where you can live, where your kids go to school. And when you're sick, government tells you what kind of care you get and when. And if you find a job, the government cuts the welfare benefits. And if you save, if you manage to put a little money away, maybe toward a home or to help your kid get through college, the government says, "Hey, welfare fraud." Every one of those things happens with the system that we have in place right now. And then we wonder why can't folks on welfare take control of their lives, where is their sense of responsibility?

*At Challenger Boys' and Girls' Club,
Los Angeles, Calif., May 8/
The New York Times, 5-9:6.*

1

Every four years [at Presidential-election time], the Democrats go around and say, hey, Republicans are going to cut Social Security and Medicare. They started it again. I'm the President that stood up and said don't mess with Social Security. And I'm not going to and we haven't, and we are not going to go after the Social Security recipient . . . What we need to do, though, is control the growth of these mandatory programs . . . Let it grow for inflation, let it grow for the amount of new people added, population, and then hold the line. And I believe that is the way you get the deficit down, not by the tax-and-spend program that we hear every four years [from the Democrats].

*At Presidential candidates' debate,
St. Louis, Mo., Oct. 11/
The New York Times, 10-12:(A)15.*

Jimmy Carter
*Former President
of the United States*

2

There are some who justify the harsh lives of the poor with claims that they are lazy, lack ambition, or care little about family values. These statements are false, either based on ignorance,

on racism, or are deliberate attempts to divide Americans one from another for political gain . . . Given a chance for a better life, we find [the poor] to be just as ambitious, just as willing to work, and just as concerned about their children and grandchildren as we are.

*At Democratic National Convention,
New York, N.Y., July 14/
The New York Times, 7-15:(A)12.*

Margaret Catley-Carlson
*Deputy Minister of Health
and Welfare of Canada;
Director-designate,
Population Council*

3

The decade ahead offers extraordinary promise in bringing better family health, including fertility management, to substantially greater numbers of the world's families. We now have the biggest-ever crop of teenagers on the planet, and it will be their decisions about the size of families that will help determine whether the population doubles in size again, as it has done since 1950. Teenagers are anything but stupid. They look around and understand that smaller families can mean a better life. They recognize they have access to contraceptives their parents did not.

*Interview/
The New York Times, 6-12:(A)13.*

Bill Clinton
*Governor of Arkansas (D);
Candidate for the 1992
Democratic Presidential nomination*

4

Entitlements are now more than 40 per cent of the annual [Federal] budget. So anybody would be right to say we can't let entitlements increase at the rate they did in the '80s and hope to get control of the budget. What are your options for doing that, and when do you bring them in? Why have entitlements increased? Because we have cost-of-living increases, and everybody gets them. You also have to say entitlements increased because poverty exploded, and the more poor people you have, the more entitlement spending there will be, which is why we need an

(BILL CLINTON)

anti-poverty strategy, which is why I have called for investments in welfare reform and the earned-income tax credit to lift the working poor above the poverty line. There is also the untrammeled growth of health-care costs, which are ripping back through the entitlement programs. They are breaking the bank on Medicare and Medicaid.

Debate with former U.S. Senator
Paul Tsongas, Chicago, Ill./
Time, 3-23:20.

1

"Family values" can't simply be Washington code for Beltway Republicans who really mean "you're on your own," or Beltway Democrats who want to spend more of your tax money on programs that don't embody your values . . . [We must find] a third way, beyond the traditional politics of both parties. Family values alone won't feed a hungry child, and material security cannot provide a moral compass. We must have both.

At Cleveland City Club,
Cleveland, Ohio, May 21/
The New York Times, 5-22:(A)10.

2

Think back 10 or 11 years ago when we didn't have much of a homeless problem. It was really unusual, wasn't it, to see someone sleeping on the street? Now you see it in all cities of all sizes. That is because we've gone for more than a decade without a national housing policy. Housing is not much different than highways. You've got to have some sort of investment policy—except, in America, we have both public and private dollars going into housing. I favor a homeless strategy that would give more funds to cities to design their own homeless programs, and would emphasize the lowest possible cost in solving the problems—which is to take these buildings that the government owns, like we foreclosed on all these savings-and-loan properties. HUD has a lot of buildings, other Federal agencies. We own houses. Those houses ought to be rehabilitated and made available for home-

less shelters. We ought to take people who are out of work and let them work in return for public assistance and have them rehabilitate houses and then open them for the homeless.

Call-in question-and-answer broadcast,
Pittsburgh, Pa./NBC-TV, 6-12.

Bill Clinton
Governor of Arkansas (D);
1992 Democratic
Presidential nominee

3

I'm fed up with politicians in Washington lecturing Americans about "family values." Our families have values. Our government doesn't. I want an America where "family values" live in our actions, not just in our speeches. An America that includes every family. Every traditional family and every extended family. Every two-income family and every single-parent family, and every foster family . . . The thing that makes me angriest about what went wrong these last 12 years is that this government has lost touch with our values, while politicians continue to shout about them.

Accepting the Presidential nomination
at Democratic National Convention,
New York, N.Y., July 16/
The New York Times, 7-17:(A)12.

4

[I want] an America where we end welfare as we know it. We will say to those on welfare: You have the opportunity through training and education, health care and child care, to liberate yourself. But then you have a responsibility to go to work. Welfare must be a second chance, not a way of life.

Accepting the Presidential nomination
at Democratic National Convention,
New York, N.Y., July 16/
The New York Times, 7-17:(A)13.

Bill Clinton
Governor of Arkansas (D);
President-elect
of the United States

5

For the last seven years, for the first time in our history, our retiree population is less poor than

(BILL CLINTON)

the rest of the population; it never happened before. And that's because of some of those entitlements: Social Security, Medicare, SSI— and I think some adjustments may be in order, particularly for upper-income people who are getting a lot more out of it than they ever paid in.

At economic conference he convened,
Little Rock, Ark., Dec. 15/
The New York Times, 12-16:(A)10.

Mario M. Cuomo
Governor of New York (D)

1

[President Bush] says we cannot afford to do all that needs to be done. He says we have the will but not the wallet . . . [But] we have the wealth available—we've proved it over and over, when the dramatic catastrophes strike. Remember the savings-and-loans? Governors and Mayors had gone to Washington to plead for help for education, for job training, for health care, for roads and bridges. "Sorry, there is none," said the President. "We're broke. We have the will but not the wallet." Then Americans discovered that wealthy bankers—educated in the most exquisite forms of conservative, Republican banking— through their incompetence and thievery, and the government's neglect, had stolen or squandered everything in sight . . . *Mirabile dictu*—all of a sudden—the heavens opened and, out of the blue, billions of dollars appeared. Not for the children. Not for jobs. Not for the ill. But hundreds of billions of dollars to bail out failed savings-and-loans. Billions for war. Billions for earthquakes and hurricanes. If we can do all this for these spectacular catastrophes, why can't we find the wealth to respond to the quiet catastrophes that every day oppress the lives of thousands, that destroy our children with drugs, that kill thousands with terrible new diseases like AIDS, that deprive our people of the sureness of adequate health care, that stifle our future?

Nominating Bill Clinton for President
at Democratic National Convention,
New York, N.Y., July 15/
The New York Times,
7-16:(A)12.

Sheldon Danziger
Professor of social work
and public policy,
University of Michigan

2

[On calls for a WPA-type public jobs program]: For all the rhetoric about welfare, the nation has not been committed to coming up with the bottom line—an actual job. By now we've learned that if we really want to tackle the welfare problem, the government has to act as an employer of last resort.

The New York Times, 3-13:(A)8.

Jim Florio
Governor of New Jersey (D)

3

Our goal is to wean people off welfare, and the way to do that is to force them to be responsible for their actions. It's time we stopped selling poor people short. They don't need a cradle-to-grave system that treats them like children and gives them absolutely no credit for being able to make decisions.

Before Senate Finance Subcommittee
on Social Security and Family Policy,
Washington, D.C., Feb. 3/
The Washington Post, 2-4:(A)13.

Benjamin L. Hooks
Executive director,
National Association for the
Advancement of Colored People

4

Any objective, unbiased observer would agree that when there was segregation, the only way to end it was to have integration; you could be laser sharp. [But] if you're talking about solving the problems of the poor, there's no way under God's sun you can have the same kind of agreement and focus.

The New York Times, 7-11:8.

Wade F. Horn
Commissioner,
Federal Head Start program

5

Over the long term, it will not be government programs, no matter how richly funded or well

(WADE F. HORN)

designed, that will solve the problems children face. The solution lies in strengthening the American family. And not just any kind of family. What children need to thrive is a two-parent family, in which a mother and a father, bound in marriage, commit themselves to the health and welfare of their children.

Interview/
Christianity Today, 4-6:72.

Jack Kemp
Secretary of Housing
and Urban Development
of the United States

1

The $2.5-trillion that have been spent on social-welfare programs since, say, 1965, have really empowered a bureaucracy instead of empowering people. It's redistributed wealth instead of creating wealth. And it's been aimed at the wrong recipient. It was aimed at government, to trickle down on the poor, instead of allowing people some boots and some straps and some property and some seed corn and jobs and good education that can help them out of welfare onto the ladder of opportunity that we call the American dream.

May 5/
The Washington Post, 5-6:(A)27.

Daniel Langan
Spokesman, National Charities
Information Bureau

2

The character of American giving is that people are always willing to help those worse off than themselves. The lower you go on the economic ladder, the truer that is.

Newsweek, 1-13:23.

Daniel Patrick Moynihan
United States Senator,
D-New York

3

If you eliminate the Social Security payroll tax and treat Social Security as part of general revenue, you pull out the cornerstone of the Social Security system. Take away payroll contributions, and Social Security becomes welfare.

Before the Senate,
Washington, D.C., March 26/
Los Angeles Times, 3-27:(A)11.

Ross Perot
Industrialist;
1992 independent
Presidential candidate

4

If I had to solve all the problems that face this country and I could be granted one wish . . . I would say a strong family unit in every home, where every child is loved, nurtured and encouraged. A little child before they're 18 months learns to think well of himself or herself, or poorly. They develop a positive or negative self-image. At a very early age they learn how to learn. If we have children who are not surrounded with love and affection—see, I look at my grandchildren and wonder if they'll ever learn to walk because they're always in someone's arms. And I think, my gosh, wouldn't it be wonderful if every child had that love and support. But they don't. We will not be a great country unless we have a strong family unit in every home. And I think you can use the White House as a bully pulpit to stress the importance of these little children, particularly in their young and formative years, to mold these little precious pieces of clay so that they, too, can live rich full lives when they're grown.

At Presidential candidates' debate,
St. Louis, Mo., Oct. 11/
The New York Times, 10-12:(A)14.

5

Let me talk to the men [who father babies and then abandon the mothers]: I've got no respect for you at all. As far as I'm concerned you're dirt if you create a baby and walk away from it. That's not a man, that's not a boy, that's a jerk . . . You young people need to stop just thinking about getting high, getting drunk, getting laid and getting pregnant.

Broadcast interview/MTV, 11-1.

Diane Piktialis
*Vice president
of elder care services,
Work/Family Directions,
Boston, Mass.*

1

[On families who are caring for both their young children and their older parents]: We call this the sandwich generation, which refers to people who are caught between the middle of two groups of dependents: children on the one hand and aging parents on the other. It's becoming a much more common occurence, particularly with the baby-boom generation that often postpones child rearing. They now find themselves with young children, and they also are now facing parents who are aging and need their help . . . This trend is definitely going to change society in a fundamental way because we are definitely going to have more older people. They are going to need more resources, not just health, but also long-term care. And we as a society have not really addressed how to plan for an aging population.

Interview/USA Today, 4-9:(A)11.

Alvin F. Poussaint
*Associate professor of psychiatry,
Harvard University
Medical School*

2

The family is not like it was a hundred years ago, when families had total control over their environment and their children and could work to support them and have adequate income. The times have changed, and that's why families are in trouble—not because values have changed, but because society has changed in many ways, putting more demands, bringing more pressures and bringing more stresses on families and people trying to raise children. Families can't exist on family values alone. They need economic support. They need social support from their community and society. If you don't have a job, and if you don't have a job that pays a living wage, it's very hard to support a family. If you don't have money, you're less likely to want to be married or to take on the responsibility of a family.

Interview/USA Today, 7-8:(A)9.

Dan Quayle
*Vice President
of the United States*

3

Marriage is a moral issue that requires cultural consensus, and the use of social sanctions. Bearing babies irresponsibly is, simply, wrong. Failing to support children one has fathered is wrong. We must be unequivocal about this. It doesn't help matters when primetime TV has Murphy Brown—a character who supposedly epitomizes today's intelligent, highly paid, professional woman—mocking the importance of fathers by bearing a child alone and calling it just another "lifestyle choice." I know it is not fashionable to talk about moral values, but we need to do it. Even though our cultural leaders in Hollywood, network TV, the national newspapers routinely jeer at them, I think most us in this room know that some things are good, and other things are wrong. Now it's time to make the discussion public. It's time to talk again about family, hard work, integrity and personal responsibility. We cannot be embarrassed out of our belief that two parents, married to each other, are better in most cases for children than one.

*Before Commonwealth Club,
San Francisco, Calif., May 19/
The New York Times,
5-20:(A)11.*

4

Children who do not live with two parents are more than five times as likely to live in poverty than children who do. We also know that children who are raised without fathers are more likely to do poorly in school and, indeed, to drop out. If they drop out of school, they are more likely to join gangs, to break the law and to have babies out of wedlock. Single parents, especially single mothers, who raise their children alone do a tremendous job against the odds . . . It is the men who need to be reminded that they have a responsibility for the children they have fathered.

*Before Chamber of Commerce,
Kansas City, Mo.,
Sept. 2/
The Washington Post,
9-3:(A)15.*

Robert Rector
Senior policy analyst,
Heritage Foundation

1

[Criticizing a Census Bureau report on in-creasing poverty in the U.S.]: If they don't count food stamps, Medicaid and public housing, then they must not think that such income is im-proving the condition of the poor and we can presumably cut them out and do the taxpayer a huge favor . . . The real problems are not hunger and over-crowded living but that the welfare state *per se* rewards non-work and single parenthood. Because the welfare state rewards single parent-hood and non-work, the more we spend on welfare, the more government fuels the be-havioral problems.

The Christian Science Monitor,
9-8:8.

Linda Rush
President,
Formerly Employed Mothers
at the Leading Edge

2

The more we can update the image of home-based mothers and make it realistic, the more respect will be gained for parents, and the more comfortable people will be in their role as the primary care-giver of their children. In the media we still see references to how easy it is to be at home—that life is under control, that there is a great deal of idle time available to turn on the television and contemplate household cleaners.

The Christian Science Monitor,
8-18:14.

Patricia Schroeder
United States Representative,
D-Colorado

3

I'm getting tired of the President [Bush] mouthing his great concern for children, families and babies. He loves them to death up to the door of the budget office; then he drops them like a hot rock.

May 11/The New York Times, 5-12:(A)10.

Louis W. Sullivan
Secretary of Health
and Human Services
of the United States

4

There have been a number of things that the President [Bush] has done and others that he has wanted to do where we haven't gotten the Congress's support. You must remember that the President proposes legislation, but the Congress disposes. For example, my colleague in the Cabinet, [Housing] Secretary [Jack] Kemp, has tried to get enterprise-zones legislation passed in the Congress that would enable the development of small businesses in our inner cities. The Congress has not passed that legislation. I have proposed, for example, legislation to address our high infant-mortality rate. The Congress is very vocal in criticizing our high infant-mortality rate, but when I asked for $171-million to initiate a program, I received only $25-million after much speculation in the Congress. So we must have joint leadership to address these problems. Not only from the President, but from the Congress.

Broadcast interview, May 4/
The Washington Post, 5-5:(A)24.

Transportation

Bernard Attali
Chairman, Air France

1

[Criticizing the idea of "open skies," a policy of allowing more U.S. airlines access to more European cities in exchange for European carriers being granted routes to more U.S. destinations]: Those who advocate "open skies" today should say that they feel the time has come to conquer Europe in the name of the American carriers. Be aware that this is a game where everyone loses.

The Christian Science Monitor,
11-20:8.

Edward R. Beauvais
Chairman,
America West Airlines

2

Large [air] carriers continue to muscle smaller carriers out of business . . . I don't think [the public] believe they're getting the best airline industry can produce. We have de facto regulation going on right now, but American [Airlines] is the regulator. It sets the stage, it imposes the new fare formula on the industry and then it punishes those who don't go along. That's a sign that the oligopoly is at hand. After the 50 per cent [fare] sale expires, people are going to be paying more than they should for commercial aviation. Let the consumer beware. It's coming. You either have regulation by a monopolist, or you'll have government regulation. You have to deal with it now, and I don't believe that we as a nation have a choice.

Interview/Newsweek, 6-15:45.

Andrew H. Card, Jr.
Secretary of Transportation
of the United States

3

There are private-sector solutions to high-speed [rail] transportation. All solutions do not emanate from the Federal government and Federal dollars. But I think there are opportuni-

ties for the Federal government to be partners. We are not abrogating any responsibility in this area . . . But is there a huge infusion of Federal dollars for high-speed rail? No, there isn't.

Interview,
Washington, D.C., March 11/
The Washington Post, 3-12:(A)25.

Gilbert E. Carmichael
Administrator,
Federal Railroad Administration

4

People are under the impression that railroads are on the fence, teetering on the edge of bankruptcy. They see abandoned lines with grass growing between the rails and they think the railroads are a 19-century technology, obsolete . . . It's just not true.

Los Angeles Times, 8-12:(A)17.

W. Graham Claytor, Jr.
President, Amtrak

5

We [Amtrak] have laid off several hundred people around the country. We have 80-year-old facilities that we are using to maintain all of our equipment. We've got detailed plans for making those modern up-to-date facilities that would provide more productivity. We are ready to start that instantly. Where would the money come from? This will take about a billion dollars to get our national railroad passenger system in first-class shape. Long-term solutions don't come about unless there's short-term action.

At economic conference convened
by President-elect Bill Clinton,
Little Rock, Ark., Dec. 15/
The New York Times, 12-16:(A)10.

Bill Clinton
Governor of Arkansas (D);
1992 Democratic
Presidential nominee

6

We've wrecked the airline industry already because—well, there's all these leveraged buy-

(BILL CLINTON)

outs and all these terrible things that have happened to the airline industry. We're going to have a hard time rebuilding it, but the real thing we've got to have is a competitive economic strategy. Look what's happening to McDonnell Douglas, even Boeing is losing market share, because we let the Europeans spend 25 to 40 billion dollars on Airbus without an appropriate [U.S.] response.

At Presidentail candidates' debate,
East Lansing, Mich., Oct. 19/
The New York Times, 10-20:(A)13.

Robert L. Crandall
Chairman,
AMR Corporation
(American Airlines)

1

Our business is the closest thing we have in this country to a perfect marketplace. The prices are always equal [among airlines] because there's nowhere to hide. You make one telephone call to your travel agent, and all of our prices come up on the computer. Anybody who offers a higher price for the same thing loses your business, so we all keep matching the competition. And when the prices are the same, people pick an airline according to the quality of its service. It is foolish to call yourself a discounter and throw away good service. Because the way this business works, the guy who offers superior service at the same price always comes out ahead.

Interview/Time, 5-4:53.

2

By every measure of profitability, airlines consistently rank dead last among major U.S. industries. Only once during the last 10 years—in 1988—did the airline industry earn a net profit margin of as much as 3 per cent. The average margin was actually negative.

At National Press Club,
Washington, D.C./
The New York Times, 7-6:(C)1.

3

[This summer's] half-price [airline-ticket] sale was a monstrous stupidity. A monstrous stupidity perpetrated by Northwest [Airlines].

Interview/
The New York Times, 9-12:1.

John H. Dasburg
Chief executive officer,
Northwest Airlines

4

[Criticizing American Airlines' fare restructuring earlier this year]: What American Airlines did was predatory and very damaging. It clearly cost the industry hundreds of millions of dollars, apparently on the basis of some long-term notion of how the customer is supposed to buy airline tickets.

Interview/
The New York Times, 9-12:1.

Gerald Hirshberg
Vice president,
Nissan Design International;
Former head of design,
Buick division,
General Motors Corporation

5

[On his now working for a Japanese car manufacturer]: I have evenings when my wife and I look at each other and I think, "I wish I could be doing this for an American company." But I do not, when I think critically, think I have done anything but help America. Detroit has never made cars as well as it's making them now, and it's not because they wanted to. And when I finish designing a vehicle like the [new minivan designed by Nissan and built by Ford], I defy anybody to tell me what culture that car represents. To me, that's wonderful.

Interview/
Los Angeles Times, 3-11:(A)7.

William Hoglund
Executive vice president,
General Motors Corporation

6

We've [GM] been severely criticized, inside and out, for taking five years to bring out new

(WILLIAM HOGLUND)

cars. Now we're down to 30 months, 36 months. It's the decision to *get* to the decision to do the new product—that's where we're going to be faster . . . [Also] in the past, we tried to increase market share at all costs. We were selling cars to rental fleets and making "deal-of-the-month" offers, where we ended up putting no money in the cash register. No more. And the decision to change that strategy was made within five days . . . not five or six months.

Interview, New York, N.Y./
Newsweek, 11-23:47.

Lee A. Iacocca
Chairman,
Chrysler Corporation

1

[On the decrease in U.S. market share of the big three American auto-makers]: This is the most lucrative, biggest market in the world, and we're down to three manufacturers. I mean, we invented the goddam car and we have trouble keeping three guys with their head above water.

Newsweek, 1-6:32.

2

[On his company's opening of a plant in Detroit that will build Jeep vehicles]: We're going to show the world that an American-owned company, smack in the middle of urban American, building an American product with American components—and, most importantly, using American workers—can build the best sport-utility vehicle in the world.

At dedication of new plant,
Detroit, Mich., March 31/
The New York Times, 4-1:(A)8.

William E. Jackman
Vice president, Air Transport
Association of America

3

It seems we can't get passengers back on planes without cutting fares to the bone, making it unprofitable for the carriers, who have about

$150-billion invested in more than 2,000 new jet planes. We hear from economists that this industry isn't going to take off in the near future, but will just grow slowly. Our biggest challenge is somehow to convince people not to sit around waiting for the next discount [fare] to come along.

The New York Times, 9-12:21.

Yutaka Kume
President,
Nissan Motor Company (Japan)

4

[On problems faced by U.S. car-makers who want to sell in the Japanese market]: The solution is straightforward. If the big three [U.S. manufacturers] are to expand in the Japanese market, they first and foremost have to offer a car that is the right size and the right feel for Japanese consumers. They have to improve their marketing. [Most important,] they have to realize that no one else will help them sell while they are sitting on their hands.

The New York Times, 1-6:(A)5.

Jim Landry
President, Air Transport Association
of America

5

[On the ICAO's suggestion that its member airlines phase out smoking on all their international flights by 1996]: This is about as strong a resolution as you can get out of the International Civil Aviation Organization on a matter of this level of controversy. It is a very strong resolution. But it is not mandatory . . . U.S. carriers will certainly join in support of the development of a worldwide ban, but our position to date has been that it has to be implemented by all . . . If we reach the position where we have a critical mass of nations with competing cariers willing to take this step, then we'll reach the common goal.

The Washington Post,
10-13:(Health)6.

Colin Marshall
Chief executive officer,
British Airways

6

Over time—and it may be the middle of the first decade of the next century—we will have

(COLIN MARSHALL)

open skies for the airline industry. And there will, in the end, be relatively few—maybe eventually only half a dozen—airlines, that will have come about through alliances or partnerships, in due course leading, no doubt, to mergers and take-overs when the rules and regulations permit such. If you look at every other substantial industry in the world, you will find very rarely more than half a dozen truly global competitors in each of those industries. I do believe that the airline industry, once it is freed from all the shackles that encircle it at the present time, is going to formulate itself along the lines of almost every other industry. Clearly there will be some regulation that will remain. One would encourage that in terms of safety and security.

Interview/Newsweek, 8-24:59.

Federico Pena
Chairman, President-elect
Bill Clinton's transition team
on transportation

1

Many of the international [air] carriers are working in partnership with their respective governments, and that kind of partnership does not exist here in the United States, where our carriers are left to their own devices as they compete globally . . . [Under the new Clinton Administration,] there's going to be much closer attention on the part of the Federal government to the U.S. airline industry, to assure the ulti-mate survival of the industry.

Interview/
The New York Times, 12-25:(C)1.

Ross Perot
Industrialist; 1992 independent
Presidential candidate

2

[Calling for a 50-cent-per-gallon gasoline tax phased in over five years]: Some of our interna-tional competitors collect up to $3.50 a gallon in taxes, and they use that money to build infra-structure and create jobs. We collect 35 cents and we don't have it to spend. I know it's not

popular . . . but the people who will be helped the most by it are the working people who will get the jobs created because of this tax.

At Presidential candidates' debate,
St. Louis, Mo., Oct. 11/
The New York Times, 10-12:(A)13.

3

I did everything I could to get General Motors to face its problems in the mid-'80s while it was still financially strong; they just wouldn't do it. And everybody now knows the terrible price they're paying by waiting until it's obvious to the brain-dead that they have problems. Now, hun-dreds, thousands of good decent people, whole cities up here in this state are adversely impacted because they would not move in a timely way.

At Presidential candidates' debate,
East Lansing, Mich., Oct. 19/
The New York Times, 10-20:(A)12.

4

[Criticizing proposed financial arrangements between certain U.S. airlines and foreign air-lines]: We're getting ready to dismantle an airlines industry in our country, and none of you know it. And I doubt, in all candor, if the Presi-dent [Bush] knows it. But this deal that we're doing with BAC and USAir and KLM and Northwest . . . This deal is terribly destructive to the U.S. airline industry. One of the largest industries in the world is the travel and tourist business. We won't be making airplanes in this country 10 years from now if we let deals like this go through . . . We hammerlock the American [airline] companies—American Airlines, Delta, the last few great [ones] we have—because we're trying to do this deal with these two European companies [BAC and KLM]. And never forget, they've got Airbus over there and it's a government-owned, privately-owned con-sortium across Europe. They're dying to get the commercial airline business. Japan is trying to get the commercial airline business. I don't think there are any villains inside [the U.S.] govern-ment on this issue, but there sure are a lot of people who don't understand business. And maybe you need somebody up there [in Wash-

(ROSS PEROT)

ington] who understands when you're getting your pocket picked.

At Presidential candidates' debate,
East Lansing, Mich., Oct. 19/
The New York Times, 10-20:(A)13.

John V. Pincavage
Partner,
Transportation Group, Ltd.

1

We should not allow airlines to go into Chapter 11 [bankruptcy] and dissipate creditor assets while they [the airlines] continue to operate and not have to pay their bills. That's what has led to continued over-capacity in the industry. The day a company declares bankruptcy we should padlock the doors and put it out of business. This would help reduce excess capacity and help the remaining airlines, which would get the traffic from the bankrupt airlines.

The New York Times, 12-25:(C)2.

Seth Schofield
Chairman, USAir

2

[On the proposed investment by British Airways in USAir, which has caused a controversy over foreign ownership of U.S. airlines]: There will be consolidation [in the airline industry]. It's a matter of do you want to get down to three domestic airlines? Or would you rather have five or six domestic airlines offering service internationally as we propose? This investment by British Airways is to ensure the long-term viability of USAir as a major domestic competitor against the Big Three [American, United and Delta]. They have 60 per cent of the international and U.S. market. That is getting to the point of an oligopoly that will eliminate competition.

Interview/USA Today, 12-2:(B)5.

Robert C. Stempel
Chairman,
General Motors Corporation

3

The American [car] buyer is very sharp when it comes to spending his money. And I think he perceives Japanese cars as the best product. We're challenging that. Our cars generally cost less than Japan's. And then there's fuel economy. The media have done a great job of talking about our [U.S.] gas guzzlers and Japanese fuel economy. But we're actually better in fuel economy than Japan . . . I haven't seen anything anywhere—TV, print media—that suggests *any-thing* done in the U.S. is good. Certainly the auto-makers haven't had good press on quality, gas mileage, transmission smoothness. I am pleased at the reaction on the new [Cadillac] Seville. Finally we've seen some breakthrough.

Interview, Detroit, Mich./
Time, 1-27:45.

Urban Affairs

Donald J. Borut
Executive director,
National League of Cities

1

Essentially what is happening is the Federal government is shifting costs onto local government. It's what we call shift and shaft Federalism.
July 8/
The Washington Post, 7-9:(A)21.

Joseph Boskin
Director, urban-studies
public-policy program,
Boston (Mass.) University

2

Cities have not been treated very well over the last two decades by Presidents. [Yet] they are crucial to the economic and psychological viability of this nation.
The Christian Science Monitor,
12-2:8.

Bill Bradley
United States Senator,
D-New Jersey

3

Above all, the city to me was never just what I heard my white liberal friends say it was. In their world, people of color were all victims. But while my teammates [when he played in professional sports] had been victimized, their experience and their perception of the experience of black Americans could not be reducible to victimization. To many, what the label of victimization implied was an insult to their dignity and discipline, strength and potential. Life in cities was full of more complexity and more hope than the media and the politicians would admit, and part of getting beyond color was not only attacking the sources of inequity but also refusing to make race an excuse for failing to pass judgment about self-destructive behavior. Without a community, there could be no commonly held standards; and without some commonly under-

stood standards, there could be no community. The question is whether in our cities we can build a set of commonly accepted rules that enhances individuality and life chances but also provides the glue and the tolerance to prevent us from going for each other's throats.
Before the Senate,
Washington, D.C., April 30/
The Wall Street Journal, 5-4:(A)20.

Edmund G. "Jerry" Brown, Jr.
Candidate for the 1992
Democratic Presidential nomination;
Former Governor
of California (D)

4

The priorities of this country are out of whack. Too much has been spent on "Star Wars" [the proposed space defense system] and not [on] star cities. The engine of civilization is in urban America and its connection to suburban America. As one dies, so does the other.
Campaign debate,
New York, N.Y., March 31/
The New York Times, 4-2:(A)14.

5

[Criticizing President Bush and Democratic Presidential candidate Bill Clinton]: When it was time for tax breaks, when it was time for pay raises, when it was time to bail out the S&Ls, when it was time for foreign aid, they talked tens of billions. When it's time to invest in American cities like Oakland and San Francisco and Los Angeles, it's crumb time.
Campaigning,
Oakland, Calif., May 22/
Los Angeles Times, 5-23:(A)31.

George Bush
President of the United States

6

Every hour of meetings yesterday [in Los Angeles on conditions in poor black areas of the city]—and they were for me very emotional, very moving—confirmed why I believe in the plan that

(GEORGE BUSH)

we have proposed for urban America. I kept hearing words like "ownership," "independence," "dignity," "enterprise," a lot of times from people who never had a shot at dignity or enterprise or ownership. And it reinforced my belief that we must start with a set of principles and policies that foster personal responsibility, that refocus entitlement programs to serve those who are most needy and increase the effectiveness of government services through competition and through choice ... Families can't thrive, children can't learn, jobs can't flourish in a climate of fear, however. And so first is our responsibility to preserve the domestic order. And a civilized society cannot tackle any of the really tough problems in the midst of chaos [such as the recent street riots in Los Angeles].

> *At Challenger Boys' and Girls' Club,*
> *Los Angeles, Calif., May 8/*
> *The New York Times, 5-9:6.*

1

Our enterprise zones, that we hear a lot of lip service about in Congress, would bring jobs into the inner city. There's a good program, and I need the help of everybody across the country to get it passed in a substantial way by the Congress. When we went out to South Central in Los Angeles [after this year's riots there] ... I went to a boys club and every one of them—the boys-club leaders, the ministers, all of them were saying, "Pass enterprise zones." We go back to Washington and it's very difficult to get it through the Congress. But there's going to be a new Congress [following this year's election] ... and then you can sit down and say, "Help me do what we should for the cities; help me pass these programs."

> *At Presidential candidates' debate,*
> *Richmond, Va., Oct. 15/*
> *The New York Times, 10-17:11.*

Stuart Butler
Director of domestic policy,
Heritage Foundation

2

[On the idea of enterprise zones in inner cities]: The first people setting up [in] an enterprise zone are likely to be ... retailers, check cashers, small businesses and so forth. And as they get established, as the community begins to stabilize, then you start getting the next wave of people, who are less inclined to take risks at the beginning, the franchises, and in time you get the more middle-class businesses ... The model I use is the wave of movement west. If you look at inner-city America, it's not all that different from the frontier. You get the hunters and trappers and the small settlers and the farmers, and the towns develop and you have to think about it that way. The pioneers in the South Bronx [N.Y.] are the first wave [in the enterprise zones], and they're the ones who stabilize the community—and that's what the enterprise zone is designed for. Once they get in and start stabilizing a community, the incentives become less important. We're trying to set in motion all kinds of people to try out their ideas. They're more likely to succeed than someone in city hall.

> *Interview, Washington, D.C./*
> *The Washington Post, 10-24:(D)7.*

Henry G. Cisneros
Former Mayor
of San Antonio, Texas

3

Bring people together [in the inner cities] on a more consistent, systematic, tireless and structured way than ever before. That means informal as well as formal leaders, not just people who head organizations or run corporations, but people who work in the neighborhoods and have churches in the area and speak for community organizations—and even some of the gang structure. At a minimum, take the temperature of the community regularly and try to understand what people are thinking and saying.

> *Interview/Los Angeles Times, 5-15:(T)6.*

Henry G. Cisneros
Secretary-designate of
Housing and Urban Development
of the United States;
Former Mayor
of San Antonio, Texas

4

I sense that we have limited time for America; that we cannot talk about the economy and not

(HENRY G. CISNEROS)

talk about our cities and towns, about the poor of all races. It breaks my heart every time I'm in a meeting and hear people talk about writing off neighborhoods or entire cities or, worst of all, a generation of our youth.

News conference,
Little Rock, Ark., Dec. 17/
The New York Times, 12-18:(A)16.

Bill Clinton
Governor of Arkansas (D);
Candidate for the 1992
Democratic Presidential nomination

1

Urban America's problems are America's problems. They're America's problems not only because the fate of the cities determines in some measure the fate of the nation as a whole, but also because those problems can be found even in smaller volumes in the smaller towns.

Campaign debate,
New York, N.Y., March 31/
The New York Times, 4-2:(A)14.

David N. Dinkins
Mayor of New York, N.Y.

2

[On Vice President Dan Quayle's criticism of the way Democratic liberals have run New York City]: I think it is rather sad that this person, who is a heartbeat away from the Presidency, who could, like that, become the leader of the free world, would occupy himself in such a fashion. Would that he would spend that same energy to try to find a resolution to some of the problems that beset our cities and our country, and we've got a lot of them.

June 15/
The New York Times, 6-16:(A)10.

3

[On his being a black Mayor]: There are some people in this town who believe that when a chief executive is elected, in addition to whatever title you may hold, you are ex-officio the head of the ethnic group to which you happen to belong. Well, I have news for them. It's not true and it's demeaning. I am the Mayor of all the people of our city.

At Jewish Theological Seminary,
New York, N.Y., Nov. 17/
The New York Times, 11-18:(B)12.

Christopher J. Dodd
United States Senator,
D-Connecticut

4

[Saying his reaction is lukewarm to Secretary of State James Baker's call for U.S. financial aid to Russia, Baker saying this is a defining moment in U.S.-Russian relations]: Let me suggest that for an awful lot of people in this country, defining moments are happening every day. I've introduced legislation to deal with [American] cities—far less than what we're talking about here [for Russia] over five or six years. I'll guarantee you that there'd be no rush to deal with [that] legislation by July or August to provide some assistance and encourage economic development in the Bridgeports, the Hartfords, the Detroits or San Franciscos. I would guess public support for this [aid to Russia] is not very high, because people are disappointed that we're not doing enough on the domestic agenda.

Washington, D.C., April 9/
The New York Times, 4-10:(A)6.

Osborn Elliott
Chairman, Citizens Committee
for New York City;
Former editor,
"Newsweek" magazine

5

If the cities die, our society dies. The cutbacks [in aid to cities by the Federal government] have been brutal. They've sort of happened without anybody paying much attention. It's time for the country to wake up. The cities are the engines of our society. It's in them that the commerce and art and culture and medical science and higher education . . . take place.

The Christian Science Monitor,
4-10:3.

Jeff Faux
President,
Economic Policy Institute

1

Enterprise zones are a very secondary issue. The reason why no one is investing in the inner cities has nothing to do with the tax rate and everything to do with conditions. It's dangerous and lacks consumers with money.

The Christian Science Monitor,
5-7:2.

Raymond L. Flynn
Mayor of Boston, Mass.;
President, United States
Conference of Mayors

2

The [recent] riots in Los Angeles show what happens when billions of tax dollars are annually drained from a city [for Federal military spending]. There is plenty of tax money to rebuild the roads, bridges, schools and public housing of our great [cities]. It is in the military budget and must be converted to productive use.

May 11/
The New York Times, 5-12:(A)11.

Stephen Goldsmith
Mayor of Indianapolis, Ind.

3

[Saying he favors direct grants to cities without strings attached by the Federal government]: The bottom line is that simply throwing more money into the current system will have, at best, a brief and unremarkable effect on urban problems and economic recovery. We must understand that all the grant programs in the guide to Federal domestic assistance cannot overwhelm the impact of a sick economy . . . A sudden windfall of Federal assistance tied up with mandates on how to use it, when to use it and where to use it is doomed from the start. It is unlikely that local government can respond to this kind of surprise in a quick and effective way.

Before Senate Budget Committee,
Washington, D.C., Jan. 8/
Los Angeles Times, 1-9:(A)16;
The Washington Post, 1-9:(A)23.

Arnold Hiatt
Chairman,
Stride Rite Corporation

4

[Saying business should help the troubled inner cities]: I think businesses now have to realize that unless they get involved in those communities and reversing that growth, those are 38 million fewer consumers of their products, 38 million people who consume corporate taxes and aren't paying taxes themselves. That's why it's good for business to get involved.

Interview/
The New York Times, 4-20:(C)8.

Donald A. Hicks
Professor of political economy,
University of Texas, Dallas

5

The idea of a city simply does not compute as demonstrably as it did in the 1960s or early '70s. Cities are politically invisible [in a national election] because they became economically invisible.

The Christian Science Monitor,
3-4:7.

Jesse L. Jackson
Civil-rights leader

6

[We must] recognize the analogy between the needs of urban America and what was done to get Europe and Japan back on their feet after World War II. It means the same kind of funding and training now being proposed for the former Soviet republics. It means that folks who live [in the inner cities] will have priority on loans, debt forgiveness, jobs and training. It means that the new enterprise zone exists for the benefit of those who live there, not for somebody else's benefit. This is not to create an incentive for America's wealthiest top 1 per cent. You need to create an incentive for those locked out in the first place . . . We obviously need a long-term urban plan. It is in our national interest to do so.

Interview/
Los Angeles Times, 5-15:(T)8.

229

Sharon Pratt Kelly
Mayor of Washington, D.C.

1

[Saying people in her city should come together and support her in efforts to better the city]: I may have won [election] as the lone outsider, a crusader with a band of volunteers fighting for change, but I will never lead this city to its real potential if I try to govern that way. When I was a child, there were many things I wanted to be when I grew up. But never in my life did I ever want to be the Lone Ranger.

State of the District address,
Washington, D.C., Feb. 5/
The Washington Post, 2-6:(A)1.

Jack Kemp
Secretary of Housing
and Urban Development
of the United States

2

It is hypocritical for America to preach democracy to the rest of the world and Eastern Europe and not make it work better in East L.A., and East St. Louis and East Palo Alto and East Harlem and the other East Harlems of America . . . I think we have to rise above party and politics and narrow partisanship gain in an election year and prove to the American people that we can get something done in urban America and in housing and economic development and get this country growing again.

At National Housing Conference,
Washington, D.C., June 23/
The Washington Post, 6-24:(A)18.

John F. Kerry
United States Senator,
D-Massachusetts

3

Tragically, the fact is that the majority of the white majority in this country does not want to invest more of their scarce tax dollars in minority neighborhoods or what many believe to be predominantly minority problems. Tragically, too, the crisis in our urban centers has come to be viewed by many people as simply a question of

"us" versus "them," thereby preventing real dialogue and real progress.

Before the Senate,
Washington, D.C., April 2/
The Washington Post, 4-8:(A)21.

Vincent Lane
Chairman, Chicago (Ill.)
Housing Authority

4

There are about five things that make for good neighborhoods; and that's what got this country where it is—strong neighborhoods. One is public safety. Another is decent and clean housing . . . Economic incentives to encourage people to put into place public safety and clean and decent housing will start the rebuilding of that, our communities.

At economic conference convened
by President-elect Bill Clinton,
Little Rock, Ark., Dec. 15/
The New York Times, 12-16:(A)10.

William O'Hare
Director of population
and policy research,
University of Louisville (Ky.)

5

Who is moving from rural areas [to metropolitan areas]? It's clearly the younger, the better-educated, the ones in managerial occupations. It's a push-pull. The jobs are seldom available in rural areas and more available in metro areas. That drains the people who might revive the rural areas.

The Washington Post, 7-31:(A)1.

David Osborne
Senior fellow,
Progressive Policy Institute

6

[On enterprise zones for inner cities]: Targeting poor areas for economic development is a good idea, and I think the tax code can play some role in that . . . [But] I don't think tax incentives are quite as powerful as some [enterprise-zone enthusiasts] do. The fundamental issue is, who

(DAVID OSBORNE)

are you going to help? Are you helping poor people or redeveloping a piece of geography?

The Washington Post, 10-24:(D)7.

Ross Perot
Industrialist;
1992 independent
Presidential candidate

1

The facts are the American people are hurting. These people are hurting in the inner cities. We're shipping the low-paying jobs—quote "low-paying jobs"—overseas. What are low-paying jobs? Textiles, shoes, things like that that we say are yesterday's industries. They're tomorrow's industries in the inner cities. Let me say in my case, if I'm out of work, I'll cut grass tomorrow to take care of my family. I'll be happy to make shoes. I'll be happy to make clothing. I'll make sausage. You just give me a job. Put those jobs in the inner cities instead of doing diplomatic deals and shipping them to China where prison labor does the work.

At Presidential candidates' debate,
Richmond, Va., Oct. 15/
The New York Times, 10-17:11.

Dan Quayle
Vice President
of the United States

2

Here is what's right with New York [City]: the decent, hard-working people who live here. Here's what's wrong with New York: the entrenched government establishment and its liberal ideology that have failed them. In so many ways the liberal Democrats chose the perfect site for their [1992 Democratic National Convention]—almost as if they feel a strange compulsion to return to the scene of the crime. And as we watch this spectacle on our televisions, I suspect many Americans from around the country will be left with this conviction: We must not let them do to the rest of America what they have done to the people of New York City.

Before Manhattan Institute,
New York, N.Y., June 15/
The New York Times, 6-16:(A)10.

William Schneider
Political analyst

3

New York is the ultimate folly of liberalism to most Americans. New York is wretched excess . . . For most Americans, New York is Mars. It's another planet. It's not America; it's the Third World, with [a] Third World gap between the very rich and the very poor. There's no middle class. [Suburban voters] have a lot of problems of their own, and they're not quite ready to spend a lot more money taking on the problems of the cities.

The Christian Science Monitor,
7-13:2.

Billy Tidwell
Director of research,
National Urban League

4

[President-elect Bill] Clinton has to deal with the [Federal budget] deficit. But the economic conditions that feed into it, such as the costs associated with the neglect of inner cities, need a high priority. There will be a good deal of pressure from reasonable people to move the Clinton Administration in that direction.

The Christian Science Monitor,
12-2:8.

Peter V. Ueberroth
Businessman; Chairman,
Rebuild Los Angeles Committee

5

[Referring to the recent riots in minority sections of Los Angeles]: For 40 years, corporate America, and I'm part of that, has moved every decent job out of the inner city. I had 300 offices and not one was in the inner city . . . I live in Laguna Beach, a mostly white area. But I know that the people of South-Central [Los Angeles, where most of the rioting occurred] must have a chance to have jobs, hope, to pay fair prices for food, everything the suburbs have but that the inner city does not have.

At National Urban League convention,
San Diego, Calif., July 28/
Los Angeles Times, 7-29:(A)3.

231

PART TWO

International

Foreign Affairs

Norman Anderson
*Former United States Ambassador
to Sudan*

1

Foreign affairs has become so complicated and multilateral—with issues like drugs, the environment and famine, as well as trade and military—that Washington can't know exactly how its policies are to be carried out in each individual country in every specific case. That is the job of the [U.S.] Embassies [in those countries]. And it's hard to gather information on a country and do all this without knowledge of the language . . . In the same year in which we dispatched 500,000 troops to the Arab world [as a prelude to the Persian Gulf war of 1991], the Foreign Service field school in Tunis could graduate only half a dozen Arabic-speakers.

The Atlantic, August:61.

James A. Baker III
*Secretary of State
of the United States*

2

The community of democratic nations is larger and more vigorous than at the end of World War II. That is why we plan to build a democratic peace by pursuing a straightforward policy of American leadership called "collective engagement." Germany, Italy and Japan are now strong and prosperous allies. By working with our other allies and the international institutions we created in the aftermath of World War II—the United Nations, the World Bank, the International Monetary Fund—we need not go it alone. Instead, we can build a democratic peace together . . . As the most powerful democracy on earth, we must act the catalyst, driving forward where we can. As President Bush has said, "The world trusts us with power. They trust us to do what's right." Because of this American record, we are able today—if we will—to work with our partners to share responsibilities and costs, and to advance together on common problems.

That's American leadership through collective engagement.

*Before Chicago Countil on Foreign Relations,
April 21/The New York Times, 4-22:(A)6.*

3

[Comparing his previous role as Treasury Secretary with his current position as Secretary of State]: One thing you could do there that you can't do here is pick your shots. You could decide what you wanted to concentrate on because you were not held hostage to what was happening in the world every day. Here you have a lot more stuff coming at you, a lot more traffic in terms of written things you have to deal with. Your role, in particular the negotiating aspects of it, is highly political—international policies is not politics in the electoral sense. This is a much more political job than the job of Secretary of the Treasury.

*Interview/
The Christian Science Monitor,
5-5:6.*

Michael Bar-Zohar
*Member of Israeli Knesset
(Parliament);
Former member of Israeli
military intelligence*

4

[On foreign intelligence agents who have been affected by the fall of the iron curtain]: Many of them are scared out of their minds and are capable of anything. They are dangerous men without anyone to curb and control them. They are one more fermenting ingredient in this world's boiling cauldron of instability . . . [Local nationals who have served as moles for foreign spy organizations] are panicky. They don't know where to run. New identities are all but impossible without the help of some powerful official institution. Some of the people involved may be Presidential aides, heads of ministerial bureaus, senior CIA staffers, top bankers or industrialists. All they can do is hope that no one will open some

WHAT THEY SAID IN 1992

(MICHAEL BAR-ZOHAR)

hidden safe somewhere and remember them. The helplessness and fear will not leave them as long as they live.

World Press Review, March:10.

Herbert L. Beckington
Lieutenant General,
United States Marine Corps (Ret.);
Inspector General, Agency
for International Development
of the United States

1

I am the Inspector General of an agency responsible for the management and accountability of billions of dollars of U.S. taxpayers' resources annually in what is arguably the most vulnerable environment conducive to fraud, waste, abuse and mismanagement that routinely confronts any Federal agency: the Third World.

The Washington Post,
7-30:(A)25.

Joseph R. Biden, Jr.
United States Senator,
D-Delaware

2

[Criticizing a Defense Department plan to maintain the U.S. as the world's only remaining superpower]: What these Pentagon planners are laying out is nothing but a *Pax Americana*. Where threats to our stability need to be destroyed, the notion that it can only be done by American military power is outmoded.

Los Angeles Times, 3-9:(A)6.

Boutros Boutros-Ghali
Secretary General
of the United Nations

3

We are seeking to create a new world order. To achieve such an order, we will need new world laws to regulate it. But these laws must be brought about in the same way that new laws are created within nations. That means that everyone who will be affected by such legal changes

should have a say—not just a few rich, powerful people. I could name, for example, a "new environmental order," a "new diarmament order," a "new economic order." It is unthinkable that nations and peoples would accept such fundamental changes if they had had no say in their development. I see getting these people involved in those debates as one of the most important tasks facing the UN.

Interview/
World Press Review, February:23.

4

The [UN] Secretary General can have an impact on the world only when the five permanent members of the Security Council want him to and support him. In the end, he is just an official, acting at the behest of the Security Council and the General Assembly. No one should overestimate the role of the Secretary General. Suppose that he wanted to clean house at the UN, to carry out some much-needed reforms— he could do so only with the consent of the member states. But I know from my work with the Organization of African Unity how reform proposals fare in the face of opposition from members of international organizations.

Interview/
World Press Review, February:22.

5

United Nations operations in areas of crisis have generally been established after conflict has occurred. The time has come to plan for circumstances warranting preventive deployment [of UN forces]. In cases where one nation fears a cross-border attack, if the Security Council concludes that a United Nations presence on one side of the border, with the consent only of the requesting country, would serve to deter conflict, I recommend that preventive deploymnent take place.

UN report, June 18*/
Los Angeles Times, 6-19:(A)4.

6

The importance of the United Nations comes from its moral value, from its credibility. I cannot

(BOUTROS BOUTROS-GHALI)

take the risk of having young soldiers killed in Sarajevo [in the current ethnic conflict in what used to be Yugoslavia] and then having the Security Council order the other soldiers out. You cannot jeopardize the many other [UN] operations. I have the rest of Yugoslavia and Cambodia and El Salvador. I have 10 other operations . . . Public opinion wants to see quick results, and there are no quick results in solving international disputes. They take months and years of negotiations. But the public just wants quick results, and they accuse us of not doing what needs to be done.

Interview/
Los Angeles Times, 8-10:(A)18.

Abdel-Madjid Bouzidi
Economic adviser to
Algerian President Ali Kafi

1

Twenty years of debt experience in the Third World shows us that restructuring, as practiced [and imposed] by international institutions, results in a snow-plow effect. You just push everything off farther down the road and never do get rid of it . . . Not only are objectives imposed [from the outside], but so are the means for achieving them. National independence and authority are the victims.

The Christian Science Monitor,
12-9:7.

Seyom Brown
Chairman, department of politics,
Brandeis University
(United States)

2

[Criticizing U.S. President George Bush's handling of foreign affairs]: In general, I think there's been a squandering of opportunity for constructive leadership in the dramatically changed international system. What you have, unfortunately, is petty electoral considerations and small-mindedness masquerading under his favorite term, "prudence." With the end of the Cold War, it was really a great opportunity for

leadership that was handed down to Bush by [former President Ronald] Reagan on a silver platter . . . Well, Bush wasted most of the first year of his Administration with what the Administration said was a review of Soviet policy, and from my perspective he played to the conservative gallery with postures of diplomatic toughness toward [then-Soviet President Mikhail] Gorbachev.

Interview/
The New York Times, 6-26:(A)12.

Zbigniew Brzezinski
Counsellor, Center for
Strategic and International
Studies (United States);
Former Assistant to the
President of the United States
(Jimmy Carter) for
National Security Affairs

3

A *Pax Americana* simply won't work anymore. Our economic difficulties simply make it impossible . . . Somebody has to take a leadership role, and it ought to be the United States— but we aren't in any shape to do it.

Los Angeles Times, 2-1:(A)7.

Patrick J. Buchanan
Political commentator;
Candidate for the 1992
Republican U.S.
Presidential nomination

4

[Criticizing a Pentagon proposal to keep the U.S. as the world's only remaining superpower]: This is a formula for endless American intervention in quarrels and war when no vital interest of the United States is remotely engaged. It's virtually a blank check to all of America's friends and allies that we'll go to war to defend their interests.

To reporters, March 9/
The New York Times, 3-10:(A)10.

5

[Saying his foreign-policy position is not isolationist]: We simply do not want to fight other

WHAT THEY SAID IN 1992

people's wars. It is those who would spill the blood of American soldiers in a quest for empire, or empty our Treasury to buy the transitory friendship of distant emirs and despots, who are the true isolationists. They would isolate America from her dreams, her traditions and her true national interest.

Before World Affairs Council,
Beverly Hills, Calif., May 19/
Los Angeles Times, 5-20:(A)11.

George Bush
President of the United States

1

Right now, across the globe the UN is working night and day in the cause of peace. And never before in its four decades have the UN's blue helmets and blue berets been so engaged in the noble work of peacekeeping, even to the extent of building the foundation for free elections. And never before has the United Nations been so ready and so compelled to step up to the task of peacemaking, both to resolve hot wars and to conduct that forward-looking mission known as preventive diplomacy.

At UN Security Council summit meeting,
United Nations, New York, Jan. 31/
The New York Times, 2-1:5.

2

[On whether the U.S. should move more toward a system of collective security in international affairs or continue itself to bear most of the burden for policing the world]: I think the United States has a burden to bear. But we have worked effectively through multilateral organizations. The clearest example of that is what happened in the [Persian] Gulf war . . . But we are leaders and we must continue to lead, we must continue to stay engaged. So it isn't a clear-cut choice of either-or.

News conference,
Washington, D.C., March 11/
The Washington Post,
3-12:(A)18.

3

Whether the lands of the old Soviet empire move forward into democracy or slide back into anarchy or authoritarianism, the outcome of this great transition will affect everything [in the world], from the amount of resources government must devote to defense instead of domestic needs, to a future for our children free from fear.

At U.S. Naval Academy commencement,
May 27/Los Angeles Times, 5-28:(A)4.

4

Four years ago, I spoke . . . of our urgent mission—defending our security and promoting the American ideal abroad. Just pause for a moment to reflect on what we've done. Germany has united—and a slab of the Berlin Wall sits right outside this Astrodome. Arabs and Israelis now sit face-to-face and talk peace. Every hostage held in Lebanon is free. The conflict in El Salvador is over, and free elections brought democracy to Nicaragua. Black and white South Africans cheered each other at the Olympics. The Soviet Union can only be found in history books. The captive nations of Eastern Europe and the Baltics are captive no more. And today on the rural streets of Poland, merchants sell cans of air labelled: the last breath of Communism. If I had stood before you four years ago and described this as the world we would help to build, you would have said: "George Bush, you must be smoking something, and you must have inhaled."

At Republican National Convention,
Houston, Texas, Aug. 20/
The New York Times, 8-21:(A)16.

5

While the U.S. post-war strategy was largely bipartisan, the fact remains that the liberal, McGovern wing of the other [Democratic] Party . . . consistently made the wrong choice. In the '70s, they wanted a hollow army. We [conservatives] wanted a strong fighting force. From Angola to Central America, they said, "Let's negotiate, deliberate, procrastinate." We said, "Just stand up for freedom." Now the Cold War is over and they claim, "Hey, we were with you

(GEORGE BUSH)

all the way." Their behavior reminds me of the old con man's advice to the new kid. He said, "Son, if you're being run out of town, just get out in front and make it look like a parade."

At Republican National Convention,
Houston, Texas, Aug. 20/
The New York Times, 8-21:(A)16.

1

The community of nations and the United Nations face three critical, interrelated challenges as we enter the 21st century. First, we face the political challenge of keeping today's peace and preventing tomorrow's wars. As we see daily in Bosnia and Somalia and Cambodia, everywhere conflict claims innocent lives, the need for enhanced peace-keeping capabilities has never been greater, the conflicts we must deal with more intractable, the costs of conflict higher. And second, we face the strategic challenge of the proliferation of weapons of mass destruction, truly the fastest-growing security challenge . . . And third, we face the common economic challenge of promoting prosperity for all, of strengthening an open, growth-oriented, free-market international economic order, while safeguarding the environment.

At United Nations,
New York, Sept. 21/
The New York Times, 9-22:(A)7.

2

[On whether he knew at the time about the Iran-contra affair, in which the U.S. sold arms to Iran in return for hostages and in which monies from the sale were illegally diverted to Nicaraguan contras]: In terms of the contra part of it, absolutely not. And no one has suggested that I did. Diversion of arms for support for the contras, no. And no one's challenged that . . . What was asked was whether I knew that [then-U.S. President Reagan's Defense Secretary] Caspar Weinberger and [Secretary of State George] Shultz, how strongly they opposed it. And I said to that there were two key meetings where they almost got into a shouting match, I'm told, that I did not

attend. But I said all along that I knew about the arms going [to Iran] and I supported the President [Reagan] . . . I've said so all along, given speeches on it.

Broadcast interview,
Washington, D.C./
"Today," NBC-TV, 10-13.

3

We will have a continuing responsibility as the only remaining superpower to stay involved [in the world]. If we pull back in some isolation and say we don't have to do our share or more than our share anymore, I believe you can just ask for conflagration that we'll get involved in the future . . . And we're going to stay engaged, as long as I'm President, working to improve things. You know, it's so easy now to say, "Hey, cut out foreign aid; we got a problem at home." I think the United States has to still have the Statue of Liberty as a symbol of caring for others . . . So the new world order, to me, means freedom and democracy, keep engaged. Do not pull back into isolation. And we are the United States and we have a responsibility to lead to guarantee the security. If it hadn't been for us, [Iraqi President] Saddam Hussein would be sitting on top of three-fifths of the oil supply of the world and he'd have nuclear weapons. Only the United States could [put together the coalition that it led to oust Iraq from Kuwait in the 1991 Persian Gulf war].

At Presidential candidates' debate,
Richmond, Va., Oct. 15/
The New York Times, 10-17:12.

4

History is once again summoning [the U.S.] to lead. The new [post-Cold War] world could, in time, be as menacing as the old . . . A retreat from American leadership, from American involvement, would be a mistake for which future generations . . . indeed our own children, would pay dearly . . . In 36 days we will have a new President [Bill Clinton]. And I am very confident that he will do his level best to serve the cause that I have outlined here today. He's going to have my support. I'll stay out of his way.

At Texas A&M University, Dec. 15/
USA Today, 12-16:(A)4.

WHAT THEY SAID IN 1992

(GEORGE BUSH)

1

The alternative to American leadership [in the world] is not more security for our citizens, but less; not the flourishing of American principles, but their isolation. Destiny, it has been said, is not a matter of chance. It's a matter of choice. Our choice as a people is simple: We can either shape our times, or we can let the times shape us. And shape us they will, at a price frightening to contemplate—morally, economically and strategically.

At Texas A&M University, Dec. 15/
The New York Times, 12-16:(A)1.

Jimmy Carter
Former President
of the United States

2

The world cries out for peaceful resolution of conflict, but our country is seen as more warlike than peace-loving. We celebrated a great victory over tiny Grenada and later invaded Panama, where hundreds of our friends were killed. We promoted and financed the contra war that caused 35,000 casualties in Nicaragua. There are even second thoughts about [last year's Persian] Gulf war, where Saddam Hussein still reigns supreme in Iraq, Kuwait is no closer to democracy and the Kurds and other refugees endure terrible hardship . . . In none of these cases was Camp David or any other avenue used to avoid conflict. Our country should seek greatness in peace, not war.

At Democratic National Convention,
New York, N.Y., July 14/
The New York Times, 7-15:(A)12.

Henry E. Catto
Director,
United States Information Agency

3

[The USIA is] the best-kept secret in America. Nobody here knows what the USIA is or does. In case you can't tell, I think it's the most exciting agency in the whole world.

Interview/Nation's Business, April:59.

Dick Cheney
Secretary of Defense
of the United States

4

The [recent U.S. Presidential] election has ended with this idea that foreign stuff doesn't matter, that we have to focus on domestic issues. I think that's absolutely dead wrong . . . The revolution . . . under way in what used to be the Soviet Union has just begun. [The potential] for violence, for continued collapse of their economy, for ethnic unrest, is very great. And all of this is going to take place on top of stockpiles of 30,000 nuclear weapons.

Interview, Washington, D.C./
USA Today, 11-27:(A)2.

Warren M. Christopher
Secretary of State-designate
of the United States

5

[The] world is still a dangerous place [despite the end of the Cold War]. While the risk of nuclear threat has diminished, the new era has produced a new set of dangers. Ethnic and religious conflicts threaten to ignite widespread hostilities in Central and Eastern Europe. Weapons of mass destruction may reach the hands of untested and unstable powers, and new threats spring from old rivalries in the Middle East, in Europe and in Asia. At the same time, we face a world where borders matter less and less, a world that demands we join with other nations to face challenges that range from overpopulation to AIDS, to the very destruction of our planet's life-support system . . . In contrast to the well-understood goals of the Cold War era, it will be difficult to measure our success as we deal with these new challenges. No doubt the surest test will be the well-being of the American people and the unfailing concern that they have always had for others. In confronting these new challenges, we must remain cognizant that a great power requires not only military might but a powerful economy at home, an economy prepared for global competition. In today's world, that means that foreign policy and domestic policy must be addressed simultaneously, not

(WARREN M. CHRISTOPHER)

sequentially, or else neither will be successful for very long.

News conference,
Little Rock, Ark., Dec. 22/
The New York Times, 12-23:(A)10,9.

Jeffrey Clark
Consultant to the
United States Committee
on Refugees

1

The United States is now showing leadership by sending troops into Somalia [to enforce distribution of food supplies to the starving population]. But this is also the moment for America to lead a wholesale reform of the UN so that, next time, 300,000 people won't have to die before nations find the will to act.

USA Today, 12-7:(A)2.

William R. Clines
Senior fellow,
Institute for International
Economics (United States)

2

What could emerge [in the world] is a period of competition between different capitalist models which all accept the premise that you have a right to private ownership and would acknowledge that private incentive is necessary for development. But there will be a debate between the Japanese model which gives a bigger role to government planning, the U.S. model which is essentially *laissez-faire,* and the European model which gives more emphasis to social welfare.

The New York Times, 4-29:(A)7.

Bill Clinton
Governor of Arkansas (D);
Candidate for the 1992
Democratic U.S.
Presidential nomination

3

America has to take care of its own problems . . . but America cannot withdraw from the world. Protectionism is not an option. Isolationism is not an option. We have to organize ourselves and develop our people so we can compete and be successful in the world . . . We can't withdraw from it.

At Concord (N.H.) High School,
Feb. 5/
The Washington Post, 2-6:(A)16.

Bill Clinton
Governor of Arkansas (D);
1992 Democratic U.S.
Presidential nominee

4

[U.S. President Bush has an] eagerness to befriend potentates and dictators [around the world], [and] in the long run [Bush's] neglect of our democratic ideals abroad could do as much harm as his neglect of our economic needs at home. He simply does not seem at home in the mainstream, pro-democracy tradition of American foreign-policy. He shows little regard for the idea that we must have a principled and coherent American purpose in international affairs— something he calls "the vision thing." Instead, President Bush seems too often to prefer a foreign policy that embraces stability at the expense of freedom—a foreign policy built more around personal relationships with foreign leaders than consideration of how those leaders acquired and maintained their power. It is almost as if this Administration were nostalgic for a world of times past when foreign policy was the exclusive preserve of a few aristocrats.

Campaigning,
Milwaukee, Wis., Oct. 1/
The Washington Post, 10-2:(A)12.

Bill Clinton
Governor of Arkansas (D);
President-elect
of the United States

5

[On his approach to foreign policy]: We can either try to focus on these problems, get ahead of them, come up with a decent policy and aggressively pursue it, or we can ignore it for a while, wait for it to explode. Then the problems will

WHAT THEY SAID IN 1992

swarm on us and I might have to spend all my time on foreign policy. I don't want that . . . We're trying to develop a disciplined, aggressive approach that will permit us the freedom to focus on America's problems at home.

To reporters,
Washington, D.C., Dec. 8/
USA Today, 12-9:(A)3.

Saul B. Cohen
Former president,
Association of
American Geographers

1

[On technological and political changes taking place in the world]: It's like a circuit board. You can now move from one point to another without having to go through all the middle points. The world's going to be like that, which means the old ideas of hierarchy and hegemony will become obsolete. Nations of all sizes, shapes and manners will be able to reach out to other nations of all sizes, shapes and manners without having to ask for permission from larger powers or without having to go through intermediaries.

Los Angeles Times, 8-25:(H)4.

George Demko
Geographer; Director,
Rockefeller Center,
Dartmouth College
(United States)

2

The current changes in the political and economic geography of the world are as significant as what the world went through after the Treaty of Westphalia [in 1648]. As we're challenging the traditional ideas of state sovereignty, globalizing economies and communications, and breaking up the last empires, the geography of the world is unhooking old connections and hooking up new ones. Along with borders, the dynamics and functions of states will change too.

Los Angeles Times, 8-25:(H)4.

Milovan Djilas
Author; Former Vice President
of Yugoslavia

3

I get the impression, and in this maybe I am not right, that the United States is becoming a little weaker, a little less able to play its role in the world; and if this is so, if the power of the United States declines, then the way is open to everything bad. It will be a tragedy, not only for America but for the rest of the world, if you [the U.S.] lose your capacity to lead.

Interview, Belgrade, Yugoslavia/
The New York Times, 3-27:(A)4.

Lawrence S. Eagleburger
Deputy Secretary of State
of the United States

4

What is peculiar to the United States is that every generation or so we debate not only the merits of this or that [foreign] policy, but the existential purpose of American foreign policy itself. Such a debate would be almost unthinkable in most other countries, where foreign policy is deemed to serve national interests, which themselves are seen as timeless and immutable.

Speech/
The New York Times, 2-7:(A)7.

5

Any Ambassador or Foreign Service officer who has his or her head screwed on right knows that the U.S. position in the world is . . . dependent on our ability to compete in world markets . . . We are going to have to shift away from the stuff we spent the last 40 years doing. The world has changed. A guy who spent his life in NATO is going to have to adjust because that's not where we are. The United States will rise or fall in the next 50 years on its ability to compete in international trade, and we had better get in the business of making success possible.

Interview/
The Washington Post,
3-20:(A)19,20.

J. James Exon
United States Representative,
D-Nebraska

1

[Arms exports are] the way you get to be a superpower. You surround yourself with a lot of your supporters, you give them a lot of nuclear armaments and then you become Mr. Big.

Interview,
Washington, D.C., Feb. 25/
The New York Times, 2-26:(A)5.

Mark Falcoff
Scholar,
American Enterprise Institute

2

From the perspective of practitioners of the international arts, [U.S. President George] Bush is highly regarded . . . Bush is seen as a man who in a very dignified way closed down the Cold War and allowed our adversaries to hang up their weapons without humiliating them.

The Christian Science Monitor,
8-18:7.

Dante B. Fascell
United States Representative,
D-Florida

3

This is no longer a unipolar world, even though the United States is a superpower. We have to exercise our responsibility. We have to show the leadership . . . We are now in an era in this world where leadership and partnership go together, and the United States must continue to take that lead and demonstrate the capability that we can forge the partnerships that are necessary to make this a better world, have more stable political systems, have greater freedoms for individual people, greater respect for human rights. We have a proud record in this country. We, the people, have a proud record. And we have to continue that struggle whether we're inside or outside.

News conference,
Washington, D.C., May 27/
The Washington Post, 5-28:(A)20.

J. William Fulbright
Former United States Senator,
D-Arkansas

4

[On his Fulbright Scholar Program]: I introduced the legislation two weeks after we dropped the atomic bombs on Japan [in World War II]. I understood then that atomic weapons would make war intolerable. In a sense, that's dictated everything I've tried to do in the [Fulbright Scholar] exchange program. The main purpose is not academic—it's political. I had a theory that if you go live in another country, if you get acquainted with other people, if you realize that they have families and children just like you do, you won't be inclined to go to war with them.

Interview, Washington, D.C./
The Christian Science Monitor,
11-27:14.

Robert M. Gates
Director of Central Intelligence
of the United States

5

[On his plans for more openness at the CIA]: The purpose for greater openness is to make CIA and the intelligence process more visible and understandable [to the public]. We must try to help people understand better what CIA does and how we do it . . . [But] there will be no press room at CIA, and our employees will be expected to maintain discipline and refer all press inquiries to our public-affairs office. In short, we still must be able to keep secrets in order to do our work.

News conference,
Tulsa, Okla., Feb. 21/
The New York Times, 2-22:7.

6

Many of our new requirements can be satisfied only by human intelligence [gathering]. Our problem in estimating Iraqi nuclear progress was that we had to depend primarily on technical intelligence, and that's why we underestimated. This is true for a lot of areas—narcotics, terrorism. But we know human intelligence is very difficult in terms of the recruitment of agents, staying in touch with them and assuring that their information is valid.

Interview, Washington, D.C./
Time, 4-20:62.

1

Every major [U.S.] intelligence failure over the last 20 or 40 years has been because the analysts tended to accept the conventional wisdom. The problem has not been a lack of dissent by the various agencies. The problem has come about when they all signed up to a view that was in fact wrong ... The point is that we see a world of more, not fewer, mysteries. It seems imperative to change our approach to doing intelligence estimates by building in our judgments alternative possibilities—what if we're wrong? We must help the policy-makers think through the problems, in addition to supplying our best judgment. There is, for example, really no way of knowing for sure how reform in Russia is going to turn out.

Interview, Washington, D.C./
Time, 4-20:61.

Alixe Glen
Spokesman for U.S. President
George Bush's re-election campaign

2

[Criticizing U.S. Democratic Presidential nominee Bill Clinton's charge that U.S. President Bush's foreign policy is to support dictators and not to promote democracy]: Since 1989, some 43 countries have moved toward democratic government, a movement that is unparalleled in history. President Bush's policies have taken the rhetorical support for democratic government and put it into practice, encouraging these democratic movements around the world.

Oct. 1/
The Washington Post, 10-2:(A)12.

Mikhail S. Gorbachev
Former President
of the Soviet Union

3

It is quite clear that the enhanced integration and interdependence of the world at the same time creates new tensions, both domestically and internationally, unleashing processes which earlier were hidden from view. The very fact that the two world blocs are no longer in confrontation and that the collapse of totalitarian regimes has released centrifugal forces which had been temporarily frozen—territorial and intergovernmental contradictions and claims—has encouraged and exaggerated nationalism, and this has already led to much bloodshed. The ending of the global confrontation of the nuclear superpowers and of the ideological opposition between the two world systems has rendered even more visible today's major contradictions between the rich and the poor countries, between the North and the South.

At Westminster College,
Fulton, Mo., May 6/
The New York Times, 5-7:(A)6.

Albert Gore, Jr.
United States Senator,
D-Tennessee;
1992 Democratic U.S.
Vice-Presidential nominee

4

[Criticizing U.S. President Bush for taking credit for winning the Cold War]: I want to tell you, President Bush, [that] the people of the United States of America [won the Cold War]. This wasn't a partisan victory that came suddenly a few months after you took the oath of office. This started with [the late Democratic President] Harry Truman, and it was a bipartisan effort from the very beginning. George Bush taking credit for the Berlin Wall coming down is like the rooster taking credit for the sunrise.

At Vice-Presidential candidates' debate,
Atlanta, Ga., Oct. 13/
The New York Times, 10-14:(A)13.

Porter Goss
United States Representative,
R-Florida

5

[On current testimony by Alan Fiers against former CIA employee Clair George in connection with alleged CIA improprieties carried out

(PORTER GOSS)

by George in the past]: I have tremendous sympathy for both Mr. Fiers and Mr. George. I think this is a tragedy being played out. It's a little bit like *Death of a Salesman* in some ways. We're dealing with human nature here, being asked to do things in an imperfect world using imperfect tools. [In foreign-intelligence operations,] there are no exact lines in the sand.

The Washington Post, 8-22:(D)5.

Alexander G. Granberg
Adviser to Russian President
Boris Yeltsin

1

It is a well-known rule of international relations that if [a country's leader's] actions cause harm to his neighbors, then, in the final analysis, he will be the loser.

Los Angeles Times, 3-31:(H)6.

Mahbub ul Haq
Former Minister of Finance
of Pakistan

2

Developing countries can graduate out of foreign assistance in the 21st century and take their chances in the international market. But they can only do so if global markets are open—if capital, labor and goods are allowed to flow freely around the world . . . After World War II there was tremendous creativity; the Marshall Plan, the World Bank, the UN, the idea of the single European market. But where are the sources of creativity now? In the last five years we've seen [world political] events unfold that one could only have dreamed about a few years ago. Who's thinking about the 21st century?

The Christian Science Monitor,
4-24:2.

Vaclav Havel
President of Czechoslovakia

3

A global revival of Communism, a turnaround of history to the times of [former Soviet leaders]

Leonid Brezhnev or Joseph Stalin, is out of the question. Today's process [the fall of Communism] is irreversible. Local resuscitations are possible; I can imagine that Communist governing methods could come back under a flag of a different color. For instance, in one of the former Soviet republics, previous [Communist] Party hierarchy could be used to remodel the old system. However, an empire or a bloc will be excluded from our epoch. You cannot set back the clock of history.

Interview/
World Press Review, March:14.

4

[With the spread of democracy and the rise of nationalism in the world,] all the ancient conflicts, wrongs, injustices and animosities are suddenly coming back to life and back to mind. The sudden outburst of freedom has thus not only untied the straitjacket made by Communism, it has also unveiled the centuries-old, often thorny history of nations.

At conference on Security and
Cooperation in Europe,
Helsinki, Finland, July 9/
The New York Times, 7-11:4.

Vaclav Havel
Former President
of Czechoslovakia

5

In the entire post-Communist world there exists an imminent danger of nationalistic and ethnic conflict. In some cases nations were not able to search freely for and find their own identity and form of statehood and gain their independence for tens or even hundreds of years. We cannot be surprised that now, when the straitjacket of Communism has been torn off, all the countries wish to establish their independence and self-determination. A second reason is that for many years the individual citizen was not used to living in freedom. The people got used to a certain structure of guarantees, albeit unpleasant ones. The people are shocked by the freedoms to a certain extent. They are looking for replacement guarantees. And the guarantees of one's own tribe seem to be the most accessible.

Interview, Prague, Czechoslovakia/
Time, 8-3:47.

Stanley Hoffmann
European specialist,
Harvard University
(United States)

1

[Saying the U.S. claims to be the only remaining superpower, but also says it can't afford to do much in international affairs]: During the first few years, I think the [U.S. President] Bush people thought they saw the future almost the way it looked in 1945: We would be clearly the Number 1 superpower, [and] the Soviet Union would follow our lead. The two great powers and a few lesser ones would do things together. That is not going to happen. Now we have to shut up or put up, and since we don't want to put up, we may have to shut up.

The New York Times, 6-26:(A)12.

Richard C. Holbrooke
Former Assistant Secretary
for East Asian and Pacific Affairs,
Department of State
of the United States

2

[The Cold War] was the defining issue in our political discourse and public policy from 1947 until last year. It made "national security" the justification for everything—the interstate highway system, the National Defense Education Act, the Vietnam war, the foreign-aid program. [The late Senator] J. William Fulbright used it to sell his scholarships, and [the late FBI Director] J. Edgar Hoover used it to sell his wiretaps.

The New York Times, 2-6:(A)1.

Hume Horan
Former United States Ambassador
to Saudi Arabia

3

There is a "Kleenex" quality to Ambassadors. We're policy instruments, not policy-makers,

there to take the blame, to be wiped away so the process can continue.

Interview/
The Atlantic, August:44.

James Ingram
Executive director,
United Nations
World Food Programs

4

There has grown up a certain dependency on [foreign] aid . . . in both the donor community and the recipients. I think that too much of it is ill-directed. I'm not talking now about the failure of policies and so on in developing countries. I'm talking about the misdirection on the part of the developed countries of so much of their aid. I don't agree very much with the new conditionality which is being applied. That doesn't mean that I believe one should give aid when it's manifestly ill-used. But I think it's better not to give aid in bad situations than to be always trying to establish conditions.

Interview, Rome, Italy/
The Christian Science Monitor,
4-22:7.

Geoffrey Kemp
Senior associate,
Carnegie Endowment for
International Peace
(United States)

5

[Saying there will be a withdrawal of U.S. involvement in many areas of the world]: It's inevitable. In the absence of a global threat [since the end of the Cold War], democracies do not respond well to a patchwork quilt of regional threats. Aside from issues in our own back yard, our primary interests can now be narrowly defined along a fault line through the Eurasian landmass—an arc from Berlin to Beijing, via Baghdad and the Balkans. That's the only area where we'll have vital interests and not be able to wash our hands.

Los Angeles Times, 6-15:(A)11.

Jeane J. Kirkpatrick
Senior fellow,
American Enterprise Institute;
Former United States
Ambassador/Permanent Representative
to the United Nations

1

UN institutions only work in hard cases, like invasions and war, where some country or countries are willing to assume leaderhip and take on heavy burdens, including putting together a coalition and maintaining that coalition. The United States and [its President] George Bush did that in the case of the [1990] Iraqi invasion of Kuwait . . . [But] the United Nations is not a country or an independent actor in world affairs; it is an arena in which the member states make policy. They make decisions. They provide money. They provide troops. What the UN can do depends above all on the decisions of the member states. The Secretariat is responsible for the administration of some permanent agencies of the UN, but these permanent agencies of the UN cannot take on the peace-making and peace-keeping functions.

Interview/USA Today, 8-11:(A)11.

Helmut Kohl
Chancellor of Germany

2

[Saying the U.S. should not pull away from international affairs]: The destiny of the world is being decided on the foreign-policy front, and . . . each people that does not understand and follow this lesson of history will pay very dearly for it. For a people such as the American people, whether it wants it or not, that has a decisive role to play in world politics and will have to play this role, this is even more valid.

News conference, Washington, D.C.,
March 22/The Washington Post, 3-23:(A)10.

W. Anthony Lake
Assistant-designate to the
President of the United States
(President-elect Bill Clinton)
for National Security Affairs

3

Our daily headlines suggest that not since 1968 has a new Administration faced more diffi-

cult foreign problems. But I am convinced that out of these nettles we can pluck progress and greater security. I look forward to making sure as best I can that [President-elect Clinton] gets the wide array of alternatives, the concise information and the broad range of advice that he rquires, and that his decisions are carried out with dispatch. And I hope to see a year from now and beyond a group of senior national-security officials who are as collegial and amicable as they are today.

News conference,
Little Rock, Ark., Dec. 22/
The New York Times, 12-23:(A)10.

Li Peng
Prime Minister of China

4

Human rights and fundamental freedoms of the entire mankind should be universally respected. Human rights covers many aspects. They include not only civil and political rights, but also economic, social and cultural rights. As far as the large number of developing countries are concerned, the rights to independence, subsistence and development are of paramount importance. In essence, the issue of human rights falls within the sovereignty of each country. A country's human-rights situation should not be judged in total disregard of its history and national conditions. It is neither appropriate nor workable to demand that all countries measure up to the human-rights criteria or models one or a small number of countries . . . [We are] opposed to interference in the internal affairs of other countries using the human-rights issue as an excuse.

At UN Security Council summit meeting,
United Nations, New York, Jan. 31/
The New York Times, 2-1:5.

Edward Luck
President, United Nations Association
of the U.S.A.

5

Making sure there is not interstate aggression is very different from making sure that everyone behaves [within their own borders]. There is a

WHAT THEY SAID IN 1992

movement toward interventionism . . . but there's a real question as to whether the UN's job now is to make sure there is no violence anywhere at any time. That is an endless task.

The Christian Science Monitor,
5-18:6.

Richard G. Lugar
United States Senator,
R-Indiana

1

The [U.S. Bush] Administration came to a conclusion that it was vulnerable [in this election year] to the charge that it was paying too much attention to foreign affairs . . . [But] we've tried to remind people all the way through that the rest of the world is still out there, and it's not only a dangerous place, but there are specific dangers . . . [President-elect Bill Clinton has] governed a state [Arkansas] of 2.4 million people . . . You try to extrapolate that kind of administrative activity to this country and to the world and it's sort of a breathtaking leap.

Interview,
Washington, D.C., Nov. 12/
The Christian Science Monitor,
11-13:3.

John Major
Prime Minister
of the United Kingdom

2

All around the world, socialism is being ditched—across the whole of Eastern Europe, in Latin America, wherever you go . . . In Russia, what are they doing now? They are privatizing companies as fast as they possibly can. In India, what have they just done? Cut the top rates of tax dramatically. Both [are] ideals pioneered essentially in the United Kingdom under [former Prime Minister Margaret] Thatcher's leadership in the early 1980s. That is the drift of history.

Interview, London, England/
Newsweek, 3-23:39.

Michael Mandelbaum
Foreign-policy specialist,
School of Advanced
International Studies,
Johns Hopkins University
(United States)

3

We [the U.S.] have a foreign policy today in the shape of a doughnut—lots of peripheral interests, but nothing at the center. There is no one central problem from which all others emanate and which can be used to galvanize the public.

The New York Times, 2-7:(A)1.

Ian Martin
Secretary general,
Amnesty International

4

We have, I think, largely gotten away from the case where there's any resonance for the argument that human-rights criticism [of foreign countries] is interference in internal affairs. We still get that a bit from the Chinese government. But it sounds more and more anarchronistic each time you hear it. Even the Chinese are beginning to shave that position and to say, yes, we are going to engage in human-rights dialogue. What's particularly important . . . is that people don't give up on human rights as an issue because they think it's sort of taken care of, with the trend to democracy, with Western governments making human rights more central in their foreign policies. Because, positive as those things are, it's not very hard to see that democracy from elections is only the beginning . . . of improving the protection of human rights.

Interview,
Boston, Mass., March 23/
The Christian Science Monitor,
4-2:5.

R. Bruce McColm
Executive director,
Freedom House (United States)

5

[On the current trend toward democracy around the world]: These significant gains are fragile. The 21st century will again challenge

(R. BRUCE MCCOLM)

liberal democracy with questions concerning its ability to produce prosperity and a just social system. Democratic values are clearly resurgent today. Viewed over the long course of human history, however, most democracies have been short-lived.

Los Angeles Times, 2-25:(H)1.

Robert S. McNamara
Former Secretary of Defense
of the United States

1

I'm not so naive as to believe this post-Cold War world would be without conflict. There have been 125 wars leading to 40 million deaths, largely in the Third World, after World War II and before the [1991 Persian] Gulf war. These were not a function of ideological differences between East and West. They were a function of the age-old causes of war—boundary disputes, economic conflicts, ethnic tensions.

Interview/
The New York Times, 2-3:(A)6.

Kiichi Miyazawa
Prime Minister of Japan

2

The world needs American leadership. An isolationist America would be everyone's nightmare.

At National Press Club,
Washington, D.C., July 2/
Los Angeles Times, 7-3:(A)8.

Sibjhatullah Mojadedi
President of Afghanistan

3

The weakest nations in the world are those that had a woman as a leader. It doesn't mean that Islam [his religion] is against women. On the contrary, it respects them and says they are equal to men. But [history shows] that weak nations are led by women.

Newsweek, 5-11:23.

Brian Mulroney
Prime Minister of Canada

4

As political leaders, our job is to force the pace and stretch out the limits of international cooperation. The nations gathered here today have the human genius to create a world free from deprivation and secure from degradation. What remains is for governments to provide the leadership the world so desperately needs . . . Our children, the Rio generation, will be our judges and our beneficiaries.

At UN Conference on Environment
and Development,
Rio de Janeiro, Brazil, June 12/
Los Angeles Times, 6-13:(A)23.

Paul H. Nitze
Former Special Adviser to the
President of the United States
(Ronald Reagan)
for Arms-Control Negotiations

5

Who are our [the U.S.'s] enemies? Certainly the old U.S.S.R. is a changed country altogether. But there are enemies. [Iraqi President] Saddam Hussein has been our enemy for some time. There are cases, such as Hitler or Saddam Hussein, where there's a danger to the world community which does involve some breach of the sanctity of sovereign nations. We shouldn't shy away from interfering with that. We should try to do it through the United Nations. If the UN is recalcitrant, we should try to do it ourselves or try to form a coalition outside the UN. There's a temptation to say, "Let's turn everything over to arbitration by the United Nations and not act without the consent of the UN." I think that's dangerous. I've always believed in the great-power veto. It's a fundamental protection that we as the leading countries need to have so people don't gang up against us.

Interview/The New York Times, 2-4:(A)4.

Richard M. Nixon
Former President
of the United States

6

Even some of those who have been the strongest supporters of a strong foreign-policy

WHAT THEY SAID IN 1992

(RICHARD M. NIXON)

role for the United States now say it's time to turn our efforts inward . . . What they fail to realize is that foreign and domestic policy are like Siamese twins: Neither can survive without the other . . . We can't be at peace in a world of wars, and we can't have a healthy American economy in a sick world economy.

At conference sponsored by
Richard M. Nixon Library,
Washington, D.C., March 11/
Los Angeles Times, 3-12:(A)6.

Joseph Nye
Professor of international affairs,
Kennedy School of Government,
Harvard University (United States)

1

Reducing foreign policy to "jobs, jobs, jobs" not only trivializes it, but it puts the focus on only one aspect of American interdependence with the rest of the world. There has to be a better way of defeating isolationist arguments and justifying an international policy.

The New York Times, 2-7:(A)7.

David R. Obey
United States Representative,
D-Wisconsin

2

The American people never really endorsed [the late President] Harry Truman's support for NATO, Bretton Woods or the Marshall Plan. They acquiesced in them, though, because they knew he was engaged at home, because they were animated by the Cold War and because Truman was operating in the context of a balanced budget and rapidly rising family income. All of those are absent today . . . What many internationalists don't understand is that if they insist that we stay involved up to our elbows in all corners of the world, they will experience a backlash from the American public that will make it difficult to stay involved anywhere.

The New York Times, 2-7:(A)7.

Turgut Ozal
President of Turkey

3

Regional concepts, rather than national strategies, have become the focal point of international attention. The emergence of commonly shared values such as democracy, human rights and free enterprise creates favorable conditions for new forms of economic partnership.

To representatives of Black Sea Economic
Cooperation Region, Istanbul, Turkey,
Feb. 3/
Los Angeles Times, 2-7:(A)10.

Connie Peck
Senior research fellow,
Institute for Peace Research,
La Trobe University
(Australia)

4

[On the UN's new policy of trying to stop violence before it starts in vulnerable areas of the world]: If "preventive diplomacy" is effective 10 per cent of the time, it is still going to be more cost effective in terms of picking up the pieces afterwards and the huge devastation that occurs in armed conflict . . . [UN representatives should regularly visit potential trouble spots,] meeting with leaders and the actors in the capital cities and the hot spots in the region to get in-depth understanding of what the issues are in the disputes and to offer "quiet diplomacy."

The Christian Science Monitor,
11-3:12.

Claiborne Pell
United States Senator,
D-Rhode Island

5

The new cooperative relationship between the United States and Russia has enabled us to resolve an astonishing array of regional conflicts. Working under the umbrella of the United Nations, settlements have been reached to such longstanding and divisive conflicts as those in Namibia, Angola, El Salvador, Western Sahara, Cambodia, Iran-Iraq, as well as the more recent wars between Iraq and Kuwait and within the

(CLAIBORNE PELL)

former Yugoslavia. Now, however, having won our battles with the Marxists at great expense, the [U.S.] Congress appears unwilling to spend the relatively small sums required to win the war. I am dismayed at the apparent unwillingness of many in Congress to pay the relatively modest sums required for the peace-keeping forces needed to consolidate our victories. I read in the press of complaints at the skyrocketing cost of United Nations peace-keeping. Of course the costs have gone up. It is entirely a function of how many of the world's conflicts have been resolved and of how many victories America has won. And may I remind my colleagues that however costly UN peace-keeping is, it is far less costly to the United States than the price we paid for our earlier involvements in these regional conflicts ... Both the [U.S.] Bush Administration and the Congress have been counting the pennies while missing the prize.

Before the Senate,
Washington, D.C., March 12/
The Washington Post, 3-18:(A)20.

Ross Perot
American industrialist

1

[Saying that, if he runs for and wins the U.S. Presidency this year, he would want to restructure the Embassy system]: Embassies are relics of days of sailing ships. At one time, when you had no world communications, your Ambassador spoke for you in that country. But now, with instantaneous communications around the world, the Ambassador is primarily in a social role. If some American walks in with a problem, at least in all my experience, you're treated like a nuisance. I would recommend we redo the whole Embassay structure.

Broadcast interview/"20/20,"
ABC-TV, 5-29.

Dan Quayle
Vice President
of the United States

2

The starting point for any discussion these days has to reference the end of the Cold War.

Today, in place of one great threat, there are many smaller, less recognizable threats. And today, more than ever before, other nations look to America for leadership. Who will take up this responsibility if we refuse it? Germany? Japan? China?

Before Economic Club of New York,
Feb. 27/
The New York Times, 2-28:(A)7.

3

[On 1992 Democratic Presidential nominee Arkansas Governor Bill Clinton]: Bill Clinton's foreign-policy experience is a summer internship with the Senate Foreign Relations Committee. In the area of foreign policy, we ought to compare the experience of Bill Clinton with the experience of [President] George Bush, and it is no comparison at all.

At forum sponsored by American
Israel Public Affairs Committee,
Aug. 17/
The New York Times, 8-18:(A)6.

4

The President of the United States deals on the international scene. He's got to deal with the President of Russia; he's got to deal with the Chancellor of Germany, Prime Minister of Britain, President of France, Prime Minister of Japan; he's got to deal with a whole host of leaders around the world. And the leaders sit down and they will negotiate and they will come to agreements with people that they trust ... [Democratic U.S. Presidential nominee] Bill Clinton has trouble telling the truth, and he will have a very difficult time dealing with somebody like [Russian] President [Boris] Yeltsin or [German] Chancellor [Helmut] Kohl or [British] Prime Minister [John] Major or [French] President [Francois] Mitterrand—because truth and integrity are prerequisites to being President of the United States.

At Vice-Presidential candidates' debate,
Atlanta, Ga., Oct. 13/
The New York Times, 10-14:(A)13.

P. V. Narasimha Rao
Prime Minister of India

1

We inhabit a single planet, but one of many worlds. Such a fragmented planet cannot survive in harmony with itself . . . We must assure that the affluence of some is not derived from the poverty of many.

At UN Conference on Environment
and Development,
Rio de Janeiro, Brazil, June 12/
Los Angeles Times, 6-13:(A)23.

Ronald Reagan
Former President of the United States

2

It was not so long ago that the world was a far more dangerous place. It was a world where aggressive Soviet Communism was on the rise and American strength was in decline. It was a world where our children came of age under the threat of nuclear holocaust. It was a world where our leaders told us that standing up to aggressors was dangerous, that American might and determination were somehow obstacles to peace. But we stood tall and proclaimed that Communism was destined for the ash heap of history. We never heard so much ridicule from our liberal friends. The only thing that got them more upset was two simple words: "evil empire" [the phrase Reagan used to describe the Soviet Union]. But we knew then what the liberal Democrat leaders just couldn't figure out: The sky would not fall if America restored her strength and resolve. The sky would not fall if an American President spoke the truth. The only thing that would fall was the Berlin Wall.

At Republican National Convention,
Houston, Texas, Aug. 17/
The New York Times, 8-18:(A)6.

Rozanne L. Ridgway
President, Atlantic Council;
Former Assistant Secretary
for European and Canadian
Affairs, Department of State
of the United States

3

During the Cold War, we [the U.S.] got used to a world of "Either you're for us or you're against us." We expected 100 per cent support [from allies] . . . The major challenge for the United States is learning to deal with people who on some issues are partners but on other issues are competitors. We will find that discomfiting—to put it politely . . . We need to get used to a world in which we don't pay 100 per cent of the bill and we don't control 100 per cent of the outcome. It's going to be very difficult for the United States to handle that, psychologically and emotionally.

Los Angeles Times, 6-9:(A)16.

Gordon Ritchie
Former Canadian Deputy Trade
Negotiator during U.S.-Canada
free-trade talks

4

[On Canada's trade negotiations with various countries]: When the Americans are at their most bloody-minded, they still are better than the Europeans at their best. And the Europeans at their worst are better than the Japanese at their best.

Los Angeles Times, 5-18:(D)2.

Bert Rockman
Political scientist,
University of Pittsburgh (Pa.)
(United States)

5

The world is going to be a far more dangerous place [even with the end of the Cold War], not less dangerous; but the danger will be the pocket wars, the brush fires with regional implications. We [the U.S.] can choose to sit them out, but we'll be called on often to intervene.

The Christian Science Monitor,
8-21:6.

Frank A. Rubino
Chief defense attorney
for former Panamanian leader
Manuel Noriega in his
U.S. trial on drug and
racketeering charges

6

[On Noriega's being convicted by a U.S. jury on 10 drug and racketeering charges]: A new

(FRANK A. RUBINO)

page has been written in American history. The U.S. government, in its role as world policeman, saw fit to invade a country [Panama] and seize its leader [and bring him to the U.S. for trial]. The jury has condoned that action and sent a message to the rest of the world's leaders that you too may soon be in our courthouse . . . The United States will now trample across the entire world, imposing its will upon so-called independent, sovereign nations. Unless leaders of foreign governments are willing to kneel once a day and face Washington and give grace to [U.S. President] George Bush, they, too, may be in the same posture as General Noriega.

Miami, Fla., April 9/
Los Angeles Times, 4-10:(A)1;
The New York Times, 4-10:(A)14.

Michael J. Sandel
Professor of government,
Harvard University
(United States)

1

The challenge for the [forthcoming U.S. Bill] Clinton Presidency will be twofold. On the one hand, he will have to articulate clearly the principles on behalf of which we may need to intervene [with force in foreign countries]—whether it is upholding human rights, averting starvation or promoting democracy . . . [On the other hand,] Clinton will have to be honest with the American people about both the principles justifying intervention and the practical considerations that might restrain such action. Otherwise he will seem inconsistent and hypocritical and ultimately undermine the domestic consensus for intervention.

The New York Times, 12-5:1,4.

James R. Sasser
United States Senator,
D-Tennessee

2

[On U.S. financial support for UN international peace-keeping operations]: We are in a dilemma here in Congress. Many of us recog-

nize the importance of these peace-keeping efforts around the world and recognize our responsibility to pay our share. But at the same time, we are being whipsawed by domestic urgencies. Our constituents are saying that they have borne the burden as long as they intend to.

Interview,
Washington, D.C., March 5/
The New York Times, 3-6:(A)6.

David Scheffer
Senior fellow,
Carnegie Endowment for
International Peace
(United States)

3

In a sense, self-determination [for the world's peoples] has taken on a level of importance comparable to individual human rights in the 1960s. It is now the linchpin of U.S. foreign policy.

The Christian Science Monitor,
10-21:4.

Philippe Seguin
Deputy,
French National Assembly

4

[On the G-7 industrial countries]: When you have seven leaders from seven different nations, what you really have are seven different competitors, all of whom are thinking about their own national interests. The question is whether we need a new organization with the power to make decisions on a worldwide level . . . Because we now live in a world where the least decision in Italy or Hong Kong has consequences here [in France].

Interview/
USA Today, 11-27:(B)3.

David Smock
Senior program officer,
United States Institute of Peace

5

Any significant UN military intervention [to help the starving people in Somalia] will raise the general issue of whether to intervene for humani-

(DAVID SMOCK)

tarian purposes, with or without local permission, to a new level of salience and immediacy. If the UN force gets sucked into a morass, the international community will think twice before it commits itself again. If the operation is a marvelous success, that will also have an impact on future action.

The Christian Science Monitor,
12-4:1.

Abraham D. Sofaer
Former Legal Adviser
to the Department of State
of the United States

1

[On criticism that the U.S. acted improperly in bringing former Panamanian leader Manuel Noriega to trial on drug and racketeering charges by kidnaping him and taking him to the U.S. during the 1989 American invasion of Panama]: This is not a precedent for going into countries and grabbing heads of state. We never recognized him as a head of state. After the election [of current President Guillermo Endara], we gave [Noriega] no recognition whatsoever. That was the reason he was indicted—he was not a head of state in our view.

Los Angeles Times, 4-10:(A)28.

Ronald Spiers
Former Under Secretary
for Management,
Department of State
of the United States

2

[Criticizing the Presidential practice of appointing U.S. Ambassadors based upon their monetary contributions to the cause of the President's party]: Ambassadors are the eyes and voice of America abroad. If these jobs are just regarded as perks, something you can buy, it demeans the whole proposition.

Los Angeles Times,
7-6:(A)4.

John D. Steinbruner
Director of foreign-policy studies,
Brookings Institution
(United States)

3

[Criticizing a U.S. Defense Department plan to maintain the U.S. as the world's only remaining superpower]: This is an overt attempt to preserve very stark U.S. superiority, and that is going to raise fears of American hegemony all over the world. [The authors of this plan] are people who have yet to see the nature of the new world and are trying to justify a confrontational security policy in the absence of an enemy. It's not appropriate and it's self-defeating. If others think we're trying to maintain this position, they'll program to hedge against us.

Los Angeles Times, 3-9:(A)6.

Paul E. Tsongas
Candidate for the 1992
Democratic U.S.
Presidential nomination;
Former United States Senator,
D-Massachusetts

4

We [the U.S.] cannot intercede in every case where clashes have broken out. That temptation is a snare and must be resisted. No American blood should be casually spilled taking sides in the international affairs of woeful nations.

Los Angeles Times, 3-17:(H)6.

Brian Urquhart
Scholar-in-residence,
Ford Foundation (United States);
Former Under Secretary
for Special Political Affairs
of the United Nations

5

We've bumbled into a world where everything affects everybody. We've got to stop looking at the UN only in terms of day-to-day emergencies and start seeing it as the only organization that can foster institutions for a global society.

Time, 2-3:28.

Paul C. Warnke
Former Director,
Arms Control and
Disarmament Agency
of the United States

1

What we have to do over a period of years is to devalue nuclear weapons, deprive them of their value as a status symbol, because you've got a lot of countries that feel, "I'm not in the big leagues unless I have a nuclear weapon." I think this is the way in which we would have a real risk of nuclear war . . . For one thing, [we should] go along with a test ban. Russia has declared a one-year moratorium. The French have stopped testing. The British couldn't test if we stopped because they test at our Nevada test site. So we have China and the United States that are the only ones in the nuclear-testing club. When we try to justify continuing to test, we give a certain glamour to nuclear weapons.

Interview/USA Today, 6-17:(A)13.

Ben Wattenberg
Senior fellow,
American Enterprise Institute

2

[In the past,] we needed a [U.S.] President who knew what a sword was, who believed in a strong national defense. But now [with the end of the Cold War] the test of an American President is not going to be whether he can play defense but whether he can play offense. The prime goal of American foreign policy should be to purvey American democracy, and [Democratic Presidential nominee Bill] Clinton just may be better at that [than his challenger, President Bush]. It's the best single issue in American politics, telling Americans that we should stand for something great.

The Christian Science Monitor, 10-7:9.

Marvin Wilson
Professor of Biblical studies,
Gordon College (United States)

3

The number-one obstacle to peace is nationalism, because so often it insists on the denial of the other guy.

Christianity Today, 3-9:50.

William Julius Wilson
Professor of sociology
and public policy,
University of Chicago
(United States)

4

In the international arena, nationalism can prove to be destructive in the long run. Given that, the United States should work to curb the excesses of nationalism by promoting forms that buttress the mutual cooperation of nations. I think you can become a powerful giant if you lead by example.

Interview/The New York Times, 2-7:(A)7.

R. James Woolsey, Jr.
Director-designate
of Central Intelligence
of the United States

5

The problem posed by one enemy with a worldwide reach is gone with the end of the Cold War; but the problems posed by the proliferation of weapons of mass destruction, terrorism, drugs, ethnic and national hatreds, ecological damage and tough economic competition all give American intelligence a full agenda. In a number of ways it is a more complex and difficult agenda even than that which existed before.

News conference,
Little Rock, Ark., Dec. 22/
The New York Times, 12-23:(A)10.

Boris N. Yeltsin
President of Russia

6

For many years, [the U.S. and Russia] were the two poles, the two opposites. They wanted to make us implacable enemies. That affected the destinies of the world in a most tragic way. The world was shaken by the storms of confrontation. It was close to exploding, close to perishing beyond salvation. That evil scenario is becoming a thing of the past. Reason begins to triumph over madness. We have left behind the period when America and Russia looked at each other through gun sights, ready to pull the trigger at any time.

Before joint session of U.S. Congress,
Washington, D.C., June 17/
The Washington Post, 6-18:(A)36.

Africa

Dennis Avery
Senior fellow,
Hudson Institute
(United States)

1

[On the civil war and famine in Somalia]: This year we've got a famine in Somalia with no drought, and drought in southern Africa with no famine. And the difference is guns.

The Christian Science Monitor,
10-21:10.

Abrahim Babangida
President of Nigeria;
Chairman, Organization of
African Unity

2

Africa cannot and should not be immune from the political developments taking place in the world. The quest for democracy and freedom is so universal that no amount of repression can hold it in check for too long.

At Organization of African Unity summit,
Dakar, Senegal/
The Washington Post, 7-2:(A)32.

Roelof F. Botha
Foreign Minister of South Africa

3

We [in southern Africa] want to form an economic bloc. We are small compared to the giant America, or to the giant Europe, or that giant that is rising in the Far East and the Pacific Rim, but we want to be your partner. Your ships are passing here, one way or the other, and we want to make a deal. We want firm prices for our minerals, metals and raw materials. And we also want to become a manufacturing area, where we can build parts for your cars, as well as your cameras and radios. I am working beyond apartheid and beyond the new Constitution. I'm working on what I call the southern Africa platform, because I realize that unless this comes into being as soon as possible, we will quite literally miss the boat. The necessity for regional Africa to succeed has never been greater, and we have to work hard together with all the nations of this continent, to plan properly, to stimulate economic growth, to interact with one another so we can save Africa.

USA Today, 9-8:(Our World)13.

George Bush
President of the United States

4

[Announcing that U.S.-led military forces will go to Somalia to ensure food supplies get to the starving population]: For many months now, the United States has been actively engaged in the massive international relief effort to ease Somalia's suffering. All told, America has sent Somalia 200,000 tons of food—more than half the world total. This summer, the distribution system [in Somalia] broke down. Truck convoys from Somalia's ports were blocked [by roving armed gangs]. Sufficient food failed to reach the starving in the interior of Somalia. And so in August, we took additional action . . . [But] the security situation has grown worse. The UN has been prevented from deploying its initial commitment of troops. In many cases, food from relief flights is being looted upon landing. Food convoys have been hijacked, aid workers assaulted, ships with food have been subject to artillery attacks that prevented them from docking. There is no government in Somalia. Law and order have broken down. Anarchy prevails . . . Last night, the United Nations Security Council, by unanimous vote, and after the tireless efforts of Secretary General [Boutros] Boutros-Ghali, welcomed the United States' offer to lead a [military] coalition to get the food through. After consulting with my advisers, with world leaders and the [U.S.] Congressional leadership, I have today told Secretary General Boutros-Ghali that America will answer the call. I have given the order to [U.S. Defense] Secretary [Dick] Cheney to move a substantial American force into Somalia . . . Only the United States has the global reach to place a large security force on the

(GEORGE BUSH)

ground in such a distant place quickly and efficiently and thus save thousands of innocents from death. We will not, however, be acting alone. I expect forces from about a dozen countries to join us in this mission.

Broadcast address to the nation,
Washington, D.C., Dec. 4/
The New York Times, 12-5:4.

Frederick Chiluba
President of Zambia

1

The map of Africa is almost a complete tale of *coups d'etat* and other forms of military insurrection. Peaceful change of government is a concept we are only now beginning to grasp . . . While [the OAU] has championed the cause of freedom from foreign and racist domination, African nations chose to be blind to the many inequalities and injustices existing within our own borders.

At Organization of African Unity summit,
Dakar, Senegal/
The Washington Post, 7-2:(A)31,32.

Herman J. Cohen
Assistant Secretary for African Affairs,
Department of State
of the United States

2

There were always priorities related to the Cold War that kept us [the U.S.] from doing what I wanted to do in Africa. If we wanted to do something in the Horn of Africa, the first question was how it related to our need for bases there. Now [with the end of the Cold War] we don't need bases there . . . Until recently, everything we did in Africa was dependent on some external factor. Everything was related to some non-African issue. Now we don't have that anymore . . . During the Cold War, we would tolerate many things among our friends because we had other things in play. Now we can show greater impatience, telling them their behavior is wrong, that it's going to result in trouble with [the U.S.] Congress.

Interview/
The New York Times, 3-23:(A)12.

3

It is the civic associations, it is the independent judiciary, it is the free press that will make democracy work [in Africa]. I think you will see more and more aid and the whole scope of U.S. government assistance [to Africa] aimed essentially at the "governance" that is so important for the good working of democracy . . . When new people come to power [in Africa], we are telling them, "No democracy, no assistance." The new regimes do not have any grace period.

Speech/
Los Angeles Times, 5-2:(A)28.

Frederik W. de Klerk
President of South Africa

4

We [whites] have to live together with the other people of South Africa [the blacks]. They are as South African as we are. They have been living here for more than three centuries. We have to live together with them because it's in the Bible. We have to bring them justice. It's what the Bible says.

Campaigning on a forthcoming
referendum on black-white relations,
Johannesburg, South Africa/
Los Angeles Times, 3-10:(H)2.

5

[Acclaiming the results of a referendum in which white South Africans approved of his moves toward dismantling apartheid]: Today will be written up in our history as one of the most fundamental turning-point days in the history of South Africa. Today we have closed the book on apartheid—and that chapter is finally closed . . . The massive positive result sends out a powerful message to all South Africans that those who have the power in terms of the present imperfect Constitution really mean it when they say, "We want to share power" [with the black majority].

Victory statement and news conference,
Cape Town, South Africa, March 18/
The New York Times, 3-19:(A)1.

6

Communism is dead—otherwise I would not have come to Russia, and I don't believe they

(FREDERIK W. DE KLERK)

would have invited me. And there is acceptance here in this big and important country of the irreversibility of the process of change in South Africa—we have turned our back on apartheid, and there will be no return.

News conference,
Moscow, Russia, June 1/
Los Angeles Times, 6-2:(A)8.

1

[On whether foreign countries should try to help restore anti-apartheid negotiations between the South African government and the ANC, which have broken down because of recent violence against blacks]: [We reject] foreign interference [in South Africa's affairs. But] advice, yes, we are open to advice. Recommendations, yes, we will seriously consider any constructive recommendations. Fact-finding commissions, yes, they are welcome. We have no hesitation to say that we recognize the interest which the international community has in South Africa.

To reporters,
Pretoria, South Africa, June 24/
The New York Times, 6-25:(A)7.

2

It is becoming increasingly clear that the Communists in the ANC are making deliberate attempts to render further constitutional negotiations [between whites and blacks in South Africa] impossible. They have evidently taken the ANC in tow at the expense of those in the ANC who are not in favor of violence.

News conference, Sept. 9/
The Washington Post, 9-10:(A)24.

3

[On protecting the minority white population in a black-majority-run government in a future apartheid-free South Africa]: I don't just represent a minority. I'm fighting to represent the majority . . . [But] we must have a constitution which will prevent the misuse of power by any

majority. That is not equivalent to continued minority domination—it is not equivalent to apartheid or to asking for a blank veto for minorities. In my party's proposals, we're leaning heavily on many principles enshrined in the American Constitution, [such as] the two-chamber system. We believe in strong regional government. We believe in a strong bill of rights. We believe that the British system, where with 51 per cent of the vote you have 100 per cent of the power, is a good system for a homogeneous society but not for a complicated country like ours. Some black South Africans are as different from other black South Africans as Frenchmen are from Germans. The best way to accommodate this is devolving meaningful power and authority to regions.

Interview/
Newsweek, 9-28:30.

Abdelkader Djeghloul
Algerian sociologist

4

Traditionally Algeria hasn't used injections of fresh money for making crucial investments . . . Algeria has to put aside the source of its pride for the past 30 years, its jealous independence, and ask others to come help us. With that and only in this way is there a little hope.

The Christian Science Monitor,
3-3:6.

Jose Eduardo dos Santos
President of Angola

5

We are living in a time of democracy instead of dictatorship. We have to construct a new life and undergo reconciliation in Angola. We have to install and consolodate democracy and we cannot do this by practicing the old ways.

At MPLA rally, Namibia, Angola/
The Christian Science Monitor,
9-30:3.

Thomas Franck
Professor of international law,
New York University

6

[On the current U.S.-led military intervention in Somalia aimed at protecting and distributing

(THOMAS FRANCK)

food to the starving population]: There's a very big question in everybody's mind as to what the second phase of this operation is going to look like . . . If the Somalis are determined—after we've restored law and order and brought in some food—to have a genocide among themselves, there's very little the world can do about it. Civil wars are messy and awful . . . but sooner or later somebody wins and history moves on.

The Christian Science Monitor,
12-11:6.

Chris Hani
Chairman, Communist Party
of South Africa

1

[Accusing the South African government of being involved in violence against blacks]: It's not the first time that a government fights and talks at the same time. They want to prolong [anti-apartheid] talks [with the ANC] while they weaken and destabilize our movement, so that, by the time we win the right to elections, the ANC will be exhausted. [But] our main strategy is negotiatioins. We have to defend the process against violence, because we can't afford to have the negotiations derailed.

Interview/
Mother Jones, July-Aug.:27.

Abdelqader Hashani
Acting president,
Islamic Salvation Front
of Algeria

2

[On his party, which made large gains in the recent Parliamentary election in Algeria]: We guarantee freedom of opinion in Algeria. Our purpose is to persuade, not oblige people into doing what we say. I challenge anyone to prove that so far we have repressed any other political tendencies. You must remember we have won control of some 800 municipalities in elections more than a year ago. We have a record of tolerance that no one can deny. This is the essence of Islam.

Interview, Algiers, Algeria/
The New York Times, 1-7:(A)3.

Iddi Pandu Hassan
Minister of State and
Attorney General of Zanzibar

3

In Africa, you cannot allow people to go completely free, otherwise you will have chaos. We are going to be extra careful. We are going to take our time. We have learned a lot from Kenya—and we don't want to follow that example. We are determined to control the changes. We are not going to be like the Soviet Union. [Former Soviet President Mikhail] Gorbachev tried to do everything at the same time—he wanted *glasnost* [openness], he wanted *perestroika* [reform]. You should only open the door a little bit, and let people come through one at a time.

The Washington Post, 3-24:(A)14.

Douglas Hurd
Foreign Secretary
of the United Kingdom

4

[On air and arms sanctions imposed against Libya for its refusing to turn over suspects in the 1968 bombing of a Pan Am flight over Scotland]: These are not punitive sanctions. They tackle exactly those areas of Libyan life which are part of the trouble. The trouble arose from air terrorism, so the action is against air traffic. It arose from arms, and therefore the action is against Libyan purchase of arms.

BBC radio interview, April 15/
The Washington Post, 4-16:(A)33.

Edmond Keller
Professor of political science,
University of California, Los Angeles
(United States);
President,
African Studies Association

5

The United States should encourage the forces of democratization [in Africa], but not necessarily tie that support to any kind of rigid ideological concerns. The [Bush] Administration should realize that foreign policy can sometimes be driven by humanitarian and social considerations, not only strategic ones. A peaceful

259

WHAT THEY SAID IN 1992

Africa that can feed itself would be in the strategic interest of the United States.

Broadcast interview/
Los Angeles Times, 5-2:(A)28.

Thomas W. Kelly
Lieutenant General (Ret.),
United States Army;
Former Chief of Operations,
Joint Chiefs of Staff

1

[On the U.S. sending troops to Somalia to enforce the delivery of food to the starving population]: I have reservations about every operation where you load the guns and send the troops in. But duty is duty. In the case of Somalia, I really don't see how anybody could see what has happened and not make some decision to try to stem it. The naysayers are saying that other [critical] situations exist. And while the naysayers are saying their nays on TV, probably 10, 20 or 30 people die of starvation [in Somalia]. I do know [U.S.] casualties will be very, very low. You've got a bunch of thugs running around [in Somalia]. They're playing for pay, working for warlords. This is not Vietnam, where they were committed to a cause. A cause is the difference between fighting hard and not fighting hard. So I think we'll do it. We've got to do it.

Interview/
USA Today, 12-3:(A)13.

Mansour Kikhia
Exiled former Foreign Minister
of Libya

2

There are now pressures in Libya to change policies, but the larger truth is that [Libyan President Muammar] Qaddafi holds all the strings, playing one group against the other. If there is one thing Qaddafi truly believes, it is that if you plant more confusion you defer problems . . . We are opposed to the [Qaddafi] regime but not to our own country. We worry about [new UN sanctions against Libya] or military actions that can only hurt the Libyan people. The issue in Libya is

that people in this case think the West is out to get Libya, not Muammar Qaddafi and his clique.

Paris, France/
The New York Times, 4-1:(A)6.

Sadiq al-Mahdi
Former Prime Minister
of Sudan

3

[On the current regime in Sudan]: This regime is even worse, from a democratic point of view, than other military dictatorships. They say we will elect a new assembly, but when you know of the security forces and intimidation, you know they will weed out all opposing views. Because there are no longer human rights here, you can ensure that this assembly will sing one tune. The problem for this regime is not foreign isolation, but internally having to keep their own people at bay.

Interview, Khartoum, Sudan/
The Christian Science Monitor,
3-31:5.

4

[Criticizing the current Islamic government of Sudan]: Whatever difficulties were faced by a [previous] democratic system, the failures of this [present] system are greater and more dangerous. I say very clearly, any system which does not respect Islam's political imperatives can't call itself Islamic. Unless you are based on the consent of the governed and remove compulsion from the equation, you can't call yourself Islamic.

Los Angeles Times, 4-6:(A)10.

Nelson Mandela
President, African National Congress
(South Africa)

5

[On criticism of the ANC's close and friendly relationship with the South African Communist Party]: We don't intend doing anything about our alliance with the Communist Party of South Africa until democratic changes in this country

(NELSON MANDELA)

have been introduced. After all, it was the West which, during the last World War, formed an alliance with the Soviet Union. The West did not hesitate to form an alliance with a country which also had a common enemy, an enemy which could effectively be fought by pooling the resources of all those countries. If that had not happened, it is very likely that the history of the world would have been totally different. Why should we be expected to do anything different from what the West has done?

Broadcast interview/
CNN-TV, 1-7.

1

We [South African blacks] have been concerned right from the beginning about allaying the fears of whites [when apartheid is ended]. We understand their fears, because democracy is going to mean that they are going to lose their privileged position. It will be stabilized in due course, but nobody can deny that in the beginning they will have to lose.

Interview,
Johannesburg, South Africa, February/
Newsweek, 3-2:42.

2

We have announced in the ANC Freedom Charter that we would nationalize the mines, the banks and other monopolies, but the rest of the economy is based on private enterprise. Not even the land is nationalized, which is normally the first sector of the economy which socialist [governments] nationalize. [But] it is reasonable to nationalize an organization like the mines.

Interview,
Johannesburg, South Africa, February/
Newsweek, 3-2:42.

3

[On the breakdown in black-white negotiations in South Africa in the wake of renewed violence]: I can no longer explain to our people why we continue to talk to a government which is

murdering our people. The negotiations process is completely in tatters.

At rally, Evaton, South Africa,
June 21/
The New York Times, 6-22:(A)1.

Sam Motsuenyane
Executive president,
National African Federated
Chamber of Commerce
(South Africa)

4

South Africa has to take significant strides toward integrating blacks meaningfully into the economy, the formal economy, in our country. We would like to see more blacks on the boards of corporations. We would like to see more black people owning a greater stake of the nation's wealth. We would also like to see a lot of manufacturing involvement by blacks, going into the manufacturing and producing of goods and selling more than just their hands to the economy. But of even greater importance is the question of management. Black people constitute some 80 per cent of the country's population, yet they amount to only four per cent of all managers. We'd like to see that number up around 60 per cent within the next 10 years.

USA Today, 9-8:(Our World)13.

Makau wa Mutua
Director of the
human-rights program,
Harvard University
Law School
(United States)

5

Effectively, [rebel leader] Charles Taylor's control over most of Liberia creates a new nation in the region. This situation is most tragic because the West, which is consumed by changes in Eastern Europe and the Soviet Union, has abandoned this small nation as its social and political fabric slowly dies.

The New York Times,
4-14:(A)3.

Jayaseelan Naidoo
General secretary,
Congress of South African
Trade Unions

1

We are not scared to say we are socialist. Business must understand that our members are attracted to socialism out of their daily experiences and sufferings. [But] we are available to compromise, to reach agreements and to honor those agreements.

Interview/
Los Angeles Times, 8-4:(H)2.

Andrew Natsios
Assistant Administrator,
Agency for International Development
of the United States

2

[The current war in Somalia] is the worst humanitarian crisis in the world right now, with no exceptions. We are facing not a civil war, but anarchy. Even if there were peace between the two sides that are fighting, there are several other clans just in Mogadishu and other clans in other areas in the south that are fighting among themselves. So there's no two forces you can write an agreement with to protect relief workers or to have a cease-fire to bring in food. It's anarchy. There's just no other way of putting it.

Feb. 3/
The Washington Post, 2-4:(A)14.

Robert B. Oakley
United States Special Envoy
to Somalia

3

[On the difficulty in disarming gunmen in famine- and strife-torn Somalia]: There are three things important to a Somali—his wife, his camel and his weapon.

Newsweek, 12-28:11.

Randall Robinson
Executive director,
TransAfrica (United States)

4

You look across the board, you see a marked pattern of racial discrimination. There is no ques-

tion about it that the life of whites is more highly prized and valued than the life of blacks. Even when you look at media, there is more attention paid to parts of Africa where there are whites in concentrarion than to the rest of Africa ... There was democratization going on at the same time in Africa as in Eastern Europe. People would kill for a chunk of the Berlin Wall, but little or no attention was paid to what was going on in Africa.

Interview/
USA Today, 9-9:(A)15.

Harry Schwarz
South African Ambassador
to the United States

5

There is no doubt that there are white South Africans who want to maintain apartheid, and who are opposed to change. There's no question about it. The question is how many. And I think it would be remarkable if you had a period of change—with dramatic change, with a movement toward democracy after you'd had this white oligarchical government for so long—if some people wouldn't want [apartheid] to continue. It would be most remarkable. But ... the majority of whites in South Africa want to move toward non-racial democracy ... There may be a few obstacles in the road. There may be a few difficulties. But I don't believe this process can be stopped.

Broadcast interview,
Washington, D.C./
"Evans and Novak," CNN-TV, 2-29.

6

[On charges that South Africa's security forces are trying to undermine efforts to end apartheid in that country]: I think that the security forces are engaged in activities that they should not be in. The extent of it is open to question and debate. The difficulty that exists is that it doesn't require large numbers of people to undermine a situation. A few people in key positions can also do a lot of damage ... I've always been against apartheid. But what about the person who's been brought up from childhood believing

(HARRY SCHWARZ)

that apartheid is the right thing? Being then in the police force, enforcing the apartheid rules, and suddenly on February 1990 being told, "Look here, from now on it's different. You're going to have a different approach to learn [as apartheid is phased out]." It's not so easy to deal with that situation. I don't rationalize it and I don't justify it. But I understand why they're doing it.

Interview, Boston, Mass., Aug. 24/
The Christian Science Monitor,
8-31:6.

Sydney Sekeramayi
Minister of National Security
of Zimbabwe

1

Whereas, in the past, the greatest threat to our security was external, the current threat emanates from some commissioned individuals masquerading as human-rights activists, ivory-tower intellectuals, and some foreign mass-media correspondents. They are dedicated to sowing the seeds of national despondency [and] racial and ethnic hatred and conflict through sections of the local anti-government press . . . Appropriate administrative, political and security measures will be taken to nip these destabilization maneuvers in the bud.

October/
The Christian Science Monitor,
12-2:7.

Steven Stedman
Professor, School of Advanced
International Studies,
Johns Hopkins University
(United States)

2

[Expressing reservations about sending U.S. troops to Somalia to enforce the delivery of food to the starving population]: Some Somalis are going to welcome troops. Some are going to try to kill the people who come in. And in these kinds of wars, it's often not easy to find out who's who. The 20,000 troops on the ground are going to be very visible—and very vulnerable. The loss of

[U.S.] life won't be in battles; it will be from snipers. It's not going to be a lot of lives that will be lost; but it could be fairly constant, like a couple a day . . . [And] as soon as [the troops] pull out, without a solution to the civil war, the war will resume, and you'll be back to famine. The people [in Somalia] with guns will still have guns. You'll have the same problems you have now.

Interview/
USA Today, 12-3:(A)13.

Helen Suzman
President,
South African Institute
of Race Relations;
Former member of
South African Parliament

3

[Unless racial violence in South Africa ends soon and the economy prospers again,] whoever does inherit the country—be it an ANC government or any other—will inherit a wasteland, an ungovernable country inhabited by millions of undisciplined youths to whom a culture of democracy is meaningless.

Address as president of
South African Institute of Race Relations,
South Africa/
The Washington Post, 10-24:(A)18.

4

[Saying the ANC is to blame for more racial violence in South Africa than is reported by the media]: Unfortunately, it has become fashionable in liberal circles to make excuses for the ANC, to say, oh, well, they were in exile for so long, or they were fighting a wicked regime. As far as I'm concerned, you can't exonerate the state for the violence, you can't exonerate [the anti-ANC] Inkatha, but you can't exonerate the ANC either. The real problem now is that violence has become so ingrained that even if the leaders wanted to stop it, I'm not sure they could. There are too many avengers, too many criminals, too many local warlords. Maybe you could have stopped it in the mid-1980s, when it first got out of hand, but I'm not sure you can now.

Interview, South Africa/
The Washington Post, 10-24:(A)18.

WHAT THEY SAID IN 1992

Eugene Terre Blanche
Leader,
Afrikaner Resistance
Movement
(South Africa)

1

[Calling for a "no" vote on the forthcoming referendum on democratic reforms in South Africa that would include the black majority population]: The referendum is not one between the Conservative Party and the National Party. It is a referendum between God and the Communists . . . Referendum or no referendum, this is our [whites'] land and we will see that we keep it.

At rally,
Pretoria, South Africa,
March 7/
The Christian Science Monitor,
3-9:2.

Lloyd Vogelman
Director, Project for the
Study of Violence,
University of Witwatersrand
(South Africa)

2

[On the increasing racial violence, from both whites and blacks, in South Africa]: I would say we are about 18 months away from near-anarchy and levels of violence which will take a long time to stop. The only way to halt the current trend is to move swiftly to a democratic election and a transitional government of national unity which can begin to reverse the break-down of law and order . . . In this climate there is a continual blurring of the lines between political violence and crime. Only when there is a government of national unity will it be possible to create a new social morality.

The Christian Science Monitor, 12-1:3.

Raul Alfonsin
Former President of Argentina

1

Progressive thinking . . . is going through a very difficult moment in South America, where there is a neo-conservative fashion. Because of a certain dependence [on developed countries] because of the debt problem, neo-conservative policies are being implemented, and we have to try to resist this [trend] that brings us . . . to a society lacking solidarity.

The Christian Science Monitor,
3-6:2.

Ricardo Arias (Calderon)
First Vice President
of Panama

2

[On the emergence of democracy in Panama after the U.S. invasion in 1989 that ousted dictator Manuel Noriega]: What has happened is that once democracy was installed, all the social and economic matters that had been postponed in recent years began to emerge. The overall economic figures sound good, but there is an enormous accumulation of poverty at the lower levels . . . This is more serious than normal transition problems because we have a presidential system and [with President Guillermo Endara] practically don't have a President.

The New York Times, 4-29:(A)4.

Jean-Bertrand Aristide
Exiled former President
of Haiti

3

[Saying the U.S. should help overthrow the current Haitian government, which overthrew his elected government last year in a coup led by Raoul Cedras]: How can we ask the Haitian people to remove these criminals with their bare hands? . . . The Haitian people know the power of the United States. The Haitian people remember how the American Ambassador helped us

liberate ourselves from General [Prosper] Avril [who seized the government in 1988]. They remember that we had a free, democratic election with the help of the international community. When the Haitian people think that Cedras is still there after five months, they say: "Why is it that American power cannot put pressure on these criminals?"

Interview, Caracas, Venezuela,
March 7/
The New York Times, 3-10:(A)5.

4

[On why he wants to return to lead Haiti following the coup that ousted him in 1991]: First . . . it is my responsibility. I am Haitian; it is my country; I give my life for my country, for sharing love, for fighting peacefully for justice and democracy. Second . . . I am the President, and my place is in Haiti to continue what I have accepted for five years [his elected term of office]. Third . . . how great is that people who continue to give their lives, to fight with their hands while other hands are filled with weapons? How can I accept staying far from them?

Los Angeles/
Los Angeles Times, 3-18:(E)1.

Bernard W. Aronson
Assistant Secretary
for Inter-American Affairs,
Department of State
of the United States

5

The Latins and Caribbeans are much more willing to cooperate with the United States because they recognize that the democratic game is the only game in town. But we also have an interest in relying more on multilateral approaches to prove that we are not going to be bullies, and the new world order is not going to be an American imperium. Also, we alone cannot sustain the level of resources required to address the problems of the hemisphere.

The New York Times, 2-7:(A)7.

WHAT THEY SAID IN 1992

(BERNARD W. ARONSON)

1

The future in Cuba depends on how the transition [after Cuban President Fidel Castro] is carried out. If there's a peaceful evolutionary change, your chances of creating pluralism and democracy and open markets are greatly enhanced. If there's some kind of traumatic, violent change, it depends on who comes out on top and what their agenda is.

Interview/
Los Angeles Times, 4-7:(A)13.

James A. Baker III
Secretary of State
of the United States

2

Let us be frank. There are some Salvadorans, with memories of guerrilla war and violent political struggle, who fear that the [recent] peace accords [between the FMLN guerrillas and the government] are an enormous trap—a political Trojan Horse—that will allow the FMLN to re-enter civil society only to return to the violent and destabilizing politics of the past. It is essential that the FMLN demonstrate by its actions as well as by its words that these skeptics are wrong.

Before Salvadoran National Assembly,
San Salvador, El Salvador, Jan. 17/
The Washington Post, 1-18:(A)15.

3

The time has come to negotiate an end to Guatemala's 30-year-old insurgency. When it ends—and it will end—we will be able to look across Central America for the first time in its history and see the promise of [the 1987 regional peace accord of] Esquipulas fulfilled: every nation living peacefully under a government freely chosen by its people.

Before Salvadoran National Assembly,
San Salvador, El Salvador, Jan. 17/
The New York Times, 1-18:4.

4

[On Peruvian President Alberto Fujimori's dissolving Parliament and suspending the Con-

stitution]: No nation and no people face a more daunting, dangerous, or terrible set of crises than those inherited by [Fujimori's] new democratic government of Peru less than two years ago. No nation and no people need and deserve international solidarity and support more than the Peruvian nation and the Peruvian people. They confront the deepest economic crisis of their history, the violence and corruption of narco-trafficking, and the most murderous and dangerous terrorist movement that has ever appeared in Latin America . . . [But] the actions taken by President Fujimori, whatever the justification given, are unjustified. They represent an assault on democracy that cannot and will not be supported by the United States of America. And therefore we have suspended all new assistance to the government of Peru, and we will continue to do so until constitutional democracy is restored. All of us recognize that democracy can be inefficient. All of us recognize that democracy can be slow. And all of us recognize that democracy can be frustrating. But there is no alternative. You cannot destroy democracy in order to save it. The only long-term beneficiaries of this assault on democracy in Peru will be those very terrorists and guerrillas who falsely argue that violence is the solution to the problems of the Peruvian people.

Before Organization of American States,
Washington, D.C.,
April 13/
The New York Times, 4-14:(A)7.

Keith Banting
Professor of policy studies,
Queens University,
Kingston, Ont. (Canada)

5

Health care, more than any other social program, has become an important part of how Canadians see themselves. So far Medicare has been eroded in ways that [the] public cannot see in demonstrable ways. They hear that service has been eroded, that waits are longer, but can't see it yet.

The Christian Science Monitor,
7-7:3.

Maude Barlow
Chairman,
Council of Canadians

1

I would argue that our [Canada's] biggest sense of identity, given our history, is that we're not Americans. Well, being *not* something isn't enough. We are so ethnically, regionally, linguistically and geographically diverse that one can honestly ask, "What's a Canadian?" and we've been going through that . . . People all through our history have predicted we would eventually become part of the [United] States. Today we're asking very hard questions, like, "How do we stay Canadian on the doorstep of the world's only remaining superpower?"

The Christian Science Monitor,
7-1:1,4.

Marc Bazin
Prime Minister of Haiti

2

[On being named Prime Minister during Haiti's current crisis stemming from the army's ousting of elected-President Jean-Bertrand Aristide last year, and the subsequent international trade embargo imposed on the country]: If the situation remains as it is today, the chances that Mr. Aristide might eventually return to this country are zero. As a democrat and a patriot, I believe that I can be of service to this country in trying to mediate between the two parties in order to create a new atmosphere that is conducive to democratic institutions in the future. We can't sit here waiting for the United States to decide for us what to do next . . . We need someone we can trust, someone who can sort of help genuinely to solve this, and I think that is where I come in.

Interview, Port-au-Prince, Haiti,
July 4/
The Washington Post, 7-6:(A)14.

Francois Benoit
Foreign Minister of Haiti

3

[When Francois Duvalier was dictator of Haiti in the 1960s,] I thought for a few years that

the only way to a solution was by force, to oppose and overthrow Duvalier. I prepared myself, trained myself, kept myself in tip-top shape for the day it would come. But it became more and more obvious through reflecting on Haitian history that what I was getting ready to do had been done before—people overthrowing the government, establishing a new rule. The very dynamics of the overthrow is to bear more dictatorship.

Washington, D.C./
The Christian Science Monitor,
8-3:3.

Boutros Boutros-Ghali
Secretary General
of the United Nations

4

The armed conflict [civil war] in El Salvador has come to an end. [But] democracy is an illusive goal. [Salvadorans] must become accepting of tolerance, must accept that others could have different ideas, different attitudes and different politics.

San Salvador, El Salvador,
Dec. 15/
The New York Times, 12-16:(A)4.

George Bush
President of the United States

5

Make no mistake, the future growth of the United States economy depends on expanding mutual investment and trade with our neighbors in the Americas. [It will] create new jobs and raise the quality of life for people in Syracuse and St. Louis as well as Sao Paulo and Santiago.

February/
The Christian Science Monitor,
4-3:10.

6

[On his decision to send Haitian refugees, who are trying to enter the U.S. after last year's coup in their country, back to Haiti]: We still open our arms to . . . the politically oppressed. But we cannot and I will not open the doors to economic

(GEORGE BUSH)

refugees from all over the world . . . Not to be mean about it, we're trying to say, listen, we've got to live by the [immigration] laws of the land.

At Mount Paran Christian School,
Atlanta, Ga., May 27/
The Washington Post, 5-28:(A)8.

Kim Campbell
Minister of Justice of Canada

1

I think so much of what people went through in talking about the various aspects of the Charlotte-town Accord [the failed proposed rewriting of Canada's Constitution] related to their attempt to define the country, what it is we are as a country, what are the things that unify us. It sometimes seems to boil down to nothing more than our social programs, and I think no, no, no . . . We have a social and political culture that's quite remarkable. We have ways of doing things . . . certain senses of historical connectedness that gave us a sense of obligation to one another.

Interview, Boston, Mass./
The Christian Science Monitor,
12-2:6.

Shirley Carr
Former president,
Canadian Labor Congress

2

The U.S.-Canada free-trade agreement certainly has fully confirmed our fears that free trade with a country [the U.S.] that has lower social standards such as medical care and lower wages leads to a large job loss in our country . . . So far, we have lost about 325,000 jobs since the agreement was passed in 1989 . . . and the massive majority of those are lost forever . . . We only have 26 million people in Canada compared to 250 million in the United States. So what is happening is that Canada is becoming a branch plant economy for the multinationals and our government now is finding out that what they have done to the country as a whole with the agreement is not what even they expected.

Interview/
Los Angeles Times, 6-28:(M)3.

Fidel Castro
President of Cuba

3

[Criticizing the long-standing U.S. trade embargo against his country]: Cuba loses with the blockade, but the United States also loses. We, as . . . a small country, lose in a much higher proportion. The United States loses in a much smaller proportion; but I think that it loses morally and politically before the world, because there is no political or moral justification to sustain the blockade against a small country . . . It constitutes a giant hypocrisy to speak of human rights while they deprive a population of 11 million of the possibility of acquiring medicine and food from the United States. This did not have . . . nor will it ever have, justification, much less now when one cannot speak of the Cold War or tensions between West and East [since the Soviet Union has ceased to exist as an adversary against the West]. Furthermore, it implies enormous cynicism to say, as many North American leaders have said, that commerce with Cuba does not interest them because Cuba is a small country, and yes they are interested in commerce with a large Communist country like China because it constitutes an enormous market. Such ways of conceiving politics and ethics are truly repugnant.

Interview/
Current History,
February:61.

Dick Cheney
Secretary of Defense
of the United States

4

[On the U.S. decision to return to Haiti Haitians who are seeking asylum in the U.S. following a coup in their country]: The reason they fled Haiti is primarily for economic, as opposed to political, reasons. The charge that somehow their lives are threatened back inside Haiti has not been substantiated.

Broadcast interview/
"Newsmaker Sunday,"
CNN-TV, 2-2.

Bill Clinton
Governor of Arkansas (D);
President-elect
of the United States

1

With regard to the Haitians [who are trying to come to the U.S. following the coup ousting their elected President, Jean-Bertrand Aristide], I think my position on that has been pretty clear all along. I believe that there is a legitimate distinction between political and economic refugees. But I think that we should have a process in which these Haitians get a chance to make their case. I think that the blanket sending them back to Haiti [as U.S. President Bush has done] under the circumstances which have prevailed for the last year was an error and so I will modify that process. I'm not in a position to tell you exactly how we're going to do it or what the specifics will be, but I can tell you I'm going to change the policy.

News conference, Little Rock, Ark.,
Nov. 12/
The New York Times, 11-13:(A)8.

Fernando Collor (de Mello)
President of Brazil

2

[On a forthcoming Congressional vote on his impeachment on charges of corruption]: We will win the vote. In 10 days, they're going to try to break the mandate of the President of the republic, one made legitimate by the popular vote. Those who think they can break the President's mandate are fooling themselves . . . Of course, I made mistakes—but who doesn't? I erred by trusting too much in people who later proved not to be worthy of this trust.

Broadcast address to the nation,
Aug. 30/
The New York Times, 8-31:(A)2.

John Conyers, Jr.
United States Representative,
D-Michigan

3

[Saying the U.S. should get tougher with those who took over Haiti last year by ousting its

democratically elected government]: What the military thugs down there understand is that they have got a nod and a wink from the U.S. government. If you wanted to see an end to this mobster rule, ban air travel to the United States, impose a blockade on Haitian ships into Miami, ask for a United Nations task force.

Interview,
Washington, D.C., Feb. 25/
The New York Times, 2-26:(A)3.

Guillermo Endara
President of Panama

4

[Applauding the conviction in the U.S. of former Panamanian leader Manuel Noriega on drug and racketeering charges]: This act of justice closes a disgraceful chapter of Panamanian history. It would have only been just to find him guilty and this is what they did . . . Panamanians . . . knew perfectly well that we were witnessing the first narco-military dictatorship in history.

Panama City, Panama, April 9/
Los Angeles Times, 4-10:(A)29.

Alberto K. Fujimori
President of Peru

5

[On his dissolving the Peruvian Congress and suspending the Constitution]: Our objective is to achieve . . . a prosperous and democratic society. The current democratic system is deceptive, false; its institutions routinely serve the interests of the privileged groups . . . Peru cannot indefinitely continue postponing fundamental socioeconomic changes. It is for that reason that today, more than ever, Peru needs not a patch or a partial reform but a profound transformation. Peru cannot continue weakening itself at the hands of terrorism, drug trafficking, corruption.

Broadcast address to the nation,
Lima, Peru, April 5/
The Washington Post, 4-7:(A)1,20.

6

[On his decision to dissolve the Peruvian Congress and suspend the Constitution]: For the

(ALBERTO K. FUJIMORI)

people, what has happened—instead of a break in democratic order—is a break in the chain of corruption. Our final objective is democracy. Peru will not stop belonging to the democratic family of the continent. Have no doubts, democracy is the best of systems, when it works authentically as such—not when it is only a formality used precisely to consecrate anti-democratic privileges. Therefore, when we [re-] open the national Congress, the people are going to want authentic renovation.

Broadcast address to the nation,
Lima, Peru, April 8/
Los Angeles Times,
4-9:(A)9.

1

In no more than five months we will see the establishment of a democratic constitutional Congress [in Peru], including the direct representatives of the people. With this, Peru will have achieved full constitutional legitimacy.

Before OAS foreign ministers,
Nassau, Bahamas, May 18/
The New York Times,
5-19:(A)6.

2

[On whether his dissolving the Peruvian Parliament and assumption of dictatorial control may help the Shining Path rebels]: That is a fallacy. Shining Path would have a greater chance of infiltration if Peruvian society were distanced from its government. But an extraordinary event has occurred. We no longer have a state with an immense gulf between it and the population. On the contrary: Something close to an identification with the government has occurred. The support of 90 per cent of the population is going to allow us to stand up better against Shining Path. The government will be counting on that support. The proposal for a struggle against terrorism is going to strike a chord.

Interview/
World Press Review,
July:17.

Cesar Gaviria (Trujillo)
President of Colombia

3

[On the export of drugs from Latin American countries]: As long as there is such a huge demand for drugs in industrialized nations, drug trafficking will remain a problem that will be very difficult to reduce in size, no matter how great our efforts or the sacrifices our nations make to face it.

Interview, Feb. 24/
The Washington Post, 2-25:(A)5.

Robert Gelbard
Deputy Assistant Secretary,
Department of State
of the United States

4

I have established that Haitians have one less chromosome, that of compromise and consenses, and on the other hand, one additional chromosome, that of conflict and dissension.

To Haitian political and business
leaders, Port-au-Prince, Haiti/
Los Angeles Times, 5-1:(A)31.

Stuart M. Gerson
Assistant Attorney General,
Civil Division,
Department of Justice
of the United States

5

[Criticizing those who say the U.S. is not accepting enough Haitian refugees because of racism in the U.S. Bush Administration]: The charge of racism is a hell of a lot easier to make than it is to document. If you take a balanced view of everything we're trying to do, not only is the charge not supportable, but it's not true . . . All [Haitian refugees] get hearings or the functional equivalent of hearings. Some don't fit into the category of well-founded fear of persecution [at home in Haiti]. [The policy of U.S.] interdiction [of Haitian boat people] was designed to be a humanitarian policy, upon which the nations of the hemisphere agreed. You can debate that policy. But we don't want to see black folks dying at sea.

Interview/
USA Today, 9-9:(A)15.

Jorge Gonzalez (Izquierdo)
Dean, College of Economists
(Peru)

1

[On Peruvian President Alberto Fujimori's dissolving of Congress and suspension of the Constitution last April]: Some people don't understand what the niceties of politics have to do with the economy. But only if we create real democracy here will we eliminate the obstacles to a fresh influx of resources from abroad.
The Christian Science Monitor,
12-3:9.

Ricardo Israel
Political scientist,
Institute of Political Science,
University of Chile

2

Democracy is more efficient for politics. The market is more efficient for the economy. What do we [in Latin America] want to do with this efficiency? . . . You still have not solved the problems between the poor and the rich, done anything about the environment or about moral problems . . . There is an ethical debate now about how far you can go with these huge social differences . . . Before, people saw democracy only as a right. Now they also see it as a duty, with responsibilities.
The Christian Science Monitor,
2-18:2.

Antonio Lacayo
Minister of the Presidency
of Nicaragua

3

As soon as [President Violeta de Chamorro] was elected, she stopped being a candidate of one group, and became the President of all Nicaraguans. Always in the past, we governed as one group against another, and we never progressed. Now we are governing for all Nicaraguans, so the country can be stable and democracy can take root.
The Washington Post, 8-22:(A)14.

Myles Malman
Assistant United States Attorney
prosecuting the trial
against former Panamanian
leader Manuel Noriega

4

Manuel Antonio Noriega was a man of great, great power [who used that power] to trick the DEA, the CIA and the gringos. He sold his uniform, his army and his protection to a murderous international [drug] gang known as the Medellin cartel. For millions and millions of dollars, they bought that man and his uniform. He was a classic military dictator.
Trial summation, Miami, Fla.,
March 31/
The Washington Post, 4-1:(A)3.

Michael N. Manley
Prime Minister of Jamaica

5

There is quite a widespread view that we would like to see some measure of reintegration of Cuba [into hemispheric affairs]. We are a democracy and they are not, but we have always felt it was good to cooperate in ways that do not compromise our principles.
The New York Times, 3-11:(A)6.

Rigoberta Menchu
Guatamalan peace activist;
Winner, 1992 Nobel Peace Prize

6

[Saying foreign tourists to Guatemala do not see the other, negative side of the country]: The other face of Guatemala is the face of repression, of the war, of many dead. But in the end it seems insignificant in the lives of other people. I mean, they are amazed when they hear that 46,000 people have disappeared in Guatemala. They say, "How horrible," and they are very impressed. But it does not go beyond that.
Interview,
Guatemala City, Guatemala,
Oct. 18/
The New York Times, 10-19:(A)7.

Carlos Saul Menem
President of Argentina

1

Nothing can be achieved outside the framework of democracy and freedom. Peace, justice, dignity and freedom: This is what the world has the right to expect of Latin America.

At Ibero-Latin American summit,
Madrid, Spain, July 23/
Los Angeles Times, 7-24:(A)10.

Desmond Morton
Historian, University of
Toronto (Canada)

2

[On the recent defeat by voters in Canada of the Charlottetown Accord, which would have reshaped the country's Constitution]: This is the first time I can remember that most Canadians believe their future will be worse than their past. It will be harder for their children to have careers and security than it was for them . . . and they resent it . . . Being a compromise, the Accord required a little discomfort, and Canadians weren't prepared to put up with any more discomfort from their leaders.

The Christian Science Monitor,
10-24:4.

Brian Mulroney
Prime Minister of Canada

3

[Saying he is confident of re-election next year because he has done the right things rather than the politically expedient things]: I've paid a hell of a price [in the public-opinion polls], but I'm not concerned at all about the outcome, because I'm absolutely satisfied, having led my party in two election campaigns from way behind and having won substantial victories in both. I believe Canadians will respond to that . . . What Canada needs is a Prime Minister who won't listen to popularity polls, who'll bloody well go out and do what he thinks is right and to hell with popularity, but just tackle those things that are right.

Interview,
Ottawa, Canada, March 4/
The Washington Post, 3-5:(A)31.

4

[Criticizing new U.S. duties on cars and lumber imports from Canada]: These disputes constitute vexatious harassment and are not based in international trade law. They are based on pure politics at a lower level in the United States of America . . .

Before Canadian Parliament,
Ottawa, Canada, March 9/
Los Angeles Times, 3-10:(D)3.

5

[Criticizing new U.S. duties on cars and lumber imports from Canada]: If you told me that some tin-pot dictator in some tiny little country somewhere was engaging in this kind of harassment, I'd say, "So what else is new?" But for the United States, this is most unworthy.

Interview/
Los Angeles Times, 3-10:(D)3.

Joseph Nerette
President of Haiti

6

[On his provisional government, installed after the overthrow of President Jean-Bertrand Aristide last September]: I am chief of the state, the free, sovereign and independent state of Haiti. My mission is to follow the Constitution and [exercise] the public powers of the Presidency until an election of a new President . . . [Meanwhile,] any solution [to the current crisis] has to be a Haitian solution, negotiated by Haitians. It is time to take our own destiny into our own hands. We will never surrender. The solution is in our own hands and no negotiated settlement will be forced on Haiti from the outside.

Before Haitian National Assembly,
Port-au-Prince, Haiti, Jan. 13/
Los Angeles Times, 1-14:(A)4.

Leo Panitch
Chairman,
Department of political science,
York University (Canada)

7

[On the Charlottetown Accord, which would have altered the Canadian Constitution]: By far

(LEO PANITCH)

the most important reason Canadians voted against the deal was they felt it was insufficiently democratic. I think voters realized that what the Charlottetown Accord would have done was put in place a process of executive Federalism forever, whereby these [provincial] Premiers and Prime Ministers would sit down and make decisions behind closed doors.

The Christian Science Monitor,
11-4:3.

Jacques Parizeau
Separatist leader of Quebec,
Canada

1

[On his support of sovereignty for Quebec]: After a lot of discussion, everyone in Quebec defines sovereignty the same way. It means all our taxes, all our laws, all our treaties. Does it mean a Quebec army? Indeed it does. A diplomatic service? Of course. Concerning the currency, I have never opposed a Quebec currency. But I seem to be one of the few who don't. People say it will collapse in three weeks. So this time I say we keep the Canadian currency . . . We have been committed since the notorious—some would say—bill of 1977 [declaring French to be the official language of Quebec] to set up a society that functions in French. Does that mean Quebecois should not learn English? By God, I'll boot the rear end of anyone who can't speak English. In our day and times, a small people like us must speak English.

Interview/Time, 4-13:38.

Marifeli Perez-Stable
Specialist on Cuba,
New School for Social Research
(United States)

2

Looking at the Soviet experience [an attempted coup last year prior to that country's disintegration], you might have expected somebody or a small group from within to challenge the leadership [in Cuba]. It didn't happen. The ruling elites seem to be uniting around [Cuban President] Fidel [Castro] . . . That's an important factor in preventing radical change.

The Christian Science Monitor,
5-6:10.

Douglas Peters
Chief economist,
Toronto Dominion Bank
(Canada)

3

Canada has achieved a low inflation rate, but that has been attained at a cost of two years of recession, the destruction of Canada's manufacturing industries, and $100-million increase in international debt. While I applaud the low inflation, I deplore the method of achieving it and the destruction of the Canadian economy that has resulted.

The Christian Science Monitor,
4-15:7.

Charles B. Rangel
United States Representative,
D-New York

4

[Criticizing the U.S. Bush Administration's decision to return to Haiti Haitians who have fled the turmoil there]: It's an outrage that conditions in Haiti are so dangerous and the military so violent that we should recall our Ambassador [in protest of a police beating of politicians] and then only days later force civilians to return to the same dangerous place.

The Washington Post, 2-4:(A)11.

Judy Rebick
President,
National Action Committee
on the Status of Women (Canada)

5

"Multi-culturalism" . . . is the [Canadian] government's term to make racial diversity a song and dance. The government doesn't want to say there is racism [in Canada]. But there is. And I think increasingly it will become a central issue.

Interview, Toronto, Canada/
The Christian Science Monitor, 9-4:6.

Iqbal Riza
Chief, United Nations Observer Mission
in El Salvador

1

On every human-rights report [we issue on El Salvador], we've received strong criticism from the government for being anti-government. And we've received criticism from NGOs [non-governmental organizations] for not being anti-government. NGOs expect us to work as they do. We can't possibly do that. They publicize cases, appear in court. They're more crusaders than verifiers.

The Christian Science Monitor,
9-2:7.

Randall Robinson
Executive director,
TransAfrica (United States)

2

Since 1975—from 1975 to '91—we accepted in this country a million Asians, 250,000 Soviets, 100,000 Eastern Europeans. From 1981 to 1990, those fleeing persecution in Haiti, we picked up on the open seas 22,940 Haitians of whom we allowed only 11 to apply for political asylum. Of the Soviets who applied in the '80s, we accepted 76 per cent. Of the Haitians, 1.9 per cent. I think there's a clear pattern of egregious and patent racism here.

Broadcast interview/
"Today," NBC-TV, 9-9.

Manuel Saavedra
Director, Peruvian Company
for the Investigation of Markets
(public-opinion firm)

3

[On polls showing the majority of Peruvians approving President Alberto Fujimori's assumption of almost dictatorial powers]: The feeling of Peruvians is that we have had 12 years of democracy and what we have gotten for it is corruption, ineptness, chaos, poverty, disorder, hunger and malnutrition. So the public is saying: "What good is democracy to us? Let's try a government willing to use a strong hand."

The New York Times, 4-9:(A)3.

Carlos Salinas (de Gortari)
President of Mexico

4

[Saying his country should not be afraid of high imports, as long as they are mostly in the form of capital goods that can help build its economy]: Mexico should have a trade deficit of $30-billion [it is about $17-billion now]. That's what it needs to modernize its production plants to be competitive. A current-account deficit of 6 to 8 per cent of GDP is a typical pattern for an under-capitalized economy. Look at South Korea, Taiwan, post-war Japan and Germany.

The Christian Science Monitor,
12-14:8.

David Simcox
Executive director,
Center for Immigration Studies
(United States)

5

In some of the smaller countries [of the Caribbean], if you measure emigration as a portion of their total population, the numbers you come up with are just incredible. Tiny states like St. Kitts and Nevis, Grenada and Belize are sending 1 per cent to 2 per cent of their citizens to the United States every year, meaning they are basically exporting all of their population growth to us.

The New York Times, 5-6:(A)8.

Richard Simeon
Authority on
the Canadian Constitution,
University of Toronto (Canada)

6

The standard analogy of the difference between Canadians and United States citizens is that Canadians are much more willing to defer to their elites in government, and to toe the line of authority, compared with traditional American hostility toward authority. That may have been true once; it is not anymore.

The Christian Science Monitor,
11-4:3.

Wayne Smith
Professor,
Johns Hopkins University
(United States);
Former chief U.S. diplomat
in Cuba

1

The age of the romantic revolutionary linked with Marxist-Leninist ideology is finished. [But] movements such as the FMLN [in El Salvador], who champion the poor but who do it through electoral means, are going to have a growing place in Latin America.

The Christian Science Monitor,
5-6:10.

Margaret D. Tutwiler
Spokesman for the
Department of State
of the United States

2

[Defending the U.S. Bush Administration's decision to return to Haiti Haitians who have fled the turmoil there]: In the last 11 years, there is no evidence . . . not a single case, in which a Haitian who was repatriated was targeted for persecution by the regime. So we just don't have any evidence of it.

To reporters, Feb. 3/
The Washington Post,
2-4:(A)11.

Arturo Valenzuela
Director, Center for
Latin American Studies,
Georgetown University (United States)

3

[On Peruvian President Alberto Fujimori's dissolving of the Peruvian Congress and suspending the Constitution]: The tragedy of Peru is that he's going to find out that if he couldn't govern with Congress, he'll have a lot more difficult time governing without any political support at all. He needs the institution more than he realizes.

The Christian Science Monitor, 4-17:3.

Alexander Watson
Deputy United States Representative
to the United Nations

4

[On Cuba's appeal to the UN to get the U.S. to end its economic embargo]: The government of Cuba is using these lofty sentiments as a pretext. What it really wants is to involve the international community in one aspect of its bilateral relations with the United States: the United States economic embargo against Cuba, [which is in effect because, among other reasons, Cuba] in violation of international law, expropriated billions of dollars worth of private property belonging to U.S. individuals and has refused to make reasonable restitution. [The U.S. embargo is] a legitimate response to the unreasonable and illegal behavior of the Cuban government.

At United Nations, New York, Nov. 24/
The New York Times, 11-25:(A)5.

Asia and the Pacific

Mohammed Ashgar
Leader, National Salvation Front
of Afghanistan;
Former Mayor
of Kabul, Afghanistan

1

We have been trying to convince [Afghan President] Najibullah indirectly, through our writings, that the Communist Party is responsible for the problems of Afghanistan. The Communist Party has changed its name and its constitution, but the leaders are the same, the leaders who are responsible for the tragedy of Afghanistan. There is a crisis of confidence now. Dr. Najibullah says one thing and does another. That is the difficulty. Time is short. It is 11:55, or possibly later.

The New York Times, 3-13:(A)4.

Rafidah Aziz
Minister of Trade and Industry
of Malaysia

2

Anybody who's too concerned about what happens in other countries better not venture out of their own country. We don't want people to impose their human-rights values on us. These great busybodies of the world, who don't bother with their own problems, their back yards are full of dirt.

At Malaysian investment seminar,
Los Angeles, Calif./
Los Angeles Times, 6-15:(D)3.

Upendra Baxi
Vice chancellor,
Delhi University (India)

3

[On a proposed law to ban beggars in India and to impose jail terms for begging]: The government doesn't want these people lying around. A lot of middle-class people, of course, regard them as a nuisance, and as committing criminal acts. The base of this is simply the unpleasantness of it

all. We have a situation in Delhi where there is a lot of push of migration from semi-urban and rural areas searching for livelihood. In a situation here where one becomes destitute because of fate—a riot, my house is burned down, some catastrophic act that leaves me destitute, where there is no social security—I am suddenly a beggar. The point is that destitution is being systematically created. The victims of misuses of power or catastrophe are not compensated or rehabilitated. So in a society that specializes in creating destitution, it can only do one thing, which is ban begging.

The New York Times, 12-4:(A)4.

Barton Biggs
Chairman,
Morgan Stanley Asset Management
(United States)

4

Japan is no longer a super-country with a super-economy. It's another mature, developed industrial country just like the U.S., Germany or France. There's nothing wrong with that. It's just no longer a super-economy. The real bear is that this is an end of an era for Japan. And the [falling] stock market [there] is signaling it. Just as there is a crescendo of screaming about how Japan is killing us everywhere, Japan is coming right back down with everybody else. I really think this could be signaling the end of the Japanese miracle. The end of Japan, of course not. But Japan is going to be just like the rest of us.

Interview/USA Today, 4-6:(B)3.

Leon Brittan
Commissioner for Competition
of the European Community

5

My immediate concern is to emphasize the very perception that Japan's economic system gives it an unfair advantage in world trade that is destroying the confidence of open trading relations. The simple fact is that Japan retains a busi-

(LEON BRITTAN)

ness culture and elements of economic regulation which have the effect—whether by accident or design—of discouraging imports except in certain niche markets . . . [The strength of the Japanese economy] has been part of the cause of the present questioning of economic liberalism both in Europe and the United States. There has arisen a perception that the Japanese economy is not so much a friendly locomotive of world trade, but a hostile steamroller.

To Japanese business executives,
Tokyo, Japan, Feb. 19/
The Christian Science Monitor,
2-20:1.

George Bush
President of the United States

1

We [the U.S.] are going to stay totally involved in this part of the world. We won't let you down. And we will stay involved right up until the very end of eternity because we know it's fundamentally in our own interests. And we hope like hell it's in yours.

At New Year's Day luncheon,
Sydney, Australia, Jan. 1/
The Washington Post, 1-2:(A)16.

2

I will do my level best as President of the United States to preserve and strengthen the important relationship between Japan and my country. It has a lot to do with world peace. It has a lot to do with world economic stability. It has a lot to do with two great economic and democratic countries working together, setting an example for other countries around the world.

Japan, Jan. 7/
The New York Times, 1-8:(A)1.

3

[Criticizing the U.S. Congress and his Presidential opponent Bill Clinton for wanting to limit U.S. most-favored-nation trade status toward China]: I am the one that said let's keep the

MFN, because you see China moving toward a free-market economy. To do what the Congress and Governor Clinton is suggesting, you'd isolate and ruin Hong Kong. They are making some progress, not enough for us . . . But Governor Clinton's philosophy is isolate them [because of China's human-rights record]. He says don't do it, but the policies he's expounding of putting conditions on MFN and kind of humiliating them is not the way you make the kind of progress we are getting . . . You isolate China and turn them inward, and then we've made a tremendous mistake.

At Presidential candidates' debate,
St. Louis, Mo., Oct. 11/
The New York Times, 10-12:(A)14.

John Clammer
Specialist on Southeast Asia,
Sophia University (Japan)

4

In much of Asia, active politics is seen as elitist. Below that is a culture of jokes, cartoons and satire, which are a way for people to send signals as a form of criticism. If you're not allowed to say many things in public, you're forced to read between the lines.

The Christian Science Monitor,
6-3:3.

Bill Clinton
Governor of Arkansas (D);
Candidate for the 1992
Democratic U.S. Presidential
nomination

5

The [U.S. Bush] Administration continues to coddle China, despite its continuing crackdown on democratic reform, its brutal subjugation of Tibet, its irresponsible export of nuclear and missile technology, its support for the homicidal Khmer Rouge in Cambodia, and its abusive trade practices. Such forbearance on our part might have made sense during the Cold War, when China was the counterweight to Soviet power. It makes no sense to play the China card now when our opponents have thrown in their hand.

Los Angeles Times, 3-17:(H)6.

Bill Clinton
Governor of Arkansas (D);
1992 Democratic U.S. Presidential
nominee

1

There is no more striking example of [U.S. President] Bush's indifference toward democracy than his policy toward China. Today we must ask ourselves, "What has the President's China policy really achieved?" The Chinese leadership still sells missiles and nuclear technology to Middle Eastern dictators who threaten us and our friends. They still arrest and hold in prison leaders of the pro-democracy movement. They restrict American access to their markets, while our trade deficit with China will reach $15-billion this year. I do hope that our nation has a higher purpose than to coddle dictators and to stand aside from the global movement toward democracy.

Speech, Milwaukee, Wis., Oct. 1/
The New York Times, 11-20:(A)11.

2

I think our relationships with China are important and I don't think we want to isolate China, but I think it is a mistake for us to do what this [U.S. Bush] Administration did when all those kids went out there carrying the Statue of Liberty [demonstrating for democracy] in Tiananmen Square [in Beijing in 1989]. Mr. Bush sent two people in secret to toast the Chinese leaders [who crushed the pro-democracy demonstrations] and basically tell them not to worry about it . . . I would be firm [with the Chinese]. I would say, "If you want to continue most-favored-nation [U.S. trade] status for your government-owned industries as well as your private ones, observe human rights in the future. Open your society. Recognize the legitimacy of those kids that were carrying the Statue of Liberty." If we can stand up for our economics, we ought to be able to preserve the democratic interests of the people in China, and over the long run they will be more reliable partners.

At Presidential candidates' debate,
St. Louis, Mo., Oct. 11/
The New York Times,
10-12:(A)14.

Bill Clinton
Governor of Arkansas (D);
President-elect
of the United States

3

[On U.S. trade with China in light of China's poor human-rights record]: I noted with satisfaction that in the last several months, when the [U.S.] Bush Administration, for whatever reason, maybe because of the changing political climate, took a tougher line on [Chinese] goods made with prison labor, on unfair trade practices, we began to have more moderation [in China]. China now has a $15-billion-a-year trade surplus with us. I know we create a lot of jobs with trade with China, but they've got a $15-billion surplus. They have a big stake in that. We have a big stake in not isolating China, in seeing that China continues to develop a market economy. But we also have to insist, I believe, on progress in human rights and human decency. And I think there are indications in the last few months that a firm hand by our government can help to achieve that.

News conference,
Washington, D.C., Nov. 19/
The New York Times, 11-20:(A)11.

Tran Quang Co
Deputy Foreign Minister
of Vietnam

4

It was very unfortunate for us that Vietnam was put in the focus of superpower conflicts for many decades, and [now that the Soviet Union has broken apart] it is good for us not to be tied into the framework of bipolar confrontations. We would like to have the same fate as other Southeast Asian countries—independence, peace and stability. But unhappily for Vietnam, there is still an enormous gap.

Interview, Hanoi, Vietnam/
The New York Times, 6-19:(A)1.

Kenneth S. Courtis
Chief strategist,
Deutsche Bank Capital Markets
(Japan)

5

America is in retreat [in Asian markets]. There are exceptions—Proctor & Gamble and a few

(KENNETH S. COURTIS)

others. But by default and design, Japanese money is going into the mega-market of the future [in Asia].

Los Angeles Times,
5-19:(H)12.

Seth Cropsey
Director,
Asian Studies Center,
Heritage Foundation
(United States)

1

I am not sure that the current security relationship we [the U.S.] have with Japan, which is characterized by the United States being in a superior role and Japan in a subordinate one, is not something we would like to see continued. It makes Asia more stable, because the other Asian countries feel more secure that way. World War II is still a raw nerve with them. It is nice to have one area where we are still Number 1, still superior, and I don't think there is one Asian country that would like to see it otherwise.

The New York Times,
1-8:(A)6.

J. William Fulbright
Former United States Senator,
D-Arkansas

2

[On his being against U.S. involvement in the Vietnam war of the 1960s and '70s]: It cost a lot of money, it cost a lot of harm, and what did it accomplish? Even now, after all these years, I don't think we had any business going halfway around the world to intervene. They had their revolution, and they should have been allowed to decide for themselves. I don't have any reservations about my position. The only thing wrong with it was that I didn't reach it soon enough.

Interview,
Washington, D.C./
The Christian Science Monitor,
11-27:14.

Thomas B. Gold
Sociologist and
specialist on China,
University of California, Berkeley
(United States)

3

I believe the [Chinese] Communist Party is going to concentrate on the things it thinks it can do best—presumably political control, media, education—and allow the economy to function by some of its own logic. As the society becomes increasingly complex, and as a new type of person moves into the Party hierarchy, there has to be some kind of loosening. One question is the degree to which they can guide it and avoid an explosion.

The New York Times, 10-19:(A)4.

Joseph T. Gorman
Chairman, TRW, Inc.

4

The Japanese must change their system of [foreign trade] competition and change . . . to bring them into material alignment in all respects with those in North America and those in Europe. It is simply unacceptable to have one of the three major trading regions of the world with a different set of rules.

Los Angeles Times, 1-7:(H)2.

Jawhar Hassan
Defense analyst,
Institute of Strategic and
International Studies
(Malaysia)

5

[Saying people in Southeast Asia are not confident of U.S. military protection]: For us, it's not just vacillation but a lack of clarity to the U.S. commitment to peace and stability in the region. No one really thinks the U.S. will go for a major showdown. There is a feeling that the U.S. is less interested in this region than in other parts of the world.

The Christian Science Monitor,
7-6:4.

Richard E. Hawley
Lieutenant General,
United States Army;
Commander,
U.S. forces in Japan

1

Russia is still [a threat in Asia and the Pacific]. You don't see the same changes in the Russian military structure when you sit in Japan and look west as you do when you sit in Berlin and look east. China is a major power center, and that alone is ample justification for continued U.S. presence in this part of the world.

The New York Times, 5-5:(A)6.

Shigezo Hayasaka
Japanese political analyst

2

[In Japan,] it's not a matter of voters punishing the party in power because of the economy, the way they do in America. Here, when the economy is weak, people gravitate to the [ruling Liberal Democratic Party] because they think it is the only party strong enough to do anything.

The Washington Post, 7-24:(A)31.

Gerald Hensley
Minister of Defense
of New Zealand

3

The more respectable argument is not that Japan will re-militarize in the absence of America but simply that if America pulls back, the Japanese will slowly move to fill the gap. Everyone [in the area] will feel uncomfortable. Not because of memories of World War II—most people are too young to remember it—but because America and Great Britain, while they have made mistakes in Asia, have thought and acted globally. They pay into the system as well as take out. And so far, the Japanese have not paid in.

The New York Times, 5-5:(A)6.

Hiroshi Hirabayashi
Acting Japanese Ambassador
to the United States

4

Japan is an ally, perhaps the single most important ally of the U.S. In the post-Cold War era,

there are so many problems which cannot be solved without the two biggest economies' cooperation. We must jointly address those problems in the future. So to think Japan is an enemy [because of the economic difficulties between the two nations] is entirely out of context and does not serve anybody, including Americans.

Interview/USA Today, 3-23:(A)9.

Hun Sen
Prime Minister of Cambodia

5

It is not correct to call me a [former Soviet President Mikhail] Gorbachev of Cambodia. I have a different approach. He started his reforms from the top and hoped it would go down. We started form the bottom to force change in the top, and we did.

Interview,
Washington, D.C., March 26/
The Washington Post, 3-27:(A)24.

Lee A. Iacocca
Chairman,
Chrysler Corporation

6

[Saying the U.S. should be tougher with Japan on the issue of fair trade]: I think it is high time our government faced up to their government—be polite about it but tough—and said we can't continue this way . . . To say we are coming to Japan to get a souvenir or we're going to sit around and accept whatever favors they can bestow on us, that's not the game. The game is, you've got to change the basic trading relationship between these two countries. We don't have to apologize to anybody.

To reporters, Jan. 7/Los Angeles Times,
1-8:(A)6.

Jiang Zemin
Chairman,
Communist Party of China

7

Practice in China has proved that where market forces have been given full play, there the

(JIANG ZEMIN)

economy has been vigorous and has developed in a sound way. We must continue to intensify the market forces . . . The goal . . . is to build a socialist democracy suited to Chinese conditions and absolutely not a Western, multi-party, parliamentary system.

At Chinese Communist Party Congress,
Beijing, China, Oct. 12/
The Washington Post, 10-13:(A)14.

Chalmers A. Johnson
Specialist on Asia,
University of California, San Diego
(United States)

1

There's no doubt that the military arrangements today are totally anachronistic. The U.S.-Japan Security Treaty is based on the idea that Japan has unlimited strategic significance and no economic significance—but the situation today is precisely the reverse.

Los Angeles Times, 6-9:(A)16.

Shin Kanemaru
Vice president,
Liberal Democratic Party
of Japan

2

Some Japanese politicians have caused misunderstandings as a result of their remarks [criticizing the U.S.]. I told my colleagues that you have to be extremely cautious when you make remarks, that you have an impact on people overseas. If we belittle the United States, there is no future for Japan. Japan can exist because the United States exists, but it is not the other way around. We owe our prosperity to the United States. Many Japanese forget this fact.

Interview, Tokyo, Japan, Feb. 12/
The New York Times, 2-13:(A)1.

Kang Young Hoon
Former Prime Minister
of South Korea

3

North Korean Communist leaders haven't changed their basic orientation. They say they

don't have a nuclear-weapons program, but the [U.S. and South Korean] intelligence community are agreed that they have reached the final stage of producing a bomb. This will only heighten the tension on the Korean peninsula and in this part of Asia as well.

The Christian Science Monitor,
3-31:1.

Kim Il Sung
President of North Korea

4

We do not possess nuclear weapons. We are not making any nuclear weapons. Nor do we have a need to make any. We have no intention to confront the bigger nations around us with nuclear weapons. And it is unimaginable to develop nuclear weapons that could obliterate our brethren [in South Korea].

To visiting South Korean Prime
Minister Chung Won Shik,
Pyongyang, North Korea, Feb. 20/
Los Angeles Times, 2-21:(A)8.

Kim Tal Hyon
Deputy Prime Minister
of North Korea

5

The Cold War and socialist market have disappeared from this globe. The world is changing and times progress. We welcome foreign investment from any side . . . Because of the quick destruction of the socialist markets, we are facing difficulties. We can't import oil and other resources in time, and we can't export our goods.

News conference,
Pyongyang, North Korea/
Los Angeles Times, 5-8:(A)1,47.

Kim Woo Choong
Chairman, Daewoo Group
(South Korea)

6

If [North and South Korea were] reunited, we could emerge as one of the greatest economic zones of the world. Think of this: Unified, we will have a population of more than 70 million people. There are more than 1 million ethnic Koreans in China, about 300,000 ethnic Koreans in Russia . . . [With] many Chinese and Russian inhabitants [joining in], we could easily build an economy around 200 million people and become a center of the Asian economy.

January/
Los Angeles Times, 5-19:(H)8.

Kazuhiro Kobayashi
Director,
Child Development Office,
Ministry of Health and Welfare
of Japan

1

What did we [Japanese] get [for economic progress]? We produced the highest [per capita] gross national product in the world. In a macroeconomic sense, we are extremely prosperous. But are our individual lives the richest in the world? No one thinks so.

Los Angeles Times, 6-8:(A)6.

Toru Kusukawa
Chairman,
Fuji Research Institute Corporation
(Japan)

2

[On the current downturn in the Japanese economy]: Up to now, we had a myth . . . that the Japanese economy would have unlimited growth. We said that we were perfect. Now it happens that we are like one of you [non-Japanese]. Now we are coming to some sobering realizations.

The Christian Science Monitor,
12-3:8.

Lee Kuan Yew
Former Prime Minister
of Singapore

3

[Saying he prefers a U.S. military presence in Asia rather than a resurgent Japanese military

power]: The American presence, in my view, is essential for the continuation of international law and order in East Asia. We'd all be happier if the American security alliance remains, leaving Japan to concentrate on high-definition television.

Interview/
Los Angeles Times, 1-3:(A)4.

4

[On the economic success in some Asian countries with authoritarian governments and the economic failure in some Asian countries with democratic governments]: I think it's not just the constitution. It is also the culture. They're authoritarian in a positive sense — Taiwan, Korea, maybe even Japan. Look at the way authority is respected in Japan. Two persons meet and they bow to each other, and the man with the higher standing bows less deeply. There is a certain sense of order and discipline, and that is favorable for growth, because when you get down to work, to get a factory going, you can't keep on discussing and contradicting. Somebody has got to make decisions to go this way or that way. And I think it's not soft democracy that has made the Philippines and India less successful, but the nature of their cultures . . . They accept lower standards because they don't consider high standards or hard objectives worth the effort. They're prepared to make do with less.

Interview, Singapore/
Los Angeles Times, 5-19:(H)15.

Li Peng
Prime Minister of China

5

The issue of human rights falls within the sovereignty of each country. A country's human-rights record should not be judged in isolation from its history and culture . . . We are opposed to using human-rights issues as an excuse for interference in our affairs.

At United Nations Security Council
summit meeting, United Nations,
New York, Jan. 31/
The Washington Post, 2-1:(A)19.

(LI PENG)

1

To make China a powerful, socialist country standing firm as a rock in the East, we must concentrate on our domestic affairs—above all, on more rapid economic development . . . We should aim high, work hard, pay attention to economic results and bring about sustained, coordinated growth to raise our economy to a new stage every few years. That is the only way to prevent a peaceful evolution toward capitalism and to consolidate the foundation of the socialist system . . . It is impossible for us to proceed with reform and expand the economy amid social upheaval. Order leads to prosperity and chaos to decline.

Before National People's Congress,
Beijing, China, March 20/
Los Angeles Times, 3-21:(A)10.

James R. Lilley
Assistant Secretary for
International Security Affairs,
Department of Defense
of the United States;
Former United States Ambassador
to China

2

To talk about an American decline of interest [in Asia and the Pacific] is both wrong and dangerous. It gives potential predators a false sense of opportunity and an inducement to be aggressive. Let's not give [North Korean heir-apparent] Kim Jong Il any ideas.

The New York Times, 5-5:(A)6.

Lim Dong Won
Vice Minister of the
National Unification Board
of South Korea

3

[On the lack of progress in getting North Korea to change its ways]: It takes time. North Korea is not so weak that it will collapse suddenly. North Korean people have been poor for so many years that they are accustomed to it. They can eat one meal a day and not be tempted to revolt. You can't use a Western yardstick of progress. You have to use a North Korean yardstick.

The New York Times, 12-16:(A)6.

Alex Magno
Political scientist,
University of the Philippines

4

There's a very cynical view that elections [in the Philippines] are a way to distribute the wealth. It should make the rich a little poorer, and the poor a little richer . . . There's a Robin Hood mentality.

Los Angeles Times, 2-10:(A)6.

Tran Cong Man
Vietnamese government spokesman

5

The collapse of the Soviet Union was a devastating blow for us [Vietnamese]. The Soviet Union was our support, ideologically and psychologically, also militarily and economically. It was our unique model. Now we find it was a false model.

The New York Times, 6-19:(A)1.

Kiichi Miyazawa
Prime Minister of Japan

6

[On U.S.-Japanese relations]: It is incumbent upon us to create a new world order of peace and democracy from this Cold War era. We want to demonstrate to the world that the U.S. and Japan can manage their bilateral relationship, even as economic relations become more prominent in the post-Cold War era . . . For 40 years, Japan has benefitted from the friendship of the U.S. We would like to be a friend in need.

To reporters, Tokyo, Japan, Jan. 6/
Los Angeles Times, 1-7:(A)4.

7

[Supporting the idea of sending Japanese troops to participate in UN peacekeeping in Cambodia]: We are a country that has focused our foreign policy on the United Nations. Now the United Nations is carrying out the biggest peacekeeping mission in its history. The UN Secretary General's personal representative in Cambodia is a Japanese, and so is the UN Commissioner for Refugees. In the midst of these circumstances, no matter how you look at it, it would be strange for us to do nothing at all.

News conference,
Tokyo, Japan, April 13/
Los Angeles Times, 4-14:(A)6.

1

[Saying the West should understand China, despite its human-rights problems]: We need to appreciate that for a country like China, with more than 1 billion people and a low national income, the expansion of its national economy is indispensable for its domestic stability. Economic reforms should pave the way for political reforms.

At National Press Club,
Washington, D.C., July 2/
Los Angeles Times, 7-3:(A)8.

Roy D. Morey
Resident representative in China
of the United Nations
Development Program

2

[On China's experimentation over the years with various methods of market economics and foreign investment]: Years ago, there was an attitude that you should simultaneously release a number of the horses from the corral and let them run. The horses have run. It's true, some have run faster than others. But they certainly have run. The notion that you're ever going to put these horses back in the same corral you had 15 years ago is nonsense.

Interview, Beijing, China/
Los Angeles Times, 5-19:(H)12.

Ronald A. Morse
Authority on Japan;
Formerly at the
Woodrow Wilson Center of the
Smithsonian Institution
(United States)

3

A nuclear-armed Japan could be a benefit to the United States. It would strengthen the U.S.-

Japan partnership, because we'd be dealing with each other as equals. And we need at least one [nuclear power] in Asia that's on our side.

Los Angeles Times, 6-9:(A)16.

Richard W. Mounce
General manager,
Hong Kong operations,
Chase Manhattan Bank

4

[On concern about Hong Kong's future when, in 1997, control over it passes from Britain to China]: People say, what's going to happen in 1997? And a lot of the business community says, Lord knows. But that's only asking half the question. The other half is, what if things go positively? In the view of a lot of us here, the upside is stunning. South China may become the premiere light-manufacturing center of the world over the next 20 to 30 years.

The Washington Post, 5-25:(A)22.

Najibullah
President of Afghanistan

5

We have a common task, Afghanistan, the United States of America and the civilized world, to launch a joint struggle against [Islamic] fundamentalism. If fundamentalism comes to Afghanistan, war will continue for many more years. Afghanistan will turn into a center of world smuggling for narcotic drugs. Afghanistan will be turned into a center for terrorism.

Interview,
Kabul, Afghanistan, March 9/
The New York Times, 3-10:(A)3.

Nursultan A. Nazarbayev
President of Kazakhstan

6

We don't know today what will happen to the Commonwealth of Independent States [made up of now-independent former republics of the Soviet Union]. We don't have a normal state-to-state treaty with Russia. Nobody knows what will happen to the leadership of Russia in the future. Seventy kilometers from this place, China is testing her nuclear weapons . . . We are prepared to proceed with the [total] reduction of nuclear weapons, but we want to be a participant in the negotiating process . . . I want America, with all its economic and technological might, to establish a presence in Kazakhstan. We are prepared for a far-reaching and mutually beneficial relationship . . . to create economic, political and possibly military relations.

Interview, Alma-Ata, Kazakhstan/
The Christian Science Monitor,
4-27:4.

Richard M. Nixon
Former President
of the United States

1

Don't write [China] off . . . because over 50 per cent of Chinese GNP is from private enterprises, and you cannot have free markets without having, eventually, political freedom.

Broadcast interview/
U.S. News & World Report,
1-20:19.

Michel Oksenberg
President,
East-West Center
(United States)

2

[On China]: You simply cannot postpone political reform and assuage political demands through economic prosperity alone. You have the beginnings in China of an urban middle class, and we see no movement in the political sphere to cope with the increasing occupational differentiation, the changing locus of where a people live.

The New York Times, 10-19:(A)4.

Martha Brill Olcott
Specialist on Central Asia,
Colgate University
(United States)

3

Central Asia is a place where China, Iran, Turkey and, to a lesser extent, Pakistan and Afghanistan are now defining their strategic

interests. So even if we [the U.S.] decide it's not worth our direct intervention, we have to deal with the consequences of other people intervening . . . What happens in Central Asia will also eventually affect the balance of power in the Persian Gulf, South Asia, the Mideast and, to a lesser degree, China.

Los Angeles Times, 2-10:(A)29.

Robert D. Orr
United States Ambassador
to Singapore

4

We [the U.S.] spend so much time trying to open up the Japanese market that we almost totally overlook the fact that the Japanese are everywhere selling their products. They consider the world as their marketplace.

The Washington Post, 3-20:(A)19.

William H. Overholt
Executive director,
Bankers Trust Company
(Hong Kong)

5

The Asian system [will get] to a market economy and a democracy, even if the leaders don't intend to. Economic success creates a broad middle class and a huge education system, and it creates factories filled with large numbers of educated workers who form unions. Economic success also forms ties with the outside world, so that liberal foreign ideas penetrate. These social glaciers break up any dictatorship.

The New York Times, 5-22:(A)2.

Christopher Patten
Governor of Hong Kong

6

[On the scheduled turnover of control of Hong Kong from Britain to China in 1997]: Our task for the future is as momentous as your achievements in the past. It is a task that will require all the qualities you have already shown—resilience, determination, drive—only in still greater measure. It is a task which, when we accomplish it successfully . . . will provide a shining example

(CHRISTOPHER PATTEN)

to the world of partnership and cooperation between peoples and nations for the good of all.

Addressing the people of Hong Kong
at his swearing-in ceremony,
Hong Kong, July 9/
Los Angeles Times, 7-10:(A)5.

1

Hong Kong is sometimes described as crassly materialistic and motivated solely by a search for personal gain. The truth is very different. Democracy [in Hong Kong] is more than just a philosophical ideal. It is . . . an essential element in the pursuit of economic progress.

Speech/
The Christian Science Monitor,
10-8:3.

Claiborne Pell
United States Senator,
D-Rhode Island

2

[Criticizing the U.S. for not contributing enough funding for UN peacekeeping operations in Cambodia]: I am dismayed at the apparent unwillingness of many in Congress to pay the relatively modest sums required for the peacekeeping forces . . . However costly UN peacekeeping is, it is far less costly to the United States than the price we paid for our earlier involvements in these regional conflicts . . . Both the [U.S.] Bush Administration and the Congress have been counting the pennies while missing the prize.

Before the Senate,
Washington, D.C., March 12/
The Washington Post, 3-14:(A)18.

Ross Perot
American industrialist;
1992 independent
U.S. Presidential candidate

3

China's a huge country, broken into many provinces. It has some very elderly leaders that

will not be around too much longer. Capitalism is growing and thriving across big portions of China. Asia will be our [the U.S.'s] largest trading partner in the future. It will be a growing and a closer relationship. We have a delicate tightwire walk that we must go through at the present time to make sure that we do not cozy up to tyrants, to make sure that they [in China] don't get the impression that they can suppress their people. But time is our friend there, because their leaders will change in not too many years, worst case, and their country is making great progress.

At Presidential candidates' debate,
St. Louis, Mo., Oct. 11/
The New York Times, 10-12:(A)14.

Fidel V. Ramos
President of the Philippines

4

Let us begin by telling ourselves the truth. Our nation is in trouble. And there are no easy answers, no quick fixes for our basic ills. Once we were the school of Southeast Asia. Today, our neighbors have one by one passed us by. The immediate future will be difficult. In some areas, things could get worse before they get better. Sacrifices will be asked of every sector of society.

Inaugural address,
Manila, Philippines, June 30/
Los Angeles Times, 7-1:(A)6.

Barnett R. Rubin
Associate professor
of political science,
and director of the Center
for the Study of Central Asia,
Columbia University
(United States)

5

The situation [in Afghanistan] is quite similar to Somalia. There are large numbers of armed men in a variety of groups representing political parties or ethnic or tribal affiliations. Over the last decade, they have been hyper-armed, mainly because of the Cold War, but also because of competition for influence between Saudi Arabia and Iran. There is no central political authority. As in Somalia, armed groups [in Afghanistan]

(BARNETT R. RUBIN)

are fighting over power and food. You can't have food unless you have power, and you can't keep power unless you can feed your followers.

Interview/
The New York Times, 10-14:(A)6.

K. S. Sandhu
Director,
Institute of Southeast Asian Studies
(Singapore)

1

No matter what kind of nice face they put on it, people are still suspicious as hell of the Japanese. The fact is that they are perfectionist about everything they do, and if they decide again to become influential politically or militarily, they will do it to a fine art.

The New York Times, 5-5:(A)6.

Leticia Ramos Shahani
Head of Foreign Affairs Committee,
Philippine Senate

2

Philippine relations with the United States are at an all-time low. I think many people feel that the special relationship is gone. But closing this chapter may be good. It will make us less obsessed with the American relationship, make us look more to Europe and Japan and force us to be more competitive.

The New York Times, 6-29:(A)5.

David Shambaugh
China specialist,
School of African and
Oriental Studies,
London University (Britain).

3

The world view of China's leadership is out of synch with reality. There is an extreme disjuncture between the Chinese elite that clings to the idea of state sovereignty and anti-hegemonism and the simple fact of life today that money, trade, missiles and human rights transcend national borders.

The Christian Science Monitor,
2-26:11.

Norodom Sihanouk
Former Chief of State
of Cambodia

4

I don't mind about my personal power. I just wish to enjoy a good reputation—not just as the father of national independence [for Cambodia] and the father of peace and reconciliation, but also a third title, which I wish to get from my people spontaneously—the father of liberal democracy. In the economic sphere, if we want to develop quickly, we should imitate Thailand. Why? Because you see the results there. Their people are happy and are enjoying an economic boom, with a very high per-capita income. It is true there exists corruption, but we cannot avoid it. Cambodia must become a free-enterprise, free-market nation, attracting investment from the wealthy nations. Not just joint venture, but 100 per cent investment from America, France, Japan, Thailand and Singapore and others, with a guarantee of non-nationalization.

Interview, Phnom Penh, Cambodia/
Los Angeles Times, 1-5:(M)6.

Stephen J. Solarz
United States Representative,
D-New York

5

[Criticizing U.S. President Bush's decision to extend MFN trade status to China for another year]: It's *deja vu* all over again. Nothing has changed in China or in Washington. The President sticks to his view that the best way to facilitate change in China is a policy of constructive engagement. He apparently agrees with the philosopher Hegel that if theory and fact disagree, so much for the facts—because the facts simply don't sustain Mr. Bush's views.

June 2/
The New York Times, 6-3:(A)6.

Yasunori Sone
Political scientist,
Keio University (Japan)

6

[On the just passed legislation in Japan permitting its troops to be used overseas as part of a limited combat role in conjunction with UN forces]: Two years ago, nobody would have dreamed that Japan could pass this bill. But then came the [Persian] Gulf war. The Japanese people heard criticism from around the world of our passive role. Of course, the devotion to pacifism is still very strong... But the reaction to the Gulf war is stronger. Japan is desperately looking for a way to make an international contribution.

Tokyo, Japan, June 9/
The Washington Post, 6-9:(A)10.

Maurice Strong
Secretary General,
United Nations Conference
on Environment and Development

1

What I call Japan's second miracle is the way in which it has so dramatically reduced air and water pollution in Japan itself. The rest of the world doesn't know much about that. They look at Japan's environmental record in terms of fishing, damage to the tropical forest, whales— the kind of things for which the Japanese have been widely criticized. But . . . Japan is in the process of developing a national consensus to project its national performance into its international activity.

Interview, Geneva, Switzerland/
The Christian Science Monitor,
5-29:3.

Bertrand Tsai
Political scientist,
National Taiwan University

2

[On China's relations with Taiwan]: In the past, Beijing has always tried to divide and rule. They will probably try to play one faction off against another and create a crisis. But if they're

smart, they'll keep quiet. A stable Taiwan is more beneficial to China just as a stable China is better for Taiwan.

The Christian Science Monitor,
12-22:6.

Haji Akbar Turajonzoda
Spiritual leader of Tajikistan

3

Our society isn't prepared to live according to Islamic law. We've strayed far from Islam over the past 70 years. We will become an Islamic state, but it will take 40-50 years. We have to train a new generation. Introducing any ideology by force is a mistake.

Interview, Dushanbe, Tajikistan/
The Christian Science Monitor,
9-30:10.

Frank Wisner
Former United States Ambassador
to the Philippines

4

There may never be a day when the Philippines is under the kind of focus in America that it had in the 1930s and before. But there is still a lot to make this relationship special. The history has a dynamic to it.

The New York Times, 6-29:(A)5.

Paul D. Wolfowitz
Under Secretary of Defense
of the United States

5

There's no question that the North Koreans will sell anything they have to anybody who has money to pay for it—and about all they have are weapons of mass or considerable destruction, so they're dangerous people.

To reporters/
Los Angeles Times, 3-13:(A)8.

Europe

Giovanni Agnelli
Chairman, Fiat S.p.A. (Italy)

1

[On Italy's precarious economic situation]: Italy cannot go on this way. The state is out of money, the stock exchange stagnant. We will have to accept sacrifices and discipline. But the problem is that Italy is a country of people whose affluence is recent, and they do not want to give up anything.

The New York Times, 6-25:(C)2.

Ramiz Alia
President of Albania

2

There is no other alternative [for Albania] but a free-market economy. Undoubtedly I have my own ideals, but I'm a realist.

Interview, Tirana, Albania/
The New York Times. 3-16:(A)7.

Giuliano Amato
Prime Minister of Italy

3

We must make radical changes. Or else Italy risks being viewed as the Disneyland of Europe.

Before Italian Senate,
Rome, June 30/
The Washington Post, 7-21:(A)14.

Yevgeny Ambartsumov
Deputy Chairman,
Foreign Affairs Committee,
Russian Parliament

4

[Russian President Boris] Yeltsin sometimes behaves like a bull in a china shop. But I don't have any qualms about him controlling the nuclear button. He may have an impulsive nature, but he is an orderly, decent person. He is basically a civilized person who does not always behave in a civilized way. There is nothing psychopathic or paranoid about him.

The Washington Post, 2-1:(A)18.

Ernest Ametistov
Russian Constitutional Court
Justice

5

[On Russia's Constitutional Court giving President Boris Yeltsin a partial approval of his ban on Communist Party activity in Russia]: It was a compromise. The crucial point of the whole trial was the examination of the juridical and social nature of the Communist Party in this country: Was it some kind of state or was it a political party?

Interview, Moscow, Russia/
The Christian Science Monitor,
12-1:1.

David Anderson
Director, Berlin Office,
Aspen Institute;
Former United States Ambassador
to Yugoslavia

6

There's never been a Europe-wide debate about what this new [united] Europe is supposed to look like. The Germans only just got their full sovereignty back with unification. Are they now supposed to give it up for Europe? It's an issue just sitting there, waiting for debate.

The New York Times, 5-13:(A)4.

7

[On the ethnic conflict in what used to be Yugoslavia]: The world was supposed to be a better place after the Cold War's end. This terrible little war leaves Europeans feeling very edgy, very unhappy, but still sitting on the sidelines, doing nothing, not knowing what to do.

The Washington Post, 5-16:(A)1.

James A. Baker III
Secretary of State
of the United States

8

[Supporting U.S. aid to Russia to help prevent an economic collapse that could bring on a less-friendly government there]: This is a once-in-a lifetime opportunity. I think we must find a way to be there. We have spent trillions and trillions of dollars over the last 40 years in winning the Cold War and we really should be willing . . . to spend the millions or maybe billions that it takes to secure the peace—because otherwise, we'll find ourselves right back in another Cold War.

Congressional testimony,
Washington, D.C./
Los Angeles Times, 3-7:(A)9.

1

[On the ethnic conflict in what used to be Yugoslavia]: As this nightmare drags on, the willingness of countries around the world to see it happen or stand by as it does happen is going to diminish . . . It's hard to believe, in this day and age, that armed forces will fire artillery and mortars indiscriminately in the heart of a city [Sarajevo, Bosnia], flushing defenseless men, women and children out into the streets and then shooting them. The world has condemned the Belgrade [Serbia/Yugoslavia] government for these outrages. It has imposed sanctions on the regime there, but in our view more must be done.

Before Senate Foreign Relations Committee,
Washington, D.C., June 23/
Los Angeles Times, 6-24:(A)4.

Martin Bangemann
Vice President,
Commission of the
European Community

2

[On polls that show younger people in Germany are not as enthusiastic about European unity as are their parents]: The European Community was much more "in" with younger people when it was just a vision, a dream that couldn't be realized. They accused their fathers of not doing enough. Well, now the fathers—who were once those young people—are doing what they dreamed of in their younger days and making the dream into a reality. Europe has entered into the reality of life's daily problems

[and] the new generation has discovered something else. This is normal.

Interview, Bonn, Germany/
Los Angeles Times, 6-9:(H)4.

3

[On the recent public vote in Denmark rejecting the Maastricht treaty on European unification]: I do not belong to those who look at the Danish decision as some kind of traffic accident. It is a crisis. It shows there is an underlying crisis of a European dimension; but in the past, the European Community has not only always survived such crises but has come out stronger in the end. I believe the public debate on European unity after the decision in Denmark will be based much more on fact and judgment than emotion and feelings.

Interview, Bonn, Germany/
Los Angeles Times, 6-9:(H)4.

Sergei Barburin
Member, Russian Congress
of People's Deputies;
Leader, Russian Unity

4

[On the office of Prime Minister of Russia]: What matters is not just personalities. What matters is whether we continue the processes which I personally call the destruction of Russia, the destruction of her economy, the extermination of her people, or we demand change. As Prime Minister, we need a person who knows how to work both with the state sector of the economy and the sector of new market structures, a person who knows not only what to do but how to do it.

At debate in Congress of People's Deputies,
Moscow, Russia, Dec. 9/
The Christian Science Monitor,
12-10:6.

Robert L. Barry
United States State Department coordinator
for U.S. assistance
to Eastern Europe

5

Poland is going through the kind of political confusion that comes from weariness with

(ROBERT L. BARRY)

austerity. People don't understand that there's no way to take the pain out of a profound economic transformation [from Communism to the free market]. But sooner or later, the Poles, and those who balk at austerity elsewhere in the region, will have to recognize that there is no third way—that trying to pump up the dead dinosaurs of inefficient industries with government subsidies leads nowhere but a sure move to the poorhouse.

The Washington Post, 5-23:(A)27.

Enzo Bartocci
Italian political scientist

1

What we [in Italy] have come down to is a basic identity question. Over recent years, "Italy" has degenerated to a pejorative identification, with both the rise of the European Community and the "leagues" [a political movement in the north of the country] encouraging a turn to the local dimension . . . My feeling is that people will find their national identity is important, and that will work in favor of substantial reform.

The Christian Science Monitor,
10-28:3.

Silvio Berlusconi
Italian industrialist

2

I am an optimist with regard to Italy. Working as I do in contact with thousands of protagonists of the Italian economy, I only see signals of this nature. Those looking in from outside see only the evident shortcomings and think everything is over. I have just come back from a "Tour of Italy." I've visited 14 cities and met some 5,000 protagonists of the Italian industry. It was the moment when the newspapers were full of pessimism. The protagonists of our economy always were coming out with statements full of doubts and pessimism such as "the party's over, we have to tighten our belts and make sacrifices"—I personally rebuked them for spreading a climate of pessimism which is the exact opposite of what is needed. Instead I found a great deal

of optimism based on the results being achieved. Hence, we've been only marginally affected by the slow-down in the world economy.

Interview, Arcore, Italy/
USA Today, 9-8:(Our World)8.

Joseph R. Biden, Jr.
United States Senator,
D-Delaware

3

Right now, the [U.S.] aid package for [Russia] is stalled, because there is little momentum in the Senate, outright opposition in the House and a tepid effort by the President [Bush]. Consequently, there is little prospect that the bill will pass by the time of [Russian President Boris] Yeltsin's visit [to the U.S.]. Without a bipartisan bill, we will make it harder to secure democracy in Russia.

The New York Times, 6-5:(A)1.

Carl Bildt
Prime Minister of Sweden

4

We've [Sweden] been under-funding our defense forces for 10 years. Russia remains the strongest single power on the continent. Even after all the [Russian] cutbacks, there is no rival to it. The uncertainty is there and a small nation must be aware of that.

Interview, Washington, D.C./
The Christian Science Monitor,
3-3:9.

Vernon Bogdanor
Professor of government,
Oxford University (England)

5

[There is] a debate over the evolution of the [British] monarchy. At the root of it, I believe, is a recognition of the need to move toward a monarchy that is more rational and more modern. [Buckingham] Palace must now deal with a society that is less deferential and demands more accountability.

The New York Times, 12-16:(B)1.

Bill Bradley
United States Senator,
D-New Jersey

1

[Russian President] Boris Yeltsin's [arrival] in Washington . . . should signal the beginning of a new era of friendly, cooperative, Russo-American relations. The new reality is that Russia and the other republics are not the [former] Soviet Union. They are new countries, distinct from each other and from their common predecessor. We have to stop talking about them as if they carry the taint of the old union. The old system was controlled by a few who had power, but no legitimacy. Now forces that are democratic, market-oriented, national and spiritual seek institutional arrangements through which they can build for a better tomorrow. I believe [the U.S.] Congress and the American people should help make this change irreversible. A new beginning is at hand.

At National Press Club,
Washington, D.C., June 11/
The Washington Post, 6-16:(A)20.

Patrick J. Buchanan
American political commentator;
Candidate for the 1992
Republican U.S. Presidential
nomination

2

If people are starving in [what was the old Soviet Union and is now the Commonwealth of Independent States], we will be the first there with food aid. But taxing American workers to send billions of dollars to politicians in the [C.I.S.] works against everybody's interests. Private capital will pour into the resource-rich C.I.S. so long as C.I.S. policies make the C.I.S. an attractive place to invest. If the vestiges of socialism survive there, no amount of American aid will help.

Los Angeles Times, 3-17:(H)6.

George Bush
President of the United States

3

[Supporting U.S. financial aid for Russia and the other former republics of the Soviet Union]:

The revolution in these states is a defining moment in history, with profound consequences for America's own national interest. The stakes are as high for us now as any that we have faced in this century. And our adversary for 45 years, the one nation that posed a worldwide threat to freedom and peace, is now seeking to join the community of democratic nations. A victory for democracy and freedom in the former U.S.S.R. creates the possibility of a new world of peace for our children and grandchildren. But if this democratic revolution is defeated, it could plunge us into a world more dangerous in some respects than the dark years of the Cold War. America must meet this challenge, joining with those who stood beside us in the battle against imperial Communism: Germany, the United Kingdom, Japan, France, Canada, Italy, and other allies. Together we won the Cold War, and today we must win the peace. This effort will require new resources from the industrial democracies, but nothing like the price we would pay if democracy and reform failed in Russia and Ukraine and Belarus and Armenia, and the states of Central Asia.

News conference,
Washington, D.C., April 1/
The New York Times, 4-2:(A)7.

4

[On the spread of nationalism and the resulting ethnic conflicts in parts of Europe since the end of the Cold War and the breakup of the Soviet Union]: During the Cold War, we saw the denial of human rights as a primary source of the confrontation that scarred Europe and threatened global war. Now a new ideology—intolerant nationalism—is spawning new divisions, new crimes, new conflicts.

At Conference on Security and
Cooperation in Europe,
Helsinki, Finland, July 9/
Los Angeles Times, 7-10:(A)12.

5

[On the ethnic conflict in what used to be Yugoslavia]: We're trying to help on a humanitarian basis. And now we have some people

(GEORGE BUSH)

coming at me saying, "Commit American [military] forces." Before I'd commit forces to a battle, I want to know what's the beginning, what's the objective, how's the objective going to be achieved and what's the end.

Interview, Aug. 4/
USA Today, 8-5:(A)9.

1

[On the ethnic conflict in what used to be Yugoslavia]: Those who understand the nature of this conflict understand that an enduring solution cannot be imposed by force from outside on unwilling participants. The blood of innocents is being spilled over century-old feuds. The lines between enemies and even friends are jumbled and fragmented. Let no one think there is an easy or a simple solution to this tragedy. The violence will not end overnight, whatever pressure and means the international community brings to bear. Blood feuds are very difficult to resolve. Bringing peace again to the Balkans will literally take years of work.

News conference,
Colorado Springs, Colo., Aug. 6/
Los Angeles Times, 8-7:(A)1.

2

For some 40 years we kept the peace [in Europe]. If you look at the cost of *not* keeping the peace in Europe, it would be exorbitant. We have reduced the number of [U.S.] troops that are deployed and going to be deployed. I have cut defense spending [in the wake of the end of the Cold War]. And the reason we could do that is because of our fantastic success in winning the Cold War. We never would have got there if we'd gone for the nuclear-freeze crowd; never would have got there if we'd listened to those that wanted to cut defense spending. I think it is important that the United States stay in Europe [militarily] and continue to guarantee the peace. We simply cannot pull back.

At Presidential candidates' debate,
St. Louis, Mo., Oct. 11/
The New York Times, 10-12:(A)12.

3

The Soviet Union did not simply lose the Cold War. The Western democracies won it. And I say this not to gloat but to make a key point. The qualities that enabled us to triumph in that struggle—faith, strength, unity and, above all, American leadership—are those we must call upon now to win the peace.

At Texas A&M University, Dec. 15/
The New York Times, 12-16:(C)18.

Fidel Castro
President of Cuba

4

[On the demise of the Soviet Union]: They carried out colossal achievements, although they did not know how to design a good pair of shoes . . . They paid attention to research but they totally neglected the application of scientific advances and technology in many sectors; they had to invent many things that had already been invented; in general, their equipment used excess steel and energy, and they did not pay sufficient attention to computerization, at least in the civil field . . . But these are not errors of the system; they are errors of economic management . . . A large part of those resources was absorbed in the arms race. This could occur in any system, socialist or capitalist. There were political errors, such as the abuse of power and the cult of personality . . . I mention this only so that you will understand that when I point out the great successes achieved by socialism in that country, I do not ignore the errors they committed.

Interview/
Current History, February:61.

Hikmet Cetin
Foreign Minister of Turkey

5

[On the current ethnic conflict in what used to be Yugoslavia]: The problem we are facing in Bosnia is no civil war, nor is it a humanitarian crisis. It is one of [Serbian] aggression, the unbridled use of force, the attempt to gain territory through the use of force and "ethnic cleansing." It also involves crimes against humanity and a deliberate design to wipe out an entire community through murder or forced displacement.

At conference on the Balkans,
London, England, Aug. 26/
Los Angeles Times, 8-27:(A)12.

Charles
Prince of Wales

1

[Arguing against strict central regulations over EC countries exercised by Brussels, such as proposed common health standards for cheese, which would particularly affect the French]: The very phrase "minimum hygiene standards" should strike terror into the hearts of any true-born Frenchman. It certainly frightens me, and all other people in my country who find that life is not worth living unless you have a choice of all the gloriously unhygienic things which mankind—especially the French portion of it—has lovingly created.

The Washington Post, 9-25:(A)23.

Aleksandr Chikvaidze
Foreign Minister of Georgia

2

What's very important now for the previous [now independent] Soviet republics, especially for Georgia, is not [foreign] humanitarian help. Humanitarian help will never solve any problems. It is necessary to help us create some kind of economic infrastructure. It means we have to build things that give us products, that give us goods, which we can use for ourselves and also sell to get some hard currency.

To reporters, en route from Lisbon
to Tbilisi, Georgia, May 25/
The New York Times, 5-26:(A)5.

Anatoly B. Chubais
Deputy Prime Minister
of Russia for Privatization

3

[On his government's issuing vouchers to its citizens entitling them to own shares in state-owned industries]: This is the starting point of the capitalist education of the Russian people. The first thing we have to do is start the process ... If the Communists say we have to stop, that means we have to [start] it as soon as possible. Their motives are crystal clear and they pursue only one goal. The Communists and those who stand behind them understand full well that the distribution of property to the people, popular privatization, signifies the death of the command economy and the political system which was built on the basis of total state property ownership.

Interview,
Moscow, Russia, Sept. 30/
The New York Times, 10-1:(A)1,6.

Bill Clinton
Governor of Arkansas (D);
Candidate for the 1992
Democratic U.S. Presidential nomination

4

[Supporting the idea of U.S. financial aid for Russia]: I know it isn't popular today to call for foreign assistance. It's harder when Americans are hurting, as millions are today. But I believe it is deeply irresponsible to forgo this short-term investment in our long-term security. Let me be clear: Our nation can afford this. This is not an exorbitant price to pay for a chance to create new American markets and anchor a revitalized Russia firmly in the democratic camp.

Before Foreign Policy Association,
New York, N.Y., April 1/
The New York Times, 4-2:(A)16.

5

[On what the U.S. should do about the ethnic conflict in what used to be Yugoslavia]: If we are going to risk the lives of Americans to save hundreds of thousands of people in Central Europe, we have to have some clear notion of what we are doing and whether we can succeed. We don't want to just put a bunch of people into a quagmire and risk their getting killed for nothing ... We have to know we have achievable objectives and that other nations closer to the scene of action are doing their part too.

July 15/
Los Angeles Times, 8-8:(A)18.

Bill Clinton
Governor of Arkansas (D);
1992 Democratic U.S.
Presidential nominee

1

[On the ethnic conflict in what used to be Yugoslavia]: History has shown us that you can't allow the mass extermination of people and just sit by and watch it happen. I think the United Nations, with the United States' support, needs to consider doing whatever it takes to stop the slaughter of civilians, to investigate under international law whether there have been any human-rights violations. We may have to use military force. I would begin with air power against the Serbs to try to restore the basic conditions of humanity.

At East St. Louis (Ill.) High School,
Aug. 5/
Los Angeles Times, 8-6:(A)8.

2

I disagree that we need 150,000 [U.S.] troops to fulfill our role in Europe. We certainly must maintain an engagement there. There is certainly dangers there. There is certainly other trouble spots in the world which are closer to Europe than to the United States. But two former [U.S.] Defense Secretaries recently issued a report saying that 100,000 or slightly fewer troops would be enough . . . I simply don't believe we can afford nor do we need to keep 150,000 troops in Europe given how much the Red Army, now under control of Russia, has been cut. The Arms Control Agreement concluded between [U.S.] President Bush and [Russian President Boris] Yeltsin is something I have applauded. I don't think we need 150,000 troops.

At Presidential candidates' debate,
St. Louis, Mo., Oct. 11/
The New York Times, 10-12:(A)13.

Dobrica Cosic
President of Yugoslavia

3

Neither Serbia nor the Federal Republic of Yugoslavia is involved in the Bosnian war. That war is not a result of Serbian aggression. It is a religious, inter-ethnic civil war.

Interview, Dec. 17/
The New York Times, 12-19:6.

Edith Cresson
Prime Minister of France

4

[Criticizing the center-right opposition to France's long-in-power socialist government]: Most of them have contracted in this long abstinence such an appetite for position, honor and money that it is easy to predict that on the first occasion [that] they would throw themselves into power with a kind of gluttony, not bothering to choose the time nor the morsel.

Before French National Assembly,
Paris, France, Feb. 7/
Los Angeles Times, 2-12:(A)4.

Hans Daniels
Mayor of Bonn, Germany

5

[Criticizing plans to move Germany's capital from Bonn to Berlin]: Today just as strongly as ever, I think this decision was wrong, not only for Bonn but for all of Germany. It is dangerous to concentrate political power in a country's biggest city, as the Americans wisely recognized when they moved their capital out of New York. We are abandoning the place where Germany built its most stable democracy, in favor of a megacity that has a much different history. Berlin is overwhelmed with other challenges, and the costs [of moving] are far beyond what we can truly afford.

Interview/
The New York Times, 4-14:(A)6.

Jacques Delors
President,
Executive Commission,
European Community

6

[On the planned economic and political unification of the EC countries]: We are facing 12 sovereign nations that have long traditions, that have geopolitical interests that are sometimes different, sometimes contrary. Little by little, they have to learn to think in common and act in common . . . Thanks to McDonald's, you have lunch in 10 minutes. But you can't build a grand political system in a year.

Los Angeles Times, 2-4:(H)4.

Philip Dimitrov
Prime Minister of Bulgaria

1

Until the late 1980s, Bulgaria exhibited all the essential characteristics of a Communist society; indeed, some were even more pronounced in our country than elsewhere. The majority of the people were deprived not only of the right to property and political freedom, but also of almost all possibilities for individual initiative and moral choice. The dictatorship seemed so stable, entrenched and invincible that even those who desired change could only conceive of it as a gradual and slow process that should take into consideration and accommodate the views and interests of the ruling class . . . The Communist authorities had indoctrinated people to feel vulnerable and dependent on the state, and not only in the sense that it could violate their rights at will. By imposing a great number of impractical and often illogical restrictions and limitations, which were inevitably and routinely breached or disregarded, they also cultivated in the individual a feeling of being an offender in any case. This served to not only blur the line between the permitted and the forbidden, the acceptable and the unacceptable, but negatively affected the moral standards of society, for instance, by stripping, cheating, theft and dishonesty of their moral repulsiveness.

Washington, D.C., March 5/
The Washington Post, 3-10:(A)16.

Milovan Djilas
Author;
Former Vice President
of Yugoslavia

2

[On the current conflict over borders between the republics of what used to be Yugoslavia]:

Criticism of the Communists for the manner in which they resolved the national questions [in 1946] is coming only from Serbian and Croatian nationalists, and it is not correct or truthful. They have national pretensions to enlarge their own states . . . The Communists didn't just sit in some office and draw these borders from nothing. They are the product of long experience, of history and ethnic principles, not just the desires of the Communist Party.

Interview, Belgrade, Yugoslavia/
Los Angeles Times, 7-7:(H)2.

Jerko Doko
Minister of Defense
of Bosnia and Herzegovina

3

[On the ethnic conflict between Serbia and Bosnia]: Until [the Serbs] are forced to stop this, civilians [in Bosnia] will continue dying, no matter whether the Americans bring food or not. To end this suffering, I make this plea to the United States: Realize that the only solution is to deploy the Sixth Fleet in the Adriatic, impose an air blockade over Bosnia and Herzegovina, and deliver an ultimatum to Serbia that it must withdraw all Yugoslav Army and Air force units from our territory, with all their equipment. If they don't do it within the prescribed time limit, let them suffer the consequences—[a U.S.] air attack on Belgrade [the Serbian capital], which is the source of all this evil.

Interview, June 24/
The New York Times, 6-25:(A)4.

Roland Dumas
Foreign Minister of France

4

[On the forthcoming French referendum on the Maastricht treaty on European union]: A "no" [vote] would turn things upside down, it would be an earthquake, everything would be put into question. When there is an earthquake, you cannot tell how the houses will fall down or how the ground will open up. You simply know that it is a catastrophe.

Hatfield, England,, Sept. 13/
The New York Times, 9-14:(A)8.

Lawrence S. Eagleburger
Secretary of State
of the United States

1

[On the ethnic conflict in what used to be Yugoslavia]: Yugoslavia is a shocking reminder that barbarity exists within our midst, and that we cannot call the new Europe either civilized or secure until we have developed stronger mechanisms for dealing with this and similar crises. We must seek early enough to prevent the outbreak of conflict, or else find ourselves, as in Yugoslavia, constantly reacting to new horrors.

At Conference on Security
and Cooperation in Europe,
Stockholm, Sweden, Dec. 14/
The New York Times, 12-15:(A)7.

2

[Saying Serbian leaders in Yugoslavia may be war criminals for their actions in the ethnic conflict in Bosnia]: We know that crimes against humanity have occurred, and we know when and where they occurred. We know, moreover, which forces committed those crimes, and under whose command they operated. And we know, finally, who the political leaders are and to whom those military commanders were—and still are—responsible . . . In waiting for the people of Serbia, if not their leaders, to come to their senses [and stop the war against Bosnia], we must make them understand that their country will remain alone, friendless and condemned to economic ruin and exclusion from the family of civilized nations for as long as they pursue the suicidal dream of a Greater Serbia, They need, especially, to understand that a second Nuremberg awaits the practitioners of "ethnic cleansing," and that the judgment and opprobrium of history awaits the people in whose name their crimes were committed.

At conference on the Balkan conflict,
Geneva, Switzerland, Dec. 16/
The New York Times, 12-17:(A)1,10.

Abdulfaz Elchibey
President of Azerbaijan

3

It is common to all these former Soviet [now-independent republics] that leaders having a peaceful, evolutionary thinking have difficulty in governing their states because the Communist, Bolshevik psychology is still very alive. We need an evolution in the social psychology of the people.

Interview,
Baku, Azerbaijan, Nov. 12/
The Christian Science Monitor,
11-30:6.

Elizabeth II
Queen of England

4

[On being part of Britain's Royal Family]: If you live in this sort of life, which people don't very much, you live very much by tradition and by continuity. I find that's one of the sad things, that people don't take on jobs for life. They try different things all the time . . . As far as I'm concerned, you know exactly what you are going to do two months hence, even beginning to know about next year. I think that this is what the younger members [of the Royal Family] find difficult, the regimented side of it.

British TV documentary, Feb. 6/
Los Angeles Times, 2-7:(A)5.

5

[On the personal troubles the British Royal Family has endured this year]: 1992 is not a year on which I shall look back with undiluted pleasure.

At banquet honoring her 40th year
on the throne, London, England/
USA Today, 11-27:(A)11.

6

[On calls for reform in how Britain deals with its Royal Family]: There can be no doubt that criticism is good for people and institutions. No institution—city, monarchy, whatever—should expect to be free from the scrutiny of those who give it their loyalty and support, not to mention those who don't. [But it should be scrutiny] with a touch of gentleness, good humor and understanding.

At banquet honoring her 40th year
on the throne, London, England/
The Christian Science Monitor, 11-27:1.

Stanley Fischer
Professor of economics,
Massachusetts Institute
of Technology (United States);
Former chief economist,
International Bank for
Reconstruction and Development
(World Bank)

1

Germany and Europe have gained in economic strength relative to the U.S., hastened by the weakening of the U.S. fiscal situation in the 1980s. With the decline of the Soviet threat, the tendency of Europe to do what the United States wants, and make strategic concessions on the economic front, has definitely declined . . . The U.S. no longer has the money to put into various international agencies and efforts that it used to have. It leads from financial weakness.

The New York Times, 4-29:(A)7.

Barbara Hackman Franklin
Secretary of Commerce
of the United States

2

[On the U.S. decision to provide financial aid to Russia]: This is not altruism. It is an investment in our future. Helping build strong economies in the new [former Soviet] states will contribute to their political and economic stability, and these efforts will also create new export markets for American goods and services and will generate jobs for Americans.

April 1/
Los Angeles Times, 4-2:(A)10.

Yegor T. Gaidar
Deputy Prime Minister
for Economic Reforms of Russia

3

[Saying the reforming Russian economy needs Western aid]: Touch and go; everything [in Russia] is touch and go . . . We need help, not to bail us out but to steady us on our course. Where do the West's interests lie? Certainly not in a return to past oppression [in Russia], certainly not in re-establishment of an ideologically aggressive political and economic system, cer-

tainly not in another battle for world supremacy. But still the West hesitates.

Interview, New York, N.Y./
Los Angeles Times, 2-3:(A)7.

Yegor T. Gaidar
Acting Prime Minister
of Russia

4

It is very easy to skid toward the road of underdevelopment [in Russia]. To achieve this, one doesn't even have to oppose reforms. One simply has to slow down changes that can help us form a normal market infrastructure.

Before Congress of People's Deputies,
Moscow, Russia, Dec. 2/
The New York Times, 12-3:(A)6.

5

[On whether Russia should model its economy on the U.S. or the Scandinavian system of capitalism]: We are not on a spacious square where we can stand and decide what way to take toward a radiant future. We are on a narrow footpath, and the task is not to step away from it. Of course, if we work very hard and very successfully, if we really manage to create a multi-sector economy, to privatize at lease 50 per cent of the domestic economy, to put an end to the power of the bureaucracy, to really open a broad path for entrepreneurship, to pave the way for integration into the world market, only then, maybe in three to five years, [can we] seriously discuss what kind of society we want to have, Scandinavian or American.

Before Congress of People's Deputies,
Moscow, Russia, Dec. 2/
The Christian Science Monitor,
12-3:4

John R. Galvin
General, United States Army;
Supreme Allied Commander/Europe

6

I think the U.S. presence in Europe is seen by Europeans as a stabilizing element. American military power is not oppressive. The United

(JOHN R. GALVIN)

States feels that with a commitment to Europe, it gains something it lacked in the first half of the century—the ability to have an influence in shaping events rather than being drawn into them willy-nilly. The question is: What is the best way to have influence in Europe that is less costly than what we're doing now? In fact, what is the minimum commitment?

Interview/
U.S. News & World Report,
6-1:40.

John R. Galvin
General,
United States Army (Ret.);
Former Supreme Allied Commander/
Europe

1

[On the ethnic conflict in what used to be Yugoslavia and what the outside world can do about it militarily]: I don't think the U.S. should ever go in there alone. I would like to see it be a NATO effort, and I'll tell you why: Because the mission can change over and over. You could be doing peacekeeping; you could be doing humanitarian assistance; you could be in conflict; you could be in peace enforcement. There are big logistical problems. There are command, communication and intelligence questions. NATO is more set up to be the basic backbone of that than anybody else. Obviously, NATO could work with other countries. The Russians are already in there. But not the U.S. by itself. That is really not a feasible option.

Interview/USA Today, 8-10:(A)7.

Fabrizio Garimberti
Italian economist

2

[On the possible sale of government-owned assets and industries to the private sector in Italy because of the economic crisis there]: If you sell state assets, you strike at the heart of the Italian political system. But politicians will be dragged kicking and screaming into privatization because it is the only way to solve the crisis of our public

finances. And therefore it is the only way for Italy to remain in Europe.

The New York Times, 6-25:(C)2.

Filipe Gonzalez
Prime Minister of Spain

3

[Saying Spain must adjust its economy so that it can fit into the coming European economic unification]: I'm ready to fight to the bitter end to carry out policies that I believe are in Spain's best interests. The [labor] unions have simply not understood European integration. For a country like ours, so historically isolated, no effort should be spared to climb aboard this train.

The Washington Post, 6-3:(A)27.

4

[On criticism that he has abandoned his socialist policies and become capitalistic]: I'm proud of what we did [in Spain since he became Prime Minister 10 years ago]. I'm proud of it because we had a responsibility to carry out a blueprint for Spain and not for the [Socialist] Party . . . The problem is that this country lacks confidence in itself. After hosting the Mideast peace conference last year, after the [1992] Olympics and Expo [which were both held in Spain], let's for once say we have done something well—despite the government, if you like.

Interview/
The New York Times, 10-26:(A)6.

Mikhail S. Gorbachev
Former President
of the Soviet Union

5

I have turned out to be too much of a prophet [regarding the breakup of the former Soviet Union], one whose prophecies have begun to come true within a few weeks. The country is being torn apart, economic ties are being broken. They are even talking about dividing up the contents of the Hermitage and Tretyakow [museums]. This is sheer madness. It reminds me of the atmosphere in an insane asylum. After all,

(MIKHAIL S. GORBACHEV)

politicians can be crazy, but society cannot be crazy.

Interview,
Moscow, Russia, March 23/
The Washington Post, 3-24:(A)1.

1

[Calling for U.S. economic aid for Russia]: This is a historic moment and a historic opportunity. It should not be allowed to slip by . . . We're now at the most difficult stage of these [democratic and economic] reforms [in Russia]. In fact, we still haven't reached the bottom of the crisis. The peoples of Russia are courageously bearing up under these burdens . . . When Russia emerges from the present crisis, the national memory will forever remain cognizant of the magnanimity displayed by Americans at this moment of difficulty.

To U.S. Congressional leaders,
Washington, D.C., May 14/
The New York Times,
5-15:(A)3.

Albert Gore, Jr.
United States Senator,
D-Tennessee;
1992 Democratic
U.S. Vice-Presidential nominee

2

[U.S. President] George Bush wants to maintain at least 150,000 American soldiers in Europe, even though World War II ended 50 years ago. [Democratic U.S. Presidential nominee] Bill Clinton and I agree with so many military experts who believe that it is time for the Europeans, who are so much wealthier now and more powerful than they were at the end of World War II, to start picking up a little more of that tab themselves and not rely so exclusively on the United States taxpayers for the defense of Europe.

At Vice-Presidential candidates' debate,
Atlanta, Ga., Oct. 13/
The New York Times,
10-14:(A)13.

Pavel Grachev
Minister of Defense of Russia

3

The establishment and strengthening of the Russian Army is one of the nation's most urgent tasks now. Russia should have an armed force commensurate with its status as a great power . . . [But Russian nuclear weapons] would be used only to ensure sufficient defense if there is a threat from the outside, a threat that cannot be met by political means and by conventional forces.

News conference, May 22/
The Christian Science Monitor,
6-9:7.

Gunter Grass
German author

4

[In Germany,] politics is not always *the* reality, but it's always very hungry and wants to be the reality. We are, in Germany and in Europe, formed or misinformed, punished by politics, getting older by politics. I see it in my children. Whether they want or don't want, they are involved in politics, even if they are not engaged in a political party . . . Someone traveling from Sweden will be asked about beautiful blond women. Or from the U.S., they will be asked about the Empire State Building. But when you say you're from Germany, immediately people want to know about the skinheads and firebombing the foreigners' hostels. There is no escape from it.

Interview, New York, N.Y./
The New York Times, 12-29:(B)1.

Helge Hansen
Lieutenant General
and Chief of Staff,
German Army

5

[Saying Germany did not send combat troops to join the U.S.-led coalition in last year's Persian Gulf war against Iraq because of a decision by Germany's political leaders that there was a lack of constitutional basis under law for sending such troops]: Subjectively, our allies had

(HELGE HANSEN)

the feeling that we were looking for reasons not to participate. They diagnosed our attitude as malingering or even cowardice before the enemy, and of course for a military force that is very damaging. But we have to live with it, and to make clear that these were political decisions that we had to support, and work on the weaknesses which they revealed.

Interview/
The New York Times, 6-23:(A)5.

Vaclav Havel
President of Czechoslovakia

1

Judging by what is beginning to appear in Czechoslovakia, the most menacing demons are anti-Semitism, ethnic intolerance and xenophobia . . . Other demons can feed on our still-uncertain conditions. Democratic government, in comparison with the previous totalitarian one, seems at times to be indecisive and insufficiently strong or energetic. People who had lived under a totalitarian authority now have that feeling. It is fertile soil for those who dream of a strong-arm regime. There is a desire for so-called strong personalities to come forward and instill order. I believe that this type of peril exists in all post-Communist countries.

Interview/
World Press Review, March:15.

2

[The people who lived under Communism in Eastern Europe] did in fact hate it, the totalitarian regime. But at the same time, they spent their whole life in it, and in spite of their will [to break away from Communism], got accustomed to it. They became used to the fact that there is an omnipotent state over them that can do everything, take care of everything and is responsible for everything. One cannot just lose this habit overnight.

Interview/
The New York Times, 4-8:(A)6.

Vaclav Havel
Former President
of Czechoslovakia

3

[On the possible breakup of Czechoslovakia into two independent countries]: If we become two stable democratic states, then the fact that we are not a large state is not a tragedy. If the breakup of our common state should lead to inner instability, chaos, poverty and suffering, then it would start to become a tragedy. The fact in itself that two states shall emerge out of one is not a tragedy. I do not feel any sentimental ties to the Czechoslovak state. I do not place the highest value on the state, but rather on man and humanity.

Interview, Prague, Czechoslovakia/
Time, 8-3:47.

Robert E. Hunter
Director of European studies,
Center for Strategic and
International Studies (United States)

4

[On the ethnic conflict in what used to be Yugoslavia]: This is the new world order where [those outside countries wishing to stop the conflict] have to mix your carrots and sticks. The Serbs are sitting there watching to see whether the [foreign] cavalry is coming, and it isn't. We in the Western world have sent the message that we're not going to do anything.

The Christian Science Monitor,
8-26:2.

Douglas Hurd
Foreign Secretary
of the United Kingdom

5

[On the ethnic conflict in what used to be Yugoslavia]: I don't think you can impose peace by military force [from the outside]. This is valley against valley, village against village, fighters mixed up with civilians, no clear targets; and I think the idea of achieving peace through air strikes [by outside forces] would involve a lot more people being killed So I regard that idea as very extreme.

Aug. 3/
The New York Times, 8-7:(A)5.

WHAT THEY SAID IN 1992

Ion Iliescu
President of Romania

1

[On the widespread mistrust of his government]: I see all of this as the result of ideological intoxication, which dominates all of us, here and abroad . . . Compare the evolution now. After the "velvet revolution," Czechoslovakia is being dismembered. In Romania, progress was difficult and encountered problems, but I think Romania now is an area of greater calm, balance and stability.

Interview, Bucharest, Romania/
The New York Times, 12-17:(A)11.

Alija Izetbegovic
President of Bosnia
and Herzegovina

2

[Saying the U.S. should supply weapons to Bosnian forces to help fight the Serbs in the current civil war in what used to be Yugoslavia]: I would like to say that I completely agree with [U.S. President] Bush's statement that American boys should not die for Bosnia. We have hundreds and thousands of able and willing men ready to fight, but unfortunately they have the disadvantage of being unarmed. We need weapons. We need them urgently, and I ask this of the United States in the name of our fundamental right to self-defense, since we are being attacked by a very-well-equipped [Serbian] army with hundreds of tanks, thousands of artillery pieces and several tens of thousands of well-armed men.

Interview,
Sarajevo, Bosnia, Aug. 7/
The New York Times, 8-8:5.

Hans-Gerd Jaschke
Political scientist,
Institute for Social Research
(Germany)

3

Small neo-Nazi groups have existed [in Germany] since the end of [World War II]. What is new is that these neo-Nazi groups have a new generation of leaders and followers who did not live through the Third Reich. Opinion surveys show a quite high level of acceptance of racism and violence among German youth right now, and these neo-Nazi groups are creating a climate that justifies violence. If a *Fuehrer* type were to come along in Germany, we could very realistically expect a fusion of the various right-wing factions.

The Washington Post, 3-2:(A)12.

Geza Jeszenszky
Foreign Minister of Hungary

4

I think it would be very important for the U.S. public to see that . . . helping the former [East European] Communist countries is not only sound policy from the political angle but even from the business angle . . . Every U.S. taxpayer will profit if these countries succeed in overcoming the legacy [of Communism] and become good buyers of U.S. products; and there is an insatiable demand . . . This region continues to be very important. This region has a better chance to accomplish this transition and become a prosperous market-economic region. The Commonwealth of Independent States [made up of republics of the former Soviet Union] can and will succeed very largely only once Central Europe is in order and with our collaboration.

Interview, Budapest, Hungary/
The Christian Science Monitor,
4-16:5.

Juan Carlos I
King of Spain

5

We [in Spain] have known moments of splendor and of decadence. We have lived epochs of profound respect for freedom and others of intolerance and persecution for political, ideological or religious reasons. What is important is not an account of mistakes or successes but the willingness to project and to analyze the past in the context of our future.

At ceremony marking 500th
anniversary of Spain's expulsion of Jews,
Madrid, Spain, March 31/
Los Angeles Times, 4-1:(A)4.

Sergei Karaganov
Deputy director,
Institute of Europe (Russia)

1

Washington may be shocked, but it will find that Kiev [the capital of Ukraine] is now more important to us [Russians than is the U.S.]. The Germans will find that, yes, Minsk [capital of Belarus] matters more [to us] than Bonn. The changes proceed from there. East-West relations are less important than the shape of the new Commonwealth of Independent States and our 10 partners in it.

Los Angeles Times, 1-30:(A)10.

George Kenney
Former Acting Chief
of Yugoslav Affairs,
Department of State
of the United States

2

[On the current ethnic conflict in what used to be Yugoslavia]: The Bosnians are really the poor innocents who got mugged [by the Serbs]. What we [the U.S.] could do, what we should do, is arm the Bosnians, allow them to defend themselves, allow them to protect their remaining territory and allow them to try to recover territory which has been forcibly taken from them . . . I do not understand at all why the [U.S. Bush] Administration will allow Serbian military aircraft to bomb towns in Bosnia . . . Everyone who has been there will agree that a tragedy is taking place and that the Serbs are responsible, and many people will agree with me that what is going on is genocide.

Interview,
Washington, D.C., Aug. 28/
Los Angeles Times, 8-29:(A)4.

Ruslan Khasbulatov
Speaker of the
Russian Parliament

3

[On Western promises of financial aid for Russia]: I don't believe too much in these billions. The American economy is hit by a serious crisis. The West, including the United

States, has no source for such major financing [for Russia] . . . The entire world economy is not enough to drag Russia out of its crisis.

News conference/
The Christian Science Monitor,
4-8:3.

Robert M. Kimmitt
United States Ambassador
to Germany

4

Let me state, clearly and unequivocally, that we welcome and value this German assertiveness in collective actions designed to achieve common goals and objectives. With whom could the U.S. better pursue effective collective action than Germany, a trustworthy, reliable ally?

Speech/Time, 4-13:36.

Klaus Kinkel
Foreign Minister of Germany

5

We need European union because individual states are no longer able to resolve the political, economic and social challenges we face. The era of exclusively national politics is over, even and especially in Europe. Only together do we have a future.

Before German Parliament,
Bonn, Germany, Dec. 2/
The New York Times, 12-3:(A)9.

Neil Kinnock
Leader,
Labor Party of Britain

6

[On his Party's loss to the Conservatives in the recent election]: We have to recognize we lost by 7.5 per cent. Our defeat cannot be attributed to individuals or individual events, to the campaign, the conduct of the campaign or the last week in the campaign. The plain truth is that too many voters had memories of the problems in the Labor Party of years gone by.

Los Angeles Times, 7-7:(H)2.

Helmut Kohl
Chancellor of Germany

1

For a long time to come, there will be enormous stocks of nuclear, biological and chemical weapons in the successor republics of the former Soviet Union. They remain a source of danger against a background of political instability and hence conflict.

*Before American Newspaper Publishers
Association, United Nations, New York,
May 5/The New York Times, 5-6:(A)1.*

2

[On fears of the French and others that European union would cause the individual nations to give up their sovereignty to a European Community dominated by Germany]: We all will conserve our identities, our histories, our cultures. It would be absurd to think that tomorrow we are no longer French or Italian . . . I don't understand this fear in the French point of view. Why would you suddenly want to have an inferiority complex?

*Broadcast debate, Sept. 3/
The Washington Post, 9-4:(A)29.*

Andrei Kortunov
Russian foreign-policy analyst

3

Russia will regain a sense of itself as a European nation, first of all. Its horizons will be continental, not global. The issues will be practical, such as ecology and trade and not things like the "new world order." Compared with the past, we will even seem isolationist. Central America, Africa, Southeast Asia, for example, will likely disappear from policy-makers' maps. Our de-globalization is not only inevitable, it is under way.

Los Angeles Times, 1-30:(A)10.

Krzysztof Kozlowski
*Member, Polish Senate;
Former Minister of the
Interior of Poland*

4

There's a little Communist in all of us [Poles]. For me, it's very banal things: the fear of risks, of

something new, the fear of competition [all of which are occurring in the now non-Communist Poland]. People think that if someone is successful in business, it must have been done immorally or illegally. Sometimes I catch myself thinking about someone: "You've been doing real well, there must be something wrong with you.'

The New York Times, 4-8:(A)1.

Andrei V. Kozyrev
Foreign Minister of Russia

5

One of the priorities of our foreign policy is our comeback in the ranks of our natural partners and allies. At the turn of the century, Russia occupied a worthy place in the foreign relations of such states as France, Germany and the United States. We should regain this place. It is also important that our foreign policy should be guided not by some global schemes but by normal economic interests. Our foreign policy will be based on all that contributes to our economic progress and to the normal life of the people of Russia.

Los Angeles Times, 1-30:(A)12.

6

The renewed Russia sees no need in maintaining [military] parity and does not want to have as many weapons as the United States or any other power. We have no strategic designs against anyone. But it is difficult to translate this political will into action . . . The problem today is not what to do, but how.

*At Geneva Institute
of International Affairs,
Geneva, Switzerland, Feb. 12/
Los Angeles Times, 2-13:(A)11.*

7

We see, with various permutations, persistent attempts by NATO and the Western European Union to develop plans to strengthen their military presence in the Baltics and other areas of the former Soviet Union, and interference in Bosnia and in the internal affairs of Yugoslavia . . . We demand [that Western sanctions against Yugo-

(ANDREI V. KOZYREV)

slavia due to the ethnic conflict in that area] be lifted, and if this does not happen we retain the right to take the necessary unilateral measures to preserve our interests, the more so since we are suffering economic damage. The present government of Serbia [Yugoslavia] can count on the support of Great Russia in its struggle.

At Conference on Security
and Cooperation in Europe,
Stockholm, Sweden, Dec. 14/
The New York Times, 12-15:(A)7.

1

[Saying the speech he just gave, taking a hard line against the West, was only a joke to show what might happen if Russian President Boris Yeltsin were defeated by his opposition in Russia]: Neither President Yeltsin, who remains leader and the guarantor of Russian domestic and foreign policy, nor I as Minister of Foreign Affairs will ever agree to what I read in my previous speech.

At Conference on Security
and Cooperation in Europe,
Stockholm, Sweden, Dec. 14/
The New York Times, 12-15:(A)7.

Mark Kramer
Fellow,
Russian Research Center,
Harvard University
(United States)

2

[On the ethnic conflict in Yugoslavia]: Many [foreign] people and organizations hoped to get involved and settle things promptly. What they found was all their best efforts were for nought. It is a classic case of conflict between ethnic groups whose main desire is to kill one another. It is not amenable to outside mediation.

The New York Times, 5-15:(A)7.

Leonid M. Kravchuk
President of Ukraine

3

The status of the Black Sea Fleet [of the now-defunct Soviet Union] will determine the future

not only of the fleet but will have a great importance for the future status of Ukraine. I think that no one doubts that Ukraine should be a maritime state. It has all the basis for it. Scores of kilometers of sea coast. More than one-fourth of Ukrainian citizens live in the Black Sea area. It has huge economic potential. Ukraine has a genuine desire for a maritime military force.

At meeting with military officers,
Kiev, Ukraine, Jan. 9/
The New York Times, 1-10:(A)6.

4

The creation of a joint armed forces on the territory of the Commonwealth [of Independent States], which has 11 [former Soviet republics], would mean an end to everything. Who is going to head such an army? A military person. And what civilian officials will be placed in charge of it? . . . The brass hats will concentrate formidable power in their hands, and they will frog-march you where you don't want to go. Army institutions should be localized and should be subordinated to their respective Presidents.

The Washington Post,
2-13:(A)33.

5

[On the Commonwealth of Independent States, made up of former Soviet republics]: The situation continues to worsen, and events since the Minsk summit [in February] force us to express extreme concern over the fate of the Commonwealth and its member states. Economically, we are no longer on the edge of the abyss but are actually sliding down into it. People place great faith in us, but we have not been able to resolve a single issue, military, economic or other, within the Commonwealth framework. Public opinion is growing that the Commonwealth has become a screen behind which each member state looks after its own needs and problems quite separately from the common needs and interest.

At C.I.S. meeting,
Kiev, Ukraine/
Los Angeles Times, 3-23:(A)8.

Vlodymyr Lanovy
Former Deputy Prime Minister
for Economic Reform
of Ukraine

1

[On his being fired from his job as Ukraine's top economic reformer]: At the moment, both economically and politically, Ukraine reminds me of a house that is supposedly under major reconstruction, but only the facade has been renovated. It was clear from the very beginning that they wanted to use me as a cover . . . If the President has removed one of the few leaders of economic reforms in the government, then my conclusion is that he has no intention of realizing radical economic reforms. In fact, I am certain that [Ukraine President Leonid] Kravchuk is not fully convinced that Ukraine's economy can emerge from its crisis using purely market methods . . . There are attempts on many occasions to renew old command-administrative ways. Their real goal is to support the existing economic system and by no means allow its transformation based on new forms of property ownership.

Interview/
The Christian Science Monitor,
7-21:5.

Tom Lantos
United States Representative,
D-California

2

[Criticizing the U.S. Bush Administration for not taking military action against Serbia, which he says is committing atrocities against residents of Bosnia-Herzegovina in the current ethnic conflict in that area]: There is [taking place in Bosnia] what is called "ethnic cleansing," a most sickening, despicable, disgusting term, and we are [doing no more than] talking about discussing the possibility of the need for additional United Nations resolutions. Well, let me tell you what the problem is. The problem is that there is [a Presidential] election [in the U.S.] in 90 days, and this election paralyzes the [U.S. Bush] Administration.

At House European Subcommittee hearing,
Washington, D.C., Aug. 4/
Los Angeles Times, 8-5:(A)14.

Patrick J. Leahy
United States Senator,
D-Vermont

3

[On $24-billion in proposed multinational aid for Russia]: [It is] a Rube Goldberg hodgepodge of current and new money, technical and humanitarian assistance and massive loan guarantees . . . lumped together without theme, theory or consistency.

Los Angeles Times, 5-8:(A)44.

Jaak Leimann
Minister of Economics
of Estonia

4

In a way, [when Estonia was part of the Soviet Union] we lived in a very closed world. We had access to resources from the Soviet empire, getting them for rubles at very cheap prices. We also sold almost all our products to the rest of the Soviet empire, also for very cheap prices . . . We wouldn't have minded if the Soviet Union had gone on for a little longer [after Estonia became independent and the Soviet Union disintegrated]. A very messy neighbor is worse than a predictable one . . . Unfortunately, Russia, being on the verge of hunger right now, is not interested in buying our clothes. It only wants food. When you're hungry, you don't buy furniture. You want meat or dairy products or fish [which Estonia must keep for itself or sell to the West].

Interview, Tallinn, Estonia/
The Washington Post, 1-28:(A)16.

Francois Leotard
Former Minister of Culture
of France

5

[On French President Francois Mitterrand]: One man alone governs France today. Combatted by his rivals, irritated by the press, outflanked by his likely successor [former Prime Minister Michel Rocard], ignored by his party, surrounded by unknown fears.

Before French National Assembly,
Paris, France, Feb. 7/
Los Angeles Times, 2-12:(A)4.

Jean-Marie Le Pen
Leader, National Front party
of France

1

[On his far-right party]: The pendulum of history is swinging in our direction. For many years world politics was dominated by notions like internationalism and socialist utopias. Now it is being shaped by concerns like order, nationhood and family . . . We can no longer be considered just an accident in French political life. We are succeeding in winning over new voters, while the other parties are losing them. That's what they cannot stand.

Interview, Lyons, France/
The Washington Post, 3-10:(A)13.

John Major
Prime Minister
of the United Kingdom

2

[On the forthcoming national elections in Britain]: We [Conservatives] favor reducing taxation; [Labor Party leader Neil Kinnock] wants to increase it. We favor strong defense; he would cut defense. We would continue with health reforms to give more people more choice; he would stop the health reforms . . . We have a clear view that we want to be leaders in Europe but not in a United States of Europe; he doesn't have any such view. We take a particular view about our position in the world that would differ sharply from his . . . The Labor Party would cut defense expenditures by 25 per cent. That is a gulf between the two parties, an absolute gulf. Twenty-five per cent off expenditure would mean that the United Kingdom would no longer be the allies of the United States and the other allies that NATO needs.

Interview, London, England/
Newsweek, 3-23:39.

3

It is not necessary [for the U.K.] to choose between Europe and America . . . It is in the interests of Europe and the United States that we are the bridge. Why should we tear down that bridge? It would be folly—folly for Europe, folly

for the United States, and plain daft for us . . . It is the American presence in Europe over the past 40 years that has kept Europe safe. Europe knows that, and the United States knows it as well. But in these days of potential interglobal war, it is also in the interests of the United States to make sure there is peace in Europe . . . Let me make clear what I am saying: I am not saying that the United States has got to come here and defend Europe. Europe should do more in its own defense . . . But I cannot foresee the day in which American troops would leave Europe, or that any conceivable American President would consider it right that they should.

Interview, London, England/
Newsweek, 3-23:39.

4

[On Western aid to Russia]: Just simply saying "Here is the money" will not really be of help to the Russians except in the very short term. There are structural changes necessary [in Russia]. There is a complete culture change from the command economy, that they had thus far, to the market economy. Many decrees and parliamentary changes have been made—and they are very welcome—but they have to be implemented . . . We have an obligation to assist, and it is in our self-interest to assist, but it has to be on the basis of our assistance with tangible resources, with advice and in other ways and [with] a Russian response that is tangible in moving down toward a proper, enforceable reform program that actually meets the demands that are necessary if it is to be successful.

At Group of Seven summit meeting,
Munich, Germany, July 8/
Los Angeles Times, 7-9:(A)8.

5

[Saying European unity is not as important as each country's domestic priorities]: Just as the interests of France and Germany will come first for them, so should the interests of Britain come first for us. [I do not] share the belief in the desirability or the inevitability of a centralized Europe.

Before British House of Commons,
London, England, Sept. 24/
The Washington Post, 9-25:(A)27.

(JOHN MAJOR)

1

It is announced from Buckingham Palace that, with regret, the Prince [Charles] and Princess [Diana] of Wales have decided to separate . . . The Queen [Elizabeth] and Duke of Edinburgh, though saddened, understand and sympathize with the difficulties which have led to this decision. Her Majesty and His Royal Highness particularly hope that the intrusions into the privacy of the Prince and Princess may now cease.

Before British House of Commons,
London, England, Dec. 9/
The New York Times, 12-10:(A)9.

Mikhail Malei
Adviser on defense conversion
to Russian
President Boris N. Yeltsin

2

[On Russian arms sales to other countries]: The [economic] situation we are in forces us to penetrate the international market. The lives of [Russian] people depend on it. This winter will be cold and the spring will be hungry . . . If we have to choose between the life of a child and the sale of a cannon to [Libyan leader Muammar] Qaddafi, we will choose the life of the child [and make the sale] . . . The military-industrial complex has to earn money on the international market from the sales of weapons, no less than $5-billion to $7-billion a year. There is no other source of financing for conversion [of the industry to civilian use] left.

Interview, Moscow, Russia/
The Christian Science Monitor,
11-25:6.

Denko Maleski
Foreign Minister
of Macedonia

3

[Criticizing Greece's insistence that the world not recognize Macedonia unless that former Yugoslav republic changes its name, which Greece says is exclusively Greek]: We have said to the Greeks, let us talk about the content of our relations. But the Greeks say no, you change your name and then we will talk . . . [But Macedonia] is not only the name of our state, it is in our books, our tales, our songs. How do you tell a people to change their name? All this would be funny if it were not a tragedy. History tends to repeat itself in the Balkans. If the European Community and the U.S. government leave this land in a state of limbo, I'm afraid that our neighbors will get ideas.

The Washington Post, 6-10:(A)28.

Laurence Martin
Director, Royal Institute
of International Affairs (Britain)

4

[On Britain's continuing buildup of nuclear weapons]: Russia and the United States are moving into a world in which they are de-emphasizing the need for nuclear weapons. There will be a problem over whether Britain, as one of America's foremost allies, can go on maintaining a deterrent with no really plausible utility. The Americans, who are supplying the Trident missiles, are now talking about collaborating with our former target [Russia], and that poses further serious questions.

The Christian Science Monitor,
6-19:1.

Margarita Mathiopoulos
Senior vice president,
Norddeutsche Landesbank
(Germany); Political scientist

5

[On the emphasis in Germany on a strong currency]: All the other things were swept under the rug, such as the past and what went wrong here. We are finally learning that the mark is not the remedy to all our ills. Americans like to make money too, but they are equally obsessed with their democratic institutions and how to preserve them. We need, especially now in eastern Germany, to talk about our democracy, especially in light of all these [anti-foreigner] riots of the past month.

The Washington Post, 9-19:(A)16.

Howard M. Metzenbaum
United States Senator,
D-Ohio

1

[On calls for U.S. aid to the new reformist government in Russia]: Sure, we need to be concerned about stability in Russia. But it angers me that Russian recovery is viewed as more of a threat to [U.S.] national security than the rot from within that threatens our own nation.

Washington, D.C., July 2/
Los Angeles Times, 7-3:(A)6.

Slobodan Milosevic
President of Serbia,
Yugoslavia

2

The United Nations sanctions against Serbia and Montenegro [because of their involvement in the ethnic conflict in Bosnia] are unjust and must soon be canceled. All those who imposed these sanctions will very soon be ashamed of their decision against this country and its people, who wish to be the masters of their own home and refuse to bow down . . . Serbia has the power to withstand and survive the United Nations Security Council's sanctions. People in capitals across the wide world are trying to tell us how to behave in our land. In our land, we will behave as a free people behaves and not according to the dictates of world politicians.

Campaigning for re-election,
Krusevac, Yugoslavia, Dec. 15/
The New York Times, 12-16:(A)4.

Francois Mitterrand
President of France

3

[On the referendum in France in which the Maastricht treaty on European unity narrowly passed]: France has insured its future, reinforced its security and consolidated peace in a region of the world so cruelly torn by war. Just imagine now the joy of member countries of the [European] Community, our closest friends, who were waiting for this necessary signal from us. Imagine the joy of the other European countries, almost all of whom aspire to join [the EC], above all those [in Eastern Europe] who were deprived of liberty for so long.

Sept. 20/
The New York Times, 9-21:(A)6.

Jurgen Mollemann
Minister of Economics
of Germany

4

We [Germans] have to demonstrate some political leadership, and that includes drastic measures to reduce [Germany's budget] deficit. With tax revenue falling because of slower growth, that means cutting expenditures. At the same time, we need to set new priorities. And the absolute priority now is creating incentives for additional investment, both public and private . . . We are going to turn [the eastern part of Germany, what used to be East Germany] into one of the most modern production areas in Europe. It will take some time—25 years or so—and cost a lot of money. But it is an investment in our national economic future. Everything has taken longer than we thought.

Interview/
USA Today, 11-27:(B)3.

Jorgen Ostrom Moller
Undersecretary of State
of Denmark

5

[On the forthcoming public vote in Denmark on whether to accept the Maastricht treaty on European unity]: Most of the arguments against the treaty are emotional. Some people don't like the word "union." Some people are afraid of the Germans. Some people are afraid of immigrants. Some people fear Brussels [headquarters of the European Community]. Most of the arguments in favor [of the treaty] are based on reason. We should be confident of our sovereignty. For 1,000 years, Denmark has been a sovereign nation. A small country like ours cannot exist without close links to other nations.

The Washington Post,
5-29:(A)27.

WHAT THEY SAID IN 1992

David Morrison
Chief European economist,
Goldman Sachs

1

The ERM is a disastrous agreement that guarantees recessionary effects all over Europe as long as it exists. The United States and Japan have been cutting interest rates, and they're still trying to get their economies going. How are they going to do it in Europe with interest rates so much higher?

The Washington Post, 9-18:(A)32.

Andrew Morton
Biographer of the
British Royal Family

2

[On his writings about the Royal Family]: I believe it is far healthier to know what really goes on in the big chief's wigwam than not. And what disappoints me is that so many people say you shouldn't write about members of the Royal Family [in such detail] and to kindly leave them alone. Well, [the Royals] are incredibly influential in our society. They are part of the warp and weft of our social fabric . . . And it seems to me wrong-headed not to want to understand more about your society. Indeed, it is almost criminal neglect for a journalist not to want to understand how that institution works and what motivates the people behind it, if that is your specialization. And it always strikes me that what we see in the monarchy tells us as much about ourselves as it does about the institution.

Interview, London, England/
The Christian Science Monitor,
12-18:13.

Anatoly Z. Moskalenko
Ukrainian historian
and journalist

3

Russians love to refer to the relations between Russia and Ukraine as the relations of an older brother and a younger brother. But in reality, the relationship was like that of a horse and a rider. The rider—Russia—always did everything to prevent the horse—Ukraine—from getting free

. . . Now this horse and rider have become like Siamese twins. The very painful process of dividing Siamese twins is going on.

Los Angeles Times, 5-1:(A)32.

Brian Mulroney
Prime Minister of Canada

4

It is rare in history that there has been such a victory for an idea—the idea of democracy. The defeat of Communism opened the door to democracy. But it also brought economic hardship to 425 million people throughout Central and Eastern Europe. The task the world's democrats face now is to secure that victory and to insure that it is neither hollow nor short-lived.

At Johns Hopkins University
commencement, May 21/
The New York Times, 5-22:(A)12.

Bolodymyr Naumenko
Economic adviser
to Ukrainian President
Leonid M. Kravchuk

5

Because of political factors, without a doubt we [Ukrainians] lag behind Russia in the pace of economic reform . . . The inertia here has its roots in many fears: the mentality; the unprofessional level of the government, still full of old [Communist] Party functionaries; populist politics in Parliament; and the fact that Ukraine has only started building its state institutions. Russia simply took over the Soviet Union's.

The Christian Science Monitor,
5-7:3.

Hans Jorgen Nielsen
Political scientist,
University of Copenhagen
(Denmark)

6

[On the recent public vote in Denmark rejecting the Maastricht treaty on European unity]: We are a country with an Anglo-Saxon tradition of self-governance by elected laypersons at a low level. We are mistrustful of central governments

(HANS JORGEN NIELSEN)

and we have no past to run away from into a European identity.

The Washington Post, 6-4:(A)22.

Thomas M. T. Niles
Assistant Secretary for
European and Canadian Affairs,
Department of State
of the United States

1

[On the ethnic conflict in what used to be Yugoslavia and charges that atrocities are being committed by Serbia in Bosnia-Herzegovina]: It is an . . . almost poignant tragedy that the Serbian people, who suffered so terribly at the hands of the Nazi occupiers of Yugoslavia during the Second [World] War, are engaging in practices which are in some respects reminiscent of some of the things that happened during the [Nazi] occupation . . . It's not a question of reluctance by the United States [in using military force to stop the fighting]; it's a question of building a coalition in the [UN] Security Council where you have nine votes for the resolution . . . That's what we're engaged in right now. Members of the Security Council . . . are understandably reluctant to commit themselves to use military force . . . So they're approaching this with a certain amount of care and caution. This does not depend solely upon the United States. If it did, I can assure you that the action would have already been taken.

Before House European Subcommittee,
Washington, D.C., Aug. 4/
Los, Angeles Times, 8-5:(A)1,14.

Richard M. Nixon
Former President
of the United States

2

[Russian President Boris] Yeltsin will survive because he believes in the right things. He has a characteristic that every leader should have . . . He isn't afraid to have people smarter than he is around him.

Broadcast interview/
U.S. News & World Report,
1-20:19.

All of the pollsters are telling their candidates [in the current U.S. Presidential primary elections], don't tackle foreign policy, and particularly not foreign aid, because foreign aid is poison as a political issue. They're wrong and history proves it. In 1947, I recall vividly as if it were yesterday what [then-President] Harry Truman did . . . I remember Harry Truman—jaunty, some said a little cocky—coming down before a joint session of the Congress and asking for millions of dollars in aid to Greece and Turkey to prevent Communist subversion and possibly Communist aggression. It was a very tough vote for two very young and both, as history later indicated, rather ambitious young Congressmen [Nixon and John F. Kennedy] . . . Under the circumstances, however, after considering it, we both voted for it, and a majority in that Republican House and the Senate voted for that program which later was developed into the Marshall Plan and later into NATO, which not only contained Communism but bought the time that was essential for Communism to fail . . . And then you have a situation at the present time, where we have a Republican President [Bush] with a Democratic Congress with the opportunity to take action which would provide aid to [the new democracy in] Russia and the other [newly non-Communist European countries] which would assure the victory of freedom. This is the question, then, that Americans must face today, political Americans, all Americans, and I think we know what the answer should be.

At conference sponsored by
Richard M. Nixon Library,
Washington, D.C., March 11/
The New York Times, 3-12:(A)6.

Jan Olszewski
Prime Minister of Poland

4

[On the transition in Poland from a centrally planned economy to a free-market system]: We are dealing here with quite a different system, a system where there was no free market at all. It was annihilated [under Communism], and one has to recreate it from the ground. This requires a new look, and a very pragmatic one in which

(JAN OLSZEWSKI)

there is analysis of concrete results of each move and readiness to correct it if it turns out the results are not what we expected.

Interview,
Warsaw, Poland, Feb. 28/
The New York Times, 3-2:(A)4.

Turgut Ozal
President of Turkey

1

Germany changed a lot after [its recent] unification. It is as if it is trying to intervene in everything, interfere with everyone, trying to prove it is a great power. In the past, Hitler's Germany did the same thing.

March/Time, 4-13:35.

Milan Panic
Prime Minister-designate
of Yugoslavia

2

I will come to Yugoslavia [from the U.S.] with a brand-new view, which in my case is an American view with all that implies—constitutional democracy, a system of checks and balances on power, civilian control of the police and, most fundamentally, pluralism, respect for diversity and opposing points of view, political parties contesting for and transferring power based on free, democratic elections. My task is very large. Democracy must be built from scratch. And that starts with the basics—respecting someone else's property, and not killing them or putting them in prison whenever there is disagreement. Of course, that doesn't mean America is the be-all and end-all, and that Yugoslavia's experience is simply to be negated. But America's constitutional model has been tested in very diverse environments and has proven highly successful. [The late U.S. General Douglas] MacArthur wrote Japan's Constitution based on the American model, and look how successful Japan is today. Why not Yugoslavia?

Interview,
Los Angeles, Calif., July 2/
Los Angeles Times, 7-3:(B)7.

Milan Panic
Prime Minister of Yugoslavia

3

[Criticizing Serbian President Slobodan Milosevic for the poor economic conditions in Yugoslavia and the war against areas, such as Bosnia, that used to be part of Yugoslavia]: There has been enough destruction, enough death, enough impoverishment. No longer, at the end of the 20th century, can cannon be used to solve problems. This is a rich land, and someone has made it poor. This is not a struggle between two men [himself and Milosevic], but between two systems. We're here to build.

Campaigning for the Presidency,
Nis, Yugoslavia, Dec. 11/
The New York Times, 12-12:8.

Geoffrey Pattie
Vice-chairman,
Conservative Party of Britain,
in charge of relations
with Europe

4

[Albania's President] Ramiz Alia had one of the most appalling Communist regimes [in Europe]. What these people need is a big change, one they can see. They won't get any investment until they have a democratically elected government, until Albania gets rid of the stained and discredited Communist and crypto-Communist regime. The last election was free but not fair. People now are much more aware of what's going on in the country. The freeing up of the broadcast media has had a great effect.

The Christian Science Monitor,
3-19:5.

Ross Perot
American industrialist;
1992 independent
U.S. Presidential candidate

5

[Saying the U.S. should reduce its spending on defense of countries that can afford to defend themselves]: If I'm poor and you're rich, and I can get you to defend me, that's good. But when the tables get turned, I ought to do my share.

(ROSS PEROT)

Right now we spend about $300-billion a year on defense; the Japanese spend about $30-billion in Asia; the Germans spend about $30-billion in Europe. For example, Germany'll spend a trillion dollars building infrastructure over the next 10 years. It's kind of easy to do if you only have to pick up a $30-billion tab to defend your country. The European Community is in a position to pay a lot more than they have in the past . . . When they couldn't, we should have. Now that they can, they should. We sort of seem to have a desire to try to stay over there and control it. They don't want us to control it, very candidly. So it's, I think, very important for us to let them assume more and more of the burden and for us to bring that money back here and rebuild *our* infrastructure.

At Presidential candidates' debate,
St. Louis, Mo., Oct. 11/
The New York Times, 10-12:(A)12.

Simon Petermann
Professor of
international relations,
Brussels Free University
(Belgium)

1

Indisputably, Germany is going to occupy a totally dominant position in the years to come. That's a position that, in many respects, the Germans have long held. The difference now is that the old formula casting Germany as an economic giant and a political dwarf no longer holds true.

Time, 4-13:35.

Sergei M. Plekhanov
Deputy director,
U.S.A. and Canada Institute
(Russia)

2

[On the warm response received by Russian President Boris Yeltsin during his address to the U.S. Congress in Washington]: Yeltsin would never get such a rapturous response from the Russian Parliament, and this he had better not

forget . . . Too many people hold Yeltsin responsible for what has gone wrong in their daily lives, and too many of our deputies are out to get him in any way they can. Washington was a stunning triumph for Yeltsin—here was a leader you could identify with—but he must still win in Moscow.

Los Angeles Times, 6-19:(A)1.

Mikhail Poltoranin
Minister of Information
of Russia

3

[Russian President Boris] Yeltsin does not like standard, typical moves. Sometimes when people are waiting around for him and expecting him to come in through a certain door, he will deliberately come in through another door. He is unpredictable.

The Washington Post, 2-1:(A)18.

Dan Quayle
Vice President
of the United States

4

During this [U.S.] Presidential-election year, you will hear voices from the left and right [in the U.S.] saying, "Come home, America." Well, Europe is our home, and as long as we are welcome, we will stay.

At Conference for Security Policy,
Munich, Germany, Feb. 9/
The New York Times, 2-10:(A)3.

Burkhard Rauber
Deputy Mayor
of Neubrandenburg, Germany

5

[On the young generation of what was formerly East Germany and is now part of a reunited Germany]: Two years ago, my daughter was being taught that God did not exist and that anyone who was religious was a fool. This year, the very same teacher led the class in religious instruction and Christmas songs, without ever explaining how or why she could make such a change. When kids see things like that, they naturally lose faith in adults and in institutions.

WHAT THEY SAID IN 1992

(BURKHARD RAUBER)

They become prone to violence, alcoholism and right-wing radicalism. It's worrisome. German unification is going to succeed in economic terms, but as far as for what is inside people's heads, that will be a more complicated problem.

Interview,
Neubrandenburg, Germany/
The New York Times, 4-18:4.

Albert Reynolds
Prime Minister of Ireland

1

[On the recent vote in Ireland in favor of the Maastricht treaty on European unity]: [It is] a great day for Ireland and a great day for Europe. It shows that the Irish people want a place in the front rank of European nations and to close the prosperity gap, and they see this treaty as a means of doing this . . . We have succeeded in putting European union back on the rails.

News conference, June 19/
The Washington Post, 6-20:(A)18.

Bert Rockman
Political scientist,
University of Pittsburgh (Pa.)
(United States)

2

[On the West's failure to put an end to the ethnic conflict in what used to be Yugoslavia]: It's inevitable that any leader of a major Western power looks bad right now, because it's a horrible situation and an extremely complicated one. It's a hard call to make for any incumbent, because, morally, everybody wants to do something. The question is, practically: What can they do? None of these things are the least bit clear.

The Christian Science Monitor,
8-21:6.

Pier Luigi Romita
Member of Italian Parliament;
Former Minister
of European Affairs of Italy

3

Our [Italy's political] system resulted in a frozen democracy where only one majority—that

of the Christian Democrats and the Socialists—was possible. Many of our problems result from our having no majority alternative. But now the pressures [for reform] are too great to resist.

The Christian Science Monitor,
10-28:3.

Volker Ruhe
Minister of Defense
of Germany

4

When one talks of leadership, one must think of the very successful system in the EC, where every country has just one vote. We [Germans] don't like to lead from the front. We like to lead from the middle of the crowd.

Time, 4-13:36.

Oleg Rumyantsev
Leader, Social Democratic Party
of Russia

5

Some serious changes in the composition of this [Russian] government must be made. The shock period of this economic reform is moving to its end and the second stage must stabilize the results . . . Stability can be achieved only by a mixed government, [with] mixed approaches to economic reform.

The Christian Science Monitor,
9-24:3.

Alex Salmond
Leader, Scottish National Party
(Britain)

6

[On an opinion poll showing half of Scotland's population favoring independence from Britain]: When we [his Party, which favors independence] claimed in September [1991] that we would be challenging to win in Scotland, the response from the unionists was loud guffaws. Now, far from laughing, we have a state of near hysteria from those trying to halt our surge. When we win, we would want a general election in Scotland, held under proportional representation for an independent Scottish parliament.

(ALEX SALMOND)

That will give the people of Scotland the chance to decide who should be the first Prime Minister of an independent Scotland.

Interview,
Edinburgh, Scotland/
Los Angeles Times, 2-25:(H)3.

Ionel Sandulescu
Secretary of State
for External Affairs of Romania

1

We [Romanians] cannot understand why the Western world divides the region of Central and Eastern Europe in two. I do not refer to the countries that made up the former Soviet Union, but the countries that were satellites of the former Soviet Union. I cannot understand why Romania, an island of Latinity in a Slavic sea, is taken aside. I do not understand this permanent discrimination and marginalization of our country . . . The difference that is made between Czechoslovakia, Hungary, Poland, Bulgaria, even Albania, is really evident—the difference that is made between these countries and Romania. How can we find an explanation for this? . . . I consider it a moral duty of the Western world, including those who sold us to Moscow in '43, to be closer to us . . . Again, I come and ask you the question: Why? I do not understand why we are today left aside.

Washington, D.C., April 16/
The Washington Post, 4-18:(A)22.

Poul Schlueter
Prime Minister of Denmark

2

[On the recent public vote in Denmark rejecting the Maastricht treaty on European unity]: We have no intention of leaving the EC. We will try to keep Danish cooperation with the EC in as many areas as possible. Can anyone seriously believe that our small nation with 5 million people can stop the great Europe Express of 300 million people?

June 3/
The Washington Post, 6-4:(A)22.

Nikolai P. Schmelev
Russian economist

3

[On the sudden large increase in consumer prices in Russia as the economy changes to a free market]: The government, the state, society want to correct its 70-year-old [economic] mistakes at your [consumers'] personal expense, and to pull the economy out of the hole it fell into [under Communism]. Someone has to pay for that. If you want our millionaires to pay for it, that will be enough to last for about two weeks. Until *you* are ripped off, nothing can be accomplished.

Russian TV broadcast/
Los Angeles Times, 1-3:(A)6.

Helmut Schmidt
Principal editor,
"Die Zeit" (Germany);
Former Chancellor
of West Germany

4

[On the ethnic conflict in what used to be Yugoslavia]: If you want to stop the slaughter in the Balkans, you have to send troops in, and stay for years. Germans should not take part in this, because they have committed enough crimes on Yugoslav territory already, during Hitler's time.

Interview, Hamburg, Germany/
The New York Times, 12-25:(A)4.

5

No other country in Europe has as many neighbors as the Germans have, and historically, whenever Germany has been either too strong or too weak, there has always been turbulence . . . Germany, with 80 million people after unification, is half again as big as Italy or Great Britain, five times as big as Holland and twice as big as Poland. On top of that there is Auschwitz and the rest of our terrible history. So all our neighbors look at us with concern and alarm when things seem to be going wrong. Sometimes they overreact.

Interview,
Hamburg, Germany/
The New York Times,
12-25:(A)4.

Andrew Scott
Economist,
London School of Economics
(Britain)

1

The lack of [educational] training is the main reason why Britain is in such a [bad] state and will eventually become a poor country. Education remains geared toward the elite, and market forces cannot sort this problem out. We've got to spend an awful lot more money on education and we've got to change the way society looks at education.

The Washington Post, 8-4:(A)16.

Brent Scowcroft
Assistant to President
of the United States
George Bush for
National Security Affairs

2

[On possible U.S. financial aid to Russia]: We have to be very careful that we don't pour large amounts of money into a system where there's no expectation that it will be used profitably. That is a very large economy. Unreformed, it can absorb unbelievable amounts of money with no change, which it's done in part already.

Broadcast interview/
"Meet the Press," NBC-TV, 4-12.

3

[On the ethnic conflict in what used to be Yugoslavia]: It's already out of control . . . As the conflict goes on and defies attempts at solution, the risks of it directly impinging on the interests of the Euro-Atlantic community increase . . . Yugoslavia is a painful case study for all of us . . . On the one hand, there is the trepidation of involvement in the stickiest kind of conflict possible. On the other, there is the painful vision of slaughter going on while we all stand aside and watch. I don't really know what the answer is here. I think we need to recognize that not every conflict in the world has to be taken on by multilateral institutions . . . But the Balkans are the Balkans, and Sarajevo [the Bosnian capital currently under siege] has a history that we should forget only at our peril.

Before Euro Group and Atlantic Council,
Washington, D.C., June 22/
Los Angeles Times, 6-23:(A)1,10.

Peter F. Secchia
United States Ambassador
to Italy

4

The Italians have a marvelous sense of balance. They always land on their feet—a country of many political parties, of many governments, but of continuity in policies. It has maintained a steady course in foreign affairs since the inception of its Constitution in 1948. It would be difficult to argue that nothing has changed in Italy for over 40 years, but I think those who are accustomed to think of Italy as a country of constant political crisis, of turmoil or perennial instability, are missing the larger picture. The difference in perception is due to Italy's political system of multi-party coalitions and shifting internal alliances, something which confounds most Americans.

Interview, Rome, Italy/
USA Today, 9-8:(Our World)8.

Eduard A. Shevardnadze
President of Georgia

5

The entire territory that used to constitute the Soviet Union is in a quagmire today. These countries have not had independence for a long, long time. Georgia was part of Russia for 2½ centuries, and now that it has started building a new independent society, it encounters many difficulties. We sometimes have a sense that there are no prospects. We have an economy that is absolutely ruined . . . The disintegration of the Soviet Union was unexpected by everyone. That includes those who received independence; they were not ready for it. That is why elections held in various [newly independent] countries, including Georgia, were held by naive people who trusted the words they heard. They were deceived. But these mistakes seem to be unavoidable in any newly independent country.

Interview, New York, N.Y./
Time, 10-5:64,65.

Andre Shleifer
Economist,
Harvard University (United States);
Adviser to the government
of Russian President
Boris N. Yeltsin

1

[On new Russian Prime Minister Viktor S. Chernomyrdin]: A very bad man became Prime Minister of Russia. Mr. Chernomyrdin's fundamental view is that the revival of the economy will take place through the revival of major state companies. But the country does not need more steel or more weapons or more airplanes that sit at airports because they cannot fly.

Interview/
The New York Times, 12-22:(A)8.

Stanislav Shustov
Member, Russian Congress
of People's Deputies

2

[Criticizing Russian President Boris Yeltsin for dropping his choice for Prime Minister, Yegor Gaidar, under pressure from his opposition]: The price for this will be paid by Russia. To save Gaidar would have taken real courage [by Yeltsin]—not like the courage when he stood on the turret of a tank surrounded by supporters, but the courage of a politician among adversaries.

Moscow, Russia, Dec. 14/
The New York Times, 12-15:(A)1.

Haris Silajdzic
Foreign Minister
of Bosnia and Herzegovina

3

[Calling on Europe to help his country in its current ethnic war with Serbia]: The government of Bosnia-Herzegovina . . . is a democracy, committed to human rights and a free-market economy. It is only just that peace should be imposed after so many sanctions, so many appeals, so many attempts at dealing with the expansionist policies of the [Serbian] Milosevic regime. For the 5,200 people who have died, it is too late. For the 20,000 wounded, the damage is

done. For the million more homeless, life is hell. For the thousands of little children waiting for a piece of bread and a cup of water, starvation creeps up . . . Let us try our very best to stop the suffering of the people of Bosnia-Herzegovina. Let us by our actions prevent despotic regimes, now and in the future, from fomenting their fanaticism.

Speech, Helsinki, Finland, June 8/
The Washington Post, 6-9:(A)14.

4

[On the ethnic conflict in what used to be Yugoslavia]: Islamic countries have a responsibility [to help Bosnia against the Serbs] . . . because there are Muslims in Bosnia-Herzegovina and also because the world community, and Europe in particular, did not take adequate steps to stop the slaughter in Bosnia . . . We shall accept arms from anyone, because it is our right. We shall do whatever is in our power to stay alive . . . This [ethnic war] could put relations between the West and the Islamic world on the wrong track or on the right track. If people are looking for a confrontation between Islam and the West [because of the West's not helping Bosnia], this is a chance. If they want cooperation, this is also a chance.

Interview, Nov. 30/
The Christian Science Monitor,
12-1:2.

Dmitri K. Simes
Senior associate,
Carnegie Endowment for
International Peace
(United States)

5

[Russian President Boris] Yeltsin's first months in office form a complex, contradictory but generally encouraging picture. What is encouraging is his commitment to reform. He was not frightened by the first resistance to higher prices. He demonstrated flexibility, yet toughness, with other Commonwealth [of Independent States] members. The buck stops with him. And in

(DMITRI K. SIMES)

foreign policy, his heart is certainly in the right place. But he is still Boris Yeltsin. He is from the old [Soviet Communist] Party apparatus, and when the going gets tough he still has a tendency to rely on people of his type, people he knew, people he is comfortable with. The sense is that he is determined to proceed with reforms, but that very often he's bigger on intentions than on appreciation of nuance and complexity.

The New York Times, 1-31:(A)6.

Immo Stabreit
German Ambassador
to the United States

1

[On the current outbreak of violence against foreigners in Germany]: The roots are social, not political. The uncontrolled influx of foreigners [fleeing conflicts elsewhere] is one element. Young [east Germans] are disoriented, afraid for the future; they have no jobs; they have no guidance from parents who are also out of work. There is no centrally organized movement behind all this. It is wrong to say that we have a neo-Nazi movement that endangers the German state. The young people have found out that if they say "Heil Hitler" they will get into the newspapers; 70 per cent of the perpetrators of these attacks are under 20. We will get hold of this in a very short time. Some 300,000 people demonstrated [against violence] in Munich, 350,000 in Berlin. The public is getting mobilized.

Interview, Boston, Mass./
The Christian Science Monitor,
12-11:3.

Robert S. Strauss
United States Ambassador
to Russia

2

[Supporting U.S. financial aid to Russia]: I think the American people need to understand that this is a rather unique opportunity. That's an understatement. I don't think any American generation has had a better opportunity to make a major move toward what people used to call

"peace in our time." I think the American people think they are being called upon to make some great sacrifice to provide foreign aid—charity—to what was once known as the evil empire. And I just don't see it that way. We have an opportunity to do something for ourselves here. It's enlightened self-interest.

Interview/
The Christian Science Monitor,
3-31:18.

3

I think [Russian] President [Boris] Yeltsin has matured into one of the more astute political leaders I have been around in my time. He's fiercely anti-Communist, intelligent; he's faced problems that are far more complex and difficult than any politician I have known. He's totally loyal to the people. He has handled nationality problems and former republics with skill and restraint, and more patience than I ever thought he had . . . I see so many positive things [in Russia] every day—little shops, women manufacturing jackets at home, shoe-shine stands, sidewalk cafes opening up, people doing things and making money. I know there are dangerous forces lurking. One has to be naive not to recognize them. You can make a case as good as my case that the glass is half-empty. It may be easier to make that case. [But maybe] I believe they're going to make it because I can't conceive them not making it. I think every day Yeltsin stays in place the process becomes more irreversible.

Interview, Moscow, Russia/
The New York Times, 11-7:5.

4

[Urging U.S. President-elect Bill Clinton to provide financial and technical aid to Russia]: The issue is not between a strong Russia and a weak Russia. The question is whether, is it going to be a democratic Russia that belongs to the civilized world or is it going to be one that falls into the hands of the first real demagogue who comes along. It's getting made to order for one.

Interview, Nov. 18/
The Christian Science Monitor,
11-19:3.

Hanna Suchocka
Prime Minister of Poland

1

The last three years have shown beyond any doubt that the Polish people have lived up to the challenge posed before them by their regained freedom. Despite their errors, the last three Cabinets ruled Poland in a sovereign way, determining the fate of the country and remaining free from any foreign dictate. No force, domestic or foreign, has managed to take control over the Polish state for its own end. Gone are the times of [economic] shortages and queues everywhere, inflation is falling and the Polish zloty, until recently the butt of vicious jokes, is becoming a real currency, which is confirmed by the fact that people are keeping their savings in zlotys, and not in foreign currency . . . We now live in a state neighboring countries toward which Poland can pursue a friendly policy. An international situation such as this is an opportunity we must not waste.

Before Polish Sejm (Parliament),
Warsaw, Poland/
USA Today, 11-30:(Our World)2.

Horst Teltschik
Former National Security Adviser
to German Chancellor
Helmut Kohl

2

Germany is suffering from anxiety about the future. There is a widespread impression that we have terrible problems—unification [of east and west Germany], [what to do about the ethnic conflict in what used to be] Yugoslavia, immigration—and a government unable to find solutions. The past 10 years were Germany's best, but unfortunately, people believe we have reached the end of the Golden Age.

The Washington Post, 10-2:(A)42.

Margaret Thatcher
Former Prime Minister
of the United Kingdom

3

[Supporting the re-election of the Conservative Party in Britain's forthcoming national elec-

tions]: Everything we have gained could so easily be lost unless we are returned for a fourth term under [Prime Minister] John Major's leadership . . . [The Labor Party] are still socialist and they deliberately set out to impose more government control over people's lives. That's where their whole belief starts—with the power of government over people's lives.

At rally, London, March 22/
Los Angeles Times, 3-23:(A)7.

4

[On the current ethnic conflict in what used to be Yugoslavia]: What is happening in Bosnia is not a civil war. It is a Communist war of aggression [by the Serbs against Bosnia]. Every time we [in the West] say that force will not be used [by the West against Serbia] we encourage the aggressor, who has already caused 2.5-million people to flee their homes. The Bosnians need military help within days unless an even greater catastrophe is to occur.

Switzerland/
The Christian Science Monitor,
8-10:2.

Wolfgang Thierse
Member of
German Parliament

5

[On the animosity some west Germans have toward east Germans following the reunification of the country]: I haven't gotten over the feeling that we [of the former East Germany] are somehow a nuisance. Apparently, if your background is wrong, if your history was in the wrong nation, you have nothing serious to contribute, especially if it challenges the status quo of the Federal Republic of [the former West] Germany.

The New York Times, 4-18:4.

Franjo Tudjman
President of Croatia

6

[On the ethnic conflict in what used to be Yugoslavia]: The world has been looking for an alibi not to take action against Serbia in Bosnia, and it found it by blaming Croatia as well. But objectively, this guilt does not exist. Croatia encouraged Croats in Bosnia to participate in the referendum that approved Bosnia's independence, and we were the first to recognize Bosnia as an independent state. Where we have fought in Bosnia, it has been to defend those areas where Croats are a majority. How can anybody call this a crime?

To reporters, Zagreb, Croatia/
The New York Times, 12-18:(A)8.

Rainer Veit
First vice president,
Deutsche Bank Research
(Germany)

1

[On the current problems with the European Monetary System]: We [Germans] still believe that the best solution for the EMS would be a realignment, with these elements: a moderate devaluation of the [Spanish] peseta and the [Irish] punt, to avoid interventions, and the fixing of a new parity for the [Italian] lira. Something like this could stabilize the EMS. In such realignment, the [German] Bundesbank would be able to reduce short-term interest rates . . . For more than five years, we have been so proud of our well-functioning EMS that we postponed a realignment. The stabilization of the EMS, and getting those others who have dropped out of the system back into it, should be a prime objective.

The Christian Science Monitor,
10-8:3.

Dragan Veselinov
Leader,
National Farmers Party
of Vojvodina, Serbia
(Yugoslavia)

2

[On the current ethnic conflict in what used to be Yugoslavia]: Keep in mind that his [Serbian President Slobodan Milosevic's] aim is Greater Serbia, not because he believes in it—he doesn't believe in anything. He uses the idea of Greater Serbia to provoke war and keep himself in power. He's a bloody pragmatist and a man without

morality . . . The party in power in this country is not ready to withdraw its primitive elite forces. The rulers will stay in power through criminal ways, by enriching those closest to the leadership. No more than 100 people will suck the blood of the other 8 million.

Los Angeles Times, 8-25:(H)2.

Karsten Voigt
Member of the Bundestag
(German Parliament)

3

With the changes that have taken place [in Germany], we have a stronger impact in whatever we do. It is not that we are being more assertive, but that even with continuity in our policies and behavior we have more influence. The apprehension felt by other countries will fade away in perhaps 10 or 15 years when people will see that a united Germany is a stabilizing factor in Europe. Meanwhile, we have to live with the criticism.

Time, 4-13:36.

Paul A. Volcker
Former Chairman,
Federal Reserve Board
(United States)

4

[On the recent popular vote in Denmark rejecting the Maastricht treaty aimed at European unity]: I think [the EC] has a bit of a problem. I wonder how the Danish reaction will rub off on other countries? We don't know how much the problem is a unified currency, or how much is federation, too much strength in Brussels [the EC headquarters] or Germany getting too dominant. I am a true-blue European. I think a common currency makes sense.

Interview, New York, N.Y./
Los Angeles Times, 6-14:(D)8.

Dmitri Volkogonov
Colonel General,
Russian armed forces;
Adviser to Russian President
Boris N. Yeltsin

5

[Saying Russia needs Western aid to keep its economic and political reforms on track]: Con-

(DMITRI VOLKOGONOV)

sider what happens if we fail. Those who succeed us will not say that we weren't radical enough, that we didn't go fast enough . . . To the contrary, to the contrary. If we fail, and we could, those who succeed us will say that the error was in abandoning socialism, in forcing out the Communist Party, and they will restore the Soviet system, perhaps in a reformed model but still very much a threat to the freedom of our people and everyone else in the world.

Los Angeles Times, 2-3:(A)7.

George Walden
Member of British Parliament

1

By and large, the entire [British school] system is designed to perpetuate class—it provides a leg up for the children of the people who run the country. The fact is that these people—politicians, editors, doctors, professionals—may talk a lot about what's wrong with the schools, [but] wouldn't touch a state school with a barge pole.

The Washington Post, 8-4:(A)16.

William Wallace
Historian,
Oxford University (England)

2

[Saying that, with the end of the Cold War, U.S. influence in Europe is on the wane]: The August, 1991, [attempted] coup [in the Soviet Union] is as fundamental to European-American relations as the Berlin crisis of 1947-48 . . . There is no longer a reason for the U.S. to stay . . . The United States hasn't yet learned that if there's no money [due to the U.S. economic decline], there's no leadership. The perception [in the U.S.] that America can have a free ride because it's protected Europe for 40 years just won't wash much longer . . . We've always seen America as our natural partner, and the horrifying part of what is happening now is that there's no alternative being articulated. We haven't yet woken up to just how fundamental a shift is under way.

Interview/Los Angeles Times, 2-4:(H)2.

Heiner Wegesin
Christian Democratic Party
domestic-policy specialist
in the German Bundestag

3

Germans in this rich society aren't willing to take on low-income jobs, or jobs where you have to touch dirt, or where you have to work at night. Just look at the restaurants. Who is washing dishes? Not Germans anymore.

The Christian Science Monitor,
11-25:3.

Robert Worcester
British public-opinion analyst

4

The [British] Labor Party [which lost the recent election to the Conservatives] faces a series of barriers. First, the Boundary Commission will redraw electoral constituencies before the next election—resulting in the net gain of from 16 to 24 Tory [Conservative] seats. Second, the public is getting older and more conservative. Women are living longer and leaning toward the Conservative Party. Third, many working-class voters are moving up to the middle class, which works against the Labor Party. Trade-union strength is falling and members are getting more conservative. The situation for Labor is, in a word, bleak. I don't think the Labor Party can win the next election. The Conservative Party has to lose it—as they would have if [former Conservative Prime Minister] Margaret Thatcher ran in the last election.

Los Angeles Times, 7-7:(H)2.

Boris N. Yeltsin
President of Russia

5

The measures that we are taking in the sphere of disarmament are not undermining in any way the defense potential of Russia and member states of the Commonwealth [of Independent States]. We are seeking to achieve the reasonable minimum sufficiency of nuclear and conventional weapons. This is our main principle in the establishment of the armed forces. Sticking to this principle will make it possible to save considerable resources. They will be channeled to meeting civilian needs and implementing the [economic] reform . . . I want to emphasize that we are not talking about our unilateral nuclear disarmament. The United States is taking parallel steps in a gesture of good will. It is now possible and necessary to move much further along this road.

Broadcast address to the nation,
Moscow, Russia, Jan. 9/
Los Angeles Times, 1-30:(A)14.

1

[Calling for more Western aid to support reforms in his country]: The only thing that can impede our progress will be general unrest [in Russia], and general unrest will happen if our reforms fail. Should the reforms fail, we shall face a new leadership and Russia will fall into the habits which tortured us for 74 years . . . Deeds we need [from the West], not words.

London, England, Jan. 30/
The New York Times, 1-13:(A)6.

2

I am grateful to the world community for its support of our efforts and for the understanding that not only the future of the people of Russia, but also that of the entire planet, largely depends on whether or not the [economic and political] reforms [in Russia] are successful. I am also grateful to Russians for their courage and patience. They should take a great deal of credit for the fact that the world community is breaking with its totalitarian past. Democracy is one of the major assets of human civilization. All times and all countries have known people who stood up to defend it without sparing themselves. The people of Russia defended democracy near the walls of our Moscow White House.

At UN Security Council summit meeting,
United Nations, New York, Jan. 31/
The New York Times, 2-1:5.

3

[On a new treaty aimed at cementing good relations among the various republics in Russia]:

Today we can tell our fellow citizens, our peoples who have lived together for centuries, and the world community that Russia was, is and will be united. By signing the federation treaty, we each seal the will of our peoples to preserve Russia, its spiritual treasure, its unique place in the world community. Decades of violence and tyranny have not separated our people nor exterminated their desire to live in a unified country . . . The treaty . . . will put an end to the domination of the so-called Moscow bureaucracy. At the same time, it will protect Russia from chaos, anarchy and the raging of selfish provincialism.

At treaty signing,
Moscow, Russia, March 31/
Los Angeles Times, 4-1:(A)1,15.

4

[Saying there may be Vietnam-era U.S. POWs who have been held in Russia]: The archives of the KGB and the Communist Party Central Committee are being opened. Moreover, we are inviting the cooperation of the United States and other nations to investigate these dark pages. I can promise you that each and every document in each and every archive will be examined in order to investigate the fate of every American unaccounted for. As President of Russia, I assure you that even if one American has been detained in my country and can still be found, I will find him. I will get him back to his family.

Before joint session of U.S. Congress,
Washington, D.C., June 17/
Los Angeles Times, 6-18:(A)7.

5

The world can sigh in relief. The idol of Communism, which spread everywhere social strife, animosity and unparalleled brutality, which instilled fear in humanity, has collapsed. I am here to assure you we [in Russia] will not let it rise again in our land . . . For us, the ominous lesson of the past is relevant today as never before. It was precisely in a devastated country, with an economy in near paralysis, that Bolshevism succeeded in building a totalitarian regime, created a gigantic war machine . . . and an insatiable military-industrial complex. This

(BORIS N. YELTSIN)

must not be allowed to happen again. That is why economic and political reforms are the primary task for Russia today . . . I will not go back on the reforms. And it is practically impossible to topple Yeltsin in Russia. I am in good health, and I will not say "uncle" before I make the reforms irreversible.

Before joint session of U.S. Congress,
Washington, D.C., June 17/
Los Angeles Times, 6-18:(A)6.

1

[On his proposal to issue vouchers to all Russians with which they can buy shares in what are now state-owned assets in a massive privatization move]: We need millions of property owners, and not just a handful of millionaires. These vouchers are a ticket to the free-market economy. The more owners and entrepreneurs we have—people for whom actions mean more than words—the sooner we will have prosperity in Russia.

Broadcast address to the nation,
Moscow, Russia, Aug. 19/
The Washington Post, 8-20:(A)1.

2

The tragedy of 20th-century Russia is that it did not manage, despite many attempts, to fully carry out any reform. And this was due not as much to reaction from the opposition but more due to the weakness of the reformers.

Before Russian Congress of People's Deputies,
Moscow, Russia, Nov. 30/
The Christian Science Monitor, 12-2:4.

3

The transformations in Russia have lately become a subject of controversy and fierce struggle. Colossal political overloads and confrontations among various political forces have become an evil plaguing Russia's economy. The inability and the unwillingness to look for compromise is turning into a serious factor impeding the reform . . . We must say directly that for the majority of the population, the reforms are for the moment only increasing the problems and difficulties . . . Against the background of considerable deterioration of living standards of most of the population, a rapid and in many aspects unjustified social differentiation is making itself acutely felt.

Before Russian Congress
of People's Deputies,
Moscow, Russia, Dec. 1/
The New York Times,
12-2:(A)1,8.

4

[Criticizing members of the Russian Congress of People's Deputies for fighting against or blocking his initiatives and proposals]: The walls of this hall reddened from the endless insults, the hatred and the rudeness, from the filth that flows over at the Congress because of the morbid ambitions of bankrupt politicians.

Before Russian Congress
of People's Deputies,
Moscow, Russia, Dec. 10/
The New York Times,
12-11:(A)8.

The Middle East

Magdi Abeid
*Scholar, Center for Political
and Development Studies
(Egypt)*

1

There is [currently] no power regulating the relations between the smaller states in the [Persian] Gulf. The competition between Iraq and Saudi Arabia and the competition between Iran and Iraq—these competitors were very important to guarantee the security in the Gulf. Now Iraq is excluded from the balance of power [having been defeated in 1991's Persian Gulf war], so every state . . . has the freedom to assert its aims.

*The Christian Science Monitor,
10-9:7.*

Abdul Amir Anbari
*Iraqi Ambassador
to the United Nations*

2

[On a possible use of force by the U.S. or UN against Iraq because of its refusal to allow UN weapons inspectors to search the Iraqi Agriculture Ministry building]: Throwing a bomb or two in Baghdad or here or there is not going to change Iraq's position.

*To reporters, July 21/
Los Angeles Times, 7-22:(A)7.*

Yasir Arafat
*Chairman,
Palestine Liberation Organization*

3

If there is going to be peace [between the Arabs and Israel], it will not be because Israel decides to give up land but because America and the West push the Israelis to make concessions. There are no Soviets to cause instability in the area anymore, and the industrialized nations like America must have stability in a region where most of the world's energy is stored. Israel used to be of vital strategic importance to America,

but not now. It [still] has some value, but we have reached a historic point where the interests of today's Israel and America do not coincide.

*Interview, Tunis, Tunisia/
Newsweek, 5-4:40.*

Moshe Arens
Minister of Defense of Israel

4

[On U.S. President Bush's reluctance to grant $10-billion in loan guarantees to Israel]: We will not beg or crawl for help. We hope our friends in Washington will help us shoulder the guarantees burden . . . But if that is not to be, without rancor and with continuing friendship for the United States, we shall have to do it ourselves.

*To National Jewish Appeal volunteers,
Washington, D.C., March 16/
The Washington Post, 3-17:(A)14.*

Hanan Ashrawi
*Palestinian representative at
Middle East peace conference*

5

We [Palestinians] start with the assumption that we are human beings with rights, national rights and rights on the ground. [The Israelis] start with the assumption that we are inhabitants of the [occupied] territories with no rights whatever.

*Washington, D.C., Feb. 26/
The Washington Post, 2-27:(A)32.*

6

[On the current Middle East peace conference involving the Arabs and Israel]: We are accomplishing long-term political and public relations achievements, but in terms of real change it looks as if we are not accomplishing much. People measure by the price they are made to pay . . . If the peace process can produce any concrete changes to alleviate people's suffering, that would give us a real push. But instead, the Israelis are escalating the pressure. That condenses our time frame.

The Christian Science Monitor, 4-6:4.

Hafaz al-Assad
President of Syria

1

[Israel's separate] peace with Egypt did not put an end to the [Arab-Israeli] conflict in the region. Moreover, Egypt, and in particular [then President Anwar Sadat, who was later assassinated], paid a very high price. Any Arab leader who does what Sadat did [make a separate peace with Israel] would pay no less. Separate deals do not achieve peace; they may in fact lead to the opposite result. I am surprised that some people would like to cut peace into pieces—one piece now, another later. What is the use of solving a problem in a way that creates a larger problem? When we speak of a comprehensive peace, we do not mean that everybody marches shoulder to shoulder, like soldiers on parade. A little progress may take place on one front, a little delay on another. All the Arab parties understand that there are certain peculiarities regarding each of the issues. As long as they are satisfied that we are proceeding toward a comprehensive solution, progress on one issue can be made more speedily than on others.

Interview, Damascus, Syria/
Time, 11-30:49.

Shlomo Avineri
Israeli political scientist

2

[On Yitzhak Rabin's Labor Party's victory in the recent Israeli election]: I call it mini-Gaullism. Rabin has been able to present the Labor point of view from the proposition of national interest. He couches a peace intitiative [with the Arabs] in centrist terms, not in terms of civil and human rights expressed by the peace camp. We don't give up the [Israeli-occupied Arab territories] because we love Arabs but because it benefits us. It's a tactical approach to get the same result without left-wing language.

Los Angeles Times, 7-4:(A)6.

Tarik Aziz
Deputy Prime Minister of Iraq

3

[Criticizing UN-imposed sanctions and inspections aimed at ending Iraq's development

and possession of weapons of mass destruction]: The question constantly asked by 18 million Iraqis, together with millions more of honest free people in the world, is: For how long will this iniquitous siege continue to be imposed upon Iraq? Iraq is a country which has made an outstanding contribution to the establishment of human civilization. [Yet, Iraq is now] prohibited from importing the chlorine it needs to sterilize its drinking water . . . Iraq has been fulfilling its obligations month after month. What obligations has the [UN Security] Council, for its part, fulfilled toward the people of Iraq? The answer is: Nothing whatsoever.

At United Nations, New York,
March 11/
Los Angeles Times, 3-12:(A)11.

4

[Saying that, despite threats of military action against it, Iraq will not open its Agriculture Ministry building to UN inspectors looking for Iraqi weapons records as called for in the Persian Gulf war cease-fire accords]: [Iraq] will never abandon its sovereignty and will never accept any insult and will never allow a UN inspection team to threaten its internal security. [Iraq] is sticking with its rejection stand concerning any demand that will involve an insult to Iraq. The Iraqi people and Iraqi command are ready to face all consequences.

News conference, Baghdad, Iraq,
July 23/
Los Angeles Times, 7-24:(A)1.

5

[On 1990's Iraqi invasion and takeover of Kuwait and 1991's Persian Gulf war in which U.S.-led forces ousted Iraq from that occupation]: We didn't have any false illusion about the position of the United States. We knew the United States would have a strong reaction against [the Iraqi invasion]. So we didn't have any false expectations the United States would sit and watch [the invasion]. At that stage we knew that it would lead to a conflict. And later on, when they sent troops, we knew it would lead to a war.

Interview, New York, N.Y./
USA Today, 11-27:(A)2.

James A. Baker III
Secretary of State
of the United States

1

[Supporting new Israeli Prime Minister Yitzhak Rabin's policy of stopping or limiting the establishment of further Jewish settlements in the occupied territories]: It's a pleasure to be going to Israel under circumstances in which I anticipate that we will not be met with the opening of a new settlement or settlements, but rather a suspension of contracts for the construction of new houses or settlements activity—something that I think can only inspire trust and confidence [beteween Israel and the Arabs].

To reporters enroute to Israel,
July 19/
The Washington Post, 7-20:(A)1.

Eliahu Ben-Elizar
Chairman, Foreign Affairs
and Defense Committee,
Israeli Knesset (Parliament)

2

[On the current chill in U.S.-Israeli relations]: It happens that there are differences of opinion that become deeper. It is not easy to have such a long romance and always keep it at its peak. Any responsible U.S. decision-makers with a choice between basing long-term policy on Iran or Iraq or on any of the other dictatorships in the region, and basing it on Israel, they will try to find an equilibrium, but in the end they will trust Israel.

The Christian Science Monitor,
3-20:4.

Howard L. Berman
United States Representative,
D-California

3

[Criticizing a U.S. Bush Administration policy of allowing sales of high-tech equipment—which could have military applications—to non-military entities in Syria]: What the Administration did with Iraq, they are now doing with Syria. Syria's continued harboring of terrorism is being overlooked for geopolitical reasons; whether they relate to the [Arab-Israeli] peace process or

hostage release I don't know . . . The military dominates all aspects of life in Syria. There is no independent, free, private sector in that country at all . . . Our capacity to know that any item which has military capabilities stays with the civilian-end user is minimal, at best. It's just like Iraq. We're going down the same road all over again.

Los Angeles Times, 2-13:(A)1,14,15.

Richard A. Boucher
Deputy Spokesman,
Department of State
of the United States

4

[Criticizing Iraq's handling of UN weapons-inspection teams who have been investigating that country's military programs]: As we've seen many, many times throughout this process, going back over a year now, Iraq has made various disclosures and allowed certain things to be destroyed, allowed certain things to be inspected, allowed certain things to be documented, and then has tried to stop the process. [When inspections began again,] we found more. [Iraq is playing a game of] cheat and retreat.

July 15/
The New York Times, 7-16:(A)6.

Edmund G. "Jerry" Brown, Jr.
Candidate for the 1992
Democratic U.S.
Presidential nomination;
Former Governor
of California (D)

5

American policy must ensure a strong, secure and democratic Israel, and at the same time, vigorously pursue a Middle East peace process which addresses the legitimate interests of all the parties concerned. We need a policy of realism which recognizes that Israel is an ally, a friend, and that we stand behind her security. But at the same time, the people who live in the West Bank and the Gaza Strip have their rights, their interests and their dignity.

Los Angeles Times, 3-17:(H)6.

Patrick J. Buchanan
American political commentator;
Candidate for the 1992
Republican U.S.
Presidential nomination

1

[U.S.] President Bush's policy toward the Arab-Israeli conflict is basically sound. The United States has a moral commitment to guarantee the security and survival of the state of Israel. Israel is entitled to secure borders, a lifting of the Arab boycott and recognition by her neighbors. But there will be no lasting peace in the region until the longing of the Palestinian people for a homeland is satisfied. What they want is a homeland, a flag and a state of their own.

Los Angeles Times, 3-17:(H)6.

George Bush
President of the United States

2

[On current U.S. relations with Jordan, following Jordan's siding with Iraq in the recent Persian Gulf war against U.S.-led coalition forces]: I just want to make sure that people know across this country how pleased I am to see His Majesty [Jordanian King Hussein]. For years we've had strong relations with Jordan. We know there were difficulties. He is my friend . . . So we're looking to the future.

Welcoming visiting King Hussein,
Washington, D.C., March 12/
The Washington Post, 3-13:(A)19.

3

[On last year's Persian Gulf war between Iraq and U.S.-led coalition forces]: The UN resolutions [authorizing the war] never called for the elimination of [Iraqi President] Saddam Hussein. It never called for taking the battle into downtown Baghdad, and we have a lot of revisionists [in the U.S.], who opposed me on the war, now saying, "How come you didn't go into downtown Baghdad and find Saddam Hussein and do him in?" We have all but removed the threat of Saddam Hussein to his neighbors . . . Am I happy Saddam Hussein is still there? Absolutely not. Am I determined he's going to live

with these [UN-imposed disarmament] resolutions? Absolutely. But we did the right thing, we did the honorable thing, and I have absolutely no regrets about that part of it at all.

At American Society of Newspaper Editors
convention,
Washington, D.C., April 9/
Los Angeles Times, 4-10:(A)12.

4

[On charges that he knew that between 1985 and 1990 Iraq was diverting U.S.-supplied technology to its nuclear-weapons program]: We didn't know that. The State Department didn't know that . . . We did not . . . enhance [Iraqi President] Saddam Hussein's] nuclear, biological or chemical capability. I have an executive order out on specifically that. And you have repeated something that isn't true.

Broadcast discussion,
Washington, D.C./
"This Morning," CBS-TV, 7-1.

5

Iraq has refused to participate in the work of the Iraq-Kuwait border commission. Iraq has refused to account for Kuwaiti citizens seized during the occupation [of Kuwait by Iraq in 1990-91] and to return property that was stolen by the occupiers. Iraq has not renewed the memorandum of understanding with the UN and has stepped up its harassment of UN officials and humanitarian agencies operating in the country. [Iraqi President Saddam Hussein] has stepped up his persecution of the Iraqi people in flagrant violation of UN Security Council Resolution 688, including recent use of jet fighters against the Shiites in maintaining a blockade of the Kurds. Iraq has refused to accept UN Security Council Resolution 706 and 712, which would allow for the sale of oil for food and medicine . . . The international community cannot tolerate continued Iraqi defiance of the United Nations and the rule of law, and there's too much at stake for the region, for the United Nations and for the world.

News conference,
Washington, D.C., July 26/
The New York Times, 7-27:(A)4.

327

(GEORGE BUSH)

1

[On criticism that he stopped the Persian Gulf war of 1991 too soon and that U.S.-led forces should have continued into Baghdad to depose Iraqi President Saddam Hussein]: Look, we had an international mandate . . . to kick Saddam out of Kuwait. Now we have a lot of second-guessing. There are people that I had to drag to support our objectives [who are now] criticizing that we stopped too soon. I'm very interested at this historical revision, but I also know the facts, and I know we were right . . . [If we had decided to carry the war to Baghdad to get Hussein,] first place you'd have had the [U.S.-led] coalition fall apart . . . The United States would've been alone. Secondly, I could make a case that we would still be bogged down in an urban guerrilla war in Baghdad, and I'd like to hear somebody honestly refute that case.

Interview, Aug. 4/
USA Today, 8-5:(A)9.

2

[On criticism by some Jews of his refusal to grant Israel loan guarantees as long as Israel continues to build settlements in occupied territories]: To accuse those [like himself], who may come to different conclusions on one or another public issue, of harboring anti-Semitism is to cheapen the term. And when those words, without justice have been aimed at me, I can tell you they cut right to the heart.

Before B'nai B'rith, Sept. 8/
USA Today, 9-9:(A)10.

3

[On criticism that, before the 1991 Persian Gulf war, his Administration helped build up the military forces of Iraq]: It's awful easy when you're dealing with 99 hindsight. We did try to bring [Iraqi President] Saddam Hussein into the family of nations. He did have the fourth-largest army. All our Arab allies out there thought we ought to do just exactly that. And when he crossed the line [and invaded Kuwait, which precipitated the Persian Gulf war] I stood up and looked into the camera and I said this aggression

will not stand. And we formed an historic coalition [through the UN against Iraq] and we brought him down. And we destroyed the fourth-largest army. And the battlefield was searched and there wasn't one single iota of evidence that any U.S. weapons [supplied to Iraq] were on that battlefield, and [Iraq's] nuclear capability has been searched by the United Nations and there hasn't been one scintilla of evidence that there's any U.S. technology involved in it. And what you're seeing, on all this "Iraqgate" [blaming the U.S. for Iraq's military buildup] is a bunch of people who were wrong on the war trying to cover their necks here and [trying] to do a little revisionism. And I cannot let that stand because it isn't true. Yes we had grain credits for Iraq, and there isn't any evidence that those grain credits were diverted into weaponry. None. None whatsoever.

At Presidential candidates' debate,
East Lansing, Mich., Oct. 19/
The New York Times, 10-20:(A)15.

Shoshona S. Cardin
Chairman, Conference of
Presidents of Major American
Jewish Organizations

4

[Criticizing the U.S. Bush Administration for refusing loan guarantees for Israel unless that country stops its Jewish settlement activities in the occupied territories]: There may be divisions in the American Jewish community about whether Israel should continue to build settlements, but the community is totally united on the need for granting these guarantees. In pursuing its political objective, the Administration seems to have lost sight of the humanitarian issues— that the futures of thousands of men, women and children are jeopardized by this linkage.

To U.S. Secretary of State James Baker/
The Washington Post, 3-10:(A)13.

Dick Cheney
Secretary of Defense
of the United States

5

[On why U.S.-led forces did not go to Baghdad and capture Iraqi leader Saddam

(DICK CHENEY)

Hussein after his forces were defeated in 1991's Persian Gulf war]: Let's assume for the moment that we would have been able to do it—we've got Saddam now . . . Then the question comes [of] putting a government in place of the one you've just gotten rid of; you can't just sort of turn around and walk away—you have now accepted the responsibility for what happens in Iraq. What kind of government do you want us to create in place of the old Saddam Hussein government? Do you want a Sunni government, or a Shia government, or maybe it ought to be a Kurdish government, or maybe one based on the Ba'ath Party, or maybe some combination of all of those? How long is that government likely to survive without U.S. military forces there to keep it propped up? If you get into the business of committing U.S. forces on the ground in Iraq, to occupy the place, my guess is I'd probably still have people there today instead of having been able to bring them home . . . The bottom-line question for me was: How many additional American lives is Saddam Hussein worth? The answer: not very damn many.

Before Detroit Economic Club,
Detroit, Mich., Sept. 14/
The Washington Post, 9-15:(A)22.

1

[On criticism that the U.S. built up Iraq's war machine by supplying it with military-applicable materials before 1991's Persian Gulf war, in which U.S.-led forces pushed Iraq out of Kuwait]: That's revisionism, generated and promoted especially by people who were wrong on the war, who voted against us when it was time to back the [U.S.] President [Bush] and support the use of force to liberate Kuwait. I think there's an enormous amount of Monday-morning quarterbacking. We sold scrap metal to the Japanese before Pearl Harbor, too . . . What the country [the U.S.] saw in Desert Storm [the war]— because they got to see it direct with their own eyes instead of having it interpreted for them [by the media]—was that we had the finest military in the world, that the equipment was phenomenal and the troops were even better. After the fact,

the revisionism starts. I expect to pick up the newspaper any day now and be told we lost.

Interview, Washington, D.C./
USA Today, 11-27:(A)2.

Bill Clinton
Governor of Arkansas (D);
Candidate for the 1992
Democratic U.S.
Presidential nomination

2

I am deeply concerned by the damage done by the [U.S.] Bush Administration [to U.S.-Israeli relations. Bush] has pressured Israel to make one-sided concessions [to the Arabs] in the peace process . . . The Administration will spend the next four months hoping you will forget the last four years. But we cannot forget the cold shoulder—and even the back of its hand—the Administration gave to Israel.

Before Jewish community leaders,
Washington, D.C., June 30/
Los Angeles Times, 7-1:(A)18.

Bill Clinton
Governor of Arkansas (D);
1992 Democratic U.S.
Presidential nominee

3

Let's give [U.S. President Bush] the credit he deserves for organizing Operation Desert Storm and Desert Shield [during 1991's Persian Gulf war against Iraq's occupation of Kuwait]. It was a remarkable event. But let's look at where I think the real mistake was made. In 1988, when the war between Iraq and Iran ended, we knew [Iraqi President] Saddam Hussein was a tyrant. We had dealt with him because he was against Iran— the enemy of my enemy may be my friend. All right, the war is over. We know he's dropping mustard gas on his own people. We know he threatened to incinerate half of Israel. Several [U.S.] government departments, several, had information that he was converting our aid to military purposes and trying to develop weapons of mass destruction. But in late '89, [U.S. President Bush] signed a secret policy saying we were going to try to improve relations with [Hussein], and we sent him some sort of communication on the eve of his invasion of Kuwait that we still wanted better relations. So I think that was wrong. I give credit where credit is due, but the responsibility was in coddling Saddam Hussein when there was no reason to do it and when people in high levels in our government knew he was trying to do things that were outrageous.

At Presidential candidates' debate,
East Lansing, Mich., Oct. 19/
The New York Times, 10-20:(A)15.

Suleyman Demirel
Prime Minister of Turkey

1

[On whether the U.S. should try to topple Iraqi President Saddam Hussein]: Many people aren't happy with Saddam. We are not happy with Saddam. But he is there, and it's the business of his country what to do with him . . . When it comes to pushing out a man at the top of a country, you have got to consider world public opinion. World public opinion is not the same thing as your own public opinion. An action might be right and correct in spirit and essence, but if it is not going to be well received by world public opinion, it could do harm.

Interview,
Washington, D.C., Feb. 12/
The New York Times, 2-13:(A)6.

Lawrence S. Eagleburger
Deputy Secretary of State
of the United States

2

[On criticism of the U.S. Bush Administration's aiding Iraqi President Saddam Hussein before he invaded and took over Kuwait, which led to last year's Persian Gulf war]: It is clear that [U.S.] policy did not work. We tried. Because we tried does not mean that we created [in Hussein] a Frankenstein monster. He was his own monster. We tried to contain him. We did not succeed . . . [But] quite frankly, the selective disclosure [by Bush critics]—out of context—of classified documents has led—knowingly or otherwise—to distortions of the record, half

truths and outright falsehoods, all combined into spurious conspiracy theories and charges of a [Bush Administration] coverup.

Before House Banking Committee,
Washington, D.C., May 21/
The Washington Post, 5-22:(A)1.

Rafael Eitan
Member of the Knesset
(Israeli Parliament)

3

All we [Israelis] want is quiet, and quiet is not tied to a peace agreement with Syria, but to Israel's ability to crush any military threat against it.

Sept. 13/
The New York Times, 9-14:(A)8.

Fahd ibn Abdel Aziz al-Saud
King of Saudi Arabia

4

The democratic system prevailing in the world does not suit us in the region. Islam is our social and political law. It is a complete constitution of social and economic laws and a system of government and justice.

Interview/
The New York Times, 3-30:(A)6.

Robert M. Gates
Director of Central Intelligence
of the United States

5

[Iraqi President Saddam Hussein's control of his country's] territory and people is eroding, mainly because he has not been able to extract his country from the grip of UN sanctions, [despite his] cynical manipulation of food and medical supplies. Even so, fear and intimidation continue to prevent his opponents from acting individually, while disunity and the pervasive security system impede the formation of a collective resistance. Consequently, it is difficult to say when public frustration or political and military defections will lead to his overthrow.

At conference sponsored by the
Richard M. Nixon Library,
Washington, D.C., March 12/
The Washington Post, 3-13:(A)19.

Sam Gejdenson
United States Representative,
D-Connecticut

1

[On U.S. President Bush's denial that he knew that between 1985 and 1990 Iraq was diverting U.S.-supplied technology to its nuclear-weapons program]: The Administration's own [newly declassified] documents tell us the President's denials are not true. As early as 1985, the Defense Department said we cannot trust the Iraqis with nuclear technology because they are diverting it from other programs to their nuclear effort.

Interview, July 1/
Los Angeles Times, 7-2:(A)1.

Dore Gold
Authority on U.S.-Israeli relations,
Jaffe Center for Strategic Studies,
Tel Aviv University (Israel)

2

In the old days of the Cold War, the United States and Israel did have a difference of view over what was the principal threat. While the United States focused on the Soviet Union, Israel focused on its Arab enemies. While the United States had a mostly global orientation, Israel's was regional. In the post-Cold War period, both are going to be focusing on regional problems. As long as the United States cannot conceive of a role for Israel in [Persian] Gulf security matters, Israel has to find strategic relevance for the relationship in the Mediterranean theatre, and in non-Soviet related scenarios.

The Washington Post, 7-28:(A)12.

Henry B. Gonzalez
United States Representative,
D-Texas

3

[Criticizing the Reagan and Bush Administrations for allowing U.S. technology that could be used for military purposes to be exported to Iraq, which the U.S. later fought in the Persian Gulf war]: [Between 1985 and 1990,] the Commerce Department approved at least 220 export licenses for the Iraqi armed forces, major [Iraqi] weapons complexes and enterprises identified by the [U.S.] Central Intelligence Agency as diverting technology to weapons.

At Senate hearing,
Washington, D.C., Oct. 27/
USA Today, 10-28:(A)4.

Albert Gore, Jr.
United States Senator,
D-Tennessee;
1992 Democratic U.S.
Vice-Presidential nominee

4

[On U.S. President Bush's handling of 1991's Persian Gulf war against Iraq's invasion and occupation of Kuwait]: He deserves credit for calling the fire department, but we should understand it was he who started the blaze. Once the fire has started, you don't say, "Wait a minute; we shouldn't put it out because this fire shouldn't have been set in the first place." I would cast that vote [in the Senate supporting the war] all over again. [But] I started making speeches against [Bush's] Iraq policy back in 1988. I think it was an extremely serious mistake by Bush [to supply Iraq with material that could be used to make armaments], and one for which he ought to be held accountable.

Interview/Time, 10-19:36.

David Hannay
British Ambassador
to the United Nations

5

[On Iraq's refusal to cooperate with UN demands that it report and destroy its facilities for weapons of mass destruction]: A year ago, Iraq was expelled from Kuwait by force of arms under the authority of the United Nations. The use of force was required because Iraq miscalculated and believed that this [UN Security] Council was bluffing . . . There is an opportunity again now for Iraq to comply. I hope she will not again miscalculate.

At United Nations, New York,
March 11/
Los Angeles Times, 3-12:(A)1.

David A. Harris
Executive vice president,
American Jewish Committee

1

[On the current tougher U.S. Administration stance toward Israel]: What I am finding when I travel around the country is American Jews who feel caught between a rock and a hard place. People are not fully happy with some of the ways Israel is behaving, but they don't have confidence in the script being written by the [U.S. Bush] Administration either. We are not only missing the violins in the relationship, we are missing the whole orchestra. What you have here are two countries that have so much in common but are increasingly losing sight of it. It worries us. It troubles us. It scares us, because many of us can see what happens down the road if this continues.

The New York Times, 3-2:(A)1.

Hussein ibn Talal
King of Jordan

2

[Saying Jordan is not breaking UN economic sanctions against Iraq]: We accept and have adhered to the UN sanctions. We are doing the best we can to get the Iraqi people food and medicine. But as to non-humanitarian goods, I want to say that our credibility is very important to us, and we are not engaged in sanctions-busting.

News conference, Amman, Jordan,
July 21/
The Washington Post, 7-22:(A)21.

Saddam Hussein
President of Iraq

3

[Addressing Iraqi educators]: Give special attention to sanitary facilities for students. These should be clean and functional . . . The student who cannot go to the bathroom all day because it is dirty and in awful condition cannot concentrate. Some people might ask why this man is speaking about such an issue and preoccupying himself with it. I speak about it and preoccupy myself with it because although manufacturing a

missile is important, this issue is more important to me than manufacturing a missile. This is because when society achieves balance in its development, then we can expect from it all big and mature things.

June/
The Washington Post, 7-28:(A)14.

Faisal Husseini
Palestinian nationalist;
Director, Arab Studies Center,
Jerusalem, Israel

4

Israelis are celebrating [the 25th anniversary of its reunification of Jerusalem] under the slogan of a unified Jerusalem. But everyone sees this is not a unified city in any way, shape or form. One part is under occupation and another part is not.

Los Angeles Times, 6-6:(A)3.

Martin Indyk
Executive director,
Washington Institute
for Near East Policy
(United States)

5

[The Arab-Israeli] peace process is a snake pit for American involvement. That might argue for staying away, but for [U.S. Secretary of State James] Baker it was like Mount Everest for the best climber in the world.

The Christian Science Monitor,
5-5:7.

Abdul-Karim Iryani
Foreign Minister of Yemen

6

[On the recent merging of North and South Yemen and the forthcoming democratic elections]: There is no doubt that a unified Yemen is a greater country than a partitioned Yemen. But in my view, Yemen unity has removed one of the hotbeds of conflict in the Arab world. The trend, the mode today, is for democracy, a multi-party system. This is the language of the age. I'm proud that we are speaking it. I don't think anybody should be worried. If that worry exists, I think it's very old-fashioned thinking.

Los Angeles Times, 6-1:(A)8.

Khalil Jahshan
Executive director,
National Association
of Arab Americans

1

[On the Middle East peace talks between the Arabs and Israelis]: The way this peace process has been structured, it's very vulnerable and highly personalized. Any change in the terms of reference or any drastic change in personnel managing the peace process could cause the process to implode.

The Christian Science Monitor,
11-10:2.

Abdullah Kabaa
Professor of political science,
King Saud University
(Saudi Arabia)

2

I would say that [Saudi] King Fahd has lived up to his promises. Fundamental changes are taking place in Saudi Arabia . . . The King's decree for the first time deals with a legal constitutional framework, which is almost a constitution. That would put Saudi Arabia for the first time as a constitutional monarchy.

March 1/
Los Angeles Times, 3-2:(A)7.

Robert W. Kasten, Jr.
United States Senator,
R-Wisconsin

3

We [the U.S.] have two long-standing policies. One long-standing policy is that we have a responsibility to Soviet Jewry, to seek their safety and to allow them to freely emigrate from the Soviet Union. We have another U.S. policy [against Jewish] settlements [by Israel in the occupied territories]. Those two policies are now in a collision course [as more and more Soviet Jews are settling in the occupied territories]. We have to choose. I believe the United States' responsibility to Soviet Jewry is at least as compelling, possibly more compelling, as the U.S. policy vis-a-vis the settlements.

At Senate Foreign Operations Subcommittee
hearing, Washington, D.C., Feb. 25/
The New York Times, 2-26:(A)6.

David Kay
Former United Nations
weapons inspector

4

[On UN requirements that Iraq destroy its offensive military equipment]: The resolution requires that [Iraqi President] Saddam [Hussein] destroy equipment only in front of UN inspectors. He insists on destroying it before calling the inspectors in, and you're looking at a bunch of debris, and you have no idea what you are looking at . . . That's the great difficulty. You don't know whether you are looking at the debris of maybe three Scuds [missiles] and 85 crushed Buicks, or whether you're looking at, really, all the Scuds . . . I think it is typical Saddam strategy of buying time, hoping the world will lose interest, or some other event will intervene and Iraq will get off the hook . . . You do, indeed, hope that the Iraqis have turned over a new leaf. But as an inspector or former inspector, I much prefer to see what is actually there. Behavior that is promised six weeks from now doesn't count.

Broadcast interview/
"Good Morning America,"
ABC-TV, 3-23.

Geoffrey Kemp
Senior associate,
Carnegie Endowment
for International Peace
(United States)

5

[On the recent and to-be-continued negotiations between Israel and its Arab adversaries]: If you compare where we are in January 1992 to January 1991 and every other January going back to the birth of Israel in 1948, you have to conclude that something of a miracle has happened. Everyone knew that [these negotiations] would be an extraordinarily tortuous process with lots of posturing and setbacks. But the fact that no one shows any real sign of saying, "The heck with it," and walking away is very encouraging.

Jan. 17/
The Washington Post,
1-18:(A)16.

Abdul Wajeed Khuraibet
Chief, Statistics,
Planning and
Criminology Division,
Kuwaiti Police

1

[Saying the current upsurge in violent crime in Kuwait is attributable to Iraq's invasion and occupation of the country in 1990-91]: Not many societies have experienced a total occupation, as happened here in Kuwait. We are witnessing a new phenomenon of human society, and of our society's behavior . . . The Iraqi occupation was a time of complete lawlessness. During that time, people witnessed so much killing [by the Iraqis], so much looting—even the traffic lights were stolen. And the people lived in that environment for so long. We are just now beginning to see its full effects.

Los Angeles Times,
8-10:(A)14.

Edward Luck
President,
United Nations Association
of the U.S.A.

2

[On the possibility that the U.S. might use military power to enforce the UN's demand that Iraq destroy its facilities for weapons of mass destruction]: Either the U.S. is part of the multilateral decision-making on this or it's not—you can't just be a partner to the UN when it's convenient. If you push too hard on the question of using force [against Iraq], you might risk losing some of your support for enforcing sanctions and the disarmament of Iraq. I don't think the U.S. wants to do that . . . I think [U.S. officials are] not sure that politically it's so desirable either with the American public or internationally or so certain that it's going to work . . . As long as [Iraqi President Saddam Hussein and his people] are in power in Baghdad, they're going to want to acquire weapons of mass destruction. It's going to require having a UN presence there for a long, long time.

The Christian Science Monitor,
3-23:6.

Abdul Rahim Malouh
Member, executive committee,
Palestine Liberation Organization

3

[On the effect of the disintegration of the Soviet Union on the PLO]: It was a shattering blow. The PLO was stripped of its major international ally, while at the same time Israel's ally, the U.S., has emerged stronger than ever.

The Christian Science Monitor,
5-6:12.

Abdul-Aziz Masaeed
Speaker,
Kuwaiti National Council

4

[Criticizing American suggestions that, following the U.S.-led Persian Gulf war that pushed Iraq out of its occupation of Kuwait in 1991, Kuwait should become more of a democracy]: America did not bring us back to our country. If it weren't for the wisdom of our government and the help of Saudi Arabia, the Gulf Cooperation Council, Egypt and Syria, we wouldn't have been liberated.

Newsweek, 6-15:17.

Taher Masri
Former Prime Minister
of Jordan

5

[On the current Arab-Israeli peace talks]: No practical progress has been made, but psychological progress has been made. First, the peace negotiations are still going on. Second, the Arab population and the Israeli population are dealing with that event as a fact now. People are watching the news. They are seeing things that used to be taboo—Arabs and Israelis sitting around a table, smiling and shaking hands. They may believe in it or not believe in it, but there it is in front of their eyes.

The Washington Post, 2-24:(A)13.

Abdel-Jabbar Mohsen
Press aide to
Iraqi President Saddam Hussein

6

[On the UN's inspection team that is combing Iraq for evidence of that country's weapons of

(ABDEL-JABBAR MOHSEN)

mass destruction]: We owe nothing to the [UN] Security Council. We have nothing else to do but despise them . . . and march ahead, trampling on their decisions and the resolutions of their council under our feet.

Los Angeles Times, 7-28:(A)8.

Richard W. Murphy
Former Assistant Secretary
for Near Eastern and South
Asian Affairs,
Department of State
of the United States
1

We [the U.S.] have a flat-out, frank, up-front disagreement with Israel, because the way it's proceeding on [Jewish] settlements [in the occupied territories] is destructive to the [Arab-Israeli] peace process. But the ties that bind are still very real. There's no basis for speculating that the U.S. is turning its back or pulling the plug on Israel.

The Christian Science Monitor,
3-20:2.

Ghanem al-Najjar
Director, Kuwaiti Association
for the Defense of War Victims
2

[Saying many Kuwaitis are still concerned about Iraq, which invaded and took over Kuwait in 1990 and was pushed out by U.S.-led forces in the Persian Gulf war of 1991]: Kuwaitis don't feel secure at all. [Iraqi President] Saddam Hussein showed us what "secure borders" mean. They don't mean anything.

The Christian Science Monitor,
10-13:3.

Ali Akbar Nategh Nuri
Former Minister of the Interior
of Iran
3

Our hatred toward crimes committed by the U.S. in Iran and in the Islamic world is immense.

Speculation about a possible resumption of ties with the U.S. is ridiculous.

The Christian Science Monitor,
5-7:2.

David R. Obey
United States Representative,
D-Wisconsin
4

[On the controversy over whether the U.S. should provide loan guarantees to help Israel settle immigrants in the occupied territories]: I do not feel any particular obligation . . . to enforce the agenda of any set of Israeli politicians within their own country . . . If we are to move in the teeth of [U.S.] taxpayer concern, we had better be sure . . . that the [guarantees] are provided in the context of [Israeli] policy that is consistent with American interests and policy.

At House Appropriations Subcommittee
on Foreign Operations hearing,
Washington, D.C., Feb. 21/
The Washington Post, 2-22:(A)14.

John Cardinal O'Connor
Roman Catholic Archbishop
of New York
5

Israel-bashing [by some in the U.S.] is not only disgraceful, it is not only a betrayal and is not only morally irresponsible, but is very dangerous . . . If the rug is pulled out from under Israel, and if suddenly the whole world is given to understand that the United States might even be washing its hands of Israel, I would be surprised if [the Israelis] didn't get very edgy, if the situation didn't become very volatile and that dreaded first shot of a pre-emptive war [against the Arabs] might not begin in Israel.

Before International Jewish Committee
for Inter-religious Consultations,
New York, N.Y., March 31/
The New York Times, 4-1:(A)7.

Ehud Olmert
Minister of Health of Israel
6

It is almost impossible for Israel to do anything to satisfy the U.S. [Bush] Administration, which has set out to do almost everything to antagonize the interests of the state of Israel.

To American Jews visiting Israel/
The Christian Science Monitor,
3-20:1.

Yossi Olmert
Director, Israeli Government
Press Office

1

There is no "new order" in the Middle East. In some countries there is more repression. In Algeria, you have a rise of Islamic fundamentalism and a military reaction that has sent tremors through the region. Meanwhile, Iran has Iraq as the new monster, arming itself and trying to extend its influence at the expense of the United States. It's therefore a testimony to the diplomatic brilliance [of U.S. Secretary of State James Baker] that the United States was able to create a post-[Persian Gulf] war peace process out of nothing. The Americans have created a good framework. But can they change the nature of these countries? How can you change [Syrian President] Hafez Assad?

The Washington Post, 2-24:(A)11.

Daniel S. Papp
Professor of international affairs,
Georgia Institute of Technology

2

[On last year's Persian Gulf war, in which a U.S.-led coalition forced Iraq out of Kuwait]: I would argue that the Persian Gulf war was worth the price we paid because it did have two positive outcomes aside from getting [Iraqi President] Saddam Hussein out of Kuwait. First, it illustrated the American capability to put together a very diverse coalition. It was one of the most adroit diplomatic, political maneuvers of recent years. Second, it was a crucial factor in bringing the Israelis and the Arabs to the peace table. The Persian Gulf war was not a war fought purely for oil. For one thing, it was appropriate to demonstrate that in the 1990s invading one's neighbor [as Iraq did with Kuwait] is not the way

to solve one's problems. The international community did come together in strong support of getting Saddam out of Kuwait. At the same time, had we left Saddam there, he would have had control of something like 38 per cent of the world's known oil reserves and he would have been sitting there menacing Saudi Arabia. On that basis, it had to be done.

Interview/
The New York Times, 6-27:8.

Shimon Peres
Foreign Minister of Israel;
Former Prime Minister
of Israel

3

[On U.S.-Israeli relations now that the Cold War between the East and the West is over]: We remain the same partners with the same strengths, but with different goals. Previously we had to balance the world; now we have to advance the people, economically and politically, which is even more difficult. If previously we had to confront the Russians, now we have to confront the situation. Because the best peace paintings, hung on deteriorating walls, will fall down. We need different walls, not just different paintings. And I think it is in the interests of the U.S. to see the Middle East reconstructed.

Interview, Jerusalem, Israel,
Aug. 4/
The Christian Science Monitor,
8-5:4.

4

[On current Syrian-Israeli negotiations]: Today, the problem is not to negotiate frontiers, but to defend your civilian population, and the Syrians know the Russians are out, and no longer can a country in this region [survive by prolonging conflicts] . . . Until now, the Middle East was concerned about how to please its leaders. The time has come to think how to please its people, and to take care of their economies, their shortages. The leaders won't be able to control the present situation forever . . . [Syrian President Hafez al-Assad has learned from the experience of deposed Romanian dictator Nicolae

(SHIMON PERES)

Ceausescu that] you can have all your might and all your secrets and all your armies and all your control, and then 400 undisciplined students start to boo, and put an end to all your powers.

To reporters,
Jerusalem, Israel,
September 14/
The Washington Post,
9-15:(A)20.

Edward Perkins
United States Ambassador/
Permanent Representative
to the United Nations

1

[On the UN-imposed embargo against Iraq, except for food and medicine]: If food is not reaching the needy in Iraq, it is because the Iraqi regime has diverted food imports to the military and security forces which allow [President] Saddam [Hussein] to maintain his brutal dictatorship.

At UN Security Council session,
United Nations, New York,
Nov. 23/
The Christian Science Monitor,
11-25:2.

Ross Perot
American industrialist

2

[Criticizing the U.S. Bush Administration for building up Iraq, which invaded and took over Kuwait resulting in the U.S.-led Persian Gulf war against Iraq in 1991]: For 10 years, we created [Iraqi President] Saddam Hussein with your taxpayer money. [Shortly before Iraq's invasion of Kuwait,] our President was sending delegations over to burp and diaper and pamper Saddam Hussein and tell him how nice he was . . . [Iraq's invasion of Kuwait threatened Bush's] manhood, [and] off we go into the wild blue yonder with the lives of our servicemen at risk because of 10 years of stupid mistakes.

Broadcast interview/
"Today," NBC-TV, 6-11.

William B. Quandt
Senior fellow,
Brookings Institution
(United States)

3

[On U.S. relations with Israel now that the Cold War is over]: In the Cold War, the rules of the game [for the U.S.] were you didn't lean too hard on your friends. Israel played it to the hilt. What you see now is that [U.S. President] Bush has none of that sort of sentimental attachment to Israel that Presidents [Ronald] Reagan and [Lyndon] Johnson had. He has a more distant personal style, and the strategic rationale [for supporting Israel 100 per cent] which developed in the 1980s is essentially gone.

The Washington Post, 3-23:(A)12.

Yitzhak Rabin
Chairman,
Labor Party of Israel;
Former Prime Minister
of Israel

4

[Comparing himself with Israeli Prime Minister Yitzhak Shamir, against whom he is running for Prime Minister in the forthcoming elections]: I believe that our position on the substance of the peace negotiations [with the Arabs] is different. [I] will focus on negotiations with the Palestinians from the [occupied] territories on the creation of autonomy offering, first, general elections in the territories. Second, [I] will freeze all of what I call the political [Jewish] settlements [in the territories]—that no doubt, in my mind, are in contradiction with the bona fide negotiation for [Palestinian] autonomy. [I] had opposed settling in the densely populated [Arab] areas. At the same time, [I] would not freeze building in greater Jerusalem and its vicinity and along the confrontation lines in the Jordan Valley and the Golan Heights. [I] will change the order of national priorities. I believe that Israel faces a period in which the threat to our security—to the very existence of Israel—has been reduced as a result of the change on the international scene [the breakup of the Soviet Union] . . . [I] do not see as our ultimate goal the whole land of Israel under Israel's sovereignty. We are willing to compromise, including territorial compromise.

Interview, Tel Aviv, Israel/
Los Angeles Times, 6-16:(H)2.

Yitzhak Rabin
Prime Minister of Israel

1

[Addressing Palestinians]: [You are] our foes today and partners in peaceful coexistence tomorrow. We have been fated to live together on the same patch of land, in the same country. We lead our lives with you, beside you and against you. You have failed in the war against us. One hundred years of your bloodshed and terror against us have brought you only suffering, humiliation, bereavement and pain. You have lost thousands of your sons and daughters, and you are losing ground all the time. For 44 years now, you have been living under a delusion. Your leaders have led you through lies and deceit. They have missed every opportunity, rejected all our [Israel's] proposals for a settlement, and taken you from one tragedy to another. Listen to us, if only this once. We offer you the fairest and most viable proposal from our standpoint today: autonomy, with all its advantages and limitations. You will not get everything you want. Neither will we . . . Don't lose this opportunity that may never return.

Before Israeli Knesset (Parliament),
Jerusalem, Israel, July 13/
The Washington Post, 7-14:(A)9.

2

As [the new Israeli] Prime Minister, I changed Israel's polition on peace negotiations [with the Arabs]. I made it clear that we are ready to go along with Resolution 242 of the UN Security Council, which specifies withdrawal to secure and recognized boundaries in the context of peace. The former government of Israel stressed "peace for peace" and nothing else. But I also said that the dimension of the territorial concession should not be negotiated before we know that Syria is ready for a full-fledged peace, with open boundaries for the movement of people in

groups, diplomatic relations including embassies, and at least an agreement in principle for the normalization of relations. Secondly, I said that a peace treaty between Syria and Israel should not be influenced by the success or lack of success of negotiations with the other Arab delegations. I don't feel that Syria is ready for a full-fledged peace and a peace treaty that will stand on its own. Many Israelis wonder how Syria can be involved in the peace negotiations while allowing rejectionist Palestinian organizations with headquarters in Damascus to call for the Palestinians to withdraw from those negotiations.

Interview, Jerusalem, Israel/
Time, 11-30:50.

3

[Defending Israel's deportation of 415 Palestinians who Israel claims are anti-Israeli Islamic militants]: Just as the state of Israel was the first to recognize the Iraqi nuclear danger [when it attacked and destroyed an Iraqi nuclear reactor years ago], thus we stand first today in the line of fire against the danger of extremist Islam . . . I will admit there is no pity in my heart for [the deportees]. The protesting and advice-giving world that is flinging criticism at us is the same world that didn't say a word when 300,000 Palestinians were thrown out of Kuwait. And this is the same world that day by day and night by night sees thousands die—slaughtered, butchered, raped—in Bosnia and doesn't lift a finger.

Before Israeli Knesset (Parliament),
Jerusalem, Israel, Dec. 21/
The New York Times, 12-22:(A)1.

Elie Rekhkess
Specialist on Israeli Arabs,
Dayan Center for
Middle Eastern Studies,
Tel Aviv University (Israel)

4

[On the deportation of 415 Palestinians from Israel because of their alleged terrorist ties]: The vigor and determination of the protests by Israeli Arabs in recent days is unprecedented. The mass deportation touched on one of the most sensitive

(ELIE REKHKESS)

issues for any Palestinian—the fear, real or imagined, of being deported.

The New York Times, 12-31:(A)3.

Reuven Rivlin
Member of Israeli Knesset
(Parliament)

1

We believe here in Israel in miracles. We have a direct line to God. It's a local call.

The New York Times, 4-6:(A)6.

Henry Schuler
Director,
energy security program,
Center for Strategic and
International Studies
(United States)

2

As long as we [the U.S.] have a nice, friendly regime in Riyadh [Saudi Arabia] that is beholden to the United States, there shouldn't be any threat to oil prices or supplies. Nobody else matters.

The Christian Science Monitor,
4-1:4.

Charles E. Schumer
United States Representative,
D-New York

3

[Criticizing the U.S. Bush Administration for tilting toward and aiding Iraq prior to that country's invasion and take-over of Kuwait, which resulted in last year's Persian Gulf war]: Certain aspects of this affair bear the marks of a major scandal involving at best improper [Administration] conduct, and at worst criminal activity by U.S. government officials. We already know [President Bush's] biggest foreign-policy success, the Persian Gulf war, was made necessary by his most enormous foreign-policy failure, his tilt toward Iraq.

The New York Times,
5-22:(A)6.

Brent Scowcroft
Assistant to President
of the United States George Bush
for National Security Affairs

4

I think [the children of Iraq] ought to tell their mothers and daddies to get rid of [Iraqi President Saddam Hussein] . . . [During the current international embargo against Iraq,] we are not keeping any food, medicine, any of those things from the Iraqi people. Saddam Hussein is. He's stockpiling it in different places. He's distributing it only to his friends. That's the problem.

Broadcast interview/
"Meet the Press," NBC-TV, 4-12.

Ibrahim Majid al-Shaheen
State Minister for
Municipal Affairs of Kuwait

5

[The late] King Faisal of Saudi Arabia used to say there are three great powers in the world: America, Russia and Kuwait. Indeed, we [Kuwaitis] had an opinion and a unique position on every international issue. But now, a lot of Kuwaitis say we should have policies that match our real size.

The New York Times, 5-6:(A)4.

Yitzhak Shamir
Prime Minister of Israel

6

The Arab delegations [at the current Arab-Israeli peace conference] are making all kinds of difficulties. The Syrians are not interested in any success in the region. The Jordanians have an interest, but they are very weak and they are afraid to act independently. They are afraid of the Syrians. They are afraid of the Palestinians. The Palestinians do not understand the realities of the situation. They don't understand the care with which they have to negotiate and the limits that they originally accepted. They are not united. They have 14 members that give you the impression they have 14 delegations.

Interview, Jerusalem, Israel/
U.S. News & World Report,
2-3:40.

339

(YITZHAK SHAMIR)

1

Everybody must understand that Israel cannot always perform miracles to absorb so many people without help from the outside. We cannot absorb hundreds of thousands of [Jewish] immigrants from the Soviet Union—whom no other country would accept—without getting some support. We are not asking for grants. We are not asking for loans. We are only asking for [loan] guarantees [from the U.S.] to help us raise only a part of the money we will need, and we will repay every penny of it.

Interview, Jerusalem, Israel/
U.S. News & World Report,
2-3:40.

2

We are concerned about all that is tied with our future borders because this is the basis of our security. We have to take into account the dimensions of our country. We are a very, very small country, and in our country not miles but kilometers count. It has to be clear to everybody that going back to the [border] lines of '67 is a suicidal process for Israel.

Interview, Jerusalem, Israel/
The New York Times, 4-3:(A)5.

3

[Saying Israel has permanent sovereignty over the whole of Jerusalem]: Jerusalem is not a subject for [Arab-Israeli] bargaining. Just as a person does not bargain over his heart, so the people of Israel will not bargain over its nations's heart of hearts. The Parliament will never again be a gunshot away from the border, and residents of the city will never again walk the streets under the stare of the enemy's binoculars.

At ceremony marking the 25th anniversary
of Israel's reunification of Jerusalem,
May 31/
The New York Times, 6-1:(A)3.

4

We need more, more [Jewish settlements in the occupied territories] to prevent forever the

establishment of this calamity called the state of Palestine. It will not rise. It will not be.

Pesagot, Israeli-occupied West Bank/
The New York Times, 6-15:(A)4.

Zalman Shoval
Israeli Ambassador
to the United States

5

[Criticizing the U.S. reticence to provide loan guarantees for Israel]: Israel has the potential within a few years to become one of the new economic miracles, like Hong Kong, like Singapore, like Taiwan. We have the will to work, we have the knowledge. What we don't have is the capital. The problem is that the rest of the world is looking to Washington for the right signal [on the issue of loan guarantees]. They are saying: If Israel is not good enough politically or economically for America, its closest ally, why should we go ahead and jump into the cold water?

Interview, Boston, Mass./
The Christian Science Monitor,
3-25:9.

Steven L. Spiegel
Historian of
Israeli-American affairs,
University of California,
Los Angeles

6

[On the recent election in Israel in which the Labor Party headed by Yitzhak Rabin won over the incumbent Likud Party headed by Yitzhak Shamir]: Neither American politicians nor American Jews feel comfortable in a state of constant conflict with the Israelis, and that has been the case to some degree since the 1982 Lebanon war, and was really accelerated under the last Likud government. Now there is more than a sigh of relief out there. American officials and American Jews are now so convinced that life will be easier under [new Prime Minister] Rabin, that it is going to be a self-fulfilling prophecy. He will really have to work to mess it up. Likud had its stalwarts in the American Jewish community, but the overwhelming majority wanted Rabin to win this election. It is more than relief that people

(STEVEN L. SPIEGEL)

are expressing—it is a sense that our Israeli friends are back.

June 24/
The New York Times, 6-25:(A)6.

Ehud Sprinzak
Political scientist,
Hebrew University (Israel)
1

[On the Israeli government's expansion of Jewish settlements in the occupied territories under pressure from religious groups]: The ultra-Orthodox and the extreme right, the very religious, have never been so powerful in Israeli politics. Because of their audacity and the *chutzpah* of the religious settlers, [Prime Minister Yitzhak] Shamir may soon have to make a decision about whether he is prime minister of a state that has settlers or head of a religious fundamentalist movement which has a state.

Los Angeles Times, 1-14:(H)1.

Kenneth W. Stein
Associate professor
of Middle Eastern history
and political science,
Emory University (United States);
Director of Middle Eastern studies,
Carter Presidential Center
2

[On last year's Persian Gulf war, in which a U.S.-led coalition forced Iraq out of Kuwait]: After the war, the [U.S.] Bush Administration took the attitude that one of two things would happen: either there would be a coup within the [Iraqi] military that would oust [Iraqi President] Saddam [Hussein], or that economic sanctions would cause internal turmoil that would bring him to his knees. But Saddam is the quintessential survivor. Saddam lives to fight another day. And the irony is that he may well outlast in power the man [U.S. President Bush] who defeated him militarily.

Interview/
The New York Times, 6-27:8.

Gerald Steinberg
Authority on defense issues,
Bar Illan University (Israel)
3

The Cold War is over. The United States doesn't need Israel to keep the Soviet Union out of the Middle East. It doesn't need to know about the results of weapons in Arab-Israeli wars because it is no longer competing with another superpower that supplies Israel's enemies. It had a problem with Iraq, but it didn't need Israel for that. The old security rationale for maintaining the relationship with Israel has largely evaporated. Now what we're seeing is a struggle in the United States over whether Israel ought to be given access to the next generation of U.S. military technology. Without a security rationale, Israel could lose that argument.

The Washington Post, 3-18:(A)16.

Paul E. Tsongas
Candidate for the 1992
Democratic U.S.
Presidential nomination;
Former United States Senator,
D-Massachusetts
4

[On proposed U.S. loan guarantees for Israel]: The U.S. should not erect obstacles to [Soviet Jews who wish to immigrate to Israel] by politicizing this humanitarian issue. The loan guarantees don't detract from U.S. domestic priorities. Israel has a perfect record of repaying its loans. Tying the settlements [by Israel in the occupied territories] to the loan guarantees was wrong. Settlements are an issue to be negotiated at the peace conference.

Los Angeles Times, 3-17:(H)6.

Harry Wall
Jerusalem director,
Anti-Defamation League of B'nai B'rith
5

[On the current chill in U.S.-Israeli relations]: For the first time, there is political legitimacy to using U.S. aid as a sanction [against Israel]. Everything points to a separation between the two states—not a divorce, but growing alienation and separation. The warmth has gone.

The Christian Science Monitor, 3-20:4.

PART THREE

General

Robert Altman
Motion-picture director

1

[Greed for money is] a terrible thing that's happened to our country, to our culture—and I'm talking about *all* of Western culture. And it's crushing the artists. People are avariciously out there . . . It's like what they did to the art market, selling paintings for $93-million and all that. It's just ridiculous . . . There's no time or room for this wonderful stuff [art] that really entertains the population of this earth—not in terms of just entertaining them but it gives them pause to think, gives them reason to feel important, to be important, to put their own ideas together with existing ideas. It's a reason for being, the reason for it all.

Interview/
Film Comment, May-June:28.

Bill Clinton
Governor of Arkansas (D);
President-elect
of the United States

2

The cumulative impact of this banalization of sex and violence in the popular culture is a net negative for America. I think the question is, what can Hollywood do, not just to entertain, but to raise the human spirit?

Interview/
USA Today, 11-13:(D)2.

William E. Dannemeyer
United States Representative,
R-California

3

[On whether the NEA is in danger of losing its Federal funding]: I would hope so . . . At a time when we're adding to a $480-billion national debt, to think that we can afford to spend $173-million on the NEA is a luxury that, in my judgment, we can no longer afford. The arts contribute a great deal to our society, and private

sources fund them to a great extent, and that's the way it ought to be.

Interview/
The Christian Science Monitor,
3-23:9.

David Emmes
Producing artistic director,
South Coast Repertory,
Costa Mesa, Calif.

4

More and more corporations are saying that they want their monies to go into arts education, to make up for the lack of it in public schools. But what they have to realize is that our educational programs are fueled by the main artistic work we do. My concern is that if monies become so restricted to educational outreach programs, if it becomes all the more difficult to fund the art purely, that eventually the institution becomes inhibited and compromised.

Daily Variety, 2-26:12.

Ernest Fleischmann
Managing director, Los Angeles
Philharmonic Orchestra

5

It sounds rather grandiloquent, but we must bring back a message to the average American about the importance the arts can occupy in anybody's life. We've done nothing. We've had no leadership in the arts for a long time. And I think some of that is due to the namby-pamby leadership in Washington at the National Endowment for the Arts.

Interview/
Connoisseur, February:94.

John E. Frohnmayer
Chairman,
National Endowment for the Arts
of the United States

6

When the [NEA's] reauthorization was passed in 1990, it was made very clear that it could not

WHAT THEY SAID IN 1992

fund obscenity, and we never would in the first place. And yet it's so galling to have people continue to talk about the Endowment and pornography in the same breath. And for Congress to feel it has to genuflect with each new piece of anti-obscenity legislation is disproportionate to what the situation requires . . . People who favor the arts should be cross-examining [NEA] critics. Find out what they find offensive and why. They certainly are quick to condemn but slow to ask what an artist is trying to accomplish . . . and most artists are trying to get a message out . . . Arts education in public schools has been on a decline since the early 1960s. The result has been a generation of adults who know little about the arts and who have little appreciation of them.

Los Angeles, Calif., Jan. 16/
Daily Variety, 1-17:2.

1

[Announcing his decision to resign as head of the NEA amid controversy over NEA funding of what some see as objectionable art]: I leave with the belief that this eclipse of the soul [new Congressional restrictions on what the NEA can fund] will soon pass and with it the lunacy that sees artists as enemies and ideas as demons.

At NEA staff meeting,
Washington, D.C., Feb. 21/
The Washington Post, 2-22:(A)1.

2

[What] has gone wrong [at the NEA are] the politicians who demand that the only art that be funded is that which will not offend a mainstream person. That perspective turns our whole system upside down. The First Amendment protects the speaker, not the listener. It protects the right to articulate an idea which may be offensive to some. And if we are going to fund the arts, we've got to be able to deal with ideas that are not mainstream. Otherwise, the funding of art is going to be elevator music, pablum. So for those who claim it's not a First Amendment issue, I think it is *more* than a First Amendment issue—it goes to the very soul of what this country is, being

able to accommodate differences and live with them. The government doesn't sponsor the ideas of any of the artists that we fund; it is merely the enabler that allows these things to happen. The analogy is that the government is the provider of the Hyde Park soapbox, and the artist is the provider of the ideas. The ideas can be in the whole spectrum of beliefs and values that are encompassed in the American people. But to hear some of our critics, you'd think there is a unified American value that somehow everybody can sign on to. That's not the case.

Interview/Newsweek, 3-16:69.

Philip Glass
Composer

3

What do we have against entertainment [being combined with art]? Is it the old American puritanism? The world of the flesh and the world of entertainment go together, and we have residual misgivings about the world of the flesh. As a people, we're not comfortable with that—you see it coming up in our right-wing politics all the time—and this gets into the American soul. We're suspicious of entertainment . . . and this is one of our problems as a culture.

Interview, New York, N.Y./
The Christian Science Monitor,
11-16:14.

Malcolm MacKay
Head of the non-profit division,
Russell Reynolds Associates,
executive-placement firm

4

The job of directing a museum has become so complex and demanding that it's important for museums to cast their nets as broadly as possible [when looking for a director]. In the old days, there was an old boys network. The problem was that it was too narrow. Art historical and curatorial qualifications—having an eye—was all that was required of a director in the past. That is still essential, but other qualities are needed now . . . It's no secret in 1992 that the biggest problem facing museums is funding. Many museums are just dying.

Interview/
Los Angeles Times, 8-5:(F)6.

Ian McKellen
British actor

1

I myself am entirely a product of the English system of public funding for the arts. Without such funding, the arts wouldn't exist in the national-kingdom. The Royal National Theatre was built by an act of Parliament. Every theatre outside of London is owned and run by public funding . . . Because the nation funds the arts doesn't mean to say that it can tell the artist what to do. It's only in Communist countries where artists are funded and told by the government what to produce . . . [The theatre] never has been [self-supporting]. When you're creating a body of work, a repertory company, it's a very, very expensive way to put on plays. It requires a permanence of actors, directors, writers. Yet in return, it allows for the creation of a certain style of work, the protection of new work, the exploration of new ways of presenting theatre. And the commercial sector eventually feeds off of this effort.

Interview,
San Francisco, Calif./
Daily Variety, 9-15:18.

Michael Medved
Film critic; Co-host,
"Sneak Previews," PBS-TV

2

We are now seeing the popular culture taken over by the same nihilistic mentality that has already wrecked classical music, the visual arts and the world of poetry. Once upon a time, people had the vision—in the most general sense—that what made art worthwhile, lasting and praiseworthy was that it was created for the greater glory of God, in one sense or another. That is what inspired Shakespeare and Tolstoy and Beethoven and Mozart and Dickens, even though there is obviously social protest in a lot of his work. But there was some sense of the larger purposes of art. And that was also true to a great extent in the so-called Golden Age of American movies. In the latter part of the 20th century, we have accepted increasingly this idea that any kind of art that emphasizes human happiness or

human possibilities—that has an optimistic tenor to it—can't be taken seriously.

Interview/
Christianity Today, 4-27:40.

Charlotte Murphy
Executive director,
National Association of
Artists' Organizations

3

[On the resignation of John Frohnmayer as head of the NEA]: I just think it's really regrettable that what Frohnmayer leaves behind is an NEA that has been compromised and no longer has the trust of the American artists. All along, the NEA has been a political target for the far right, and [President] Bush never once tried to fully support either Frohnmayer or the NEA.

Feb. 21/
Los Angeles Times, 2-22:(A)16.

Anne-Imelda Radice
Acting Chairman,
National Endowment for the
Arts of the United States

4

[On NEA funding of controversial art projects]: If we find a proposal that does not have the widest audience . . . even though it may have been done very sincerely and with the highest intentions, we just can't afford to fund that. The concerns of the taxpayers, the concerns of the Congress . . . have as much weight [as artistic merit] . . . To me, when the obvious sexual nature, sexual message, is the only thing you see or the first thing you see or the overwhelming thing that you experience, the American public has given us a lot of guidance on this, and Congress has given us a lot of guidance, saying they don't want us to spend money on that particular type of art.

Before House Interior Appropriations
Subcommittee, Washington, D.C., May 5/
The Washington Post, 5-6:(A)1,7.

5

[On criticism of the way the NEA decides which art projects get its funding]: The arts

WHAT THEY SAID IN 1992

endowment is a Federal agency—your tax dollars, my tax dollars. It has to follow legislative mandates and guidelines. There are rules. These rules are different than private foundations, private money, personal investment choices in the arts, and for 27 years the arts endowment has done a magnificent job in this country. For the past three years, it has taken it on the chin, oftentimes very unfairly. All the good work it has done and continues to do gets little attention; a minuscule number of grants or possible grants or things we didn't fund that we get credit for have captured the American people's attention. They've been upset, they've told their Congressmen, and their Congressmen have told us.

At Governor's Conference on the Arts,
Sacramento, Calif., May 27/
Daily Variety, 5-28:13.

Peter Sellars
Artistic director,
Los Angeles (Calif.) Festival

1

The arts are the opportunity to open a frank, public discussion [of urban problems] without violence. The arts are a way to work out our problems without having to kill someone . . . The arts are a bridge we can create to let you venture into a part of the city where you would never have dreamed of going . . . Art is value and it is values, and those are two things we need now. America has got it wrong—the arts are not the add-on line to the budget. Without a cultural life, you have no economic life; society breaks down. It is the glue that holds us together . . . Remove it and nothing functions.

At Governor's Conference on the Arts,
Sacramento, Calif./
Daily Variety, 5-29:26.

2

Art is about doing, rolling up your sleeves and doing something in an atmosphere of generosity and moral acuity. Most people look at things as they are, and are stymied. An artist never looks at

something for what it is, but what it might become.

Interview, Toronto, Canada/
The Christian Science Monitor,
10-2:13.

Michael Shapiro
Director-designate,
Los Angeles County Museum
of Art,
Los Angeles, Calif.

3

Museums display examples that are picked by people who have devoted their lives to them. The question is, once they are selected, how are they explained to someone who has no experience? We probably need a place in the entrance areas of the museum that tells you where you are in the world, what you are able to see and how it relates to other areas and to your own experience.

Interview/
Los Angeles Times, 8-28:(F)20.

Jean Sousa
Associate director,
department of museum education,
Art Institute of Chicago (Ill.)

4

[On her museum's project making art more accessible, especially to young people, by using videos, puzzles and other hands-on techniques]: We've combined masterpieces of art with a learning environment . . . We're trying something new. I don't know of other [art museums] that are doing this. Parents and kids can start here and then go to other parts of the museum with a better understanding of the works of art . . . It helps them feel more comfortable . . . Museums are trying to become more accessible. It's a mandate.

Interview, Chicago, Ill./
The Christian Science Monitor, 12-7:11.

Robert Storr
Curator of contemporary art,
Museum of Modern Art,
New York, N.Y.

5

Art is no longer an elite activity, in the same way it once was. Now the audience is large . . .

(ROBERT STORR)

Anyone can look and think. That's not just the preserve of people who are [art] professionals . . . People should feel that [art] is there for them to think about, and that the process of doing that is far more important than the specific conclusions drawn—that having an answer to a show as you leave it is not only not important, it's in general terms antithetical to the experience of the show. It's okay for people not to know what they're looking at. The reason they're there is to spend time with the installation and to let their own imaginations click in . . . Curators are there to be intermediaries but not to be decisive voices. That robs people of their experience.

At museum tour and interview,
Newport Beach, Calif./
Los Angeles Times, 6-12:(A)14.

Kirk Varnedoe
Director of painting and sculpture,
Museum of Modern Art,
New York, N.Y.

1

Politicians right and left are both busy these days warning you that imagined worlds—from [photographer Robert] Mapplethorpe to [TV character] Murphy Brown, and from rap music to Romantic poetry—will enslave your thoughts, determine your politics or morals, and guide your deeds in some specific way, for good or evil . . . [But art is most powerful] when it orchestrates perplexity, fails to confirm what you already know, and instead sends you away temporarily disoriented but newly attuned to experience in ways that are perhaps even more powerful because they are vague, rogue and indeterminate.

At Stanford University commencement,
June 14/
The New York Times, 6-15:(A)11.

Ben Wattenberg
Senior fellow,
American Enterprise Institute

2

Today, only the American democratic culture has legs. Only Americans have the sense of mission—and gall—to engage in global cultural advocacy . . . We run the most potent cultural imperium in history.

The Christian Science Monitor,
3-30:13.

Journalism

Arthur Ashe
Former tennis player

1

[Criticizing the press for revealing he has AIDS]: Are you [in the press] going to be cold, hard, crass purveyors of the facts just for the sake of peoples' right to know, under the guise of freedom of the press—or are you going to show a little sensitivity about some things? . . . I really wish to question your values [and] tweak your journalistic sensibilities. I am not easily rattled, as most friends would tell you about me, but I was very irritated and disappointed at being put in what amounted to a no-win situation: that is, to protect what I thought and assumed was a right any American had to keep personal matters private.

At National Press Club,
Washington, D.C., May 26/
Los Angeles Times, 5-27:(C)2.

Merv Aubespin
Associate editor for development,
"Louisville (Ky.) Courier-Journal";
Former president, National Association
of Black Journalists

2

[On being a black journalist]: Even if they [white management] promote you, they're condescending. Even if they send you out on a story and you do it, it's an exception . . . They think they're doing you a favor, when in fact they're doing themselves a favor, because they're tapping into a constituency out there that's dying for some attention.

The Washington Post, 8-22:(D)7.

Richard Bergenheim
Editor-in-chief,
Christian Science
Publishing Society

3

[Our] newspaper has had 85 years to learn what it means to be *The Christian Science*

Monitor—and it is still learning. Our radio and television activities have had far less time. They have the benefit of the paper's experience, but new lessons need to be learned . . . We need to master these tools of the 20th century if we are to be ready for the work that lies ahead in the 21st; otherwise we are in danger of becoming an artifact of the 19th century.

At annual meeting
of First Church of Christ, Scientist,
Boston, Mass., June 8/
The Christian Science Monitor,
6-10:9.

David Brinkley
Journalist; Host,
"This Week With
David Brinkley," ABC-TV

4

[On the state of U.S. network-TV news commentary]: I would say that it is very sad, weak, wan, sick, and almost not there.

Los Angeles Times, 5-16:(F)1.

Barbara Bush
Wife of President
of the United States George Bush

5

[Speaking to Hillary Clinton, wife of President-elect Bill Clinton]: Avoid this crowd [journalists] like the plague. And if they quote you, make damn sure they heard you.

During Mrs. Clinton's visit
to the White House,
Washington, D.C., Nov. 19/
The New York Times, 11-20:(A)11.

George Bush
President of the United States

6

[On the press' use of "anonymous sources" for articles about his Administration]: What I'd say to the American people is: Please ask for a name

(GEORGE BUSH)

to be placed next to the source so I can get mad at the guy who's doing this. It's strange out there. It's strange.

News conference,
Washington, D.C., March 11/
The Washington Post, 3-13:(A)23.

1

[On whether a Presidential candidate's behavior in his private life should be an issue in the election campaign]: I think private lives basically should be off the agenda, and I think public trust should be on the agenda . . . If there's evidence that someone has betrayed the public trust, well, then ask him about it. But I just think there's too much sleaze [in today's campaigning]. I think you've [the press] gone too far in your profession. I think the magazines have gone too far . . . People's lives are just destroyed by sleaze and it's not worth the candle. I think for years there were better guidelines on that whole question of sleaziness. It's yellow journalism, people waiting to jump on something—"Oh, well, I had to write this because somebody else did." That's sick. And I don't like it.

Interview, Washington, D.C./
Time, 8-24:24.

2

I don't believe [the news media] has the right to disrupt a family just to get a news story. Character is important, but if reporters must tear up a family and destroy family privacy to get a story— that story isn't worth printing.

USA Today, 10-30:(A)11.

James Carville
Senior strategist,
Bill Clinton's 1992 Democratic
Presidential-election campaign

3

[News editors are] a bunch of drunks who get together after a [political] campaign and you talk and say, "We are not going to do this [pay atten-

tion to alleged scandals in candidates' personal lives] again." It's like detox. And then everybody gets out of detox and, wow, here comes Gennifer Flowers [who claimed she had an affair with now-President-elect Bill Clinton] and it was just like a jigger of whiskey for everybody at the bar and everybody's killing each other to get it. And all of a sudden everyone's got a giant hangover and says, "I don't like this." And that accounted for better coverage [of the just-concluded Presidential campaign].

Before Associated Press Managing Editors,
Honolulu, Hawaii, Nov. 21/
USA Today, 11-23:(A)4.

Bill Clinton
Governor of Arkansas (D);
Candidate for the 1992
Democratic Presidential nomination

4

One of the things that amazes me [in the Presidential campaign] is, if I don't say something, they [the press] say I'm not being candid, and if I tell the whole truth I'm [also] not being candid. You've got to calculate not what the truth is, apparently, but what the press will think the truth is, and what they will make jokes about. It's a terrible way to live.

At Florida A&M University,
April 23/
The New York Times, 4-24:(A)11.

Stanley Cloud
Washington bureau chief,
"Time" magazine

5

[On newly agreed guidelines for press coverage of future wars]: [The agreement] requires an act of faith on our part that the Pentagon negotiated in good faith, and I assume they did. But I am not naive and I don't assume there won't be continued tugs of war between the Pentagon and the press. This is certainly not the Ten Commandments, or even the Bill of Rights.

May 21/
The Washington Post, 5-22:(A)23.

Jeff Cohen
Executive director,
Fairness and Accuracy
in Reporting

1

[On revelations in the press that former tennis star Arthur Ashe has AIDS]: There is a long-standing journalistic rule that a public figure's private life should remain private unless it impacts his or her public responsibilities . . . Instead of investigating the private sphere regarding this or that celebrity with AIDS, mass media could be deploying investigative resources aimed at the public arena—the AIDS research effort, inadequacies in the public health-care system, and how homophobia has slowed the effort.

Los Angeles Times, 4-10:(A)26.

Kent Conrad
United States Senator,
D-North Dakota

2

I think the media also bear substantial responsibility for the frustrations people feel about government. Reporters are chasing every rabbit of scandal, and it's not healthy. Journalists have gone from a healthy skepticism to a destructive cynicism. The House-bank [scandal] has got far more attention than it deserved. Meantime, virtually no attention is being paid to the $400-billion worth of hot checks being written by the Federal government. I think the media fail to deal with substance in favor of any minor scandal that comes along.

Panel discussion,
Washington, D.C./Time, 6-8:65.

Thomas J. Downey
United States Representative,
D-New York

3

[Saying the press over-dramatizes its coverage of the scandals involving Congressional perks, check-bouncing at the House bank, etc.]: You have some of the best reporters in America in a frenzy, trying to make sure someone else hasn't gotten something first. There's a certain amount of righteousness in all this coverage that I find a little disturbing. You know what it's like to go home and have people look at you and think you're some sort of criminal? The country is in serious trouble, and it's not because of the House bank or the House post office or the perks.

The Washington Post, 4-9:(A)4.

Tom Farmer
Senior producer,
"Larry King Live," CNN-TV

4

[On the use of call-in TV interview shows by this year's U.S. Presidential candidates]: With the average sound bite on the evening newscasts trending below the nine-second range, voters are fed up and candidates look for another way to reach people. If you sit down and watch a guy for an hour, you will see him hit issues, cope with curve-ball phone calls. You will see how he reacts to a joke, to an unexpected question. You will get a full measure of the candidate.

The Christian Science Monitor,
10-8:14.

Fred W. Friendly
Former president, CBS News

5

Television news . . . has lost its way. I watch the nightly news. They're not really remembering what it is their job to do. If you don't make television important, there's not going to be any reason to be in the television business.

Interview, March 5/
Los Angeles Times, 3-7:(F)14.

Jack Germond
Journalist,
"The Baltimore Sun"

6

[On newspapers compared with TV news]: You could write your damn fingers off for 25 years and never have the same reach as television. Television is just a monster. Much as we [in the print media] hate to admit it, what the networks play is so much more influential than what we print. We really are writing for an elite. If

(JACK GERMOND)

I write 35 or 40 inches on what's happening in Pennsylvania, the people who are going to read that in *The Baltimore Sun* are people who are pretty damn interested in politics.

Interview, Philadelphia, Pa./
The Washington Post, 10-5:(C)4.

Al Gollin
Vice president
and director of research,
Newspaper Association of America

1

[A newspaper strike is] like a bolt of lightning that suddenly illuminates the landscape of readers' interests and commitments. It highlights for people their degree of reliance on the newspaper across the board.

USA Today, 7-29:(B)2.

Katharine Graham
Publisher,
"The Washington Post"

2

[On the effects on journalism of the press investigation that led to the Watergate scandal of the 1970s]: I think everybody in the world, all the young people in the world, went to journalism school and wanted to investigate everything. And I think they overdid it. I think that you have to investigate things, you have to be skeptical, but you shouldn't be vengeful. You have to be fair and you have to be careful.

Radio interview/
"Newsweek on the Air,"
AP Radio Network, 6-14.

Daniel C. Hallin
Political scientist,
University of California,
San Diego

3

[On the short "sound bites" used in today's newscasts when reporting statements by politicians]: It is hard to see what viewers gained by hearing [former President] Richard Nixon ramble in 1968 for 43 seconds about his Aunt Olive. But often it was extremely interesting—or so it seems to me, with 20 years' hindsight—to hear a politician, or occasionally a community leader or ordinary voter, utter an entire paragraph. One gained an understanding of the person's character and the logic of his or her argument that a 10-second sound bite could never provide.

The New York Times, 1-23:(A)10.

Tom Hannon
Political director,
Cable News Network

4

We're [CNN] a general news organization. That's what we do for a living, cover news. They [the other TV networks] cover news, do entertainment, sports events. In general, [other] network news has retrenched, given us an opportunity to serve the audience better. It's good news for us.

The Christian Science Monitor,
7-10:4.

Don Hewitt
Founding producer,
"60 minutes," CBS-TV

5

When there was a disaster, it used to be that people went to church and all held hands. Then television came along, and there was this wonderful feeling that while you were watching Walter Cronkite, millions of other Americans were sharing the emotional experience with you. Now the minute anything happens, they all run to CNN and think, "The whole *world* is sharing this experience with me."

Time, 1-6:24.

Jim Hoagland
Pulitzer Prize-winning reporter,
"The Washington Post"

6

The effect of CNN should be to persuade newspapers that the stenographic mode of reporting is obsolete, a real dinosaur. The simple

(JIM HOAGLAND)

news account of an event that much of our audience has already witnessed [on TV] is no longer sufficient. We've got to shift to a more analytical mode or find the story that TV couldn't or didn't cover.

Time, 1-6:26.

Brit Hume
White House correspondent,
ABC News

1

[Saying the press has been soft on Democratic U.S. Presidential nominee Bill Clinton and hard on U.S. President Bush during the current election campaign]: Some reporters are smitten with Clinton. There are things written about Bill Clinton and [his Vice Presidential running mate] Al Gore that I've never seen written, even by opinion reporters. I think there has been a double standard . . . Suddenly there's this wave of media concern, expressed with Victorian grimness, that seems only to apply to Republicans.

The Washington Post, 9-1:(A)7.

Bernard Ingham
Former Press Secretary
to the Prime Minister
of the United Kingdom
(Margaret Thatcher)

2

I don't think we want analysis [in news reporting]. What we want is reporting of the facts. People can form their own judgments. There are too damn many journalists analyzing the news.

Time, 1-6:26.

Walter Isaacson
Editor, "Time" magazine

3

I think one of the little secrets of journalism is that if you ask often enough, people aren't going to say no [to an interview]. They always resist giving an interview at first, they'll give you a couple of excuses, but you just keep going back

and saying, "Okay, how about now?" I've never had it happen that you start to work on a story and proceed with it and are unable to get the cooperation of the subject at hand. If you ring the doorbell often enough, people will want to talk about themselves—because, after all, their own life is the most interesting topic in the world to them.

Interview, New York, N.Y./
Publishers Weekly, 9-7:72.

Landon Jones
Managing editor,
"People" magazine

4

[On the success of his magazine]: We've tapped into a universal interest—that people are interested in people. It's so basic and fundamental that the appetite for it is enormous. I don't want to put down my sister publication, *Time*, at all. But suffice it to say that I think there are probably more people interested in personalities than issues.

Los Angeles Times, 2-13:(A)16.

Marvin Kalb
Director, Barone Center on
the Press, Politics and
Public Policy,
Harvard University

5

[On the plan by the TV networks to share pool coverage of the forthcoming New Hampshire Presidential primary]: There's certainly a potential for this kind of cut to have an impact on the quality of coverage. It's true that a pool is just as good for routine coverage of speeches, but any arrangement that diminishes the competitive fires of the networks worries me. This is yet another illustration of the power of economics to determine campaign coverage.

The New York Times, 1-10:(A)10.

6

[On the cooperation of TV news organizations with government law-enforcement agencies in the apprehension of criminals]: I've seen this on the air many, many times. Whenever

(MARVIN KALB)

there's a drug bust, there's a need for television to get pictures . . . It's great footage. But to do that, there has to be a deal [between the media and the government agency]. This may be a time when reporters ought to sit back and reflect on the degree to which they allow themselves to get caught up in a government operation.

The Washington Post, 1-18:(A)3.

Jeane J. Kirkpatrick
Senior fellow,
American Enterprise Institute;
Former United States Ambassador/
Permanent Representative
to the United Nations

1

There has been less attention on the misery in Somalia in the public focus. Ask the media why. It's the media that have failed to focus on them, just as there has been for so long so much less focus on human-rights violations in Burma, and in Vietnam for that matter, and in China. There's an element of arbitrariness about where the media focus and where the international institutions focus. It's very important that these major disasters be brought into international focus and international attention.

Interview/
USA Today, 8-11:(A)11.

Brian Lamb
Chief executive officer and host,
Cable-Satellite Public Affairs Network
(C-SPAN)

2

People seem to be concerned about the economy and their future, and the haves versus the have-nots. An awful lot of people seem to have the impression that some of the haves are [working] in TV [news], making big money and pontificating about what the world should be about . . . The politicians are beginning to respond because they have to if they want to get elected, but the media have been slow to respond to this mood of throwing the in's out . . . When people get into the journalism business, they

usually get into it because they love information and wanted to impart that. But today, TV news is agents, contracts and salaries. I'm not condemning them, because they're living in the world that was presented to them, but one of the motivations of C-SPAN was to present an alternative. I grew up in a three-network environment, and I always felt there was room for more.

Interview,
New York, N.Y./
Los Angeles Times, 7-13:(F)10.

David Laventhol
Publisher and chief executive,
"Los Angeles Times";
President,
Times Mirror Company

3

These are bad days for the newspaper industry in general. An industry evolution has been taking place since the advent of television, and we're seeing the end of head-to-head competition of metro dailies in most regions . . . We're in a several-front war. There are still a lot of niche positions, but there is only one spot per niche now.

The New York Times, 12-21:(C)3.

Jim Lehrer
Co-host, "MacNeil/Lehrer NewsHour,"
PBS-TV

4

[Criticizing news-media coverage of the current U.S. Presidential campaign]: I think we're in really serious trouble. I think we're losing our credibility. I think [people] don't understand why we ask nasty questions . . . why we play "gotcha" . . . why we ask about political strategy and polls and sex . . . As [his "NewsHour" co-host] Robert MacNeil says, it takes courage to be dull.

At forum sponsored by Harvard
University's Barone Center on the
Press, Politics and Public Policy,
New York, N.Y., July 12/
The Washington Post, 7-13:(A)11.

Suzanne Braun Levine
Editor,
"Columbia Journalism Review"

1

People are getting saturated with undigested news. They want more context, substance, more thought-out information . . . There's an assumption that people have no attention span. This assumes that if you try to get serious, people will tune out. [That's not true,] even self-defeating. If you assume people aren't going to pay attention, you throw things at them in disconnected globs, and then they really don't pay attention. But if complicated material is presented in a meaningful and accessible way, people will take the time to read it.

Interview, New Brunswick, N.J./
The Christian Science Monitor,
7-2:13.

Jerry L. Martin
Assistant Chairman for
Programs and Policy,
National Endowment for the
Humanities of the United States

2

The history of the country is really contained foremost in its newspapers. If you think of the original reports of the Lincoln-Douglas debates, or job lists that appeared in newspapers in the Great Depression—that's really the record of the life of the people.

The Christian Science Monitor,
7-2:12.

John McLaughlin
Political commentator

3

[On the free-for-all format of his TV discussion program *The McLaughlin Group*]: Does this depreciate journalism? Not one damned bit. Journalists can get very pompous, especially in the formalized days of *Meet the Press,* when they took themselves so damned seriously. This show demythologizes the press, and I think people like that.

Interview, Washington, D.C./
The New York Times, 12-16:(B)6.

Joshua Meyrowitz
Professor of communication,
University of New Hampshire

4

[On CNN's world-wide audience]: Many of the things that define national sovereignty are fading. National sovereignty wasn't based only on power and barbed wire; it was based also on information control. Nations are losing control over informational borders because of CNN.

Time, 1-6:26.

John Morton
Newspaper analyst,
Lynch, Jones and Ryan,
securities dealers

5

The daily-newspaper business in the 1990s is probably not going to be two to three times more profitable than other manufacturing industries [as it was in the 1980s]. But it will probably still be one to two times more profitable . . . The industry is healthy, even though economically inefficient newspapers are closing down. It is not a happy trend for someone who works [for a troubled newspaper] or someone like me who loves [newspapers], but it's inevitable.

The Christian Science Monitor,
7-23:13.

Rupert Murdoch
Owner, News Corporation

6

[On the time he owned the *New York Post*]: For all its inadequacies, and the things we didn't do, the resources we didn't have, we still had a real influence on that city. To be involved, hands on, in the issues of the streets and the city every day—it was a lot of fun. Absolutely! And it was a heartbreaker. Mission impossible. Afterward [when he sold the paper], I was lost and kind of depressed.

Interview, Los Angeles, Calif./
The New York Times, 7-21:(B)9.

Lisa Myers
Journalist, NBC News

7

[Saying she prefers doing political analysis in a studio than traveling around the country with

(LISA MYERS)

political candidates]: I don't miss the road one bit. The logistics have become so difficult when you're on a bus. The physical grind is awful because you're brain-dead half the time. You cannot go night after night on four or five hours' sleep and be able to think. I found listening to rhetoric day after day an enormous turnoff. So much of it is garbage. I think I have a better sense from a distance. I can't tell you every word [President] George Bush and [his Presidential opponent] Bill Clinton have said, but I probably understand the difference between their economic programs much better than I ever would have being on the road.

The Washington Post, 10-5:(C)4.

Gary Omernick
Publisher,
"The Journal-News,"
Hamilton, Ohio

1

[On the trend toward morning newspapers at the expense of afternoon papers]: The good old days where Ward Cleaver came home from work and everyone read the newspaper has all changed. To compete for [readers'] time, we have to provide them with a greater window of time to read the paper. It starts first thing in the morning and goes for the entire day now.

USA Today, 9-8:(B)3.

Norman J. Ornstein
Fellow,
American Enterprise Institute

2

[On criticism of press coverage of Congress]: It's not just that the messengers are bringing bad news. Coverage has gotten shrill and irresponsible. The editors, major anchors and correspondents have completely lost their moorings.

USA Today, 5-8:(A)9.

Geneva Overholser
Editor, "Des Moines Register"

3

[On criticism that the press has become too much involved in personal exposes and invasion of privacy of public figures]: As rough and unruly and uncomfortable as it is, this is what we're supposed to be doing. If you think about the things that are the most difficult for people—rape victims' names or [tennis star] Arthur Ashe's AIDS—this is how society makes change. Our role is not to suppress difficult information. We've got to be willing to offend people. We should be in the business of telling people what we know.

The Washington Post, 4-23:(D)4.

Ross Perot
Industrialist

4

[On negative articles about him, a possible contender for the Presidency this year]: They don't matter. I'm not sure how much people read anymore. What happens on TV is what really impacts on people. I think you could print any story you want on the front page of *The New York Times* and there's no reaction. It just blows away. What's even weirder, there will be a print story that carries some fairly serious allegation—that has nothing to do with the truth, nothing at all—but fairly serious, and you would think that at least the other print guys would pick it up and ask questions. But no. It just dies on its own legs . . . That's the game the press plays. It doesn't bother me.

Interview/
The New York Times, 5-26:(A)10.

James Pinkerton
Deputy Assistant to
President of the United States
George Bush
for Policy and Planning

5

Just at the moment when all the do-gooders and professional tut-tutters are telling us we need to take our longer [political] sound bites like we need to take our medicine or our vegetables, the market came along with a better solution: freedom of choice. The invisible media hand has given cable viewers a range of MTV to network news to CNN to C-SPAN. They can watch one-and-a-half-second sound bites or entire speeches.

The New York Times, 1-23:(A)10.

Byron Scott
Professor of journalism,
University of Missouri,
Columbia

1

The death of big-city newspapers is due to the continuing tendency of Americans to put their media loyalties in more specialized [print] media, such as suburban weeklies and dailies and specialized magazines. And advertisers are following them.

The Christian Science Monitor, 7-23:13.

Alfred C. Sikes
Chairman,
Federal Communications Commission

2

Our public discourse is too often defined by [TV news] pictures or by the incredible shrinking sound bite. And what "news" are we treated to? Infinite replays of Rodney King being beaten by policemen in Los Angeles; nightly parades of grisly disaster and crime scenes; guaranteed evening-news coverage of summit meetings in picturesque locations; or heated exchanges in Congressional hearings that are often only so much empty grandstanding . . . If, as some say, we get the government we deserve, perhaps it's partly because the media is not helping to educate a constituency for something better. How many citizens—and how many TV correspondents, or evening-news producers, or news-division presidents, for that matter—are aware that interest payments are now their Federal government's largest line-item expense? If few Americans understand these elementary contours of our current situation, and most Americans get their news from television, then it has to follow that television news is not achieving what we must ask of it.

At Edward R. Murrow Symposium,
Washington State University, April 24/
Daily Variety, 4-27:5.

Jim Snyder
Former vice president of news,
Post-Newsweek Stations, Inc.

3

Sound bites are a part of [TV news] coverage. Counting how many bites are used in each nightly newscast leads to sweeping conclusions about coverage. Each network should be judged by everything it does, not just by people with stop-watches . . . You can't weigh sound bites by the pound. Some wonderful things have been said in far less than 30 seconds. Perhaps the greatest sound bite of all time—"give me liberty, or give me death"—took maybe three seconds.

Daily Variety, 9-22:12.

Robert M. Teeter
Chairman of President
George Bush's re-election campaign

4

I'm not . . . anxious to get into a fight with the press. But I do think press coverage, not only of the President, but particularly of the conditions in the country, has been much more negative . . . than actual conditions warrant . . . The country, at least in my view, is in nowhere near as bad a shape as those numbers [indicating high voter dissatisfaction with the country's direction] indicate. I think a lot of that is attitudinal, and not real experience.

To reporters/
The Christian Science Monitor,
8-25:1.

Seymour Topping
President,
American Society of
Newspaper Editors;
Director of editorial development,
The New York Times Company

5

Involvement [by newspapers] in [local community] civic affairs, grappling with the central issues, is critical not only to the health of our society, but also to the survival of newspapers.

The New York Times, 4-11:9

Ed Turner
Vice president in charge
of news gathering,
Cable News Network

6

[On MTV's foray into news programming]: It's not news in a traditional sense. It's a polemic,

(ED TURNER)

with a point of view that tends to come from the liberal side. What's worrisome is that they're using the cache of news on an unsuspecting, non-reading [young] generation. I fear that not only will [audiences raised on news from MTV] have an appetite for news at a frenetic pace, with all the glitter of entertainment—but that they won't be able to discern between opinion as news and news as news.

Los Angeles Times, 2-16:(Calendar)79.

G. Cleveland Wilhoit
Professor of journalism,
and associate director
of the Institute for
Advanced Study,
Indiana University
1

Ideological critics of the media, left and right, agree on one thing—that the press is too arrogant, too ready to tell people what to think. [But] by its very structure, CNN is populist. It provides the raw materials of the story and lets the viewers form their own opinions.

Time, 1-6:26.

Pete Williams
Assistant Secretary
for Public Affairs,
Department of Defense
of the United States
2

[On newly agreed guidelines for press coverage of future wars]: The military believes it must retain the option to review news material to avoid the inadvertent inclusion of news reports of information that would endanger troop safety or the success of a military mission. Any review system would be imposed only when operational security was a consideration. [These principles] will help us both do our jobs better in the future.

May 21/The Washington Post, 5-22:(A)23.

George Wilson
President,
"The Concord (N.H.) Monitor"
3

[On the trend toward morning newspapers at the expense of afternoon papers]: With an afternoon publishing slot, you're giving people about two hours to read your paper or it becomes stale. It's a very narrow time slot, and [the afternoon newspaper] just doesn't read quite the same way the next morning.

USA Today, 9-8:(B)3.

Thomas Winship
Editor emeritus,
"The Boston Globe"
4

CNN has put a tremendous strain on the print press. During the past five years, print has been clobbered by television and has generally failed to respond by emphasizing the analytic and investigative stories that TV cannot do so well.

Time, 1-6:26.

Timothy E. Wirth
United States Senator,
D-Colorado
5

Many journalists feel they are somehow a culture unto themselves. It's as if they can't have any patriotism, they can't have any friends in Congress, they can't be committed to an idea or make a judgment that one idea is better than another idea. They're detached, very little involved in the process. There's enormous economic pressure put on reporters to do the short, *USA Today*-style piece, and that does not serve the hard work of government.

Panel discussion,
Washington, D.C./
Time, 6-8:65.

Literature

Douglas Adams
British author

1

[On writing about serious subjects in a witty manner]: "Popularizing" is a word which carries with it all sorts of pejorative connotations. I believe that the art is in concealing Art.

Interview/
Publishers Weekly, 2-1:63.

Maeve Binchy
Irish author

2

[On her romance novels with realistic characters]: I don't have ugly ducklings turning into swans in my stories. I have ugly ducklings turning into confident ducks.

Interview, Cork City, Ireland/
Publishers Weekly, 10-26:42.

Sven Birkerts
Literary critic

3

As far as my sense of human nature goes, we have an absolute and fundamental appetite for narrative. What I think is happening is that we are getting our narrative much more expeditiously elsewhere [other than books] these days. I think the idea of the novel as being the carrier of extended and complex narrative that shows us our world used to be its reason for being. That has been taken over and eclipsed by the narratives everyone gets by going to movies or turning on TV at night. The price of entry for a reasonably demanding novel is a certain willingness on the part of the reader to make a sacrifice, to say, "I believe this narrative is going to be worth my time." This has to be seen within the larger context of reading itself, which is moving a little bit to the margins. It's a sad thing because it speaks to a change in our culture away from certain habits of being.

Interview, Arlington, Mass./
The Christian Science Monitor, 8-17:14.

Barbara Taylor Bradford
Author

4

[On delivering a finished manuscript for publication]: I'm a bit sad for a few days. I get attached to the characters in the book. They become very real to me. Journalists laugh when they ask me about someone in a book, because I talk about that character as if that person is actually alive and living around the corner.

People, 3-16:90.

Joseph Brodsky
Poet Laureate
of the United States

5

[The] assumption that the blue-collar crowd is not supposed to read [poetry] or a farmer in his overalls is not [supposed] to read poetry seems to be dangerous, if not tragic.

The Writer, June:5.

Edna Buchanan
Author; Former Pulitzer
Prize-winning journalist

6

Fiction is wonderful because it allows you to tie up loose ends. The problem with real life is non-resolution. Murders go unsolved, missing people are never found, unidentified bodies keep turning up. And if something does go to court, you'd better hang on for a long ride.

Interview, Miami, Fla./
Publishers Weekly, 9-28:55.

James Lee Burke
Author

7

I don't think up the stories. I'm convinced they're already written in my unconscious. My work is simply a day-to-day discovery. I never see more than two scenes around the corner and I don't know a book's ending until the last pages.

(JAMES LEE BURKE)

The best metaphor I know for how it happens comes from Michelangelo, who said he didn't carve his sculptures, he released them from the marble. I see my characters as living people inside me, almost whole populations that live in my unconscious. They come out of my dreams too. I wake up in the middle of the night and see them clearly. I believe this is a gift. If a writer convinces himself that he generated his talent out of his own willpower, he'll lose it. Such a person may be visible on TV or panels for a while, but not for long. He's living yesterday's box score.

Interview, New Orleans, La./
Publishers Weekly, 4-20:34.

Tim Cahill
Author

1

I sometimes speak to college writing courses, and I find that if the students are not actually writing at the time, then anything I can tell them about technique and craft seems simple and obvious and essentially meaningless. If they *are* writing, then what I have to say becomes vital to them; they'll come up afterwards and tell me I've been talking about problems they've encountered that same day. So the old cliche is true: The only way to learn about writing is to write. You can't allow yourself to get bogged down in peripherals—"I need to get a word processor, sharpen my pencils." If you want to be a writer, you have to sit down and start writing. Now.

Interview/Writer's Digest, April:46.

Jonathan Carroll
Author

2

I feel that writers nowadays don't have any courage. They have cleverness but they are clevering themselves to death. "Do you *mean* this?" is what I want to ask. With these wiseguys . . . well, you feel the way a woman does when she is given a line in a bar: "Does this guy really mean this?" Writing, I think, has never been less serious.

Interview/
Publishers Weekly, 1-27:77.

Scott Donaldson
Biographer

3

Literary reputations are notoriously hard to forecast. A hundred years ago, Herman Melville died in oblivion, Mark Twain was merely a funny fellow, and Emily Dickinson's just-published poems were dismissed as the work of a New England eccentric. The stature of those writers has risen dramatically, but the process cuts both ways. Who today reads Henry Wadsworth Longfellow, a giant of the time?

The Writer, September:5.

Katherine Dunn
Author

4

I am a writer and I've always been a writer. I'm a writer like a dog's a dog. It may not be a good dog. It may not be a pretty dog. It may not be a fashionable dog. But it is a dog from the tip of its tail to the tip of its nose, and that's the way I'm a writer.

Interview, Oregon/
Writer's Digest, February:37.

Deborah Eisenberg
Short-story writer

5

I like the bristling, sparky, kinetic effect you can get from condensing something down to the point where it almost squeaks.

The Writer, September:5.

Harold Evans
Publisher,
adult trade division,
Random House publishers

6

[On the cutback in the number of titles issued by major book publishers]: Before, [publishers] used to ask, "Why shouldn't I publish this?" Now the question they are asking is, "Why do I have to publish this?" People say there are too many books out there, and it's probably a fair observation. The conventional wisdom is that all publishers should publish fewer titles.

Interview/
The New York Times, 3-30:(C)1.

WHAT THEY SAID IN 1992

Clare Ferraro
Editor-in-chief,
Ballantine Books publishers

1

[Saying publishers of paperback books cannot just buy rights to best-sellers, publish them in paperback and expect them to be successful]: The days of sending out a book and just assuming they will stick are over. It's always been true that you have to know the market you're trying to reach. But now more than ever, if you don't communicate through packaging and promotion what you are selling and if you don't find out whether what you're selling is what the public wants to read, then you are in big trouble.

The New York Times, 6-10:(B)5.

Ken Follett
Author

2

Newspaper writing requires the bare facts. In writing novels, I had to learn to linger at climactic scenes.

The Writer, May:3.

Russell Freedman
Author

3

If an 88-year-old can't read a book that an 8-year-old can enjoy, then there's something wrong with it. I think that a good children's book can't have an upper age limit.

The Writer, August:5.

Sue Grafton
Author

4

My goal in life is to write one perfect mystery, which I don't think is possible, but it certainly gives me something to try for each time out.

The Writer, August:5.

Phyllis E. Grann
President,
Putnam-Berkley Group publishers

5

[On the cutback in the number of titles issued by major book publishers]: I really believe a book that is really good will be published, even if it's a print run of only 4,000 or if it ends up with a smaller house. But there's a lot of junk that won't get published, and I think that's good.

Interview/
The New York Times, 3-30:(C)1.

Gunter Grass
German author

6

[On the influence of politics on literature]: What is deadly dangerous to literature is that in politics you have to repeat yourself. And literature and art are about the new and the innovative, about the undiscovered and the unvoiced. We must find ways to show responsibility to both.

Interview, New York, N.Y./
The New York Times, 12-29:(B)2.

Linda Gregg
Poet

7

I want my poetry to be effective, and sometimes one method does it better than another. I use whatever I can find, both abstract statement and image. For me, poetry is not just surface, it's about things. It's trying to communicate a feeling, communicate knowledge. And it's important to remember that a statement can have a wildness that's as good as an image.

Interview/The Writer, March:5.

Seamus Heaney
Irish poet

8

My sense of poetry is based as most people's is, I think, on reading the traditional canon. When I read Shakespeare or Marlowe or Hopkins or Keats or Eliot or Yeats, the extra voltage in the language, the intensity, the self-consciousness of the language was what I associate with poetry ... It mightn't be rich diction, but it's a principle of over-languaging the language. I mean, poetry is born under the superfluity of language's own resources and energy. It's a kind of overdoing it. Enough is *not* enough when it comes to poetry ...

(SEAMUS HEANEY)

This extra may be subtle and reticent, you know. Or it may be scandalous and overdone. But it is *extra*.

Interview/
The Christian Science Monitor,
10-7:16.

Janette Turner Hospital
Australian author

1

Ideas and subjects just grab me by the scruff of the neck. I get the abstract central conception of the novel first, and a vivid sense of place and locale comes early on. Then the characters, and last of all the plot. It's just something I simply discover. Once I've got my central conception, my place, my characters, I set out, and I literally don't know where I'm going. I find out when I've written the novel what's going to happen.

Interview, Kingston, Ont., Canada/
Publishers Weekly, 9-14:81.

Erica Jong
Author;
President, Authors Guild

2

You read in the papers about the multimillion-dollar book deals that a handful of writers are fortunate enough to get. You don't read about the canceled contracts, the writers sued to pay advances back with interest, the writers who worked 4 years or 7 years or 10 years only to have it orphaned when some fancy new Japanese or German conglomerate bought the publishing house and fired the editors who were the authors' only contact.

At conference of writers' groups,
New York, N.Y., June 9/
The New York Times, 6-10:(B)5.

3

I came to a place in my life where I understood that there were really only two subjects in poetry—love and death—and that if you didn't confront your own mortality, you couldn't grow as a poet.

The Writer, September:5.

William Kennedy
Author

4

I've always believed that a writer has to have an ability to manipulate you with language in order to catch you up in the story. It's like what Hemingway said, that he was trying not to describe emotion but the events that created the emotion. Of course, you need the analytical element of anybody's life to get at the real complexities, but then you go into the poetry of their existence.

Interview/
"Interview" magazine, May:62.

Stephen King
Author

5

The best work that I've ever done always has a feeling of having been excavated. I don't feel like a novelist or a creative writer as much as I feel like an archaeologist who is digging things up and brushing them off and looking at the carvings on them. Sometimes you get a little pot out of the ground, and that's a short story. Sometimes you get a bigger pot, which is a novella. Sometimes you get a building, which is like a novel. When I feel like I'm "creating," I'm usually doing bad work.

Interview/
Writer's Digest, March:24.

Jayne Ann Krentz
Author

6

[The romance novel] has got to be the most misunderstood of all genres. It's got a lot of power, subtlety and complexity, but it's widely ignored because the books are "women's books." Romance is the quintessential women's literature. It's written by women, edited by women, sold to women. It gives us tales that feature women at the center of the book, tales that provide a female world view and stress the qualities that women think are the most important in themselves—honor, courage, determination, as well as our female characteristics like gentleness and compassion. The bottom line on romance is

(JAYNE ANN KRENTZ)

it's the one area of literature in which the woman always wins. That, in a nutshell, is the appeal of the books. It's a very life-affirming sort of victory. In a romance, a new family is formed and that has got to be the most essential sort of survival fantasy. The books are so 100 per cent female in orientation that it's easy to dismiss them in the same way that society dismisses everything that's 100 per cent female.

Interview/
The New York Times, 11-16:(D)4.

Elmore Leonard
Author

1

The difficulty [as an author] is getting tired of situations done before. You're always looking for something new . . . [The characters] have to be able to talk. I audition them, and if they don't hold up, either they get a less-important role, or they're out . . . [Ernest] Hemingway made it look so easy. He's easy to copy, and you learn to write by imitating. But I realized that I didn't share his attitude, and style comes out of attitude. I don't take myself as seriously as he did—I see more humor in life.

Interview, San Francisco, Calif./
The Washington Post, 9-8:(B)3.

Robert MacNeil
Co-host, "MacNeil/Lehrer
NewsHour," PBS-TV

2

The fun of writing is the fun *in* writing—all those little moments of excitement, when the perspiration starts running down your sides inside your shirt. I don't have that fun doing television.

The Writer, May:3.

David McCullough
Biographer, Historian

3

I must immerse myself in a subject. I reach the point where I know the people I'm writing

about—not only the subject, but the full cast of characters—better than I know people around me. I know who said what; I know exactly what their rooms looked like. It's not until I reach this state that I'm ready to write. When someone says, "I hear you're working on a book," I often think the preposition is wrong; I'm working *in* a book.

Interview, New York, N.Y./
Publishers Weekly, 6-8:44.

4

[As a writer of history,] I see the past as my territory. I'm a foreign correspondent who goes there instead of to India or South America.

Interview/
U.S. News & World Report,
6-22:76.

Alice McDermott
Author

5

We have to remember that fiction is in its own world—it's a new world every time you open a book, and what its relationship is to the real world is almost beside the point. And isn't that wonderful? It's giving you an opportunity to see life not actually portrayed but as something else entirely. Not to get highfalutin, but it's a work of art that's complete in some way.

Interview/
Publishers Weekly, 3-30:86.

Charles Melcher
Publisher,
Callaway Editions, publishers

6

[On books that also utilize today's electronic innovations, such as CDs, etc.]: This is an attempt to revitalize the medium of books and have it appeal to a younger audience. When I was a child, a book was an afternoon of entertainment. These days, an afternoon of entertainment is usually focused around [the electronic] Nintendo [games] or a movie. It is not focused around a book.

The Christian Science Monitor,
12-1:12.

Paul Monette
Author;
Winner, 1992 National Book Award
for non-fiction

1

[On his winning the National Book Award as a gay writer who wrote about his homosexuality]: I think this award sends a very happy message. Some people will see it as just a politically correct decision in a year filled with political hatred and intolerance toward the gay and lesbian community. But I think, among other things, including what I think is appreciation for my book, this award is for all of us . . . a whole group of young gay and lesbian writers who are writing now. It's an acknowledgment that our literature is significant. We are finding voices that are not just shrill with anger and wracked with pain. We're finding an elegance and a dignity in our writing that we didn't have when we started writing about ourselves 15 or 20 years ago. We now have a revolution behind us and a tragedy within us that has given us a new power in our writing.

Interview, Los Angeles, Calif./
The New York Times, 11-25:(B)2.

Phyllis Reynolds Naylor
Children's-book author

2

[On writing for young people]: It's like having another child and introducing him to the world. That's the joy of parenthood, and it's also the joy of writing for children. Your book may be the first one in which they've met this problem or laughed about this particular thing. What can you tell an adult he doesn't know already?

Interview/
The Washington Post, 1-28:(E)8.

Edna O'Brien
Author

3

I think I write under a shadow, so to speak. I don't quite know what that shadow is, but the shadow is en route to suffering. And suffering is not a gratuitous ingredient in fiction; it's very central to it. I think pain deepens people. It can make for profundity, definitely.

Interview, New York, N.Y., March/
Publishers Weekly, 5-18:48.

4

I don't think an academic upbringing is necessarily the best soil to become a writer, because so much of academia is meant to do dissection. And creation is creation; it has to be pure and instinctive; it comes from deep within the self, from a place one doesn't know. So, to forge my own little way through the books that I wrote, maybe it was better that I didn't have help. It was lonelier; it was harder. But it made one more severe. I think I'm very severe about writing. I'm very severe with myself. I take writing as seriously as religion.

Interview, New York, N.Y./
Publishers Weekly, 5-18:49.

Mary Oliver
Pulitzer Prize-winning poet

5

[On writing poetry]: I never have felt yet that I've done it right. This is the marvelous thing about language. It can always be done better. But I begin to see what works and what doesn't work. I begin to rely more on style, which is, as I say, apparatus or method, than on luck, prayers or long hours of work. I worked privately, and sometimes I feel that might be better for poets than the kind of social workshop gathering. My school was the great poets; I read, and I read, and I read. I imitated—shamelessly, fearlessly. I was endlessly discontent. I looked at words and couldn't believe the largess of their sound—the whole sound structure of stops and sibilants, and things which I speak about now with students! All such mechanics have always fascinated me. Still do!

Interview/
The Christian Science Monitor,
12-9:16.

Michael Reagan
Publisher, Turner Publishing

6

[Saying publishers have to branch out into the various new electronic media]: The Nintendo generation has grown up an interactive, visually intensive generation, and they don't go into books. There has to be a way to reach out to them. In 10 years, this [books on compact discs

WHAT THEY SAID IN 1992

with visuals and sound] will be a $100-billion business. We're on the threshold of something absolutely profound.

At American Booksellers Association
convention, Anaheim, Calif./
Los Angeles Times, 5-26:(E)4.

Carolyn Reidy
President, trade division,
Simon & Schuster publishers

1

[On the competition to books by new electronic literary media]: I think people like the physical heft of a book. This 19-century medium is never going to go away.

At American Booksellers Association
convention, Anaheim, Calif./
Los Angeles Times, 5-26:(E)4.

Jeremy Rifkin
Author

2

There are two types of editors [at book-publishing companies], I find—those who are really acquisitions people and those who have a deep sense of commitment to intellectual ideas and to popularizing those ideas. Not that the acquisition people don't, but many of the younger people don't have the depth of knowledge.

Interview, Washington, D.C./
Publishers Weekly, 2-24:34.

Paul Roche
Poet-in-residence,
Centenary College

3

Education systems today are designed to crush imagination, to turn students into machines. I try to return them to their origins, help them see that poetry is all about them. You start with love poems. Then, little by little, you make your students feel more, think more and read more, of course. But above all, to feel more. You see, if you don't have the resonances of the imagination through literature, you cannot know your own feelings. People today, not only students, fear feeling.

Interview, Hackettstown, N.J./
The New York Times, 12-18:(A)24.

Judith Rossner
Author

4

The most important thing that I can say about my writing voice, or voices, is that they're the smartest voices I have, often teaching me things I didn't know I knew.

The Writer, June:5.

Sandra Scofield
Author

5

I'm interested in people whose will isn't necessarily greater than the circumstances of their lives, and I know that violates really important rules about contemporary fiction, [according to which] our taste is for characters who grow like spider plants—or the therapy model of fiction, where characters finally face some huge trauma and overcome it.

Interview, Ashland, Ore./
Publishers Weekly, 11-9:63.

Richard Selzer
Author; Former surgeon

6

As a patient is anesthetized on the table, a surgeon too has to be anesthetized in order that he be at some emotional remove from the white heat of that event—which is, after all, the laying open of the body—in order to do his work dispassionately and coolly. The surgeon/writer—which I had become—must not only perform the operation but must report it back in the most compelling language. What had happened [becoming a writer while being a surgeon] . . . was that little by little I had stripped off my carapace, and I had begun to perceive these events with the third eye of the artist. A surgeon can unmake himself by simply stopping. A writer cannot unmake himself. Once that third eye is opened, it can never be shut.

Interview/
Publishers Weekly, 8-10:49.

Charles Simic
Poet

1

I think poets have always been incredible historical witnesses. There's a way in which they take the pulse of the age better than anybody else. I've said this before: Future historians, if they want to know the truth of our age, will find it more faithfully rendered in the work of many poets or novelists than in the pages of daily newspapers. Poetry has to be close to some kind of daily reality. [It's] the place where individuality, an individual's experience, is defended, protected. That's why it survives.

Interview/
The Christian Science Monitor,
7-14:17.

Donald Spoto
Biographer

2

The field of biography drew me. I think there's nothing so rich as the exploration and assessment of a human life, particularly a creative human life . . . Academics are always making judgments—they have to *rate* people. But the biographer's task is not to judge; rather, he must open for the reader the complexities of another life and leave us with an understanding of how the subject coped.

Interview, Los Angeles, Calif./
Publishers Weekly, 8-24:56.

Roger Straus III
Managing director,
Farrar, Straus & Giroux publishers

3

[On the cutback in the number of titles issued by major book publishers]: This is one of those trends that everyone starts talking about when times get tough. The trouble with downsizing as a concept is if someone could tell up front which books would sell and which wouldn't, it would be brilliant. But since most of us can't really tell, it becomes a dangerous idea that could make things worse.

Interview/
The New York Times, 3-30:(C)8.

Graham Swift
British author

4

A lot of novel-writing is precisely that—you're *fired* to write. Writing is a thing of passion. I *do* believe in inspiration, however you actually define that. There is something that occurs, something rather ecstatic. That's what makes you do it. But it's not what makes you do it week in, week out, month in, month out, for perhaps years. Something else has to take over—call it stamina. That stamina has to preserve the original flame. It is very difficult to keep that happening. You have this enormous familiarity with what you're doing, and familiarity breeds a kind of apathy or indifference to what once might have been astonishing. You have to somehow keep reminding yourself that the astonishing thing is still there and that it's going to astonish your reader.

Interview, London, England/
Publishers Weekly, 2-17:44.

Anne Tyler
Author

5

The most appealing short-story writer is one who is a wastrel. He neither hoards his best ideas for something more important [a novel] nor skimps on his material because "this is only a short story."

The Writer, August:5.

Mona Van Duyn
Poet Laureate-designate
of the United States

6

[There is] an enormous audience for poetry in America, [but most of that audience doesn't buy poetry books]. They come to poetry readings by the hundreds and the thousands and watch the poet's lips move and the words come out. Perhaps it's the influence of television. They're used to seeing it and hearing it. They're just not used to sitting by themselves and reading it.

Interview, June 14/
Los Angeles Times, 6-15:(A)4.

WHAT THEY SAID IN 1992

Nicholas von Hoffman
Author, Journalist

1

Novels are always a pitfall for journalists, because you have to keep telling yourself to lie. My last one, *Organized Crimes*, was set in Chicago in the 1930s, so anything I had picked up in journalism was useless. I read a lot of microfilm of things from the period to make it convincing, but it's all a trick. There are all sorts of little things that make you feel that you're in Chicago in the early '30s, but it's all smoke and mirrors. If you want to read social history, buy yourself a social-history book—fiction is very different.

Interview,
New York, N.Y./
Publishers Weekly, 9-21:73.

Derek Walcott
Poet; Winner,
1992 Nobel Prize
for Literature

2

Poetry, which is perfection's sweat but which must seem as fresh as the raindrops on a statue's brow, combines the natural and the marmoreal; it conjugates both tenses simultaneously: the past and the present, if the past is the sculpture and the present the beads of dew or rain on the forehead of the past. There is the buried language and there is the individual vocabulary, and the process of poetry is one of excavation and of self-discovery. Tonally the individual voice is a dialect; it shapes its own accent, its own vocabulary and melody in defiance of an imperial concept of language; the language of Ozymandias, libraries and dictionaries, law courts and critics, and churches, universities, political dogma, the diction of institutions. Poetry is an island that breaks away from the main . . . For every poet it is always morning in the world. History a forgotten, insomniac night; History and elemental awe are always our early beginning, because the fate of poetry is to fall in love with the world, in spite of History.

Nobel lecture,
Stockholm, Sweden, Dec. 7/
The New York Times, 12-8:(A)19.

Brigitte Weeks
Editor-in-chief,
Book-of-the-Month Club

3

[On large advances paid by publishers to some authors]: The fact is that if a book blows your socks off, you want it and you're willing to pay big bucks for it. And the dirty little secret of this industry is that a lot of times emotions get away from you and you pay more than logic or a financial analysis would justify. And then you just pray.

The New York Times, 5-18:(C)8.

Elie Wiesel
Author; Winner,
1986 Nobel Peace Prize

4

[On his writings about the Holocaust]: I believe mainly in memoir. Memoirs are important; witness accounts, testimonies, children's songs are important—but not novels. Always with exceptions: John Hersey's *The Wall* is one. But novels, even literary criticism of the novels, are beside the point. From the literary viewpoint, they may be right, but from the viewpoint of authenticity, truth, they are wrong.

Interview/
Publishers Weekly, 4-6:39.

A. B. Yehoshua
Israeli author

5

My foreign readers cannot understand the codes and nuances fully, because in translation we gain something and lose something. But they can see something that we cannot see, above the political and cultural codes. This is the pleasure I have from being translated and published in foreign countries. It makes you believe that your book has merit as a story and not as a political allegory . . . In a foreign country you are over-praised 30 per cent, and in your own country you are under-praised 10 per cent.

Interview/
Publishers Weekly, 3-9:38.

Medicine and Health

Lonnie R. Bristow
Physician; Trustee,
American Medical Association

1

Doctors have a responsibility to treat patients, and they fulfill that responsibility. Anybody who chooses the profession of medicine because it's safe and clean has made the wrong decision.

The New York Times, 4-7:(A)19.

Edmund G. "Jerry" Brown, Jr.
Candidate for the 1992
Democratic Presidential nomination;
Former Governor
of California (D)

2

There is no will to deal with the [U.S.] health-care crisis except in trivial ways. "Pay or play" is dead on arrival. It has too many different tiers, too many problems and it requires taxes. There is the corporate-managed approach that I believe doctors are going to fight just as hard as a national health-care system. The other system is the Canadian single-payer plan, which the insurance companies are going to fight because they're eliminated from most proposals. I believe a national health-care system is the only way to go. It's the only way to control prices through a single payer that could then have the leverage to hold down fees, hospital costs and provider costs.

Interview/USA Today, 5-7:(A)11.

George Bush
President of the United States

3

Some say nationalized health care would serve everyone. Sure, it would—just like a restaurant that serves bad food, but in very generous proportions.

Before San Diego Rotary Club,
San Diego, Calif., Feb. 7/
Los Angeles Times, 2-8:(A)18.

4

[Comparing his health-care plan with that of his Democratic opponent for the Presidency, Arkansas Governor Bill Clinton]: The other plan will dump 52 million Americans into a new government bureaucracy—and my plan will help 90 million Americans afford private insurance to take care of their health-care needs. The other plan would slap at least a 7 per cent payroll tax on middle-income Americans—and my plan would provide tax relief to Americans, to help them pay for their own health care . . . The other plan will create lines at hospitals so long you'll think they were selling [Chicago] *Bears* [football team] tickets inside. My plan attacks the root cause of rising [medical] costs: faulty insurance, too much paperwork, far too many frivolous lawsuits out there. Understand what is at stake here. If the Governor of Arkansas is elected [President] with a Democratic Congress . . . within a year the government will run health care in this country. Our health-care system will [then] combine the efficiency of the House post office [which recently went through a scandal] with the compassion of the [Soviet] KGB. I'm not going to let that happen.

At Republican fund-raising luncheon, Chicago, Ill.,
Aug. 2/Los Angeles Times, 8-3:(A)14.

5

[AIDS is] one of the few diseases where behavior matters. And I once called on somebody, "Well, change your behavior; if the behavior you're using is prone to cause AIDS, change the behavior." Next thing I know, one of these Act-Up groups is out saying, "Bush ought to change *his* behavior." You can't talk about it rationally; the extremes are hurting the AIDS cause. To go into a Catholic mass, in a beautiful cathedral in New York, under the cause of helping in AIDS, and start throwing condoms around in the mass—I'm sorry, I think it sets back the cause. We cannot move to the extreme.

At Presidential candidates' debate,
St. Louis, Mo., Oct. 11/
The New York Times, 10-12:(A)15.

369

(GEORGE BUSH)

1

[On criticism that he isn't doing enough in the fight against AIDS]: We have increased funding for AIDS, we've doubled it, on research and on every other aspect of it. My request for this year was $4.9-billion for AIDS, 10 times as much per AIDS victims as per cancer victim. I think that we're showing the proper compassion and concern, so I can't tell you where [the criticism] is coming from; but I am very much concerned about AIDS and I believe that we've got the best researchers in the world out there at NIH working [on] the problem. We're funding them. I wish there was more money, but we're funding them far more than any time in the past, and we're going to keep on doing that.

At Presidential candidates' debate,
St. Louis, Mo., Oct. 11/
The New York Times,
10-12:(A)15.

2

One thing to blame [for the high cost of medical care in the U.S.] is these malpractice lawsuits. They are breaking the system. It costs 20 to 25 billion dollars a year and I want to see those outrageous claims capped. Doctors don't dare to deliver babies sometimes because they're afraid somebody's going to sue them. People don't dare—medical practitioners—to help somebody along the highway that are hurt, because they're afraid that some lawyer's going to come along and get a big lawsuit. So you can't blame the practitioners for the health problem. And my program [for health care] is this: Keep the government as far out of it as possible. Make insurance available to the poorest of the poor through vouchers. Next, range in the income bracket through tax credits. And get on about the business of pooling insurance. A great big company can buy . . . insurance cheaper than [a] mom-and-pop store on the corner. But if those mom-and-pop stores all get together and pool, they too can bring the cost of insurance down. So I want to keep the quality of health-care—that means keep government out of it . . . And part of our plan is to make it what they call "portable." A big word, but that means, if you're working for the

Jones Company, you go to the Smith Company, your insurance goes with you.

At Presidential candidates' debate,
Richmond, Va., Oct. 15/
The New York Times, 10-17:11.

Joseph A. Califano, Jr.
Director, Center on Addiction
and Substance Abuse,
Columbia University;
Former Secretary of Health,
Education and Welfare
of the United States

3

[Substance] addiction is the loss of control, it's the loss of free will, it's the loss of human dignity that tells you that you're no longer a creature of God, in the sense that you have the ability to live in His image and likeness . . . You lose the ability to be yourself, to be whatever you can be . . . I did a book on health care in '86, but gradually I became convinced the problem was abuse and addiction. It wasn't legal versus illegal drugs, it was everything! Smoking. Pills that doctors prescribe. Alcohol, pot, heroine, cocaine. Everything. Roughly speaking, 54 to 55 million are hooked on cigarettes, 18 million are alcoholics . . . Substance abuse and addiction are the largest single causes or exacerbators of cancer, cardiovascular disease, AIDS.

Interview, New York/
The Washington Post, 10-13:(E)8.

Arthur L. Caplan
Director,
Center for Biomedical Ethics,
University of Minnesota

4

[Supporting increased use of pain-killing drugs in medical treatment]: We've been scaring people into the arms of the euthanasia movement because they fear they won't get adequate pain relief. We've made people terrified of words like "cancer," because it sounds like a sentence to suffer. Across the board, we've had too many people frightened of too many treatments be-

(ARTHUR L. CAPLAN)

cause they worry that they're going to hurt—and that is intolerable at a time when we've got the means to prevent it. We've had a puritanical attitude that says not only does pain build character but that pain is redemptive . . . that pain is deserved. It's time to separate our morality from our medical response to pain.

Los Angeles Times, 3-6:(A)22.

Bill Clinton
Governor of Arkansas (D);
Candidate for the
1992 Democratic
Presidential nomination

1

Every American ought to have a comprehensive package of affordable health care. You ought to be able to get [it] either through your job or, for the self-employed, the poor and small business who can't buy insurance, the government ought to offer an affordable insurance package. And every American ought to be guaranteed a comprehensive package. Then the payment ought to be the same, state by state, whether the government provides it or whether the employer provides it. And everybody ought to be involved in the system. There ought to be some incentives for cost controls, but the main thing we have to do is to take on the big insurance companies and the health-care bureaucracies, drug companies that are raising [prices of drugs] at three times the rate of inflation. These things are unforgivable. You need to know that your country spends, conservatively, $70-billion to $80-billion on health care totally unrelated, unrelated, to providing you health care because we don't have a system. And let me say, listen, I'm very suspicious of government. I know that there are things government can't do. But no nation has solved this problem without government taking the lead and controlling costs and guaranteeing health care. I will do that, if I'm elected President. We have to do that. I will do that.

Call-in question-and-answer broadcast,
Pittsburgh, Pa.,/
NBC-TV, 6-12.

Bill Clinton
Governor of Arkansas (D);
1992 Democratic
Presidential nominee

2

Yesterday, he [President Bush] compared [my] common-sense effort to control health-care costs, with the police-state tactics of the KGB. He called [the late] President [John] Kennedy's plan for Medicare "socialized medicine." Mr. Bush displays no passion for solving the health-care crisis, but when someone else has an idea for making health care available and affordable, he goes ballistic. For the past dozen years, he's done nothing while health-care costs have risen like a patient's fever chart. The average cost of individual health insurance rose from $1,000 to $3,000 a year, but he did nothing. Our country's annual spending on health care increased in the decade of the '80s until last year, from $250-billion to $809-billion, but he did nothing. Thirty-five million Americans, mostly workers and their families, have no health insurance. Another 35 million don't have adequate coverage. Millions more live in fear that they'll have to pay more for less insurance or lose their insurance completely. And he's done nothing.

News conference,
Little Rock, Ark., Aug. 3/
The New York Times, 8-4:(A)9.

3

Both parties in Washington, the President and the Congress, have cut Medicare. The average senior citizen is spending a higher percentage of income on health care today than they were in 1965 before Medicare came in. The President's [Bush] got another proposal that will require them to pay $400 a year more for the next five years. But if you don't have the guts to control costs by changing the insurance system, in taking on the bureaucracies and the regulation of health care in the private and public sector, you can't fix this problem. Costs will continue to spiral. And just remember this, folks—a lot of folks on Medicare are out there every day making the choice between food and medicine—not poor enough for Medicaid, not wealthy enough to buy their medicine . . . When we talk about cutting

WHAT THEY SAID IN 1992

(BILL CLINTON)

health-care costs, let's start with the insurance companies and the people that are making a killing instead of making our people healthy ... We are spending 30 per cent more on health care than any country in the world, any other country. And yet we have 35 million people uninsured. We have no preventative and primary care ... I say if Germany can cover everybody and keep costs under inflation, if Hawaii can cover 98 per cent of their people at lower health-care costs than the rest of us, if Rochester, New York, can do it with two-thirds of the cost to the rest of us, America can do it, too. I'm tired of being told we can't. I say we can. We can do better and we must.

At Presidential candidates' debate,
St. Louis, Mo., Oct. 11/
The New York Times, 10-12:(A)15.

1

[On AIDS]: We must remember, for all of its terror and far reach, it is still a disease. It is not a vengeance or punishment or just desserts. It is an illness. We have fought illnesses before. And we must fight this one.

Speech, Jersey City, N.J./
USA Today, 10-30:(A)3.

Howard B. Dean
Governor of Vermont (D)

2

I don't want a national health-insurance system that's administered by the Federal government. The Federal government already administers Medicare, and it's one of the worst programs that's ever been devised. We need a system that's like the Medicaid system, which is administered by the states, so that it's possible to deal with the state capital instead of calling Washington to solve your problems.

Interview/USA Today, 2-10:(A)11.

Jim Florio
Governor of New Jersey (D)

3

Our exclusive reliance on hospitals as the health-care provider for people without insur-

ance is bad medicine and bad economics. We can't solve our health-care crisis just by pouring money into a broken system. Money spent on prevention and keeping well is a much better investment than money spent the way we spend it now.

At symposium of New Jersey
Public Health Association,
North Brunswick, N.J., Oct. 28/
The New York Times, 10-29:(A)14.

Janet Flynn
Spokesman,
Distilled Spirits Council

4

[Criticizing proposed government requirements that alcoholic-beverage advertisements carry health warnings]: [The bill] is inappropriate at best, harmful at worst, in the critical objective of reducing alcoholic abuse. The facts need to be understood that the U.S. is not awash in alcohol. According to the United States' own statistics, under-age drinking is at its lowest level since 1974, fatal accidents involving teen-age drunk drivers are down 39 per cent since 1982. Our industry already has a highly self-regulating code. We voluntarily don't advertise [on radio and television]. We're a legitimate industry and a legal product and have every right to First Amendment rights.

The Christian Science Monitor,
4-30:7.

John Fung
Chief, division of
transplantation surgery
and associate professor of surgery,
University of Pittsburgh

5

[On the recent transplantation of a baboon liver into a human being, at which he was one of the surgeons]: [Transplantations of animal organs into humans] offer a potential solution to a very difficult problem, which is accessibility to organs. Now, animal-rights activists will argue that it's not fair to kill an animal to save a human. I personally don't agree with that. In some responsible way we may be able to at least relieve

(JOHN FUNG)

part of the organ shortage now . . . The real reason this whole thing has proceeded is because of the organ shortage. If there were more people who were responsive to the call for organs in terms of being aware of the critical need and signing donor cards, we probably wouldn't have to do this—at least not for awhile. It seems to me that the Number 1 area to expand prior to getting into these very controversial issues is to look at ways to educate the public and say: "Look, organ donation isn't going to hurt you. It's not going to hurt your family. It benefits mankind."

Interview/USA Today, 7-6:(A)11.

Booth Gardner
Governor of Washington (D)

1

My preference would be to take the elderly and disabled populations out of Medicaid and move them into Medicare on the thesis that those categories have social-service needs, as well as medical. Then turn Medicaid into an income-based or needs-based system that basically provides health care.

Interview/USA Today, 2-10:(A)11.

Helena Gayle
Chief, AIDS Division,
Agency for International Development
of the United States

2

We're now in the second decade of an [AIDS] epidemic that is continuing to expand and to cause major human suffering and loss of life. So it's hard to feel the battle is won. On the other hand, we have more knowledge of the virus and there have been advances in learning how to change the behavior that leads to the transmission of AIDS, at least in the short run. We go into the second decade armed with important information and with people who are extremely committed to halting the epidemic.

The Christian Science Monitor,
7-31:2.

Willard Gaylin
President, Hastings Center
(for biomedical ethics)

3

In our attempt to constrict the rise of health-care costs, we are going to be forced to redefine what is desirable. Like the Western frontier, we have an expanding concept of health—and we can no longer afford it. There's been too much of a readiness to redefine pleasure, youthfulness and aesthetics as health issues. Half of what we call health today would not have been considered health 50 years ago . . . Fertility problems are now defined as diseases . . . So is fixing a knee, orthopedic surgery and plastic surgery. Before the invention of the lens, nobody worried about old people not being able to read. People who don't know medicine assume that there's a sickness and we discover a cure. Today, we frequently discover a cure and try to find a sickness to go with it . . . [Consequently,] the power to define something as a disease is crucial.

The Washington Post, 6-26:(F)3.

Alixe Glen
Spokesman for
U.S. President Bush's
re-election campaign

4

[Saying President Bush's health-insurance proposals are better than those of his Democratic Presidential opponent Bill Clinton]: We have the best health-care system in the world. Some 220 million people have insurance and can get immediate care from the doctor of their choice. The Bush bill would cover the other 30 million people. We should not throw the baby out with the bath water.

The Washington Post, 9-25:(A)21.

Bernadine P. Healy
Director,
National Institutes of Health
of the United States

5

I don't think biomedical research in the United States can continue its preeminence at home and abroad if we continue [because of funding problems] to turn down 75 per cent of meritorious research that comes before us. At the present time, we are *not* funding as much excellence as we [should be] funding. That means numerous opportunities are not being pursued that need to be pursued. Something has to be done. Obviously, that something requires a broader consensus beyond the scientific community . . . If we can accomplish one thing directed toward that issue, it would be to elevate NIH and biomedical research as a priority for the American public. One, and primarily one, because it is of great importance to their health. Secondly, NIH is of growing importance to this nation's economy. That cannot be minimized.

Interview, Los Angeles, Calif./
Los Angeles Times, 7-26:(M)3.

Edward M. Kennedy
United States Senator,
D-Massachusetts

1

The [Bush] Administration refuses to bite the bullet on tough, effective [medical] cost containment. They have never been willing to bite that bullet in the past. They are not prepared to do that now. Without doing that, any [health-care] reform is not worth the paper it's printed on.

USA Today, 2-4:(A)4.

David A. Kessler
Commissioner,
Food and Drug Administration
of the United States

2

People don't understand how we [the FDA] operate. This agency doesn't test drugs; we don't develop them; we don't do research on them; we don't collect the data. We have to rely on data that comes into this agency. What is the FDA's job? It may sound corny, but we end up almost being the arbiter of truth.

Interview/USA Today, 2-4:(D)1.

3

[On the controversy over the safety of silicone-gel breast implants]: We know more about the life span of automobile tires than we know about longevity of these devices . . . I am highly conscious that some women need these implants for reconstruction after cancer surgery or traumatic injury, or for certain congenital disorders. While this policy [of permitting limited use of the implants] is meant to be compassionate toward these patients, it is not to be interpreted as "business as usual." Our primary goal is to put in place a process to obtain adequate information about the safety of these devices . . . The public needs to understand that when a device is implanted, there is no such thing as zero risk. We have to be willing to expect that there will be problems 15 or 20 years down the road.

April 16/
The Washington Post, 4-17:(A)2.

Daniel J. Klass
Project director,
standardized patient project,
National Board of Medical Examiners

4

When we make a statement that someone is licensed to practice medicine, that should mean more than knowing multiple-choice answers from a book. They should have skills that allow them to relate to patients well, to listen properly, to hear what's said, so the patient leaves the encounter thinking, "Hey, I just saw a real doctor."

The New York Times, 6-4:(A)1.

C. Everett Koop
Former Surgeon General
of the United States

5

Seventy to 75 per cent of our [American] people already enjoy the best health care in the world because they are insured through an employer or an employed family member. But that leaves the other 30 per cent in real trouble because they are on Medicaid or Medicare, which is not responsive to all the needs of the elderly, especially in pharmaceuticals. What good does it do you if you're 70 and get a marvelous medical workup and a great regimen prescribed but you don't have the money to buy

(C. EVERETT KOOP)

the drugs to make it work? What do we do about long-term care for people who can't be cared for at home? There is no provision in Medicare for long-term hospitalization or long-term nursing care. As for Medicaid, it's an absolute fraud. It's supposed to be the health-care system for the poor, but it takes care of less than half of them . . . The most pitiful are the 33 to 37 million people too proud to go on welfare, trying to make it, maybe working two jobs, neither one of which has a health plan. The combined salary from both doesn't give them the money to buy health insurance. They are disenfranchised. When these people go to the hospital uninsured, they have three times the mortality of people with the same diagnosis who go into the hospital insured; the reason being that they postpone, postpone until, when they get there, they're too far gone to be pulled back.

Interview, New York/
Lear's, April:22.

Joseph Liu
Senior health associate,
Children's Defense Fund

1

The simple reason infant mortality rates have gone down [in the U.S.] is that medical technology has gotten better and better. [But] we have done absolutely nothing to make sure pregnant women can get prenatal care. We are relying on the miracle of modern technology to save very sick babies, while failing to provide up-front preventive care to make sure more babies are born healthy.

The Washington Post, 2-7:(A)3.

Jonathan Mann
Former director,
International AIDS Center,
Harvard University

2

To date, we have not been confident enough— bold enough—to do what we know is needed to be more effective against AIDS: to confront . . . the problems deeply embedded in the status quo of societies worldwide which fuel the spread of HIV, interfere with care for affected people and underlie the major causes of ill health worldwide. To control AIDS . . . we must proclaim a bold demand: that health . . . take its rightful place as . . . a universal aspiration, a common good of humanity.

At International Conference on AIDS,
Amsterdam, Netherlands, July 19/
Los Angeles Times, 7-20:(A)6.

Walker P. Merryman
Vice president,
Tobacco Institute

3

This trend [of decreased smoking in the U.S.] has been evident for several years. Smoking is fundamentally a matter of an individual adult's right to choose, free of harassment from the government or anyone else. Nearly 50 million adults in this country have chosen to continue smoking. No one would seriously suggest that the American public is uninformed of the possible risks of smoking. [But] adults should be free to make their own decisions based on their beliefs.

Los Angeles Times, 5-22:(A)4.

Antonia C. Novello
Surgeon General
of the United States

4

I have asked [the alcohol industry] to stop using any ads that lead our youth to think they can ski, swim, scuba dive or race cars better if they drink. In short, we are doing everything we can to change the way Americans think and act with regard to the use and misuse of alcohol . . . It is no coincidence that sports such as boating, swimming, skiing, surfing, car racing and mountain climbing—which have strong links to alcohol-related injuries—are the very activities glamorized in alcohol-beverage ads and promotions.

At conference on alcohol-abuse prevention,
March 23/
The Washington Post, 3-24:(A)8.

Ross Perot
Industrialist;
1992 independent
Presidential candidate

1

We [in the U.S.] have the most expensive health-care system in the world; 12 per cent of our gross national product goes to health care. Our industrial competitors who are beating us in competition spend less and have better health care. Japan spends a little over 6 per cent of its gross national product; Germany spends 8 per cent. It's fascinating. You bought a front-row box seat and you're not happy with your health care, and you're saying we've got bad health care but very expensive health care. Folks, here's why. Go home and look in the mirror. You own this country but you have no voice in it the way it's organized now. And if you want to have a high-risk experience comparable to bungee jumping, go in to Congress some time when they're working on this kind of legislation, when the lobbyists are running up and down the halls. Wear your safety-toe shoes when you go.

At Presidential candidates' debate,
Richmond, Va., Oct. 15/
The New York Times, 10-17:12.

Robert Petersdorf
President, Association
of American Medical Colleges

2

The disparity in incomes [among doctors in the various areas of practice] now is too great, and there are some that are enormous. That's why we can't get people to go into family medicine, when they have to try to raise a family and pay off a large [medical-school] debt on maybe $80,000 a year. Many surgeons can expect figures four and five times that. I think we have to begin to appeal to altruism, rather than looking on medicine as a big money-maker.

The Washington Post, 6-9:(Health)11.

Harold Poling
Chairman,
Ford Motor Company

3

Ford spends as much on health care as it does on steel. Health-care providers are our largest

supplier. To accomplish effective reform, we must address the following five principles . . . Universal coverage; I'm sure everyone here today agrees that health-care coverage should be afforded to every American. Quality assurance; studies have indicated that unnecessary operations and procedures are running as high as 30 per cent. Administrative simplicity; there are more than 1,000 insurance companies with 1,000 different claim forms; can you believe that over four billion insurance claims were processed last year? Cost containment; with health-care costs in the United States approaching $3,000 for every man, woman and child, neither large nor small companies nor individuals can afford to continue their health care; purchasers, providers and government must cooperate to develop a plan to contain these growing costs. Inequitable financing; costs should be spread fairly among all participants in the health-care system and cost-shifting must be eliminated.

At economic conference convened
by President-elect Bill Clinton,
Little Rock, Ark., Dec. 14/
The New York Times, 12-15:(A)14.

Ron Pollack
Executive director,
Families U.S.A.

4

Medicare has helped our parents and grand-parents, but despite Medicare, older Americans today are being squeezed much harder by health costs than during [the late President] John F. Kennedy's time . . . The two most important changes that need to occur include serious system-wide cost containment and protection against the bankrupting costs of long-term care. Growing old and growing sick should not mean growing poor, but increasingly it does.

Feb. 25/
The Washington Post, 2-26:(A)3.

5

[On Americans who cross the border into Mexico for medical treatment and prescription drugs because of the lower costs there]: The hemorrhage at the Mexican border is a symptom of the fundamental sickness of the American

(RON POLLACK)

health-care system. What greater embarrassment could we have than the spectacle of tens of thousands of Americans leaving our country to get affordable health care? If you want to know why comprehensive health reform is certain to pass in 1993, this disgrace at the border gives you part of the answer.

Nov. 20/
The New York Times, 11-23:(A)8.

Douglas Richman
AIDS researcher,
University of California,
San Diego

1

[Criticizing the U.S. Congress's decision to spend a larger share of government AIDS funds on pediatric AIDS research, thus reducing the amount spent on adult AIDS]: I have nothing against doing research on AIDS in young people. But what I don't like is that the adult programs have been attacked in order to find the money for it . . . That is a cheap political trick. And Congress doesn't deserve credit for compassion or sympathy for pediatric AIDS by doing it . . . Everybody likes kids, everybody has compassion for them, everybody can get good press for being sympathetic to children. Gay men and drug users and minorities just are not as important influence groups in Washington.

The Washington Post, 10-5:(A)10.

Martin A. Russo
United States Representative,
D-Illinois

2

Insecurity about health care affects decisions to buy a house or a car or to make other major expenditures, which would spur economic growth. It also affects our international competitiveness because every one of our trading partners uses this more efficient manner [national health-care systems] of paying for its citizens' health-care costs. All Americans, whether they're rich or poor, deserve the peace of mind of knowing that their children and their parents will live in dignity.

Interview/USA Today, 2-6:(A)9.

Robert St. Peter
Pediatrician,
University of California-San Francisco
Medical School

3

It is hard to understand how, in this country, we can have the most expensive and sophisticated health-care system in the entire world—spending more than one out of 10 dollars in our economy on health care—and yet more than one-fifth of our children do not receive even basic, preventive care. It's absolutely baffling to me and seems completely unacceptable.

Los Angeles Times, 6-23:(A)20.

William B. Schwartz
Professor of medicine,
Tufts University

4

[Criticizing Oregon's health plan which rations care based on a list of medical priorities]: Nearly every low-ranked activity on Oregon's list has some very highly valued uses. And the highly ranked activities on Oregon's list have a great many low-valued uses. The expected value or payoff from any procedure depends on the particular characteristics and severity of an illness in a particular patient. Those variables are generally not reflected in Oregon's list of priorities.

The New York Times, 8-5:(A)8.

Louis W. Sullivan
Secretary of Health
and Human Services
of the United States

5

[On new government recommendations that doctors provide post-surgery painkillers to patients faster and more aggressively]: We can do more, and we can do better, to control pain after surgery. This guideline discusses the actual physical damage which a patient can sometimes suffer as a result of pain, and it shows that inadequately managed pain can inhibit recovery, prolong hospitalization and thus potentially contribute to higher-than-necessary costs.

News conference,
Washington, D.C., March 5/
The New York Times, 3-6:(A)1.

(LOUIS W. SULLIVAN)

1

We [in the U.S.] are on a course now where we'll be spending 20 per cent of our gross national product on health care by the year 2000. That's something we cannot afford. We're spending far more than any other nation on health care and we do have 13 per cent of our citizens who are locked out of the system. We have a number of things causing the cost of health care to be so great. That cost gets built into our goods and services and makes us less competitive with other nations. So there are a number of adverse consequences we really can foresee but can avoid if we make changes now.

Interview/USA Today, 3-25:(A)11.

2

[On the new food-labeling law which will require nearly all packaged foods to indicate specific nutritional information]: The Tower of Babel in food labels has come down, and American consumers are the winners.

News conference,
Washington, D.C., Dec. 2/
The New York Times, 10-3:(A)1.

3

The health care of America's citizens must include increased emphasis on health promotion and disease prevention. As many as 900,000 of the 2.2 million deaths that occur in the United States each year could be prevented. Personal decisions by Americans to control fewer than 10 common risk factors—including use of tobacco, abuse of alcohol and illegal drugs, careless eating habits, failure to wear seat belts, ignoring necessary medical examinations and vaccinations, and unsafe sexual practices—could prevent between 40 per cent and 70 per cent of all premature deaths, a third of all cases of acute disability and two-thirds of all cases of chronic disability ... The simple fact is, improved health behavior by every American would have a far greater impact on preventing disease, increasing life span and reducing the cost of health care than any government-sponsored program or other activity.

Interview/
USA Today, 12-30:(A)11.

Mark H. Swartz
Director, Morchand Center
for Clinical Competence,
Mt. Sinai Hospital,
New York, N.Y.

4

In all the years of training, doctors are rarely, if ever, observed while examining a patient and even more rarely are they critiqued. How do you rate a doctor's interaction with a patient? There are always too many variables.

The New York Times, 6-4:(A)13.

James S. Todd
Executive vice president,
American Medical Association

5

[On the health-insurance proposals of President Bush and his Democratic Presidential opponent Bill Clinton]: The Bush plan does not go far enough, the Clinton plan goes too far, and no one tells us how much [their plans] are going to cost. The Democrats, in general, are closer to the average person and are more sensitive to trends in this country. I guess I part company with their solutions.

At AMA-hosted dinner, Sept. 23/
The Washington Post, 9-25:(A)21.

E. Fuller Torrey
Psychiatrist; Senior author of
study on the mentally ill
sponsored by Public Health
Research Group and National
Alliance for the Mentally Ill

6

[Criticizing the placing of mentally ill persons in jail cells until space opens up in psychiatric facilities]: The criminalization of the seriously mentally ill is a national disgrace. It is a remarkable return to conditions which existed 200 years ago. It mocks our pretense of being a civilized nation ... [Mental] hospitals have long waiting lists because the whole mental-health system in [for example] Indiana has broken down. It is routine practice in Indiana, and many other states, to use local jails as [holding] facilities for mentally ill patients awaiting a hospital bed.

(E. FULLER TORREY)

How would you feel if you were told that jails are being used as [holding] facilities for persons with other diseases—say diabetes and multiple sclerosis—while waiting for hospital beds?

Sept. 9/
The Washington Post, 9-10:(A)2.

Reed Tuckson
President, Drew University
of Medicine and Science

1

Each day we read stories about hospitals that turn people away because they don't have the right insurance and because they are more interested in the *business* of health care as opposed to being sensitive to the special needs of special people. [But] black hospitals have traditionally served the neediest among us. Daily, they treat the under-served and uninsured and do the work other hospitals have been unwilling to do.

Ebony, March:24.

Kenneth E. Warner
Professor,
University of Michigan

2

[Saying magazines that carry tobacco advertizing do not print sufficient articles warning about the dangers of smoking]: Magazines have not done the job they might have, had they not been dependent upon this [advertising] money . . . Cigarettes kill more people than the sum total of . . . cocaine, heroin, alcohol, auto accidents, AIDS, fires, homicide and suicide. Aren't you a little surprised by this? That's the point. We don't appreciate the magnitude.

Interview/
Los Angeles Times, 1-30:(A)27.

Henry A. Waxman
United States Representative,
D-California

3

As part of this year's budget, the [Bush] Administration proudly announced that Federal AIDS spending is growing rapidly, up by 13 per cent over last year, and 118 per cent over 1989. What they didn't say is that the growth in these numbers is almost all in the cost of caring for the sick. The growth in the Bush AIDS budget is not because of investments in research or prevention or expanded health services. The growth is because more and more Americans are dying of AIDS, and they are eligible for basic safety-net programs because they are elderly, disabled, veterans or poor. Calling this "AIDS spending" is a deliberate and cynical sham. This is health and welfare spending, and it is growing because AIDS makes people poor, sick and disabled. Such increases are no more related to research than spending for iron lungs is to immunization programs. Such increases are the mark of a failed plan. This budget is not an agenda of research opportunities; it is a body count.

Before House Health and Environment
Subcommittee, Washington, D.C.,
Feb. 24/
The Washington Post, 2-25:(A)16.

The Performing Arts

Mary Helen Barros
President, American Hispanic Owned
Radio Association

1

[Criticizing proposed changes in FCC rules that would permit ownership of more broadcasting stations by one entity than is now allowed]: When you're a small broadcaster, especially a woman or a minority broadcaster, and you're trying to get a foothold, you are placed at a tremendous disadvantage by big broadcasters who have deep pockets. Deregulation upsets the economic balance within a marketplace. It only helps the larger companies stay large.

The Washington Post,
2-7:(F)4.

Gary Bauer
President,
Family Research Council

2

[Saying audiences are influenced by the messages contained in TV programs]: The whole concept of advertising is based on the notion that powerful television images can affect what a person buys and the beer they drink. It stands to reason that if kids are getting a message that out-of-wedlock childbirth is fine, or the way to solve problems is through violence, it is going to have an impact in a society that is media-dominated.

The Washington Post,
5-21:(A)17.

Meredith Baxter
Actress

3

[On her decision to produce her own movies for TV]: I don't want to make run-of-the-mill films. I want quality and high interest. I want to

make movies that have a passion. I realize that everyone in (Hollywood) is a "producer." My hairstylist is a producer. The guy who pumps gasoline is a producer . . . I was fortunate to have some hot television movies. But as soon as a clunker comes along, who will be told to answer Meredith's calls? Somebody's underling.

Interview,
Los Angeles, Calif./
Los Angeles Times, 5-28:(F)7.

David Blankenhorn
President,
Institute for American Values

4

We can't blame the media alone for the declining well-being of children and families . . . [But] we talk with hundreds of parents on a regular basis about family values and it is a virtually unanimous opinion that TV is a negative influence because of TV's glamorization of violence, consumerism and promiscuous sexuality.

Interview/
USA Today, 6-17:(D)1.

Alfred Blumstein
Dean, John Heinz School
of Public Policy and Management,
Carnegie-Mellon University;
President, American Society
of Criminology

5

The glorification of violence on television has little effect on most folks, but it has a powerful effect on kids who are poorly socialized. It dehumanizes them and becomes a self-fulfilling process.

The New York Times,
10-19:(A)8.

L. Brent Bozell III
Chairman,
Media Research Center

1

Network primetime television is promoting a host of positions anathema to traditional family and social values. When it comes to traditional American family values like teenage sexuality, homosexuality, illegitimacy, abortion or role models like law-enforcement officials and religious figures, Hollywood addresses them in terms of "political correctness." [Although 90 per cent of Americans] identify with religion, [on TV] priests are perverts and characters with strong religious convictions are "Bible-thumpin' hayseeds."

News conference,
Washington, D.C., May 28/
Daily Variety, 5-29:26.

Daniel Burke
President,
Capital Cities/ABC, Inc.

2

[Saying the costs of switching to HDTV could threaten the economic health of small TV stations]: My concern is the possibility of undermining the universal over-the-air system of television by not thinking through every possible consequence of changes now being planned . . . Could this mean the end of a universal, free over-the-air delivery system as we know it? And if a significant number of stations do close their doors, could the loss of coverage cripple the networks, which are already fragile financially despite their size? Could we become a nation of urban "haves" and small-community "have-nots"?

Before Association for Maximum
Service Television,
Washington, D.C., Oct. 1/
Daily Variety 10-2:4.

Robert C. Byrd
United States Senator,
D-West Virginia

3

[I am] increasingly disturbed by the smutty language [on TV programs. Children are more

and more exposed to] profanity, vulgarity, violence and crudeness. Such television programming is teaching our children that gutter speech and anti-social behavior are acceptable, even preferred, norms of cool, hip, sophisticated speech and conduct . . . [TV] can be compelling, vital, life-changing and history-changing. [But TV is mostly] not just bubble gum for the mind, [but] packaged corruption for the soul.

Before the Senate,
Washington, D.C., June 2/
Daily Variety, 6-3:13.

Ted Capener
Chairman,
Public Broadcasting Service

4

[On the viewer competition PBS receives from cable-TV channels]: These Johnny-come-latelies cannot keep up [with PBS's ability] to educate, enlighten and fulfill minority and other interests in local and national markets . . . Not everyone is with the content of our programming . . . But that's okay. We are and should be open to scrutiny and evaluation every minute and every day . . . Ours is an open, democratic institution with democratic goals . . . and education as its main mission.

At PBS annual meeting,
San Francisco, Calif., June 21/
Daily Variety 6-23:20.

Gilbert Cates
Producer, Director

5

I think it's really outrageous and disgusting when you tune in TV shows in primetime and you rarely find things that don't deal with murder, rape and robbery. I'm deeply troubled by watching TV with my 13-year-old son. But I'm absolutely against censorship in any form. I *am* befuddled by [the problem]—I think at some point it stems from a lack of respect for what people like to watch.

Interview/
Daily Variety, 5-28:19.

Dick Cavett
TV talk-show host

1

I still don't have the remotest idea what's the best way to do a talk show. I've done good shows where I've hated the guest [beforehand] and turned out to like them; or vice versa; or when I prepared over or under . . . There doesn't seem to be any *rule*.

Interview, Boston, Mass./
The Christian Science Monitor,
6-18:13.

Peggy Charren
President, Action
for Children's Television

2

[On her decision to cease operations of her organization after more than 20 years]: We didn't set out to make sure that everything on the air was gorgeous. We started out to enforce the law as it applies to children. What we got was a mandate: We got Congress to say to the FCC, who said to the stations, "You have to provide programs specifically designed to meet the education and information needs of children as a condition of license renewal." When you think about it, that's sort of a miracle . . . ACT thinks that the time has come for these issues to be handled by, first of all, the national PTA, which has 7 million members who care about what their kids see on television. It's up to the pediatricians of the country to educate their patients' parents that children's television is as important an issue to worry about as what you say to kids and the schools that they go to.

Interview,
Cambridge, Mass., Jan. 8/
Los Angeles Times, 1-9:(F)1,10.

Matty Chiva
Director,
Child Psychology Center,
University of Paris (France)

3

Certainly, television contributes at least to opening up the world for children, making them more aware of the world's problems. It makes it possible to reach out to many things while staying in one place. You sit there, you zap, and you have the world at your feet.

World Press Review, March:27.

Bruce Christensen
President,
Public Broadcasting Service

4

Congress, the Federal Communications Commission and other policy-makers have given public television the latitude to go to the market-place for funding, but [in doing so] it runs the risk of making us more commercial. We've been very careful to isolate and insulate the production process from our underwriters.

The Christian Science Monitor,
11-13:12.

Robert J. Dole
United States Senator,
R-Kansas

5

[Arguing against Federal funding for public TV]: [Public-television viewers are] affluent, highly educated, the movers and shakers, the socially conscious and the well-informed. What about the rest of us?

Newsweek, 6-15:17.

Leonard Eron
Chairman, Commission on
Violence and Youth,
American Psychological Association;
Research professor emeritus,
University of Illinois, Chicago

6

There can no longer be any doubt that heavy exposure to televised violence is one of the causes of aggressive behavior, crime and violence in society. This finding of a causal link between the watching of violent television and subsequent aggressive behavior is not an isolated finding.

Before Senate Committee on
Government Affairs,
Washington, D.C./
The Christian Science Monitor, 4-7:8.

Sandra J. Evers-Manly
President,
Beverly Hills/Hollywood (Calif.)
chapter, National Association
for the Advancement of Colored People

1

African-American images on television are centered in comedy and are often one-dimensional. After 9 p.m. on TV, African-Americans and others of color are non-existent. African-American dramas have yet to be seen as extensively, in film or television, as they should. The plight of African-American women has remained unchanged. Positive roles for women of color are too few.

At meeting with entertainment-industry
executives, Oct. 28/
Daily Variety 10-29:3.

Albert Gore, Jr.
United States Senator,
D-Tennessee

2

[Criticizing those who want to cut government support for public broadcasting because of alleged sexual and political content]: The American people don't want to see public broadcasting made into a political football [by those who want to cut funding]. If we start coming into this chamber and seeking to review the editorial judgment of those who decide what programming goes on, it won't be long before we see the right wing insisting that [public-TV personality] Mr. Rogers change his lesson plan to include a right-wing agenda.

Before the Senate,
Washington, D.C., March 3/
The Washington Post, 3-4:(C)10.

Bill Haber
Television agent,
Creative Artists Agency

3

In the 1980s, the escape we all wanted [in TV programs] was pleasant—*Love Boat, Fantasy Island.* Now it's a time of reality. People want to see some semblance of truth. The comedies now are meaner, edgier. The shows are grittier.

The New York Times, 10-19:(B)5.

Takaaki Hattori
Professor of communications,
Rikkyo University (Japan)

4

[Saying many Asian leaders fear the advent of direct satellite broadcasting around the world, which permits uninvited programming from foreign countries to reach the populace]: A new type of nationalism is forming against this intrusion. Direct satellite broadcasting is like the Black Ships [U.S. Commodore Matthew Perry's arrival in Japan in 1853] all over again—something unknown and uncertain from abroad.

The Christian Science Monitor,
10-2:1.

Jesse Helms
United States Senator,
R-North Carolina

5

[Criticizing certain aspects of public broadcasting]: We're not talking about [the public-TV character] Big Bird and we're not talking about *Sesame Street* . . . [One program, for example,] blatantly promoted homosexuality as an acceptable lifestyle. It showed homosexual men dancing around naked. A lot of decent Americans called my office . . . and said, "What the hell is going on when the taxpayers are required to fund such garbage as that?"

Before the Senate,
Washington, D.C., March 3/
The Washington Post, 3-4:(C)1,10.

Andrew Heyward
Executive producer,
"48 Hours," CBS-TV

6

[On the plethora of TV news-magazine programs]: I think these news shows fit the pattern of the way people now watch television. People are busier. They work harder and longer. They can't sit in front of the set every week. We have an advantage because on a news show you can get the full measure every week, even if you haven't watched in a month. You missed nothing with any character as you would in a drama show.

The New York Times, 10-19:(C)6.

Marilyn Horne
Opera singer

1

[On whether the televising of opera is a boon or a detriment]: It's both. It's a boon for the obvious reasons that a couple of million people can watch at one time, that people who could never get to an opera house see it . . . And yet, the tradeoff is that we begin to worry more about television than we do just about regular performances. Opera, basically, is a larger-than-life art form, and I think it should be viewed from afar. Things that fit into the big proscenium and look wonderful don't necessarily look wonderful on television, especially when they're doing closeups.

Interview, New York, N.Y./
The Christian Science Monitor,
3-2:11.

Larry King
Television and radio
talk-show host

2

Today, if [politicians] do the full swing of radio and TV [talk shows, they] are going to reach 80 per cent of the public in a week. You could run a whole [election] campaign on TV and move right to the public . . . The [talk-show hosts] Larry Kings and Phil Donahues make citizens feel connected.

Los Angeles Times, 5-23:(A)20.

Everett Ladd
Professor of political science,
University of Connecticut;
Executive director,
Roper Center for
Public Opinion and Research

3

The television age produces more volatility in mood swings [among the public]. It puts the country on an emotional roller coaster given the inherent ways it covers national events. It says this is what is important. Here's crisis one. Here's crisis two. Bang, bang, bang. Full color. We have found that a generalized dissatisfaction about certain things remote has been an increasing characteristic of the television age.

Interview/USA Today, 6-23:(A)11.

Norman Lear
Producer

4

[On the new practice of TV networks showing reruns of old hit series in primetime]: There's little surprise in anything here. This is happening in difficult financial times. It's impossible to take television out of the context of the rest of American business. We always wish to do that—would that it were an art form. But it isn't. It's a business, and it reports to Wall Street the way every other American business does. As long as the climate dictates concentration on immediate success over long-term thinking, the networks will respond like every other business.

Los Angeles Times, 1-9:(F)11.

Matthew McAllister
Professor of communication studies,
Virginia Polytechnic
Institute and State University

5

The [TV] medium is now 50 years old and is running out of viable ways to permute and combine. [The networks] are trying to find a specific niche to appear special, broaden the appeal to attract enough audience to stay on the air, and react to the diversifying pressure of cable all at the same time.

The Christian Science Monitor,
9-3:14.

Michael Medved
Film critic; Co-host,
"Sneak Previews," PBS-TV

6

The notion that television has no impact on the people who watch it directly contradicts the basis on which television executives solicit thousands of dollars for 30 seconds of [advertising] time. Don't they see the inconsistency in arguing that a 30-second commercial for floor polish will change people's behavior at the supermarket and then turning around and saying that a 30-minute program showing violence and rape and horror has no influence on people's behaviors?

Interview/
Christianity Today, 4-27:39.

Bill Miller
President,
Hearst International

1

There will be more and more international [TV] co-production. We are determined to create films and programs that appeal internationally, but also have a chance on American TV. The future lies in that combination.

The Christian Science Monitor,
12-1:13.

Dennis Potter
British television writer

2

[On writing for TV]: It's that chalice that you carry, that sense of what pictures can do, which jumps over all the hierarchies of print that say, "You're a bum, you're uneducated," or, "You're educated, how wonderful." The fact that all kinds and conditions of human being can be watching the same thing at the same time made the hairs on the back of my neck prickle.

At seminar sponsored by
Museum of Television and Radio,
New York, N.Y., Jan. 15/
The New York Times, 1-18:11.

James H. Quello
Commissioner,
Federal Communications Commission

3

[Saying the FCC should consider easing its rules limiting the number of TV stations one organization can own]: I think it is time for some practical, prudent deregulation. We've gone from an era of broadcast spectrum scarcity to an era of multi-channel abundance, even over-abundance.

The New York Times, 5-15:(C)2.

Jeff Sagansky
President, CBS Entertainment

4

[On entertainer Johnny Carson leaving the *Tonight* show after hosting it for 30 years]: The idea that one man, basically unscripted, could last on TV for 30 years—it's a freak of television.

Time, 3-16:64.

Paul Simon
United States Senator,
D-Illinois

5

[On violence in TV programming]: I think the American people are not going to simply sit by and say, "Well, if they're not going to regulate themselves, we're just not going to do anything about it." I think there is going to be a demand for some type of action. And I think we have to be very careful in this field because we don't want violations of the First Amendment . . . Congress doesn't have the power to institute a ratings system [for violent TV programs], but the industry could begin it with voluntary standards . . . The problem is one of will. What we need is the CEOs of ABC and NBC and CBS saying to their people, "Let's be responsible citizens. Let's get together and establish standards."

The Christian Science Monitor,
8-26:9.

Aaron Spelling
Producer

6

While there should be [TV] programs aimed at the Emmys [awards], there should also be something for the people who just want to sit down and watch some TV after work. It seems in some circles that if you have a show that's just warm and entertaining, that's a no-no. But glamour and dreams . . . that's why I came out here [to Hollywood] in the first place.

Daily Variety, 1-17:(P)14.

David Thorburn
Director,
Cultural Studies Project,
Massachusetts Institute
of Technology

7

Television programs . . . are part of what amounts to the national conversation, and the conversation involves in the broadest sense the problems that we're concerned with. The cultural work of television, even the most apparently banal of sitcoms, is to carry on a tentative dialogue about continuity and change.

The Washington Post, 5-22:(A)23.

WHAT THEY SAID IN 1992

Grant Tinker
Producer;
Former chairman,
National Broadcasting Company

1

The economics of the [independent TV production] business no longer allow you to be in business as I was [when he headed his own production company] and [producer] Norman Lear was and Lorimar [Productions] was, where you're in effect living off your own proceeds. You were self-supporting on the basis of the projects that you sold and that succeeded. You can't do that anymore. In fact, the more you succeed today with programming, the worse shape you're in because of the accumulating deficits [of production costs]. So unless you have the deep pockets and the interacting divisions and international sales arms of the big studios, you really can't be in the independent production business.

Interview/
Los Angeles Times, 1-14:(F)1.

Peter Tortorici
Senior vice president
of programming,
CBS-TV

2

[On the new practice of TV networks showing reruns of old hit series in primetime]: Programming a network is like sending an army into battle, and you can only protect so many flanks at one time. [If] you try and fight on too many fronts and spread your resources too thin, you create such high risk that you may lose it all ... Is it an alarming trend to see [the movie] *Casablanca* 20 times? There are very few great, great works in any medium. That's why they become true classics. That's why compositions from the 17th and 18th century are playing on the radio today. That's why movies from the '30s and '40s are on laser disc today. There are only so many great works the creative community is capable of producing. There's no reason in our mind why television would be exempt from that.

Los Angeles Times, 1-9:(F)11.

Dean Valentine
Executive vice president
of network television,
Walt Disney Company

3

[On the new practice of TV networks showing reruns of old hit series in primetime]: The networks are looking for more and more ways to save money. The danger is, and I'm not the first person to say it, you wind up with the situation where the snake swallows its own tail for survival and eventually disappears. You put on more old stuff and more old stuff, pretty soon you don't have a network, because a network depends on original, quality programming.

Los Angeles Times, 1-9:(F)11.

Harold M. Williams
President, J. Paul Getty Trust

4

Television is the dominant medium today. What does television tell us about our values? Primarily, violence of one form or another. Isn't there something more constructive that TV can tell us?

Interview/
Los Angeles Times, 5-15:(T)7.

Alan Wurtzel
Senior research executive,
American Broadcasting Companies

5

[On the TV industry's reliance on audience ratings, which have sometimes proven not as reliable as previously thought]: The thing we've always had has been this set of numbers. It's the foundation upon which program decisions are made, deals are made, advertising dollars are spent. When those numbers became unreliable, inconsistent, inaccurate, unexplainable, they just threw into chaos almost everything we did, because they were the basis on which the business was built.

The Atlantic, March:67.

MOTION PICTURES

Percy Adlon
German director

1

My general experience is that Germans don't like their own films . . . The sad truth is that the German critics are extremely hateful to most German films. Instead, they embrace anything American, even mediocrities . . . They can't distinguish between good and bad Hollywood movies. And the German audience never gets taught.

Interview, Los Angeles, Calif./
The Washington Post, 1-18:(G)4.

Woody Allen
Actor, Writer, Director

2

People always used to think that I was some poor little schnook who lived in Greenwich Village, who was physically weak and so on, and I always tried to explain that this is the natural material of a comedian, whether it's Charlie Chaplin or Bob Hope. Charlie Chaplin was not inept; this was part of his art. The same with Bob Hope; he's not just a girl-chasing fool and a coward's coward. The same with me. I did a certain kind of character publicly, but in real life I lived on the Upper East Side in a nice apartment. I was an athletic kid when I grew up and was not what people thought I was. I thought there was something wrong with the culture for wanting to think that. You don't want to think that John Wayne would walk around with two six-shooters. That's silly to me.

Interview, New York/
Los Angeles Times, 3-15:(Calendar)87.

Pedro Almodovar
Spanish director

3

I don't want to become an expensive director. For me, the special effects are the faces of the actors and the good line to say. This is as powerful as the thousand special effects of *Terminator 2.*

Interview/
"Interview" magazine, January:80.

Robert Altman
Director

4

I collaborate with everybody, but mostly the actors. You could point out any really good thing that happened in any of my films [and ask], "Whose idea is that [and] it is almost invariably somebody else's. And I don't even know whose.

Time, 4-20:80.

5

[Today, the major motion-picture companies] have all these executives, and they keep adding them on, but none of them can make a decision. The decision goes upstairs. Upstairs, there's nobody in that room—it's empty. And what comes back is something based on computer data: "We don't find a place for what you tell us this picture is going to be. We don't find an example of where that will succeed." There's nobody there who can have a hunch. Not even a bad guy. People don't work on feelings or hunches [anymore]. They work on what they think is intellect. And you cannot intellectualize art.

Interview, New York, N.Y./
"Interview" magazine, May:31.

Richard Attenborough
Actor, Director

6

[On why he cast a relatively unknown actor to play Charlie Chaplin in the film he is now directing on Chaplin's life]: If you have a box-office name, then the persona, the baggage that that actor brings is significant. If you want to convince an audience they're witnessing somebody's life demonstrated by a particular performance, a life that people know about, then if you can bring in someone with other connotations you start at a disadvantage. By finding someone . . . with [a] relative lack of familiarity on screen, you bring an opportunity for suspension of disbelief. Whereas if you start off by saying—well, I'm sure Mr. [Robert] Redford would dye his hair . . .

Interview, Fillmore, Calif./
Los Angeles Times, 1-26:(Calendar)34.

William J. Bennett
Former Secretary of Education
of the United States;
Former Chairman, National
Endowment for the Humanities
of the United States

1

I say, too bad about foreign films. If they can't make it [economically], tough. I stopped going [to foreign films] at the same time I threw away my black turtleneck and I hated them, I hated America, I just gave it all up. I think they died in the '80s when people decided that life was not meaningless and that we were going to adopt a different posture toward the world. Now, I'm unfairly typifying foreign films. But I went to those [Ingmar] Bergman things and felt bad, and felt good about feeling bad, and the '80s was good medicine for that.

At forum sponsored by
American Enterprise Institute/
The Washington Post, 3-19:(C)3.

Tim Burton
Director

2

Movies are very hard to make and all you want are people to help you. And you don't care if it comes from the studio head or the guy cleaning the toilet. Maybe they are one and the same. But

a lot of people don't help you and a lot of times those are the people giving you money. That's where the struggle is, this generic "us versus them"—the film-makers versus the studios—which is unfortunate because it doesn't need to be that way. But it's getting harder and harder.

Interview, Los Angeles, Calif./
Los Angeles Times, 6-14:(Calendar)78.

Vincent Canby
Film critic,
"The New York Times"

3

[On critics who are used by the film industry to promote their films or act in their behalf]: Critics are not part of the industry. We are reporters, period. The danger is for film companies or producers to somehow charm the reviewers and say, "You're so smart, so bright, that we need your input." Whether or not a producer pays a critic or charms them with confidences about what's going on, the critic can cross the line. It's very difficult to write a devastating review of the work of someone you like, so you try to avoid having much contact with them.

Interview/
The New York Times, 3-11:(B)3.

Gilbert Cates
Producer, Director

4

So many students at graduate film schools know all about the lenses and hardware of making films, and the grammar of films, but they have nothing to say. It's as if you went to journalism school and spent all your time learning to use a computer rather than learning how to write a story. We cannot be led by our technology.

Interview/Daily Variety, 5-28:19.

Sean Connery
Actor

5

The American film industry is like Broadway—it's always dying. But it's still got an entrepreneurial sense. I think what's hurting it

(SEAN CONNERY)

now is that they're locked into sequels, and the energy that should be channeled into product is now channeled into making money back as soon as possible. It used to be that people were more willing to let time go by before turning a profit and concentrated on the nuts and bolts of making the movie. But now you have a lot of people in positions of control who have absolutely no idea of what film-making is about.

Interview, Los Angeles, Calif./
Los Angeles Times, 7-24:(F)8.

Kevin Costner
Actor

1

[When acting,] I don't need to always wear the white hat. I'm interested in a character larger than life, who's strong and decisive, someone who stirs the juices. I'm not in this business to protect my image. Hell, I have no idea what my image really is. The characters I play are frequently better than I am personally. They're more heroic, more honorable. I try to honor the world of character by being as accurate and truthful as I can. I think I'm about what's gone before me. Not just myself but what Hollywood represents. Those earlier stars like Henry Fonda and Spencer Tracy helped teach me about becoming the kind of man I'd like to be. You learn a lot from watching heroes act. Henry Fonda once said, "I've played enough great men on screen that I feel I should've learned something from them."

Interview/
Cosmopolitan, March:199.

Andrew Davis
Director

2

People want to see action [films]. Life is boring for a lot of people and they want to be excited. But if you make these, you've got to like the people in it. You've got to have some irreverent humor. Audiences want to cheer for the good guys and hiss the bad guys, and really love the hissing. Look, it's so dark out there for a lot of people. You want to give people some hope without turn-

ing it into a diatribe. Every successful action movie has a guy who's a nobody, who gets messed up by the big guys in the system and then comes back and does right. It's Robin Hood. It's hope for the little guy. That's what it's all about.

Interview, Los Angeles, Calif./
The New York Times, 10-26:(B)2.

Brian De Palma
Director

3

In a different era, I would love to have been a silent-film director. If you are dependent on words, you aren't using what makes movies movies. In thrillers, images—dark corners, people following each other, intense close-ups—are used to create tension, emotion, ambience. Those directors driven more by character and ideas should spend time making thrillers to get a better grip on the medium they're working in.

Interview, Los Angeles, Calif./
Los Angeles Times, 8-2:(Calendar)25.

Olympia Dukakis
Actress

4

[On winning the Academy Award]: People think of an Oscar as the culmination of your life, payment for many sacrifices. To me, it's less about reward than evolution.

Interview/
Los Angeles Times, 3-29:(Calendar)48.

Robert Duvall
Actor

5

[On his playing the role of the late Soviet leader Joseph Stalin in a new film]: How do you find in the scenes the overall arc of a character like this without thinking, "I am playing an evil guy"? As an actor, you hang back, you take it down to zero, to nothing. It's always a little more dangerous that way. You never get ahead of the guy, you don't anticipate, you play it moment to moment and you don't know what the results will be. It's like [Marlon] Brando at his best. Or [Gene] Hackman. Or George C. Scott. Or Kim

WHAT THEY SAID IN 1992

(ROBERT DUVALL)

Stanley. Certain actors do it. You start from nothing, from zero, and not embroider at all. You reveal the guy slowly, naturally.

Interview, Beverly Hills, Calif./
The New York Times, 11-5:(A)12.

Clint Eastwood
Actor, Director

1

[Saying successful film-makers shouldn't take themselves too seriously]: All the things you've attempted, where they fall, has a lot of fate involved with it. It's like a wheel in motion— where it goes, we don't know. The only thing you can hope for is to keep your balance, your head screwed on straight, and improve instead of degenerating into somebody that says, "This is American culture." Big deal! Big deal! You haven't done anything that great, haven't found a cure for heart disease or AIDS or solved the disassembly of nuclear weapons. You've created a certain amount of entertainment. That's fun for people, but that's about all you can say for it. Maybe you've cast a little message here and there.

Interview, New York/
Los Angeles Times, 8-2:(Calendar)82.

Michael D. Eisner
Chairman,
Walt Disney Company

2

You look at the future landscape of the entertainment business, and I'm convinced more and more that our company's leverage is in software. Software is managed by people as opposed to machines, and the creation of intellectual product is what we do well.

The New York Times, 11-3:(B)4.

Nora Ephron
Screenwriter, Director

3

There are three things about directing a movie. One is, you better have a pretty good script. The

second is, you better not screw up the casting, because you can't survive that. The third is knowing where the shot is. And if you [also] write the movie, you know where the shot is.

Interview, Beverly Hills, Calif./
Los Angeles Times, 2-16:(Calendar)28.

Jodie Foster
Actress, Director

4

Personally, I'd like to see more good films made in Hollywood. I'm not sure why the studios seem convinced that a great literate story can't be entertaining. Because movies are so expensive to make, decisions are made for the wrong reasons: "Will millions of people like this?" I think there should be room for more than just stabs at mass popularity. Without taking risks, without addressing the complexities of life, you're doomed to mediocrity and dishonesty. I don't believe that that's such a sure bet at the box office anymore anyway.

Los Angeles Times, 3-29:(Calendar)7.

Brian Grazer
Producer

5

I trust my [creative] judgment, and I don't equivocate. I'm totally impervious to rejection. When someone says "no" to me, it has no relevance to my reality. I just keep trying . . . [To be a producer,] you have to be a doer personality. You have to be the person who sees the top of the mountain and is always pushing toward it. He sees something on the side, [but] he doesn't walk over to get it. He just keeps going. You don't get deviated on little fire trails. You don't trip on a rock. You just keep pushing up the hill. No matter how incremental.

Interview/
Los Angeles Times, 2-16:(Calendar)30.

Peter Guber
Chairman,
Sony Pictures Entertainment

6

This [movie] business depends on people picking themselves up out of their couch, putting

(PETER GUBER)

fuel in their tanks, loading up the vehicle, parking and putting themselves in seats with 600 other people to share a communal experience. Movies basically have an allure that staying at home with a frozen chicken dinner and a video can't achieve. While entertainment isn't a panacea for problems, it certainly has a palliative effect.

Interview, Aspen, Colo./
The New York Times, 1-2:(B)1.

Katharine Hepburn
Actress

1

[On acting]: I think you either can do it or you can't do it. Usually if you want to do it very much you can do it. Sometimes you want to do it very much and you can't do it. But I don't think it requires any special brilliance. It took a lot of nerve in the theatre. I don't think it takes any nerve in the movies.

Interview, New York, N.Y./
The Saturday Evening Post, Jan.-Feb.:43.

2

[On comedy]: I like to make people laugh, and I like to laugh. I was brought up in that era of the '30s and '40s when the writing had a great deal of wit. Now it doesn't. It's rather heavy on the witty side. Comedy today is visual, it's not literary, and ours were both literary and visual.

Interview, New York, N.Y./
The Saturday Evening Post, Jan.-Feb.:43.

Walter Hill
Director

3

[On whether violence in motion pictures inspires violence in real life]: I somehow think the notion that if you disarm Clint Eastwood or Arnold Schwarzenegger you can change the world in some positive way is probably a little naive. The real question to ask, in terms of motion pictures, is: Do they avoid social issues? The answer, on the whole, is pretty clearly yes.

Los Angeles Times, 5-18:(F)12.

Anthony Hopkins
Actor

4

Some directors say: "Okay, let's talk about *character*." But, really, what is there to talk about? On stage, sure, you have to establish what the character is. But on film you can put it together like a jigsaw puzzle. It seems to fall into place without thinking.

Interview, Dartmouth, England/
Los Angeles Times, 3-1:(Calendar)8.

Jeremy Irons
Actor

5

[Saying he carries something of his roles with him off-screen]: I used to say I sloughed it off when I got home, but I don't think I do. A bit of it stays. I think I'm like a room in which a cigar isn't actually being smoked, but you can still smell the cigar. And then I go into work, and I light up the cigar again.

Interview, New York, N.Y./
The New York Times, 11-20:(B)6.

Irving Lazar
Literary agent

6

I admire a lot of the guys who run things [at the major studios] today. They're fantastically bright and quick. But they're not much fun. You're not going to get a laugh out of Peter Guber [the head of Sony Pictures], I can tell you that. In the old days, humor and eccentricity were appreciated . . . Most people who run the studios today are just interested in the bottom line. You have MBAs who might as well be making manure. Their point of view is only money. Now, nothing's wrong with making money. But I deplore the lack of dedication to making good movies.

Interview, Beverly Hills, Calif./
"W" magazine, 5-25:18.

Spike Lee
Director

7

[His new film about civil-rights leader Malcolm X] is going to be a big hit, and it's really going to

WHAT THEY SAID IN 1992

(SPIKE LEE)

crumble that old, tired Hollywood axiom that the white movie-going masses are not going to see a black film that's a drama, or a film that's not a comedy and musical, or that doesn't have Eddie Murphy in it. Because no matter what lip service those executives say, that is still their belief. Just look at TV: Every single show that is about black folks, they're all situation comedies. I mean, you can't get drama out of their lives? But that's because they feel that white people won't be interested. I really think they're underestimating the intelligence of the white movie-going masses, who will see anything if it's done good.

Interview/Time, 11-23:66.

Li Shaohong
Chinese director

1

The basic steps of getting a [Chinese] film made are still the same. Many people must approve the script at different stages of production . . . and there's a whole series of other censorships after the film is finished. Still, the opportunities to make films [in China] are increasing, since foreign money is coming in. The overall atmosphere—in choosing what you'll shoot and how you'll arrange and organize a production—is a little easier and more relaxed then it used to be.

Interview/
The Christian Science Monitor,
10-14:14.

Paul Mazursky
Director, Screenwriter

2

[On the current trend toward mainstream films with "family values"]: The word "mainstream" is what I hear a lot. Will it last? I doubt it. None of these cycles last. The mindless pictures just seem to make more money. In the 20 years I've been making movies, there have been so many trends. Today, it's this one; two years from now it'll be something else.

Interview/
The New York Times, 11-12:(B)4.

Michael Medved
Film critic; Co-host,
"Sneak Previews," PBS-TV

3

Lately in movies there is an increasing tendency to show people urinating. What if we took that a little further, to include a lot of scenes showing people defecating? The fact that something occurs in real life doesn't mean that it must be up there on screen in all movies.

Interview/
Christianity Today, 4-27:40.

4

[Movies] took a fateful turn in the late '60s, reacting in part to the removal of the [Production] Code in 1966. Much of what Hollywood did [after that] was self-destructive and alienated audiences. I'm not a swami—I'm a film critic—but I couldn't believe that no one had ever written [as he does] about what happened to those missing movie-goers. [Audiences] went from 44 million a week in 1965 to 16 million a week in 1968. And it [the bottom figure] stayed down there. What happened? Something went wrong with the movies.

Interview, Santa Monica, Calif./
Publishers Weekly, 10-12:55.

Robert Mitchum
Actor

5

Anybody, as long as they can speak—even if they can't—can get into a drama school. And they will "teach" you to act. Now, if you go to Juilliard to study music, if you don't have an ear you can't make it. If you're not a natural musician, they won't let you in. So there's no mystery about acting. But you've got to have the basics. It's a matter of timing, talent, mimicry. Some pictures you get to use all these to the full. Others, the best you can do is speak the lines believably. I've been accused of "coasting" through movies. But there are some parts you cannot do anything else. There is literally nothing to do but to be there.

Interview/
Film Comment, July-Aug.:35.

Donald M. Morgan
Cinematographer

1

The lovely thing about [making a] film is that you can tell someone exactly what you did, but they can't do the same thing because part of *you* is on that film. It's like leaving fingerprints.

Daily Variety, 12-15:12.

Rupert Murdoch
Chairman, Fox, Inc.
(20th Century Fox Film Corporation)

2

The impulse is for you, the studio, to take all the risk [in making a film], and if you clear something [a profit] at the end of the day, good luck to you, and if you don't, forget it, let's go on to the next thing. I'm not frightened of the risk. I'm looking at the risk and the reward. There's not enough reward for the risks involved. The secret is you don't have to make expensive movies to be successful. Look at Disney and *Sister Act*. It looks like it was made on half a sound stage. But it works.

Interview, Los Angeles, Calif./
The New York Times, 7-21:(B)9.

Eddie Murphy
Actor

3

[On his latest film, *Boomerang*]: *Boomerang* is a very political film. Because it is black and yet it's about nothing to do with being black and it cost $40-million. So if it's successful, then it will prove that you can do [mainstream] movies about blacks that are not just set in the [black neighbor-] 'hood. Those movies are good, but if that's all we [blacks] did—if every time a movie came out and it was "hey man, it's going down"—then we'd be right back into black exploitation films again.

Interview/
Los Angeles Times, 6-28:(Calendar)76.

Lynda Obst
Producer

4

[On Hollywood]: There's the nature of this place. Sociopathically competitive, status-con-scious, hierarchal, flavor-of-the-month-oriented and glamour-struck. [The Oscar award] is the brass ring at the end of the rainbow. You become crazy.

The New York Times, 3-31:(B)4.

Jack Palance
Actor

5

[On his being nominated for an Academy Award this year]: I sure hope they celebrate serious acting . . . The only reason I'm around at all this year is that I had a great role. You see people getting nominated over and over again for Oscars because they get the best roles of the year . . . It wasn't me; I don't kid myself about that.

Los Angeles Times, 3-29:(Calendar)6.

Anna Hamilton Phelan
Screenwriter

6

To write a screenplay and not be admitted to the psychiatric ward at Cedars [Hospital], it helps to be emotionally secure as a human being and have no attachment to the outcome [of the script after you finish it]. You get pregnant, gestate the baby, go through a live birth, cut the umbilical cord and have to let everyone [at the studio]—including wives, lovers, aunts, uncles—take the baby and do what they want with it.

Los Angeles Times, 4-5:(Calendar)22.

Sydney Pollack
Director

7

Before they can be anything else, American movies are a product. This is not good or bad; this is what we've got. A very few may become art, but all of them, whatever their ambitions, are first financed as commodities. They're the work of craftsmen and artists, but they're soon offered for sale. Whether we say that we're "creating a film" or merely "making a movie," the enterprise itself is sufficiently expensive and risky that it cannot be, and it will not be, undertaken without the hope of reward. We have no Medicis here. It

WHAT THEY SAID IN 1992

(SYDNEY POLLACK)

takes two distinct entities—the financiers and the makers—to produce movies, and there is a tension between them. Their goals are sometimes similar, but they do different things . . . If you operate in a democracy and you're market-supported and -driven, the spectrum of what you will get is going to be very wide indeed. It will range from trash to gems. There are 53,000 books published in this country every year. How many of them are very good? Tired as I may be of fast-food-recipe, conscienceless, simple-minded books, films, TV and music, the question remains: Who is to be society's moral policeman?

Speech,
Washington, D.C., March 10/
The Washington Post, 5-20:(A)22.

Richard Price
Screenwriter

1

It takes about three times as long as you think [to write a screenplay]. You sit down and write a first draft in three months. Then everybody's panicky, time's passing, they get a director, the director asks for changes, you put in the changes, the director goes off and does another movie instead, you get a new director, and the new director doesn't like what the other director wanted. This guy goes off and does another movie, and then you've got to wait six months. He gets a new script. They hire an actor. The actor says, "I can't say this. The way I see this character is blah, blah, blah." And it becomes like one of those lamb carcasses that the Tartars played polo with. Every time you start, you get naive all over again. You think, this one's going to be different. "Hurry up and wait" is the expression that I use to describe the pressure in Hollywood.

Interview, New York, N.Y./
Publishers Weekly, 5-4:38.

Satyajit Ray
Indian director

2

Cinema is a great compendium of the arts, requiring everything I am good at—storytelling,

visual design, camera work, acting, ingredients theatrical and dramatic, and, finally, musical elements. Advertising techniques, illustration and calligraphy are involved in planning the scenes, their composition, credit sequences, posters, decor and costumes. Yes, I had been good at my job as the director of a British advertising agency, but soon realized that an advertising artist is never free. He has to contend with the winds of time. Cinema is the only medium where I could have total creative independence.

Interview/
"Interview" magazine, June:22.

Del Reisman
President,
Writers Guild of America West

3

We don't believe there is a causal relationship [between violence in motion pictures and real-life violence]. And the cure [government censorship] is horrendous.

Los Angeles Times, 5-18:(F)12.

Joe Roth
Chairman,
20th Century Fox Film Corporation

4

We've [film-makers] become obsessed with the business of the movies and not the movie business. The fact of the matter is, if someone has a good idea, a good story, it doesn't matter who's in it or, frankly, who directs it. People will come and revenues will go up.

At entertainment-industry conference
sponsored by Variety and
Wertheim Schroder, New York, N.Y./
Daily Variety, 3-30:12.

Paul Schrader
Director, Screenwriter

5

[On finding an idea when screenwriting]: The more you force it, the harder it is. It just comes to you at a certain point and knocks at your door and says "Write me." Plot and execution are rela-

(PAUL SCHRADER)

tively easy after that, particularly if what you're doing is a character study. The kinds of stories I write are not plot-driven. Events happen and the plots do coalesce, but they're primarily studies of a kind of life.

Interview/
"Interview" magazine, March:52.

1

It's nice when films have hidden language . . . It's not good that audiences understand everything. There's a certain level of a film where audiences get 90 per cent of it, and then another level where they get 50 per cent, and then there's always some things that maybe only 10 per cent get. And unless you layer the film that way, it doesn't feel complex. If you're watching a movie and you're getting everything, in a way I find it a little disappointing.

Interview/
Film Comment, March-April:59.

Ron Shelton
Screenwriter

2

[Lamenting a trend at the major studios toward mainstream films with "family values"]: It's discouraging. Studios are going the way of television networks. What "mainstream" really means is the lowest common denominator. The reason for this is that television people are now running a lot of the studios. You sit with these people and they don't know what a movie is. [To them,] it's television on a large screen. People who used to run studios were different. Sure, you couldn't talk about life experiences because they didn't have any. But you could talk in terms of movies. You could say, "I have an idea that's a cross between *Sunset Boulevard* and *Straw Dogs*," and they'd know what you're talking about. These people today have never heard of Billy Wilder. Or Sam Peckinpah. They don't know movies!

Interview/
The New York Times, 11-12:(B)4.

Terry Southern
Author, Screenwriter

3

[On the immediacy of film compared to the written word]: You step off a curb and you're hit. That's a primary experience. A secondary experience is you're standing on the curb, you don't step off but someone next to you steps off and so you see it happen in a vicarious way. It's very impressive. You hear the screech of the brakes, the thud of the body. To this extent, film is stronger than prose, because film is much closer to the primary experience. If you read in a newspaper, "So-and-so was hit by a car," even if it's well written, like a feature story, you still have to visualize it. Seeing it in the cinema medium, on the other hand, is very powerful and irresistible.

Interview, East Canaan, Conn./
The Washington Post, 3-17:(B)1.

James Stewart
Actor

4

When I came out [to Hollywood] in 1935 under contract to MGM, this was the ideal way to make pictures. You learned your craft by working at it. Unlike so many now, you didn't sit at home and wait for something you liked and reject everything you disliked. As soon as you were through with one thing, it was "Okay, now you play George. Go down to costuming and get fitted for what you'll wear. You'll start Tuesday." You either got a big part in a small picture or a small part in a big picture, but all the time you were learning. It was a great system.

Interview, Beverly Hills, Calif./
Los Angeles Times, 5-10:(Calendar)80.

Barbra Streisand
Actress, Director

5

[On criticism that she is too controlling when she directs or produces a film]: You don't ask a *man* do you want to be in control—you *assume* he wants control. Why should a woman be any different? . . . People see it as some ego trip; it's the weirdest thing. What does producing mean? It means getting it on the screen, watching over it like it's my baby. What's wrong with a woman doing that? How could anyone *not* want to be in control of their work? It's a very anti-feminist thing we're talking about here.

Interview, New York, N.Y./
Ladies' Home Journal, February:150.

Bertrand Tavernier
French director

1

There are two or three types of directors who write. The directors who write their own screenplays—[Joseph L.] Mankiewicz, Delmer Daves, many people—*are* writers. And sometimes they are writers on the screenplays where they are not [credited as writers] . . . The second type greatly influences the writer, in different ways. It's not as though these directors are actually writing, but they give a kind of direction. That's Hitchcock, Hawks, Lubitsch . . . It's *nearly* like writing. Then you have the director who does not write but whose style will change certain things, and whose style, therefore, becomes almost like writing.

Interview/
Film Comment, March-April:15.

Liv Ullmann
Actress

2

I never made a "big" box-office picture . . . Yet at the film festivals I have won awards for every film I have done in recent years; but that is not widely known . . . Yet the work has meaning, wherever it falls. It is not how many seeds you plant. If I have planted one, I am happy. Our craft was never meant to be about big stars. Our craft was to *act*.

Interview/Lear's, February:86.

Jack Valenti
President, Motion Picture Association
of America

3

If the movies are there, they [the audience] will come. I don't care whether it's a depression, a

recession or an earthquake . . . There is only one constant value in our mesmerizing business: If we make movies that have high entertainment quality, the audience will come. If we make movies that just don't have it, the audience stays away in droves.

At NATO/ShoWest convention,
Las Vegas, Nev., Feb. 18/
Daily Variety, 2-19:20.

4

[On the Cannes Film Festival]: In ancient times in the Middle East, caravans would trek across the desert and gather at an oasis, where the leaders would catch up on business. Cannes is the oasis where the movie caravans gather.

Los Angeles Times, 5-13:(D)2.

5

Each year, over 450 movies are produced and released in the U.S.A. Unhappily, some of them won't be very good. Movie-making is an unpredictable art form and, between the idea and the finished print, much can go wrong and often does. [But] American movies are the U.S.A.'s most-wanted exports, returning to this country more than $3.5-billion in surplus balance of trade. The year 1993 will be no different. American movies are the toast of the world.

Interview/USA Today, 12-30:(A)11.

Christopher Walken
Actor

6

There is something cathartic about watching a performance—not just acting, but dancing or singing. There is a little shift, a little change. I think that's what people mean when they say, "I was moved." It doesn't necessarily mean "I was moved to tears" but "I was moved in my mind." I call it emotional power and it's a very valuable thing for an actor to have. There are people who are very stoic, very unrevealing about what they think and feel, and yet they have something about them that you take very seriously—and that's what I mean. As time goes by, I'm less interested in emotion and more interested in that. The

(CHRISTOPHER WALKEN)

ability to laugh and cry and get angry at the drop of a hat becomes less interesting—it's a facility, a technique, an interesting gift, but [one] that can be abused.

Interview/
Film Comment, July-Aug.:58.

Brian Walton
Executive director,
Writers Guild of America West

1

[On the relationship between the screenwriter and the film industry]: There's either an inherent conflict—or an approved one. Writers don't do what they do unless they believe in the art; companies don't do what they do unless they believe in the business. What you need is a capitalist who believes in art or an artist who believes in commerce.

Los Angeles Times, 4-5:(Calendar)22.

Wim Wenders
German director

2

I think American movies have become, for the most part, "entertainments." Films in Europe still start with ideas that allow film to be an expression. In most American movies now, the only reality is the reality of other movies.

Interview, New York, N.Y./
"Interview" magazine, January:76.

3

Hollywood films are made from recipes. Movies that come out today only pretend to be telling stories. It's that whole business of story conferences and going through the script three times with different writers. The ingredients and the special effects and show values are more important. The story is only there to create a certain chain of excitement—it's no longer a living thing.

Interview, New York/
Connoisseur, January:18.

Debra Winger
Actress

4

Don't you think it's silly when women talk about power in Hollywood? Let's talk brass tacks. I haven't seen a chick bring in what [actor] Arnold Schwarzenegger does in the first week of a *Terminator* movie. When *you* [an actress] can open a movie like that, *you* can make $11-million, too. It's all ridiculous. After a while, actors forget they're making a huge amount of money. That's something you have to learn, not to be identified with how much money you make. We all operate under that illusion for a time. Then you wake up. Hopefully you pay attention, and that empowers you as a human.

Interview/
Harper's Bazaar, June:80.

WHAT THEY SAID IN 1992

MUSIC

Rockwell Blake
Opera singer

1

If the Metropolitan Opera is marketing itself nationwide, it must produce a product that's capable of being understood and appreciated by entire audiences. Especially in America, the marketing that goes on is a necessary evil. [As a singer], one can get caught in the cogs of these machines. One has to be very aware of what one is doing, be capable of self-recognition, self-determination, self-evaluation. Without that, one can be convinced on one's own publicity . . . The art itself lives outside of the bounds of the media, except as a carrier or fodder for criticism. The difficulty is that we are all entertainers, and that is quite true of the media.

Interview/Opera News, 2-29:21.

Garth Brooks
Country-music singer

2

This business has a way of changing you . . . picking at you until you are a different person. I want to give people the best show we can, but more than anything I want the people who came to see us a long time ago go away from the show thinking: "That guy was real then and he's real now. He hasn't changed."

Interview, Reno, Nev./
Los Angeles Times, 6-28:(Calendar)62.

Jose Carreras
Opera singer

3

What originates everything (for a singer) are the emotions, the feelings, what we call soul. Then the brain commands these feelings to the voice. The voice is just the vehicle, it's the very last step in the chain.

Interview, Los Angeles, Calif./
The Christian Science Monitor, 9-30:14.

Alain Coblence
Director, Prague Mozart Foundation
(Czechoslovakia)

4

Young musicians today are trained in a very superficial, highly specialized, highly technical, highly dehumanized way. We need to train them in the cultural context of the music they are making, at its birthplace here in Central Europe.

The New York Times, 10-22:(B)1.

John Corigliano
Composer

5

[On writing new operas]: In the concert world, if you write a piece and it gets knocked by the critics, another conductor in another city who believes in it can put it on the program, and it can be successful. But it's rare today that another opera company will give a [new operatic] work a second chance, because of the incredible expense involved. Puccini and Verdi operas that were not successful initially got second chances.

Interview/Opera News, 1-4:10.

David DiChiera
General director,
Opera Pacific,
Orange County, Calif.

6

In the next 10 years, you're going to see many opera companies creating works which build bridges into groups in the community which have not heretofore played a great part in the makeup of opera audiences. In the 21st century, opera companies will no longer be simply the repositories of European-style works. They're going to reflect the changing makeup of our cities. There's no doubt we're going to have a very different repertoire—one that's reflective of our times.

Los Angeles Times, 4-19:(Calendar)59.

Christoph von Dohnanyi
Music director,
Cleveland Orchestra

1

There are certain things that I think are indispensable priorities [in the making of great orchestras]. The first thing is, you try to create a spirit where the musicians and the conductor try to achieve the same goals. There are orchestras where the conductor does his "pirouette," so to speak, and the orchestra does their "pirouette." Then what you need is discipline, and a real understanding of democracy. That's why I think there are lots of good orchestras in [the U.S.], because the social structure makes it possible to acknowledge authority without feeling dominated.

Interview, Cleveland, Ohio/
The Christian Science Monitor,
5-18:13.

Christoph Eschenbach
Music director,
Houston Symphony Orchestra

2

Being a music director of an orchestra has a very human side . . . You develop a mutual understanding with the orchestra, and you learn to supply the musical ideas, the passion that they need. You can develop a wonderful rapport and you learn what you can draw out of people, the way you can communicate with their musical sensibilities, the excitement you share with a musician who sees himself doing what he didn't think he could do.

Interview/
The Washington Post, 3-2:(B)10.

Valery Gergiev
Artistic director,
Kirov Theatre (Russia)

3

Classical music is more than temporary pleasure. Rock music is a short passion; it lasts two, three years—then some new trend comes along. *Don Giovanni* exists forever . . . The music existed before us and will exist after us. We should remember that beauty, reality, the depth of the characters, the depth of the relationships—

maybe we respond to them because we do not have such beauty, such depth in our lives, no matter how much we love our families and friends. We sometimes don't *have* real lives in music, because we are so involved in "business." We have the opportunity in opera to show these characters who are deeply involved. We have the *responsibility*. If we deny the beauty, the depth, the seriousness that touches you so much in the opera, we have failed. And we must not fail.

Interview/Opera News, June:57.

Tom Harrell
Jazz saxophonist

4

Music can be a lot of things. It can reflect what people are directly experiencing. It rethinks the industrialization of our lives. The subway in New York is a beautiful instrument. I listen to my refrigerator and try to figure the chords it generates, the higher and higher partials of its harmonic series. The first music was imitations of the sounds of nature—birds, thunder, rivers rushing. It's based on the heartbeat. Music can be soothing, but it also expresses what drives us.

Interview. Los Angeles, Calif./
Los Angeles Times, 6-13:(F)1.

Joe Henderson
Jazz saxophonist

5

I think of playing music on the bandstand like an actor relates to a role. I've always wanted to be the best interpreter the world has ever seen . . . I've always tried to recreate melodies even better than the composer who wrote them. I've always tried to come up with something that never even occurred to them. This is the challenge: not to rearrange the intentions of the composers but to stay within the parameters of what the composers have in mind and be creative and imaginative and meaningful.

Interview/Down Beat, March:16.

Marilyn Horne
Opera singer

6

I still believe that American [opera] singers should have the European experience. The

WHAT THEY SAID IN 1992

theatres over there are maybe not what they were, the provincial theatres. I think the standard has probably fallen a bit, but I really still feel that American singers need to be immersed in those languages [Italian, German, French], because those three languages are what they are going to be singing their whole career. The thing I don't understand is how the people can make careers without speaking the languages. But we do have some very startling examples [of that].

Interview, New York, N.Y./
The Christian Science Monitor,
3-2:11.

Michael Jackson
Rock singer

1

Deep inside I feel that this world we live in is really a big, huge, monumental symphonic orchestra. I believe that in its premordial form all of creation is sound and that it's not just random sound, that it's music . . . I think music soothes the savage beast. If you put cells under a microscope and you put music on, you'll see them move and start to dance. It affects the soul.

Interview, Africa/Ebony, May:40.

Christopher Keene
General director,
New York City Opera

2

[On alternative versions and stagings of traditional operas]: One opera has a traditional mold, and you play it until you can't stand the sight of it any longer. Then somebody comes along with an idea, say, about *Carmen* that you feel does no injustice to the work, indeed illuminates it in an interesting way. So you try it out. This seems to me the whole value of a theatre like ours, which is not heavily indebted to tradition. We talk about European traditions, but the Europeans are the pioneers, simply because they've seen these operas so many times that they have to do something different just to get themselves through yet another *Figaro*. I probably take more heat from my subscribers about these alternative visions

than about any other thing we do. Our *Traviata*, which sold extremely well, aroused the most passionate anger from people for whom these pieces are relics, I think, of their ancestry—relics of a vision of the world order that has vanished, representing a kind of harmony and orderliness that are increasingly difficult to envision as part of our current lives. Our *Boheme* and *Butterfly* productions are threatening to vaporize at the rise of every curtain. They've seen thousands of performances. They continue to sell extremely well, and one says if something's not broken, why fix it? But they simply will have to be replaced, just as a bridge or a road has to be replaced. So I'm open at those moments to consider any unusual idea.

Interview/Opera News, August:10.

Lesley Koenig
Stage director,
Metropolitan Opera,
New York, N.Y.

3

I worry about [the future of] directors like me who want to ground their productions in the words and the music. I'm not one of those directors who put a "concept" on an opera. People say to me, "What's your style?", and I say, "What's your opera?" Directors like us are endangered.

Interview/Opera News, 3-14:44.

Ardis Krainik
General director,
Lyric Opera, Chicago, Ill.

4

Opera is hot. We have many more performances than last year. We have many more people in the audience. Of all the arts right now, opera is doing the best of them all. I'm bullish on opera in America.

Los Angeles Times, 4-19:(Calendar)8.

Branford Marsalis
Jazz musician

5

Jazz has an underlying logic that can't be denied . . . In interviews that I read, there had

(BRANFORD MARSALIS)

been those people who constantly tried to pretend as though the lineage didn't exist. They always used the coinage "new" as in "the new sound," as if previous generations had no cumulative influence on this new music. I was a history major in college and I never once heard a history teacher say that in order for us to progress as a nation we must destroy the past. Nor were historians ever labeled neo-classicists. But it seems in jazz there's an obsession with new versus good. It seems like new is much more important than being good, and I don't agree.

Interview/Down Beat, January:18.

1

[On his soon becoming musical director of NBC-TV's *Tonight Show*]: I'm not trying to bring jazz to the masses. You can't. Jazz is too difficult, too intellectual a music for the masses to deal with. I'm not going to turn the average person on to jazz. I'm not trying. What you can bring to the masses is a sensibility of good musicianship.

Interview/Down Beat, May:27.

Wynton Marsalis
Jazz musician

2

Jazz deals with what goes on between a man and a woman. The difference between jazz and pop music is that pop looks at love on the level of teenagers. When you're a teenager, you just want to get you some, and that music deals with that level of emotional involvement.

Interview/Cosmopolitan, April:98.

Johnny Mathis
Singer

3

That's the whole thing about performing: You have to come up with this magical moment every night, to sing the same songs you've been singing for 30 years, and somehow make it sound as though it's fresh and new; that's really the burden you carry over the years. The audience may

sympathize, but they're not going to let you off the hook—they've got to hear [you sing your old hits] . . . I got all crazy for a couple of years, and I wouldn't sing my hit songs, because I wanted to do some other, newer stuff. But I remember going to see Gladys Knight at some venue in New York, and I just sat there waiting, waiting, waiting for this one particular song that I wanted her to sing, and she finally sang it. And after I heard her, I thought, well, my God, people probably feel the same about *my* music. They're sitting waiting to hear one of my popular songs and if I don't sing it, they're going to get disappointed, So anyway, I got off my high horse. And now I'll sing anything; it doesn't matter.

Interview, Los Angeles, Calif./
The Washington Post, 7-24:(Weekend)11.

John Mauceri
Conductor,
Hollywood Bowl Orchestra;
Music director, Scottish Opera

4

[On the mix of material he uses in his Hollywood Bowl concerts]:You're like somebody in an art gallery who is choosing which art will be shown and how it will hang in combination with other artworks. How you hang pictures changes them, and the same is true of [music] programming. When you choose a major work and put two other works near it, you make new music of all of it.

Interview, Los Angeles, Calif./
Los Angeles Times, 8-23:(Calendar)4.

Gian Carlo Menotti
Composer

5

I moved to Scotland for a very simple reason: I wanted to live in a country where silence is not too expensive. You see, in Italy you have to be a millionaire to buy silence. People think composers are looking for music, but what a composer wants most is silence.

Interview, Edinburgh, Scotland/
The Christian Science Monitor,
12-4:12.

WHAT THEY SAID IN 1992

Sinead O'Connor
Irish rock singer

1

Shall I tell you why I wouldn't [appear on] the Grammys [record awards]? I wanted to voice my objection to the use of the music business as a means of controlling information and honoring artists for material success rather than artistic expression or the expression of truth, which I consider to be the job of artists.

Interview/Time, 11-9:79.

Luciano Pavarotti
Opera singer

2

An opera singer should take risks constantly. If you don't take the risk, who is challenging you? Who is inspiring you? Who is making you do something different, something alive?

Interview, Washington, D.C./
The Washington Post, 7-1:(C)2.

David Randolph
Conductor, Masterwork
Chorus and Orchestra,
New York, N.Y.

3

My [rendition of Handel's] *Messiah* is not romantic. The romantic approach is slow and dull. I go for Baroque drama and grandeur, and I think the work is as dramatic as an opera. It's silly to give an entirely authentic performance. The original, in 1742, was performed for 600 people in a small hall in Dublin, and there were nearly 3,000 in Carnegie Hall [a few days ago].

The New York Times, 12-29:(B)3.

Esa-Pekka Salonen
Music director,
Los Angeles Philharmonic Orchestra

4

Concerts should be provocative, irritating maybe, and satisfying. We can't just sit there and play over symphonies as before. The orchestra should play a role in everyone's spiritual growth.

To supporters of the
Philharmonic, Los Angeles, Calif./
Los Angeles Times, 2-16:(Calendar)5.

Marc Scorca
Executive vice president,
Opera America

5

We hear from the theatre world of significant numbers of companies closing. We hear from the orchestra field of numerous multimillion-dollar deficits and closings. But I cannot report on any opera companies going out of business or any huge, multimillion-dollar deficits . . . There's been some impact from the recession, but opera companies have structures that other kinds of companies don't. Opera companies tend—in order to survive and grow—to have institutional structures that allow for flexibility when the going gets tough.

Los Angeles Times, 4-19:(Calendar)8.

Pyotr Shchenkov
Manager,
State Symphonic Kapelle
of Moscow (Russia)

6

I have always admired how much support for American orchestras comes from private benefactors. But the basic money for Russian orchestras still comes from the state. There are some big businesses in Russia, but they are not interested in supporting the cultural sphere as yet. Other countries give corporations a tax incentive to donate money to national culture. Unfortunately, we haven't reached that point in Russia.

Interview, New York, N.Y./
The Wall Street Journal,
2-13:(A)16.

Leonard Slatkin
Music director,
St. Louis Symphony Orchestra

7

I'm known for doing a lot of [American] music that other people don't do. But my choices have nothing to do with the fact that the repertory is unusual. I conduct works that I think deserve a place in the repertory. We're coming up on a century of original American music, yet as Americans we can't define what our basic repertory is yet. It's time to look back and ask ourselves who

(LEONARD SLATKIN)

our Brahmses and Beethovens are, whose music means that to us. It's time to define an American orchestral legacy that can be translated to the rest of the world.

Interview/
The New York Times, 1-4:10.

Sanford Sylvan
Opera singer

1

[On the expanding horizons of the music world]: At this point, everything is up for grabs. Things are less narrowly defined than they were, which might be a way of saying that the musical Establishment is being opened up to accept a wider variety of forms . . . We must augment the masters with the work of our time. What will break down the barriers [of classical music and opera] even more is the opening up of the boundaries of the forms themselves.

Interview/
Los Angeles Times, 4-5:(Calendar)52.

Renata Tebaldi
Former opera singer

2

I suppose we were more ambitious in [the old] days and worked harder. The [voice] schools today give a couple of hour lessons a week. Not enough. We worked six hours a day. The conductors today don't understand voices. They don't rise through the ranks of *repetiteurs*, assistant conductors, chorus masters and the like, the way Bellezza, Capuana, Cleva, Erede and Febritiis did. [Today] they're instant stars. Promising singers don't have the chance to mature. They want to sing everything right away in the big houses. I hardly go to the opera at all anymore. I suffer. I suffer when I see and hear what they put onstage.

Interview/Opera News, 2-1:18.

Franz Welser-Most
Music director,
London Philharmonic Orchestra
(England)

3

Music has to be and is related to anything else—nature, science, whatever. It's very strongly related to science, especially today; I mean, if you read about physics, chemistry, cosmology—always, especially in the last 20 years, you meet musical terms again. Harmony, just to take one. And music has a lot in common with mathematics. So if you start to work on that more and more, it gives you a wider prospect, really. And that is very important to me.

Interview, London, England/
The Christian Science Monitor,
7-8:18.

THE STAGE

Brooke Adams
Actress

1

[Comparing acting in films with acting on stage]: In films, you are a commodity. You are a look, something that the camera really likes, something that has struck an audience in a certain way. It's not really so much about transforming yourself the way actors do onstage. I think there's a difference between the skill of acting in movies and onstage. For a trained actor, I believe, acting in movies is much more difficult; it is like sight-reading music. While acting in plays is like being with a band that you've played with before and you know all the music and then going off on a riff.

Interview, San Francisco/
Los Angeles Times, 6-28:(Calendar)82.

JoAnne Akalaitis
Artistic director,
New York Shakespeare Festival

2

If critics really understood what goes into a production, if they could go to rehearsals and watch people at work, they would be less dismissive of what they feel is a faulted work. The faulted work should be allowed to happen if it's developing art. Around my productions, we never talk about reviews—good or bad. We are not validated by the reviews. We are validated by the knowledge that we have tried our best. I think honesty is important, and if critics don't like a production they should say so; but it's just as important to nurture and support the passion and integrity that goes into the work.

Interview/"W", 4-27:33.

Nina Ananiashvili
Russian ballerina

3

[On classical ballet]: Art like this will never die, certainly not in Russia, England and Denmark, where it is a very natural part of the national culture. Artistry will change as it has over the past 40 years—the ballerinas of today cannot be compared with the dancers of the '50s, and the next generations will dance even higher, faster, sharper.

Interview/Dance Magazine, July:41.

Reid Anderson
Artistic director,
National Ballet of Canada

4

I was lucky enough to be brought up surrounded by the creative process. At Stuttgart, new work of all kinds was being made all around us, incessantly. It is the height of heights and nothing can match it. If I'm able to convey some of that feeling to our dancers now, I think it comes out in the way they are getting to be real daring risk-takers. It's the only route to that electrifying quality great dancers have, the sensation of not always having to be in complete control.

Interview/
The Washington Post, 9-29:(B)2.

Warren Beatty
Actor

5

[On why he concentrates on working in film rather than the theatre]: There are three things. One is that fame and fortune are seductive. The second thing is that the medium of movies is very exciting and seductive, and it is not temporal as the theatre is; the film lasts, for a while anyway. And the third thing would be that in certain forms of drama, in the darker-spirited stuff, I found it masochistic to have to be in a negative frame of mind night after night [in the theatre], this kind of enforced and repeated unhappiness. I'm very dependent upon the attitude of other actors to

(WARREN BEATTY)

keep the ball in the air—let's call it a volleyball. And what I found, working in the theatre, was that I really was not in control of who those other players were and whether we were all playing volleyball in the same way.

Interview/
Film Comment, Jan.-Feb.:32.

Annette Bening
Actress

1

In theatre, part of your ability, your tool, is you don't have to face yourself and how you really are. You can imagine yourself to be short or tall or thin or fat, blonde or black-haired, with a cane, with a moustache, with high heels. You can use your imagination about how you look to feed your behavior. You delude yourself purposefully. In film there is no lie. *Oh! That's what my face does when I'm feeling that?* I'm very critical when I see myself on film.

Interview, Los Angeles, Calif./
Vanity Fair, June:156.

Gordon Davidson
Artistic director/producer,
Mark Taper Forum,
Los Angeles, Calif.

2

What I love best [about the theatre] is to go into unknown territory and see how I can swim in it. On one level, I love being in the rehearsal room. At the same time—and this has been a dichotomy in my own personality—I like that burden of being on the phone. But I don't like it forever because it's not the real food. It's the cashew nuts in the bowl . . . The act of making of theatre is extremely rewarding for me, to stand at the back of the house, to get on a plane to go see a production, to give a few notes, just even peripherally being involved in the journey, it is all in my blood.

Interview/
Los Angeles Times, 5-31:(Calendar)73.

Jeremy Gerard
Theatre editor and chief critic,
"Variety"

3

[On the many film stars appearing in Broadway plays this season]:I think there's an undeniable cachet to working on Broadway. Hollywood really does love the theatre and does perceive it as its noble cousin . . . [But] as much as it's great to have the stars here, it's not what Broadway's about. Hollywood is still about stars and Broadway is still about the written word. And that gets lost in all the hoopla.

Los Angeles Times, 2-9:(Calendar)5,55.

Moses Goldberg
Artistic director,
Stage One: The Louisville (Ky.)
Children's Theatre

4

The same things that make good adult theatre make good children's theatre: a good script, good acting, good directing, a feeling that there is harmony among all the elements, and characters the audience cares about. There certainly is a difference in subject matter. But the way we approach the theatrical material is exactly the same as in adult theatre . . . And it starts with respect for the children.

Interview, Louisville, Ky./
The Christian Science Monitor,
5-26:11.

Benjamin Harkarvy
Dance teacher,
Juilliard School,
New York, N.Y.

5

My ideal is that the dancer's execution comes out like he's speaking a natural language, like it's being *sung* out of the body. A lot of dancers stutter and mumble and scream. We must not make dancers feel inadequate because they don't have powerhouse technique. I often say to a dancer, "You will always find someone in your vicinity with higher legs, higher jump—in other words, with *more*. But no one has your upper body, your head and your face."

Interview/Dance Magazine, April:55.

WHAT THEY SAID IN 1992

Erick Hawkins
Choreographer

1

I've tried to go a little bit into what you might call metaphysical thinking. And I guess I've always been trying to find out more. But I've had a vision that modern dance should be mature and adult and not go in for the gimmicks. I see modern dance going into popular culture, which is okay, but it's not probing deeply into the poetic experiences that everybody needs to have. If artists don't partake of this, then they've just missed the boat.

Interview, New York, N.Y./
The New York Times, 2-11:(B)1.

Marcia Haydee
Prima ballerina and director,
Stuttgart Ballet (Germany)

2

I think the mistake most [ballet] dancers make today is to develop a role, and they don't understand that you don't develop a role, you develop yourself. And it's how you develop as a human being that the role develops. They're all looking for technical ways of how to grow in your role. Your role is exactly the same as you did it the first day. So I don't even think about how I'm going to do the role differently. The curtain goes up and I go out on stage and do it, and so of course each time [it] is different. That is what is difficult to make dancers understand. They try to read books and to think about what to do, where to look, how to look, and how to lift that finger, and that doesn't make the role better. It just makes it more and more artificial.

Interview, Washington, D.C./
The Christian Science Monitor,
5-5:10.

J. Daniel Herring
Education director,
Stage One: The Louisville (Ky.)
Children's Theatre

3

Passing on the culture [to young audiences] is part of what we do. We're not trying to make theatre artists out of everyone. We're primarily

trying to open them up to the art-form, to experience and appreciate it. Then, too, we expose them to other parts of the culture they may not have been exposed to. It may be in the socialization of coming to the theatre or it may be in the script. We give them a broader look at the world they live in.

Interview, Louisville, Ky./
The Christian Science Monitor,
5-26:11.

Judith Jamison
Artistic director,
Alvin Ailey American Dance Theatre,
New York, N.Y.

4

[I look for dancers who are] not tunnel-visioned and who don't live, breathe, think, eat and sleep dance, because then they don't have anything to bring on the stage. You get a lot of technique and no soul and no passion . . . We ask for their vulnerability, and we ask for their innermost thoughts, And we ask for their spirit, and we ask that they remember why they started dancing in the first place, because if you forget that, you forget it all.

Interview, New York/
The Christian Science Monitor,
3-24:14.

Darci Kistler
Ballerina,
New York City Ballet

5

When you're first starting out [as a dancer], you try to put so much in. You want to do *everything*, because you want people to see that you know what you're doing. You want to be liked. But the more I dance, the more I see that the thing is just to listen to the music and do the steps the way it says to . . . Dancing breathes life into you. The more you do it, the more you have to do it. And it becomes easier, because you become simpler. Things in you get chipped away— mannerisms, attitude, things where, before, you couldn't admit you were wrong. And by giving up those things in yourself, you end up doing more. You become part of the ballet. You're not it—

(DARCI KISTLER)

you're part of it. And so you just do it, and pretty soon it's all you want to do.

Interview/
"Interview" magazine, May:121.

Bella Lewitzky
Modern-dance choreographer

1

Modern dance is such a maverick. It has always been an iconoclastic form. It will change . . . There's always going to be some visionary. Change for me is the only constant in life, and we're in a period of change.

Interview/
Los Angeles Times, 1-26:(Calendar)53.

Ian McKellen
British actor

2

[On winning a 1980 Tony award]: I've got to be very careful of what I say, because I know in this country [the U.S.] how important the Tony award is. When I picked it up I told the audience that it had been the most wonderful year of my life, and that this Tony award would be a marvelous souvenir for me to take home with me. About a week later, my dresser got up the courage to say to me, "You should never have called the Tony award a souvenir, as though you sort of assume it's something you got from Atlantic City and put with the clock on the mantelpiece." Did the Tony change my life? I'm very glad to say it didn't. If I thought that that was going to be it, and that somehow all the problems of being an actor were solved by winning the Tony, I'd probably have been out of the business by now.

Interview, Washington, D.C./
The Christian Science Monitor,
8-5:13.

Harold Prince
Director

3

[On his currently directing an Off-Off-Broadway show]: This is the least-pressured, most

joyful and satisfying theatre experience I can remember. It's wonderful that there aren't millions of dollars at stake. It's nice to stay up nights worrying about the material, and not about the investors who gave you $10-million to do your musical [on Broadway] . . . Aiming for Broadway—I can't think that way anymore. Of course, Broadway will always be important. But it's not the focus of everything that you do. You know, I'm very happy I was born when I was, so I got [to Broadway] in time—when it was time to get there.

Interview, New York/
The New York Times, 2-13:(B)2.

Isabel Stevenson
President,
American Theatre Wing

4

It's amazing how many [film stars began their careers on the New York stage]. I often ask them why they come back [to play on Broadway] when they've got to face tough critics and make far less money than they can make in Hollywood. They always say the same thing—it's the live theatre experience. There's nothing like it, for an audience and for an actor.

The Christian Science Monitor,
5-29:12.

Julie Taymor
Director

5

One of the things that attracts me to the theatre is that it is about personal transformation. A play isn't a play unless it has that evolution of character. And making physical that evolution through the power of the visual image, I think, is the reason to do theatre.

Interview, New York, N.Y./
The Christian Science Monitor,
11-13:11.

Twyla Tharp
Choreographer

6

I'm just interested in dancing. I'm no longer interested in these arbitrary categories of so-

(TWYLA THARP)

called ballet, so-called modern. And someplace this poor word *classical* fits in. Classical art is an art that has a way and a reason for going on for more than just its generation. Classical demands certain verities. It looks to acquire a kind of clarity. It demands that certain things are right. What is classical existed before the 19th-century ballets and will exist after 20th-century post-modernism. Classical has been very badly served by connecting it so closely to the ballet. Americans get very nervous about the word *classical*. They are not quite ready for that yet. They don't want to be the parents; they still want to be the kid. And parents are the ones who have to be responsible for what's classical.

News conference,
Ohio State University-Columbus/
Dance Magazine, January:53.

Jim Thesing
Executive director,
National Alliance
of Musical Theatre Producers

1

The New York theatre has an enormous impact on regional musical theatre. American audiences across the country have an insatiable appetite for the latest Broadway musical hit, so regional companies have traditionally built their seasons around the new shows.

The Christian Science Monitor,
5-29:12.

Dale Wasserman
Playwright

2

I just *loathe* Broadway. I have no desire to have my shows on Broadway. I can safely say that because I've been there . . . I think Broadway is doing damage to the future of theatre. The fact is, only the elite can attend Broadway shows because of the pricing process. It may be good for the tourist industry in New York, but I can't think what else it's good for. It's become prohibitively expensive, both to produce and for ticket buyers. It has become very elitist.

Interview/
Los Angeles Times, 8-11:(F)4.

Garland Wright
Artistic director,
Guthrie Theatre,
Minneapolis, Minn.

3

[On his theatre's successful campaign for funding, which resulted in an endowment of over $23-million]: The money is endowing in perpetuity the programs that were put into place four years ago, chief among which is to extend the acting company and to increase their remuneration, so the actors can make a commitment like this, as well as have homes and families and vote and do the things other human beings get to do.

The Christian Science Monitor,
4-7:11.

Philosophy

Robert Altman
Motion-picture director

1

A guy like [actor] Paul Newman starts a company [selling salad dressing], makes $54-million in profits last year, and it all goes to a charity; you don't hear a lot about that. A guy like [corporate CEO] Steve Ross makes $63-million a year, a guy like [corporate CEOs] Michael Eisner, Lee Iacocca, Barry Diller, those guys don't feed that money back. They gather as much as they can, and the profits don't have any real meaning. They can't spend that money. All they've got, they can say on their record they have the most chips in front of them when they die.

Interview/
Film Comment, May-June:28.

Corazon C. Aquino
President of the Philippines

2

It is true that you cannot eat freedom and you cannot power machinery with democracy. But then neither can political prisoners turn on the light in the cells of a dictatorship.

Speech/
The Washington Post, 6-29:(A)12.

William P. Barr
Attorney General
of the United States

3

[Saying the country's moral fiber is weakening, and citing actor Woody Allen's affair with the adopted daughter of his lover Mia Farrow as an example]: Seemingly genuinely puzzled by all the fuss [about the affair in the media], Mr. Allen explained to *Time* magazine that he was in love with the girl. And having fallen in love, Mr. Allen implied, it must follow as night follows day that the two of them would consummate their love in sexual intimacy. After all, he said, "the heart wants what the heart wants." There you have it. In seven words Mr. Allen epigrammatically

captures the essence of contemporary moral philosophy. The heart is presented as an unreasoning tyrant over which reason, and therefore morality, has no influence. Try that as an instruction for your children when they ask you if a particular course of conduct is good or bad.

Before Catholic League for
Religious and Civil Rights, Oct. 5/
The New York Times, 10-8:(A)10.

George Bush
President of the United States

4

Democracy, human rights, the rule of law, these are the building blocks of peace and freedom. And in the lives of millions of men and women around the world, its import is simple. It can mean the difference between war and peace, healing and hatred, and where there is fear and despair it really can mean hope.

At UN Security Council summit meeting,
United Nations, New York, Jan. 31/
The New York Times, 2-1:5.

5

We need, as [former U.S.] President [Richard] Nixon once said, an open world, open cities, open hearts, open minds, and only then can we not merely trade with other nations, but profit from other nations.

At AmeriFlora '92 show,
Columbus, Ohio, April 20/
USA Today, 4-22:(A)4.

Jimmy Carter
Former President
of the United States

6

The worst discrimination on Earth is the rich and powerful against the poor and weak.

Interview,
Anaheim, Calif., May 25/
Los Angeles Times, 5-26:(A)26.

WHAT THEY SAID IN 1992

Bill Clinton
Governor of Arkansas (D);
1992 Democratic
Presidential nominee

1

I think serious people, the older they get, try to achieve a certain integrity in their lives. You try to put your mind, your body and your spirit in the same place at the same time. There's a great difference in that sense between integrity and honesty. Honesty is not lying in the moment, but integrity is much more difficult to achieve because you have to decide what you believe. The older you get, the more you want to actually confront the areas of doubt in your life, and you get to the point where you don't want to disappoint yourself anymore. You realize that the time you have is limited, and you want to live like a laser beam instead of a shotgun.

Interview/
U.S. News & World Report,
7-20:30.

2

The cause of change is always difficult to make. It is always easy to stay with a proven path, even if it is failure. It takes courage to change.

Campaigning, Boston, Mass./
The Christian Science Monitor,
9-28:2.

Hillary Clinton
Wife of Arkansas Governor
and 1992 Democratic Presidential
candidate Bill Clinton

3

People miss the boat when they say [about me], "Gosh, if only she weren't married." They read into my life their own interests and projections. I don't know if I would ever run for office. People think so much is planned when, in truth, life has a way of just happening. You are who you are, not who you're married to. At the core is your own identity, and the challenge is to discover who *you* are. And I know who I am.

Interview/
Working Woman, August:72.

Dan R. Coats
United States Senator,
R-Indiana

4

When a choice is torn by moral conflict, an odd courage is needed—the courage to walk in an unfamiliar land without landmarks. After the facts are collected, after the principles are defined, after the prayers are offered, a decision is required. Those who make them carefully are left drained of self-righteousness. Moral choice begins with surrender. It completes itself in humility.

At Wheaton (Ill.) College commencement/
Christianity Today, 7-20:92.

Sean Connery
Actor

5

I thought so many of those [highly educated, intellectual, lettered] people were so bloody marvelous, but they turned out to be not so smart. If an expert on something can't give you an answer in relatively simple terms, he usually doesn't know what he's talking about. That's the hardest thing I've had to learn, as well as trust. There's no measure to trust; either you trust or you don't. Once you get into bed with somebody—I don't mean literally—there's nothing you can do. Learning to trust wisely has been my toughest lesson.

Interview, Los Angeles, Calif./
Los Angeles Times, 7-24:(F)9.

Midge Decter
Distinguished fellow,
Institute on Religion
and Public Life

6

That we should nowadays be discussing something called "family values" is itself a symptom of our pathology. Families are not mere arrangements of things to be defended or criticized—or, above all, "redefined"—they are nature, like rocks and rivers. It takes one man and one woman to produce a child. There ought to be a message in that, and when we were a civilization that could make its way even in the dark, we knew

(MIDGE DECTER)

it. Families are not meant to make you happy; they are meant to make you *human* . . . [If we don't recognize] our arrogance in believing we could tamper with nature itself, there will be no hope.

Interview/USA Today, 7-8:(A)9.

Marian Wright Edelman
President,
Children's Defense Fund

1

Kids need a counter-voice. They really want to know what we [parents] feel strongly about and what we value . . . We need to challenge all the cultural signals that glorify violence and careless sex . . . A lot of kids are not engaging in too-early sex. We need to say, "That's terrific. That's pretty cool." Most kids are staying in school. More kids are making it than not. We need to create a new set of heroes and heroines around them.

Interview, New York, N.Y./
The Christian Science Monitor,
6-9:14.

Suleyman Demirel
Prime Minister of Turkey

2

I don't think you can take democracy away from people with Western values. They will give up bread, but not democracy. But I also don't think that you can sell democracy to those people who don't know its value. That is today's problem.

Interview,
Washington, D.C., Feb. 12/
The New York Times, 2-13:(A)6.

Alexander Dubcek
Former First Secretary,
Communist Party of Czechoslovakia

3

Politics opens the door for economics and economic reforms . . . Politics is everything. Politics includes housing problems, the issue of

whether or not we can travel—politics is everything you touch in the place you live. Politics is always here in one form or another. The point is only: What should it be like? Our idea is that politics should be for people, that it should encourage democratic development and social welfare, culture and all that is related to man's life. This is my understanding of politics.

Interview, Prague, Czechoslovakia/
Los Angeles Times, 8-9:(M)3.

Claire L. Gaudiani
President, Connecticut College

4

Leaders need to be primarily in service to the people and values of the organization that they lead. Leaders almost never need to exercise power. They need to lead in ways that create a vision that motivates people.

The Christian Science Monitor,
2-28:14.

Andre Glucksmann
French philosopher

5

Democracy requires change to function well, because ideas of government need to be refreshed every so often.

The Washington Post, 4-14:(A)18.

Mikhail S. Gorbachev
Former President
of the Soviet Union

6

Decisiveness [in a political leader] is regarded in a very primitive fashion, both by you Americans and us Russians. If someone commits himself to reforms, and does not give way no matter what the pressure but keeps maneuvering, that is not [regarded as] decisiveness. That is "being slow"; that is "maneuvering"; that is indecisiveness. But if he moves his tanks into Budapest and wipes away half the city—or invades Grenada and strangles it—that is "decisiveness."

Interview,
Moscow, Russia, March 23/
The Washington Post, 3-24:(A)16.

David Hamburg
President,
Carnegie Corporation

1

People my age [66] need to understand that our well-being depends on the workers of the next generation. Moreover, as a society, we've got to stop concentrating on the short-time horizons— the next election, budgetary cycle or quarterly report—and start taking stock of the long term. Children are a long-range investment.

Interview/Time, 3-23:59.

Vaclav Havel
President of Czechoslovakia

2

Personally, I do not share the view that the free-market mechanism is the magic solution to all of our problems. I do not believe that it is a world outlook or the meaning of life. I differ on this subject with some rightist politicians and publishers and have frequent disputes with them. The validity of the law of supply and demand is clear to me. But I do not treat it as an ideology but as something that has been tested for centuries. One does not have to be a scientist to know that if one calls in a private electrician, he will do his job better than an employee of a state enterprise, because he is personally interested in the results of his work, as reflected in the pay he will receive for his services. From that standpoint, then, I support the fastest restoration of natural property rights, pluralism and competitive enterprises. I treat market mechanisms as a reality.

Interview/
World Press Review, March:16.

John Hume
Member of British Parliament
from Northern Ireland

3

Humanity transcends nationality. We're human beings before we're anything else. It's only an accident of birth wherever we were born. So it shouldn't be a source of conflict or hatred. The essence of unity is the acceptance of diversity.

The New York Times, 4-1:(A)5.

Henry J. Hyde
United States Representative,
R-Illinois

4

[The leaders of media and academia] admire and implement the Enlightenment ethic, the notion that [theological] revelation has nothing to teach us. In their view, the obstacles to a good society are simple ignorance. "If only we could educate everybody," they cry, "not only would racism, sexism and crime disappear, but we'd have a wonderful life—Utopia itself!" Ask them about sin, and they reply, "Sin? There's no such thing. *Society* is the cause of evil and crime." Somehow, it appears, society has "failed" the rapist, the dope dealer, the mugger, the murderer. [To them society's] to blame, not the individual responsible for his choices.

Interview, Washington, D.C./
Christianity Today, 3-9:30.

Jesse L. Jackson
Civil-rights leader

5

Cynicism is a luxury and is something that people who have real needs can't afford. I can't afford to be cynical because it is hope that keeps the people alive. When your job is gone, and your electricity is turned off, and your loved ones are injured or dead, and your job is gone, and you are down to your irreducible essence, only hope stands between you and collapse. It can't collapse. That's why we have to keep hope alive. It's so fundamental to the human spirit. The very least that leaders can do, when they can't supply the material goods yet, is to sustain imagination and hope.

Interview/
Los Angeles Times, 5-15:(T)8.

Elton John
Singer, Musician

6

In this business [entertainment], I don't care who you are; there are Jekyll and Hyde characters in us all. There's not one performer who can't be an absolute animal at times. You have to be pretty strange to be a performer.

Interview, Atlanta, Ga./
Los Angeles Times, 8-23:(Calendar)81.

Lee Kuan Yew
Former Prime Minister
of Singapore

1

How is it that only in Britain, and subsequently overseas Anglo-Saxon communities, has the democratic system of government succeeded? The British exported it to their white colonies in North America, Canada, Australia, New Zealand and South Africa. Why was it not universal, even in Europe? Not the Germans, not the Spaniards. The French attempted it and were not very successful; they went through five republics since the storming of the Bastille . . . The British were more phlegmatic, less volatile. They had a knack for compromise. They were willing to accept that since you've won [an election], then [the] next four or five years, you run it, and I will obey your rulings. It will come back to my turn some other time. This was not part of the Latin temperament: Having lost, you begin immediately to fight and thwart the winner from the day you've lost . . . So the question I would ask is, why is it that only the Anglo-Saxon temperament led to the development of parliamentary democracy?

Interview, Singapore/
Los Angeles Times, 5-19:(H)15.

Bernard Lewis
Professor emeritus
of Near Eastern studies,
Princeton University

2

The West is often blamed for African slavery, yet this institution has existed in virtually all human societies. Western slavery is unique in only one respect: its abolition.

Lecture at American Enterprise Institute/
The Wall Street Journal,
7-23:(A)12.

Bella Lewitzsky
Modern-dance choreographer

3

I am plagued with perfectionism. I used to think it was a backward manifestation of ego. But another part of me said that it's healthy. Since perfection can never be achieved, you'll never stand still.

Interview/
Los Angeles Times, 1-26:(Calendar)8.

Mark Lowenthal
Senior specialist in
U.S. foreign policy,
Congressional Research Service

4

In times of trouble, authoritarians provide the easiest answers. It reflects a certain immaturity in the body politic. They abdicate rights in return for trains that runs on time, three meals a day, and law and order. It's like reverting to childhood. They think returning power to the government will mean taking care of them again.

Los Angeles Times, 2-25:(H)4.

Mahathir Mohamad
Prime Minister of Malaysia

5

It is the height of arrogance to claim that only a particular system is right and just. The fact is that even democracy can bring misery to a lot of people . . . Democracy is not the universal cure it is made out to be.

At meeting of Association
of Southeast Asian Nations,
Singapore, Jan. 27/
The Washington Post, 1-28:(A)14.

Wynton Marsalis
Jazz musician

6

The world is a great place to live in, even with all the terrible things in it. Because you're poor or you have to deal with ignorance or you're afraid somebody's going to shoot you doesn't make the sunset less beautiful, doesn't make you less in love with your old lady, doesn't make the food you like to eat taste less good. Everybody's life has deep pain and sorrow, but you don't see people going through terrible things rushing out to commit suicide.

Interview/Cosmopolitan, April:98.

413

Paul Mellon
Philanthropist

1

Nothing in a list of my charitable contributions is really terribly coherent. You see, they're based on intuitions. The hunches that I act upon, whether good or bad, just seem to rise out of my head like those word balloons in comic strips.

Interview, Washington, D.C./
The Washington Post, 4-7:(E)1.

Demi Moore
Actress

2

Who I am today is not who I was even six months ago. I think that's good. We should always keep changing. Following a path is everything. I don't think we ever get to the end of it. And if we did, how sad. How sad to have nowhere left to go.

Interview, Los Angeles, Calif./
Harper's Bazaar, June:125.

Brian Mulroney
Prime Minister of Canada

3

The problems in industrial democracies today are so intractable and so complex that if a leader leaves office on a wave of popularity, he or she should be disqualified from any consideration of greatness. The reason for that is that it means he has chosen popularity over priniciple.

Interview, Ottawa, Canada, March 4/
The Washington Post, 3-5:(A)37.

Ross Perot
Industralist

4

The most successful people in the world aren't usually the brightest. They are the ones who persevere. Thomas Edison is one of my heroes. He tried everything to make an electric light until he finally hit it. And as a result of that brutal experience, inventions poured out of his head. I don't mean to compare myself with the Wright brothers, but they are a role model of sorts. If you read about them and study their work, you see they just *had* to fly. They didn't believe those who said it couldn't be done. It was just inside them.

Interview/
U.S. News & World Report, 6-29:32.

Dan Quayle
Vice President of the United States

5

As I discovered recently, to appeal to our country's enduring, basic moral values is to invite the scorn and laughter of the elite culture. Talk about right and wrong and they'll try to mock us in newsrooms, sitcom studios and faculty lounges across America. But in the heart of America, in the homes and workplaces and churches, the message is heard . . . The cultural elites respect neither tradition nor standards. They believe that moral truths are relative and all "lifestyles" are equal. They seem to think the family is an arbitrary arrangement of people who decide to live under the same roof, that fathers are dispensable and that parents need not be married or even of opposite sexes. They are wrong . . . We cannot, as the sophisticated folks are always reminding us, "turn back the clock" to the America of Norman Rockwell and the small-town values he celebrated. And yet those values are still there. These values live because they are invaluable. They stand as our essential guide to a good and honest life . . . We defend the rights of all Americans. We are for compassion and tolerance. We are, after all, commanded to love our neighbor. But we do not believe that being compassionate and tolerant means abandoning our standards of right or wrong, good or bad . . . Such moral values represent the consensus of humanity about what makes for a good life and a good society. [And while] moral cynicism is an easy out, a sneer is never an answer. The elite's culture is a guilt-free culture. It avoids responsibility and flees consequences. [But] those who imagine an America without clear moral values yearn for something that could never be. If America ever lost its moral vision, it would cease to be America.

At Southern Baptist Convention,
Indianapolis, Ind., June 9/
Los Angeles Times, 6-10:(A)1;
The New York Times, 6-10:(A)1,13.

Arnold Schwarzenegger
Actor; Chairman,
President's Council on
Physical Fitness and Sports

1

We are in a very fast world now, and we're always looking for a shortcut. We always want to get rich the fastest way, we want to get famous the fastest way, we want to get strong and be competitive the fastest way. But really there is no shortcut. It all comes down to one thing, and this is why sports and fitness activities are so important: The more hours we put in and the more we struggle, the more we fight against resistance and obstacles, the better we will get and the more it will pay off for other activities in life.

Interview/
U.S. News & World Report,
6-1:63.

Gloria Steinem
Women's-rights activist;
Former editor, "Ms." magazine

2

This society, Western culture in general, has devoted itself to externalizing everything, whether it's obeying the demands of the church to win rewards after death, or the secular heaven of consumerism that makes us feel insecure if we don't buy endless things—all the vast array of external hierarchies that depend for *their* authority on weakening *our* authority—especially women's.

Interview,
New York, N.Y./Time, 3-9:57.

Suharto
President of Indonesia

3

Ultimately, the purpose of development is the achievement of the human being to his fullest potential, in a manner that is in balance with the environment. National development must be people-centered. National development must be of the people, by the people and for the people.

At Non-Aligned Movement summit meeting,
Jakarta, Indonesia/
The New York Times, 9-24:(C)24.

Lionel Tiger
Anthropologist

4

One of the fascinating things about the United States is that, notwithstanding its Puritan heritage, it is a place where people can probably find as wide an array of pleasures legitimately enjoyed as anywhere in the world. I think that is one of the peculiar, unexamined political results of the Constitution and the Bill of Rights. I believe that there is some reason for evaluating a society on the basis of how much domestic personal pleasure it allows its citizens. The lack of personal pleasure in the Soviet system may explain why the whole Communist scheme was doomed. And I think that the Japanese are going to have a major intellectual task in trying to reassess the value of private, as opposed to public, experience. It is interesting to speculate on what would happen if we looked at countries not in terms of their gross national product, but in terms of a different GNP, their gross national pleasure.

Interview/
U.S. News & World Report,
2-3:54.

Ted Turner
Chairman,
Turner Broadcasting System

5

[Saying people should not set goals they can achieve]: My father told me he wanted to be a millionaire, have a yacht and a plantation. And by the time he was 50 he had achieved all three, and he was having a very difficult time. *I'm* not going to rest until all the world's problems are solved. Homelessness, AIDS. I'm in great shape. I mean, the problems will survive me—no question about it.

Time, 1-6:39.

Nicholas von Hoffman
Author, Journalist

6

Unfortunately, both liberals and conservatives in America have come unconsciously to think of society very much like a virgin forest:

(NICHOLAS VON HOFFMAN)

"That's what it is; it's natural." But that is not so. The human being is a tool-maker, and the greatest of all human tools is society. This is all *made by people*: every convention, every belief, every arrangement. Nature had nothing to do with it!

Interview, New York, N.Y./
Publishers Weekly, 9-21:72.

Willie L. Williams
Chief of Police
of Los Angeles, Calif.

1

We must begin today the process of talking to each other, and not just at each other. Each and every one of us has to realize that we cannot exist for very long without the help and/or assistance of our brothers and sisters, or our neighbors. We cannot remove the tensions that hang in the air like dark glooming storm clouds if we are afraid to meet our neighbors, both old and new. Tensions cannot be removed, nor will we see justice prevail, if we continue to run back across the street, lock our door or speed up our cars whenever we come upon one who is a stranger.

Speech upon his inauguration as Chief,
Los Angeles, Calif., June 30/
Los Angeles Times, 7-1:(A)1,21.

Lois Wilson
Former president,
World Council of Churches

2

I think we would be greatly improved if we all wore fish-eye lenses on our eyes because that way we could see the world at 180 degrees. We could see the world whole and as it really is instead of only our own little part of it. I think if we wore good hearing aids and perhaps a clothespin for the mouth, that would help too because we might then listen to people of the Third World and people who are very different from ourselves . . . I think it would help if we had flippers for our feet such as scuba divers wear, because those of us who are attempting to create and sustain authentic human community in our world really need a little extra propelling.

At Ripon (Wis.) College commencement/
The Christian Science Monitor,
6-22:11.

Boris N. Yeltsin
President of Russia

3

There is no people on this earth who could be harmed by the air of freedom. There are no exceptions to that rule. Liberty sets the mind free, fosters independence and unorthodox thinking and ideas. But it does not offer instant prosperity or happiness and wealth to everyone. This is something that politicians in particular must keep in mind. Even the most benevolent intentions will inevitably be abandoned and committed to oblivion if they are not translated into everyday efforts. Our experience of the recent years has conclusively pointed that out. Liberty will not be fooled. There can be no coexistence between market economy and powers who control everything and everyone. There can be no coexistence between a civic society, which is pluralist by definition, and Communist intolerance to dissent. The experience of the past decade has taught us: Communism has no human face. Freedom and Communism are incompatible.

Before joint session of U.S. Congress,
Washington, D.C., June 17/
The Washington Post, 6-18:(A)36.

Karl Zinsmeister
Adjunct scholar,
American Enterprise Institute

4

Strong, healthy values are critical to national prosperity. They are not a frill. Today, national riches are measured in . . . personal behaviors and productive habits.

The Christian Science Monitor,
9-22:4.

Religion

Adam Boniecki
Editor, "Tygodnik Powszechnie"
(Polish Catholic weekly)

1

Many [in Poland] don't know what the real role of the church is—to lead people to God, to faith. This is the real role of the church, not politics. People don't understand what the church is, what they can expect from the church, how the church functions. The church was always well organized. People are suspicious now. They think, "We're finished with the Reds [Communists], now we have blacks [clergy]." The press has been very anti-clerical.

The Christian Science Monitor,
9-8:13.

Patrick J. Buchanan
Political commentator;
Former candidate for the 1992
Republican Presidential
nomination

2

There is a religious war going on in this country for the soul of America. It is a cultural war as critical to the kind of nation we shall be as the Cold War itself, for this war is for the soul of America. And in that struggle for the soul of America, [Democratic Presidential nominee Bill] Clinton . . . [is] on the other side and [President] George Bush is in our side.

At Republican National Convention,
Houston, Texas, Aug. 17/
The New York Times, 12-12:7.

George Carey
Archbishop of Canterbury
(England)

3

We ought to be less interested in sexuality and more interested in life. People get the idea that most Christians are talking about only two things: homosexuality and women's ordination. But these take up less than 5 per cent of my time.

We tend to exaggerate the fleshy passions instead of thinking in global terms. And the church is just as guilty as any other section of the community in thinking sexual sins more significant than other sins.

Interview/
The New York Times, 4-18:8.

4

We [in the church] are in danger of not being heard if women are exercising leadership in every area of our society's life save the ordained priesthood.

Time, 11-23:58.

Bill Clinton
Governor of Arkansas (D);
1992 Democratic
Presidential nominee

5

We all have the right to wear our religion on our sleeves. But we should also hold it in our hearts and live it in our lives. And if we are truly to practice what we preach, then Americans of every faith and viewpoint should come together to promote the common good.

At University of Notre Dame,
Sept. 11/
The New York Times, 9-12:7.

6

My faith tells me that all of us are sinners, and each of us has gone in our own way and fallen short of the glory of God. Religious faith has permitted me to believe in my continuing possibility of becoming a better person every day. If I didn't believe in God, if I weren't, in my view, weren't a Christian, if I didn't believe ultimately in the perfection of life after death, my life would have been that much more difficult.

Broadcast interview/
The New York Times, 10-8:(A)15.

Jerry Falwell
Evangelist

1

I am not a "televangelist." Billy Graham is an evangelist who uses television to preach his message—that's a televangelist. The press just refuses to use his name as a televangelist because they know he's a man of integrity, and the word "televangelist" for them is meant to be pejorative. Charles Stanley, Jerry Falwell, James Kennedy—I could list a dozen more—are not televangelists. They are pastors of local churches that allow cameras to look in on their local church services. I would say these "telepastors" are here to stay because they are personally above reproach, and they pastor local churches where they have very, very strong accountability. Televangelists in the truest sense of the word include Robert Tilton, Kenneth Copeland, Richard Roberts, Ernest Angley, W. V. Grant, Larry Lea—the list is long. Most of them, in my opinion, are defrauding the public. They are preaching that it is God's will for everyone to be healthy and wealthy. That is anti-scriptural.

Interview/
Christianity Today, 2-10:46.

Kirk Fordice
Governor of Mississippi (R)

2

[On his statement that the U.S. is a "Christian nation"]: It means that Christianity is the predominant religion in America. We all know that's an incontrovertible fact. The media always refer to the Jewish state of Israel. They talk about the Muslim country of Saudi Arabia, of Iran, of Iraq. We talk about the Hindu nation of India. America is not a nothing country. It's a Christian country . . . Christianity is the predominant religion. That can't possibly be construed as denigrating the Jewish faith.

Broadcast interview/
"Crossfire," CNN-TV, 11-19.

Carl F. H. Henry
Theologian; Founding editor,
"Christianity Today" magazine

3

Talk of a "new world order" is empty political talk unless the basic right of religious freedom is addressed in all the nations of the world . . . Religious rights of some minorities are non-existent in some countries.

Before Southern Baptist Christian
Life Commission, March 3/
The Washington Post, 3-7:(G)11.

Bradley P. Jacob
Executive director,
Christian Legal Society

4

[On a recent Supreme Court ruling prohibiting prayer at public-school graduations]: The bad news is that prayer at public-school graduation is pretty much outlawed as of today. I don't think that, if a rabbi utters a short prayer that mentions God, that most students in their heart of hearts think they are being coerced into taking part in a religious service.

June 24/
The Washington Post, 6-25:(A)25.

John Paul II
Pope

5

I do not believe that one can talk about a "political" role [for the Pope] in the strict sense, because the Pope has as his mission to preach the gospel. But in the gospel there is man, respect for man, and, therefore, human rights, freedom of conscience, and everything that belongs to man. If this has a political significance, then, yes, it applies also to the Pope. But always speaking of man and defending man.

Interview, Vatican City/
Los Angeles Times 3-8:(M)5.

6

[On the fall of Communism in Eastern Europe and elsewhere]: The collectivist Marxist crisis is not due solely to economics, but has shown that the truth about man is intimately and necessarily tied to the truth about God.

At Latin American Episcopal Conference,
Santo Domingo, Dominican Republic,
Oct. 12/
The Washington Post, 10-13:(A)14.

James Turner Johnson
Professor of political science,
Rutgers University

1

Religion is subject to being used politically in the search for a rationale or for identity during times of change, whenever there is a cultural vacuum or when the old order is falling apart. Religion is always there in the subculture and relatively easy to grab onto for political use.

Los Angeles Times, 1-14:(H)4.

Arthur J. Kropp
President,
People for the American Way

2

[Agreeing with the Supreme Court decision banning organized prayer at school ceremonies]: The decision is a remarkable win for church-state separation in the schools and an embarrassing rebuff to President Bush. His Administration went out of its way to embrace the religious right and their school-prayer agenda. With today's decision, they all took a very big and very public fall.

June 24/
Los Angeles Times, 6-25:(A)12.

Martin E. Marty
Professor of church history,
University of Chicago
Divinity School

3

With modern nationalism called into question in so many places, the large-scale trend will be toward tribalism or massive convulsive ingatherings of peoples who consider themselves to have mythic and historic roots that radically separate them from all others. Religion comes into the political picture here because it's almost always the reinforcer of the tribal habit and ethos.

Los Angeles Times, 1-14:(H)4.

4

The American people are very friendly to religion in general in their [political] candidates— and very nervous when it gets too specific. Every President acts on the basis of his or her religious outlook. You don't leave your religion at the door. But if you're a smart one, you'll be judicious about how you use it.

USA Today, 6-15:(A)2.

Michael Medved
Film critic; Co-host,
"Sneak Previews," PBS-TV

5

The way [motion pictures today] portray religion. You know this is a profoundly religious country. Seventy-eight per cent of us pray at least once a week, according to a *Newsweek* survey. And you never see this stuff in movies. The only time you ever see people in films as religious is as crooks or crazies.

Interview/
Christianity Today, 4-27:40.

Warren Rudman
United States Senator,
R-New Hampshire

6

[On Mississippi Governor Kirk Fordice's recent reference to the U.S. as a "Christian nation"]: It may be that the Governor of Mississippi didn't intend it . . . [But] with all due respect, he offends not only Jewish people but Muslims, those who have other kinds of beliefs. This is a nation made up of many groups of individuals, and we ought not to be talking about any particular set of values . . . Maybe he didn't mean anything by it, but it's deeply offensive to many Americans, frankly, including me.

Broadcast interview/
"Face the Nation," CBS-TV, 11-29.

Aziz Shukri
Head of the law faculty,
Damascus University (Syria)

7

[Islamic fundamentalism] is going back to the roots of Islam, to the Holy Koran, to the traditions of the Prophet . . . to see if they can provide a good response to the problems we face. Islam might not be complete, it might need updating.

(AZIZ SHUKRI)

But it is definitely more likely to suit my life than any imported ideology.

The Christian Science Monitor,
4-1:10.

Stephen J. Sidorak, Jr.
Executive director,
Christian Conference
of Connecticut

1

[On his group's support for an Ecumenical Baptismal Certificate, a uniform evidence of baptism covering that rite in all Christian churches]: We're not trying to create a super-church. The distinctive contributions, emphases and the historical uniqueness of all the churches must be preserved. Nevertheless, when we talk about baptism, we should no longer talk about being baptized into the United Methodist church or the Episcopal Church or the Catholic Church but into the Christian Church.

The New York Times, 2-8:5.

Donna Steichen
Author;
Specialist on religion

2

[On the movement toward allowing women to become priests]: [The movement's goal is] the overthrow of Christianity. It's not about advancing women in positions in the church. It's about a complete change in theology. Are we talking about a church founded by the Son of God made man? Or are we talking about simply a social gathering that we can rebuild as we wish?

Time, 11-23:54.

Hassan Abdullah Turabi
Islamic leader of Sudan

3

[On the anti-Islam feeling in many areas of the Western world]: Most of what the West is afraid of is subconscious, historical backlog. You know, Islam was a target of antagonism and hostility during the Crusades and the colonial wars. Most of these [Western] powers had to fight their way in Muslim territories, and, during the liberation wars, they were thrown out by force in Algeria and many other countries, and they developed some antipathy toward Islam . . . They came to realize that the revival of Islam would correct the equation between West and East, the Third World . . . The other factor, I think, there is a vacuum now, a threat vacuum, with Russia out of the scene. You [in the West] need an empire of evil to mobilize against.

Interview/
Los Angeles Times, 4-6:(A)9.

Boris N. Yeltsin
President of Russia

4

[On his attendance at church services, as he used to be an atheist]: I am acquiring a different world outlook which is probably connected with my psychological state and situation in society . . . In church I feel I can become cleaner. This is the only place where you don't worry that something is happening somewhere else. It is difficult to explain this state, but for me it has become necessary and not only from my personal and spiritual point of view . . . [I was] born into a farmer's family; my great-grandfathers and grandfather, my parents were believers. I have something in my genes—love of the land and a natural faith. Of course, while I was a Communist, I was a sincere atheist.

Soviet broadcast interview/
Los Angeles Times, 6-15:(A)1,6.

Science and Technology

Roger Angel
Astronomer,
Steward Observatory,
University of Arizona

1

[Saying the U.S. is losing its leadership in astronomy to other countries]: I feel terrible about this trend. Astronomy was the first physical science in which America became pre-eminent. That happened in the 19th century at a time when Europeans led in almost all other fields of science, including chemistry. In the early 20th century, Europe was blazing trails in chemistry, relativity theory, quantum mechanics and many other sciences, but the United States could still claim to be first in astronomy, and it remained preeminent for a century. It really hurts to see Europe taking that lead away.

The New York Times, 8-18:(B)7.

Norman R. Augustine
Chairman,
Martin Marietta Corporation

2

[On the 1986 Challenger space-shuttle explosion that killed all the astronauts on-board]: You can't build a machine with millions of parts, with hundreds of thousands of gallons of liquid hydrogen and oxygen, made by human beings, and expect that things won't happen. But when it happens, you buckle your belt up, get on with life and see it doesn't happen again.

USA Today, 11-25:(B)4.

John Billingham
Program Chief,
Ames Research Center,
National Aeronautics and
Space Administration
of the United States

3

[On NASA's increased interest in searching for extraterrestrial life]: More searching [via radio telescopes] will be accomplished than in all previous searches combined. We have never really listened in the past with search systems of the sort of sophistication and capability we now have . . . The vast majority of scientists today believe it is likely that extraterrestrial life exists. If there is another star like the sun and going around it is a planet like Earth, which is likely to be the case, then the odds of life beginning and evolving are high. It's not some random chance.

USA Today, 10-9:(A)2.

D. Allan Bromley
Assistant to President
of the United States
George Bush
for Science and
Technology Policy

4

We've [the Bush Administration] done a lousy job of telling the public what the Administration has done in science and technology. I happen to be convinced that George Bush has been more supportive of the science and technology base of this country than any President in recent memory . . . In every budget that has been submitted, science and technology has been a first or second priority . . . Actions always speak louder than words; George Bush's actions, in terms of investments, are greater and more sustained than any President in memory.

The Washington Post, 10-2:(B)10.

Arthur C. Clarke
Science-fiction writer

5

Mars is the next frontier, what the Old West was, what America was 500 years ago. It's been 500 years since Columbus. It's time to strike out anew. There's a big argument at the moment. The Moon is closer, and we've got to go back there sometime. But whether it will ever be *settled* on a large scale is a question. But Mars—there's no doubt about it . . . Everything you need is on Mars.

Interview, Sri Lanka/
The Washington Post, 3-9:(B)1.

Bill Clinton
Governor of Arkansas (D);
1992 Democratic
Presidential nominee

1

America cannot continue to rely on trickle-down technology from the military. Civilian industry, not the military, is the driving force behind advanced technology today. Only by strengthening our civilian technology base can we solve the twin problems of national security and economic competitiveness.

Document issued Sept. 21*/
The New York Times, 11-10:(B)6.

Jean-Loup Cretien
French astronaut

2

We are now in a situation where we must say "yes" or "no" [to continuing space exploration] . . . Future generations will remember those who say "yes" to going farther [in space] . . . If we say "no," no one will remember the end of the century. If there is a key to eternity, it's probably in space.

The Christian Science Monitor,
9-23:13.

Hubert Curien
Minister of Technology and Space
of France

3

It's a mistake to think of space uniquely in terms of manned flight. For us it is really several other areas—telecommunications, Earth observation, launch technology, scientific research—that represents the fundamental program . . . The fact is that the issues of prestige are much less important in the world today.

The Christian Science Monitor,
6-17:14.

Edward E. Davis
Former science adviser
to former President
of the United States
Richard M. Nixon

4

[On cases of science fraud]: The pressures for success are inexorable. Personal advancement, economic survival and political advantage often are at stake, even as personal curiosity and the joy of discovery still are widespread. In this climate of mixed motivations, it is essential to act responsibly and to strengthen research ethics.

April 22/
Los Angeles Times, 4-23:(A)23.

Riccardo Giacconi
Chief scientist,
Hubble Space Telescope

5

We [in the U.S.] have very poor management [in science]. We just don't seem able to exploit our intellectual and technological resources. Take my own particular field, X-ray astronomy. We Americans founded the field and were the world leaders in X-ray astronomy. But it's come to the point where everything new in the field is either Japanese or German. It's not that we didn't spend the money. It's just that we spent it wrong, we spent it poorly.

Interview/
The New York Times, 8-18:(B)7.

Daniel S. Goldin
Administrator,
National Aeronautics and
Space Administration
of the United States

6

[On the recent manned space-shuttle flight that corrected the orbit of a stranded communications satellite]: What we have done is demonstrate that humans can and should operate in space. [There is the] brilliance of the human mind that's able to adapt and react and do the things that machines just can't do. In front of the eyes of the world, they [the shuttle astronauts] performed the impossible . . . [It] brought the magic back to our space program.

May 14/Los Angeles Times, 5-15:(A)4.

7

I believe the people in Congress understand the criticality of the space station in the future. The space station is going to be the first interna-

(DANIEL S. GOLDIN)

tional research laboratory in space, and the main purpose of that space station is to understand how the human body interacts in a space environment—bone and muscle growth, fluid buildup in the body, the heart, the sensor system. If we want to go out in space, we have to understand that.

Interview/USA Today, 7-28:(A)11.

1

This search for life [on other planets]—this urge to explore to the very limits of our technology—is not idle curiosity. It's a biological imperative . . . It's what defines us as human beings . . . Exploration is what we live for. It's how we grow as intelligent beings.

The Christian Science Monitor,
10-28:15.

2

I believe we can build a spacecraft in three years weighing hundreds, not thousands, of pounds, and costing a few hundred million dollars, not billions—and have it arrive at Pluto, the last unexplored planet, in the first years of the 21st century . . . [We] space professionals . . . must revolutionize the culture of our organizations to carve money for new projects out of existing budgets. We must . . . *make* ourselves build spacecraft smaller, faster and cheaper.

At World Space Congress/
The Christian Science Monitor,
11-4:14.

David Hamburg
President,
Carnegie Corporation

3

As a nation, we need to turn our attention to the long term, to try to relate scientific and technological innovations to societal goals. Science and technology are now fundamental to modern life, and new technologies and advances in basic science are essential to the continued strength and progress of American society.

The Christian Science Monitor,
9-30:12.

Bernadine P. Healy
Director,
National Institutes of Health
of the United States

4

We need to have a sense that there is great opportunity in science, and have the excitement of that opportunity conveyed to young people. I think we do have to address some of the public-trust issues that have eroded the sense of scientific pursuit as a profession of dignity with high goals associated with it. We do have to tackle with the regulatory environment surrounding science and, I think, make sure that the scientific community's voice is appropriately heard, that they are party to the debate. They may not be able to dominate the debate, particularly when you are dealing with issues that transcend science—like issues of animal rights, socially contentious issues, moral or ethical issues. But I think the scientist ought to be viewed as a respected and vital part of the policy debate. I think there are issues of academic freedom that have to be addressed, particularly for scientists who work for the government.

Interview, Los Angeles, Calif./
Los Angeles Times, 7-26:(M)3.

James E. Katz
Staff sociologist,
Bellcore (research division of
the regional Bell companies)

5

[On the advent of ultra-small portable telephones]: One thing we know about PCS is that it will provide people the electronic equivalent of butlers and secretaries. It spreads to the middle class what only robber barons once enjoyed.

The New York Times, 11-12:(A)1.

Leon M. Lederman
President,
American Association for the
Advancement of Science

6

The [employment] opportunities for scientists in general are tremendous. A physicist may not always find opportunity in his original narrow

423

research specialty, but only 2 or 3 per cent of physicists are actually unemployed. The need for scientists to contribute to the defense of the environment is growing, and physicists will also star in the quest for alternative energy sources and many other social needs. There's no question that the nation will need more physicists.

The New York Times, 3-10:(B)9.

Barbara A. Mikulski
United States Senator,
D-Maryland

1

The goal of any joint venture in space exploration or space science with members of the former Soviet Union should be the generation of additional U.S. jobs. Any budget savings from joint projects with the Russians should be reinvested in our own space program and the technology that will keep us the world leader in this area.

At Senate Appropriations
Subcommittee on Veterans Affairs,
Housing and Independent Agencies
hearing, Washington, D.C., Feb. 21/
The Washington Post, 2-22:(A)6.

Nathan Myrthvold
Vice president of
advanced technology and
business development,
Microsoft Corporation

2

IBM as the IBM that defined computing is over; it's gone. As a result of new technology developments during the past 10 years, IBM's role in the computer industry has fundamentally changed.

The New York Times, 12-16:(A)1.

Robert Park
Director,
American Physical Society

3

[On the vote in the House to eliminate funding for the U.S. super collider]: If I were pressed, I would have said that the space station was more likely [than the super collider] to go. There is very little science to come out of the space station, which competes directly with the National Science Foundation—which is critical to every field of science, including high-energy physics. [The House vote] certainly indicates how deeply the problem with the Federal deficit is going to affect some of our most important institutions.

June 17/Los Angeles Times, 6-18:(A)17.

Frank Press
President,
National Academy of Sciences

4

A fundamental feature of the [new scientific] era . . . will be the ascendancy of the research technologies—those technologies seeded in advance in fundamental research rather than refinements to the existing processes and products.

The Christian Science Monitor,
4-29:1.

Roland Schmitt
President,
Rensselaer Polytechnic Institute

5

There continues to be a steady erosion of U.S. industrial R&D. At danger is our ability to generate pioneering discoveries and pioneering inventions. If you look back at the record, most of [the discoveries] that have led to new industries have come out of corporate laboratories or research universities. Both of those institutions are under stress today.

News conference, Aug. 12/
The Christian Science Monitor,
8-14:8.

Alfred C. Sikes
Chairman,
Federal Communications Commission

6

1993 will be seen by consumers as the beginning of the personal-communications revolution. New, powerful digital technologies will give consumers more choice and more control over

(ALFRED C. SIKES)

their communications. They will be able to communicate on the go, from more places, and have access to vast stores of information and entertainment. Mobile communications will become easier and less expensive. Cellular phones will become smaller, lighter and cheaper. The majority of cellular phones sold will be for carrying around rather than installed in cars . . . While the personal-communications revolution won't be fully realized until later this decade, 1993 will be the beginning for consumers.

Interview/USA Today, 12-30:(A)11.

Bill Spencer
President, Sematech
(U.S. government-industry
consortium for the
semiconductor industry)

1

The big science projects we [in the U.S. are] thinking about are good ones. But they should be global projects. The human genome. The superconducting super collider. The manned exploration of Mars is something we can't pass up. But those are things we ought to do as a planet. We don't have to be macho and do it ourselves anymore.

Interview/The New York Times, 2-5:(A)8.

Paul E. Tsongas
Candidate for the 1992
Democratic Presidential nomination;
Former United States Senator,
D-Massachusetts

2

If you don't have the ideas, you don't get products. The fact is that basic science in this country is devalued. So I would increase the National Science Foundation and the basic life-science agencies, in essence say to young people around this country, "Science and technology is the future. If you have a bent in that direction, stay there. We are going to assure you a future." Second is to provide funding for research into process technologies. Where we do well is we come up with ideas. What the Japanese do well is

they take those ideas and take them to market. So *we* end up with a Nobel Prize; *they* end up with a cash cow of production. Once you have those ideas, you have strategic technologies in which the government is going to have to come in and help finance in the pre-development stages.

Debate with Arkansas Governor
Bill Clinton, Chicago, Ill./
Time, 3-23:17.

Boris N. Yeltsin
President of Russia

3

[The U.S. and Russia just signed] a very important agreement concerning joint space-exploration . . . projects between the United States of America and Russia. After all, what sense does it really make to reinvent the bicycle? Why do we have to pursue parallel efforts doing exactly the same thing in Russia and in the United States? . . . [We should establish] some sort of joint centers, where our young people who are interested in science and research and development could join their efforts . . . in designing spacecraft and possibly even in manning our future giant space stations. It is only by that common endeavor that we can achieve meaningful results.

At Wichita (Kan.) State University,
June 18/
The Washington Post, 6-19:(A)26.

John Young
Former president,
Hewlett-Packard Company

4

[On whether the government should contribute to the research and development costs of technology]: Is the support of research and development broadly legitimate public policy? The answer to that is, clearly, yes. Every economist will agree . . . that the private sector will invest . . . less in research and development than [what] is in the public interest, because no private firm can capture [all of] the benefits of research and development.

Interview/
The Christian Science Monitor,
11-19:8.

Sports

Greg Aiello
Spokesman,
National Football League

1

[On the elimination this season, after five seasons, of the use of instant-replay in officiating at NFL games]: There's a very noticeable lack of interruptions without instant-replay reviews, which 90 per cent of the time led to calls of "inconclusive" or "play stands." Consequently, there's less emphasis on the role of officiating in the games, which is a positive. It's a perception. Everyone accepts when a game is stopped for a timeout. Instant replays irritated people. And so far, in the first three weeks, there's been no controversy, knock on wood.

USA Today, 9-23:(C)9.

Kevin Allen
Hockey reporter,
"USA Today"

2

[Today, hockey is] a real high-level skill game played at a much-faster pace. It's almost warp speed at times. They talk about how goaltenders used to play without masks, but players shoot so much harder now and skate so much faster. Back then, the puck was floating up there like a knuckleball. [Now,] skaters let go with 90-m.p.h. slap shots while skating at 25 m.p.h. It's pretty amazing.

Interview/
The Christian Science Monitor,
3-20:14.

Davey Allison
Auto-racing driver

3

[On auto-racing accidents]: This stuff happens in everyday life, not just stock cars. It happens to everyone. In racing everyone thinks, "It's not going to happen to me." You know it can, but you feel like it won't and you do the best you can from that point on. Anyway, do you quit something just because things go wrong? I didn't quit football when the big guys squashed me. I stayed in because I got away from them once in a while and that was fun.

Interview/
The Washington Post, 9-15:(E)7.

Mario Andretti
Auto-racing driver

4

The cars are as safe as they've ever been, but there will never be a safe race car. It's the nature of the beast.

USA Today, 5-18:(C)11.

Bill Arnsparger
Defensive coordinator,
San Diego "Chargers"
football team

5

Your defense or offense is made up of individuals. If you have 11 people carrying out those assignments, you have a good chance of making something happen. If your defense is split, a long run will develop; if your coverage is split, a long pass will develop. Of course, people beat people individually. But for a person to be beat individually, something else happened up front; for instance, a line that would enable the quarterback to have that much time. That's the team concept that I think you have to have if you're going to be successful.

Interview, San Diego, Calif./
The New York Times, 11-25:(B)7.

Charles Barkley
Basketball player,
Philadelphia "76ers"

6

Anyone can lead the [NBA] in scoring. All you have to do is shoot enough. Rebounding is the stat that really counts. If you can lead the league in rebounding, then you can say you've really done something.

USA Today, 2-18:(C)1.

Walter Byers
Former executive director,
National Collegiate
Athletic Association

1

The corrupting influence in intercollegiate athletics is those inflamed, undeveloped alumni and boosters who have enlarged egos and retarded maturity [and] who seem to get a kick out of bribing 18-year-olds to come play for their institutions.

Los Angeles Times, 3-13:(C)2.

Jennifer Capriati
Tennis player

2

What made [playing in this year's] Olympics so special was that it was something fresh . . . I saw all those other athletes who train four years to maybe have just one crack at a 10-second race and I realized how lucky I am to be in a sport that's so publicized, where you can earn a living, and where you have chances to win big matches all year. [The amateurs at the Olympics] really have just one big chance at being the best athletes, and it made me respect them so much.

Interview/
The New York Times, 8-31:(B)10.

M. L. Carr
Community-relations director
and former player,
Boston "Celtics"
basketball team

3

Every player has the right to be a pro athlete, and with that comes responsibilities to take that high-profile life and try to better the lives of somebody else along the way. Most players take it as an obligation because they know from where they've come, understand how fortunate they are, and they love to give back something. It's not just going out to give. It's rewarding. It makes them feel good to give.

The Christian Science Monitor,
5-1:14.

Michael Chang
Tennis player

4

When [tennis player] Jimmy Connors was 20, I don't think the game was quite as intense. I think it is much more demanding on your body and on your mind now. Back then, maybe through the first couple of rounds [you] kind of walked a little bit, then you started to get the tougher matches. Nowadays, every match is tough.

The Christian Science Monitor,
9-11:14.

Mary Ellen Clark
Olympic diving champion

5

In a lot of ways, the mental game in the sport is so much [more] than the physical aspect. When you are standing up there or you are ready to do your race, it's me against you. And I think, for me, it took a long time to figure that out.

Panel discussion, New York, N.Y./
The Christian Science Monitor,
11-6:14.

Bob Cohen
Sports agent

6

[On free-agent baseball players]: When you're a free agent, you want to look around. Then you start comparing organizations. What you realize is, when you're with a good organization that has treated you well, the grass is not always greener somewhere else.

The New York Times, 12-25:(B)10.

Jimmy Connors
Tennis player

7

[Criticizing the change to "power tennis" in men's matches]: Is the way the game is played hurt the game? I think it has. It's taken a lot away from the all-court game. The way people used to watch the game being played—the angles, hitting one ball short, one long, being able to sneak in behind a good shot, hit a good volley, play baseline and also serve-and-volley. There's just one way now—bang, bang, bang.

USA Today, 3-12:(C)16.

(JIMMY CONNORS)

1

[Today's top young players] all play great tennis, they do the job; but, I mean, at [age] 39 I shouldn't be beating these guys [as he is]. What disappoints me is that's all there is to them, doing the job, and there's nothing else behind that. They say they're players, not salesmen. [But] they don't realize those people in the stands are paying good money during a serious recession to be entertained, to be made to feel like they're part of something . . . That was something I tried to do for the whole 20 years of my career, to take my tennis, put it on the high burner, turn on the crowd and make the place sound like a football or basketball game was going on.

Interview, New York, N.Y./
The New York Times, 8-31:(B)10.

Jim Courier
Tennis player

2

I think for me tennis is not about rankings, but about winning titles. That's what I cherish the most. I much prefer the Australian or French title to being Number 2 on the computer. The computer can be imperfect . . . [but] tournaments don't lie. If you win, you win.

The Washington Post, 1-31:(D)2.

Paul Dupont
Hockey reporter,
"Boston Globe"

3

The big brawl [in hockey] is very much out of the norm now, but there are still one-on-one fights. I don't like it, but I think a lot of people do. And that's what probably prevents the [NHL] from outlawing it. To an extent, they're giving people what they want.

Interview/
The Christian Science Monitor, 3-20:14.

Donald Fehr
Executive director,
Major League (baseball) Players
Association

4

[Player] salaries are related to [club] revenues, and regardless of what you hear from the owners,

revenues still are increasing at a rapid rate. That's a fact that always gets lost. I mean, when revenues level off, salaries will level off. When revenues fall, salaries will fall. We're in the midst of a phenomenon that hasn't run its course yet.

Florida/
Los Angeles Times, 3-9:(C)9.

5

[Criticizing baseball-team owners who say they are in economic difficulty and may have to reduce or cap player salaries]: When people cry doom and gloom, it suggests to me their motives aren't to talk about the state of baseball but to set the stage for some new bargaining venture, with the [TV] networks or the players or whomever. I have been here for 15 years. I have never heard anybody with the sole exception of [former Baseball Commissioner] Peter Ueberroth, when he wanted to look good, say that things were good. What astonishes me is the pervasive notion that the natural and only recourse to solve the problem is to ask for subsidies from the employees [reductions in player compensation]. They have to get past that.

The New York Times, 10-19:(B)8.

Jim Finks
General manager,
New Orleans "Saints"
football team

6

[On the NFL's decision to stop using instant replays during games]: I personally am very disappointed. I think it's a step backwards for the National Football League. I think it was something we had that was very unique, very effective . . . I think we're going to regret the day we voted it down and I think we'll have it back in, very frankly. That's my own personal view.

March 18/
The Washington Post, 3-19:(A)1.

Mike Gartner
Hockey player,
New York "Rangers"

7

[On the current NHL players strike]: How do you explain a strike to the fans? Do we expect the

(MIKE GARTNER)

fans to feel sorry for us? I don't think they will feel sorry for players who are making an average salary of $350,000 a year. But by the same note, I don't think people will necessarily feel sorry for some owners who are making several million dollars a year. We're not trying to get sympathy from the fans, although the fans are the people that are generally going to get hurt. What we are trying to do is say to the people that there are some very important issues that are on the table that are extremely important for our players association and for us to continue as a players association.

News conference,
Toronto, Canada, April 1/
The New York Times, 4-2:(B)7.

Joe Gibbs
Football coach,
Washington "Redskins"

1

[On teams that lose their motivation the year after winning a championship]: You're dealing with people and human nature. Sometimes having a great year ruins you for the next one. Maybe it's just that you start thinking you're better than you are. It could be anything. You get off on the wrong foot. Guys don't like each other. They don't like their contracts. The next thing you know you're in a mess. That's the challenge of coaching.

Interview, Jan. 27/
The Washington Post, 1-28:(C)4.

Jerry Glanville
Football coach,
Atlanta "Falcons"

2

My coaching career is marred by two regrets. The first is I never met [coaches] George Halas or Vince Lombardi. The other is that I *have* met so many of the guys who are coaching now.

Los Angeles Times,
1-2:(C)2.

Thomas Hearn
President,
Wake Forest University

3

The integrity of intercollegiate athletics depends on a very simple principle: that we educate our student-athletes. These are our best guarantee.

USA Today, 1-6:(C)1.

Steve Howe
Baseball pitcher,
New York "Yankees"

4

I always feel free on a baseball field. Baseball's awesome. Baseball's not a realistic world. It's something where I can escape. It's a neat time for solitude. You can have 50,000 people around you but not notice them. It's awesome. It's excellent.

Los Angeles Times, 2-28:(C)2.

Magic Johnson
Former basketball player,
Los Angeles "Lakers"

5

[On what he misses about playing basketball, now that he has retired because he contracted the HIV virus]: You know, you miss a couple things. The first thing you miss is being one of the boys. You don't know about that until you're actually in team situations. You get to see people grow up. You get to be part of their family. You get to see kids being born. You get to be there in the low points, like when a family member dies. You get to have secret names only the team can call you. Only my team calls me Buck, and only my team can call me Buck.

Orlando, Fla./
Los Angeles Times, 2-8:(C)12.

Michael Jordan
Basketball player,
Chicago "Bulls"

6

My opinion about the greatest basketball player ever is that there isn't one. When I retire,

(MICHAEL JORDAN)

I'd like to be called one of the greatest. That could mean one out of a hundred.

Los Angeles Times, 6-12:(C)2.

Jackie Joyner-Kersee
Olympic track-and-field champion

1

[Athletes should not take] winning for granted. When I was in high school, [our team was] very dominant. So one time they tallied up all the points [and] we took our victory lap, and then they came back and said they made a mistake, and we finished second. From that point on, even in my career today, I make sure that they've tallied up the points correctly. It's hard for me to get excited. Even though I might be excited on the inside, I'm reluctant to show that because I'm afraid they're going to come back and say, "We made a mistake."

Panel discussion, New York, N.Y./
The Christian Science Monitor,
11-6:14.

Chuck Knox
Football coach,
Los Angeles "Rams"

2

The message [to players] is: Come prepared. Work in [the] off-season. The message is: If you're going to make 99 per cent of your money for the whole year playing professional football, then you ought to devote a large part of your time in the off-season to conditioning, training, because this is where you make your livelihood.

Interview, Phoenix, Ariz./
Los Angeles Times, 3-24:(C)7.

Marcel Lachemann
Pitching coach, California "Angels"
baseball team

3

In some ways we've made it easier [for starting pitchers today]. The starters don't have to throw all the complete games [pitchers in the past had to]. They only have to go six or seven innings to

get a win, but the way the money [high salaries] is, I don't see guys staying in the game as long. They can make it and get out.

Los Angeles Times, 6-18:(C)9.

Tom Lasorda
Baseball manager,
Los Angeles "Dodgers"

4

The manager of yesteryear cannot manage today; you have to change, and I've changed. It's not like it was when I took over the [*Dodgers*] in 1977. Back then, 17 of the 25 players had played for me in the minor leagues, and four more had come through our farm system. They were all my children. They bled *Dodger* blue. Then last year, I would look out on the field and . . . sometimes all eight position players would be from other organizations. They are all my adopted children now. And while I love them all, deep down you can never love anyone more than you love your real children.

Interview/
Los Angeles Times, 2-22:(C)11.

William Lombardy
Chess International
Grand Master

5

[On chess champion Bobby Fischer's emergence from retirement to play Boris Spassky]: I hope he doesn't retire again. Fischer may be controversial, people may disagree with his philosophy or his actions, but everybody loves his chess. He's a great favorite to serious players, casual players—even people who don't play at all. He makes chess go. He's an exciting personality. We need Bobby Fischer.

Interview, New York, N.Y./
The Christian Science Monitor,
8-28:14.

Andy MacPhail
General manager,
Minnesota "Twins"
baseball team

6

All teams aren't created [financially] equal. We can't compete in a bidding war [for players]

(ANDY MACPHAIL)

with teams like the *Mets, Dodgers* and *Blue Jays.* We've done well, so there's no use crying. In fact, by forcing us to run a lean operation with an emphasis on young players, those teams seem to have done us a favor.

Fort Myers, Fla./
Los Angeles Times, 3-22:(C)8.

Bruce McNall
Owner, Los Angeles "Kings"
hockey team

1

[Criticizing the current NHL player strike]: I don't appreciate when somebody is paid to do a job and they leave with that job half done. I don't think that's fair. I'm stunned at the walkout. They should give the fans what they've already been paid for and honor their contracts. God forbid if I didn't honor a contract, if I said, "I'm not going to honor your contract because I don't like the way you're playing."

April 1/
Los Angeles Times, 4-2:(C)1.

Alison Muscatine
Tennis writer,
"The Washington Post"

2

[On the possibility of technology replacing line judges in tennis]: I think human fallibility is one of the things that makes the game interesting. It's a game of a certain amount of precision. But we are human beings, and line calls have always been controversial. I think it's the nature of the game. You get a bad bounce, a bad line call, and to be a great player you have to overcome that. To make it so scientific that it reduces it to a sport of perfection would be a shame.

Panel discussion,
Wimbledon, England/
The Christian Science Monitor,
7-3:14.

Martina Navratilova
Tennis player

3

[On whether she is thinking of retiring because of age]: Not to compare myself to any great artist,

but should Van Gogh stop painting at a certain age? I heard an Elton John interview the other day on the radio, and he said that music was his connection to life. For me, it's tennis. I'm fitter at 35 than most players are in their 20s. They've been retiring me every year. "This is Martina's last Wimbledon [tournament]"—I've been reading that for a long time. Some people are burned out at 25; I'm alive at 35. Age is a state of mind, and I'm defying it as well as I possibly can.

USA Today, 7-2:(C)2.

Don Nelson
Basketball coach,
Golden State "Warriors"

4

Coaching is kind of like golf. The harder you try to succeed at it the worse you're likely to get. It's a fine line between over-coaching and under-coaching, and now I'm just trying not to step over it.

The Washington Post, 2-26:(D)8.

Peter O'Malley
President,
Los Angeles "Dodgers"
baseball team

5

The fact that players are moving from one team to another more than ever before creates a totally different chemistry on the club than [the chemistry of] an infield that came up through the minors together and played a long time at major-league level. You will not see that happen again. You will not only not see it happen in Cleveland, you will not see it happen in Los Angeles because of the conditions of the industry . . . Last year, the two teams in the World Series both finished last the previous year. Last year we spent more than 100 days in first place, and this year we might spend more than 100 days in last place. That's what baseball is today. There is an extraordinary movement up and down with teams.

Interview/
Los Angeles Times, 8-4:(C)14.

WHAT THEY SAID IN 1992

Dave Phillips
Baseball umpire,
American League

1

I know this is going to sound funny. But the players and managers create the strike zone. Obviously, we [umpires] are in charge of the game. But we call what they will accept. The batter won't swing at the [ball at the chest]. The pitcher won't throw it there because most of them are taught to throw at the knees. So we never call it. If they want us to call that higher strike, it would make our jobs easier. But they have to demand we do it; none of this, "Let's experiment."

USA Today, 7-29:(C)4.

Gary Player
Golfer

2

Most people are surprised about my devotion to [horse] racing. but there's a similarity to championship golf and racing. Most people think the top golfers win all the time. It's not so. We win about 10 per cent of the time. In racing, it's about the same. You lose 90 per cent of the races. It takes determination, perseverance and a lot of patience to succeed in golf or racing. It also takes some luck.

Interview, Indian Wells, Calif./
Los Angeles Times, 3-20:(C)4.

Richard Pound
Canadian member,
International Olympic Committee

3

One of the reasons [the Olympics] draw a lot of static when they don't work is that people are so disappointed. It's kind of a microcosm of the world. People think if the Olympics can work, then maybe there's a chance that the world can work.

Interview,
Montreal, Canada/
The Christian Science Monitor,
5-29:14.

Tom Reich
Baseball-player agent

4

[On the resignation, under pressure by team owners, of Baseball Commissioner Fay Vincent]: The problem this creates, the power of the Commissioner's office was created so strong, the power was vested with such strength, more than any judicial robe that I know about, it is going to leave an unbelievable transition, controlled by ownership against players . . . The [new] Commissioner is not going to be able to adjudicate anything anymore. There's not going to be a facade about that anymore. It is going to be a relationship strictly between ownership and labor [players] where everyone is dealing strictly from self-interest . . . Their [owners] priority is going to be eliminating arbitration. That'll never happen . . . The arbitration system, with its flaws, is still a very effective system of resolving differences . . . The days for hypocrisy are growing short. Combat is coming, and it won't be initiated by players.

Sept. 7/
USA Today, 9-8:(C)3.

Jerry Reinsdorf
Owner, Chicago "White Sox"
baseball team

5

If a [Baseball] Commissioner has an obligation to constituencies other than the [team] owners, I don't think he should be involved. When we go to war with the [players] union, I want him to have an obligation only to the owners.

The New York Times, 9-11:(B)9.

Pat Riley
Basketball coach,
New York "Knicks"

6

The game of basketball is a game of patterns, and then it's a game of spontaneity. Patterns can be taken away a lot by good defensive teams. Then you get into spontaneity: pick and rolls, random situations that you have to attack. That I see, for us, as the next level we have to get to.

New York, N.Y. Jan. 2/
The New York Times, 1-4:30.

432

(PAT RILEY)

1

You just hope that you get great players who have great character, and they want to win. It isn't as much about players needing motivation as wanting discipline. Players don't want you [the coach] to waste their time. They don't want to have seven months on the set having some director or coach dilly-dally around and walk on eggshells. They want something worthwhile.

Interview/
"Interview" magazine, May:118.

William V. Roth, Jr.
United States Senator,
R-Delaware

2

In the unregulated world of professional boxing, rules are ignored or bent, young boxers fight without any protection to their health and safety, and greed is allowed to rule the ring. Professional boxing must get its house in order before it finds itself on par with mud wrestling and cock fighting. My legislation, the Professional Boxing Corporation Act of 1992, would create a governing body for boxing to ensure that the boxing ring is square, that all participants play by the same rules or they don't play at all.

The Washington Post,
6-17:(D)2.

Pete Sampras
Tennis player

3

[On the possibility of machines replacing linespersons in making calls in tennis]: I don't want to hurt anyone's feelings, but I think you'd be giving up a human part of the game for accuracy that isn't really so much better than what we've already got. I don't mind that every call isn't perfect [with human linespersons]. And I don't know what it would be like to watch [player] John McEnroe on a court with no linespeople. You can't argue with a machine.

The New York Times,
2-25:(B)11.

Ted Schroeder
1949 Wimbledon tennis
tournament champion

4

[On today's tennis stars]: Most of today's men are a bunch of bums. Their shirttails hang out, their navels are on show and, of course, they need a shave. And they should get their hair cut. If you are a champion, you should look like a champion.

Los Angeles Times, 7-7:(C)2.

Arnold Schwarzenegger
Actor; Chairman,
President's Council on
Physical Fitness and Sports

5

There is no one who has ever gone the long haul [in sports] relying on drugs. So many kids have this misconception that all you need to do is take a few pills and work out a little bit, and that will take you over the top. But that's not the way it works. That extra 20 pounds that you may lift from using those steroids is not going to be worth it. No one will know about it. But you will know when you get sick . . . It was not the drug that made me the champion. It was the will and the drive and the five hours of working out, lifting 50, 60 tons of weights a day, being on a strict diet and training, my posing and doing all the different things that I had to do.

Interview/
U.S. News & World Report,
6-1:63.

Vin Scully
Baseball broadcaster,
Los Angeles "Dodgers"

6

[Umpires are] almost always right. My [complaint] isn't with their calls. My concern is with the way they make the calls. Over the years, the way the umpires call "safe" or "out" has changed. Their [signs] aren't as clear as I'd like. They aren't as visible as they used to be in the old days . . . My theory is that it's related to television. When I first started [broadcasting] *Dodger* games [in the 1950s], television was also just then on the scene. And the old-fashioned

(VIN SCULLY)

umpires—the [pre-TV] umpires—were very good with their calls. I first noticed the change in the younger [umpires] . . . When a close call went against a player, he'd get on the umpire for showing off for TV. The [umpire] was just making a call that would be easy for everyone in the park to read—but when he turned around, the player was growling: "TV showboat!" Then you could hear it from the bench: "TV showboat!" They kept drumming it into the younger fellows . . . They're sensitive. And they're very human. That's the big forgotten thing about umpires. It's instinctive to want to make changes if you're getting a lot of criticism.

Interview/
Los Angeles Times, 5-27:(C)4.

Bud Selig
Owner, Milwaukee "Brewers"
baseball team

1

Clearly, the economic problems are the major problems facing this industry [baseball]. We have come to a moment where, I believe, there's a significant problem on the expense side. I think in the past we've all taken for granted that revenues would just keep on increasing. I don't know that any reasonable person can say that anymore . . . We need a new player-compensation system that reflects the economy we live in.

Interview/
The New York Times, 10-19:(B)8.

2

[On suggestions that baseball has become boring, outdated and filled with greedy owners and players]: There's no question that all of us are going to have to do some creative thinking, because we're in a fight for our lives. We understand we have a wonderful game that has enormous charm and tradition. But it's up to us, now, to do something . . . Baseball is not a dying sport. [But] we're not where we were in the '60s. It's a wonderful game that happens to have a significant number of off-the-field problems, and some on the field, which need to be addressed.

The New York Times, 11-25:(B)8.

Dinah Shore
Entertainer;
Sponsor of the Nabisco
Dinah Shore golf tournament

3

I got hooked on golf. I don't care if I ever go back to the tennis court. I have this beautiful tennis court in my back yard, but if anyone calls me to play golf, I'll do it . . . [Golf is] a great way to socialize. In tennis, everyone takes a shower and goes back to the office . . . [In golf,] you get to know wonderful things about people. It's a very humanizing—and humbling—sport.

Interview/
Los Angeles Times, 3-23:(C)5.

George Steinbrenner
Owner, New York "Yankees"
baseball team

4

I once told some people that free agency [for baseball players] was going to be tough, but the cancer of baseball would be arbitration. We aren't being crucified because Don Mattingly gets paid $3-million. Mattingly will put fannies in the seats. Where we're getting hurt is through arbitration cases where some guy comes along and says, "Hey, I'm not as good as Mattingly, but I'm a third as good. So pay me $1-million." That's where baseball is getting killed.

Interview/
USA Today, 3-3:(C)8.

Payne Stewart
Golfer

5

[On the mental attitude needed to play well in tournaments]: I don't think it's something you do consciously. It's just something that happens through preparation and hard work. You can prepare yourself to be there and want to win a golf tournament the best you can. But to get into this zone, I don't know how you can do that. I've talked to Dr. Coop about it and he said something just triggers it and there is no explanation. But when it does happen, you've got to go with it and allow it to germinate. When I'm in it, I don't see anything else. All the colors and all the

(PAYNE STEWART)

people are just a blur. All I'm seeing is the ball and the hole. It's like a horse with blinders on; you don't see anything on either side.

Interview/
The Wall Street Journal,
6-16:(Supplement)30.

Bob Storey
Vice president,
International Bobsled Federation

1

[On the bobsled experience]: I've flown with demonstration aerobatic teams, ridden roller coasters and done skydiving. There are elements of thrill to all those things. But [with the bobsled] it's different: There's the thrill of the force of power, the thrill of the speed, the sense of accomplishment and elation at the bottom—a big, combined package mixed in with the competitive element. But like most things of this nature, it's not easily explained.

Interview, Albertville, France/
The Christian Science Monitor,
2-18:14.

Al Strachan
Hockey reporter,
"Toronto Globe and Mail"

2

Hockey's got enough scoring to make it interesting, unlike soccer, but not so much scoring like basketball that it's just one endless parade of scoring. It's got bodily contact and it's got the best athletes of any sport as far as promoting their own sport and being accessible and accommodating and intelligent and articulate. Hockey players just seem to be genuine, down-to-earth, basic people, for the most part.

Interview/
The Christian Science Monitor,
3-20:14.

Rick Sutcliffe
Baseball pitcher,
Baltimore "Orioles"

3

To me, being in a pennant race is everything. I've won the Cy Young [Award]. I've won the

ERA title. I've been in all-star games. Those things don't mean much anymore. It's contending, the excitement of the pennant race. That's why I play the game.

The Washington Post, 9-18:(C)1.

Isiah Thomas
Basketball player,
Detroit "Pistons"

4

In terms of being an athlete, when you're 40 or 50 or 60 years old, you're always going to believe that you'll be able to continue playing your sport. Basketball is almost an addiction to an athlete. It's what makes you what you are, and it's what got you where you are. Even 10 or 20 years from now, [star player Magic Johnson, who retired because he has the HIV virus, will] probably still think he can play the game. That's what makes you good at what you do, and it's the mentality of an athlete.

The New York Times, 2-11:(B)10.

Joe Torre
Baseball manager,
St. Louis "Cardinals"

5

Every time you talk about players anymore, it's how much money they're making and they're over-paid. Everything is related to money . . . [Players today] don't have as much fun as I did because they're making this kind of money. If you don't do what you're supposed to, you're a bum. It's really tough. I base my analysis [of] players on their effort. The guy on the [pitcher's] mound, because he's making so much money, is supposed to win so many games. But don't forget there's a guy at the plate who's making that much money and he's supposed to get a hit, too. When they go against each other, who's supposed to win?

Interview,
Clearwater, Fla., March 8/
USA Today, 3-9:(C)3.

Lee Trevino
Golfer

6

[On learning to play golf]: There's no such thing as wrong in this game. If there was, I

(LEE TREVINO)

wouldn't have made it. Golf is a game of repetition, of practice, practice, practice . . . Anyone can learn the basics. It's just a matter of hard work, determination and sacrifice. A professional can teach you everything he knows in two hours. If you keep coming back, you're just rehearsing.

Interview/
USA Today, 2-6:(C)7.

Jim Tunney
Former referee,
National Football League

1

Motivation [of players] is like a bath. It doesn't last long, but you need one every day.
USA Today, 9-23:(C)10.

Gerald Turner
Chancellor,
University of Mississippi

2

The NCAA is an institutional organization, and the [more it becomes] like other higher-education organizations, the better off we're going to be. It used to be that the NCAA was simply an athletic-officials' organization. But intercollegiate athletics has gotten so big, so publicly visible, that I think the NCAA has to take its place with other higher-education organizations that oversee land-grant schools and so forth. I would certainly hope that the days of the NCAA being primarily an athletic-officials' organization are over. Intercollegiate athletics is just too important a component of the total university. [College] presidents must be involved.
Los Angeles Times, 1-6:(C)11.

Fay Vincent
Commissioner of Baseball

3

Baseball is the one American institution that a Civil War veteran returning today would recognize. One hundred years from now, if we were lucky enough to come back, I hope we would recognize it too.
Los Angeles Times, 3-5:(C)2.

4

[On his decision to realign baseball's National League by moving some teams from the Western division to the Eastern division and vice versa]: It was an extraordinarily difficult decision. I went back and forth several times, but I was very uncomfortable leaving the alignment as it is, considering 10 or 11 National League clubs favored realignment. I know that four or five of those same clubs opposed my intervention, but I didn't consider this a political exercise. I had to look at the overall support for realignment.
July 6/
Los Angeles Times, 7-7:(C)6.

5

[On his resignation as Commissioner, under pressure by team owners]: I can only hope owners will realize that a strong Commissioner, a person of experience and stature in the community, is integral to baseball. I hope they learn this lesson before too much damage is done to the game, to the players, umpires and others who work in the game, and most importantly, to the fans . . . Unfortunately, some [owners] want the Commissioner to put aside the responsibility to act in the "best interests of baseball"; some want the Commissioner to represent only owners, and to do their bidding in all matters. I haven't done that, and I could not do so, because I accepted the position believing the Commissioner has a higher duty and that sometimes decisions have to be made that are not in the best interests of some owners. Unique power was granted to the Commissioner of Baseball for sound reasons—to maintain the integrity of the game and to temper owner decisions predicated solely on self-interest. The office should be maintained as a strong institution. My views on this have not changed . . . I remind all that ownership of a baseball team is more than ownership of an ordinary business. Owners have a duty to take into consideration that they own a part of America's national pastime—in trust. This trust sometimes requires putting self-interest second.
Letter of resignation,
Sept. 7*/
The Washington Post, 9-8:(A)8.

John Wathan
Interim manager,
California "Angels"
baseball team

1

[On today's pitchers]: With [multi-year] contracts today, there's a big concern for longevity and getting them to pitch a long time rather than a lot of innings. But you look at guys . . . who have pitched a lot of innings and are still at it, and you have to think that maybe we baby pitchers too much these days. I mean, growing up I was always told that the more you throw, the stronger your arm gets; but that's not what they tell kids anymore.

Los Angeles Times, 6-18:(C)9.

2

[On his returning to coaching after serving as *Angels* interim manager]: The hardest part of managing is making the lineup out every day. That's a relief in itself, not having to write the lineup out . . . Coaching is definitely an easier job. Coaching is not a 24-hour-a-day job. When you're managing, I don't think you ever get away from the game. As soon as the game is over, you're thinking about the next day's lineup and trying to get an idea who's going to play. As a coach, you don't have that much to think about, and your duties are pretty evenly divided. You have to make sure it's all coordinated.

Interview/
Los Angeles Times, 8-28:(C)1,4.

The Indexes

Index to Speakers

C

Y

Z

Index to Subjects

A

C

---

*Many references to George Bush are not listed in this index due to the numerous routine mentions of his name throughout the book. Only references that are specifically about him, personally or professionally, are listed here.

---

*Many references to Bill Clinton are not listed in
this index due to the numerous routine mentions of
his name throughout the book. Only references
that are specifically about him, personally or professionally, are listed here.*

E

X

Y

Z